THE OXFORD HANDBOOK OF

WORLD HISTORY

THE OXFORD HANDBOOK OF

WORLD HISTORY

Edited by

JERRY H. BENTLEY

OXFORD
UNIVERSITY PRESS

OXFORD
UNIVERSITY PRESS

Great Clarendon Street, Oxford, OX2 6DP,
United Kingdom

Oxford University Press is a department of the University of Oxford.
It furthers the University's objective of excellence in research, scholarship,
and education by publishing worldwide. Oxford is a registered trade mark of
Oxford University Press in the UK and in certain other countries

© Oxford University Press 2011

The moral rights of the authors have been asserted

First Edition published in 2011

First published in paperback 2013

Impression: 1

Published in the United States of America by Oxford University Press
198 Madison Avenue, New York, NY 10016, United States of America

British Library Cataloguing in Publication Data
Data available

ISBN 978–0–19–923581–0 (Hbk.)
978–0–19–968606–3 (Pbk.)

Printed in Great Britain by
Ashford Colour Press Ltd

ACKNOWLEDGEMENTS

The professional staff at Oxford University Press provided consistent support for this handbook. Christopher Wheeler, Natasha Knight, Matthew Cotton, and Claire Thompson deserve special mention for their various efforts. It goes without saying that this volume would not be possible except for the community of world historians, who since the 1960s and especially since the 1980s have constructed new visions of the global past.

TABLE OF CONTENTS

PART III: PROCESSES

PART IV: REGIONS

Contributors

David Abulafia is Professor of Mediterranean History at the University of Cambridge.

Thomas T. Allsen is Professor Emeritus of History at the College of New Jersey.

Thomas J. Barfield is Professor of Anthropology at Boston University.

Zvi Ben-Dor Benite is Professor of History at New York University.

Jerry H. Bentley is Professor of History at the University of Hawai`i and editor of the *Journal of World History*.

Michael Bentley is Professor of Modern History at the University of St Andrews.

Rainer F. Buschmann is Associate Professor of History at Purdue University.

Luigi Cajani is Professor of Modern History at the University of Rome 'La Sapienza.'

David Christian is Professor of History at Macquarie University.

Paul d'Arcy is Fellow in the School of Culture, History and Language at Australian National University.

Edward J. Davies, II is Professor of History at the University of Utah.

Prasenjit Duara is Raffles Professor of Humanities and Director of Humanities and Social Science Research at the National University of Singapore.

Christopher Ehret is Professor of History at the University of California, Los Angeles.

Daniel R. Headrick is Professor Emeritus of History at Roosevelt University.

Dirk Hoerder is Professor of History at Arizona State University.

Marnie Hughes-Warrington is pro-Vice Chancellor for Learning and Teaching Quality at Monash University.

Alan L. Karras is Senior Lecturer in the International and Area Studies Teaching program at the University of California, Berkeley.

Donald R. Kelley is James Westfall Thompson Professor of History at Rutgers University.

Matthew J. Lauzon is Associate Professor of History at the University of Hawai`i.

Martin W. Lewis is Senior Lecturer in International History at Stanford University.

Patrick Manning is Andrew W. Mellon Professor of World History at the University of Pittsburgh.

J.R. McNeill is University Professor of History at Georgetown University.

John A. Mears is Associate Professor of History at Southern Methodist University.

Patrick Karl O'Brien is Centennial Professor of Economic History at the London School of Economics.

Jürgen Osterhammel is Professor of Modern History at the University of Konstanz.

Peter C. Perdue is Professor of History at Yale University.

Kenneth Pomeranz is UCI Chancellor's Professor of History at the University of California, Irvine and an editor of the *Journal of Global History*.

Bonnie G. Smith is Board of Governors Professor of History at Rutgers University.

Charles Tilly† was Joseph L. Buttenwieser Professor of Social Science at Columbia University.

James D. Tracy is Professor Emeritus of History at the University of Minnesota and editor of the *Journal of Early Modern History*.

John Obert Voll is Professor of History at Georgetown University.

André Wink is Professor of History at the University of Wisconsin, Madison.

THE TASK OF WORLD HISTORY

JERRY H. BENTLEY

THE term *world history* has never been a clear signifier with a stable referent. It shares a semantic and analytical terrain with several alternative approaches, some of which boast long scholarly pedigrees, while others have only recently acquired distinct identities. The alternatives include universal history, comparative history, global history, big history, transnational history, connected history, entangled history, shared history, and others. World history overlaps to some greater or lesser extent with all of these alternative approaches.

World history and its companions have taken different forms and meant different things at different times to different peoples. From ancient times, many peoples— Hindus and Hebrews, Mesopotamians and Maya, Persians and Polynesians, and countless others—constructed myths of origin that located their own experiences in the larger context of world history. Taking their cues from the Bible, Christian scholars of medieval Europe traced a particular kind of universal history from Creation to their own day. Historians of the Mongol era viewed historical development in continental perspective and included most of Eurasia in their accounts. The philosopher Ibn Khaldun conceived a grand historical sociology of relations between settled and nomadic peoples. The Göttingen Enlightenment historians Johann Christoph Gatterer and August Ludwig von Schlözer worked to construct a new, professionally grounded *Universalgeschichte* that would illuminate the hidden connections of distant events. In the twentieth century, Oswald Spengler, Arnold J. Toynbee, Karl Jaspers, and others turned world history into a philosophical project to discover historical laws by distilling high-proof wisdom from the historical record. To many others throughout the twentieth and into the twenty-first century, world history has meant foreign history—the history of peoples and societies other than one's own. Meanwhile, in schools and universities, world history has commonly referred to a synoptic and comparative survey of all the world's peoples and societies considered at a high level of abstraction.

Since the mid-twentieth century, a new kind of world history has emerged as a distinctive approach to professional historical scholarship. It is a straightforward matter to describe the general characteristics of this new world history. As it has developed since the 1960s and particularly since the 1980s, the new world history has focused attention on comparisons, connections, networks, and systems rather than the experiences of individual communities or discrete societies. World historians have systematically compared the experiences of different societies in the interests of identifying the dynamics that have been especially important for large-scale developments like the process of industrialization and the rise of the West. World historians have also analyzed processes of cross-cultural interaction and exchange that have influenced the experiences of individual societies while also shaping the development of the world as a whole. And world historians have focused attention on the many systems of networks that transgress the national, political, cultural, linguistic, geographical, and other boundaries that historians and other scholars have conventionally observed. World historians have not denied the significance of local, national, and regional histories, but they have insisted on the need to locate those histories in larger relevant contexts.[1]

This new world history emerged at a time of dramatic expansion in the thematic scope of historical analysis. To some extent it paralleled projects such as social history, women's history, gender analysis, environmental history, and area studies, not to mention the linguistic turn and the anthropological turn, which cumulatively over the past half-century have extended historians' gaze well beyond the political, diplomatic, military, and economic horizons that largely defined the limits of historical scholarship from the mid-nineteenth to the mid-twentieth century.

Yet the new world history has conspicuously engaged two sets of deeper issues that do not loom so large in other fields. These deeper issues arise from two unintended ideological characteristics that historical scholarship acquired—almost as birthmarks—at the time of its emergence as a professional discipline of knowledge in the mid-nineteenth century: a legacy of Eurocentric assumptions and a fixation on the nation-state as the default and even natural category of historical analysis. The early professional historians reflected the influence of these values, which were common intellectual currency in nineteenth-century Europe, and to a remarkable degree, their successors have continued to view the past through the filters of distinctively nineteenth-century perspectives. Because world historians work by definition on large-scale transregional, cross-cultural, and global issues, they regularly confront these two characteristics of professional historical scholarship more directly than their colleagues in other fields. By working through the problems arising from Eurocentric assumptions and enchantment with the nation-state, world historians have created opportunities to open new windows onto the global past and to construct visions of the past from twenty-first rather than nineteenth-century perspectives.

How did professional historical scholarship acquire its ideological birthmarks? How did it happen that serious scholars—who were conscientiously seeking an accurate and precise reconstruction of the past—came to view the past through powerful ideological filters that profoundly influenced professional historians' understanding of the past, their approach to their work, and the results of their studies?

Rigorous study of the past has deep historical roots. From classical antiquity to modern times, historians of many cultural traditions worked diligently to compile accurate and honest accounts of historical developments. By the seventeenth and eighteenth centuries, historians in several lands were independently developing proto-cols for rigorous, critical, evidence-based analysis of the past.[2] Yet professional histori-cal scholarship as we know it today—the highly disciplined study of the past centered principally in universities—acquired its identity and achieved institutional form only during the nineteenth century. Professional historical scholarship as we know it today derives from the efforts of Leopold von Ranke and others who worked to establish reliable foundations for historical knowledge and to enhance its credibility by insisting that historians refrain from telling colorful but fanciful stories and base their accounts instead on critically examined documentary evidence.

This essay will argue that professional historical scholarship has suffered from several serious problems from its beginnings to the present day. Let me emphasize that this argument is a critique of historical scholarship, not a rejection or condemna-tion. The critique does not imply that it is impossible for historians to deal responsibly with the past and still less that professional historical scholarship is a vain endeavor. In the absence of any alternative approach capable of achieving absolute objectivity or yielding perfect knowledge, professional historical scholarship, in spite of its pro-blems, is in my opinion clearly the most reliable, most responsible, and most construc-tive mode of dealing with the past. It is by no means the only way or the most popular way by which the world's peoples have sought to come to terms with the past. The world's peoples have more commonly relied on myth, legend, memory, genealogy, song, dance, film, fiction, and other approaches as their principal and preferred guides to the past.[3] Granting that these alternative ways of accessing and dealing with the past wield enormous cultural power, it is clear also that they do not readily open themselves to critique, revision, or improvement. They stand on the foundations of unquestionable authority, long-standing tradition, emotional force, and rhetorical power. Professional historical scholarship by contrast approaches the past through systematic exploration, rigorous examination of evidence, and highly disciplined reasoning. Some practitioners have deployed their skills in such a way as to stoke the emotions or inspire a sense of absolute certainty, but as often as not, professional historical scholarship has corroded certainty, raised doubts about long-cherished convictions, and emphasized the com-plexities of issues that some might have preferred to view as simple. More importantly, it exposes itself to review and critique in the interests of identifying problems, correct-ing mistakes, and producing improved knowledge. It enjoys general intellectual credi-bility—properly so—and it has earned its reputation as the most reliable mode of dealing with the past. Even if they left a problematic legacy, Leopold von Ranke and his collaborators bequeathed to the world a powerful intellectual tool in the form of professional historical scholarship.

Yet the habit of critique that is a hallmark of professional historical scholarship requires historians to undertake a critical examination of professional historical scholarship itself. This critical examination might well begin by considering the conditions under which professional historical scholarship emerged. It was significant that professional historical scholarship as we know it emerged in nineteenth-century Europe. The early professional historians fashioned study of the past into a rigorous and respectable scholarly discipline just as two other momentous developments were underway. First, during an age of industrialization and imperialism, Europe realized more global power and influence than ever before in world history. Second, in both Europe and North America, political leaders transformed ramshackle kingdoms and federations into powerful national states. Both developments had profound implications for historical scholarship and for the conception of history itself as an intellectual project.

Professional Historical Scholarship and the Problem of Europe

The twin processes of industrialization and imperialism created a context in which European peoples came to construe Europe as the site of genuine historical development. Michael Adas has pointed out that in the sixteenth and seventeenth centuries, European travelers found much to admire in the societies, economies, and cultural traditions of China, India, and other lands. By the eighteenth and nineteenth centuries, however, after the Enlightenment and the development of modern science, followed by the tapping of new energy sources that fueled a massive technological transformation, Europeans increasingly viewed other peoples as intellectually and morally inferior while dismissing their societies as sinks of stagnation.[4] Georg Wilhelm Friedrich Hegel articulated these views in stark and uncompromising terms. The Mediterranean basin was 'the centre of World-History,' he intoned, without which 'the History of the World could not be conceived.' By contrast, East Asia was 'severed from the process of general historical development, and has no share in it.' Sub-Saharan Africa was 'the land of childhood, which lying beyond the day of self-conscious history, is enveloped in the dark mantle of Night.' As a result, Africa was 'no historical part of the World; it has no movement or development to exhibit.' Turning his attention to the western hemisphere, Hegel declared that 'America has always shown itself physically and psychically powerless, and still shows itself so.' Like Africa, America had no history, properly speaking, although European peoples were working to introduce history there even as he wrote, so Hegel predicted that it would be 'the land of the future, where, in the ages that lie before us, the burden of the World's History shall reveal itself.'[5]

Hegel was a philosopher, not a historian, and I am well aware that his conception of history was more sophisticated than his uninformed speculations on the world beyond Europe might suggest. It is clear today that Hegel spoke from profound ignorance of the larger world, but his views were plausible enough in nineteenth-century Europe. Furthermore, as the dominant philosopher of his age, who placed historical development on the philosopher's agenda, Hegel deeply influenced both the conception of history and the understanding of its purpose precisely at the moment when it was winning recognition as a professional scholarly discipline capable of yielding accurate and reliable knowledge about the past.

Although the early professional historians bridled impatiently at Hegel's speculative pronunciamentos, their everyday practice resonated perfectly with his notion that history in the proper sense of the term was relevant almost exclusively for Europe, not for the larger world. The early professional historians faithfully reflected Hegel's views when they radically limited the geographical scope of proper historical scholarship to the Mediterranean basin and Europe, and to a lesser extent Europe's offshoots in the western hemisphere. These were the lands with formal states and literary traditions that were supposedly unique in exhibiting conscious, purposeful historical development. Hegel and the early professional historians alike regarded them as the drivers of world history—the proper focus of historians' attention. Hegel and the historians granted that complex societies with formal states and sophisticated cultural traditions like China, India, Persia, and Egypt had once possessed history. Because they had supposedly fallen into a state of stagnation, however, they did not merit the continuing attention of historians, whose professional responsibility was to study processes of conscious, purposeful historical development.

Accordingly, for a century and more, historians largely restricted their attention to the classical Mediterranean, Europe, and Euro-American lands in the western hemisphere. Study of other world regions was the province of scholars in different fields. Until the emergence of modern area studies after World War II, for example, orientalists and missionaries were the principal scholars of both past and contemporary experiences of Asian lands, which they sought to understand largely on the basis of canonical literary texts rather than historical research.[6] If the early professional historians excluded Asian lands from their purview, they certainly had no interest in sub-Saharan Africa, tropical Southeast Asia, the Americas, and Oceania. These lands without recognizable formal states or literary traditions were lands literally without history. As a result, these lands and their peoples, with their exotic and colorful but historically unimportant traditions—'the unrewarding gyrations of barbarous tribes in picturesque but irrelevant corners of the globe,' in the words of one latter-day Hegelian historian—fell to the tender mercies of the anthropologists.[7]

It is true that Leopold von Ranke echoed the language of broad-gauged Enlightenment scholars when he advocated a universal history that 'embraces the events of all times and nations.' He expansively envisioned this universal history not as a mere compilation of national histories but as an account from a larger perspective in which 'the general connection of things' would be the historian's principal interest. 'To recognize this connection, to trace the sequence of those great events which link all nations together and control their destinies,' he declared, 'is the task which the science of Universal History undertakes.' Ranke freely acknowledged that 'the institutions of one or another of the Oriental nations, inherited from primeval times, have been regarded as the germ from which all civilization has sprung.' Yet in the very same breath, he also held that there was no place for these 'Oriental nations' in his work: 'the nations whose characteristic is eternal repose form a hopeless starting point for one who would understand the internal movement of Universal History.' As a result, the horizons of Ranke's own universal history (published between 1880 and 1888) did not extend beyond the Mediterranean basin and Europe.[8] Thus, universal history meant European history, and European history was the only history that really mattered.

Over time, with accumulation of knowledge about the world beyond Europe, it is conceivable that historians might have corrected this kind of Eurocentric thinking by gradually broadening the geographical and cultural horizons of historical scholarship so as to include societies beyond Europe. But Hegel and the early professional historians were active at precisely the moment when European commentators were realizing the enormous power that mechanized industrial production lent European peoples in their dealings with the larger world. The intellectual environment that nurtured theories of pejorative orientalism, scientific racism, social Darwinism, and civilizing mission made no place for relativistic notions that Europe was one society among others. Contemporary experience seemed to demonstrate European superiority and suggested that weaker societies would benefit from European tutelage to raise them to higher levels of development.[9] Thus, Hegel and the early professional historians reinforced their Eurocentric perspectives with the assumption that Europe was the *de facto* standard of historical development and indeed of civilization itself.

In this intellectual atmosphere, the early professional historians universalized European categories of analysis, thereby ensuring, perhaps unintentionally, that societies in the larger world would look deficient when viewed in the light of analytical standards derived from European experience. Many critics have pointed out the distinctly European valence of terms like state and nation, culture and civilization, tradition and modernity, trade, labor, slavery, feudalism, capitalism, and others that have become workhorses of professional historical scholarship.[10] When professional historians began to broaden their geographical horizons after the mid-twentieth century and extend historical recognition to lands beyond Europe, they continued to employ these inherited concepts and thus viewed societies in the larger world through the lenses of European categories of analysis. The effect of this practice was to deepen and consolidate Eurocentric assumptions by producing a body of historical knowledge that evaluated the world's societies against standards manufactured in Europe.

In an influential article of 1992, Dipesh Chakrabarty offered a darkly pessimistic view of the resulting historiography and its potential to deal responsibly with the world beyond Europe. He argued that Europe had become the reference point of professional historical scholarship. 'There is a peculiar way,' he observed, 'in which all...other histories tend to become variations on a master narrative that could be called "the history of Europe".' Further, 'so long as one operates within the discourse of "history" produced at the institutional site of the university, it is not possible simply to walk out of the deep collusion between "history" and the modernizing narrative(s) of citizenship, bourgeois public and private, and the nation state.' Thus, professional historical scholarship as an intellectual project fell inevitably and completely within the orbit of European modernity. As of 1992, Chakrabarty regarded its value as a form of knowledge as dubious and possibly nil.[11]

It is not necessary to accept all the dire implications drawn by Chakrabarty and some other postcolonial critics to recognize that it is indeed problematic procedure to universalize categories of analysis that originated as culturally specific concepts in one society and then apply them broadly in studies of societies throughout the world, and to acknowledge further that capitalism, imperialism, and other elements of European modernity have profoundly influenced both the conception and the practice of professional historical scholarship.[12] Rather than throwing up hands and jumping to the conclusion that historical scholarship is a vain pursuit, however, a more constructive approach might be to entertain the possibility that professional historians are capable of transcending the original limitations of their discipline. Before exploring that possibility, though, a second problem of professional historical scholarship calls for attention.

PROFESSIONAL HISTORICAL SCHOLARSHIP AND THE PROBLEM OF THE NATION

Alongside a cluster of Eurocentric assumptions, professional historical scholarship acquired a second ideological birthmark in the form of a fixation on the nation-state as the default and even natural focus of historical analysis. This was not inevitable. From ancient times to the present, many historians sought ways to understand the experiences of their own societies in larger context. This was true of Herodotus in the fifth century BCE and Sima Qian in the second century BCE.[13] It was true in the thirteenth century CE of the Persian historians of the Mongols, Juvaini and Rashid al-Din. In the Enlightenment era, it was true of amateur historians like Voltaire, Montesquieu, and the authors of the English *Universal History* who managed to compile some sixty-five volumes on the histories of all world regions (1736–65), as well as the professional historians Johann Christoph Gatterer and August Ludwig von Schlözer at the University of Göttingen. Even throughout the nineteenth and twentieth centuries, a tradition of popular interest in world history persisted stubbornly in the face of university-based professional historical scholarship. Obscure individuals like Robert Benjamin Lewis and William Wells Brown published world histories from African perspectives, while prominent figures like H. G. Wells and Jawaharlal Nehru essayed comprehensive surveys of the global past.[14]

During the nineteenth century, however, as professional historians were narrowing their geographical horizons, they also chose a thematic focus for their studies that reflected the political environment in which their newly fortified discipline emerged. The nineteenth century was an age of heady nationalism and intense state building in Europe. Along with their contemporaries, historians witnessed the potential of the nation-state to mobilize human resources and marshal human energies. They became fascinated or even enchanted by national communities and the nation-state as a form of political organization. Notwithstanding the Rankean requirement that historians base their accounts on critically examined documentary evidence, they made the assumption that the national communities of the nineteenth century had deep historical roots reaching back into deep antiquity. So it was that they took the nation, the national community, and its political expressions, culminating in the nation-state, as the default and indeed almost the only proper focus of professional historical scholarship.

Like Hegel once again, the early professional historians regarded states—especially the nation-states of their own day—as the pre-eminent agents of history. Leopold von Ranke himself once referred to states as 'spiritual substances ... thoughts of God.'[15] (Peter Novick aptly characterized his approach to the past as one of 'pantheistic state-worship.'[16]) Ranke and his professional colleagues focused their gaze on the experiences of national communities and nation-states as viewed through their institutions, constitutions, political experiences, cultural expressions, and relations with neighbors. They took the nation as the default subject of historical scholarship, and they treated history as though it were a property attaching primarily or exclusively to national communities and nation-states. They often composed intensely patriotic accounts that served as legitimizing genealogies of national communities. This involved the retrojection of national narratives into the distant past so as to appropriate some earlier events and experiences (while excluding others) and to forge linear national narratives.[17]

For their own part, throughout the nineteenth and twentieth centuries, nation-states responded enthusiastically to historians' attention: they supported and even subsidized the discipline of history by maintaining national archives, founding societies to publish historical documents, funding universities, establishing professorial chairs in national histories, and including the study of patriotic history in school curricula. In the absence of the symbiotic relationship between historians and nation-states since the nineteenth century, professional historical scholarship as we know it is almost inconceivable. Historical scholarship became in large measure an ideological servant of that particular form of political organization known as the nation-state. Indeed, professional historical scholarship is in many ways an intellectual artifact of the nation-state era of world history.[18]

The past century has brought enormous change to the theory and practice of professional historical scholarship. Contemporary historians have broadened the thematic scope of historical analysis, and they have mostly moderated the intense nationalism of their nineteenth-century predecessors. Yet their *de facto* attachment to national communities and nation-states persists to the present day. While addressing themes quite different from those of traditional political and diplomatic history, for example, social historians and feminist scholars have cast their studies mostly within the frameworks of national communities. It is a simple matter to think of studies on topics like the formation of the English working class, the subjugation of subalterns in colonial India, or the experiences of women in American history. The metanarratives underpinning these works explicitly regard class and gender as portable categories of universal significance, but historians have rarely undertaken basic research addressing issues of class and gender in contexts larger than national communities. Historians who have attacked patriotic and hyper-nationalist narratives have focused their own critiques mostly on specifically national policies and thus have viewed the past through the lenses of the very nation-states they criticize. And even when historians have dealt with eras long before the emergence of modern nation-states, they have routinely focused their analyses on individual societies such as early imperial 'China' or late medieval 'Germany,' thus construing the past through the optic of a world divided into national communities. Fixation on the nation-state remains a prominent characteristic of professional historical scholarship to the present day.

The point here is not to attack national history *per se* and certainly not to question the historical significance of national communities or nation-states themselves. National communities and nation-states have powerfully influenced the conditions under which the world's peoples have led their lives during the past two centuries, when the organization of ostensibly coherent and distinct national communities into nation-states has emerged as a conspicuous global historical process. Furthermore, individual nation-states have played out-sized roles in world history: in light of their proven abilities to command popular loyalty and mobilize human resources, they demand attention from historians and will continue to do so for the foreseeable future.

It is not so clear, however, that historians should permit nation-based political organization to obscure the significance and roles of the many alternative ways human beings have expressed their solidarity with others by forming communities based on sex, gender, race, ethnicity, language, religion, ideology, caste, occupation, economic interest, status, taste, or many other conceivable foundations. Nor is it clear that historians should turn a blind eye toward the ways human groups, however diversely organized, have engaged other groups and the world beyond their own communities.

THE TASK OF WORLD HISTORY

How might professional historians deal constructively with the ideologically tinged discipline they have inherited? There can be no question of ignoring European history or abolishing national history, nor can there be any serious expectation that professional historians might find some privileged route to the holy grail of absolute objectivity. Having identified the issues, however, historians might work toward the construction of historiographies that mitigate even if they cannot entirely eliminate problems arising from Eurocentric ideologies and fixation on the nation-state.

To the extent that professional historical scholarship as a form of knowledge emerged as an integral element of European modernity—characterized by nation-states, mechanized industry, and global empire as well as a distinctive form of historical knowledge—it is a delicate operation to extricate the methods and analytical techniques of historical scholarship from ideological associations that have pervaded historical thinking for the past century and more. This task involves unthinking some perspectives on the world that have conditioned the foundations of professional historical scholarship itself. Yet there is no *a priori* reason to doubt that historians are able to root unhelpful assumptions out of their discipline: the historical record is full of cultural projects that started along one set of lines only to undergo radical changes of direction as later practitioners recognized problems and found ways to deal with them.

The new world history has emerged as one of the more promising disciplinary venues for efforts to deal with both Europe and the larger world without taking Europe as an unproblematic starting point or universal standard for historical analysis. World historians have not adopted any single formula or method as a general remedy for Eurocentric assumptions. Rather, they have constructed a less ideological and more transparent historiography through self-reflection, self-correction, and application of various *ad hoc* methods and approaches.

Not to attempt an exhaustive listing, several of these methods and approaches merit special mention. R. Bin Wong has advocated a method of reciprocal comparison that has the advantage of highlighting the distinctive characteristics and values of societies without comparing one invidiously against another.[19] Similarly, Jack Goody has suggested the adoption of analytical grids that would facilitate cross-cultural comparisons on specific characteristics (such as the cultural preferences and traits that some have thought were unique to European peoples), thus creating a context for the comparison of multiple societies with respect to particular traits or forms of organization.[20] Sanjay Subrahmanyam has turned less to explicit comparison than to the analysis of 'connected histories' and particularly the cultural influences that touched societies throughout the early modern world.[21] Meanwhile, moving beyond the bleak views expressed in his article of 1992, Dipesh Chakrabarty has more recently sought to redeem historical scholarship through the project of 'provincializing Europe'—locating European modernity as one local expression in a larger constellation of many alternative modernities.[22] Kenneth Pomeranz has laid a solid foundation for the effort to understand industrialization from global perspectives through careful, controlled comparison of early modern Europe and China.[23] And C. A. Bayly has advanced a complex analysis that makes generous room for local experiences while exploring the early phase of modern globalization.[24] It would be possible to mention many additional contributions, but these half-dozen will serve as salient examples of the different ways world historians have sought alternatives to Eurocentric conceptions of the global past.

The approaches mentioned here do not seek to replace Eurocentric with Sinocentric, Indocentric, or other ideological preferences—and they emphatically do not dismiss Europe altogether—so much as they strive to decenter all ethnocentric conceptions. They are not entirely free of imperfection, but in combination they nevertheless clear a good deal of conceptual ground and open the door to more constructive analysis of the global past. Further possibilities for improved analysis will undoubtedly arise as reflexive historians find additional ways to avoid Eurocentric and other unhelpful ideologies when dealing with the global past.

Remedies for fixation on the nation-state as a focus of historical analysis are more straightforward than those for Eurocentric assumptions. Two main alternative strategies have emerged to deal with the problem. One approach, which has taken several distinctive forms, involves a turn to the local in an effort to discover historical meaning in intimate contexts much smaller than the nation-state. In philosophical dress, this turn to the local found expression in the famous pronouncement of Jean-François Lyotard that the defining characteristic of the postmodern age is 'incredulity toward metanarratives' because the only meaningful narratives were intensely local.[25] In methodological dress, the turn to the local made a prominent appearance in the spirited critique of European analytical categories by Steven Feierman, who insisted that scholars must adopt African categories in order to understand African historical experience.[26] In empirical dress, the local turn informed Clifford Geertz's anthropology based on local knowledge and the project of microhistory, which has discovered historical meaning in the lives, experiences, and relationships of individual men and women rather than in their societies' political organs or larger structural elements.[27]

The turn to the local has in many ways enriched understanding of the past without making the nation-state the natural focus of historical analysis, but it is also capable of obscuring influences and connections that condition the lives and experiences of local subjects themselves. Focusing on the lives and experiences of the marginal, the rebellious, and the subaltern, history reflecting the local turn has provided a convenient foundation for political and social criticism as well as identity politics in search of a usable past. Yet the local turn comes at high cost if it ignores the larger frameworks (including the nation-state) and large-scale processes that profoundly influence the experiences of local subjects. To the extent that it declines to engage the larger world and the links that tie societies together, the turn to the local has the potential to encourage the production of unrelated micronarratives and a vision of history driven *de facto* by local cultural determinisms. As Fernando Coronil has pointed out, 'this popular trend leaves us facing a world of disjointed elements at a time when the globalization of space—marked by integrative and exclusionary processes—makes it intellectually compelling and politically indispensable to understand how parts and whole hang together.'[28]

A second alternative to nation-state history involves a turn toward the global by situating local, national, and regional histories in larger transregional, transcultural, and global contexts. The turn toward the global is not an unproblematic project. To the contrary, it is fraught with logical, epistemological, moral, and other kinds of difficulties. Some efforts at world history have assimilated readily to the familiar Eurocentric assumptions considered earlier. Others have drawn inspiration exclusively from the social theories, especially Marxist and Weberian, that were characteristic cultural productions of European modernity. Too many formulations have flattened differences between societies and homogenized peoples in the interests of grand abstractions.

In spite of all the potential problems and pitfalls, the turn toward the global is a necessary and indispensable project for purposes of constructing realistic visions and meaningful understandings of the world and its development through time. Without denying the significance of the nation-state, world historians have decentered it by focusing their analyses on networks of communication and exchange and by exploring processes of interaction between peoples of different states, societies, and cultural traditions. They have in many ways portrayed messy worlds and resisted temptations to reduce all the multiplicity and variety of historical experience to simple principles. They have sought to recognize both the claim that the world is a site of radical heterogeneity and the reality of transregional systems linking the fortunes of different heterogeneous peoples. In doing so, they have worked to construct visions of the past that are capable of accounting for both fragmentation and integration on multiple levels—local, regional, national, continental, hemispheric, oceanic, and global as well.[29]

The turn toward the global in the form of the new world history does not represent a cure-all, either for historical scholarship or for the more general effort to understand the larger world. It does not dwell on the experiences of individual communities, except insofar as they have participated in larger historical processes linking them to others. In taking long-term perspectives, it runs some risk of obscuring the contingency of history, even if it brings some large-scale processes into clearer focus. Moreover, it admittedly reflects modern cultural perspectives and might well seem impertinent to observers situated beyond the horizon of high modernity.

Yet the turn toward the historical global enables historians to address some significant issues that alternative approaches do not bring into focus. It offers a framework permitting historians to move beyond the issues that have been the principal concerns of professional historical scholarship since the mid-nineteenth century—cultural distinctions, exclusive identities, local knowledge, and the experiences of individual societies, most of them construed in fact as national communities—by making a place on historians' agenda for large-scale processes that connect the world's many ostensibly distinct and discrete societies. The global turn facilitates historians' efforts to deal analytically with a range of large-scale processes such as mass migrations, campaigns of imperial expansion, cross-cultural trade, environmental changes, biological exchanges, transfers of technology, and cultural exchanges, including the spread of ideas, ideals, ideologies, religious faiths, and cultural traditions. These processes do not respect national frontiers or even geographical, linguistic, or cultural boundaries. Rather, they work their effects on large transregional, transcultural, and global scales. In combination, they have profoundly influenced both the experiences of individual societies and the development of the larger world as a whole. If one of the goals of professional historical scholarship is to understand the world and its development through time, these processes demand historians' attention alongside the experiences of national communities and nation-states.

The turn toward the global in the form of the new world history has become an essential perspective for contemporary thinking about the past. While recognizing that local communities and national states have figured as crucial contexts of all peoples' historical experiences, this project makes it possible to bring historical focus also to large-scale, transregional, globalizing processes that have touched many peoples and profoundly influenced the development of individual societies as well as the world as a whole. Networks of cross-cultural interaction, communication, and exchange, after all, are defining contexts of human experience just as surely as are the myriad local communities and nation-states that scholars have conventionally accepted as the default categories of historical analysis. The challenge for the new world historians is to clear paths leading beyond assumptions that European modernity is the appropriate standard for the measurement of all the world's societies, beyond notions that the world is a site divided naturally into national spaces, and beyond temptations to take refuge in the individual histories of local communities as the only knowable subjects of history.

In the volume that follows, world historians take up this challenge in four groups of essays on salient topics in the new world history. The first group deals with the most basic conceptual issues of the new world history—theories of historical development, frameworks of time and space, the constructs of modernity and globalization, and the analytical tools that new world historians have inherited or devised. A second group turns attention to the most prominent themes that world historians have explored on a transregional and global basis—the natural environment, settled agriculture, nomadic pastoralism, states and state formation, gender, religion, technology, and science. Essays in the third group focus on more or less discrete processes that have worked their effects on large scales—large-scale migrations, cross-cultural trade, industrialization, biological diffusions, cultural exchanges, and campaigns of imperial expansion in pre-modern as well as modern times. The book closes with a final group of essays that locate the major world regions in global historical perspective—by tracing the distinctive lines of development within particular geographical and cultural regions while also taking note of the links connecting individual regions to others in the larger world. In combination, the essays in this volume represent contributions to the understanding of the global past from fresh perspectives, and they reflect both the creativity and the vitality of the new world history.

NOTES

1. Jerry H. Bentley, 'The New World History,' in Lloyd Kramer and Sarah Maza, eds., *A Companion to Western Historical Thought* (Oxford: Blackwell, 2002), 393–416.

2. Georg G. Iggers and Q. Edward Wang, *A Global History of Modern Historiography* (London: Pearson, 2008), 19–68.

3. For a statement along these lines, see Ashis Nandy, 'History's Forgotten Doubles,' in Philip Pomper, Richard H. Elphick, and Richard T. Vann, eds., *World History: Ideologies, Structures, and Identities* (Malden, Mass.: Blackwell, 1998), 159–78; and the critique in Jerry H. Bentley, 'Myths, Wagers, and Some Moral Implications of World History,' *Journal of World History* 16 (2005), 72–6.

4. Michael Adas, *Machines as the Measure of Men: Science, Technology, and Ideologies of Western Dominance* (Ithaca, N.Y.: Cornell University Press, 1989).

5. Georg Wilhelm Friedrich Hegel, *The Philosophy of History*, trans. by J. Sibree (New York: Dover, 1956), quoting from 79–102. Cf. slightly different formulations of these points in the more recent translation of Hegel's *Lectures on the Philosophy of World History*, trans. by H.B. Nisbet (Cambridge: Cambridge University Press, 1975), 152–96.

6. Robert A. McCaughey, *International Studies and Academic Enterprise: A Chapter in the Enclosure of American Learning* (New York: Columbia University Press, 1984).

7. The quotation is from Hugh Trevor-Roper, *The Rise of Christian Europe* (London: Harcourt, Brace, and World, 1965), 9.

8. Leopold von Ranke, 'Preface to Universal History (1880),' in Georg G. Iggers and Konrad von Moltke, eds., *Leopold von Ranke: The Theory and Practice of History* (Indianapolis, Ind.: Bobbs-Merrill, 1973), 160–4. See also Michael Harbsmeier, 'World Histories before Domestication: The Writing of Universal Histories, Histories of Mankind and World Histories in Late Eighteenth Century Germany,' *Culture and History* 5 (1989), 93–131; and Martin W. Lewis and Kären E. Wigen, *The Myth of Continents: A Critique of Metageography* (Berkeley: University of California Press, 1997), 106–15.

9. Adas, *Machines as the Measure of Men*, 133–270; Jürgen Osterhammel, '"Peoples without History" in British and German Historical Thought,' in Benedikt Stuchtey and Peter Wende, eds., *British and German Historiography, 1750–1950: Traditions, Perceptions, and Transfers* (Oxford, 2000), 265–87; Bruce Mazlish, *Civilization and Its Contents* (Stanford, Cal.: Stanford University Press, 2004).

10. For a single pointed critique out of many that might be cited, see Steven Feierman, 'African Histories and the Dissolution of World History,' in Robert H. Bates, V.Y. Mudimbe, and Jean O'Barr, eds., *Africa and the Disciplines: The Contributions of Research in Africa to the Social Sciences and Humanities* (Chicago: University of Chicago Press, 1993), 167–212.

11. Dipesh Chakrabarty, 'Postcoloniality and the Artifice of History: Who Speaks for "Indian" Pasts?,' *Representations* 37 (1992), 1–26, quoting from 1, 19. Chakrabarty later modified these views and sought to salvage historical scholarship through the project of 'provincializing Europe.' See Dipesh Chakrabarty, *Provincializing Europe: Postcolonial Thought and Historical Difference* (Princeton, N.J.: Princeton University Press, 2000), quoting from 27, 41.

12. Alongside Chakrabarty, see also the critiques of Eurocentric historiography by Samir Amin, *Eurocentrism*, trans. by R. Moore (New York: Monthly Review Press, 1989); and

Arif Dirlik, 'Is There History after Eurocentrism? Globalism, Postcolonialism, and the Disavowal of History,' *Cultural Critique* 42 (1999), 1–34.

13. Siep Stuurman, 'Herodotus and Sima Qian: History and the Anthropological Turn in Ancient Greece and Han China,' *Journal of World History* 19:1 (2008), 1–40.

14. Marnie Hughes-Warrington, 'Coloring Universal History: Robert Benjamin Lewis's *Light and Truth* (1843) and William Wells Brown's *The Black Man* (1863),' *Journal of World History* 20:1 (2009), 99–130; David Kopf, 'A Look at Nehru's *World History* from the Dark Side of Modernity,' *Journal of World History* 2:1 (1991), 47–63; Paul Costello, *World Historians and Their Goals: Twentieth-Century Answers to Modernism* (DeKalb, Ill.: Northern Illinois University Press, 1993).

15. Leopold von Ranke, 'A Dialogue on Politics (1836),' in Iggers and von Moltke, eds., *Leopold von Ranke: The Theory and Practice of History*, 119.

16. Peter Novick, *That Noble Dream: The 'Objectivity Question' and the American Historical Profession* (Cambridge: Cambridge University Press, 1988), 27.

17. See Prasenjit Duara, *Rescuing History from the Nation: Questioning Narratives of Modern China* (Chicago: University of Chicago Press, 1995).

18. For examples of states' contributions to the emerging discipline of history, see G. P. Gooch, *History and Historians in the Nineteenth Century* (Boston: Beacon, 1959); Felix Gilbert, 'European and American Historiography,' in John Higham, Leonard Krieger, and Felix Gilbert, eds., *History* (Englewood Cliffs, N.J.: Prentice-Hall, 1965), 315–87; and William R. Keylor, *Academy and Community: The Foundation of the French Historical Profession* (Cambridge, Mass.: Harvard University Press, 1975).

19. R. Bin Wong, *China Transformed: Historical Change and the Limits of European Experience* (Ithaca, N.Y.: Cornell University Press, 1998).

20. Jack Goody, *The Theft of History* (Cambridge, 2006).

21. Sanjay Subrahmanyam, 'Connected Histories: Notes toward a Reconfiguration of Early Modern Eurasia,' in Victor Lieberman, ed., *Beyond Binary Histories: Re-Imagining Eurasia to c.1830* (Ann Arbor, Mich.: University of Michigan Press, 1999), 289–316; and *Explorations in Connected History* (New Delhi: Oxford University Press, 2004).

22. Chakrabarty, *Provincializing Europe*.

23. Kenneth Pomeranz, *The Great Divergence: China, Europe, and the Making of the Modern World Economy* (Princeton, N.J.: Princeton University Press, 2000).

24. C. A. Bayly, *The Birth of the Modern World, 1780–1914: Global Connections and Comparisons* (Oxford: Blackwell, 2004).

25. Jean-François Lyotard, *The Postmodern Condition: A Report on Knowledge*, trans. by G. Bennington and B. Massumi (Minneapolis, Minn.: University of Minnesota Press, 1984), xxiv.

26. Feierman, African Histories and the Dissolution of World History.

27. Clifford Geertz, *The Interpretation of Cultures* (New York: Basic Books, 1977); and *Local Knowledge: Further Essays in Interpretive Anthropology* (New York: Basic Books, 1985); and Edward Muir and Guido Ruggiero, eds., *Microhistory and the Lost Peoples of Europe* (Baltimore, Md.: Johns Hopkins University Press, 1991).

28. Fernando Coronil, 'Can Postcoloniality Be Decolonized? Imperial Banality and Postcolonial Power,' *Public Culture* 5 (1992), 89–108, quoting from 99–100. For a similar assessment see Arif Dirlik, *The Postcolonial Aura* (Boulder, Colo.: Westview, 1997).

29. Bentley, 'The New World History'.

References

BAYLY, C. A. *The Birth of the Modern World, 1780–1914: Global Connections and Comparisons*. Oxford: Blackwell, 2004.

BENTLEY, JERRY H. 'The New World History,' in Lloyd Kramer and Sarah Maza, eds., *A Companion to Western Historical Thought*. Oxford: Blackwell, 2002, 393–416.

——. 'World History and Grand Narrative,' in Benedikt Stuchtey and Eckhardt Fuchs, eds., *Writing World History, 1800–2000*. Oxford: Oxford University Press, 2003, 47–65.

——. 'Myths, Wagers, and Some Moral Implications of World History,' *Journal of World History* 16 (2005), 51–82.

CHAKRABARTY, DIPESH. *Provincializing Europe: Postcolonial Thought and Historical Difference*. Princeton, N.J.: Princeton University Press, 2000.

DUARA, PRASENJIT. *Rescuing History from the Nation: Questioning Narratives of Modern China*. Chicago: University of Chicago Press, 1995.

IGGERS, GEORG G., and KONRAD VON MOLTKE, eds. *Leopold von Ranke: The Theory and Practice of History*. Indianapolis, Ind.: Bobbs-Merrill, 1973.

——. and Q. EDWARD WANG. *A Global History of Modern Historiography*.London: Pearson, 2008.

POMERANZ, KENNETH. *The Great Divergence: China, Europe, and the Making of the Modern World Economy*. Princeton, N.J.: Princeton University Press, 2000.

SUBRAHMANYAM, SANJAY. 'Connected Histories: Notes toward a Reconfiguration of Early Modern Eurasia,' in Victor Lieberman, ed., *Beyond Binary Histories: Re-Imagining Eurasia to c.1830*. Ann Arbor, Mich.: University of Michigan Press, 1999, 289–316.

WONG, R. BIN. *China Transformed: Historical Change and the Limits of European Experience*. Ithaca, N.Y.: Cornell University Press, 1998.

PART I

CONCEPTS

CHAPTER 1

··

THEORIES OF WORLD HISTORY SINCE THE ENLIGHTENMENT

··

MICHAEL BENTLEY

World history all but repudiates theorizing, just as it readily invites reflection on its grand, even metahistorical meaning.

(Raymond Grew)[1]

THE problem facing us is that theorizing about world history often remains under the blanket of a seemingly empirical narrative and that the investigation of it implies the scanning of hundreds of such narratives. It follows that its story cannot be told in a short introduction to the subject as a continuous chronology. In order to illuminate at least some of its more important twists, the best plan may be to present, not an outline of developments which would require an unmanageable account of authors taking the enquiry further through their own writing about specific aspects, but rather a series of snapshots aimed at clarifying the half-dozen major moods and 'turns' that have played an important part in transforming a subject which the eighteenth century invented into one that it would no longer recognize. The typology that follows is my own and may cut across those of others. Its various segments should be seen as progressive through time but overlapping *in* time rather than successive stages of an evolution. In our own postmodern culture fragments of all of them still survive together as if to heed Ernst Bloch's celebrated warning about *die Ungleichzeitigkeit der Gleichzeitigen*, the fundamental non-simultaneity of phenomena that appear simultaneous.

Universal History

This is the earliest frame into which world history may be inserted, and it took its shape originally not so much from the world as a universal as from the idea of a universal church which brought known cultures under the common rubric of Christendom, no one more so than Bishop Bossuet in his *Universal History* of 1681. Indeed it is crucial to understand that the opposite of 'universal' in this context did not reside in the local as an index of space but in the *particular* as an object of historical method and one that encompassed space, time, and subject-matter. Both the Baron Turgot and Voltaire lunged at Bossuet in a magnificent but misguided *ignoratio elenchi*. Turgot, the better critic, declared that 'Universal History encompasses a consideration of the successive advances of the human race, and the elaboration of the causes which have contributed to it'[2]—a thought that prompted ideas about all the human race, not just European Catholics, and suggested that history might become a systematic enquiry. Voltaire lambasted Bossuet for having failed to accomplish what he had never set out to do. 'This great writer,' always an ominous opening from Voltaire, 'takes but a slight notice of the Arabians who founded so potent an empire and so flourishing a religion; he makes mention of them as a swarm of barbarians. He expatiates on the Egyptians; but he is silent on the Indians and the Chinese, nations as ancient at least, and as considerable as the people of Egypt.'[3] But not as considerable as the people of Europe. Indeed, in his determination to encompass the world, Voltaire gets rid of China, India, Persia, and Islam in the first sixty pages and his five pages on India lack a certain sympathy for a people who have always lived in 'licentiousness & effeminacy.'[4] Nevertheless these critiques marked a shift in the idea of what a universal history might contain. Eric Voegelin pointed out many years ago that the idea of a 'comprehensive interpretation of man in society and history' did not exist before 1700 and that an accommodation with the New World and the more prominent contact with Asian cultures would be part of creating it.[5] No less a part was an attack on clericalism and the thought-control of the universal church. Together these initiatives rolled into a series of histories and sub-theoretical reflections that dominated the last thirty years of the eighteenth century from the writings of the Parisian encyclopaedists to the sparkling acidities of Edward Gibbon in London and Lausanne or the thoughtful proclamations of Scottish *literati* from William Robertson to David Hume, Adam Ferguson to Adam Smith. Very often these treatises did not set out to depict 'world history' in any form that modernity might think worthy of the name, but they regularly brought to all history a series of implied recommendations that colored the way in which the universal history would be conceived for the generations that followed.

What color did they lend? It is important to avoid a reduction to caricature but, no less urgent for our purpose, to think across these texts and to identify a few of their common characteristics. Perhaps three stand out. Enlightened historians concerned themselves, first, with the idea of *progress* and saw history, properly defined, as supplying the evidence of its transmission; they conceived of the sequence of cultures and civilizations, second, as *stadial* in its nature; and they placed on the historian, finally, the duty of *utility* to the reader as citizen.

Progress, in its Enlightenment formulation, did not have a spatial character, but it carried spatial implications. Dedicated to the unstoppable march of intellect and the enrichment of *l'esprit humain* as a cosmic process, the idea helped indicate which peoples and places were in the lead and which lagged behind. Europe, with Paris as its pinnacle, stood at the center of the world simply because it seemed the most 'advanced' in the progress towards enlightened civilization. Other parts of the known world were not intrinsically inferior, but they required the hand of civilization to lead them forward, and universal history showed that process unfolding:

> With the passing of time new peoples came into being. In the course of the unequal progress of nations, the civilized peoples, surrounded by barbarians, now conquer-ing, now conquered, intermingled with them. Whether the latter received from the former their arts and their laws together with servitude, or whether as conquerors they yielded to the natural empire of reason and culture over brute force, the bounds of barbarism steadily retreated.[6]

> (Turgot)

But the natural empire of reason would not emerge from a history of mere war and bloodshed: one had to move the emphasis to higher regions of progress in order, as the Göttingen historian August Ludwig von Schlözer put it, to 'perceive with enlighten-ment that greater revolutions have more often resulted from the quiet musings of the genius and the gentle virtue of wisdom than from the violence of all-powerful tyrants.'[7] So when, in the second Paris of Europe, Alexander Fraser Tytler pondered what to teach his students in the University of Edinburgh in the 1780s, his thoughts ran to a course of lectures on universal history with the express object of 'exhibit[ing] a progressive view of the state of mankind' which would assuredly explain the origins of states and empires but then go on 'to bestow attention particularly on the manners of nations, their laws, the nature of their government, their intellectual improvements, and progress in the arts and sciences.'[8] If non-European peoples came badly out of the exercise, they could look forward to doing better as progress marched in their direction.

That uneven march showed that societies made their way towards modernity in a series of stages that could be illuminated in a study of their languages and texts. No one made so stadial a picture of universal history as the Marquis de Condorcet, who chopped up the known past into three large slices: a pre-civilized period which came to an end with the ability to communicate through language; a second advance in which other arts developed and which culminated in the emergence of alphabetic script; and then an enormous swathe from the classical Greeks to modern France. He then subdivided his three slices, each into a further three, giving him stopping-off points at pastoralism, agriculture, Alexander and his discoveries, science, the crusades, printing, and the throwing off of the church as a constraint on the human mind.[9] Unlike the sublimely complacent Chevalier de Méhégan, who had seen no point in wasting time in his history on 'la Chine, le Japon, la grande Tartarie, les Indes' since they did not, as it seemed to him, touch on European experience,[10] Condorcet included the world in his mental frame but envisaged its forward motion at different speeds. Unlike Gibbon, who reassured his readers he would not require them to contemplate Byzantium except as it affected Europe and that the 'obscure interval' from the seventh to the eleventh century could be rapidly elided,[11] Condorcet gave full measure to his contrived steps towards the progress of mankind. This did not impede his patronizing disdain for those slow in the race, to be sure, but universal history meant what it said and countenanced a geography more expansive than traditional Christian histories had envisaged.

Utility, finally, came in the train of progress, enlightenment, and secularization. History should teach what was useful to man; and because man had to be understood as a phenomenon strengthening through space and time, it should instruct in the lessons of becoming a good person. Bossuet's idea of utility—the one echoed by his disciple Méhégan as knowing those parts of the past that helped readers espouse true religion and avoid false teaching[12]—went under the wheels of an aggressive anticlericalism and became a very different form of usefulness. 'The value of any science,' ran the argument in Edinburgh, 'is to be estimated according to its tendency to furnish improvement, either in private virtue, or in those talents which render man useful in society....'[13] Virtue (not religion) and utility as a social function shifted the argument about world history to a new place: it became no mere indulgence to study world civilizations but rather part of the road to becoming truly civilized oneself. The problem about so conceiving it became apparent only as the strength of the state as a social form came to dominate both present and past. During the nineteenth century— the age of state, capitalism, and empire—the terms of this 'universal history' underwent a transformation that could not be seen in 1780. The name remained, but what it connoted underwent irreversible change, and it may assist clarity to think of two modes of thought that supplanted it and which existed in nervous parallel. One of them took its inspiration from the doctrines of philosophical Idealism and saw world history as a vast conceptual speculation; the other grounded itself in a view of the world as a sphere of European domination. Both modes had their origins in German culture.

WELTGESCHICHTE

Some commentators prefer to fuse this mood with the universal history that preceded it, but it is better isolated as a nineteenth-century disposition. Drawing on a critique of Enlightenment assumptions associated with Johann Gottfried von Herder and Georg Wilhelm Friedrich Hegel, the pursuit of *Weltgeschichte* gathered strength from the rise of great powers as both a reality and aspiration, and it became characterized by an emphatic *Eurocentrism* and *imperialism* tainted by racial and cultural stereotyping of parts of the world that did not fit into the Western political order; and a justificatory *liberal theory* that deprecated difference and promoted homogeneity. The cohering of provinces and principalities and lands historically disunited into new states, each with a nationalist discourse about its origins and destiny, created the need for a usable past that legitimated the current process of state-formation; and since the historical profession in most Western countries advanced in tandem with state-formation, so the message of historical writing adopted a concern with the nation as a unit and the state as its higher representation. It reached intellectual distinction in the work of Germany's greatest historian, Leopold von Ranke (1795–1886) whose own, unfinished *Universal History* represents a high-water-mark. A second thread in this German development, the idea of *speculative world history*, began not with territories and *Weltpolitik* but rather with a sense of the past as a cumulative process tending towards a higher present, not through the advance of reason in its Parisian form but though a redefinition of reason that made history its vehicle, the world its other self and the state its highest expression. Here the line of development in world history became a retrospectively-imposed shape which might become an ascending spiral, as in Hegel, or a series of loops through which cultures rose and fell with a depressing inevitability, as in Oswald Spengler, or a progressive outline, as in the later visions of the man most influenced by Spengler, the English commentator Arnold Toynbee.

The first thread in this discourse concerned the burgeoning power of European states, and this had important implications for the theory of *Weltgeschichte* that considerations of space prevent us from following here. A second thread—that of speculative shaping of the past—differed from its grounded partner in leaving the ground at once to announce a theory. If Hegel were the progenitor of *Weltgeschichte* in its first sense, then another Hegel must also come into view—the creator of dialectical idealism. The state appeared under this rubric as it did under the other; but it emerged not as a constellation of government or power but, in Hegel's vocabulary, as 'the Idea of Spirit in the external manifestation of human Will and its Freedom.'[14] This deeply metaphysical understanding took its nature from the Hegelian insistence that reason and world have always been engaged in a process of mutual becoming and that the end of that process will be a condition in which actuality becomes rational and reason actuality. The driving force of the process was *Geist*—Spirit—which had 'the History of the World for its theater, its possession, and the sphere of its realization.'[15] Consequently, world history in Hegelian theory takes its shape from the cosmic vision that underlies it and the brilliant new mechanism that explains all change: thesis leading to a necessary antithesis and of both then becoming *aufgehoben* (literally 'raised') to a higher synthesis which will in turn become its own thesis and begin the dialectic over again until history's plan were fulfilled. It found its fulfillment in the Prussian state, Hegel believed, and so history had come to an end before his death in 1831. A philosophical world history, which was his project, existed only to show how that end had come about. It started in Persia (a synthesis of the characteristics of China and India); it progressed through the Greek world (democracy) and the Roman (despotism) which synthesized in aristocracy.[16] Every development after that plays its part in bringing about a Germanic world—not a German one—which is the building block of civilization, 'the Spirit of the new World.' What matters in that world is the emergence of a cultural dialectic that directs modernity, one traveling from *schwebende Unbildsamkeit* through *beschränkte Bildsamkeit* to the goal of *unbeschränkte Bildsamkeit*:[17] all else falls away.

When the young Karl Marx famously turned Hegel's system 'downside up' and replaced a dialectical idealism with its less metaphysical partner, dialectical materialism, he too implied a vision of world history in which much of the globe would remain of little interest. Territories became categories as they had for Hegel, but the predictor of the category into which they would fall was their mode of economic production rather than their potential for advancing Spirit. Once defined as an Asiatic mode of production, for example, the history of Asia became ironed out into an ideal type as Asia waited for economic dynamics to urge its societies, 'even the most barbarian,' toward the 'civilization' that attached to later phases.[18] Interest inevitably focused, therefore, on those later phases when a bourgeois mode of production 'created a world after its own image'[19] and on the frictions and contradictions that ultimately would produce the Communist vision of a new world order. This impression of world history is no longer one sustained by Marxist scholars, as we shall see, but the grounding of world history in its economic sub-structures remains a persistent theme.

Both of these strains—the Hegelian and Marxist—have a presence in the following century, but the Hegelian version in particular supplied electricity to theorists of world history in two generations of commentators after 1870. Within Germany the figures of Friedrich Nietzsche and Oswald Spengler command instant attention, despite their eccentric understanding of an historical process resting on recurrence. Neither wrote a *Weltgeschichte*: indeed neither claimed to be an historian. Nietzsche (1844–1900) brought a philosophical intensity to human experience that rivaled Hegel's. Spengler (1880–1936) was a half-mad schoolmaster given to prophecy. Yet both created an image of what it meant to think about the history of everything, one against which historians would react with great violence over the next century. Nietzsche was much the more important thinker, but his contribution to world history followed only from his essay on the use and abuse of history in his *Untimely Meditations*, where he called for an end to 'world-process' and the need for an heroic history based on life.[20] In Spengler, who would certainly have read him, Nietzsche's recommendation that history be left to those who have the genius to envision it certainly rang true and licensed one of the most remarkable cultural productions of the early twentieth century: Spengler's two volumes on *The Decline of the West*, mostly written before World War I though published later.[21] The vision of a West in terminal decline was made to appear a conclusion rather than a point of departure. Spengler's mission lay rather in proving three propositions: that everything in human experience is related to everything else; that this nexus creates coherent cultures whose history demonstrates a recurrent pattern of rise and fall; and that all cultures are unstable and degenerate into their bastardized, effeminate forms as 'civilizations' before toppling back into anarchy. World history becomes a Catherine-wheel which always spins on the same nail, turning downwards always through the poison of civilization.[22] None of this makes for happiness, and Spengler was an unhappy man. But despite the signs of mental imbalance in his approach to the history of the world, his propositions about the need to identify relations—between a culture's architecture and its mathematics, its religion and its dress, its domesticity and its art, and so on—have become an imperative of cultural history a century later. His disservice, in the eyes of later historians, lay rather in a procrustean bed of categories into which he forced a limited amount of empirical evidence about past cultures in order to make a pattern emerge that suited his argument and temperament.

In 1920 Spengler's book was handed by Lewis Namier to his friend Arnold Toynbee (1889–1975), who became captivated by the sheer scale of the thought in it. But Spengler was no historian: he had studied mathematics and natural sciences. Toynbee conceived the plan of bringing a historical mind and method to some of the insights that he believed Spengler had achieved. The result, *A Study of History*, his 'nonsense book' as he called it, would occupy twelve volumes between 1934 and 1961 and make Toynbee a titanic figure in Anglophone historiography, for all the contempt, and eventually ridicule, that settled on his venture. Like Spengler, Toynbee thought that he could see cyclical patterns of rise and fall in past cultures and reduce the whole of world history to a manageable number of civilizations. He rejected Spengler's dismissal of civilization as a category and saw it rather as a high-point of human achievement. A few devices helped predict which civilizations would survive and how they would flourish—'challenge and response,' 'withdrawal and return'—and he saw a common way of death in each as a 'proletariat,' previously excluded from control of a civilization, became capable of overmastering the civilized elite and ruining its constructions: a thought that obviously bore some relation to Soviet experience in the interwar period. Unlike Spengler, however, he came to think that not all perished in each of these Armageddons. Some form of organized religion, a generic 'universal church'—persisted and became the germ of the next civilization. So in his later volumes Toynbee offered a progressive account of civilization that became a vehicle 'borne along on wheels that turn monotonously round and round.'[23]

What divided Spengler and Toynbee became more important than their similarities. Spengler made no direct impact on world history as a genre; Toynbee dominated it for a generation. Spengler invented implausible categories to make his account hold together; Toynbee at least affected to think inductively. Nor did they share a similar fate. Spengler lived into the Nazi years and saw them as the inevitable outcome of the processes he had discussed. Toynbee, by contrast, lived through the era of historiographical modernism and became one of its earliest victims, only to enjoy a posthumous revival in the postmodern environment.

Modernism

While the twin supports of *Weltgeschichte*—a great power perspective and a penchant for speculative models of the historical process—confirmed a need for world history, a third element in the nineteenth-century intellectual environment militated against it. In Germany, where it began, it became known as *Historismus*, later confusingly translated into English as 'historicism.'[24] And the undertow of this idea, that history should concern itself with the precise, the detailed, the specific, and by implication the *confined*, pulled against the vast visions of *Weltgeschichte*. So long as those visions retained their attraction for capturing universal essences—the ambition of Ranke and his generation—the subversion of *Historismus* could be neglected. But with the development of a more scientific ethos in the humanities, a more austere understanding of the subject surfaced: one that that would deflate the pretensions of world history and redescribe it as a place of prophets and seers. This mood of criticism became especially powerful in the Anglophone world, moreover, which gave it special leverage because of the prestige that British, and increasingly American, scholarship had attained by the turn of the century.[25] We have no word for this constellation of theories and doctrines surrounding how history should be written in a self-conscious modern age. I have elsewhere called it 'modernism' and repeat the usage here to denote a significant ideal type in the history of modern historiography.[26] Modernist history admired parts of the Rankean heritage: its source-criticism and its narrative rigor. It did not admire Ranke's universal side. It partially admired English Whig authors of the second and third generations (S. R. Gardiner, C. H. Firth) for revising the romanticism of Thomas Babington Macaulay and Thomas Carlyle, which it emphatically did not admire. But it especially admired Frederic William Maitland and the forensic forms of legal and constitutional history that he inspired. One result of these moods affected the status of world history. Better to study the detailed history of a single state, its constitution, its parliaments, its governance (and that over a restricted period), than to make wild comparisons between states or to indulge in windy speculation about patterns in the history of the West, not to mention interactions with other parts of the globe. When the historical community acquired the *English Historical Review* (1886) and the *American Historical Review* (1895), global conjectures acquired a new enemy.

Between the two world wars modernism's self-image as the arbiter of historical truth and method became close to hegemonic, and its greatest victim turned out to be a man who had thought himself one of its exemplars. Few scholars suffered so much criticism in this new environment as Arnold Toynbee. There existed good grounds for attacking Toynbee, to be sure, for the rigidity of his concepts and his failure to import into his system a more sophisticated understanding of, for example, what it was to be a nation, a criticism noted by the significant Spanish philosopher José Ortega y Gasset.[27] Yet the modernist offensive concerned not the use of particular concepts but the employment of concepts at all: history must proceed by induction and learn its ideas from its sources. Devastating invigilation of Toynbee's *Study of History* made it a flawed attempt to force empirical evidence into spaces where it would not fit in order to satisfy a predetermined schema. One historian's love–hate relationship with Toynbee appeared in the writing of the Dutchman, Pieter Geyl, who entered into robust dialogue with his victim in *Debates with Historians* (1955) and elsewhere.[28] Perhaps the most lethal, because the most considered, of these judgments came rather from Richard Pares, the distinguished historian of the eighteenth century, who himself had written studies that ranged across oceans and knew something of the difficulties involved.

'Readers must decide for themselves,' he wrote, 'whether this is superstition or science; I can only avow my conviction that an attempt to establish laws, or statistical general-izations, about so small a number as twenty-odd imaginary entities . . . was foredoomed to failure.'[29] Whatever else he may have claimed to be, Toynbee had lost the title of historian. He himself was hurt and perplexed by the violence used against him, but he expressed his dismay, significantly, in modernist terms rather than in denial of them. Just as Marx refused to be thought of as a 'Marxist,' so Toynbee felt a similar resistance, as he wrote towards the end of his life in an important letter to Herbert Butterfield:

> As for as my own 'generalist' theories I am not, myself, a 'Toynbeean'. I mean, I do not take them as dogmas but simply as mental tools for trying to shape a structure for looking at the World's history as a unity in an age in which—so I guess—we shall have to become one family or else liquidate ourselves.[30]

Toynbee

He saw his mental tools as 'just one provisional shot' rather than a cast-iron theory. The postmodern world would listen; but Toynbee himself died without the satisfaction of knowing that he had reached an audience.

Already, however, modernism had moved closer to his conspectus even as it denied its legitimacy. For if World War I had helped generate the theories about method that restricted world-historical writing, then World War II helped loosen them in at least two ways. It bequeathed a world in which Marxists could find a respectable home. And in strengthening the credentials of the *Annales*—a radical movement in French social history revolving around the journal of that name—it catapulted Fernand Braudel (1902–85) to a position of world leadership in historical studies.[31] Marxism would later play a crucial role in fomenting postcolonial theories of world history, as we shall see. Braudel's drive to expand the boundaries of the subject (as much a geographical ambition as a disciplinary one) invigorated an empirical world history that took seriously the claims of Asia, Africa, and Latin America as significant historical cultures.

There is a certain paradox in this modernist movement after 1945. For it was one of Toynbee's own disciples, the Canadian William H. McNeill (who had been born in the same year as Eric Hobsbawm, 1917), who emerged from wartime experience wanting to move forward the frontiers of world history but in a way different from those suggested by Toynbee. Rather than confront modernist assumptions by writing a conceptual history, McNeill began at the other end by writing a world history designed to show that world history could be written in a modernist method like any other kind. *The Rise of the West* (1963) spoke to its own era by making Western civilization the motor of world development; but it also made a major statement about the ambitions of world history as an emancipated form of enquiry.[32] McNeill's own *World History* came much later and addressed different imperatives.[33] It was *The Rise of the West* which, for all its Eurocentrism and over-comfortable assumptions about Western supremacy, stimu-lated scholars who without it may never have turned to world history as an academic, rather than prophetic, engagement. Witness the remarkable 'turn' in the career of the Oxford historian, John Roberts. Always preoccupied by the larger questions in

European history, Roberts widened his lens appreciably after the mid-1970s to produce histories of the world for both Hutchinson and Penguin but more importantly, from the point of view of audience, a very successful television series in *The Triumph of the West* in 1985. He brought to these tasks a conventional Oxford training and no hint of Toynbeean excess. Together, he and McNeill, to whom Roberts had shown himself deeply indebted, transformed modernist appreciation of world history and made those interested in studying it appear less eccentric within the academy.[34]

In remembering the strength of this tendency, we do well to recall its theoretical limitations when seen through the eyes of a later generation. Theory, to begin with, remained a silent presence within this corpus of writing, leaving open spaces for cultural conditioning to dress up 'common-sense' and ingrained epistemological assumptions as though they were inevitable devices for packaging the past. Where the unspoken made most noise was in a sense that the *problem* of world history lay in explaining European dominance and the global reach of its superior technologies.[35] There was little questioning of the degree to which that dominance was mixed with, and partly dependent on, the experience of other cultures. Non-Western territories came into the story as necessary but subordinate elements, pulled along by the master-wheel of Western precocity. A second and deeper constituent hung on Toynbee's word 'structures.' These initiatives in theorizing world history ran parallel with the development of a structural anthropology and sociology (not to mention some styles of Marxism that adopted a structuralist model) and formal training in modernist historical method did little to reduce its impact on world history. The field denoted was simply too big, historians argued, to avoid major boxes and categories in which to contain a manageable past; and if 'challenge and response' or 'withdrawal and return' no longer seemed sustainable through empirical enquiry, then at least the idea of *some* organizing schema that could live with the presuppositions of modernist historiography seemed unavoidable. So when, from the mid-1970s, history took its turn towards a 'post-structural' epistemology that wanted to remove some of the corseting of modernist method and address itself to the history of plural discourses about past cultures, world history began again to look exposed and *démodée*. Some of its tendencies survived. The *Journal of World History* brought to the 1990s a language about cultural interpenetration that turned on the idea of 'encounters' of the sort portrayed by Eric Wolf, and the journal's editor, Jerry H. Bentley, and contributors have persisted with an implied theory of modernism that sometimes de-problematizes the fundamental issue of what it is to write world history. Some other tendencies have not survived, however, the aggression of postmodern and postcolonial theory.

POSTMODERNISM AND POSTCOLONIALISM

These critiques of modernism do not amount to the same thing but it is fair to argue that the first has functioned as a precondition for the second and that both have brought a range of implications to the study of world history. Decolonization after World War II naturally produced its own modernist histories—many of them distinguished—but the demands of a deep-structured postcolonialism ran far beyond offering accounts, however embarrassed, of colonial rule. At stake within this sensibility is a complexity of concepts that display not only the practices of colonial exploitation or aggrandizement but also (and more tellingly) the epistemologies that underlay claims to hegemony on the part of imperial cultures. Before postcolonialism could acquire that disclosure it required an epistemology of its own that transcended the presentation of the world as a transparent entity, as modernism had tended to assume, and reposition the nature of knowledge(s) in ways that helped understand the enduring quality of the colonial condition. It needed not merely an account of colonies and metropoles but a depiction and explanation of *coloniality* as a mental frame.[36] Postmodernism did not of itself provide it; but the questions posed by the postmodern mood in the humanities after 1975 destabilized existing certainties about what a history could produce and implied a need to 'decenter' Western discourses in order to create space for other voices in the world. As the American theorist Bruce Mazlish observes, 'we have moved towards postmodernism's privileging of heterogeneity, fragmentation, and indeterminacy, with an accompanying distrust of universalizing or "totalizing" discourse and a concern for the validity and dignity of the "other."'[37] This alterity might call for investigation within conventionally-focused historical studies, encouraging narratives of minorities or the neglected. But it could also point to the need for a world history that rejected Eurocentrism, redefined hegemony in ways unknown to *Weltgeschichte*, and concentrated attention on parts of the world—categorial as much as territorial— that previously had been denied a past because of their exclusion from the present. In its so-called 'cultural turn,' moreover, postmodern approaches could revivify the lapsed, highly-modernist project of Karl Lamprecht and create a global cultural history that transcended state and nation as its referents.[38]

Inevitably, the power of Marxism played an important role in sharpening the postcolonial critique since it offered, especially through its Gramscian analysis of 'hegemony,'[39] a vocabulary within which to identify burgeoning forms of imperialism inside the folds of a nascent capitalism. One of Braudel's pupils, Immanuel Wallerstein, showed the strength of a Marxist understanding of the early-modern period in his *Modern World-System* that displayed paths of trade and economic encounters, asserting a degree of interdependence within sub-systems that conventional writing had overlooked.[40] More recently Janet Abu-Lhugod has pushed the same logic backwards into the medieval period in a search for similar systems operating at a much earlier phase of their development; she announces the existence of 'an impressive set of interlinked subsystems in Europe, the Middle East (including the northern portion of Africa), and Asia (coastal and steppe zones)' in the thirteenth century.[41] In the postmodern years this *Marxist* perspective has colored much postcolonial writing but with interesting twists. Andrew Sartori's study of Bengali culture, for example, announces a Marxist understanding from the very beginning but speaks about the dialectic of global and local discourses in Bengal in ways that are hard to anticipate without a postmodern epistemology.[42]

Bengal, indeed, has registered itself as a signal energy center for postcolonial historical thought. Four authors of great intellectual power—K. N. Chaudhuri, Ranajit Guha, Dipesh Chakrabarty, and Gayatri Chakravorty Spivak—made a great impression on postcolonial thinking from the 1980s. Chaudhuri's *Asia before Europe* (1990)[43] drew on set theory to validate a different selection of characteristics for comparison in the history of south Asia in order to frame an understanding of Indian history that owed little to Western perspectives. The other three authors collaborated on the most successful historical venture since *Annales*. The first volume of *Subaltern Studies: Writings on South Asian History and Society* first appeared in Delhi in 1982 and launched a series of publications that have gone on to change the landscape of peasant and insurrection studies not merely in India but across the world in its commitment to what the Italian Communist hero Antonio Gramsci had labeled the 'subaltern classes' (in contradistinction to the 'hegemonic classes') and to a methodology that drew especially on indigenous cultural memory and oral discourse. Just as *Annales* gave rise to the Annales School in France, so *Subaltern Studies* has produced a Subaltern School of historiography whose members have a coherent view of how world history might be approached, by bringing, in Edward Said's words, 'hegemonic historiography to crisis.'[44] Marxism of a Gramscian stamp pervades the entire enterprise in a mood of sympathetic criticism and extension, 'arguing with Marx and not against him.'[45] But it also encapsulates postmodern understanding, most particularly in Spivak whose writing veers towards the edge of intelligibility as when she contends that it is unreasonable to ask 'the subaltern' to have a voice because if it did it wouldn't be subaltern, or in her ominous contention that Western academic practice in and of itself produces subalternity in those at whom it is directed.[46] Together, these authors have helped direct a world history that moves beyond an older typology of 'center' (the places that mattered) and 'periphery,' the site of the primitive and dominated. They insist that an acceptable world history will be decentered in its mental categories and global in its territorial compass. Yet by no means all Indian historians feel optimistic about the outcome and share Vinay Lal's anxiety that world historians 'still take as their centrepiece the history of Europe' and 'foreclose . . . those pasts which are resistant to the designs of an encroaching modernity.'[47]

GLOBAL HISTORY: PROSPECT AND CRITIQUE

Theories of world history demonstrate a relationship, inevitably, with the societies and cultural norms that give rise to them. Universal history owed much to the Enlightenment; *Weltgeschichte* provided legitimacy for European domination; the Subaltern School reflected moods following decolonization. After 1989 the collapse of the eastern bloc under Soviet tyranny and the onset of a more pervasive globalization of economies brought another 'advance' in thinking about what a world history ought to involve. Historical 'advances' invite always the danger of Whig assumptions—that the past has always been converging on the present as a force of constant progress towards liberty and enlightenment—and the new force of 'global history' often reads backwards the dynamic of globalization in ways that certainly provoke criticism from skeptics. When did this mode of thought begin? Bruce Mazlish sees its origins in the 1970s (which feels uncomfortable and may be a pre-dating of the phenomenon) but he identifies the issue of chronology persuasively: 'the argument turns on the question of whether enough synergy and synchronicity arises to justify the launch of a new periodization.'[48] For a younger generation of world historians the time had certainly arrived in the 1990s; and evangelism filled the air. The present world became the product of a 'great convergence' of cultures whose history now demanded research with none of the prejudices about territory, race, and power that had disfigured previous attempts.[49] Even William H. McNeill, once an apostle of hard-nosed modernism, turned towards an apocalyptic language resting on 'ecumenes'—places where cultures interacted and mutually absorbed one another.[50] For another writer one had to be ecumenical not only in examining the subject matter but also in academic method. One could only fashion an 'ecumenical history' within 'a more ecumenical scholarly community.'[51]

These epiphanies do not dominate the field but identify an aspiration for the future. In the immediate context of global history, the imperative has turned rather on producing collaborative research that will iron out the discrepancies between Western history and that of the rest of the planet. At the level of historiography rather than substantive history, recent single-volume treatment devotes as much space, for example, to China and India as it does to Western countries.[52] Or one might point to a large-scale collaborative enterprise. *The Oxford History of Historical Writing* intends covering virtually all territories and cultures over the globe in order to eradicate remnants of Eurocentrism in the world's historiographies.[53] On a less planetary scale, meanwhile, a current of investigation has emerged in the idea of *transnational history* which is distinguished by its reluctance to see nation and nationality as the necessary unit of analysis and the extension of its questions across national boundaries in a form of comparative history quite different from the tradition modes of 'international history' or 'international relations.'[54]

Theorizing these developments—they have not been theorized very profoundly—leaves a good deal of space for agnosticism. The language of analysis stresses terms such as 'encounters' and 'contacts' with a view to contending that the world's history reflects integration rather than isolation. The wry humor of Marshall Sahlins evoked the paradox. 'Ironic,' he wrote in 1993, 'that Western social scientists should be elaborating theories of global integration just when this "new world order" is breaking down into so many small-scale separatist movements marching under the banners of cultural autonomy.'[55] But there is a darker methodological worry concerning what counts as integration and the status to be accorded to 'encounters.' William A. Green announces it plangently:

> The burden of proof in these matters rests with the integrationists. They must demonstrate that, from an early time, the destinies of the world's peoples (or at least

some significant portion of the world's peoples) have been linked. It must be shown that engines of change operating globally have been *decisive* in propelling both the rate and direction of change across diverse and distant cultures.[56]

(Green)

This is the aspect of global and transnational history that frequently looks like a problematic searching for a question. We can all agree that it is 'interesting' to examine contacts between societies and civilizations; but a strong case for global perspectives depends on a convincing demonstration of the *function* of those contacts. Declaring a 'system' of relationships is easier than demonstrating one, far less one with explanatory power, outside the now familiar language of trade or economic penetration. On the other hand, the idea of theory itself has come to stay. Sometimes its arrival leaves one wishing that it would go away again for it is often couched in a rebarbative jargon. But only a re-theorizing of the subject of world history—an ongoing and welcome reality in the millennium—will protect it both from its bright-eyed evangelicals and those who continue to believe, as they fly in the face of experience and logic, that empirical 'research', uninformed by penetrating questions and conceptual schemata, will lead to the promised land.

NOTES

1. Raymond Grew, 'Expanding Worlds of World History,' *Journal of Modern History* 78 (2006), 878–98 at 897.
2. 'On Universal History,' in Ronald Meek, ed., *Turgot on Progress, Sociology and Economics* (Cambridge: Cambridge University Press, 1973), 63–118 at 64.
3. *An Essay on Universal History: The Manners, and Spirit of Nations from the Rise of Charlemagne to the Age of Lewis XIV*, translated by Mr. NUGENT (4 vols., 1759), vol. 1, 3.
4. Ibid., 30–5.
5. Eric Voegelin, *From Enlightenment to Revolution* (Durham, N.C.: Duke University Press, 1975), 5.
6. Turgot, 'A philosophical Review of the Successive Advances of the Human Mind,' in Meek, *Turgot on Progress*, 41–62 at 47.
7. Quoted in Peter H. Reill, *The German Enlightenment and the Rise of Historicism* (Berkeley: University of California Press, 1975), 45.
8. *Plan & Outlines of a Course of Lectures on Universal History etc.* (Edinburgh, 1782), 3–4.
9. A. N. de Condorcet, *Sketch for a Historical Picture of the Human Mind* (1955 edn.). He perceived 'an uninterrupted chain between the beginning of historical time and the century in which we live' (8).
10. M. le Chevalier de Méhégan, *Tableau de l'histoire moderne depuis la chute de l'empire occident, jusqu'à la paix de Westphalie*, 3 vols. (Paris, 1766), xxii.
11. *Decline and Fall of the Roman Empire* (ed. Bury), Preface to later volumes, I, x–xi.
12. Méhégan, *Tableau de l'histoire moderne* : 'J'appelle utile aux homes, tout événements qui peut fair connoître la véritable Religion & démasquer les fausses' (vii).
13. Tytler, *Plan & Outlines*, 1.

14. Georg Wilhelm Friedrich Hegel, *The Philosophy of History*, trans. by J. Sibree (New York: Colonial Press, 1899), 47.
15. Hegel, *Philosophy of History*, 54.
16. Hegel, *Philosophy of History*, 174–5, 278–9.
17. Unresolved absence of reflection through restricted reflection to unlimited reflection. This swapping of antithetical characteristics in a new synthesis is Hegel's central mechanism. On its implications, cf. Friedrich Brand, 'Über Hegels Anschauungen zur geographischen Grundlage der Gechichte in seiner Philosophie der Weltgeschichte,' *Geschichte in Wissenschaft und Unterricht* 10 (1965), 611–23 at 619. See in particular Brand's graphic world geography according to Hegel at 615.
18. *The Communist Manifesto*, quoted in Marshall Sahlins, 'Goodbye to *Tristes Tropes*,' *Journal of Modern History* 65 (1993), 1–25 at 2.
19. Sahlins, 'Goodbye to *Tristes Tropes*,' 2.
20. 'If only we did not have to hear that hyperbole of hyperboles, the word "world, world, world" . . . for now the history of humanity is merely the continuation of the history of animals and plants. Indeed, even in the deepest depths of the ocean the historical universalist discovers the traces of himself in living slime.' 'The Utility and Liability of History,' in *Unfashionable Observations* (Stanford: Stanford University Press, 1995), 85–167 at 147. It should be noted that Nietzsche, for all his cosmic tone, addressed himself specifically to the German mind.
21. Oswald Spengler, *Der Untergang des Abendlandes: Umrisse einer Morphologie der Weltgeschichte* (2 vols., Munich, 1918–22).
22. Spengler, *Untergang*, vol. 1, 20–4; 164–220.
23. Arnold Toynbee, *Civilization on Trial* (1948), 15. Cf. David Bebbington, *Patterns in History* (1979), 39.
24. The classic account by Friedrich Meinecke, *Die Enststehung des Historismus* (Berlin, 1936) found a helpful translator who rendered the book *The Rise of Historism*. A subsequent slide away from this usage into the morass of 'historicism' has merged Meinecke's sense of the term with those of Croce and Popper with damage to conceptual clarity. See my entry on 'historicism' for the forthcoming *Encyclopaedia of Political Thought*, ed. Gregory Claeys (forthcoming).
25. For a perspective on these years, see Michael Bentley, 'The Age of Prothero: British Historiography in the Long *fin-de-siècle*, 1870–1920,' *Transactions of the Royal Historical Society*, forthcoming 6th series, 20 (2010), 171–94.
26. See Michael Bentley, *Modernizing England's Past: English Historiography in the Age of Modernism 1870–1970* (Cambridge: Cambridge University Press, 2005).
27. 'una idea de nación tan ridicula e inconsistente e impropria de un hombre de ciencia come la emitida por Toynbee.' 'Una Interpretación de la Historia Universal,' in *Obras completas*, 12 vols. (Madrid, 1946–83), vol. 9, 11–211 at 50.
28. In some lectures delivered in America, Geyl castigated Toynbee's approach as 'a travesty of the scientific method.' 'Toynbee Once More: Empiricist or Aprorism?,' in Pieter Geyl, *From Ranke to Toynbee: Five Lectures on Historians and Historiographical Problems* (Northampton, Mass., 1952), 67–78 at 77.
29. Richard Pares in *English Historical Review* 71 (1956), 256–72 at 272.
30. Toynbee to Butterfield, 24 April 1969, Butterfield MSS 531/T114. Cambridge University Library.

31. Fernand Braudel, *La Méditerranée et le monde méditerranien à l'époque de Philippe II* (Paris, 1949; 2nd edn., 2 vols., Paris, 1966).
32. William H. McNeill, *The Rise of the West: A History of the Human Community* (Chicago: University of Chicago Press, 1963).
33. William H. McNeill, *A World History* (Oxford: Oxford University Press, 1967).
34. Mentioning two scholars as illustrations of a more general tendency inevitably omits a range of important names that emerged after 1980.
35. E. L. Jones, *The European Miracle: Environments, Economies and Geopolitics in the History of Europe and Asia* (Cambridge: Cambridge University Press, 1981).
36. I take the term from Walter D. Mignolo, *Local Histories/Global Designs: Coloniality, Subaltern Knowledges, and Border Thinking* (Princeton: Princeton University Press, 2000).
37. Bruce Mazlish, 'Global History in a Postmodernist Era,' in Bruce Mazlish and Ralph Buultjens, eds., *Conceptualizing Global History* (Boulder, Colo.: Westview, 1993), 113–27 at 116.
38. For critical remarks on Lamprecht's ideas for a cultural *Weltgeschichte*, see Manfred Kossok, 'From Universal History to Global History,' in Mazlish and Buultjens, eds., *Conceptualizing Global History*, 93–111 at 94–5; and Alfred Heuss's recommendations for a modern version in 'Möglichkeiten einer Weltgeschichte heute,' *Saeculum* 19 (1969), 3–29.
39. See, among other sources, Antonio Gramsci, 'State and Civil Society,' in Quintin Hoare and Geoffrey Nowell Smith, eds., *Selections from the Prison Notebooks of Antonio Gramsci* (1971), 210–75 esp. 245–6, 257–64, 269–70.
40. Immanuel Wallerstein, *The Modern World-System*, 3 vols. (New York: Academic Press, 1974–89).
41. Janet Abu-Lughod, *Before European Hegemony: The World System, A.D. 1250–1350* (Oxford: Oxford University Press, 1989), 352.
42. Andrew Sartori, *Bengal in Global Concept History: Culturalism in the Age of Capital* (Chicago: University of Chicago Press, 2008). 'The universalistic categories of capitalist modernity,' Sartori argues, 'do not occupy some global stratosphere that confronts the particularity of regional lifeworld from the outside, but are constituted in dialectical intimacy with those regional peculiarities' (231).
43. K. N. Chaudhuri, *Asia before Europe: Economy and Civilisation of the Indian Ocean from the Rise of Islam to 1750* (Cambridge: Cambridge University Press, 1990) and the review by R. I. Moore, 'World History: World-Economy or a Set of Sets?,' *International Review of Asian Studies* (1993), 99–105.
44. Edward Said, 'Foreword' to Ranajit Guha and Gayatri Chakravorty Spivak, eds., *Selected Subaltern Studies* (Oxford: Oxford University Press, 1988), v–x at vi.
45. Dipesh Chakrabarty, 'Conditions for Knowledge of Working-Class Conditions: Employers, Government and Jute Workers of Calcutta,' in Guha and Spivak, eds., *Selected Subaltern Studies*, 179–230 at 179.
46. For a perspective on this, see John Beverley, *Subalternity and Representation: Arguments in Cultural Theory* (Durham, N.C.: Duke University Press, 1999).
47. Vinay Lal, 'Provincialising the West: World History from the Perspective of Indian History,' in Benedikt Stuchktey and Eckhardt Fuchs, eds., *Writing World History, 1800–2000* (Oxford: Oxford University Press, 2003), 271–89 at 288.
48. Bruce Mazlish, 'Comparing Global History to World History,' *Journal of Interdisciplinary History* 28 (1998), 385–95 at 391.

49. The phrase derives from David Northrup who admits that the imperative 'comes from looking backward through time to discover the origins of the contemporary globalization.' David Northrup, 'Globalization and the Great Convergence: Rethinking World History in the Long Term,' *Journal of World History* 16 (2005), 249–67 at 252–3.
50. William H. McNeill, 'The Changing Shape of World History,' *History and Theory* 34 (1995), 8–26.
51. Dominic Sachsenmaier, 'World History as Ecumenical History,' *Journal of World History* 18 (2007), 465–89 at 489.
52. Georg G. Iggers and Q. Edward Wang, *A Global History of Modern Historiography* (London: Pearson, 2008).
53. Daniel Woolf, ed., *The Oxford History of Historical Writing*, 5 vols, (Oxford: Oxford University Press, 2010).
54. Some examples include Thomas Bender, ed., *Rethinking American History in a Global Age* (Berkeley: University of California Press, 2002); Christopher Bayly, *The Birth of the Modern World, 1780–1914: Global Connections and Comparisons* (Oxford: Blackwell, 2004); Gunilla Budde, Sebastian Conrad, and Oliver Janz, eds., *Transnationale Geschichte. Themen, Tendenzen und Theorien* (Göttingen, 2006). I am grateful for help in this matter to my colleague Dr. Bernhard Struck of the Centre for Transnational History in the University of St Andrews.
55. Sahlins, 'Goodbye to Tristes Tropes,' 4.
56. Green, 'Periodizing World History,' *History and Theory* 34 (1995), 99–111 at 101.

References

BERGER, STEFAN, and CHRIS LORENZ, eds. *The Contested Nation: Ethnicity, Class, Religion and Gender in National Histories.* Basingstoke: Palgrave, 2008.

CHAKRABARTY, DIPESH. *Provincializing Europe: Postcolonial Thought and Historical Difference.* Princeton: Princeton University Press, 2000.

CHAUDHURI, K. N. *Asia Before Europe: Economy and Civilisation of the Indian Ocean from the Rise of Islam to 1750.* Cambridge: Cambridge University Press, 1990.

GREW, RAYMOND. 'Expanding Worlds of World History,' *Journal of Modern History* 78 (2006), 878–98.

HEUSS, ALFRED. 'Möglichkeiten einer Weltgeschichte heute,' *Saeculum* 19 (1969), 3–29.

History and Theory. Theme Issue 34 (1995).

IGGERS, GEORG G., and Q. EDWARD WANG. *A Global History of Modern Historiography.* London: Pearson, 2008.

MAZLISH, BRUCE. 'Comparing Global History to World History,' *Journal of Interdisciplinary History* 28 (1998), 385–95.

MAZLISH, BRUCE, and R. BUULTJENS, eds. *Conceptualizing Global History.* Boulder, Colo.: Westview, 1993.

NORTHRUP, DAVID. 'Globalization and the Great Convergence: Rethinking World History in the Long Term,' *Journal of World History* 16 (2005), 249–67.

SAHLINS, MARSHALL. 'Goodbye to *Tristes Tropes*,' *Journal of Modern History* 65 (1993).

STUCHKEY, BENEDIKT, and ECKHARDT FUCHS, eds. *Writing World History, 1800–2000.* Oxford: Oxford University Press, 2003.

WOOLF, DANIEL, ed. *The Oxford History of Historical Writing.* 5 vols. Oxford: Oxford University Press, 2010.

CHAPTER 2

··

GEOGRAPHIES

··

MARTIN W. LEWIS

> History without Geography, like a dead carcass, hath neither life, nor
> motion.... History therefore and Geography, like two Fires or Meteors
> which Philosophers call Castor and Pollux, if joyned together, crown
> our reading with delight and profit; if parted, threaten both with a certain
> shiprack.
>
>   Peter Heylyn, *Cosmographie*, second edition, 1657

HISTORY and geography were once commonly regarded as sibling disciplines if not as
two aspects of a larger whole. By this way of thinking, historical processes can only be
understood as they literally take place, unfolding across particular landscapes and
influenced by the obdurate realities of the physical world. Correspondingly, the spatial
patterns of the geographer's purview can be considered comprehensible only as
examined through their historical development. Time and space, chronology and
chorology, era and region: the dualities of history and geography are ever intertwined.

Despite their long-recognized affinity, history and geography increasingly parted
ways as academic professionalization and specialization strengthened during the nineteenth and early twentieth centuries. Historians grew skeptical of the hard linkages that
geographers of the time posited between historical development and the natural
landscape. They also increasingly focused on national history, regarding the territories
of nation-states as holistic totalities requiring little geographical attention. Geographers, for their part, disengaged from historical concerns as they turned increasingly to
theory and method. When Harvard and other major universities dismantled their
geography departments in the 1950s and 1960s, cutting-edge geographers sought to
re-establish their field as an ahistorical spatial science.[1]

Beginning in the latter decades of the twentieth century, the two disciplines began to
shown some signs of reconvergence. Most geographers now recognize the need for
historical contextualization if not explanation, just as many historians have rediscov-
ered the importance of spatial relations while discovering the utility of geographical
methods. A basic geographical sensibility is probably more pronounced in world

history than in any other field of historical inquiry. Historical accounts framed around a single city, region, state, empire, or even civilization *can* proceed as if geography were of no account, portraying the area under investigation as a singular, undifferentiated place. Such an option is not open to practitioners of world history, who necessarily investigate relationships among distinct places differentiated over a broad terrain, examining processes of trans-regional if not global scope. To the extent that it covers the entire planet, world history encompasses global geography. Indeed, some of the more innovative recent reconceptualizations of global spatial patterning have been advanced by world historians.

The Development of Academic Geography

As originally conceived by the ancient Greeks, *geography* entails writings about the surface of the entire world.[2] According to the classical scheme, depictions of sizable sub-global regions were classified as *chorography*, those of more local concern were deemed *topography*, and those that included both the Earth and the extraterrestrial realm counted as *cosmography*. As definitions shifted over time, the scope of geography expanded, taking over the terrain yielded up as 'chorography' slipped into desuetude. Eventually, geography came to encompass depictions of place defined at any scale from that of the world as a whole down to that of an individual neighborhood.

The fact that geography includes the study of both purely natural features and those associated strictly with humankind generates definitional and institutional conundrums. In the popular imagination, 'geography' is often unduly associated with gross physiographic features—river, lakes, mountains, plains, and the like—thus slighting the human dimension. In academia, on the other hand, geography sometimes suffers from its overly expansive scope. Along with anthropology, it is the only discipline that lays claims to being simultaneously a natural science, a social science, and member of the humanities disciplines.

Owing to the diffuse nature of their study, geographers have often sought to delimit a more coherent disciplinary core. From the late nineteenth to the mid-twentieth century, a common maneuver was to center scholarship on the relationship between humanity and the natural environment, thus bridging the gap between physical and human geography. In the first half of the twentieth century, the main debates in the discipline pitted geographical (or environmental) determinists, who argued that climatic, topographic, or edaphic (soil) conditions shaped culture and social organization, against geographical possibilists, who allowed that the physical world sets constraints but insisted that culture is ultimately the product of human ingenuity.

The mainstream of geographical determinism in the late nineteenth and early twentieth centuries was expressly global, forwarding its own view of world history. Its overriding concern was to explain why Western Europe and parts of North America enjoyed political and economic dominance. The favored explanation was essentially climatic, the argument being that only temperate climes could produce active minds and vigorous bodies, although the favorable physiographic features of Europe and North America—navigable rivers, extensive coastlines, and the like—were also invoked. Such climatic determinism has a venerable intellectual heritage, having prevailed among geographers of both ancient Greece[3] and the classical Islamic world. In virtually all cases, scholars have located the prime environmental conditions in their own homelands.

Whereas geographical determinists focused on the sway of nature, geographical possibilists turned to the transformation of the natural world by human agency. Led by Carl O. Sauer, scholars of the Berkeley School took a deeply historical approach in examining such processes as deforestation, the spread of grassland and savannah landscapes, agricultural terracing, and the domestication of plants and animals.[4] Most of their studies were local or regional in scope, but their overarching concern was the transformation of the Earth's surface as a whole, as reflected in the path-breaking 1955 symposium entitled *Man's Role in Changing the Face of the Earth*.[5]

By the mid-twentieth century, the once regnant position of environmental determinism had been intellectually defeated and essentially excised from academic geography. Geographers—like most world historians—were thereby taken aback in the late 1990s to see the revival of unreconstructed geo-determinism on the global scale by such writers as David S. Landes. While Landes carefully opined that 'it would be a mistake to see geography as destiny,' he argued that Europe's exceptional environmental circumstances helped catapult it to a position of global domination.[6]

The success of Landes's work led many geographers to wonder what their efforts had accomplished over the previous half century. Geographers may have partially undermined their own position, however, by too thoroughly rejecting anything that smelled of geographical determinism. The publication of Jared Diamond's Pulitzer-prize winning *Guns, Germs, and Steel* in 1997,[7] which also argued that environmental conditions helped certain parts of the world achieve global supremacy, thus caused its own round of consternation in the discipline. Diamond's arguments, however, are far less ethnocentric and much more complex than those of Landes. He contends, for example, that it was Eurasia as a whole that was geographically advantaged, particularly by the fact that its east–west axis permitted a more rapid diffusion of day-length-sensitive crops than was possible in the north–south trending landmasses of the Americas and Africa.

Beyond the direction of continental axes, the basic differences in gross physical geography that have influenced the flow of global history are too varied to be fully recounted here. We might note, however, that natural factors ranging from the disease environment to soil fertility closely influence population density, which in turn impacts a slew of social evolutionary processes ranging from agricultural intensification to urbanization. Human societies in lightly populated areas have typically enjoyed more leisure and better health than those in densely populated zones, but they have also tended to experience lower levels of economic and political integration.[8] The large-scale polities that have emerged in such locales have faced special challenges, in part because disgruntled people have often been able to flee to unoccupied territories. Much of the historical development of sub-Saharan Africa, marked by shifting centers of political power, low levels of urbanization, and rapid ethnogenesis, can be partially explained by its environmentally linked population scarcity.[9] By the same token, the political structures of lightly inhabited Southeast Asia, where kings typically fought wars to obtain labor rather than territory, long remained distinctive from those of more densely settled lands.

Large-scale historical–geographical patterns such as those mentioned above are of little interest to most contemporary geographers. By the late twentieth and early twenty-first centuries, environmental studies had been reduced to merely one of a welter of geographical subdisciplines. Many works in this field, moreover, are local in scope and contemporary in their concerns.[10] But as geographers retreated from environmental geohistory, historians stepped into the breach. Environmental history emerged as a vibrant new field in the late 1900s, its studies infused with geographical content. But as world environmental history is examined elsewhere in this volume (see Chapter 7), the remainder of this chapter will turn to other ways in which geography intersects with world history.

THE DISCIPLINES OF SPACE AND TIME

Before exploring the geographical aspects of world history it is necessary to define more precisely the term geography as it is employed today. Rather than being the depiction of the Earth's surface or the assessment of the relations between people and the natural environment, contemporary geography focuses on the study of *areal differentiation and integration*, areal differentiation being the ways in which places differ from each other, and areal integration referring to the ways in which they are connected to each other. Places may be separated or linked through any manner of phenomena, be they unique to the human world (language, religion, economics, politics, etc.) or strictly natural (e.g. climate, vegetation, faunal assemblages).

Geography, so defined, can be regarded as the inherent counterpart of history; whereas the historian examines differences over time, the geographer focuses on differences over space. But history, as conventionally defined, cannot form the exact temporal complement to the spatial study of geography as it is too limited, restricting itself to the experiences of humankind over the past 5,000 years. Contemporary world history, however, ignores the larger discipline's methodological and chronological strictures, readily pushing its inquiries into prehistoric times. Geography's actual counterpart is the all-encompassing 'big history' championed by such noted world historians as David Christian and Fred Spier.[11] As big history takes as its starting point the origin of the Earth if not the 'big bang' itself, its pursuit is necessarily interdisciplinary.

Big history's main narrative thread is one of ever-increasing complexity, a process, ongoing for several billion years, that was driven first by organic evolution and then by socio-cultural evolution. The corresponding geographical story is one of differentiation alternating with integration. As biological evolution proceeded, different parts of the world ended up with highly distinctive flora and fauna, yet as continents collided or were linked by volcanic bridges or dropping sea levels, massive exchanges of species occurred. By the same token, humankind experienced a profound series of divergences early in its history as radiating bands spread out of Eastern Africa to populate the world, their languages and lifeways radically transforming in the process, yet subsequent developments would reduce many of these gaps, generating tight linkages between even some of the most far-flung human societies.

For recent times, the phenomenon of ever-tightening bonds of spatial integration over the entire world commands attention. The 'shrinking of the globe' and the 'contraction of time and space' resulting from improved transportation and communications technologies are common themes in a wide variety of academic and journalistic discourses, repeated endlessly in the globalization literature. What world history tells us, however, is that such processes have far deeper roots than is commonly realized. As linguistic and genetic history shows, early human societies may have diverged as they entered into new terrains, but countervailing processes long predate recorded history; as populations interacted, they exchanged cultural practices, language elements, and genes, and sometimes did so over vast distances. Consider, for example, the peopling of Madagascar, one of the last major landmasses to have been reached by *Homo sapiens*. Linguistic and archeological evidence suggests that seafarers from Borneo reached the island some 1,500 to 2,000 years ago, after they skirted the South Asian and East African coastlines, trading as they went. The end result was a hybridized population of roughly equal Southeast Asian and East African cultural and genetic background.

Madagascar may be singular in the depth of its cultural amalgamation, but wherever one looks, the development not just of human culture but also of civilization itself went hand-in-hand with the long-distance exchange of crops, pathogens, technologies, and systems of ideas. In Africa and Eurasia, integration of almost hemispheric scope had become a reality well before trade routes extended across the major ocean basins.[12]

In the standard public narrative of globalization, accelerating integration is only now bringing the final pieces of the Earth into the global system, as loggers, miners, and ranchers penetrate such remaining redoubts as the Amazon basin, undermining formerly pristine natural environments and tribal societies. Again, world history provides a subtler story. The Amazon basin itself was once the site of complex, semi-urban societies, which collapsed largely due to the introduction of extra-hemispheric diseases in the early modern round of global integration. Research by both historians and anthropologists shows that in many areas seemingly isolated hunter-gatherer peoples were actually 'professional primitives' who specialized in obtaining wild products for regional and global markets, bartering them for the foodstuffs and manufactured products of sedentary folk.[13]

THE CARTOGRAPHIC IMPERATIVE

If geography is the study of spatial relations, its hallmark product is surely the map, which functions to portray patterns of areal differentiation and integration in the most precise manner possible. The relationship between academic history and cartography remains ambivalent. On the one hand, historical mapping is a well-advanced project, with scores of historical atlases, some focused on specific places and eras others of global scope, being published each year.[14] Many of these volumes represent significant contributions to both the art of cartography and the study of historical processes.[15] Yet on the other hand, cartographic exposition remains underdeveloped in most fields of historical inquiry.

Despite its recent progress, historical cartography suffers from a number of common flaws. Most significantly, political maps of the past usually treat bygone polities as if they were twentieth-century European nation-states, exercising blanket sovereignty over territorially distinct realms marked by clean boundaries.[16] In actuality, pre-modern states were often congeries of nested and partially overlapping sovereignties that lacked clear spatial form; the territorial claims of early modern European empires, moreover, were often completely unrealized. Even such an impressive volume as the *DK Atlas of World History* depicts what are now the central and southwestern portions of the United States in the year 1800 as having been parts of the Spanish empire,[17] yet Spanish rule was then limited to a few outposts. In actuality, the Comanche empire effectively controlled much of this area—and much of what is now northern Mexico as well. Yet the vast Comanche domain, as Pekka Hamalainen shows, remains all but cartographically invisible.[18]

The development of effective historical mapping presents a number of challenges. Most maps portray a two-dimensional, static space, providing a snapshot of areal configurations as they exist at a single point in time. Historical cartographers have, therefore, long sought to activate their maps, allowing them to depict change. Movement, whether of individuals, armies, entire societies, or even of ideas and artifacts, can easily be shown with pointed lines. Shading or coloration can depict the expansion or contraction of states or cultural areas over extended periods of time. An individual polity experiencing continual enlargement or diminution, such as the Roman or Ottoman empires in particular historical epochs, can be easily mapped on a single sheet. If one wants to show multiple evolving states with fluctuating boundaries, however, an array of temporally specific maps has been necessary.[19] Recent progress in computerized cartography, however, allows more active presentations. Using Geographical Information Systems (GIS), one can construct complex map overlays;[20] with animated cartography, mapped features continually transform before one's eyes.

GEOGRAPHICAL EXPOSITION IN WORLD HISTORICAL TEXTS

One cannot expect such advanced forms of historical cartography to emerge as standard modes of world-historical exposition. GIS and animated mapping are demanding specializations, and even conventional maps can be difficult to produce and expensive to publish. But while cartography may be the most precise method of portraying spatial configurations, it is by no means the only one. Geographical patterns are ubiquitously described in prose, yielding all manner of implied mapping. As it turns out, world historians have addressed many geographical issues, contributing to a more robust understanding of global spatial patterning.

The range and depth of geographical concerns are clearly evident in the pages of the field's premier periodical, the *Journal of World History*. Consider, for example, the journal's March 2008 issue. In the lead article, Siep Stuurman compares the work of two ancient historians, Herodotus and China's Sima Qian, both of whom were fascinated by foreign land and peoples. In examining the works of these authors, Stuurman forwards a geographical thesis of the inner Eurasian frontier as a zone of creative interaction.[21] In the second paper, Stanley Burstein explores the role of Greek culture in ancient and medieval Nubia. Burstein's concerns are explicitly spatial, as he shows that the vast tract of Nubian land was not merely an insignificant appendage of Egypt, as traditional historiography had it, but an autonomous player in world history that was closely linked to the Greek-speaking eastern Mediterranean world.[22] The next offering, by Kirsten Seaver, examines both the local spatial knowledge of Norse settlers in Greenland and the models of global geography held by educated medieval Europeans.[23] In the final article, James De Lorenzi considers the hemispheric circuits of the Armenian mercantile diaspora, focusing on the experiences of one nineteenth-century merchant in Christian Ethiopia. As De Lorenzi demonstrates, changing European ideas about progress, race, and global geography greatly influenced this Armenian sojourner's understanding of Ethiopian culture.[24]

A more extensive analysis of articles published over the past two decades in the *Journal of World History* reveals an abiding concern with matters of spatial distribution. The issues covered can be as global as the spread of humanity over the face of the Earth,[25] or as regionally and topically restricted as the conversion of an Indian tribal population to Christianity.[26] In almost all cases, the areas under consideration are embedded within explicit spatial frameworks. The paradigmatic local study in world history shows how a given locale can only be understood through its relations with the wider world, as exemplified by Bin Yang's cartographically rich examination of Yunnan.[27] And if the formal spatial models of twentieth-century geography are seldom seen in world history, they are occasionally used to good effect, as in Philip Curtin's comparison of Argentina and South Africa in the nineteenth century through the lens of central-place theory.[28]

METAGEOGRAPHIES

World historians have thus contributed to our geographical understanding, examining a wide array of spatial relations over much of the surface of the planet. World history's overall contribution to geography, however, stems less from its specific studies than from its general mode of global apprehension. In an understated manner, world historians have been advancing a *meta*geographical project of their own, forwarding a fresh vision of how the world as a whole is put together. To operate successfully at this scale, they have had to break free from the standard model of global organization, devising new and more supple forms of comprehension as they go along.

'Metageography' refers to the ways in which the world is partitioned into constituent units that are imbued with supposedly intrinsic traits and ranked according to their purported significance.[29] Metageographical categorization is almost inescapable, preceding and informing most instances of global inquiry, yet it is often overlooked, its units of analysis taken for granted if not viewed as unproblematic givens of the natural world. Close examination, however, reveals that such seemingly fundamental categories as Europe and Asia are not actual physical features of the Earth's surface, but rather constructs of the human imagination that have been historically deployed to advance specific ideological or geopolitical positions.

Until recently, most forms of historical inquiry have relied on conventional metageographical schema. Continents and civilizations have served as the basic divisions of the world, with assemblages of scholars devoting themselves to such fields as European history, African history, the history of Islamic civilization, and so on. At the more local scale, nation-states have typically served as all-encompassing units of investigation, fitting not only for political history but also for the study of all manner of social, cultural, and economic issues. Scholars have, thus, arrayed themselves in correspondingly nested communities; historians of France generally interact primarily with other historians of France and secondarily with other Europeanists, while students of Japan cluster together under the larger umbrellas of first East Asian and then Asian studies.

In academia, such spatial categories have been implicitly ranked in terms of their relative importance, as is clearly reflected by the number of faculty positions allotted to their study. In the typical American university, historians are semi-officially divided into three roughly equivalent groups, devoted respectively to the examination of the United States, Europe, and the remainder of the world. Within European history, Britain, France, and Germany usually dominate, far overshadowing other states of similar size, such as Italy, Spain, and Poland. China and Japan occupy an equally leading position within Asian history, with vast reaches of the supposed continent, such as Southeast Asia, often falling off the map altogether.

On the face of it, there is little that is intrinsically objectionable about such an approach to the study of the global past. The spatial containers employed, be they subcontinental or national, are useful and often unavoidable. It is difficult to argue, moreover, that some parts of the world have not played more significant roles in global history than have others, or that responsible citizenship does not demand special attention to one's own country. The consideration lavished in American history departments on the United States, Britain, and the rest of Europe is thus understandable. But such conventional metageographical categorization cannot capture all of the dynamics of global history. Our received spatial framework for grappling with the world, moreover, becomes stultifying to the extent that it is taken as given, used exclusively and regarded as unproblematically natural.

Recent works in world history provide a corrective by examining the world through novel metageographical lenses. The signal departure of the field derives from its expressly global purview. World history adopts an encompassing mission, one that embraces all reaches of the inhabited world. As a result, certain places that have been cited in traditional historical scholarship occupy prominent positions in the corpus of world historical studies. Central Asia has hardly been central to the Euro-American historical imagination, yet as a number of world historians have shown, one of the crucial motors of the premodern global past was driven by the complementarities and contradictions existing between the pastoral societies of the inner Asian steppes and the sedentary civilizations of the Eurasian rim.[30] Likewise, the Pacific oceanic and island world has come to the fore, most prominently as world historians seek to understand how the globe came to function as a single economic system. Dennis O. Flynn and Arturo Giráldez have argued that globalization commenced when Manila—a city devoted to trans-Pacific trade—was established in 1571.[31] As a result of Manila's foundation by the Spanish Imperial crown, all of the world's major land-masses and oceans were for the first time linked together.

Beyond advancing a truly global vision, world history both challenges and complements conventional metageographical thinking by focusing on processes that cut across the borders of states, nations, civilizations, and cultural areas. Many studies in the field examine phenomena that are not only multinational in scope but that span vast reaches, revealing linkages between distant and seemingly disconnected societies. World historians thus tend to foreground a global geography of connection over that of division, stressing, in other words, areal integration over areal differentiation.

NOVEL MACRO-REGIONS

Despite this general emphasis on connection, world historians must still delineate specific spatial units. Discrete regions, differentiated from their neighbors by set characteristics, are an obligatory feature of historical analysis. Yet here too, world historians tend to see things differently, allowing them to carve out novel segments of terrain that reveal distinctive historical processes. One way they do so is by highlighting borderlands between established polities or cultural regions as regions in their own right. As Arnold Toynbee argued generations ago, such interstitial zones can give rise to new universalistic religions that sometimes become powerful enough to reorder the map of the world; more recently, the ecologist turned world historian Peter Turchin finds the edges of old empires spawning powerful new empires.[32] World historians also highlight maritime regions encompassing littoral zones conventionally located in separate geohistorical arenas, showing how they can bridge otherwise disjunctive parts of the world.[33] Such maritime regions have been located at varying spatial scales, from that of the Atlantic basin to those of such regional waterways as the Black Sea and the Western Indian Ocean.[34]

Several world historians have proposed novel global divisions of a more expansive scope. Dennis O. Flynn and Arturo Giráldez, for example, trifurcate the globe before the 1500s into the Old World (Africa, Europe, Asia, and the Indian Ocean basin), the New World (the Americas and the Atlantic Ocean basin), and the Pacific World.[35] A more established macro-region of the world history literature is the 'Afro-Eurasian ecumene,' a term associated with the late scholar of Islam Marshall Hodgson. Referring not to the entirety of Africa and Eurasia, this region delimits rather to the ambit of linked premodern societies extending from northern and Eastern Africa through the temperate and tropical reaches of Eurasia. Although rarely encountered outside of world history, the notion of an Afro-Eurasian ecumene—in which diseases, crops, and ideas freely circulated—is almost indispensable within it. Within this ecumenical zone, world historians have delimited smaller regional formations that tie together places usually classified separately. In a geographically rich paper, for example, David Christian differentiates Inner Eurasia from Outer Eurasia as basic units of world history.[36] Other novel world historical regions include the Turko-Persian sphere and Indo-Persian realm, the latter of which proves crucial to the study of early modern South Asia.[37]

Despite these departures, world history does not use a completely reformulated world map. Yet when world historians deploy conventional geographical divisions, they tend to frame them in a knowing manner, thereby maintaining a cosmopolitan vision. They tend to regard the West, for example, less as a singular civilization with distinct boundaries than as a metageographical construct that has been used to advance political and philosophical positions. World historians have thus examined how ideas of Western distinctiveness have been grappled with by intellectuals from other parts of the world seeking to derive alternative routes to modernization. Another strategy is to exhume the transcivilizational roots of Western civilization itself, thereby undermining Western/non-Western bifurcation of the word. In an intriguing work, Lynda Shaffer argues that global Westernization was preceded by a round of 'Southernization' in which ideas and practices originating in South Asia spread through most of the Afro-Eurasian Ecumene.[38]

THE HISTORY OF GLOBAL DIVISION

Thus far, world history has been discussed as if it were a new field of study propounding novel geographies. But although world history as an organized field of inquiry has only emerged in the past several decades, a global approach to historical understanding is as old as the study of history itself. World history in this larger sense is implicated in the development of the constrictive metageographies that world historians are now dismantling. Comprehensive geographical visions of how the world is organized have necessarily been entwined with historical accounts of how it has developed.

Herodotus is often credited as the first systematic historian, but he was also among the earliest of geographers. Herodotus sought to describe as much of the world as he could, examining the role of the physical environment in cultural and political evolution while seeking to understand how interactions among distinctive and far-flung polities generated the main geopolitical events of his day. In doing so, he expressed considerable skepticism toward the pre-existing Greek division of the world into the landmasses of Europe, Asia, and (sometimes) Libya (later deemed Africa). This original continental scheme, as he recognized, was based not on any recognizable cultural or political features, but rather on the maritime passageways through which the Greek trading network extended.

Despite Herodotus' well-founded reservations, the three-fold continental system continued to be used throughout the Greco-Roman classical period, although the continents themselves were seldom viewed as having much cultural or political significance. This situation would gradually change after the spread of Christianity in the late classical and early medieval periods. Now the very shape of the world came to be permeated with theological significance; in the standard T-O world emblems of the time, the three continents were depicted as forming the shape of a cross, with Jerusalem located at the crux. By the early modern period, most educated Europeans had come to regard the division of the world into the fundamental landmasses of Europe, Asia, and Africa as the basis of global geography.

Europeans were not the only people to develop a tradition of world historical writing, nor were they the only ones to do so in a geographically limited, ethnocentric manner. Chinese scholars stressed the centrality of the Middle Kingdom, finding some significance in bordering kingdoms and tribal confederations and, if they were Buddhists, in South Asia, but little in areas farther to the West. Like their Europeans counterparts, global historians from the Muslim world tended to limit their concern to the area inhabited by their co-religionists, dividing the world into the realm of submission to God (*Dar al-Islam*) and the generally dismissible realm of strife (*Dar al-Harb*).

European global models would eventually spread to the rest of the world, owing largely to the imperial success of European arms and economic production between 1700 and 1900 CE. But Western ideas about the shape of the world were themselves changing in the early modern age, forced to do so by the continuing acquisition of knowledge. The discovery of the Americas generated what Eviatar Zerubavel called 'cosmographic shock,' owing to the fact that the new lands could not easily be slotted into the historical narratives of the Bible, their very existence undermining the geo-physical trinity of Europe, Asia, and Africa.[39] The tripartite world was thus by necessity transformed into one of 'four quarters,' as the Americas joined the continental roster. Not that this maneuver settled the matter, as scholars have continued to disagree about how many continents exist.

However, while the number of continents remained unsettled, the basic scheme of division, founded on the separation of Europe, Asia, and Africa, triumphed the world over. Yet the expansion of basic geographical knowledge had already undermined the empirical foundation on which the entire edifice rests; by the 1500s it was clear that Europe and Asia were not distinct landmasses separated or almost separated by intervening waterways, the defining criterion of continental status. But the separation of Europe from Asia had to be maintained, as it formed the core geographic mode through which Europeans understood the world while differentiating themselves from others. Substantial intellectual gymnastics were required before the relatively insignifi-cant Ural Mountains and Ural River were selected as the standard continental divide.

By the late 1700s, European explorers and geographers had mapped out the main contours of global geography outside of the polar realm. At the same time, the explosion of skeptical creativity known as the French Enlightenment generated a fresh attitude toward world history and geography. Celebrated writers such as Voltaire and Denis Diderot rejected the notion that Europe contained the world's only histori-cally significant civilization. In criticizing the conservative nature of their own society, they placed other societies, particularly those of supposedly meritocratic China and sagacious India,[40] on an equal or even higher plane.

Eighteenth-century European efforts to craft an ecumenical approach to world history rapidly gave way to a more virulent ethnocentrism in the nineteenth century. European military and technological advances, coupled with the rapid weakening of China and other Asian states, led almost all European thinkers to celebrate their own homeland while denigrating all other parts of the world. Universal histories produced at the time typically relegated the entire historical development of such vast regions as East Asia or South Asia to a few perfunctory pages. Europe was held to be the land of progressive civilization, Asia the land of stagnant civilization, and Africa, the Pacific, and pre-Columbian America the lands bereft of civilization.

Nineteenth-century European thinkers also elaborated a metageography of direc-tion, one in which West was valorized and East belittled. Such ideas supported the elevation not only of Europe over Asia, but of Western Europe over Eastern Europe. By the same token, many European scholars of the time viewed Western Asia in a much more positive light than Eastern Asia. A global metageography based on an East–West continuum had particular appeal to scholars living in the far western fringe of Eurasia and especially to those located in North America. Americans had long had to contend with European vilifications of their homeland, but by stressing their membership in a common *Western* civilization they could put themselves on equal footing with their European peers. They could go a step beyond, moreover, by invoking the hoary trope of the westward course of historical development, a process that could rhetorically relocate the hot core of progress from Western Europe to the United States.

In the twentieth century, the metageographic distinction between the West and of the rest of the world gained further intellectual purchase, partly because it could excise objectionable elements from European history. Not only Stalinism but even Nazism could thus be read out of Western history and instead attached to an Eastern zone of intrinsic despotism. The very geographical imprecision of the category of the West, moreover, could be used to self-flattering effect. Thus, Germany could be excluded when it came to late nineteenth- and early twentieth-century political history,[41] but included when the topic turned to cultural issues.

The twinned distinctions between Europe and Asia on the one hand and the West and the East (alternatively, the West and the rest) on the other were eventually adopted throughout the world. In part this was a matter of the imperial powers forcing their own geographical schemes on their colonized subjects, but many non-Western intellectuals discovered that they could employ European metageographical ideas for their own purposes. The varied peoples of Asia, for example, could find a kind of anti-imperial unity in their supposed Asian commonalities; residents of the non-West similarly found that they far outnumbered the inhabitants of the West. Eventually, many non-Western thinkers, joined by dissenting Europeans and North Americans, began to invert the scheme's moral associations, denigrating the West and celebrating non-West.

But as the division between the West from the rest hardened in the global public imagination, world historians and scholars in related fields dismantled its geohistorical underpinnings. Crucial to the development of a more inclusive global understanding was Arnold Toynbee's monumental *A Study of History*. Macro-historical dynamics, Toynbee argued, did not march forward in a single line of development, with the torch of progress remaining lodged for long periods in single parts of the world. Instead, he contended that numerous interacting but relatively self-contained civilizations were born, evolved, and often perished on their own accord. For Toynbee, understanding the human past entailed grappling with all of the world's manifold civilizations.

Toynbee's historical synthesis enjoyed momentary fame, but by the 1960s its authority faded rapidly, owing in good part to the efforts of a succeeding generation of world historians. William H. McNeill and others showed that Toynbee's civilizations were not nearly as distinct—either geographically or culturally—as he had portrayed them.[42] The new vision stressed not spatial division but rather interconnection, cultural synthesis, and cross-fertilization. Henceforth, the emphasis would be on how peoples, practices, products, innovations, domesticated species, and pathogens moved over vast distances, in the process generating a coherently global history.

Toynbee's civilizational model thus helped spur the development of world history, but it did not significantly underwrite its geographical apprehension. In other intellectual quarters, however, a metageography based on a reduced list of discrete civilizations retained its appeal. Such a viewpoint received a significant fillip with the publication of Samuel Huntington's essay 'The Clash of Civilizations?' in 1993.[43] According to Huntington and his followers, the world has long been, and will continue to be, firmly divided into a handful of distinct civilization-based regions, each of which possesses its own habits of mind, social structures, and political institutions.

The Geographical Framework
of Area Studies

The positions of this neo-civilizational school are rejected not only by world historians but also by most other scholars of the global condition. The scholarly community as a whole, however, still requires a consistent set of global divisions, if only for purposes of effective communication and organization. Such world-historical macro-regions as the Afro-Eurasian ecumene will not suffice, as they are too large and have too little relevance outside of the confines of world history. As it turns out, a serviceable new metageographical system emerged in the mid-twentieth century, that of world regions. Especially in the United States, the scholarly endeavor of making sense of the world is organized around the *area studies* framework, founded on such world regions as East Asia, sub-Saharan Africa, Latin America, and so on.[44]

The world regional system originated with the efforts of the Ethnogeographical Board, a scholarly organization established by the United States government during World War II. American military planners found the existing continental system woefully inadequate, and therefore explicitly called for a new global geography. The board partitioned most of Asia into East Asia, South Asia, and Southeast Asia, appended Southwest Asia (the so-called Middle East) to North Africa, and attached North Asia (Siberia) and most of Central Asia to a Soviet-centered region. In a similar manner, it delineated sub-Saharan Africa and Latin America as distinct world regions. In 1958, the passage of the National Defense Education Act by the US Congress authorized the creation of university-based area studies centers devoted to these macro-regions. As a result, the academic community reoriented its global inquiries around a new geographical framework.

The metageographical foundation of the area studies system is obviously rooted in those of continents and civilizations. Sub-Saharan Africa is essentially the rump of the continent remaining after North Africa was excised, while East Asia can alternatively be defined as the zone of 'Confucian civilization.' The main distinction is that world regions carry less ideological baggage than either continents or civilization. From the outset, they have been defined not as transhistorical regions rooted in the physical landscape and imbued with their own essences, but rather as more or less convenient divisions based vaguely on historical and cultural commonalities. As a result, the framework of world regions has proved reasonably flexible, successfully organizing most global pedagogy and scholarship in the United States.

To be sure, the unfolding of historical events has periodically necessitated the rearrangement of world regional contours. The downfall of the Soviet Union and its informal empire, coupled with the expansion of the European Union, required both boundary adjustments and name changes. The area that had been deemed 'Western Europe' pushed eastward to become merely 'Europe,' reverting to a continental vocabulary although not to continental borders, as 'European Russia' was not attached. The epochal geopolitical transformation of the late twentieth century also allowed Central Asia to reappear on the map as a world region in its own right.

WORLD HISTORY AND WORLD REGIONS

The re-emergence of Central Asia fits well with the global vision of most world historians, who have long emphasized the pivotal role of the steppe and desert belt in Afro-Eurasian history. More generally, however, world history retains an ambivalent relationship with the now standard area studies division of the globe. As this volume shows, world historians employ the vocabulary of world regions as a convenient way of arranging their investigations and referencing particular parts of the globe; many of them, moreover, were trained in, and continue to operate within, academic communities devoted to the study of particular world regions. Yet world historians often find themselves frustrated by the tight organization of scholarly inquiry around any bounded spatial entities, as they are typically drawn to issues that span all such divisions. They, therefore, often find it preferable to frame the globe around complex, continually transforming, and often overlapping spheres of interaction. As a result, world historians are forced to invent and reinvent their own ever-fluctuating geographical schema. In the process, they greatly enrich our understanding of the world.

NOTES

1. R. J. Johnson and J. D. Sidaway, *Geography and Geographers: Anglo-American Geography since 1945*, 6th edn. (London: Hodder Arnold, 2004).
2. Claudius Ptolemy, *The Geography*, translated and edited by Edward Luther Stevenson (New York: Dover, 1991), 25.
3. See Clarence J. Glacken, *Traces on the Rhodian Shore: Nature and Culture in Western Thought from Ancient Times to the End of the Eighteenth Century* (Berkeley: University of California Press, 1976).
4. John Leighly, ed., *Land and Life: A Selection from the Writings of Carl Ortwin Sauer* (Berkeley: University of California Press, 1963).

5. William L. Thomas, Jr., ed., *Man's Role in Changing the Face of the Earth*, 2 vols. (Chicago: University of Chicago Press, 1956).

6. David S. Landes, *The Wealth and Poverty of Nations: Why Some Are So Rich and Some So Poor* (New York: W.W. Norton, 1999), 15.

7. Jared Diamond, *Guns, Germs, and Steel: The Fates of Human Societies* (New York: W. W. Norton, 1997).

8. Ester Boserup, *The Conditions of Agricultural Growth; The Economics of Agrarian Change under Population Pressure* (Chicago: Aldine, 1965).

9. Igor Kopytoff, ed., *The African Frontier: The Reproduction of Traditional African Society* (Bloomington, Ind.: Indiana University Press, 1987).

10. For a notable exception, see Michael Williams, *Deforesting the Earth: From Prehistory to Global Crisis* (Chicago: University of Chicago Press, 2003).

11. David Christian, *Maps of Time: An Introduction to Big History* (Berkeley: University of California Press, 2004). Fred Spier, *The Structure of Big History: From the Big Bang Until Today* (Amsterdam: Amsterdam University Press, 1996).

12. Jerry H. Bentley, 'Hemispheric Integration, 500–1500 C.E.,' *Journal of World History* 9, no. 2 (1998).

13. Thomas N. Headley and Robert C. Bailey. 'Introduction: Have Hunter-Gatherers Ever Lived in Tropical Rain Forests Independently of Agriculture?' *Human Ecology* 19, no. 2 (1991), 115–22.

14. Jeremy Black, *Maps and History: Constructing Images of the Past* (New Haven, Conn.: Yale University Press, 1997).

15. See Jeremy Black, ed., *DK Atlas of World History* (London: Dorling Kindersley, 2000) and Robert H. Hewsen, *Armenia: A Historical Atlas* (Chicago: University of Chicago Press, 2001).

16. For a notable exception, see Joseph E. Schwartzberg, *A Historical Atlas of South Asia* (Chicago: University of Chicago Press, 1978).

17. Black, *DK Atlas of World History*, 86, 126–8.

18. Pekka Hamalainen, *The Comanche Empire* (New Haven, Conn.: Yale University Press, 2008).

19. The underappreciated master of this art is Colin McEvedy. See, for example, *The New Penguin Atlas of Ancient History* (London: Penguin, 2002).

20. See Anne K. Knowles, *Past Time, Past Place: GIS for History* (Redlands, Cal.: ESRI Press, 2002).

21. Siep Stuurman, 'Herodotus and Sima Qian: History and the Anthropological Turn in Ancient Greece and Han China,' *Journal of World History* 19, no. 1 (2008), 1–40.

22. Stanley M. Burstein, 'When Greek Was an African Language: The Role of Greek Culture in Ancient and Medieval Nubia,' *Journal of World History* 19, no. 1 (2008), 41–62.

23. Kirsten A. Seaver, '"Pygmies" of the Far North,' *Journal of World History* 19, no. 1 (2008), 63–88.

24. James De Lorenzi, 'Caught in the Storm of Progress: Timoteos Saprichian, Ethiopia, and the Modernity of Christianity,' *Journal of World History* 19, no. 1 (2008), 89–114.

25. Patrick Manning, '*Homo sapiens* Populates the Earth: A Provisional Synthesis, Privileging Linguistic Evidence,' *Journal of World History* 17, no. 2 (2006), 115–18.

26. Richard M. Eaton, 'Comparative History as World History: Religious Conversion in Modern India,' *Journal of World History* 8, no. 2 (1997), 243–71.

27. Bin Yang, 'Horses, Silver, and Cowries: Yunnan in Global Perspective,' *Journal of World History* 15, no. 3 (2004), 281–322.

28. Philip D. Curtin, 'Location in History: Argentina and South Africa in the Nineteenth Century,' *Journal of World History* 10, no. 1 (1999), 41–92.

29. On metageography in general, see Martin W. Lewis and Kären E. Wigen, *The Myth of Continents: A Critique of Metageography* (Berkeley: University of California Press, 1997).

30. Andre Gunder Frank, 'The Centrality of Central Asia,' *Bulletin of Concerned Asian Scholars* 24, 50–74; David Christian, 'Silk Roads or Steppe Roads? The Silk Roads in World History,' *Journal of World History* 2, no. 1 (2000), 1–26.

31. Dennis O. Flynn and Arturo Giráldez, 'Cycles of Silver: Global Economic Unity through the Mid-Eighteenth Century,' *Journal of World History* 13, no. 2 (2002), 291–322.

32. Arnold Toynbee, *A Study of History*, 12 vols. (Oxford: Oxford University Press, 1934–61), vol. 8 (1954), 90; Peter Turchin, *War and Peace and War: The Life Cycles of Imperial Nations* (New York: Pi Press, 2006).

33. Jerry Bentley, Renate Bridenthal and Kären E. Wigen, eds., *Seascapes: Maritime Histories, Littoral Cultures, and Transoceanic Exchanges* (Honolulu: University of Hawai`i Press, 2007); Michael N. Pearson, 'Littoral Society: The Concept and the Problem,' *Journal of World History* 17, no. 4 (2006), 353–74.

34. Charles King, *Black Sea: A History* (Oxford: Oxford University Press, 2005); Patricia Risso, 'Cross-Cultural Perceptions on Piracy: Maritime Violence in the Western Indian Ocean and Persian Gulf Region during a Long Eighteenth Century,' *Journal of World History* 12, no. 2 (2001), 293–320.

35. Dennis O. Flynn and Arturo Giráldez, 'Born Again: Globalization's Sixteenth Century Origin (Asian/Global Versus European Dynamics),' *Pacific Economic Review* 13, no. 3 (2008), 259–87.

36. David Christian, 'Inner Eurasia as a Unit of World History,' *Journal of World History* 5, no. 2 (Fall, 1994), 173–211.

37. Robert Canfield, ed., *Turko-Persia in Historical Perspective* (Cambridge: Cambridge University Press, 1991); Muzaffar Alam and Sanjay Subrahmanyam, *Indo-Persian Travels in the Age of Discoveries, 1400–1800* (Cambridge: Cambridge University Press, 2007).

38. Lynda Shaffer, 'Southernization,' *Journal of World History* 5, no. 1 (1994), 1–22.

39. Eviatar Zerubavel, *Terra Cognita: The Mental Discovery of America* (New Brunswick, N.J.: Rutgers University Press, 1992).

40. Jyoti Mohan, '*La Civilization le Plus Antique*: Voltaire's Image of India,' *Journal of World History* 16, no. 2 (2005), 173–85.

41. Hans Kohn, *The Mind of Germany* (New York: Harper and Row, 1960), ix, 5, 10.

42. William H. McNeill, *The Rise of the West: A History of the Human Community* (Chicago: University of Chicago Press, 1963).

43. Samuel Huntington, 'The Clash of Civilizations?,' *Foreign Affairs* 72 (1993), 23–49.

44. On the area studies and world regional frameworks, see Lewis and Wigen, *Myth of Continents*.

REFERENCES

BENTLEY, JERRY H. 'Hemispheric Integration, 500–1500 C.E.,' *Journal of World History* 9, no. 2 (1998), 237–254.

——. BRIDENTHAL, RENATE, and WIGEN, KAREN E., eds., *Seascapes: Maritime Histories, Littoral Cultures, and Transoceanic Exchanges.* Honolulu: University of Hawai`i Press, 2007.

BLACK, JEREMY. *Maps and History: Constructing Images of the Past*. New Haven: Yale University Press, 1997.

BLACK, JEREMY, ed., *DK Atlas of World History*. London: Dorling Kindersley, 2000.

CHRISTIAN, DAVID. *Maps of Time: An Introduction to Big History*. Berkeley: University of California Press, 2004.

DIAMOND, JARED. *Guns, Germs, Steel: The Fates of Human Societies*. New York: W. W. Norton, 1997.

GLACKEN, CLARENCE J. *Traces on the Rhodian Shore: Nature and Culture in Western Thought from Ancient Times to the End of the Eighteenth Century*. Berkeley: University of California Press, 1976.

HODGSON, MARSHALL G. S. *Rethinking World History: Essays on Europe, Islam, and World History*, ed. by Edmond Burke III. Cambridge: Cambridge University Press, 1993.

KNOWLES, ANNE K. *Past Time, Past Place: GIS for History*. Redlands, CA: ESRI Press, 2002.

LEIGHLY, JOHN, ed. *Land and Life: A Selection from the Writings of Carl Ortwin Sauer*. Berkeley: University of California Press, 1963.

LEWIS, MARTIN W. and WIGEN, KÄREN E. *The Myth of Continents: A Critique of Metageography*. Berkeley: University of California Press, 1997.

MARTIN, GEOFFREY J. *All Possible Worlds: A History of Geographical Ideas*, 4th edn. New York: Oxford University Press, 2005.

TOYNBEE, ARNOLD. *A Study of History*, 12 vols. Oxford: Oxford University Press, 1934–61.

CHAPTER 3

....

PERIODIZATION

....

LUIGI CAJANI

HISTORY AND MYTH

....

THE first world histories originated as part and parcel of religious visions which connect Creation myths and human history, and which through the device of periodization often connect past, present, and future in the form of prophecy. These visions sometimes exhibit common features, for instance decadence and annihilation, or a numerology that explains chronology. Among the many examples, one finds the Aztecs, who believed they lived in the epoch of the fifth Sun, which had been preceded by four Suns, respectively of Earth, Fire, Air, and Water, each destroyed by a cataclysm. In their Sun they saw cycles of fifty-two years; at the end of each, the possible end of the world was feared and conjured with appropriate rites. According to the *Avesta*, the sacred book of Zoroastrianism, Ahura Mazda's Creation lasts 12,000 years, divided into four periods of equal length: the last two periods comprehend human history, which ends with the final victory of Good. In Hindu doctrine the structure of history is based on the *mahāyuga* of 12,000 divine years, divided into four *yugas* which are successively more and more degenerate and shorter (respectively 4,800, 3,600, 2,400, and the last one *kali yuga*, 1,200 divine years). Each of these divine years lasts 360 human years, so the length of the *mahayuga* is 4,320,000 years. At the end of a *mahāyuga*, a new one begins. The cycle is repeated 1,000 times, thus completing a *kalpa*, when Creation is destroyed and a new one is created.

Sumerians produced the first example of chronological continuity between myth and history with the *Sumerian King List*, whose first surviving text dates back to 2100 BCE. It is based on the idea of the unique legitimate kingship, established by the gods and passing from time to time to another Sumerian city. The list starts from the moment 'when kingship was lowered from heaven' to the city of Eridu, and presents a set of mythical kings with very long reigns, lasting from a maximum of 64,880 to a minimum of 18,600 years. After 241,000 years the Flood swept over the Earth, and following that kingship was introduced again from heaven, this time to the city of Kiš: these kings ruled for much shorter periods, from a maximum of 1,500 to a minimum of a few years. Finally the list passes from mythical to historical kings. This pattern was adopted by the peoples who ruled over Mesopotamia after the Sumerians and is found also in the work of Babylonian historian Berossos, contemporary of Alexander the Great, who wrote a Greek-language history of Babylon, where he mentioned ten kings before the Flood. A similar chronological continuity between gods and men is to be found in Egypt, as attested by Manetho (fourth–third century BCE) whose *Aigyptiaka* started with gods and continued with historical dynasties. Related with the Mesopotamian vision is also the Bible, which gives in the Book of Genesis a succession of ten Patriarchs before the Flood, who also had a mythically long life, the oldest being Methuselah, who lived 969 years. The narrative continues with the history of the Jewish people along a chronological axis without gaps.

GREEK AND ROMAN HISTORIOGRAPHY

The Greek vision of the past involves both myth and history. The former is represented by Hesiod (seventh century BCE), who in his poem *Erga* expressed the idea of decadence through a periodization in five ages based on a metal allegory: first was the golden age, followed by a silver and bronze age, characterized by decreasing morality and increasing violence. The trend of decline stopped momentarily with the age of heroes, the only one without a metal reference: heroes were semi-divine, fought at Troy and Thebes, and eventually were brought by Zeus to the Islands of the Blessed. Then decline resumed with the iron age, the current era, characterized by suffering, injustice, and hard work. This vision had a great influence on the Greek and Roman culture, as in Ovid.

Greek historiography, which developed with the logographers of the sixth century and culminated with Herodotus of Halicarnassus (fifth century BCE), was characterized, unlike the Mesopotamian and Egyptian historiography, by a broad ethnographic interest and by a scientific approach to chronology, which started from the present and went backwards through verifiable references. Herodotus observed with amazement the extraordinary length of Egyptian chronology, much longer than the Greek records. Later Eratosthenes of Cyrene (276–194 BCE) in his *Chronographiai* fixed the date of the Trojan War, 407 years before the first Olympic games (776 BCE), as the first reliable date. One of the tasks Greek and Roman historians undertook was the synchronization of their chronology with the Mesopotamian, Egyptian, and Jewish chronologies, as one can see in the works of Castor of Rhodes (who flourished in the first half of the first century BCE) and Marcus Terentius Varro (116–27 BCE). Greek and Roman historians also developed a periodization based on the succession of empires, seen as the supreme political structure. The first evidence of focus on empires is found in Herodotus, who made reference to the Assyrians, Medes, and Persians (*Histories*, I, 95, 130). The paradigm of the succession of empires became canonical in the fourth century, as attested by Ctesias of Cnidus (fifth–fourth century BCE) in his *Persika*. After Alexander the Great the Macedonian empire was added to this set by the Demetrius of Phalerum (ca. 350–ca. 280 BCE) in his treatise *On Fortune*. Later came Rome as the fifth, biggest, and last empire: as quoted by Velleius Paterculus (ca. 19 BCE–ca. 31 CE) in his *Historiae romanae* (I, 6), the Roman historian Aemilius Sura wrote that after the defeat of Carthage the height of the empire had arrived with the Romans. The Greek historian Dionysius of Halicarnassus (ca. 60 BCE–7 CE) in the prologue of his *Rhomaike arch- aiologia* (I, 2) confirmed the list of Assyrian, Medean, Persian, Macedonian, and Roman empires, emphasizing the superiority of the Roman for the extent of its dominion, the splendor of its achievements, and the length of its duration. Rome appeared, thus, as the achievement of an historical process: Polybius of Megalopolis (ca. 203–120 BCE) asserted that the time had come when it was possible to write a world history, because the Romans had brought about the political unification of nearly the whole inhabited world, an unprecedented event, and their rule couldn't fear any future rivalry (*Histories*, I, 1–3). This being his rationale, his world history was limited to the contemporary world, starting when it had become unified, with the Second Punic War.

THE CHRISTIAN SYNTHESIS

The early Christian authors operated a powerful synthesis by merging together the Greco-Roman and the Jewish historical traditions into the vision of the history of salvation, from an absolute beginning to an absolute end. A very important concern for them was chronology, which during the first centuries of Christianity had a special relevance in connection with eschatological visions. In fact, the Second Advent of Jesus was expected to happen soon by the Christians, and the analysis of biblical passages could foresee the exact time. Combining the account of Genesis, according to which the Creation was finished in six days and God rested on the seventh day, with a passage of the Psalms, according to which a thousand years are like one day for God (*Ps* 89 (90), 4), a statement confirmed in the New Testament (*2 Pet*, 3,8), the anonymous author of the *Epistle of Barnabas* (probably written in 130–132) maintained that the world would last 6,000 years, but without any calculation as to how many years were left until the end. That calculation was made by Iulius Africanus in his *Chronographiai* (written in 220–221), where he asserted that Jesus had been born in the year 5500 BCE; therefore, the Second Advent was to take place in the year 500 after his birth. Later Quintus Julius Hilarianus, in his *Chronologia sive libellus de mundi duratione*, written in 397, intro- duced the periodization pattern of the Six Ages, corresponding to the six days of the Creation. He identified the following: (1) from the Creation to the Flood; (2) to the liberation of the Hebrews from Egypt; (3) to Saul's anointment as king; (4) to the beginning of the Babylonian captivity; (5) to the crucifixion of Jesus; (6) to the end. Hilarianus calculated that the crucifixion happened in the year 5530 after the Creation;

therefore, he could foresee how many years were left before the end. The history of this short future could be learned in the Apocalypse (*Apoc*, 19–20): during these remaining years the Antichrist would come and be destroyed by the Second Advent of Jesus; then, Satan would be bound for 1,000 years, and a first resurrection of the saints would take place; finally, at the end of this seventh millennium Satan would be freed from his prison and seduce peoples into fighting the last battle, in which he would be definitively defeated, and after that the Final Judgment would take place. The history of the Jewish people and of the Christian church was thus the blueprint of the history of the world.

Saint Augustine of Hippo (354–430) firmly opposed this view, asserting that only God knew how many years were left until the Second Advent of Jesus, but he accepted the periodization into Six Ages, and thus consolidated one of the two main periodization patterns of Christian historiography. Slightly different from Hilarianus's scheme, his periodization recognized the following ages: (1) from Adam to the Flood; (2) to Abraham; (3) to David; (4) to the exile in Babylon; (5) to the birth of Jesus; (6) the present time (*De Civitate Dei*, XXII, 30.5).

The pattern of the ages of the world attracted many early Christian scholars, and alternatives to the six-fold model were introduced. Origen of Alexandria (ca. 185–254) identified five moments of the history of the church, based on the parable of the laborers in the vineyard (Mt, 20, 1–16): (1) from Adam to Noah; (2) to Abraham; (3) to Moses; (4) to Jesus; (5) from Jesus to the present (*Commentarium in Evangelium Matthaei*, ca. 32). Eusebius of Caesarea (ca. 263–ca. 339) in his *Chronicon*—very popular in Europe during the Middle Ages through the translation and continuation by Saint Jerome (347–420)—individuated a seven-fold periodization: (1) from Adam to the Flood; (2) to Abraham; (3) to the exodus from Egypt; (4) to the building of the Temple under Solomon; (5) to the restoration of the Temple under Darius; (6) to the fifteenth year of Tiberius, when Jesus began his public ministry; (7) the present time.

Biblical chronology was actually problematic because three versions of the Old Testament existed, the Hebrew, the Samaritan (limited to the Pentateuch), and the Greek translation called Septuagint, which showed relevant differences just in chronology. Eusebius of Caesarea gave a synchronistic comparison of the three versions, and calculated that according to the Septuagint the Flood occurred 2,242 years after the Creation, whilst the computation according to the Hebrew text gave 1,656 years and the one according to the Samaritan text 1,307 years (*Chronicon*, I, 16). Two main problems remained nevertheless open. A first problem was: which one of the three biblical texts was more reliable? Saint Jerome, who translated the Bible into the Latin Vulgate, which was later declared by the Council of Trent the only authorized text, originally preferred the Septuagint but eventually privileged the Hebrew text, though his choice was not definitive for historians. In fact, during the next centuries, some historians followed the Hebrew text, others the Septuagint, and some avoided the decision by simply giving parallel reckonings of both. A second problem was the lack of clarity of the chronological data inside each text: as Saint Jerome noticed, there were a lot of discrepancies, above all in the chronology of the kings of Judah and Israel (*Epistola LXXII ad Vitalem presbyterum*). Therefore, Eusebius' reckonings were not definitive, and the result was a conundrum which consumed historians' minds for centuries. A milestone in this long research was marked in the seventeenth century by the Anglican archbishop James Ussher, who produced the reference work *Annales Veteris Testamenti* (1650, followed by *Annalium pars posterior* 1654), where on the basis of the Hebrew text he fixed the Creation 4004 years before the birth of Jesus: his reckoning was introduced in the King James version of the Bible and met a large consensus both among Protestants and Catholics.

The second main periodization pattern of Christian historiography was the succession of empires, which the early Christian Fathers found not only in Greco-Roman historiography but also as an eschatological metaphor in the biblical book of Daniel. In the second chapter, probably written about 250–230 BCE, Daniel interprets the dream of the king of Babylon: a statue made of metals of successively lesser value (the head of gold, the chest and arms of silver, the belly of brass, the legs of iron and the feet partly of iron and partly of clay), which is eventually destroyed by a stone (*Dn* 2, 31–45). The theme reappears in the seventh chapter (written later, around 164 BCE) with the vision of the four beasts. The identification of the parts of the statue or of the beasts with actual empires varied consistently among the commentators. In any case, the five empires of Greco-Roman historiography were reduced to four in order to fit into Daniel's prophetic scheme, and the last had to be the Roman, which was to continue until the stone, the Second Advent of Jesus, put an end to it and inaugurated the Kingdom of Jesus on Earth. Saint Jerome replaced Assyrians with Babylonians and put Medes and Persians together, thus establishing the following set: Babylonians, Medes and Persians, Macedonians, Romans (*Commentariorum in Danielem prophetam liber unus*). Paulus Orosius (ca. 375–ca. 418), a disciple of Saint Augustine, identified a different succession, which matched with the four cardinal directions: in the East the Babylonian empire (which also included the Assyrian and the Persian), in the north the Macedonian, in the south the Carthaginian, and in the West the Roman (*Historiarum adversum Paganos Libri VII*).

The pattern of the Four Empires joined the universalistic vision of the Greek and Roman historians. Fundamental in this scheme was the role of the Roman empire, with its mundane endlessness. When the Roman empire became Christian, this idea of an everlasting Roman empire was accepted by many Christian authors, who attributed to Rome a central place in the history of salvation: Eusebius of Caesarea asserted that the peace realized by Augustus had prepared the context for the diffusion of the Christian message (*Historia ecclesiastica* I, 2, 23) and that Rome would last forever under the protection of the Cross (*Oratio de laudibus Constantini*, IX, 8).

MEDIEVAL EUROPEAN HISTORIOGRAPHY

The two periodization patterns of the Six Ages and of the Four Empires dominated medieval European historiography. The pattern of the Six Ages according to Saint Augustine was popularized through the influential *Chronicon* of Isidore of Seville (ca. 560–636), and through *De Temporibus liber* and *De Temporum ratione* by the Venerable Bede (ca. 672–735). Concerning chronology, Isidore followed the Septuagint. Bede acknowledged both the Septuagint and the Hebrew chronologies, but clarified that he considered the latter more reliable. After the birth of Jesus he put parallel to the years from the Creation the year *Christi* according to the reckoning made in the sixth century by Dionysius Exiguus. This system slowly entered European historiography. It was, for instance, adopted by Denis Pétau in his *Opus de doctrina temporum* (1627), by James Ussher, and by Jacques Bénigne Bossuet in his *Discours sur l'histoire universelle à Monseigneur le Dauphin* (1681). When the biblical chronology was dismissed, it became the standard in the form of BC (Before Christ) and AD (*Anno Domini*). In the context of world history writing in English, this denomination has been recently often replaced by BCE (Before the Common Era) and CE (Common Era), in order to avoid specific reference to Christianity and make chronology culturally neutral.

The periodization pattern of the Six Ages was the most popular during the Middle Ages, as in the case of Ado of Vienne, and others, who continued and updated the works of Isidore and Bede. The pattern of the Four Empires (also called monarchies) was adopted above all in Germany, because it supported the idea of the continuity between the old Roman empire and the new empire in German hands. This pattern is to be found in the *Annolied*, a poem probably written between 1077 and 1081 in honor of Anno II, bishop of Cologne, in the *Sächsische Weltchronik* (first half of the thirteenth century) and in the *Chronica sive Historia de duabus civitatibus* by Otto of Freising (ca. 1114–1158), uncle of Frederick Barbarossa. These two periodization patterns were not necessarily mutually exclusive; even if most historians opted for one or the other, some of them combined both, like Ekkehard of Aura, or inserted the four monarchies in the fifth age, like the English Benedictine monk Matthew Paris (ca. 1200–59) in his *Chronica maiora*, and the bishop of Florence Saint Antoninus (1389–1459) in his *Chronicorum opus*.

MUSLIM HISTORIOGRAPHY

Muslim historians had a quite different horizon than their European colleagues, stretching from Maghreb to China. They were acquainted not only with the Bible, which was the basis for pre-Islamic history, but also with Christian historiography, thanks to Christian historians working in the Islamic environment. Concerning periodization, Muslim scholars divided history into two ages, before and after the *hijra*: neither the Six Ages nor the Four Empires were relevant in this context. Great attention was paid to the synchronization of the chronologies of the many cultures they met, and for some historians this issue had also an eschatological dimension, as it did the early Christians. Abu Ja'far Muhammad ibn Jarir al-Tabari (838–923) accepted the idea that the days of Creation were equal to 1,000 years, and he concluded that Creation itself had lasted 7,000 years, and therefore the world after Adam would last 7,000 more years (*History of Prophets and Kings*, I, 54–5). On the contrary, Abū al-Hasan 'Alī al-Mas'ūdī (tenth century) explicitly refused any calculation of the time from the Creation and of the duration of Earth (*The Golden Meadows*), LXIX).

EUROPEANS DISCOVER NEW HISTORIES

European overseas travel since the end of the fifteenth century produced an unprecedented influx of knowledge that dramatically influenced the European vision of the world, which had remained almost unchanged since late antiquity. A process of secularization and widening of the historical horizon began, which lasted almost three centuries, during which the Christian periodization systems slowly declined. The pattern of the ages is still to be found, in Eusebius' version, during the seventeenth century in the works of Denis Pétau and James Ussher. But more popular was the pattern of the Four Monarchies, which played an important role in Lutheran thought. It shaped the *Chronica* written by Johannes Carion (1532) in close contact with the Lutheran theologian Philipp Melanchthon, which was continued by Melanchthon himself and by his son-in-law Kaspar Peucer and became, with the title *Chronicon Carionis*, the most diffused history textbook in Lutheran universities. Carion's book was also influenced by the strong eschatological visions of its time. Melanchthon in fact induced Carion to open the book with the so called *Vaticinium Eliae*, a passage of the Babylonian Talmud (actually 'teaching of the house of Elijahu'), which divided history into three ages of equal duration: 2,000 years of chaos, 2,000 years under the Torah, and 2,000 years of messianic age. Thus, again came the idea that the world would last 6,000 years. At the end, Carion calculated that in 1532 already 5,476 years had elapsed since Creation, but he added that the end of the world could arrive even earlier than the six-thousandth year because of great moral corruption. Martin Luther also put the *Vaticinium Eliae* at the beginning of his work on the reckoning of time, the *Supputatio annorum mundi* (1541), and he too expected that the Second Advent would come soon. He found reasons for his hope in some recent signs, like widespread syphilis and astronomical events.

BIBLICAL CHRONOLOGY CHALLENGED

A serious challenge to the Christian chronology came from the new knowledge of Chinese culture. In fact, Jesuit missionaries realized that Chinese historical records reported a greater antiquity than the Hebrew Bible. One of them, Martino Martini, in his *Sinicae Historiae Decas prima* (1658), the first history of China published in Europe on the basis of Chinese sources, thought that their chronology could not be easily disregarded as mistaken, since Chinese historians were highly reliable. This book arrived in the middle of an uproar among scholars provoked by Isaac La Peyrère, a Calvinist writer who in

1655 had published *Prae-adamitae*. His analysis of Genesis and of St. Paul's *Letter to the Romans* led him to posit the existence of men created before Adam, which accommodated the Egyptian, Chaldean, Chinese and other chronologies. The debate was heated because of its theological implications, and it involved many historians, like Isaak Vossius who published in 1659 the *Dissertatio de vera aetate mundi, qua ostenditur natale mundi tempus annis 1440 vulgarum anticipare*, where he adopted the longer chronology of the Septuagint to accommodate the Chinese chronology. In the same year Georg Horn riposted against him with the *Dissertatio de vera aetate mundi, qua sententia illorum refellitur qui statuunt natale mundi tempus annis minimum 1440 vulgarem aeram antici-pare*, where he defended the authority of the Hebrew version, following Ussher, and solved the problem of non-Christian chronologies by simply considering them as fabulous and inspired by the common vainglory of having a long past. The controversy between Vossius and Horn drew in other scholars for a long time. The Chinese issue strengthened the rising historical pyrrhonism, which shook the foundations of traditional visions of history and opened the way to reconsiderations. One of the most prominent representatives of this intellectual stream, François de la Mothe le Vayer, published in 1668 an essay under the very telling title *Du peu de certitude qu'il y a dans l'histoire*, where he pointed out, among the many contradictions and bias in ancient and recent historians' works, the problem with the Chinese chronology, which together with the Egyptian and the newly discovered Indian chronologies, challenged what 'we are obliged to believe about the Creation of the world'.

In the second half of the seventeenth century other signs of the crisis of the traditional periodizations appeared. The German historian Christoph Keller (also known in the Latinized form Cellarius) elaborated the three-fold periodization of ancient, medieval, and modern, which eventually became the standard for European historians, with the later addition of prehistory and contemporary history. Cellarius' work remained traditional in its exclusively Mesopotamian and Mediterranean horizon. The history of the rest of the world was ignored. Different in this sense was Georg Horn's approach in his *Arca Noae sive historia imperiorum et regnorum à condito orbe ad nostra tempora* (1666). In the dedication he explained the unusual title saying that the Europeans had built a new Noah's Ark because with their exploration travels they had brought again together the peoples of the world who had remained isolated since the dispersion after the Flood. Horn created an original periodization pattern, with a first division of history in the antediluvian era, from Adam to the Flood, followed by a very short diluvian era, embracing the Flood and Noah's Ark, and then the very long postdiluvian era, this last one divided in turn into ancient and recent, the former embracing the peoples and kingdoms established after the Flood, who have disappeared, the latter embracing those that are still alive. Chronological succession was, therefore, not strictly followed: for instance China, whose history began about 300 years after the Flood, but which still existed as a state, is described under the recent history and not the ancient.

The Christian vision of history was reaffirmed by the French bishop Jacques Bénigne Bossuet, a most prominent theologian and tutor of the Dauphin, who published in 1681 the *Discours sur l'histoire universelle*, where he defended the role of Providence in history. The book covers the time span from the Creation until the crowning of Charlemagne. The substance is most traditional, based on the Bible and on Greek and Roman historians. For his periodization Bossuet adopted an original scheme in twelve epochs, combining the seven ages of the world with secular events, like the foundation of Rome and the crowning of Charlemagne. His rationale was to show the course of both Christianity and worldly empires. He also took the opportunity to demolish the pattern of the Four Monarchies. He noticed that the traditional vision was mistaken, because the first Assyrian empire had not been replaced by the Medes in its entirety but had three successors: the Medean, the second Assyrian, and the Babylonian kingdoms. Bossuet followed Ussher's chronology, but he showed little concern for the chronologists' disputes, asserting that the differences between the Hebrew Bible and the Septuagint were irrelevant for understanding God's plan.

VOLTAIRE AND THE ENLIGHTENMENT

Bossuet had announced a second book to cover the remaining centuries, where he planned to deal also with Muhammad and the Arabs, but he never wrote it. In the middle of the following century this task was undertaken by Voltaire, but with a completely different, rather opposite approach. In the Foreword to his *Essai sur les mœurs et l'esprit des nations* (1756, with further revisions) he directly attacked Bossuet for his narrow vision of history, which completely ignored all Asian peoples. To correct Bossuet's shortcomings Voltaire started his work with a long synthesis of the history of the world before Charlemagne, devoting a large share to India, China, Persia, Arabia, America, and Egypt. After this introduction, the first chapter was devoted to China, followed by India, Persia, and Arabia, and only afterwards came European history, which of course had a great share of the book; further long chapters were devoted to the rest of the world. Characteristics of Voltaire's *Essai* are the refusal of Providence and of the pre-eminence of the Jewish people, the enlargement of the horizon beyond Europe and a still unstructured idea of progress. His *Essai* is organized as a comparative account of civilizations, and this approach is mirrored by the absence of periodization, which was on the contrary present when he dealt with European history, where he recognized a middle age of decadence, from the end of the Roman empire to the sixteenth century (in his entry on 'Histoire' in the *Encyclopédie* by d'Alembert and Diderot), amidst four 'fortunate' ages: in ancient Greece the age of Pericles and Alexander the Great; in ancient Rome the age of Caesar and Augustus; then the age of the Medici in Florence; and finally the age of Louis XIV in France (*Le siècle de Louis XIV*).

Voltaire's *Essai* marked an important milestone in the process of the establishment of a secular world history, which was accomplished during the Enlightenment. When it was published, the European historiographical landscape was dominated by a work of unprecedented scale: *An Universal History, from the Earliest Accounts to the Present Time*, published in London from 1736 to 1764 and consisting of twenty-three volumes with almost 16,000 pages. This enterprise was realized by a group of scholars initially lead by George Sale, an Arabist and free thinker. Sale opened the first volume with a *Cosmogony* where he expressed a skeptical attitude towards the Christian vision, comparing the Biblical account with those of other cultures and even dealing problematically with monogenism. This attitude was not shared by his collaborators, and after Sale's death in 1736 they steered the work in an orthodox direction and rewrote the original cosmogony for a new edition. Orthodoxy did not mean a return to the Christian periodization patterns. The editors adopted in fact the broad periodization in ancient and modern history already used by Horn, and with the same rationale, referring to extinct and still existing empires and peoples.

German *Aufklärung* and World History

The impact of the *Universal History* was especially fruitful in Germany, where it stimulated a new and fundamental reflection on world history among the historians of the Georg August University of Göttingen, one of the centers of the *Aufklärung*, who developed a new concept of world history. August Ludwig Schlözer criticized previous world histories for lacking unity and being mere aggregation of data, and argued in favor of a systematic vision based on the common features of the history of humanity as a whole, on the *Realzusammenhang* (actual context) of causal connections of events, and on the fundamental changes that had produced differences among nations. The plan he outlined in his *Vorstellung seiner Universal-Historie* (volume 1, 1772) presents many interesting new elements. He explicitly dismissed the pattern of the Four Monarchies, which, he wrote, excluded almost thirty others, and he based his periodization on a three-fold general subdivision into prehistory, universal history, and recent history, with further subdivisions. Prehistory lasted from Creation to the foundation of Rome, covering 3,200 years. This period is subdivided by the Flood into two sub-periods of equal duration, and the latter into three more sub-periods: from Noah to Moses (lasting 800 years), from Moses to Troy, and from Troy to Rome (both lasting 400 years). Schlözer said that prehistory cannot be organized synchronically by peoples but only chronologically, because there is only scattered and obscure information, above all in the first part. History, he averred, does not begin with Creation, but with written records. By that, Schlözer denied the Bible's historical reliability and advocated a scientific approach to the sources. Only the second period, universal history, which lasted about 2,300 years, is the object, as its name suggest, of a synchronical and universal narrative.

After the foundation of Rome, in fact, the records of all peoples, from the Mediterranean to Japan, increased significantly. Rome is the leading element of the periodization of universal history: a well deserved honor, asserted Schlözer, because no other empire had had a greater influence on the fate of the world by establishing connections with most peoples over twenty-two centuries. Universal history is, thus, divided into two sub-periods: ancient history, ending with the emperor Theodosius, and modern history. Schlözer explained that usually the end of ancient history was dated with the birth of Jesus, and this periodization would also make sense because this time marked the passage of Rome from democracy to despotism and at the same time the beginning of a world religion comparable to Islam; but he preferred to advance the caesura by about 400 years because after that moment Rome started to lose the world it had conquered, under the impact of the migration of peoples, which made the beginning of a new Europe. The second sub-period ended in the fifteenth and sixteenth centuries with the definitive end of Rome, represented by the fall of Constantinople in 1453 and the end of the 'new papal empire' around 1520. This epochal change also coincided with other events: the discovery of America, a new political map of Asia, and the development of the new European culture. Concerning recent history, Schlözer maintained that it could not be analyzed synchronically and systematically, because it had not yet come to an end, and historians could not make a significant selection of events but only give separate accounts of many peoples.

Schlözer based his narrative of the *Universal-historie* on a selection of the most relevant peoples who had influenced the world or a great part of it, and distinguished them into 'dominating' and 'merely important' peoples. Dominating peoples were those who determined the course of history by the exercise of power—such as conquerors—and by the use of reason—such as legislators. During ancient history this category included the Assyrians, Persians, Macedonians, and Romans; in modern history the Franks, Vikings, Arabs, Mongols, and Turks; and finally, more recently, the Spanish, Russians, Dutch, British, and Manchus. Merely important peoples were in Schlözer's view those who had influenced history without violence, but only through their wisdom, inventions, commerce, religion, superstition, or even by chance: during ancient history, they were the Egyptians, Phoenicians, Hebrews, and Greeks, and during modern history the Papal State, Byzantines, and Syrians. Besides the centrality of Rome, Schlözer's universal history had an essentially Eurasian bias: sub-Saharan Africa and America were completely missing.

Periodization of world history greatly absorbed the efforts of the historians of Göttingen. In a later work, the *Weltgeschichte nach ihren Haupt Theilen im Auszug und Zusammenhange* (1785), Schlözer proposed a different periodization in which Rome lost its centrality: the first two periods were the primeval world, from Adam to Noah, and the obscure world, up to Moses (both periods of imprecise length and with only fables instead of records); then historiography begins and with it preworld, from Moses to Cyrus; followed by the ancient world, whose end is marked not only by a character of the European history, Clovis, but also by Muhammad, the khazar king Bulan, and the Chinese emperor Yang Jian; the Middle Ages, up to Bartolomeu Dias, Christopher Columbus, and Martin Luther; and finally the new world, up to the present. In this work one can also observe a clear distance from the Christian tradition. For instance Schlözer doubted the long lives of the Patriarchs and advanced the hypothesis that the many years attributed to them referred not to one man's life but to his lineage. Concerning the age of Earth, whilst previously in the *Vorstellung* he accepted that it had existed for about 6,000 years and used the Flood as a chronological benchmark, in the *Weltgeschichte* he expressed deep doubts about whether the Earth was created at the same time as the rest of the Universe, or was a later product after millions of years, and whether it was directly created by God or was a natural product of time. But anyway, he concluded, the primeval state of the Earth is not a historian's concern. Here Schlözer quoted Georges-Louis Leclerc de Buffon's recent work *Les époques de la nature* (1778), which attributed the origin of Earth to an impact between a comet and the Sun 75,000 years earlier. Natural sciences had started challenging Biblical chronology.

Johann Christoph Gatterer, a colleague of Schlözer, also devoted much attention to world history periodizations. In the second edition of his *Abriß der Universalhistorie nach ihrem gesamten Umfange* (1773) he expounded an unusual division into four periods of equal duration of 1,800 years. The first extended from Adam to Nimrod, the second until Alexander the Great, the third until the discovery of America, and the fourth period was still going on. Like Schlözer, Gatterer focused on peoples, divided into 'dominating' and 'enlightened,' the latter close to Schlözer's 'merely important.' Both lists were longer than Schlözer's, and in the third period among dominating peoples Gatterer also included the Aztecs (which he called Mexico) and the Incas, thus enlarging the horizon to America. The last period was also the time of European supremacy in the world, and here Gatterer pointed out the concept of a unique body of states connected by diplomacy, something which was unprecedented. Africa was in that time a land of decadence, without dominating or enlightened peoples.

Interactions of peoples were also the core of the vision of history of Johann Gottfried Eichhorn, professor in Göttingen from 1788 until his death in 1827. In his *Welt-geschichte* (first published 1799 with the volume *Geschichte der alten Welt*) he divided history into two great periods, ancient world and modern world, both subdivided into a first era when peoples had no connections followed by an era of interactions. During the ancient world, the era of disconnection lasted from the beginning until Cyrus created the first great connection of peoples and states. The era of connections lasted to 486 CE, when Clovis defeated the last army of the Western Roman empire and founded the Frankish state. The modern world also began with an era of disconnection, which lasted until the first Crusade in 1096. Then came a phase of connection, lasting until the present and divided in turn into two periods by the discovery of America in 1492. The first was the time of Europe's regeneration, with the Pope as center of Europe. The second was characterized by the end of Papal supremacy and the establishment of a state system and by the fact that Europe connected the world through navigation and trade. Europe, thus, has the greatest share in Eichhorn's narrative, but the rest of the world is significantly present. In the first volume, dealing with the ancient world, attention is paid, beyond the traditional Mesopotamian and Mediterranean context, to Ethiopia, China, India, Arabia, and Bactria, and two out of the four volumes dealing with the modern world are devoted to the non-European world.

EUROCENTRISM IN THE NINETEENTH CENTURY

Eurocentrism dominated European historiography during the nineteenth century: the worldwide horizons opened during the Enlightenment shrank again to Europe—an expression of its political pre-eminence in the world. An important role was played by Georg Wilhelm Friedrich Hegel and his *Vorlesungen über die Philosophie der Geschichte*, first published after his death in 1837 on the basis of his lessons at the University of Berlin between 1822 and 1831. The rationale of Hegel's vision of world history is the progress of the Spirit as consciousness of freedom, embodied in the state. His history started with Asia, where the first step of this process took place, a world made up of the three oldest empires, China, India, and Persia with its components: Assyria, Babylon, Media, Syria, Judea, and Egypt, a world where only one man, the despot, was free; then the path of the Spirit went from East to West, first to the Greek and then to the Roman world, where only some were free, and finally to the German world, where all are free. This fourth period is subdivided into three parts: the time of migration and Christianization; the Middle Ages after Charlemagne and the establishment of feudalism, and modern times, from the Reformation up to Hegel's time. The medieval era does not have here, in the line of progress of Spirit, negative connotations. Very relevant in Hegel's vision is also the concept of peoples outside history—peoples who had not embodied the consciousness of Spirit, like Africans and Americans.

Eurocentrism was canonized by Leopold von Ranke, who expounded his vision of world history above all in his *Über die Epochen der neueren Geschichte* (written in 1854 but published posthumously in 1888), which went up to the French Revolution, and in his unfinished *Weltgeschichte* (9 volumes, 1881–8), which crowned his research. He definitively excluded the rest of the world from the mainstream of history, disparaging China, together with India, because he considered their ancient chronologies fabulous and their state as closer to nature than to history. His *Weltgeschichte* thus became a history of Europe: after an opening with the Ancient Near East, Egypt, and Persia, the narrative delved into Greece, Rome, the Germans, and European history until the fall of Constantinople, with the only exception being Muhammad and Islam, but only in connection with European history.

MARXIST HISTORIOGRAPHY

The nineteenth century also saw the birth of Marxist historiography, characterized by a worldwide horizon and by a new periodization paradigm based on the stages of the political organization of economy. The structure of four stages was expounded by Karl Marx in *Die deutsche Ideologie* (written with Friedrich Engels in 1845–6) and later in his *Zur Kritik der politischen Ökonomie* (1859). The first stage was that of tribal ownership, characterized by a familial structure with an elementary division of labor; the second was the ancient communal and state ownership, characterized by slavery; the third was the feudal or estate property, characterized by serfdom at land and the guild system in cities; and finally the modern bourgeois mode of production, characterized by capitalism and proletarians. These stages marked a progressive path, which was to be completed by socialist society. This succession of developmental stages had fully appeared only in Europe: in other parts of the world at least one stage was missing. European history, therefore, became the blueprint of world history, as one can observe in the relevant synthesis of Marxist historiography produced by the Academy of Sciences of the USSR (*Vsemirnaja Istorija*, edited by E. M. Žukov, 10 volumes, 1955–65). Even if it shows a good coverage of non-European history (but with an underrepresentation of sub-Saharan Africa and pre-Columbian America) the periodization is basically Eurocentric: the primitive community ends in Egypt and Mesopotamia in the fourth–third millennium BCE, antiquity ends in the third–seventh century CE with the crisis of the slavery system and the establishment of feudalism in Europe, Asia, and northern Africa, and the Middle Ages end in the Mid-Seventeenth century, with the English revolution, the last caesura being marked by the October revolution, which opened the final stage of history.

Initially adopted in the People's Republic of China, this Soviet model was challenged after the Cultural Revolution especially by Wu Yujin for its Eurocentrism. He followed a different Marxist framework which focused not only on the stages of progress but also on the processes of interconnections towards a global community. In 1994 Wu Yujin published together with Qi Shirong *Shijie shi* (*World History*) with a three-fold periodization: ancient history, from the beginning to around 1500 CE, focusing on the development of agriculture and interconnections in Eurasia; modern history, until around 1900, dealing with the development of capitalism worldwide; and finally contemporary history, characterized by the close interconnection of all parts of the world.

AFTER WORLD WAR II: UNESCO'S WORLD HISTORY

A new impetus to world history research came after World War II from UNESCO, which aimed to replace the nationalistic visions of history by using world history as a tool for peace education. In this context a general history of humanity was launched, focusing on the scientific and cultural aspects rather than on political history and emphasizing the interdependence of peoples and cultures and their contributions to the construction of a common human heritage and of human consciousness.

The product was the *History of Mankind: Cultural and Scientific Development*, published in six volumes between 1963 and 1969 by a commission directed by Paulo E. de Berrêdo Carneiro. Its periodization began with prehistory, divided into two parts, the first one encompassing the beginning of agriculture and the second the beginning of civilization, the urban revolution, and the invention of writing; next came antiquity, from 1200 BCE to 500 CE, with the end of the Western Roman empire; the two following periods, respectively ending around 1300 and 1775, are characterized as an age dominated by religions in relatively isolated regions, and as an increasingly secular age in intensively connected regions. Around 1775 many events took place that collectively marked an epochal change: among them, the independence of the Unites States of America, the beginning of the Eastern Question, the completion of the *Encyclopédie*, the publication of Adam Smith's *An Inquiry Into the Nature and Causes of the Wealth of Nations,* the invention of Watt's steam engine, and the development of modern science in chemistry, medicine, and astronomy. The next and last caesura is at the beginning of the twentieth century, opened by the European hegemony and the triumph of industrialism.

CURRENT TRENDS

During the second half of the twentieth century, world history research has experienced an extraordinary development. Three main periodization paradigms have emerged.

The first is based on the productive relation between humans and nature and is connected with the new vision of Neolithic developed by V. Gordon Childe (*Man Makes Himself*, 1936), who focused on the introduction of agriculture and husbandry as forms of food production, thus marking a significant change from the previous appropriation of food through hunting and gathering. Claude Lévi-Strauss in his *Race and History* (1952) asserted that the two main revolutions in human history had been the Neolithic and the industrial revolution. The former took place during the time span of 1,000 or 2,000 years around the Aegean, Egypt, Near East, the Indus Valley, China, and America, and this simultaneity in many and isolated parts of the world was the evidence that this revolution had depended not on the particular genius of a given race or culture, but on natural conditions 'beyond the conscious sphere of man's thought.' Then the industrial revolution started in Western Europe began to move to the USA, Japan, and Russia, and was progressing elsewhere. This scheme was fully accepted by Carlo Maria Cipolla in *The Economic History of World Population* (1962). Leften S. Stavrianos (*Lifelines from Our Past*, 1990), focusing on changes in societal structure as periodization benchmarks, used the Neolithic revolution as the first grand transformation from kinship to tributary societies, but then inserted the industrial revolution in the broader context of capitalist societies, which he further periodized through the stages of commercial capitalism (1500–1770), industrial capitalism (1770–1940), and high-tech capitalism (since 1940). A similar vision was proposed by futurologist Alvin Toffler, who in *The Third Wave* (1980) focused on the agricultural and industrial revolution (since the late seventeenth century) and added a fourth stage, post-industrial society, starting in the late 1950s and characterized by the digital and information revolution and other technological and social features like space research and the global village.

Religion and culture make the second paradigm, the Axial Age, introduced by Karl Jaspers in his *Vom Ursprung und Ziel der Geschichte* (1949), meaning the period between 800 and 200 BCE, when in Eurasia new spiritual foundations of humanity were laid simultaneously and independently by religious leaders and philosophers (in China Confucius and Laozi, in India the Upanishads and Buddha, in Persia Zarathustra, in Israel the prophets from Elijah to the Second Isaiah, and in Greece Homer, Plato, Thucydides, and Archimedes) whose consequences last up to today.

The third periodization is made up by the paradigm of relations among civilizations or societies. It is the foundation of William H. McNeill's seminal book *The Rise of the West: A History of the Human Community* (1963), where world history is divided into three periods: first the era of Middle Eastern dominance (until 500 BCE), then the era of Eurasian cultural balance (500 BCE–1500 CE), and finally the era of Western dominance (since 1500 CE). This is an obvious Eurasian structure, whose rationale is the diffusion of knowledge, customs, and techniques, a process advanced by trade and military expansion. The first caesura is represented by the expansion of Hellenism and the expansion of Indian and Chinese civilizations; the second is the European overseas explorations. This paradigm has been further developed by Jerry H. Bentley into six eras characterized by different levels of cross-cultural interactions: the age of early complex societies (3500–2000 BCE); the age of ancient civilizations (2000–500 BCE), the age of classical civilizations (500 BCE–500 CE), the postclassical age (500–1000 CE), the age of transregional nomadic empires (1000–1500 CE), and finally the modern age (1500 CE to the present). During the first age, interactions allowed the diffusion of horse domestication and bronze metallurgy in Eurasia; the second age was inaugurated by the spoke-wheeled chariot, which had a great impact on warfare, and during this age distance trade networks were established and great migrations took place, like the Bantu migration in sub-Saharan Africa; the classical civilizations differed from the ancient ones in many respects the larger scale of their political control, the development of communication networks through new infrastructures, and the development of cultural and religious traditions which had a deep and long-lasting impact, such as Confucianism, Buddhism, Greek philosophy, and Christianity; the collapse of the Han and Western Roman empires marked the beginning of the postclassical age, which saw the emergence of a new geopolitical actor, the Abbasid empire, and an increase of trade centered on the Indian Ocean; the fifth age is characterized by the expansion of the nomads of central Asia, which shook most of the existing empires, but also created with the Mongol empire a favorable environment of exchanges. Finally came the European expansion and modern age, no further periodized but seen as a whole, as the age of globalization, thanks to the unprecedented acceleration of pace and volume of exchange.

These three main paradigms can also be combined for a finer or more complex tuning, as recommended by Peter N. Stearns. An example is given by Marshall G. S.

Hodgson, who in *The Venture of Islam* (1975–7) gave a basic periodization of an agrarian age (from 7000 BCE to about 1800 CE) and a technical age (since about 1800 CE), and further periodized the last part of the agrarian age into preaxial (3000–800 BCE), axial (800–200 BCE), and postaxial age (200 BCE–1800 CE).

This overview on the main current periodizations of world history closes with its most recent elaboration: big history, which places human history within the wider framework of the history of the universe, thus starting with the Big Bang and going through the formation of the galaxies, the solar system, planet Earth, and the geological eras until the evolution of human beings, and down to the present day. The most influential books in this field are Fred Spier's *The Structure of Big History: From the Big Bang until Today* (1996) and David Christian's *Maps of Time: An Introduction to Big History* (2004). In the latter, human history is periodized into three eras: the era of 'many worlds' covering the Paleolithic (from 300,000/250,000 to 10,000 BP); the era of 'few worlds', covering the Holocene and the agrarian era (10,000–500 BP); and the era of 'one world', up to the present. Worth highlighting is the unusual chronological system used by Christian, BP, that is, Before Present, which refers to the C^{14} radiometric dating with its benchmark in 1950, which had a fundamental impact on archeological research and therefore on historiography. This is an evident sign of the role attributed to the sciences of nature and their technologies in this vision of history. This naturalistic approach actually has an antecedent in H. G. Wells, science fiction author, futurologist, and pacifist activist, who in 1920 published *The Outline of History* (for decades a most successful book). Even if Wells opened with the history of Earth and did not go further back, the basic idea is the same: the merging of natural and human history, an interdisciplinary approach which is gaining ground in world history.

REFERENCES

BENTLEY, JERRY H. 'Cross-Cultural Interaction and Periodization in World History,' *American Historical Review* 101, 3 (1996), 749–70.

BREISACH, ERNST. 'World History Sacred and Profane: The Case of Medieval Christian and Islamic World Chronicles,' *Historical Reflections/Réflexions historiques* 20, 3 (1994), 337–56.

GRANADA, MIGUEL A. 'Cálculos cronológicos, novedades cosmológicas y expectativas escatológicas en la Europa del Siglo XVI,' *Rinascimento*, n.s., 37 (1997), 357–435.

KLEMPT, ADALBERT. *Die Säkularisierung der üniversalhistorischen Auffassung. Zum Wandel des Geschichtsdenkens im 16. und 17. Jahrhundert*. Göttingen: Musterschmidt, 1960.

MANNING, PATRICK, 'The Problem of Interactions in World History,' *American Historical Review* 101, 3 (1996), 771–82.

MAZZA, MARIO. 'Roma e i quattro imperi. Temi della propaganda nella cultura ellenistico-romana,' in Mario Mazza, *Il vero e l'immaginato. Profezia, narrativa e storiografia nel mondo romano*. Rome: Jouvence, 1999, 1–42.

MOMIGLIANO, ARNALDO. 'The Origins of Universal History,' in Arnaldo Momigliano, *On Pagans, Jews, and Christians* Middletown, Conn.: Wesleyan University Press, 1987, 31–57.

KLEMPT, ADALBERT. *Die Säkularisierung der üniversalhistorischen Auffassung. Zum Wandel des Geschichtsdenkens im 16. und 17. Jahrhundert*. Göttingen: Musterschmidt, 1960.

MANNING, PATRICK, 'The Problem of Interactions in World History,' *American Historical Review* 101, 3 (1996), 771–82.

MAZZA, MARIO. 'Roma e i quattro imperi. Temi della propaganda nella cultura ellenistico-romana,' in Mario Mazza, *Il vero e l'immaginato. Profezia, narrativa e storiografia nel mondo romano*. Rome: Jouvence, 1999, 1–42.

MOMIGLIANO, ARNALDO. 'The Origins of Universal History,' in Arnaldo Momigliano, *On Pagans, Jews, and Christians* Middletown, Conn.: Wesleyan University Press, 1987, 31–57.

RICUPERATI, GIUSEPPE. 'Universal History: storia di un progetto europeo. Impostori, storici ed editori nella Ancient Part,' *Studi settecenteschi* 2 (1981), 7–90.

ROSENTHAL, FRANZ. *A History of Muslim Historiography*. 2nd edn. Leiden: Brill, 1968.

ROSSI, PAOLO. *The Dark Abyss of Time: The History of the Earth and the History of Nations from Hooke to Vico*. Chicago: University of Chicago Press, 1984.

SCHMIDT, RODERICH. 'Aetates mundi. Die Weltalter als Gliederungsprinzip der Geschichte,' *Zeitschrift für Kirchengeschichte* 67 (1955–6), 288–317.

STEARNS, PETER N., 'Periodization in World History Teaching: Identifying the Big Changes,' *The History Teacher* 20, 4 (1987), 561–80.

VAN DER POT, JOHAN HENDRIK JACOB. *Sinndeutung und Periodisierung der Geschichte: Eine systematische Übersicht der Theorien und Auffassungen*. Leiden: Brill, 1999.

WACHOLDER, BEN ZION. 'Biblical Chronology in the Hellenistic World Chronicles,' *Harvard Theological Review* 61, 3 (1968), 451–81.

XU, LUO. 'Reconstructing World History in the People's Republic of China since the 1980s,' *Journal of World History* 18, 3 (2007), 325–50.

CHAPTER 4

···

MODERNITY

···

MATTHEW J. LAUZON

THE related terms *modern* and *modernity* are notoriously wooly words with contested chronologies and debated definitions. At the most prosaic level, the words imply simply something like 'new,' 'now,' or 'of recent invention.' As Crane Brinton put it in his 1950 survey of European intellectual history, '*Modern* derives from a late Latin adverb meaning *just now*, and in English is found in its current sense, contrasted with *ancient*, as early as Elizabethan days.'[1] Many use the term 'modern' in this sense as a marker of temporal discontinuity and present a variety of different dates, such as 1492, 1648, 1789, 1914, 1945, 1989, or even 2001, as the beginning of something like a new historical period that could be described either as 'our times' or the 'modern world.' Historians have frequently used phrases like 'modern Europe' and 'modern world' without explicitly reflecting on the meaning of 'modern.' Take for example the striking fact that a handful of history books with the phrase 'modern world' in their titles each has a markedly different chronological starting point. While R. R. Palmer's *History of the Modern World* begins with the Middle Ages, William Woodruff's *Concise History of the Modern World* begins at 1500 and C. A. Bayly's recent *The Birth of the Modern World* starts, by contrast, with 1780.

MODERNITY AS A CATEGORY IN EUROPEAN INTELLECTUAL AND CULTURAL HISTORY

···

As some recent commentators have pointed out, a significant distinction can be drawn between the temporal and the substantive conceptions of 'modernity.'[2] These two conceptions, however, are related insomuch as the practice of thinking reflexively about a 'modern world' or 'modern age' is at the very least implicitly part of the substantive conception of modernity. In other words, the substantive conception of modernity has developed out of the much older European practice of marking temporal discontinuities in terms of a teleological development towards an idealized and radically different future.

The notion that modernity represents not simply an epoch but a special kind of epoch with distinct historical characteristics can be traced back to the nineteenth century. Jakob Burckhardt's *Civilization of the Renaissance in Italy* (1860), for example, established a tradition of locating the rise of modernity in the Italian Renaissance, when, Burckhardt argued, humanists developed both a new kind of subjective individualism and a new kind of objective realism and rationality that had broad cultural and political implications.[3] Giovanni Pico della Mirandola (1463–94) claimed, in his *Oration on the Dignity of Man* (1486), that human beings are distinguished from other kinds of being by their capacity, as he put it, to 'fashion [themselves] into whatever form [they] choose.'[4] Such a statement suggests the emergence of a new sense of the freedom to begin making oneself and the human world according to one's own plans.[5] This principle of reflective self-determination is frequently cited as one of the fundamental hallmarks of modernity.

A similar line of argument locates the early history of modernity in the Protestant Reformation's insistence on the freedom of an individual's conscience from potentially corrupt traditions inherited from the past. Certainly this insistence which developed through a period of unprecedented civil and religious violence from the sixteenth to the eighteenth century led a number of European thinkers to argue that religious beliefs that could not be convincingly shown to be universal, natural, and/or rational should be looked upon as indifferent to the functioning of the state so long as they did not interfere with anyone else's practice of their own religion. This contributed to the retreat of spiritual concerns from a civic and public realm into an inward and private realm. This move from religion to spirituality thus led to another of the frequently cited hallmarks of modernity: the secularization of the public sphere.[6] As much as the Renaissance and Reformation in Europe anticipated certain hallmarks of modernity, both movements looked to revive aspects of a distant past rather than to create a distinctly new future. Insomuch as modernity implies that the new epoch will be significantly different from and in fact freed from any past epoch, the Renaissance and Reformation might best be thought of as having merely anticipated significant aspects of modernity.

During the late seventeenth century, the term 'modern' acquired a distinct significance in the context of the quarrel over the question whether or not the new culture and ideas of the seventeenth and eighteenth centuries could be said to have equaled or perhaps even surpassed those of the ancient world. The moderns in this quarrel rejected the claim made by their opponents that human history was doomed to be one of either perpetual decline or endless cycles of limited progress followed by limited decline. The moderns argued that the intellectual, cultural, and technological innovations of their recent past demonstrated that human history could be a story of potentially endless progress and perfectibility.

To be modern, however, meant more than simply to see the present as equal or superior to the past; it also implied the rejection of the idea that the past should in any way constrain the present. During the seventeenth century, the spectacular and well publicized successes of the 'new scientists' who challenged ancient and therefore traditional and authoritative accounts of the workings of nature, especially Galileo's and Newton's accounts of the movements of the planets, contributed to the sense that traditional accounts inherited from the ancients were liable to be superstitious, irrational, and misleading. In helping to lay the foundation for this Scientific Revolution, the English statesman and thinker Francis Bacon (1561–1626) argued, in his 1620 *Novum Organum*, that 'it is idle to expect any great advancement in science from the superinducing and engrafting of new things upon old. We must begin anew from the very foundations.'[7] In the following generation, René Descartes (1596–1650) developed a similar argument that traditions should be skeptically scrutinized and rejected when they fail to meet standards of truth set by scientific rationality. Descartes explicitly dismissed, as he wrote, 'those things which I had been persuaded to accept by example and custom only; and in this I freed myself gradually from many errors which obscure the natural light of our understanding and render us less capable of reason.' Descartes, 'pretend[ing] that nothing which had ever entered [his] mind was any more true than the illusions of [his] dreams' believed that he had finally uncovered the one firm foundation upon which to erect a new and perfectly rational edifice of knowledge.[8] This was the indubitable idea he had of himself as a doubting and therefore thinking individual. On this foundation Descartes helped to construct and promoted the 'new science' that treated the universe objectively as a grand mechanism operating according to unchanging laws. Two important developments in the ideal of modernity, therefore, took hold during this Scientific Revolution. First, nature came to be thought of as something like a machine that operates according to discrete, regular, and consistent laws and, second, that these laws of nature can be grasped, expressed, and potentially and self-consciously manipulated by individual rational human beings. By the late seventeenth century, then, Western Europeans had adopted a thoroughly modern sense of the self along with a modern sense of the natural world as a set of objective and potentially controllable phenomena. This modern sense of self and nature implied a world of critically rational individuals freed from the constraints of potentially irrational traditions who were able to scientifically understand and technologically manipulate the principles that governed the workings of an objective natural world.

The remarkable successes of seventeenth-century European scientists in explaining the natural world, particularly in the domain of astronomy, inspired others to extend the same principles to the human world and inaugurate what some called a 'science of man' that aimed at uncovering and manipulating the laws that were supposed to govern human behavior. Thomas Hobbes (1588–1679), for example, was one of the earliest European thinkers to argue that human beings could be thought of as operating according to mechanical, regular, and explicable rules. The task was thus to discover the laws of human behavior so that people might fashion policies which would permit human beings and societies to rationally actualize their potential.

This modern conception of the human sciences, of course, significantly shaped not only the historical representations of European societies but also those of non-European societies and the human world as a totality. The Enlightenment assumption that all human beings share a single nature entailed that one of the new tasks for historians involved studying different human societies from around the world in order to peel away the layers of historical development and so uncover a primitive human 'state of nature.' From this first, primitive, or prehistoric stage of human development, the Enlightenment historians believed they could trace, often by way of conjectures, the ways in which the latent potential in human nature would actualize and perfect itself over time. For most Enlightenment historians, this progressive development through time culminated in the recognition of the superiority and greater rationality of recent ideas, practices, and institutions over earlier ones. Given that these eighteenth-century historians presumed that all people share a single nature, the expectation was that every society could be expected to develop a similar set of ideas, practices, and institutions given enough time and so to be converging toward one homogeneous form. One instance of this historical framework was the famous 'four-stage theory' that Adam Smith (1723–90) articulated in his *Lectures on Jurisprudence* (1762). On this theory, any and every human society would eventually instantiate the same social forms as they moved from primitive hunting and gathering to modern commercial society.[9] For Smith and other philosophical historians of the Enlightenment, the development from primitive to modern, or from savage to civilized as they tended to put it, 'illustrates the progress of the human mind' itself.[10]

MODERNITY CONCEIVED AS A PROJECT

On this conception, modernity is not simply the latest form of historical discontinuity; it is rather the very specific stage in a long series of progressive developments away from an unreflective starting point toward a reflexive awareness that by scientifically discovering and willfully applying natural laws and rational principles people can radically transform the world.[11] A number of late eighteenth-century European thinkers attempted to provide an account of this historical development from what Antoine-Nicolas de Condorcet (1743–94), to take just one example, called 'the state of the human race among the less civilized peoples' to 'the condition of the human race at the present day in the most enlightened countries of Europe.'[12] While Condorcet believed that 'the perfectibility of man is truly indefinite,' he nonetheless also believed that an intellectual and cultural threshold had been crossed by certain European societies that could now be expected to progress much more rapidly and certainly away from irrational traditions. The rest of the human world, he concluded, could look to Western European societies and see its future: 'emancipated from its shackles, released from the empire of fate and from that of the enemies of its progress, advancing with a firm and sure step along the path of truth, virtue and happiness!'[13] Though they differed significantly, Hegel and Marx, much like Condorcet, also believed themselves to have uncovered the historical process that demonstrated the inevitability and even immanence of the necessary unfolding of human rationality and freedom.

Calls for a self-conscious sweeping away of irrational traditions and for their replacement by a completely new set of rational, and therefore universally legitimate principles contributed to the unique character of the political revolutions at the end of the eighteenth century. Although competing interests guided the French Revolution, the fundamental ideals were consistent with this conception of modernity as implying the work of self-determining individuals to impose a rational design on an imperfect world of traditions. The French and American Revolutions have frequently been cited as inaugurating an era in which a rational remaking of societies was to be the consensual work of a mass of otherwise autonomous, rational, and self-directing individuals. Like the concepts of restoration, reformation, and renaissance, the concept of revolution implied a return to an earlier starting point, but unlike these other concepts the notion of revolution had the distinctly modern implication that something radically new would be created. The French Revolutionaries' imposition in 1793 of a rationalized and secularized republican calendar was self-consciously intended to contribute to the total regeneration of at least the French nation and potentially all of humanity as well. Like the revolutionaries' attempts to tear down any and every symbol of what they began calling the 'old order,' the imposition of the new calendar was intended to mark the radical and total obliteration of, and therefore absolute freedom from, a past which, as a collection of inherited customs and traditions, revolutionaries associated with vice, irrationality, treason, servitude, fanaticism, and persecution.[14]

To the extent that modernity can be thought of as the idealization of a new starting point from which to radically transform and perfect the world, America has served as a powerful exemplar of the supposed promises of modernity. When John Locke (1632–1704) famously declared in 1690 that 'in the beginning all the World was America,' he meant by this that the so-called New World, as it existed then, represented a much earlier, perhaps the earliest, stage of human historical development.[15] And when Hegel referred to America as the 'land of the future, where . . . the burden of the World's History shall reveal itself,' he was similarly presenting it as a place in which people could rationally reconstitute the world by stripping away the accretions of vicious traditions.[16] This pretense that America had never been stained by a historical process thus lent itself to claims that it represented modernity's ideal past as pure perfectibility and ideal future as full actualization of that potential. The primitivist obsession with the supposed uncorrupted character of so-called savages has, in fact, been one of the ironic implications of the idealization of modernity as the unfolding of human perfectibility. Not surprisingly, then, American revolutionaries and their heirs adopted the thoroughly modern belief that they were returning to a starting point from which they could re-constitute a civil society on purely natural and rational principles. The American politician and historian, David Ramsay (1749–1815), argued in a speech he delivered on 4 July, 1778, for example, that Americans 'are the first people in the world who have had it in their power to choose their own form of government. [Other] constitutions were . . . formed by accident [or] caprice.' 'But, happily for us,' he added, 'we had the example of all ages for our instruction, and many among us were well acquainted with the causes of prosperity and misery in other governments.' 'Is it not to be hoped,' he went on, 'that human nature will here receive her most finished touches? That the arts and sciences will be extended and improved? That religion, learning, and liberty will be diffused over this continent? and, in short, that the American editions of the human mind will be more perfect than any that have yet appeared?'[17] Ramsay's speech implies that by adopting a modern written constitution American revolutionaries were agreeing to free themselves from irrational customs and to adopt a new form of rational association that would permit them to complete the project of perfecting themselves and their world.

Substantive Conceptions of Modernity

These intellectual, cultural, and political changes internal to European history from the Renaissance to the Revolutionary period, which gave rise to a narrative of modernity as a project to remake the world on self-consciously rational principles, provided a framework within which to understand the profound transformations in the material and social conditions of European and North American societies. While modernity was in principle a totalizing project to be exported to and even, according to many, violently imposed on all human beings, modernity was in practice, from the eighteenth century onwards, conceived of in terms of nation-states. As Prasenjit Duara has put it, 'the nation-state is the agency, the subject of History which will realize modernity.'[18] To be modern, communities were expected to adopt the model of national statehood, along with the institutions of civil society, which developed in Western Europe from the sixteenth to the nineteenth century.

Social theorists in the nineteenth and twentieth centuries also emphasized the emergence of certain other hallmarks of modernity, besides the nation-state, such as industrialization, urbanization, commoditization, secularization, bureaucratization, routinization, the split between private and public spheres, the rise of capitalism, of constitutional democracy, of mass media, of public intellectuals and professional academic expertise, or of specific techniques of surveillance and discipline, as producing and shaping modern societies. Among these, social theorists, from Marx and Weber on, have tended to explain the rise of modernity in terms of fundamental social and economic institutions and practices of capitalism. Social theorists from Marx to Anthony Giddens, therefore, have tended to see modernity's peculiar social, cultural, and intellectual hallmarks as resulting ultimately from the emergence, articulation, and expansion of the complex of economic ideas, practices, and institutions associated with capitalism, especially industrial production and a market economy, in Western Europe during a period they locate at some point between the sixteenth and eighteenth centuries.[19] One of the most influential frameworks for making sense of the links between the rise of capitalism and modernity in early modern Europe has been

Immanuel Wallerstein's world-systems analysis. Wallerstein's framework attempts to take into account the ways in which Western Europe transitioned from feudalism to a capitalist world-economy sometime between 1450 and 1650 by incorporating other regions of the globe through domination and colonization.[20]

Like their Enlightenment predecessors, these various social theorists have thus tended to take Western European and North American societies, since at least the eighteenth century, as both their starting point and their yardstick for making sense of modernity. These societies in earlier periods, like societies in other parts of the world that do not exhibit these hallmarks of modernity, are assumed to be 'traditional' societies, implying that they are in some timeless stasis waiting for modernization to kick in either on its own or as a consequence of the influence of already modern European or North American societies.

Besides providing a theoretical justification for European cultural chauvinism and imperial hegemony, such conceptions of modernity have provided a framework for a universal or global history by classifying every society throughout the world at any given moment in history as being at one particular point in the process of modernization. Virtually every aspect of a society could be used as an index that demonstrated its stage of development. In this respect, the gaps separating ancient, medieval, and modern societies in Europe came to be conceived of as analogous to the gaps separating primitive, intermediate, and modern societies around the globe. After noting that the 'primitive condition corresponds in a considerable degree to that of modern savage tribes, who, in spite of their difference and distance, have in common certain elements of civilization, which seem remains of an early state of the human race at large,' the British anthropologist, Edward B. Tylor (1832–1917) wrote that 'the main tendency of culture from primaeval up to modern times has been from savagery towards civilization.'[21] In 1930, the British author C. Delisle Burns, arguing that there are three distinct 'mental ages' of society, wrote that 'there is the *primitive*, now to be seen most clearly in tropical Africa, the *medieval*, in China and India, and the *modern*, in most of Europe and in North America.' 'This last type of civilization,' he added, 'is Western in origin; but its most important characteristic is that it has followed upon a social experience which has already passed through the other two stages.'[22] As Michael Adas has shown, by the early 1930s, when Burns's book had appeared,

> American educators, missionaries, and engineers . . . advocated political, economic, and cultural transformations in China, the Philippines, and Latin America . . . In the interwar period, . . . industrial, democratic America was assumed to be the ideal that less fortunate societies ought to emulate. America's path to political stability and prosperity through the rational management of its resources, through the application of science and technology to mass production, and through efforts to adapt the principles of scientific investigation to the study of human behavior was increasingly held up as the route that 'underdeveloped' and unstable societies were destined to travel as they 'entered the modern age.'[23]

The same basic assumption that Adam Smith and many of his Enlightenment con-temporaries adopted in the eighteenth century, which is that all societies can be expected eventually and naturally to develop along the same rational path as had the West, tended also to underpin the modernization theories developed by Talcott Parsons (1902–79), Walt Rostow (1916–2003), and others in the second half of the last century.[24]

A Global Modernity

Scholars have begun in more recent years to question these Eurocentric accounts of the historical rise of the hallmarks of modernity by arguing that other parts of the world, notably Asia, contributed significantly to the emergence of certain key characteristics of modernity. Foremost among this group are Kenneth Pomeranz, Andre Gunder Frank, and Robert B. Marks. As Marks succinctly puts it,

> However influential Europeans may have been in the making of this modern world, they did not make it themselves, and the West certainly did not 'rise' over other parts of the world because of cultural (or racial) superiority ... Those are Eurocen-tric myths that do not help illuminate the past and obscure understanding the present ... In fact, *interactions* among various parts of the world account for most of the story of the making of the modern world, not the cultural achievements of any one part. Indeed, those achievements are not understandable *except* in a global context.[25]

These historians are not so much challenging the idea that there are discrete hallmarks of modernity as they are challenging the complacent Eurocentric chauvinism that it was Europeans and North Americans alone who discovered or invented those hall-marks. In fact, as noted above, it was a particular representation of the New World that inspired the European fantasy of returning to something like a state of nature from which to radically transform the world and create a more rational and universalizable order. Similar kinds of inspirations for the emergence of modernity came in the form of European representations of other societies as well. One of the favorite ploys of eighteenth-century Europeans, as Barbara Watson Andaya recently and rightly noted in the context of a discussion of modernity and Southeast Asia, 'was to attribute disparaging remarks about European customs to a Chinese, an Indian or Persian traveler. Even the standard bearer for the "Enlightenment," Voltaire, contended that China was the "best-governed and wisest nation on Earth." '[26] While most Western Europeans and North Americans remained confident that their societies were the most rationally organized and, therefore, most modern, this did not preclude the possibility that other societies might have ideas, practices, or institutions that could be usefully appropriated and incorporated into their modern cultures. While the countless Euro-centric thinkers who were confident that the West had become the best were no doubt increasingly convinced that the discovery of such non-Western phenomena was unlikely, the investment by Westerners in minutely studying other societies gives the lie to the commonplace that the ideas, practices, and institutions associated with modernity were purely products of Western Europe and/or North America. To the extent that the rise of modernity in the West was the result of a variety of global interactions, appropriations, and/or adaptations of materials, ideas, practices, and institutions; and that this particular set was later imposed and/or adopted in various parts of the world, it makes sense to speak of a modern world and of modernity as a global phenomenon.[27]

THE MODERNITY OF CRITIQUES OF MODERNITY

One of the earliest figures to reject the idea that Western European societies as they had developed in what we today call the 'early modern period' were approaching perfection was Jean-Jacques Rousseau (1712–78). Just as he has been called both an Enlightenment thinker and a critic of the Enlightenment, so he also has been called both one of modernity's foundational thinkers and a critic of modernity. This apparent paradox points to the tensions implicit in the difference between substantive and procedural conceptions of modernity. While Locke, Smith, and Condorcet could all agree that rational changes were still needed to complete the progressive process of perfecting the societies they inhabited, they were nonetheless confident that their societies were much closer to being perfect than they had been in the past as well as much closer to being perfect than other societies in the world. Rousseau, by contrast, firmly and infamously rejected these beliefs. In fact, he argued in his *Discourse* submitted to the Académie de Dijon in 1750 that the apparent progress that the human mind had made and which was taken to be evident in developments in the 'modern' sciences and arts had actually coincided with a decline in happiness and virtue. In his second *Discourse* (1754), Rousseau explained that this decline had been the result of a fundamental corruption of human nature and human reason and that this corruption itself had likely been the result of the introduction of faulty abstractions introduced into languages and minds at a relatively early stage in the development of human societies from savagery to civilization. Rousseau, however, held out hope that his conjectural historical inquiries might help to show that the languages and by implication reason and human nature themselves could be regenerated and perfected. Rousseau, therefore, remained 'convinced,' as he put it, 'that the divine voice called the entire human race to the enlightenment and the happiness of the celestial intelligences.' Those, like him—who believed that reason and human nature themselves needed to be regenerated in order ultimately to perfect humanity—he continued, 'will attempt, through the exercise of virtues they oblige themselves to practice while learning to know them, to merit the eternal reward that they ought to expect for them.'[28] Rousseau's writings on history, language, education, and political theory can all be thought of, therefore, as being critiques of modernity, insomuch as they were indictments of contemporary Western European cultures; and simultaneously foundations of modernity, insomuch as they were intended to contribute to a radical regeneration of reason itself, which he believed would ultimately allow the universal and natural human capacity for perfectibility to develop fully.[29]

Modernity continued to have no shortage of critics in nineteenth- and twentieth-century Europe, many of whom noted that it has hardly been the unqualified good that it promises to be. Even Marx, Durkheim, and Weber, who, on the whole, each 'believed that the beneficent possibilities opened up by the modern era outweighed its negative characteristics,' noted such problematic consequences of modernity as anomie, nostalgia, dislocation, disenchantment, and the loss of traditional values and creativity.[30] Anyone who reflects on the mass violence and disruption of the French Revolution and Napoleonic Wars, of World War II and the Holocaust, or of countless episodes of European imperial violence certainly must have profound doubts about modernity's promise to extend and amplify peace, prosperity, and freedom. While there have been critics of modernity who simply reject it on the assumption that traditions are unquestionably superior, most critics have ended up

> denouncing modern life in the name of values that modernity itself has created, hoping—often against hope—that the modernities of tomorrow and the day after tomorrow will heal the wounds that wreck the modern men and women of today. All the great modernists of the nineteenth century—spirits as diverse as Marx and Kierkegaard, Whitman and Ibsen, Baudelaire, Melville, Carlyle, Stirner, Rimbaud, Strindberg, Dostoevsky, and many more—speak in these rhythms and in this range.[31]

This tendency to criticize one substantive form of modernity in the name of a different one suggests that modernity in the West has never been a homogeneous phenomenon and in fact that it may be better to speak rather of Western *modernities* in the plural. Peter J. Taylor, for example, has argued that Western modernity itself has twice been significantly 'modernized,' as what he calls Dutch mercantile modernity was supplanted by British industrial modernity, which itself was overtaken by American consumer modernity.[32] In this way, it is possible to conceive of the *project* of modernity as being reflexive also in the sense that it is constantly and radically transforming the *substantive* conceptions of modernity as a set of discrete but totalizing hallmarks. Non-Europeans have also long criticized the conventional conceptions and instantiations of modernity and their implication that traditional cultures and values are at best quaintly irrational signs of an unchanging immature society that should be radically transformed.[33]

Michel Foucault's critique of modernity, though obviously markedly different from these others, nonetheless shares something fundamental with it. Taking modernity to be a project, Foucault explained in his essay 'What is Enlightenment?' (1984), that

> we must try to proceed with the analysis of ourselves as beings who are historically determined, to a certain extent, by the Enlightenment. Such an analysis implies a series of historical inquiries that are as precise as possible; and these inquiries will

not be oriented retrospectively toward the 'essential kernel of rationality' that can be found in the Enlightenment and that would have to be preserved in any event; they will be oriented toward the 'contemporary limits of the necessary,' that is, toward what is not or is no longer indispensable for the constitution of ourselves as autonomous subjects.[34]

Unlike other critics of modernity, however, Foucault explicitly rejected the assumption that the critique of modernity should simply lead to a new, more modern, set of totalizing ideas, practices, and institutions. Foucault's has thus been a more fundamental critique of modernity than others insomuch as it is also a critique of the totalizing reason upon which the legitimacy of modernity is normally thought to be founded.[35]

Multiple and Alternative Modernities

Shorn of its otherwise foundational assumption of universality that was embedded in the principles of a shared human nature and a totalizing rationality, modernity may be thought of as capable of a plurality of equally authentic instantiations. While it had always been possible to conceive of forms of modernity that were ultimately inconsistent with and even hostile toward one another because each laid claim to universality, some recent scholars have begun to use the expressions 'multiple modernities' and 'alternative modernities' in ways that refuse modernity's conventional claim to universality.[36] In the lead article to a recent issue of the journal *Daedalus* devoted to the theme of 'Multiple Modernities,' S. N. Eisenstadt acknowledged that

> the notion of 'multiple modernities'...goes against the view of the 'classical' theories of modernization and of the convergence of industrial societies prevalent in the 1950s, and indeed against the classical sociological analyses of Marx, Durkheim, and (to a large extent) even Weber,...[who] all assumed, even if only implicitly, that the cultural program of modernity as it developed in modern Europe and the basic institutional constellations that emerged there would ultimately take over in all modernizing and modern societies; with the expansion of modernity, they would prevail throughout the world.[37]

By contrast to the long history of conceiving of modernity, Eisenstadt's concept of 'multiple modernities' 'presumes that the best way to understand the contemporary world—indeed to explain the history of modernity—is to see it as a story of continual constitution and reconstitution of a multiplicity of cultural programs.'[38] As he rightly notes, one implication of this approach is that modernity and Westernization cease to be identical; 'Western patterns of modernity,' as he puts it, 'are not the only "authentic" modernities.'[39] This conception of multiple modernities, while rejecting in principle the idea that an authentic modernity implies universality, retains the other key principles of reflexivity, or critical rationality, and of human autonomy, or emancipation from the fetters of tradition. This opens the possibility of studying the many ways in which different communities have reflexively constructed modernity for themselves.

Rejecting the convergence principle on which mid-twentieth-century modernization theories were founded, Eisenstadt has argued that what he calls 'the civilizational religious cores' of certain societies provide sources of differing programs of modernity and continue to influence the social, economic, political, and technical characteristics of different but authentically modern societies. This pluralistic conception of authentic modernities, in fact, comes quite close to what has emerged, mainly in the field of anthropology, under the tag of 'alternative modernities.' As Dilip Parameshwar Gaonkar argued in his lead article for an issue of *Public Culture* devoted in 1999 to the theme of 'alternative modernities,' 'modernity today is global and multiple and no longer has a governing center and master-narratives to accompany it . . . [W]e have to continue to think through the dilemmas of modernity . . . from a transnational and transcultural perspective,' despite the fact that 'Modernity has traveled from the West to the rest of the world not only in terms of cultural forms, social practices, and institutional arrangements but also as a form of discourse that interrogates the present.' Gaonkar calls on scholars to recognize that, despite the conventional tendency to present it as an abstraction, modernity must be always historically embedded in every cultural site at which its elements are put together in a distinct way and in response to local circumstances. Gaonkar notes that 'Different starting points ensure that new differences will emerge in response to relatively similar changes . . . In short, modernity is not one, but many.' He adds that 'people (not just the elite) everywhere, at every national or cultural site, rise to meet [modernity], negotiate it, and appropriate it in their own fashion.'[40] Scholars, predominantly in the fields of anthropology and sociology, thus have taken up this project of articulating the emergence and meaning of a plurality of authentic modernities. Some professional historians have also begun to work on the project of exploring alternative forms of modernity. Besides some of the articles presented in the special issues of *Daedalus* and *Public Culture*, notable examples of the attempt to understand alternative modernities from distinctly historical perspectives are Leo Ou-fan Lee's study of the emergence of a new kind of urban culture in China during the 1930s and 1940s and Dipesh Chakrabarty's study of the appropriations and translations of various aspects of modernity in South Asia.[41]

GLOBAL MODERNITY PLURALIZED

The idea that modernity could be plural introduces the possibility of rethinking the history of global modernity not only as the processes by which Europeans and Americans discovered or invented modernity, either on their own or through interactions with non-European societies, and then how this modernity was either imposed or spread to the rest of the world, but also as the result of an interplay of multiple modernities, each with its own particular but nonetheless authentic character which developed in its own way. One recent ambitious attempt at writing such a history of the making of the modern world in terms of multi-centric modernities is C. A. Bayly's *The Birth of the Modern World* (2004). Bayly notes in the conclusion to his global yet multi-centric history of modernity that 'the origins of change in world history remained multi-centered throughout. We need not so much to reorient world history as to decentralize it.'[42] While some reviews of Bayly's work rightly point out that its adoption of the specific terminal dates 1780 and 1914 tends to undermine Bayly's goal of providing a multi-centric account of the 'modern' world by seeming to privilege the long nineteenth century of European imperial hegemony, it nonetheless provides a set of potentially promising suggestions for more effectively conceptualizing world history in terms of the emergence of and interactions between a multiplicity of distinctly authentic alternative modernities.[43]

CONCLUSION

Peter van der Veer has argued that 'the history of modernity is also and perhaps primarily the history of modern history writing.'[44] The field of world history, like anthropology, is a reflexive project that contributes to the articulation of modernities even as it attempts to represent them. For this very reason historians need to reflect on the meanings of modernity. Much of the confusion, misunderstanding, and disagreement surrounding the terms modern, modernity, and modernities has resulted from terminological looseness and from different uses of terms that give rise to incommensurable conceptions of modernity. For some, modernity is merely a temporal concept; for others, it is one of a variety of slightly different substantive concepts; for still others, modernity is principally understood to be a distinct kind of project. Until recently, modernity in each of these guises has functioned principally as a term of binary thinking, whether as the term of contrast to antiquity, medievality, tradition, or primitivity. The project of thinking of modernity both in plural and global terms holds out the promise of breaking free from these reductive abstractions. To be successful, this project will entail thinking not simply in global terms but in global terms that significantly concretize, complicate and challenge older ideas about modernity and about the historical processes that contribute to the emergence of multiple or alternative modernities. On the face of it, this suggestion seems to amount to little more than draining modernity of its normative content and its totalizing pretenses so that scholars might attempt to treat modernity as a set of historical phenomena that different societies in different places and at different times have conceptualized in their own ways and either realized or attempted to realize. History writing since the Enlightenment has, however, contributed to undermining or legitimizing various institutions and practices, some of which are associated with modernity. A responsibly reflexive historiography that thinks deliberately about modernity and modernities will, therefore, take seriously its role in shaping knowledge and power in the world.

Notes

1. Crane Brinton, *Ideas and Men: The Story of Western Thought*, 2nd edn. (Englewood Cliffs, N.J.: Prentice-Hall, 1955), 256.

2. See, for example, Bernard Yack, *The Fetishism of Modernities: Epochal Self-Consciousness in Contemporary Social and Political Thought* (Notre Dame: University of Notre Dame Press, 1997), 17–30 and Björn Wittrock, 'Modernity: One, None, or Many? European Origins and Modernity as a Global Condition,' *Daedalus* 129, 1 (Winter, 2000), 31–60.

3. For a recent discussion of the role of the idea of modernity in Burckhardt's thought see John R. Hinde, *Jacob Burckhardt and the Crisis of Modernity* (Kingston and Montreal: McGill-Queen's University Press, 2000).

4. Giovanni Pico della Mirandola, *Oration on the Dignity of Man*, translated by Richard Hooker. Retrieved 8 January, 2010 from <http://www.wsu.edu/~wldciv/world_civ_reader/world_civ_reader_1/pico.html>.

5. Burckhardt argued that with the Renaissance 'for the first time we detect the modern political spirit of Europe . . . often displaying the worst features of an unbridled egoism . . . But . . . a new fact appears in history—the state as the outcome of reflection and calculation, the state as a work of art.' See Jakob Burckhardt, *The Civilization of the Renaissance in Italy*, trans. by Samuel George Chetwynd Middlemore (London: MacMillan, 1904), 4.

6. Hegel argued that, ever since the Reformation, 'German thought has been characterized by an increasingly introspective and soulful inner life, by a constant deepening of inwardness (*Innerlichkeit*).' Hegel assert[ed] that 'this unique German characteristic . . . condition[ed] Germany's acceptance of modernity.' See Harold Mah, 'The French Revolution and the Problem of German Modernity: Hegel, Heine, and Marx,' *New German Critique* 50 (Spring/Summer, 1990), 8. For Hegel, however, this was merely an anticipation of an authentic modernity insomuch as Germans still needed to outwardly embody the principles of modernity in concrete institutions.

7. Francis Bacon, *The Works of Francis Bacon* (New York: Hurd and Houghton, 1877), vol. 1, 74.

8. René Descartes, *Discourse on Method and the Meditations*, translated by F. E. Sutcliffe (New York: Penguin, 1968), 33–4 and 53.

9. Adam Smith, *Lectures on Jurisprudence* (Indianapolis: Liberty Fund, 1982), 14.

10. Hugh Blair, *Lectures on Rhetoric and Belles Lettres* (Dublin: Whitestone, 1783), vol. 3, 76.

11. This conception of modernity as a European project to willfully, rationally, and radically transform a medieval Europe mired in irrational traditions has been articulated by Hans Blumenberg. See his *The Legitimacy of the Modern Age* (Cambridge: MIT Press, 1985).

12. Antoine-Nicolas de Condorcet, *Sketch for a Historical Picture of the Progress of the Human Mind*, trans. by June Barraclough (New York: Noonday Press, 1955), 12, 4, 171, 175 and 201.

13. Ibid., 171, 175 and 201.

14. According to Lynn Hunt, 'the will to break with the national past distinguished the French from previous revolutionary movements.' Lynn Hunt, *Politics, Culture, and Class in the French Revolution* (Berkeley: University of California Press, 1984), 27. On the idea that the French Revolution represented modernity's special moment of the experience of a radical discontinuity that reoriented historical consciousness, see also Peter Fritzsche, 'Specters of History: On Nostalgia, Exile, and Modernity,' *American Historical Review* 106, 5 (Dec., 2001), 1587–1618, esp. 1595–6.

15. John Locke, *Political Writings of John Locke*, ed. David Wootton (London: Mentor, 1993), 285 and 316.

16. Georg Wilhelm Friedrich Hegel, *The Philosophy of History* (New York: Dover, 1956), 86.

17. David Ramsay, *An Oration on the Advantages of American Independence, Spoken Before a Public Assembly of the Inhabitants of Charleston, in South Carolina, on July 4th, 1778*, in Hezekiah Niles, ed., *Principles and Acts of the Revolution in America* (New York: A. S. Barnes, 1876), 379 and 381.

18. Prasenjit Duara, *Rescuing History from the Nation: Questioning Narratives of Modern China* (Chicago: University of Chicago Press, 1995), 20.

19. See Anthony Giddens and Christopher Pierson, *Conversations with Anthony Giddens: Making Sense of Modernity* (Cambridge: Polity Press, 1998), esp. 94–117.

20. See Immanuel Wallerstein, *The Modern World-System* (New York: Academic Press, 1974).

21. Edward B. Tylor, *Primitive Culture* (New York: Holt, 1889), 21.

22. C. Delisle Burns, *Modern Civilization on Trial* (New York: Macmillan, 1931), 6.

23. Michael Adas, *Machines as the Measure of Men: Science, Technology, and Ideologies of Western Dominance* (Ithaca: Cornell University Press, 1989), 402–3.

24. In modernization theory this assumption is referred to as 'convergence.' For an intellectual history of the modernization movement, see Nils Gilman, *Mandarins of the Future: Modernization Theory in Cold War America* (Baltimore, Md.: Johns Hopkins University Press, 2003).

25. Robert B. Marks, *The Origins of the Modern World: Fate and Fortune in the Rise of the West* (Lanham, Md.: Rowman and Littlefield, 2002), 155.

26. Barbara Watson Andaya, 'Historicizing "Modernity" in Southeast Asia,' in *Journal of the Economic and Social History of the Orient* 40, 4 (1997), 394.

27. See, for example, Jerry H. Bentley, 'Early Modern Europe and the Early Modern World,' in Charles H. Parker and Jerry H. Bentley, eds., *Between the Middle Ages and Modernity: Individual and Community in the Early Modern World* (Lanham, Md.: Rowman and Littlefield, 2007), 22 and 25.

28. Rousseau made this clear in a long note, in which he asked, 'What then! Must we destroy societies . . . and return to live in the forests with bears?' He concluded, 'As for men like me, whose passions have forever destroyed their original simplicity, who can no longer feed on grass and acorn[s], nor get by without laws and chiefs; . . . those, in a word, who are convinced that the divine voice called the entire human race to the enlightenment and the happiness of the celestial intelligences; all those latter ones will attempt, through the exercise of virtues they oblige themselves to practice while learning to know them, to merit the eternal reward that they ought to expect for them.' See Rousseau, *Discourse on the Origin of Inequality* (Indianapolis: Hackett, 1992), 80 n. 9.

29. On Rousseau as providing a modernist critique of modernity, see Alain Touraine, *Critique of Modernity*, trans. by David Macey (Oxford: Blackwell, 1995), 19–24.

30. Anthony Giddens, 'The Nature of Modernity,' in Philip Cassell, ed., *The Giddens Reader* (Stanford: Stanford University Press, 1993), 286.

31. Marshall Berman, *All That is Solid Melts into Air: The Experience of Modernity* (New York: Simon and Schuster, 1982), 23. The same has been said of some of the more recent criticisms of modernity, like, for example, those of environmental movements. See Peter J. Taylor, *Modernities: A Geohistorical Interpretation* (Minneapolis, Minn.: University of Minnesota Press, 1999), 85–7 and 90–4.

32. Taylor, *Modernities*, esp. 20–38.

33. See among others Duara, *Rescuing History from the Nation*, 205–27.

34. Michel Foucault, 'What is Enlightenment?,' in Paul Rabinow, ed., *The Foucault Reader* (New York: Pantheon, 1984), 39 and 43.

35. Foucault thus envisaged a critical application of reason to the study of the past that would overcome or at least resist the totalizing tendency of modernity and at the same time contribute to at least a partial and provisional emancipation of certain individuals and groups. Along with Gilles Deleuze (1925–95), he argued against the modern conception of the public intellectual, who speaks on behalf of and thus represents powerless victims. In place of the modern public intellectual he suggested 'that all those on whom power is exercised to their detriment . . . can begin the struggle on their own terrain and on the basis of their proper activity (or passivity). In engaging in a struggle that concerns their own interests, whose objectives they clearly understand and whose methods only they can determine, they enter into a revolutionary process . . . In this sense, the overall picture presented by the struggle is certainly not that of the . . . theoretical totalization under the guise of "truth."' See Donald F. Bouchard, ed., *Language, Counter-memory, Practice: Selected Essays and Interviews by Michel Foucault* (Ithaca: Cornell University Press, 1977), 216–17. Stephen Toulmin's *Cosmopolis: The Hidden Agenda of Modernity* (New York: Free Press, 1990) offers a similar critique of the totalizing tradition of modernity grounded, he argues, in Cartesian rationality. Toulmin contrasted this totalizing tradition with what he argues to be a more pluralistic conception of modernity that was first articulated by Descartes' near contemporary, Michel de Montaigne (1533–92).

36. The term 'alternative modernities' arose principally in anthropology while the very similar 'multiple modernities' has been mainly used by those inspired by S. N. Eisenstadt's work in sociology.

37. S. N. Eisenstadt, 'Multiple Modernities,' *Daedalus* 129, 1 (Winter, 2000), 1.

38. Ibid., 2.

39. Ibid., 3.

40. Dilip Parameshwar Gaonkar, 'On Alternative Modernities,' *Public Culture* 11, 1 (1999), 13, 15–16 and 17.

41. Leo Ou-fan Lee, *Shanghai Modern: The Flowering of a New Urban Culture in China, 1930–1945* (Cambridge, Mass.: Harvard University Press, 1999), and Dipesh Chakrabarty, *Provincializing Europe: Postcolonial Thought and Historical Difference* (Princeton: Princeton University Press, 2000).

42. C.A. Bayly, *The Birth of the Modern World, 1780–1914: Global Connections and Comparisons* (Oxford: Blackwell, 2004), 470.

43. See Jan Nederveen Pieterse's review essay, 'The Long Nineteenth Century Is Too Short,' *Victorian Studies* 48, 1 (2005), 113–23.

44. 'If one wants to tackle the issue of "modernity," ' he added, 'I would argue that there is a substantial need for a reflexive theory of the genealogy of history and of the professionalization of the writing of history.' See Peter van der Veer, 'The Global History of "Modernity," ' *Journal of the Economic and Social History of the Orient* 41, 3 (1998), 290.

REFERENCES

ADAS, MICHAEL. *Machines as the Measure of Men: Science, Technology, and Ideologies of Western Dominance.* Ithaca: Cornell University Press, 1989.

BAYLY, C. A. *The Birth of the Modern World, 1780–1914: Global Connections and Comparisons* Oxford: Blackwell, 2004.

BERMAN, MARSHALL. *All That is Solid Melts Into Air: The Experience of Modernity*. New York: Simon and Schuster, 1982.

BLUMENBERG, HANS. *The Legitimacy of the Modern Age*. Cambridge: MIT Press, 1985.

DUARA, PRASENJIT. *Rescuing History from the Nation: Questioning Narratives of Modern China*. Chicago: University of Chicago Press, 1995.

EISENSTADT, S. N. 'Multiple Modernities,' *Daedalus* 129, 1 (Winter, 2000), 1–29.

GAONKAR, DILIP PARAMESHWAR, ed. *Alternative Modernities*. Durham: Duke University Press, 2001.

GIDDENS, ANTHONY and CHRISTOPHER PIERSON. *Conversations with Anthony Giddens: Making Sense of Modernity*. Cambridge: Polity Press, 1998.

LEE, LEO OU-FAN. *Shanghai Modern: The Flowering of a New Urban Culture in China, 1930–1945*. Cambridge, Mass.: Harvard University Press, 1999.

MARKS, ROBERT B. *The Origins of the Modern World: Fate and Fortune in the Rise of the West*. Lanham, Md.: Rowman and Littlefield, 2002.

TAYLOR, PETER J. *Modernities: A Geohistorical Interpretation*. Minneapolis, Minn.: University of Minnesota Press, 1999.

VAN DER VEER, PETER. 'The Global History of "Modernity," ' *Journal of the Economic and Social History of the Orient* 41, 3 (1998), 285–94.

WALLERSTEIN, IMMANUEL. 'The West, Capitalism and the Modern World-System.' In *China and Historical Capitalism*, edited by Timothy Brook and Gregory Blue, 10–56. Cambridge: Cambridge University Press, 1999.

——. *The Modern World-System*. New York: Academic Press, 1974.

WITTROCK, BJÖRN. 'Modernity: One, None, or Many? European Origins and Modernity as a Global Condition,' *Daedalus* 129, 1 (Winter, 2000), 31–60.

YACK, BERNARD. *The Fetishism of Modernities: Epochal Self-Consciousness in Contemporary Social and political Thought*. Notre Dame: University of Notre Dame Press, 1997.

CHAPTER 5

GLOBALIZATIONS

JÜRGEN OSTERHAMMEL

THE revival of world history towards the end of the twentieth century was intimately connected with the rise of a new master concept in the social sciences: 'globalization.' Historians and social scientists responded to the same generational experience—the impression, shared by intellectuals and many other people round the world, that the interconnectedness of social life on the planet had arrived at a new level of intensity. The world seemed to be a 'smaller' place in the 1990s than it had been a quarter-century before. The conclusions drawn from this insight in the various academic disciplines, however, diverged considerably. The early theorists of globalization in sociology, political science, and economics disdained a historical perspective. The new concept seemed ideally suited to grasp the characteristic features of *contemporary* society. It helped to pinpoint the very essence of present-day modernity. Historians, on their part, were less reluctant to envisage a new kind of conceptual partnership. An earlier meeting of world history and sociology had taken place under the auspices of 'world-system theory.' Since that theory came along with a good deal of formalisms and strong assumptions, few historians went so far as to embrace it wholeheartedly. The idiom of 'globalization,' by contrast, made fewer specific demands, left more room for individuality and innovation and seemed to avoid the dogmatic pitfalls that surrounded world-system theory. 'Globalization' looked like a godsend for world historians. It opened up a way towards the social science mainstream, provided elements of a fresh terminology to a field that had suffered for a long time from an excess of descriptive simplicity, and even spawned the emergence of a special and up-to-date variant of world history—'global history.' Yet this story sounds too good to be true. In fact, historians soon learned to dampen their enthusiasm. Rather than being blessed with an instantly usable kit of analytical tools, they had to learn to navigate the treacherous waters of globalization theory. They also came to understand that global history is not just a globalization approach projected onto the past. It demands its own intellectual foundations.

A CONCEPT FROM SOCIAL SCIENCE
APPLIED TO HISTORY

When it was invented in the 1960s and as it slowly gained currency in the 1970s and 1980s, the term 'globalization' referred to the present-day state of the world and did not imply a narrative in the *longue durée*. Its proponents neither suggested a theory of societal evolution nor an interpretation that would make sense of the last couple of centuries of world history—as Immanuel Wallerstein's world-system theory had attempted to do. In the theoretical debates exploding in the early 1990s, the primary concern lay with defining the concept and using it to describe, still in very general terms, processes of worldwide societal change that had recently brought about a rapidly increasing integration between national economies and societies. Critical undertones were present from the very beginning while at the other end of the spectrum of opinions a number of prominent authors felt confident enough to hail the arrival of a new 'global age.'[1]

In a second stage, only a few years later, the initial intuitions were put to empirical test. This turn to the data led invariably to a glance at earlier developments inaugurating the new state of affairs. Contemporary globalization could only be considered novel or unique if it was viewed against the backdrop of the worldwide social landscape as it existed before the 1970s, a decade that was generally assumed to be of pivotal importance. Globalization came to be seen as the result of transformative processes that had to be traced back to 1945, to the turn of the century, or even beyond. As the number of publications rocketed and the debate began to transcend the geographical limits of North Atlantic social science, the spectrum of positions diversified to a degree that makes it impossible to discern simple and orderly patterns. Still it can be argued, following David Held and Anthony McGrew, that the early 2000s were characterized by a 'third wave' of thinking about globalization.[2] In contrast to the earlier euphoria with unbound mobility and transformation, the literature of this wave emphasized the resilience of institutions, social structures, and localized traditions. A fourth wave then took up constructivist concerns and focused on communication, worldviews, and the normative underpinnings of globalization. It moved from globalization as a social process to globality as a state of mind. Even before the onset of the global financial crisis in September 2008, new debates flared up concerning not just the political consequences of 'real' globalization, but also the viability of the term as an instrument of theory.[3] The crisis confirmed the doubts of those critics who felt that 'globalization' still lacks the maturity to dethrone the well-established master concept of 'modernity' as the central trope of the social sciences.

Confronted with a bewildering variety of theoretical offers and with a rapid change of intellectual fashions, the historian looks in vain for a reliable synthesis that might guide his or her own efforts.[4] 'Globalization' may be the buzzword of our age, but there is still 'no clear sense—not even an approximate sense—of what this word means.'[5]

Another authority, Salvatore Babones, writing for a leading work of reference, arrives at the same kind of sober conclusion: 'Globalization means many things to many people, so many things that it hardly seems worth offering yet one more definition of the term.' And he suggests that of a wide variety of globalization indicators none 'can be judged theoretically superior to any other.'[6] Historians would be unwise to skirt the term altogether. At the same time, they should not take it for granted, and they should be careful not to employ it with a confidence and naiveté unwarranted in the light of ongoing and inconclusive debates.[7]

A number of general observations can be made. First, it is an obvious though somewhat unsurprising and trivial fact that the world has been 'growing together' and that a 'human web' has been thickening for a long time.[8] When it was originally put forward, this insight startled those who had been thinking in terms of secluded and unconnected 'civilizations' as well as those oblivious of the old Enlightenment idea of a basic unity of mankind. Moving beyond such truisms as the ever-growing number of human bonds in an expanding world population, the crucial question is: which empirical criteria have to be fulfilled for processes of growing connectivity to be labeled 'globalization'? If that concept is applied to all sorts of border-transgressing interaction across 'large' spaces, it loses the specificity indispensable for any notion of analytical value.

Second, historians have always been wary of the mega-processes so dear to evolutionists of all persuasions. They rarely deal with humankind as such. It is intuitively obvious to them that globalization manifests itself differently in the various dimensions of historical reality. Migrations, the extension of market relations, long-distance warfare, the diffusion of plants and animals and its consequences for human livelihood, the spread of religions and other worldviews, the growth of global media—these and many similar processes follow their distinctive kinds of logic and their own trajectories in time and space. 'Globalization' is not observable as such, but only as an attribute of more specific processes of change. It requires *something* to be globalized. Individual processes unfolding within concrete contexts of space and time can usually be studied in themselves. They should, however, be placed within the global arena in order to be understood more fully. Their relation to one another, for example of migration to empire-building, seems to be largely contingent or, at least, a subject of further inquiry. General theories of globalization tend to be reductionist and to privilege one field over others, most frequently the economic sphere. This renders them quite useless to historians, the avowed foes of monocausal simplicity. As Raymond Grew has warned, 'globalization is not quite a theory in itself.'[9] It should rather be seen as an epistemological framework that bundles more particular models of change and directs attention to their largest possible spatial contexts. A globalization perspective by itself provides little in the way of explanatory power, and the common objection to globalization theory, that it blurs the distinction between cause and effect, is difficult to refute. Yet such a perspective helps to restate historical problems and to frame more adequate strategies of explanation. These strategies then incorporate theories of a more limited range and of greater precision.

Third, one of the most important results of the vast social science literature on globalization has been to enrich the vocabulary available to historians. They have learned to speak a new language of 'networks,' 'flows,' 'currents,' 'transfers,' 'mobilities,' 'diasporas,' 'hybridities,' and all sorts of 'transnational' phenomena.[10] The 'spatial turn' in geography and cultural studies has enhanced their sensitivity to territories, land-scapes, distances, boundaries, and locations.[11] Not always do historians go along all the way with the theorists. To mention just one example: few words are nowadays more popular with global historians than 'network.' However, not everything that at first sight looks like a regular pattern of interaction qualifies as a 'network' in the technical sense of sociological network theory. Some of these patterns may be too loose or too thinly woven to be a network proper; others are of a complexity that cannot be reduced to flows of information and resources between nodes—the essential feature of a network.[12]

Fourth, there seems to be agreement among writers on globalization that the process should be seen as self-reflective. The debates on globalization form part of globalization itself. This may even lead to a rule of exclusion: relationships between cause and effect totally concealed to the understanding of the contemporary actors involved should not come under the heading of 'globalization.' Thus, the transfer of microbes around the planet was 'objectively' of a global nature, but it remained obscure as late as the great cholera pandemics of the nineteenth century and therefore lacked the qualities of true globalization. Even those who are not prepared to go that far are likely to support the argument that in an adequate concept of globalization increasing connectivity in the real world of migration, trade, or war should go hand in hand with a growing global consciousness.[13] Worldviews and the practice of expansion and exchange form two sides of the same coin. Therefore, the wide-spread disjunction between the study of globalization by economists, political scientists, and international relations specialists on the one hand, by sociologists, anthropologists, and cultural studies scholars on the other, is unfortunate and should be overcome in global history.

Fifth, one of the most fruitful lines of inquiry has been the link between the global and the local.[14] Historians, mostly trained in the careful examination of specific circumstances, find that idea immediately appealing. They tend to work from the bottom up, whereas sociological theorists often have to be told not to disregard the particular case. 'Glocalism,' as some prefer to call it in a somewhat pseudo-theoretical way, has found numerous successful adherents among historians. Timothy Brook's *Vermeer's Hat* (2008) is just one of several virtuoso performances where the local and the global—in Brook's case, the town Delft where the painter Vermeer lived and the forces connecting it to China and other parts of Asia—are artfully intertwined.[15] It remains to be discussed, however, whether a separate level of 'the global' ought to be presupposed as given. In such a view, the global exists beforehand and is 'appropriated' by local actors. A different way of conceptualization would regard both 'the local' and 'the global' as products of the activities of specific actors in their daily practice, of a permanent drawing and redrawing of boundaries between 'internal' and 'external.'[16] How are local worlds penetrated by forces of 'the global?' When and why do people's primary worlds cease to be local? Under which circumstances do human groups or macro-collectives arise that define themselves in terms of supra-national or global identities?[17] Questions such as these make the abstract concept of 'glocalization' palatable to historians.

Sixth, few types of globalization are likely to unfold without conflict and violence. Historians will view with a good deal of skepticism any theory that equates globalization with peaceful change. The idea of expansion is inherent in the concept of globalization. At one extreme it involves conquest, subjugation, and the destruction of existing forms of social and political life, at the other extreme, the peaceful one, the slow diffusion of elements of culture such as language, religion, or law. Expansion of any kind touches upon the interests of specific groups, unsettles equilibria, creates new asymmetries of power, and necessitates negotiation. It causes tensions and instabilities.[18]

Seventh, social science theory does not always draw a clear analytical distinction between globalization and modernization. Are these two macro-processes identical? Is globalization a special case or sub-category of modernization? Is it the defining feature of modernization in a particular period, in the sense, for example, that *contemporary* modernity is said to quintessentially global? Does it transcend a kind of modernity and modernization that is too closely identified with the European or Western model? Does 'globalization' put a stronger emphasis than 'modernization' on non-linear types of social change? Does it provide a better grasp of developments at peripheries and in-between spaces, of 'liminality' and cultural dissonance? Historians are not required to solve these problems on a theoretical plane. Yet they should not expect too much support from theorists.

GLOBALIZATION AND GLOBAL HISTORY

Many general works on globalization offer some kind of historical narrative, sometimes in briefest and most general outline. Those narratives, basically, come in two different versions:[19] according to a 'weak' version, globalization prolongs earlier long-term developments and is linked to them through a variety of 'path-dependencies.' On this view, the increasing interconnectedness between people across vast spaces, mainly driven by technological innovation, was accompanied by a growing density within sub-spheres of society. The world became gradually more complex on various levels. The horizon of personal experience widened for many people, and the consequences of localized decisions and events were felt across ever-growing distances. The 'strong' version envisages the world as a single system, originating in the final decades of the twentieth century. At that time, a radical transformation surpassed anything known in previous history. It created entirely new spatial and temporal frameworks. Faced with a condition of unprecedented novelty, 'historicist' modes of thought, self-evident to historians and many other scholars in the humanities, are rendered useless.

The strong version relegates historical scholarship to an antiquarian delight in bygone ages. Is the weak version a suitable template for global history? To put it more generally: what is the difference between the history of globalization and global history?

Global history is a distinctive perspective on the past. It does not necessarily examine long-term developments. On the contrary, one especially successful way of writing global history has been to make a cross section at one particular point in time, a procedure that is not interested in macro-processes.[20] It highlights the simultaneity of societies in various parts of the world without making any claims as to mutual influences and common causal factors operating in the background. Few literary devices have been more successful in overcoming Eurocentric habits of seeing.

A second difference between global history and the history of globalization pertains to methodology. The very idea of globalization as the growth of transgressive connectivity dissolves established units of analysis. The idiom of flows and interaction diverts attention away from settled units such as local communities or nation-states. The relations between nodes within a network become more interesting than the nodes themselves. This devalues comparison, the old master method of historical sociology and of certain forms of world history writing. Global history is to a lesser degree committed to the central idea of interaction. It therefore retains comparative methods, disengages them from an association with the 'Spenglerian' notion of concrete and clearly bounded 'civilizations,' refines them, and puts them to new uses in innovative combinations of comparative and relationist analysis.[21]

A third difference between global history and the history of globalization derives from the treatment of difference. Even if a globalization perspective takes account of conflict and contradiction, it is, at a fundamental level, wedded to the vision of a homogenizing trend in (modern) history. Convergence and the growth of shared experience are construed as the overall tendency of world development, divergence, and fragmentation, though up to a point contributing to multicultural plurality, as an aberration from the normal course of events. Global history makes no such assumptions. Characteristically, one of its most important debates has centered on the problem of a 'Great Divergence'—the observation that the 'global rift' between rich and poor parts of the world, especially between Europe and Asia, is of fairly recent origin. Few participants in the controversy surrounding this topic have suggested that the Great Divergence might be accounted for in terms of globalization. This classic *problématique* of global history is being discussed with hardly any reference to theories and histories of globalization.[22]

Yet another difference becomes obvious when we look at the more specific claims usually bound up with the concept of globalization. To give just one example: even those who shy away from predicting the imminent death of the nation-state would probably agree that globalization erodes state power and leads to a 'de-territorialization' of politics.[23] If globalization theory aims at elaborating substantial diagnoses of the present, it cannot avoid propositions like this one. Global history, however, does not require assumptions of such a kind. It is more 'neutral' and more open to specific interpretations of particular cases.

In sum, 'global history' is a more general and more inclusive concept than 'the history of globalization.' Not all global history is history of globalization, whereas the history of globalization inscribes itself by necessity into global history. If treated in a highly technical manner, for example, as a quantitative study in market integration, it can, however, lose sight of the attractions of global history and end up with an impoverished and reduced picture.[24]

EXPANSION AND CONTRACTION AS RECURRENT PHENOMENA

The plural 'globalizations' signifies a *double* plurality: the breaking down of an over-arching master process into several different fields and types of globalization, and the fact that expansion beyond the confines of locality has taken place repeatedly throughout human history. It is a moot point whether migrations, the creation of market systems and empires, or the emergence of religious ecumenes and other forms of universalism should come under the heading of 'globalization'. Especially scholars who previously tended to apply the notion of the 'world-system' to early constellations from ancient Mesopotamia, Egypt, or India onwards argue in favor of a similarly extended concept of globalization.[25] Not everyone will share the obsession with origins evident in this kind of literature. It is one thing to acknowledge the complexity of early civilizations, quite another to place such complexity into a temporal continuum linking vastly different societies across the millennia. The question of when globalization can be said actually to begin may lead to a dissipation of intellectual energies and has a taste of naive reification of what is more a matter of perspective than of real existence. As Barry K. Gills and William R. Thompson, themselves fond of the big picture, succinctly put it: 'Global perspectives yield global histories.'[26] Moreover, labeling early examples of human communities drawing together as 'globalization' does not help to *explain* anything. Only in a very general sense—*sub specie aeternitatis*—is it reasonable to see world history as a continuous process of macro-social integration. Upon closer inspection, large-scale structures behave in a much more specific and disorderly fashion.

The questions, concepts, and methods of global history can easily be applied to *all* periods of history. However, it makes little sense to speak of 'globalization' before the emergence of regular communication between the continents on both sides of the Atlantic. This kind of logistic globality did not arrive overnight, but the sixteenth century was certainly a pivotal age. It has also been argued, with good reason, that the preconditions for global trade were created precisely in the year 1571 when Manila was founded as a Spanish *entrepôt*. Only then, a 'world' market became practically possible.[27] Trans-Atlantic and trans-Pacific trade were linked for the first time, although it took three centuries for them to evolve into one unified system.

Prior to the sixteenth century, world history was full of different processes of expansion and contraction. The forces of expansion were conquest, trade, and the complicated mechanisms of religious transfer. The outcomes were empires, trading networks, and large spaces where individual religions predominated. Contemporary observers described the fate of these structures by using cyclical models of rise, blooming, and fall. All of these structures underwent permanent metamorphoses. Their external and internal boundaries changed all the time. Some of them existed for many centuries; others disappeared after a few decades. Some gave room to chaos; others to fragmented configurations of equal or greater stability. In the twentieth century, sociologists and a few historians showed a new interest in cyclical models of military and commercial hegemony. Yet they failed to establish general patterns of rise and decline. Historical scholarship uses sophisticated tools to analyze pre-modern macro-structures and has displayed a growing interest in comparing them. Laws that govern such processes of integration and fragmentation have not been discovered. Several periods have been identified when religious or commercial innovation, empire building, or state formation occurred in clusters simultaneously in different parts of the world. These tendencies do not easily add up to a long-term pass towards growing connectivity on the surface of the earth. What happened within different contexts is too complex to be subsumed under the all too general title of 'globalization.'

For those who insist on a general use of the term, A. G. Hopkins's and C. A. Bayly's category of 'archaic' globalization might offer a solution. But it adds little to the terminology already available for the analysis of pre-modern forms of political, economic, and cultural integration across vast spaces. Before the sixteenth century, the numerous processes of expansion and contraction going on in the world do not fall into a discernable pattern. From the time when the first regular trading links across all the oceans were established, it becomes easier to grasp elements of globalization. For the two centuries between 1600 and 1800, Hopkins and Bayly suggest the cautious term 'proto-globalization.' In their view it includes not only the rise of new commercial networks through the expansion of the slave trade, the activities of the European chartered companies, and the intensification of Arab and Chinese commerce in the Indian Ocean and adjacent seas, but also the reconfiguration of state power in Europe, Asia, and parts of Africa.[28]

Throughout the period conventionally dubbed as 'early modern,' a greater number of actors than before operated within an extending geographical horizon: merchants, soldiers, colonial administrators, explorers, missionaries, and pilgrims. Driven by the rise of commercial capitalism (in a Braudelian sense), by the improved management of seaborne commerce, and by increasingly globalist visions of empire, the degree of connectivity in the world rose, with the Atlantic as the most important arena. It cannot be taken for granted that this early modern proto-globalization was a radical break with the past rather than a modified continuation of earlier trends of expansion and contraction. Cyclical trajectories of empires resembled familiar patterns. Differently constructed empires like the Mughal empire and the Portuguese empire rose and declined within the fairly limited time-span of about two centuries. Claims about the peculiarity of a special early modern form of globalization face two issues that continue to be hotly debated.

First, there is the question of quantities and proportions. When do quantities cross thresholds of significance? When does a circuit become a system? When do separate economies develop a level of exchange and of the division of labor that justify them to be called 'integrated?' The contention that this already happened, at least in the Atlantic region, during the early modern period remains open to question. Pieter Emmer sums up a more detailed argument by pointing out that 'all shipping tonnage in Europe around 1500 could fit into only two present-day super tankers and that we would need five such tankers to arrive at the tonnage available around 1800.'[29] World trade did not multiply in value and volume and progress from luxury goods to bulk commodities until the nineteenth century.[30]

Second to consider is the problem of the cultural integration of the world and the universalisms that are expected to go with it. What constitutes genuine 'global' awareness? How many people are necessary to form a socially relevant group of intellectual 'globalizers?' During the early modern period, Europeans launched unprecedented projects in the cross-cultural gathering of secular knowledge. Earlier ages had seen transfers of religions and laws, of languages and scripts; the European initiatives since the early 1500s were unique in their reach and comprehensiveness. European travelers and missionaries—especially the Jesuits—collected information on languages, beliefs, customs, political systems, and the natural world and accumulated huge treasures of artifacts and manuscripts from those parts of the world that were accessible to them. They measured and mapped the surface of the planet. Early modern thought in Europe was pervaded with knowledge about other civilizations. New discourses arose, later crystallized into academic disciplines: ethnography, comparative philology, archaeology, and the various branches of 'oriental studies.'[31] But did all this amount to cultural globalization? How much of European culture was actually exported or rather adopted beyond Europe and its colonies of expatriate settlement? Even the efforts of the Jesuits to win adherents to the Christian faith remained disappointing, given the enormous human input that went into the grand missionary enterprise. Few members of the European intellectual classes gained first-hand experience of non-Christian civilizations. Leibniz never went to China, Montesquieu never visited Persia, Diderot never traveled to the South Seas. The great majority of the population of Europe had only hazy and extremely stereotyped ideas of other continents, if any. Hardly any active cultural exploration took place in the opposite direction. By 1800, the educated and the powerful in countries like China, Japan, or the Ottoman empire remained as ignorant of 'the West' as they had been 300 or 600 years before. Cultural contacts multiplied during the early modern period, but they did not assume a new quality that deserves the name even of 'proto'-globalization.

MODERN GLOBALIZATION

Attempts to find a periodization for the bundle of processes we have come to call 'globalization' should abandon all hope for an all-encompassing solution. As Raymond

Grew has pointed out, 'each periodization follows from a particular interpretation of the essence of globalization.'[32] From the insight that various types of globalization are unlikely to evolve synchronically follows the conclusion that it is impossible to posit a neatly demarcated sequence of 'stages.' Most historians and historically-minded sociologists prefer the idea of several 'waves'—short periods of intensified worldwide integration followed by intervals of reduced integrative dynamism. However, there is no consensus about the number of such waves and their place in long-term chronology. Few scholars defend the view that waves of globalization resemble the 'long cycles' of theories of economic growth in the tradition of Nicolai Kondratiev and Joseph A. Schumpeter. A recent metaphorical approach to the concept of 'waves' does not employ structural criteria, but sees them as clusters of representative *experiences* shared in distant regions of the planet.[33] Rhetorically persuasive as this suggestion may be, its charm results from a degree of impressionistic fuzziness unfit for a social science concept.

Something changed during the nineteenth century, probably since about the 1820s or 1830s: but what? Economic historians, able to draw on better statistical evidence than for the more distant past, single out three developments. First, the sheer bulk and value of long-distance trade reached unprecedented heights. Improved shipping and the beginning of the railway age created the logistic foundations for an expansion that, after the European colonization of Australia and New Zealand and the development of new export enclaves in West Africa and South Africa, left no part of the world untouched. This, of course, is a very simple empirical observation. Second, connections between markets for labor, commodities, and—much later—capital matured into integration. 'Integration' in turn is measured in terms of the long-term convergence of prices in distant markets.[34] Yet, price levels did not by any means coalesce all over the world, and the simple quantitative indicator of functional relations between prices ought to form part of a richer concept of 'convergence.' As Steve Dowrick and J. Bradford DeLong understand it, convergence means 'the assimilation of countries outside northwest Europe of the institutions, technologies, and productivity levels currently in use in northwest Europe and in the rest of the industrial core.'[35] By 1900, only Western Europe, the United States, Canada, three Latin American countries, Australia, New Zealand, Japan, and, in a way, South Africa belonged to a 'convergence club.'[36] The growth of global capitalism, evident in the last quarter of the nineteenth century, transformed the lives of millions of people on Earth—and left a greater number undisturbed in their accustomed ways of subsistence.[37] Countless peasants in India or in the interior provinces of China did not produce for export, never bought foreign consumer goods, and knew next to nothing about the outside world.

Forms of globalization other than economic globalization are even more difficult to pin down for a long nineteenth century up to 1914 or even a *very* long one until 1945. Few traces of global governance, the political scientists' main criterion for globalization, are to be found before World War I. The European 'concert of powers' was in shambles after the Crimean War of 1854–7, and the emergence of the earliest international organizations could not hide the fact that no normative consensus curbed the sovereignty of militarized nation-states. Most of the inhabitants of Asia and Africa were politically voiceless as colonial subjects or citizens of 'semi-colonial' countries. The League of Nations was not the complete failure it has often been reputed to be, but it certainly did not function as an effective guarantor of international peace. The inter-war years saw a fragmentation of the world economy into quasi-self-contained blocs (although it is at issue how dramatic economic de-globalization actually was) as well as a challenge to a peaceful world order from ultra-nationalism in Germany, Japan, and Italy.

Cultural globalization between the 1830s and 1945, a vast subject, is impossible to summarize in a few sentences. European civilization attained a maximum of its worldwide influence in the third quarter of the nineteenth century, thereafter losing much of its prestige in an age of mature imperialism and, even more so, during World War I. Still, colonialism left a long-term legacy particularly in education and the bilingualism of post-colonial elites. Europeans and North Americans remained curious about the rest of the world, but their perceptions were colored by a kind of structural arrogance that is nowadays known as 'orientalism.' Universalist programs like that of an all-embracing canon of *Weltliteratur* ('world literature'), advocated in the 1820s by the German poet and polymath Johann Wolfgang von Goethe, kindled little enthusiasm in Germany or elsewhere. 'Culture' invariably became a program of national soul-searching. The crucial difference between the period up to 1945 and the most recent decades is the absence of truly global media accessible for mass audiences. The fact that news agencies like Reuters cabled information from any major city in the world and that a daily newspaper like the *Times* of London was read by the powerful almost everywhere dwindles in importance when set alongside the impact of the electronic media today.

'Modern globalization' is a category wide enough to capture what went on in an age commonly described as that of industrialization, empire, and the nation-state, and the great economic spurt during the decades before 1914 laid the foundations for various post-1950 waves of global economic integration. At the same time, it remains to be discussed whether the various types of globalization really constituted *the* defining feature of the one and a half centuries after about 1800. Modernity before the mid-twentieth century was probably *not* quintessentially 'global.'

CONTEMPORARY GLOBALIZATION

With 'contemporary' or, to some, 'post-colonial' or 'post-Cold War' globalization we enter the realm of the social sciences. For twenty years it has been their principal thematic concern. The historian can only peddle a trivial kind of wisdom: the global-ization(s) we are experiencing today are in some respects of revolutionary novelty. They are so new and exciting that historians should spend at least as much time on the origins of recent global capitalism as on controversies about the very first stirrings of globalization at the dawn of history. On the other hand, some characteristics of contemporary globalization are not as singular as they appear to the historically innocent eye.

Not all changes that have taken place in the world during the last two or three decades can be credited to globalization. Thus, it remains an open question to what extent forces of globalization contributed to the collapse of the Soviet Union and its satellite states. Trends in the international economy and subversion by media from the 'free' or capitalist West certainly were not the only, perhaps not even the most important, causes of the disappearance of organized communism in Europe. The military logic of the nuclear Cold War, the civil rights movements in several countries of the Eastern bloc, nationality problems peculiar to the Soviet Union, and severe miscalculations on the part of the Soviet leadership both before and after Mikhail S. Gorbachev's assumption of power are just several among many factors unrelated to globalization that have to be considered when the end of bipolarity in world politics is to be explained.[38] The impact of globalization is more obvious in other fields:[39] first, innovations in communication and information technology, in particular computers, satellite telephones, and the Internet, and their rapid spread down to the individual household user; second, the affordability, for the first time in history, of cheap long-distance transport to middle- and lower-income groups in the 'developed' parts of the world and, as a consequence, the further growth of fuel-based mass transport; third, the creation of a unified global capital market working in real time; fourth, the convergence across countries and continents of preferences and patterns of consumption—although claims about a general 'McDonaldization' of the world should be taken with a pinch of salt; fifth, the massively enhanced importance of knowledge as a factor of production and a resource that confers competitive advantages on societies which cast themselves as 'knowledge societies'; sixth, the consolidation of a basic set of internationally accepted norms delegitimizing violations of human rights and a broad range of specific forms of violence and discrimination.

Historians will be inclined to see behind such novelties antecedents and continuity. While they do not claim that nothing new under the sun has been developing around the recent turn of the millennium, they will tend to restrain the wilder forms of excitement. A massive globalization of trade and investment already took place between the 1870s and 1914, and quite a number of economic analyses from the period read like current comments on globalization once the reader replaces the older terms *Weltwirtschaft* ('world economy')—the Germans were at the forefront of that kind of literature—or 'international economy' with 'globalization.'[40] In the domain of information technology, the invention and introduction of the Internet looks like a repeat performance of the installation of a worldwide cable network between ca. 1860 and 1902.[41] The two technologies differed in their carrying capacity, their economic contexts, the extent of political control attached to them, and the impact on the habits and cultural outlooks of their users. But the feeling that the new technology marked a 'revolutionary' compression of time and space was widely shared in the 1880s and the 1990s. The impression that life was accelerating is often claimed to be a singular novelty of an age when communication in real time has become a matter of course. Yet earlier generations, at least in Europe, had similar experiences. They were characteristic for the Age of Revolution since the 1780s, for the boom years of railway building, and for the *fin de siècle* between ca. 1890 and 1914.[42] In all these cases and up to the present time, it is difficult to find hard data for the alleged speeding up of life; a vague sense of going through exciting times is everything one usually discovers in the sources. A different kind of continuity is to be found where apparent rupture and advance turns out to be superficial. Thus, globalization theorists have often claimed that contemporary globalization successfully produces its own institutional underpinnings in the shape of robust transnational networks and effective global governance. The financial crisis that began in September 2008, however, revealed the fragile institutional basis of global business and reintroduced nation-states and national governments, already proclaimed obsolete or even defunct by many theorists, as indispensible actors guaranteeing the survival of transnational capitalism. History confounded an influential school of contemporary social and political thought.

The tremendous popularity of the concept of 'globalization' and the fact that oceans of ink have been spilled on it are no proof that social scientists will succeed in constructing theories of globalization that stand up to the highest standards of theory formation. Despite the work of important thinkers like Immanuel Wallerstein, Arjun Appadurai, Manuel Castells, or Saskia Sassen, a comprehensive and empirically relevant theory of globalization is nowhere to be seen. Such a theory, complete with ideas about how globalization is able to be identified and measured, would be indispensable to historians. It would help raise the concept from a cliché to an analytical tool. As things stand now, proponents of the concept do not even agree on their interpretation of the present-day world with its boundless availability of data. Is world society growing more equal or more unequal? Is world culture being homogenized, or are cultural differences mounting? Consensus on such seemingly simple empirical questions is still lacking. That does not inspire confidence in the application of the concept of 'globalization' to the past, where hard facts are much more difficult to come by. World historians and global historians will watch the further development of globalization theory. But given their own much more variegated concerns, they are not dependent on it.

Notes

1. For a good classification of concepts of globalization see William I. Robinson, 'Theories of Globalization,' in George Ritzer, ed., *The Blackwell Companion to Globalization* (Malden, Mass.: Blackwell, 2007), 125–43; on the public career of the concept and the political conflicts surrounding it see Nayan Chanda, *Bound Together: How Traders, Preachers, Adventurers, and Warriors Shaped Globalization* (New Haven, Conn.: Yale University Press, 2007), 245–69.

2. David Held and Anthony McGrew, *Globalization Theory: Approaches and Controversies* (Cambridge: Polity Press, 2007), 6.

3. David Held and Antony McGrew, *Globalization/Anti-Globalization: Beyond the Great Divide*, (2nd edn., Cambridge: Polity Press, 2007).

4. Good introductions are: Robert J. Holton, *Making Globalization* (Basingstoke: Palgrave Macmillan, 2005); Frank J. Lechner, *Globalization: The Making of World Society* (Malden, Mass.: Wiley-Blackwell, 2009); Jan Aart Scholte, *Globalization: A Critical Introduction* (Basingstoke: Palgrave Macmillan, 2000); David Held *et al.*, *Global Transformations: Politics, Economics and Culture* (Cambridge: Polity Press, 1999). The early debates are fully documented in Roland Robertson and Kathleen E. White, eds., *Globalization: Critical Concepts in Sociology*, 6 vols. (London: Routledge, 2003).

5. Michael Lang, 'Globalization and Its History,' *Journal of Modern History* 78 (2006), 899–931, at 899.

6. Salvatore Babones, 'Studying Globalization: Methodological Issues,' in Ritzer, ed., *Black-well Companion to Globalization*, 144–61, at 144.

7. See the strong warning against uncritical uses of the word 'globalization' by one of its earliest proponents: Roland Robertson and Habib Haque Khondker, 'Discourses of Globalization: Preliminary Considerations,' *International Sociology* 13 (1998), 25–40.

8. The standard statement is J. R. McNeill and William H. McNeill, *The Human Web: A Bird's-Eye View of World History* (New York: Norton, 2003).

9. Raymond Grew, 'Finding Frontiers in Historical Research on Globalization,' in Ino Rossi, ed., *Frontiers of Globalization Research: Theoretical and Methodological Approaches* (New York: Springer, 2008), 271–86, at 276.

10. A basic introduction is Robert J. Holton, *Making Globalization* (New York: Palgrave Macmillan, 2005), 55–80.

11. On the consequences of the spatial turn for the study of globalization see Warwick E. Murray, *Geographies of Globalization* (London: Routledge, 2006). An excellent over-view is Harm J. de Blij, *The Power of Place: Geography, Destiny, and Globalization's Rough Landscape* (Oxford: Oxford University Press, 2009).

12. Karin Knorr Cetina, 'Microglobalization,' in Rossi, ed., *Frontiers of Globalization Research*, 65–92, at 68.

13. Roland Robertson and Kathleen E. White, 'What Is Globalization?,' in Ritzer, ed., *Black-well Companion to Globalization*, 54–66, at 56.

14. With a slightly different meaning, the 'global' can also be conceptualized as the 'univer-sal.' See A. G. Hopkins, 'Introduction: Interactions between the Universal and the Local,' in A. G. Hopkins, ed., *Global History: Interactions between the Universal and the Local* (Basingstoke: Palgrave Macmillan, 2006), 1–38, esp. 7–9.

15. Timothy Brook, *Vermeer's Hat: The Seventeenth Century and the Dawn of the Global World* (New York: Bloomsbury Press, 2008).

16. Jonathan Friedman, 'Global Systems, Globalization, and Anthropological Theory,' in Rossi, ed., *Frontiers of Globalization Research*, 109–32, at 118–19.

17. See James N. Rosenau, *Distant Proximities: Dynamics beyond Globalization* (Princeton: Princeton University Press, 2003), 80–1.

18. A keen sense of such imbalances is to be found in the excellent textbook of Boike Rehbein and Hermann Schwengel, *Theorien der Globalisierung* (Konstanz: UVK Verlag, 2008).

19. Jörg Dürrschmidt and Graham Taylor, *Globalization, Modernity and Social Change: Hotspots of Transition* (Basingstoke: Palgrave Macmillan, 2007), 4–5.

20. A well-known example is John E. Wills, Jr., *1688: A Global History* (New York: Norton, 2001).

21. This is one of the great virtues of C. A. Bayly, *The Birth of the Modern World, 1780–1914* (Oxford: Blackwell, 2004).

22. On the debate within its wider context see Peer Vries, 'Global Economic History: A Survey,' in *Österreichische Zeitschrift für Geschichtswissenschaften* 20 (200), 133–69.

23. Roger King and Gavin Kendall, *The State, Democracy and Globalization* (Basingstoke: Palgrave Macmillan, 2004).

24. On the relation between global history and globalization see also Sebastian Conrad and Andreas Eckert, 'Globalgeschichte, Globalisierung, multiple Modernen: Zur Geschichts- schreibung der modernen Welt,' in Sebastian Conrad, Andreas Eckert, and Ulrike Freitag, eds., *Globalgeschichte. Theorien, Ansätze, Themen* (Frankfurt am Main: Campus, 2007), 7–49, esp. 19–22.

25. Andre Gunder Frank and Barry K. Gills, eds., *The World System: Five Hundred Years or Five Thousand?* (London: Routledge, 1993); see also the debate in Barry K. Gills and William R. Thompson, eds., *Globalization and Global History* (London: Routledge, 2006).

26. Barry K. Gills and William R. Thompson, 'Globalization, Global Histories, and Historical Globalities,' in Gills and Thompson, eds., *Globalization and Global History*, 1–17, at 2.

27. Dennis O. Flynn and Arturo Giráldez, 'Globalization Began in 1571,' in Gills and Thompson, eds., *Globalization and Global History*, 232–47, at 232–5; Dennis O. Flynn and Arturo Giráldez, 'Born Again: Globalization's Sixteenth-Century Origins (Asian/ Global versus European Dynamics),' *Pacific Economic Review* 13 (2008), 359–87.

28. A. G. Hopkins, 'Introduction: Globalization—An Agenda for Historians,' in A. G. Hopkins, ed., *Globalization in World History* (London: Pimlico, 2002), 1–10, at 5. See also C. A. Bayly, "Archaic' and 'Modern' Globalization in the Eurasian and African Arena, c. 1750–1850,' in Hopkins, ed., *Globalization in World History*, 47–73.

29. Pieter C. Emmer, 'The Myth of Early Globalization: The Atlantic Economy, 1500–1800,' *Nuevo Mundo Mundos Nuevos: Coloquios 2008*, <http://nuevomundo.revues.org/ index42173.html>.

30. Ronald Findlay and Kevin H. O'Rourke, *Power and Plenty: Trade, War, and the World Economy in the Second Millennium* (Princeton, N.J.: Princeton University Press, 2007), 383–5.

31. See the overview in Geoffrey C. Gunn, *First Globalization: The Eurasian Exchange, 1500–1800* (Lanham, Md.: Rowman & Littlefield, 2003).

32. Grew, 'Finding Frontiers in Historical Research on Globalization,' in Rossi, ed., *Frontiers of Globalization Research*, 277.

33. Lechner, *Globalization: The Making of World Society* (Malden, Mass.: Wiley-Blackwell, 2009), 15–32.

34. Ronald Findlay and Kevin H. O'Rourke, 'Commodity Market Integration, 1500–2000,' in Michael D. Bordo, Alan M. Taylor, and Jeffrey G. Williamson, eds., *Globalization in Historical Perspective* (Chicago: University of Chicago Press, 2003), 11–64, at 14; Jeffrey G. Williamson, *Globalization and the Poor Periphery before 1950* (Cambridge, Mass.: MIT Press, 2006), 25–36 (mainly on commodity markets).

35. Steve Dowrick and J. Bradford DeLong, 'Globalization and Convergence,' in Bordo *et al.*, eds., *Globalization in Historical Perspective*, 191–226, at 195.

36. Dowrick and DeLong, 'Globalization and Convergence,' in Bordo *et al.*, eds., *Globalization in Historical Perspective*, 198–99.

37. Jeffry A. Frieden, *Global Capitalism: Its Fall and Rise in the Twentieth Century* (New York: Norton, 2006), chapters 1–5.

38. For a genuinely global approach to the final phase of the Cold War see Odd Arne Westad, *The Global Cold War: Third World Interventions and the Making of Our Times* (Cambridge: Cambridge University Press, 2005).

39. Any observer will draw up his or her own list of globalizing innovations. Compare the following one with, for example, that in John Urry, *Global Complexity* (Cambridge: Polity Press, 2003), 50 seq.

40. A good example is the classic article by a German economist and sociologist: Moritz Julius Bonn, 'Das Wesen der Weltwirtschaft,' in *Archiv für Sozialwissenschaft und Sozialpolitik* 35 (1912), 797–814.

41. See Dwayne R. Winseck and Robert M. Pike, *Communication and Empire: Media, Markets, and Globalization, 1860–1930* (Durham, N.C.: Duke University Press, 2007).

42. See Peter Fritzsche, *Stranded in the Present: Modern Time and the Melancholy of History* (Cambridge, Mass.: Harvard University Press, 2004), a book based on ground-breaking work by the German historian Reinhart Koselleck; Stephen Kern, *The Culture of Time and Space, 1880–1918* (Cambridge, Mass.: Harvard University Press, 1983), 109–30; Bayly, *Birth of the Modern World*, 451–87. For David Christian, acceleration is the mark of the twentieth century *as a whole*: see his *Maps of Time: An Introduction to Big History* (Berkeley, Cal.: University of California Press, 2004), 440–63.

REFERENCES

BAYLY, C. A. *The Birth of the Modern World, 1780–1914*. Oxford: Blackwell, 2004.

BORDO, MICHAEL D., ALAN M. TAYLOR, and JEFFREY G. WILLIAMSON, eds. *Globalization in Historical Perspective*. Chicago: University of Chicago Press, 2003.

FRIEDEN, JEFFRY A. *Global Capitalism: Its Fall and Rise in the Twentieth Century*. New York: Norton, 2006.

GILLS, BARRY K., and WILLIAM R. THOMPSON, eds. *Globalization and Global History*. London: Routledge, 2006.

GUNN, GEOFFREY C. *First Globalization: The Eurasian Exchange, 1500–1800*. Lanham., Md.: Rowman & Littlefield, 2003.

HOLTON, ROBERT J. *Making Globalization*. Basingstoke: Palgrave Macmillan, 2005.

HOPKINS, A. G., ed. *Globalization in World History*. London: Pimlico, 2002.

LECHNER, FRANK J. *Globalization: The Making of World Society*. Malden, Mass.: Wiley-Blackwell, 2009.

OSTERHAMMEL, JÜRGEN, and NIELS P. PETERSSON. *Globalization: A Short History*. Princeton, N.J.: Princeton University Press, 2005.

RITZER, GEORGE, ed. *The Blackwell Companion to Globalization*, Malden, Mass.: Blackwell, 2007.

ROBERTSON, ROLAND, and KATHLEEN E. WHITE, eds. *Globalization: Critical Concepts in Sociology*. 6 vols., London: Routledge, 2003.

VANHOUTE, ERIC. 2008. *Wereldgeschiedenis: Een inleiding*, Gent: Academia Press.

CHAPTER 6

....

EPISTEMOLOGY

....

PATRICK MANNING

WHAT is the 'epistemology' of world history? What are the ways in which we know the world and its history? What are the categories through which we observe and perceive the world? What aspects of the world do we assume to be essential and unchanging? In what arenas do we believe change to be taking place? What are the limits on what can be known about the world?

This chapter poses questions and offers reflections on the most general type of thinking entailed in the study of world history. The chapter addresses the common and contested ways of knowing the world and its past that are shared among us. Epistemology has a history itself, but we will not attempt to review it here. This is a discussion of epistemology in world history at the present moment, with only brief and illustrative references to the development of global epistemology. It is about current issues and current debates, regardless of whether they are new debates or old debates. That is, the pronoun 'we' here represents contemporary writers and readers of world history.

How do we revise our understanding of the world in the context of the growing information overload? This problem, while it has surely arisen before, arises now with insistence: out of all the available information, how does one select appropriate information and process it to make possible an understanding of the world?

Indeed, what is the world? What are its synonyms and antonyms? In English-language noun forms, the terms world, globe, and planet are relatively synonymous. In adjective forms, the term 'global' is more widely used than 'worldly' or 'planetary.' But 'the world' can mean the entire universe. And 'world,' when modified by an adjective, can have meanings on numerous scales: 'a child's world,' 'the Islamic world.' Similarly, the adjective 'global' can refer to a totality at any scale. As a result, the terms 'world' and 'global'—and their equivalents in many other languages—have multiple and overlapping meanings, and need to be specified more closely when used in specific contexts. One can attempt a definition: 'the world' represents the outer boundaries or the entirety of that portion of the universe that we inhabit and seek to explain. Even this relatively unambiguous definition allows for variants and categories within it. Thus, the task of selecting a definition shades into that of creating an ontology, where the latter represents the set of categories through which we seek to classify, describe, and ultimately explain aspects of the world. The propensity to categorize and classify is arguably an inherent human characteristic.

What is history? The most dependable if not the most common definition of 'history' is the actual events and processes of the past. The 'historical record' consists of the currently available evidence on past events. It can expand as more evidence is added with time and as new discoveries and new methods enable the retrieval of additional information on the past. But the historical record can contract as information is lost or forgotten. Finally and most common in usage is 'history' as representations of the past—that is, the current and past writings and other representations that recall, describe, and interpret the past.

CONCEPTUALIZATION

The world as we know it is complex and multidimensional. The present exploration of knowledge about the world and its historical analysis is displayed along six dimensions. These dimensions of the world and its apprehension are topic, space, time, scale, philosophy of the analyst, and verification of interpretation.[1] The first four of these dimensions refer principally to the realities of the world itself, and the last two refer principally to human apprehension of the world—but all six, in some measure, are at once aspects of the world and aspects of human comprehension of the world. In addition, one must assume that the dynamics or forces for change that we apprehend are part of the world itself. These forces that change the world—or hold it within its existing state—include interactions of matter, of biological forms, and of ideas.

The topical subject matter of the world is infinite, and it is probably the case that any given subject, however defined, can be subdivided infinitely. The categories and sub-categories of topics or subject matter are far more heterogeneous than those of space and time. As a result, creating ontologies for topics is a complex task: for instance, not only is it difficult to describe topical categories with precision, but ranking topical categories and subcategories is a complex and often arbitrary task. The criteria for categorization may vary sharply from topic to topic, making it difficult to create an overall ontology for the topics of history.[2] For instance, the topic of textiles is sure to be categorized in far different ways from the topic of racial identifications. The heterogeneity of topics is a particular challenge to the study of world history as it is evident that, since there can be no general rules for categorizing and analyzing topics, there exists no deterministic procedure for summing aspects of history to get an overall result. This does not mean that world history is impossible; rather, it means that some constraints must be set by the analyst on the topics to be analyzed (and on space and time) in order to create an interpretation of world history within those limits.

The precise size and shape of the world has been known for some 500 years (though its spherical form was suspected by leading scholars for the previous 1500 years). The surface space of the earth is limited, and its limits can be experienced directly. The surface of the earth can, however, be infinitely subdivided. Space is three-dimensional, though it is often represented in two dimensions on maps and is also represented as the single dimension of distances between points. Further, space can be thought of in ways other than simple units of contiguous land: as archipelagos or multiple levels. Historical study has focused principally on studies of specific and limited spaces. In addition, comparisons, links, and interactions among spaces are standard aspects of spatial analysis in history.

An essential subdivision of time is given in years, which have been universally understood, often with great precision, because of the annual circuit of the earth about the sun; similarly the day has been of dependable length for all of human history. Seasons within years are more arbitrary. Time is apparently one-dimensional and one-directional, moving only forward. As with space, time can be infinitely subdivided. And just as space can be thought of in ways different from a contiguous terrain, time can be thought of not only as continuous progression but also as discrete periods, 'archipelagos' of such periods, and recurring cycles. The boundaries between events (treated as momentary) and processes (which unfold over time) are flexible, and exist as much in the mind of the analyst as in the reality of the past. Time can appear to have more complex dimensions when combined with space: an event at a given moment in one place will only be experienced in another place at a later time. Similarly, one must ask whether an event is confined to a locality, or whether it can take place worldwide.

The notion of scale addresses the question of how far along each dimension we go in our assessment of a world-historical issue. Scale is not actually a dimension but a measurement along dimensions, yet it is useful to treat it as a dimension to keep it in mind along with topic, space, and time. Scale can be considered in both quantitative and qualitative terms. That is, for each dimension of the world, the issue of scale addresses what domain along that dimension—what portion of the totality—is under consideration. It addresses variations in the extent of the world that enable us to discuss small worlds, parallel worlds, and the world as seen by a range of historical protagonists.

Knowledge of the world consists at once of evidence and also the apprehension or experience of that evidence. These basic categories are neither discrete nor straightforward; instead they are complex, overlapping, and undergo continuous interaction. For instance, this section has to account both for formal, academic knowledge of history and for informal, popular knowledge of history, as well as the knowledge and use of history by all sorts of social interests.

Evidence begins with information on the world, described in the previous section in terms of topic, space, time, scale, and dynamics. The category of 'evidence' begins with directly observable information about the world; it expands, with varying degrees of certainty, to types of information gained indirectly. Evidence created at a known time and place—for instance, written documents or artifacts of material culture or architecture—has a particular importance in providing testimony on that time and place. Testimony that is passed through time, as by oral tradition or by copying of texts, is subject to modification and transformation into myth. But just as some evidence is attenuated in value through transformation, in other cases the assembly and transformation of available records can expand the precision and value of evidence. Thus, the historian may combine retrieval of local records, interpolation to estimate missing data, and theory-based simulation to generate evidence on regional and national populations, birth rates, and death rates for past times.

For generations historians have labeled their evidence as 'primary' or 'secondary': primary evidence is assumed to be original and largely eyewitness evidence, while secondary evidence is taken to be mediated through an intermediate authority. This simple categorization, however, inappropriately suggests that most world-historical evidence is secondary and, by implication, inferior. Instead, rather than a two-level categorization of evidence, world-historical studies require a more complex system of description for data, indicating the original sources and the various types of selection and transformation that data have undergone to prepare them for use in global analysis. For instance, the transcription of a speech by an ancient orator must be translated to a living language to be understood by an audience today. The photograph taken today of an ancient monument provides a transformed view of a monument that has surely changed over time. National and continental statistics on population and income are not original observations, but are transformed and mediated through aggregation. Evidence, in sum, comprises a complex category.

What is apprehension? It is the collection and processing of evidence by an observer or analyst. Apprehension or perception of evidence depends on one's location (in time and space) and one's lens. The location of the observer is almost inevitably parochial. Since there is no way for an observer to view the world from all directions at once, the infinite possible perspectives become an important aspect of the apprehension of knowledge. Geographic and temporal location of observers provides basic elements of perspective. In addition, the notion of perspective distinguishes between local and global outlooks; between elite views of history and history from below; between the views of participants in and observers of a historical process; between views of contemporary events and views of past times.

The lens or outlook through which we perceive evidence begins most basically with the distinction between 'self' and 'other': the vision of 'self' can be restricted to an individual but can expand to a broad community; the remaining 'other' can be categorized into successively distant subgroups. In scholarly terms, lenses can be described especially through the academic disciplines (natural and social sciences, humanities and arts). Each discipline tends to focus on particular variables and on particular dynamics of change. As the experience and interaction of the various disciplines have developed, new distinctions and new commonalities in their lenses appear.[3] Thus, migration history and interdisciplinary migration studies have become gradually closer, while ecological studies and health studies have become more distinctive. Philosophy colors and shapes the lens with varying assumptions about the fundamental nature of the human situation, such as good and evil, free will and destiny, and change through simple causation or complex interaction.[4]

The results of apprehension, after further processing in the human mind, can lead to historical interpretation and analysis. These forms of knowledge, in which evidence and logical structures are combined to reveal statements about historical change, are to be explored in detail below. Modeling is an inherent aspect of interpretation and especially analysis: it is the systematic and often explicit logic of historical dynamics. Meanwhile the creator of a historical interpretation or analysis has the option of presenting it to an audience. That is, most people learn world history not as analysts but as 'readers' of representations created by others: the representation of world history is addressed in the concluding section of this chapter.

Apprehension of the world is arguably more complex than the world itself. Though the evidence through which humans perceive the world is limited, comprising only a tiny portion of all the reality from which evidence is collected and perceived, the range of locations, lenses, and philosophies through which humans apprehend the world adds many complexities to the world itself. History, as the representation of human apprehension and analysis of the past, is destined inevitably to be filled with controversy and reinterpretation.

To summarize this section, it is useful to compare the epistemology of global history with that of national and local history. In fact, the epistemology of world history is not much more complex than the epistemology of historical studies at a local or national level. The difference is that, because it remains a novel experience to explore the history of the world, there is a need for and an interest in the formal and explicit definition of the boundaries of study and the ways of knowing. For local and national history, certain limits tend to be given for the time, space, and even topic and scale of study, so that there remain fewer epistemological unknowns: the identity of the local community is easily taken for granted, as is the struggle of each nation for a place in the wider community of nations; the notions of a global human identity and of global patterns in family life have yet to gain easy acceptance among historians. With such exceptions, however, the epistemology of world history is not fundamentally different from that of history at any other level.

INTERPRETATION AND ANALYSIS

Historical analysis combines several levels of thinking and study: posing a question about the past, setting up the problem in a form intended to facilitate its solution, solving the problem, and verifying the solution or interpretation. Academic history relies on formal analysis, based on rational and systematic apprehension of relevant evidence. Yet such formal analysis can be seen as a subset of the broader category of interpretation, including responses to evidence that are impressionistic and informal rather than formal and logically structured. Indeed, the many genres of academic and popular history run the full gamut from logically systematic to impressionistic. The main lines of discussion in this section refer to academic analysis; however, most of the distinctions apply as well to impressionistic interpretation of the past.

Historians come from a widely varying range of philosophical traditions, and the varying philosophies lead to quite different ways of posing questions and answers. The distinctions among philosophical principles sketched here help to show how it is that different analytical priorities arise on the main topics proposed for analysis; they also show how historians can rely on similar data yet come to different or conflicting conclusions. Nineteenth-century philosophical outlooks remain central to world-historical analysis: most notably, the idealism of G. W. F. Hegel and the materialism of Karl Marx. Another great nineteenth-century current of thought was positivism, elaborated by Auguste Compte and focusing on study through breaking large problems into small ones, seeking deterministic relationships within the smaller problems. Philosophies of structuralism and postmodernism have developed in more recent times, rejecting the positivist separation of problems into discrete sub-problems and emphasizing interactions among aspects of a problem. Further work by specialists in philosophy has given pragmatic and interactive attention to such issues as evolution, consciousness, and objective vs. subjective views of truth, so that world historians may sharpen their interpretive choices by reading from the philosophical literature.[5]

World-historical analysis remains in consistent and expanding tension with positivistic thinking. Positivism, despite many shifts and currents in philosophy, remains the most influential philosophy of analysis, so that its terminology and categories have very great influence in analysis of any sort. Positivism allows for large-scale phenomena but focuses on breaking them down to smaller pieces and analyzing variables only a few at a time, leaving others as parameters that are assumed not to vary for purposes of the analysis. Positivistic thinking emphasizes simplified, cause-and-effect thinking; it traces incremental shifts of large systems toward equilibrium. World historians have increasingly abandoned monocausal interpretations, turning to analyses emphasizing feedback and interaction of several historical factors. Nevertheless, the majority of knowledge in the natural sciences and social sciences has been constructed on positivistic principles, so that world historians, in developing systemic approaches to the past, can be seen as eclectically balancing positivistic approaches against other approaches.

This discussion of philosophical differences is by no means exhaustive, but it should suffice to show that the categories of analysis in the remainder of this section, while they can be proposed as the core categories of world-historical analysis, will consistently produce differing and perhaps contradictory results because of the varying philosophies through which they are mediated.

The work of framing is the task of setting up a problem for historical study. In this discussion, the overall task of framing is broken down into setting the external frame or boundary conditions of a study, the internal frame or the systems and sub-systems under study, and the disciplinary frame that provides the tools of study.

The most basic step in framing the external boundaries of study is to set the topic. Then the frame is completed by setting the limits on space and time for analysis. In fact, historians often select the space and time of their analysis first, and the topic subsequently. That is, scholars defining themselves as historians of ancient China or medieval Europe or modern Africa may find that these boundaries are not the best for studying such a topic as silk textiles or monarchical government. For all of the selections and directions required for framing a historical analysis, there is need for attention to clarifying a typology of materials under study and for attention to units of analysis and scales of analysis. The topical, temporal, and even geographical scope of historical study has been expanding. The notion of 'history' has been successfully generalized so that it escapes the ancestral focus on politics and war and now is understood to apply to any arena of human activity or natural process that can be shown to have a temporal dimension. Inherited topical categories of social, political, economic, cultural, and intellectual history have now been supplemented by environmental history. In practice, the range of topics considered in historical analysis has raced far beyond the capacity of these categories. The effort to update libraries and create large-scale datasets seems likely to lead to more comprehensive ontologies that organize the topics of historical study and perhaps set them in systematic relationship to each other.

In defining limits of space and time, the historiography of the twentieth century gave primacy of place to the nation in recent centuries as the site of analysis and the object of analysis. Scholarship in the early twenty-first century gives attention to a fuller range of units of analysis. The wider range of units—each definable by space, time, topic, and scale—includes individual, family, nation, society, culture, civilization, race, religion, region, continent, oceanic basin, hemisphere, and the world as a whole. The recent expansion of studies in 'transnational' history means that, even for historians focusing principally on the national level, the unit of analysis is not a neatly defined nation but spills across boundaries to analyze as well at supra-national and sub-national levels. The problem raised by this greater variety in the units of historical analysis is that, as the author ranges across the scales of human activity, the reader may be confused as to the principal focus of analysis. Thus, a work on 'world history' might focus simply on interpretation at the planetary level alone, or it might privilege the interplay of the global whole, racial groups, and ethnic subgroups. Both author and reader must be clear on the principal unit or range of analysis for any given work.

The internal frame of analysis is as important as the external boundaries of historical studies. For global historical studies, framing the analysis in terms of systems is especially helpful. Systems are historical entities or analytical constructs for which the whole is composed of elements and sub-systems. The sub-systems generally have distinctive functions so that their interconnections enable the whole system to function. World-historical interpretation benefits greatly from a systemic framing, especially since it encourages analysis at multiple levels.[6] The particular approach to systems, however, varies rather sharply according to the philosophy of the analyst. Some historians have been critical of systemic approaches to world history, assuming that such approaches privilege a totalizing view of history that only considers interactions at the global level. World-systems analysis, for instance, is one sort of systemic approach to world history, but there are many other sorts of systemic approaches to the world.

The disciplinary frame provides a set of tools and an academic subculture within which problems are set up for study and then investigated. The principal organization of academic life is by disciplines that are studied within academic departments. The disciplines are organized for the study of certain types of phenomena; they are specific in their use of theory and method and develop literatures to publish their results. World history, while it falls most obviously within the discipline of history, also ranges across the disciplines.

The discipline of history was long categorized among the humanities. As such, history emphasized the skill of presentation as much as the depth of analysis. Historical scholarship was also parallel to studies in the arts such as art history and music history and parallel to study in such professions as religion, law, and education. As the social sciences formed in the eighteenth and especially nineteenth centuries—bringing into existence such disciplines as economics, politics, anthropology, and sociology—history took up a growing affinity to social sciences. The social sciences emphasized theoretical approaches from the beginning; fields of the humanities and the arts developed theories beginning in the late twentieth century, notably in literary theory. The discipline of history developed deep ties to the social sciences but also developed new links to the humanities, arts, and professions. In addition, historical analysis began to expand to the natural sciences and medicine. This was in response to the substantial expansion of historical studies in such fields as geology, biology, and medicine. For world history, its position as a developing subfield within the discipline of history became somewhat uncomfortable as world historians reached steadily into other disciplines and, in the same process, found themselves with an expanding need of theoretical knowledge in various fields. Meanwhile, two competing organizations of academic study—area studies and global studies—developed to provide both new support and new problems for world-historical analysis.

Area-studies analysis has been important in the development of world-historical analysis. The combination of history, anthropology, political science, sociology, and cultural studies, focusing especially on the past two centuries of experience outside of Western Europe and North America, has been the principal source of interdisciplinary analysis in world-historical studies. In somewhat parallel groupings of disciplines, American studies arose in the 1950s as a multidisciplinary framework for study of the United States, and cultural studies arose in Britain as a cross-disciplinary framework for analyzing culture and society.

As a disciplinary framework for understanding the world, 'global studies' is arguably an alternative to 'world history.' World history gives systematic attention to change over time but draws eclectically on the range of data and analytical frameworks in completing its temporally structured analysis. Global studies gives systematic attention to disciplinary and cross-disciplinary analysis but applies its analysis eclectically over time. In practice, 'global studies' has focused on some disciplines more than others, giving particular attention to international relations, economics, and environmental issues. Further, the field of global studies has tended to restrict its temporal frame to the very recent past and to the immediate future. Nevertheless, a consideration of the possibilities of world history and the possibilities of global studies suggests that there might develop, in the years to come, a more structured attempt to develop a more systematic, historical, multidisciplinary framework of analysis of human society and its interaction with the natural world. Of course it is utopian to imagine that scholars would be able to analyze everything at once. On the other hand, it is possible that consideration of the full range of possibilities will result in development of new constellations of disciplines and new domains of analysis that will explore larger realms of data and experience than are now studied. Historians, because of the relative breadth of their view, should consider taking positions of leadership in the reconfiguration of global studies.

To conclude this review of frameworks for world-historical study, it is relevant to return to the question of scale. The term 'scale' refers at once to the breadth of topical scale, the breadth of geographical scale, and the range of temporal scale. In the most elementary approach to world history, privileging the dimension of space, only studies that address a large geographic space can be considered as world or global history. In an expanded approach to world history, studies that address a long period of time, even if limited to a small region, can also be considered as contributing to world or global history. Further, historical studies considering the interaction of a wide range of topics, even within a small territory and for a short period of time, adopt a wide scale along the dimension of topics. Such studies can also be considered as global history, though many might be reluctant to use the label of 'world history' for such a study. Most historical study is limited to the past 200 years, although the experience of our species, *Homo sapiens*, is now estimated to reach back some 200,000 years and the history of the genus *Homo* to which we belong goes back some four million years. To the degree that the term 'history' is restricted to the recounting of the past (rather than the actual events of the past) its application had long been limited to the times and places for which written records were available, and thus to the past four or five thousand years. The term 'prehistory' was adopted for study of the events of times before 5,000 years ago; it was also applied to more recent but preliterate times in other areas, so that 'prehistory' could include times from two to five centuries ago for most of the Pacific world. But the field of history has expanded its source materials to include many sorts of evidence in addition to written records. For this reason the term 'prehistory' has arguably lost its relevance and should be replaced with 'history.'

All of the above is a review of framing the world-historical study: we turn now to world-historical analysis within these limits.

The work of analysis brings together the tasks of exploring historical evidence and interpreting the dynamics of change. The exploration of evidence involves locating relevant evidence and then ordering it. Evidence, as argued in the previous section, is of several sorts and levels, including direct and 'primary' evidence, indirect evidence, and calculated or estimated evidence. The term 'data' is used for evidence that is undergoing analysis. The data include previous interpretations and analyses, so that the analysis is seen to be recursive from the start. Dynamics of historical change and continuity are believed to exist in the real world. Interpreting the dynamics of change consists of creating models and theories of those dynamics, based on beliefs about the nature of stasis and change in the world and in human society and on the way traditions and innovations are passed on. Thus, terms such as statics, dynamics, interactivity, and equilibrium have been developed and applied across varying scales of time, space, and topic. The combined completion of these tasks of exploring evidence and interpreting dynamics yields, as a result, a set of historical interpretations of greater or lesser specificity, analytical rigor, or relevance to the historical situations analyzed or those in which they were composed. The direction of the interpretation can be signaled by a thesis statement or an interpretive conclusion: these are found both at the beginning and end of historical works. Such statements are presented sometimes as hypotheses to be tested and sometimes as conclusions resulting from exhaustive analysis; sometimes they are labeled as 'theory.' They can focus on the identification of a dynamic or a historical trajectory or the consequence of an origin.

Analysis is interpretation through systematic and logical study of change. But there are many sorts of logic. Analysts can choose between inductive and deductive approaches. They can give preference to qualitative or quantitative evidence. In explaining change, they can emphasize cause-and-effect mechanisms of change or feedback and change. Analysts can give most attention to finding the dominant influences and the dominant relations within a set of data, or they can focus on identifying the strongest connections and the widest range of connections. These varying approaches to interpreting the past are generally related to the philosophical approach of the investigator.

Attention to models in historical interpretation and analysis is a particular emphasis within world history. Historians, in making sense of the past, interpret or explain change—that is, the dynamic processes of human life. Inevitably, they carry simplified models of the dynamics of change. Analysts focusing on qualitative, descriptive approaches, using inductive logic, tend to be wary of the term 'model,' but nonetheless can generally be found to follow a systematic logic in their handling of data. The facts cannot speak entirely on their own, and need to be represented through authorial choices that are necessarily simplifications of reality. For this reason, it is important to emphasize that historical metaphors are models. That is, the metaphor of the ship of state provides a clear if indirect statement of the organization and dynamic character of the state.

For historians who are emphasizing formal analysis relying on deductive logic, models often take the form of theories. In certain arenas of study, specific theories have been developed to formalize analysis. The term 'theory,' as with all important words, has multiple meanings. Theories in natural sciences and social sciences have long existed; theories are being developed more recently in the arts and humanities. For the most fully developed theories in the social sciences—for quantitative work in economics, sociology, and political science—a theory identifies specific variables for analysis, data on those variables, and assumptions on the relationships among variables; it proposes a stable relationship among variables wherever the variables appear. Competing social science theories seek out improved correlation with available data by modifying variables, assumptions, and hypotheses. But for theory in the arts and humanities, where variables and relationships are more complex and interdependent, the identification of key variables is sometimes the main point of the theory.[7]

The study of connections—linking areas of human experience to each other—is the most effective and practical way to expand knowledge of world history. The practice of studying connection is that of seeking out links and parallels among events, processes, perspectives, and other aspects of the past. The systematic study of connections leads in many directions. It highlights interactions and dynamics in human affairs and leads to improved work in modeling and theorizing. It contributes to historical synthesis, in which the historian constructs an overall description of large-scale historical processes. It reveals the existence and the functioning of systems in human society and the natural world. Although most of the methodological specifics of world historical work are very similar to those of the various disciplines and other scholarly fields on which they draw, the manner of their application must be tailored to the nature of world-historical analysis. Put in simple terms, the world-historical method involves always looking for additional connections of the analysis to more places, different times, or related topics.

Here is the formulation of the full range of stages in world-historical method that I have proposed in an earlier study.[8] The process begins with the investigator selecting a topic of study; selecting a topic almost necessarily entails adopting a framework within which to explore the topic. The next step, which can be called 'exploratory comparison,' consists of looking at the topic from as many angles as possible—and comparing it with as many parallel topics as possible—to ensure that one has not neglected important aspects of the problem. The third step, once a real familiarity with the topic has been established, is to specify the precise research design, consisting of an analytical model of the historical dynamics of the topic, a method for documenting those dynamics, and a working hypothesis on what results the analysis is expected to show. This definition of the model includes setting its topical, geographic, and temporal scale. The next step is the collection of additional data and fitting them to the model: at this stage there should be particular attention to locating connections within the evidence and connections among historical sub-systems. While the specification of the project's model of historical dynamics necessarily involves simplification of the past, the attention to connections should identify complications that require further study.

Once the processes of defining and conducting a world-historical analysis have been completed, the investigator must hope to be able to confirm or verify the interpretation. How do we know about the world? How does a reader assess the validity of a historical narrative or interpretation developed by an analyst? The concept of verification was developed out of localized and experimental studies. Yet it is applied as well to cosmological studies of the universe. Is there a way to verify interpretive statements about the earth and its human history? Unfortunately there exists no dependable single process for confirming a world-historical interpretation.

Approaches to confirming interpretations vary widely. At one pole one finds works that give no confirmation beyond the simple affirmation and reaffirmation of interpretive statements. A slightly stronger approach consists of confirmation by documentation of the interpretation with examples, though this approach may stop short of testing for weaknesses in the argument. Both of these approaches rely on the plausibility of the interpretation.

Advancing the world-historical literature, however, requires that analysts go beyond asserting the plausibility of their interpretation. Two existing procedures are the testing of interpretations by hypothesis testing (for cause-and-effect analysis), requiring systematic handling of data and assumptions, and a more informal process of confirmation by feedback testing (for feedback analysis). These procedures are useful for suggesting the logic of confirmation, but world-historical analysis is generally too complex to fit the specific criteria for applying these techniques.

Perhaps the most practical approach for moving toward verification in world history is the effort to provide multiple narratives and multiple interpretations of historical processes, to pose the question of which is most satisfactory. That is, at present it seems that the best way to make progress in confirming interpretations in world history is for investigators to produce multiple interpretations of a given issue, thereby encouraging debate which will further sharpen the issue. The conduct of multiple analyses of a given world-historical topic offers the hope of locating where the real variance is.

The above steps constitute a single iteration of a world-historical research project. But an essential element of world-historical method is the reformulation of the issue and the conduct of another iteration of the research from a different perspective. That is, the investigator should shift perspectives and repeat the analysis with slightly different assumptions, to see if the results of successive analyses from different perspectives converge to give a common interpretation.

REPRESENTATION

The representation of world history is the aspect of world-historical study that gains the largest audience: it consists of the practices of writing and reading in world history. Initially the writing and reading of world history take place within national limits or within the limits of a given language. Ultimately world history takes place at a broader scope. It can include readers from multiple regional and cultural backgrounds, looking for analysis and interpretation on a global level. Fundamentally, authors are writing for a transnational audience, developing and invoking rhetorical devices calling up the global past, and portraying global dynamics.

The methods of presentation, as distinguished from methods of analysis, are equally central to the completion of a historical work. Historical works are most commonly presented in textual form: the author may choose among such forms as description, interpretation, narrative, and analysis. More broadly, the creator of a historical work may choose among such media as text, images, video, and multimedia assemblages. Most commonly in recent years, world history has been represented through textbooks. In any of these media, the creator faces the question of how to convey the logic of interpretation. As a general rule, it is best for the creator to break free of recapitulating the actual stages of discovery of the interpretation: once the conclusion is known, it may be possible to discover more elegant and heuristically comprehensible ways to read it.

Various approaches to the interpretation and representation of world history have arisen from the range of disciplines and schools of history that have taken on study of large-scale historical issues. In one description of this range of approaches, Diego Olstein has categorized current global historiography into the approaches or analytical paradigms of world history, world-systems, civilizations, comparative history, historical sociology, and area studies. He has distinguished among their substantial vs. analytical ways of crossing boundaries; study of several enclosed units vs. the world as the unit of analysis; diachronic vs. synchronic use of time; and endogenous vs. exogenous sources of causation. He argues that, taken together, these approaches have the potential to articulate the full range of approaches to large-scale or macro-historical issues in history.[9] In sum, an effort to encompass the full range of writings at the macro-historical or world-historical level can advance the breadth of discussion and the breadth of understanding.

Debate among authors is essential for developing wider understanding of an issue. For world history, as for other fields in which there are few researchers and an immense range of topics to be studied, the tendency is to allow a single scholar to become the expert in a given field of study. The result is that analytical frameworks and conclusions tend not to be challenged. Instead, there is an advantage to having multiple scholars and multiple approaches contesting the interpretive ground of the various topics of world-historical study.

To present historical interpretations at a global level, it will be necessary to communicate with readers in understandable terms at various scales of the past. Up to the present, certain conventions have dominated the world-historical literature, including continents (for space), centuries (for time), and societies (for social complexity). These conventions have undergone some useful critique, but there has been no systematic evaluation of the language for describing the past in terms most useful for assessing global patterns.

Communicating with readers depends most basically on developing a global narrative through a terminology and a style that can reach readers in many social situations. Such a narrative must convey the functioning and malfunction of social systems, and must enable readers to visualize historical processes at levels ranging from the individual to the global. In addition, authors of world history need to find ways to convey key elements of the models and theory they have adopted in conducting their analysis. Readers need to be presented with some device for assessing the validity of world-historical interpretations.

The number of readers of world history has only recently become large. Since national history has been the dominant genre of historical writing, readers have commonly applied the conventions and practices of reading national history to the works in world history that they read. This can lead to confusion or outright misunderstanding of world-historical texts, such as treating world history simply as the accumulation of national histories. In addition, for general audiences, historical writing focuses heavily on biographies, military history, and history of families and communities. Here again, the well-established practices of reading in those fields do not necessarily facilitate the reading of world history.

Readers most commonly encounter world history as presented in the narrative form. As world-historical readership has expanded, it has tended to evaluate writings in comparison to the established national historiography. World history has expanded through critique of the canons of writing national history; this scrutiny should lead to critical discussion of the rhetorical devices by which nations and their distinctive experiences are invoked. Thus, national history is not uncommonly seen through the experience of the nation's metropolis. With some adjustment, the same metropolis might serve equally well as a representation of the world. Similarly, such competing narratives might address empires in contrast to nations and religion at the global level. Classroom experience confirms that readers of history generally, including world history, like to be able to read multiple authorial views in order to clarify their own interpretation of the past.

As of the early twenty-first century, it is probably the case that most readers of world history are students reading textbooks at undergraduate and secondary school levels. While they have been surveyed by various authors and publishers, these students have not been in a position to formulate actively their responses as readers. While this is not the place to develop a full analysis of readers' reception of world history, one may note that existing theory, developed for literary studies, can be applied to assessing readers' reception of world-historical writing, including the issues of apprehension, consumption, appreciation, and appropriation.[10]

CONCLUSION

This review of the epistemology of world history has ranged across numerous issues, with the intention of setting the specifics of world-historical knowledge in broader context. This concluding section, in contrast, selects from the full discussion the epistemological issues that appear distinctive to the study of world history.

In conceptualizing world history, an emphasis on the multiple dimensions of the world itself serves to clarify both the immense extent of the field and ways to select workable topics for study. The dimensions of topic, space, time, and the varying scales of experience and analysis along each of those dimensions define the scope of the world; this scope is then linked to the multiple dimensions in our apprehension of the world. A second key conceptual emphasis is attention to multiple perspectives, including both attention to the multiple perspectives of people in the past and attention to the multiple perspectives in apprehension of the past by investigators and readers today. Thirdly, the notion of systems has shown itself to be valuable in conceptualizing the world. While there is much work to be done before notions of systems can be made sufficiently supple to be employed regularly by historians, the benefits of systems-thinking in identifying connections, hierarchies, and the interplay of sub-systems provide important contributions to rendering coherent the analysis of the global past.

In the analysis of world history, there is an advantage to distinguishing between the complex task of setting the frame for study of historical problems and conducting the analysis proper within that framework. The framework, in turn, includes three distinctive aspects: the boundary conditions of the external framework, an internal framework centering on the identification of historical systems and sub-systems, and a disciplinary framework providing the tools for study.

Attention to connections in the past remains the single most important tool in world-historical methodology. Breaking the habit of looking at events and situations on their own—learning to look over every hill in search of parallels and connections—is the first big step in world-historical study, and its application leads the investigator to address several other important analytical issues. Attention to connections helps to document the social systems and sub-systems of the past. Cross-disciplinary analysis, already a central aspect of world-historical study, is likely to grow in importance. In the many disciplines of academic analysis, we find that new knowledge, with a temporal dimension, is being developed rapidly. This knowledge is spilling into the historical arena, and historians have a particular opportunity to synthesize and connect this information. In any instance of world-historical analysis, investigators should pay explicit attention to modeling the processes under study. The model need not be elaborate, but it must be consciously chosen, applied to the historical data, updated based on experience, and articulated to the reader. More generally, world historians will benefit from a continuing discourse about their methods and a continuing revaluation of both the general principles of gaining historical knowledge and the specific needs of study of world-historical issues.

In representing the world-historical past to audiences, authors need to develop specific forms and conventions that can convey effectively the patterns of global change. Despite the complexity of modeling, disciplines, method, historical evidence, and narrative, there is a need to find ways to write on several levels. Interpretations must be presented to audiences ranging from students in the classroom to general audiences to academic specialists; ultimately these interpretations must reach people in communities varying widely by language, nation, and cultural tradition. For all of these subgroups within the global audience, interpretations of world history should be informative and entertaining, should elicit discussion and debate, and should provide the audience with ways to assess their validity and relevance.

Finally, scholars must acknowledge and come to terms with the recursive dimension of world-historical epistemology. Positivistic thinking—separating issues and situations for independent analysis—is useful as a tactic in study of world history but is insufficient to convey the overall character of the field. Thus, no historical analysis begins from the beginning. That is, an analyst of history has always participated in prior discussions about history. He or she, having read the historical literature, has become acquainted with methods and interpretations and has been induced to employ the philosophical outlook prevailing in that literature—or to contest it as a reader and develop another outlook. Interpretations become evidence in future interpretations. Similarly, evidence and apprehension interfere with each other; apprehension and modeling each involve selection and abstraction; theory governs the ontology of evidence but ontology limits and shapes theory; early events shape and limit later events but the later events color the evidence and interpretation of earlier events. The challenge of world history is to trace temporal patterns of order and disorder through clouds of interactions in evidence and apprehension, reality and interpretation, analysis and representation.

NOTES

1. These six dimensions were earlier articulated in Patrick Manning, 'Concepts and Institutions for World History: The Next Ten Years,' in *World History: Global and Local Interactions*, ed. Patrick Manning (Princeton: Markus Wiener, 2005), 236–42.
2. The general category of ontology includes, as specific types, taxonomy and typology. A taxonomy is an ontology in which the elements are assumed to be related through evolution, as with geological and biological taxa. A typology allocates evidence to categories based on similarities without assuming evolutionary links. The creation of a successful typology, by identifying similarities and differences among the instances being classified, can impart a great deal of knowledge. But the typology and accompanying classification of evidence does not by itself establish the relationships among the categories nor among the instances classified. Some of the evidence under classification can be identified as variables or factors. A factor is a typological category such as 'ethnic identity' that is asserted to have a coherent category yet which can vary both in quality and quantity. A variable is a typological category such as 'price of bread,' which is assumed to have an identified and consistent quality, but for which the quantity may vary. Variables are, therefore, defined and used in quantitative analyses, while factors are used in analyses that are qualitative and perhaps also quantitative.
3. William H. McNeill has argued that the historical sciences—notably geology, astronomy, and biology—moved steadily closer to history in their philosophy and method during the twentieth century. McNeill, 'Passing Strange: The Convergence of Evolutionary Science with Scientific History,' *History and Theory* 40, 1 (2001), 1–15.
4. The term 'perspective' is often generalized to account for both location and lens. Patrick Manning, *Navigating World History: Historians Create a Global Past* (New York: Palgrave Macmillan, 2003); Manning, 'Concepts and Institutions.'
5. John E. Wills, Jr., 'Putnam, Dennett, and Others; Philosophical Resources for the World Historian,' *Journal of World History* 20, 4 (2009), 491–522.
6. I am grateful to Eric Vanhaute for his articulation of the importance of systems in world-historical analysis.
7. Historians can be creators of theory as well as users of theory. Historians, since they typically deal with a wide range of phenomena, encounter numerous theoretical domains.

One approach to this complexity has been for historians simply to accept and appropriate the results from various disciplines and incorporate them into historical studies, without detailed review of the analysis. Another approach is for historians to learn details of the various theories applied to the materials they study, and to add to the depth of analysis. Still further, in some situations it is relevant for historians to construct theory. That is, while specialists in the disciplines are best placed to theorize within their disciplinary limits, historians can be specialists in linking various disciplines to each other, connecting not only the different types of evidence but also the accompanying theories.

8. Manning, *Navigating World History: Historians Create a Global Past* (New York: Palgrave Macmillan, 2003).

9. Diego Olstein, 'Monographic and Macro Histories: Confronting Paradigms,' in Patrick Manning, ed., *Global Practice in World History: Advances Worldwide* (Princeton: Markus Wiener, 2006), 23–38.

10. For a founding work in literary reception theory, see Hans Robert Jauss, *Toward an Aesthetic of Reception*, trans. Timothy Bahti (Minneapolis: University of Minnesota Press, 1982).

REFERENCES

CHRISTIAN, DAVID. *Maps of Time: An Introduction to Big History*. Berkeley: University of California Press, 2003.

CROSSLEY, PAMELA KYLE. *What Is Global History?* Cambridge: Polity, 2008.

HUGHES-WARRINGTON, MARNIE, ed. *Palgrave Advances in World Histories*. New York: Palgrave Macmillan, 2005.

MANNING, PATRICK. *Navigating World History: Historians Create a Global Post*. New York: Palgrave Macmillan, 2003.

——. 'Concepts and Institutions for World History: The Next Ten Years,' in *World History: Global and Local Interactions*, ed. Patrick Manning (Princeton: Markus Wiener, 2005), 229–58.

——. 'Interactions and Connections: Locating and Managing Historical Complexity,' *The History Teacher* 39, 2 (2006), 1–21.

MAZLISH, BRUCE. *The New Global History*. London: Routledge, 2006.

MCNEILL, WILLIAM H. 'Passing Strange: The Convergence of Evolutionary Science with Scientific History,' *History and Theory* 40, 1 (2001), 1–15.

OLSTEIN, DIEGO. 'Monographic and Macro Histories: Confronting Paradigms,' in *Global Practice in World History: Advances Worldwide*, ed. Patrick Manning (Princeton: Markus Wiener, 2008), 23–37.

SPIER, FRED. *Big History and the Future of Humanity*. Hoboken, NJ: Wiley-Blackwell, 2010.

WILLS, JOHN E., Jr. 'Putnam, Dennett, and Others; Philosophical Resources for the World Historian,' *Journal of World History* 20, 4 (2009), 491–522.

PART II

THEMES

CHAPTER 7

WORLD ENVIRONMENTAL HISTORY*

DAVID CHRISTIAN

How can we best manage the unpredictable and rapidly evolving relationship between human beings and the biosphere? This question provides one of the great research agendas for the early twenty-first century, and the breadth of the agenda will demand an equally broad perspective from those tackling it. No longer will it be enough to track human environmental impacts at the local or national level, a task taken up within the flourishing field of environmental history. Instead, it will be necessary to explore how each thread in this complex story is stitched into a larger tapestry woven throughout human history and covering the entire world. At its most ambitious, the new scholarly field of world environmental history aims at a comprehensive historical understanding of the complex and unstable patchwork of relations between humans and the biosphere. Insofar as it can achieve such an understanding it can help explain what makes our species so different from all other living species, and what makes human history so distinctive as a scholarly discipline. For, as I will argue in this chapter, current environmental issues have their roots in, and in some sense express, the very nature of our species and our history.

WHAT IS WORLD ENVIRONMENTAL HISTORY?

The two central themes of world environmental history are: (1) how a changing biosphere has shaped human history; and (2) how human action has shaped the biosphere. The unstable and rapidly changing balance between these two types of change gives the field its contemporary urgency. Like all forms of environmental history, world environmental history has one foot in the sciences and one in the humanities. Its distinctive combination of interdisciplinarity and a broad perspective on the past encourages a sort of triangulation on the nature of human history,

encouraging us to understand the history of our strange species through the complementary lenses of the sciences and the humanities.

HISTORIOGRAPHICAL BACKGROUND

'That tree same as me. This piece of ground he grow you.'[1] These words of an
Australian elder, Bill Neidjie of the Gagudju clan, capture a fundamental insight of
modern science: that there is a never-ending exchange of energy and resources
between humans and our surroundings. No human community has entirely lost
this sense of reciprocity between the human and the natural world. In all human
cultures, the great forces of nature have played starring roles in legends and literature,
as gods and goddesses of thunder or flood, or as weapons of the gods, or when listed,
year by year, in chronicles such as the Primary Chronicle of Rus', or used as literary
devices such as the great flood that drowns Maggie Tulliver and her brother in
George Eliot's *Mill on the Floss*. This widespread understanding of how human
destiny is intertwined with that of the natural world can be tracked in Clarence
Glacken's classic history of ecological attitudes, *Traces on the Rhodean Shore*.[2]
As Ramachandra Guha writes: 'Classical literary traditions manifest an abiding
concern with natural landscapes: in writing of the beauty of birds, animals, rivers
and farms, both the Roman poet Virgil (ca. 70–1 B.C.E.) and the Sanskrit dramatist
Kalidasa (ca. 375–415 C.E.) would qualify as "nature-lovers."'[3] In the nineteenth
century, the Romantic movement reaffirmed the ancient intuition that humans and
the natural world make up an organic whole, whose parts cannot be understood in
isolation from each other.

Yet at some point our ancestors did begin to set themselves apart from their natural
surroundings. Donald Hughes dates this change to the appearance of the first cities, the
first largely anthropogenic environments. The walls of Uruk, celebrated in the epic
poem of Gilgamesh, symbolize, he argues, 'a new view of the world, which entailed
a 'Great Divorce,' a sense of separation between culture and nature....'[4] Mark
Elvin argues that this growing sense of separateness measures the increasing distance
between human actions and their environmental consequences:

> The creation of the city began a crucial decoupling between the dominant,
> decision-making part of the human population, now living increasingly in
> a built environment, and the rest of the natural world.... [W]here and when a
> decision was made less and less coincided with where and when its environmental
> impact was felt. *Decisional distance* of this sort has the dimensions of space
> (from the point of decision to the point of impact), time (from present to
> future generations), and social rank (from decision-makers to the lower classes).
> Increasing it has progressively lessened the awareness of and sensitivity to the
> environmental effects of their policies among rulers and their advisers. This still
> holds today.[5]

From the late nineteenth century, this same sense of separateness began to generate a sort of scholarly apartheid, as historians were herded into the humanities and students of the natural environment into the natural sciences. In retrospect, the fragmentation of modern scholarship, though justified by rising standards of scientific rigor, may come to seem as absurd as Nasreddin Hodja's decision to search for his lost key only in the pool of light from a street lamp. All too often, historians have ignored themes such as the human relationship with the biosphere because they lay too far from the street lamps of modern scholarship.

In practice, of course, historians could not entirely ignore a relationship as intimate as that between humans and their natural surroundings. In newly colonized lands such as the 'neo-Europes' of the Americas, Australasia, and South Africa it was hard to miss the impact of human settlement and cultivation on what colonizers thought of (incorrectly) as pristine wilderness.[6] Such concerns, when combined with Romanticism's increasing sensitivity to the natural world, helped generate early forms of environmentalism. Guha distinguishes several strands of nineteenth-century environmentalism. Wordsworth, Thoreau, and Gandhi all represented a 'back-to-the-land' environmentalism that turned away from the modern world. The 'scientific conservationism' of writers such as George Perkins Marsh aimed, rather, to tame the excesses of industrialism. Finally, there emerged a 'wilderness' environmentalism, committed to preserving those areas that still seemed untouched by humanity.[7] Within mainstream historical scholarship, environmental perspectives never vanished entirely. The *Annales* school always retained a strong sense of how geography shaped history. In the natural sciences, the concept of a 'biosphere,' developed by the Russian scholar Vladimir Vernadsky, made it clear that the biosphere itself had a history in which our species was one of many different actors, while the new discipline of ecology teased out the complex flows of energy and resources binding humans to the natural environment.[8]

The environmental movements that emerged in the 1960s began to narrow the gulf between human history and the study of the natural environment. In the English-speaking world, the change was heralded by isolated classics such as W. L. Thomas's edited collection of essays *Man's Role in Changing the Face of the Earth* (which updated Marsh's study) or Rachel Carson's *Silent Spring*.[9] In 1976, William H. McNeill, one of the pioneers of modern world history, completed an influential world history of human relations with the microbial world, *Plagues and Peoples*.[10]

In the United States, formal recognition of environmental history as a field of scholarship can be dated to the foundation of the American Society for Environmental History in 1977. Environmental history soon flourished as a global enterprise with active scholarly communities in Europe, Africa, Asia (particularly India), Australasia, and Latin America.[11] Yet most environmental historians continued to focus on regional or local issues. Like gender history, environmental history fought for a place within the history profession by accepting traditional conventions that framed historical scholarship within particular eras, regions, or themes. Yet even in the early twenty-first century, the status of environmental history remained uncertain. David Cannadine's edited volume *What is History Now?*, published in 2002, has only one reference to environmental history, in an essay by the world historian Felipe Fernández-Armesto.[12]

World environmental history is even more marginal, perhaps because it raises such unwieldy questions. 'The first efforts in this vein,' writes John R. McNeill, 'were written in the early 1990s by geographers and in one case by a cashiered mandarin from the Foreign Office.'[13] Though there is much good scholarship that has a bearing on world environmental history the number of works explicitly devoted to the subject is tiny.[14] However, there are grounds for optimism about the future of the field, given the increasing importance of global environmental issues and the rapid growth of world history, particularly in the United States. Indeed, there is a natural alliance between world history and world environmental history because the importance of the complex relationship between humans and the natural environment is particularly evident at the large scales of world history. As Felipe Fernández-Armesto puts it, 'We are enmeshed in the ecosystems of which we are part, and nothing . . . in human history makes complete sense without reference to the rest of nature. That is why historical ecology, or environmental history, deserves a growing place in the curriculum.'[15]

A Drama in Three Acts

At the center of world environmental history is a story of constantly changing relations between humans and the environment and, consequently, between different human communities. At small scales, it is hard to see the larger shape of this story. Different problems and different regions require different, sometimes conflicting periodizations, so that, for example, the environmental history of Australia during the last millennium requires a quite different periodization from that of China, while the environmental history of the Americas requires yet another periodization. Furthermore, at small- or even middle-range scales, trends often reverse themselves. The familiar story of civilizational rise and fall dominates the story even at scales of several millennia. Yet at the scale of human history as a whole, world environmental history falls clearly into three great eras, each characterized by increasingly powerful ways of extracting energy and resources from the biosphere.

The first, or 'paleolithic' era, extends from the emergence of our species to the first signs of agriculture, some 10,000 years ago. This era is dominated by a huge diversity of lifeways all of which can be described as forms of hunting and gathering or 'foraging.' During the second or 'agrarian' era, human relations with the environment were increasingly dominated by the powerful ecological technologies we commonly describe as 'agriculture.' Agriculture enabled humans to manipulate flows of energy and resources through the environment so that more and more of those flows could be tapped by our own species. The increasing ecological power of those communities that took up agriculture explains why, in the long run, agrarian communities expanded demographically and geographically, usually at the expense of societies deploying less productive technologies. So crucial is this differential that John R. McNeill argues: 'This slow frontier process [the expansion of the agrarian frontier] is the main theme of world environmental history between the emergence of agriculture and modern times.'[16] The third great era of world environmental history began sometime in the last third of the last millennium. Human control of the biosphere increased spectacularly, first with the appearance of global networks of exchange that allowed ecological manipulation on a global scale, and then with the development of techniques to exploit the colossal energy buried beneath the earth in fossil fuels. We can call this era, with deliberate vagueness, the 'modern' era. So rapidly has human control of the biosphere increased in this brief period that Paul Crutzen has proposed that we recognize the beginning of a new geological era, the 'Anthropocene,' from about 1800 CE. The Anthropocene is the era of human history in which, for the first time in the planet's history, a single species dominates the biosphere.[17]

THE PALEOLITHIC ERA

Our distinctive relationship with the natural world can be traced back to the very origin of our species. We know much more about human evolution than we did just a few decades ago, and there is now broad agreement that our species, *Homo sapiens*, evolved in Africa, before migrating further afield in the last 60,000 years.[18] Yet controversy still surrounds the question of exactly when our species (and the ecological creativity that is our hallmark) first appeared. Richard Klein argues that we know humans started not just to *look* like modern humans but to *behave* like them when we see the sudden burgeoning of new technologies during the 'Revolution of the Upper Paleolithic', from about 50,000 years ago. In that era, evidence multiplies, particularly in European sites, of new, more delicately made stone tools, new forms of artistic and ritual activity, and of migrations into new and hitherto inaccessible environments such as Australia and ice-age Siberia. Klein writes:

> Archaeology links the expansion of modern humans to their highly evolved ability to invent tools, social forms, and ideas, in short, to their fully modern capacity for culture. We suggest that this capacity stemmed from a genetic change that promoted the fully modern brain in Africa around 50,000 years ago.

He adds that this event counts as the dawn of culture and should be regarded as

> the most significant prehistoric event that archeologists will ever detect. Before it, human anatomical and behavioral change proceeded very slowly, more or less hand-in-hand. Afterwards, the human form remained remarkably stable, while behavioral change accelerated dramatically. In the space of less than 40,000 years, ever more closely packed cultural 'revolutions' have taken humanity from the status of a relatively rare large mammal to something more like a geologic force.[19]

Other scholars have argued that the changes of the Upper Paleolithic reveal merely new human migrations into regions that archaeologists happen to have investigated with peculiar thoroughness. Sally McBrearty and Alison Brooks have argued that careful examination of the sparse scholarship on Africa in the Middle Paleolithic shows evidence of our exceptional ecological creativity as far back as 100,000, and possibly even 200,000 years ago.[20] African evidence for the crossing of a behavioral threshold includes finds of ocher and cut marks on skulls from Ethiopia dating from perhaps 150,000 years ago, both of which may indicate a heightened capacity for symbolic thought and language.[21] Until these controversies are resolved, all we can say is that our roller-coaster ride as a species began somewhere in Africa between 50,000 and 200,000 years ago.

The technologies of our Paleolithic ancestors are normally described as 'foraging' or 'hunting and gathering.' Like all other species, our ancestors collected the food and other resources they needed from their environment and used these resources with limited modifications, such as the shaping of stones to make stone tools. The main difference between the foraging of humans and that of other species was that humans foraged using an expanding repertoire of techniques stored in the encyclopedias of ecological and social knowledge painstakingly assembled within each community. This slow and often reversed accumulation of knowledge within and between communities explains why, even in the Paleolithic era, there were important changes in human adaptations and why humans began to have a significant impact on the biosphere.

Migrations into new environments provide the most striking evidence of our ancestors' accumulating ecological virtuosity, for each of these migrations required new intellectual, dietary, and technological adaptations. Most took place under ice-age conditions, which dominated climates from about 60,000 years ago, and have been the climatic norm for 90 percent of the last million years. In the northern hemisphere ice sheets covered a quarter of the earth's land surface, locking up so much water that global sea levels were well below those of today. Indeed, our knowledge of the Paleolithic era may be warped by the fact that most of our ancestors may have occupied coastal regions that are now under water.

By 10,000 years ago, as the last ice age ended, our ancestors had settled all continents apart from Antarctica. The chronology of these migrations is now reasonably clear. Some humans lived in Southwestern Asia 100,000 years ago, but this migration from Africa would prove temporary. Genetic evidence suggests that about 70,000 years ago human numbers contracted to just a few thousand individuals, bringing the species close to extinction. Then populations rebounded and we find evidence of new migrations within and beyond the African continent. In so far as these repeated earlier migrations into southern Eurasia by hominines such as *Homo erectus*, as well as by other mammal species from lions to great apes, they offer little evidence of adaptive virtuosity. More interesting is the appearance of artistic activity and new forms of technology during the so-called 'Revolution of the Upper Paleolithic.' But migrations into regions never settled by earlier hominines provide the most decisive evidence of our ancestors' increasing ecological virtuosity. Those who settled Australia, from perhaps 50,000 years ago, must have had sophisticated seafaring technologies, and a remarkable ability to adapt rapidly to new landscapes, climates, plants, animals, and diseases. No other mammal species had made this crossing before. Equally significant is the arrival of modern humans in ice-age northern Eurasia from about 40,000 years ago. Adapting to the periglacial steppes of ice-age Ukraine and Russia required mastery of fire, tailoring skills good enough to make well-fitting warm clothing, and the ability to systematically hunt and exploit large mammals such as mammoth. Sites such as Mezhirich, with its dwellings constructed of mammoth bones covered, presumably, with hides, give a vivid impression of the technological innovations these migrations required. Equally spectacular is the rapid occupation of the novel and diverse environments of the Americas from about 15,000 years ago, presumably by populations from eastern Siberia, who entered either by sea or across the land bridge of Beringia, which was exposed during the coldest phases of the ice age.

For the most part, these migrations did not lead to increasing social complexity. Ecological and technological innovations widened the range of modern humans and presumably increased their numbers, but they did not increase per capita control of energy or generate dense population centers that might have allowed or required greater social complexity. The technological ingenuity of our Paleolithic ancestors was expressed mainly in extensive rather than intensive exploitation of the environment, and this creates a misleading impression of technological stasis.

In reality, each new migration provides evidence of our species' capacity for sustained innovation and the result, for the species as a whole, was increasing collective control over biospheric resources. Striking evidence of this increasing ecological power is the impact that Paleolithic humans had on animal and plant life in some regions. That many large animal species (megafauna) died out towards the end of the last ice age is clear. In the Americas extinct species included mammoth, horse, several species of camelids, and giant sloth and armadillo; in Siberia, they included mammoth, woolly rhinoceros, and giant elk; in Australia they included giant species of kangaroo, wombat (including the *Diprotodon*, a hippo-sized creature), and many other species. It has been estimated that in Australia and the Americas, 70–80 percent of all mammals over 44 kilograms in weight may have vanished. More controversial is the role of humans in their disappearance. Paul Martin has argued forcefully that over-hunting by newly arrived humans accounted for much of the process in the Americas, and Tim Flannery has argued a similar case for Australia.[22] Particularly striking is the fact that the extinctions seem to have occurred soon after the first arrival of modern humans in these regions. Unfortunately, the dating is not yet quite precise enough to clinch the argument, and direct evidence of human hunting of these species is sparse, which is why some scholars have argued that climatic factors or even new diseases were as important as human predation in explaining these megafaunal extinctions. Tim Flannery has also demonstrated the importance in Australia and elsewhere of what Australian archaeologists have called 'fire-stick farming': the regular firing of the land to limit uncontrolled fires, stimulate new growth, and attract grazing species that could be hunted.[23] In Australia, at least, fire-stick farming may have transformed landscapes and plant life over much of the continent, accounting, in particular, for the predominance of fire-loving flora such as Eucalypts.

Here is clear evidence that the ecological virtuosity of *Homo sapiens* was already apparent in the Paleolithic. Our ancestors were transforming the biosphere well before they started farming. It goes without saying that such trends, unlike those of today, were invisible to those who lived through them. The environmental history of the Paleolithic era is apparent only from a significant historiographical distance.

THE AGRARIAN ERA

The agrarian era extends from the appearance of the first farming communities, about 11,000 years ago, to the beginning of the modern era, within the last five hundred years. The multiple technologies of agriculture gave human communities increasing control over biospheric flows of energy and resources. Intensification typifies growth in the agrarian era just as 'extensification' typifies growth in the Paleolithic era. Using the powerful new technologies of agriculture, farming communities diverted biospheric flows of energy and resources with increasing efficiency and on an increasing scale to the use of our own species. In the long run, increasing flows of energy and resources would increase per capita control of biospheric energy and resources, accelerate population growth, encourage increasing social complexity, and intensify human impacts on the environment.

Though this chapter focuses mainly on human impacts on the biosphere, this section must begin with a reminder of biospheric impacts on human history, for the appearance of agriculture coincided with, and was closely linked to, profound changes in global climates. From about 16,000 years ago, climates in much of the world began to get warmer and wetter as regular changes in the Earth's orbit and tilt increased the amount of solar radiation received at the Earth's surface, generating more warmth, more evaporation, and more rainfall. The great northern glaciers that had occupied 25 percent of the land surface of the Earth retreated until today they occupy a mere 10 percent. The water they released raised sea levels in middle latitudes by about 100 meters, drowning the land bridges between Siberia and Alaska, between Tasmania, Australia, and Papua New Guinea, and between Britain and Europe, while turning Indonesia into an island archipelago. (In northern latitudes, however, land freed from the weight of ice-age glaciers rose even faster than sea levels.) Armies of cold-adapted species such as firs marched north into what had once been tundra, and behind them advanced deciduous trees such as oak and beech. The warming was erratic, and there were brief returns to ice-age conditions, the most important lasting from about 12,800 to 11,600 years ago and known as the 'Younger Dryas.' By 8,000 years ago, average temperatures had peaked. Then, in a pattern predictable from knowledge of changes in the Earth's orbit and tilt first worked out by Milutin Milankovitch in the early twentieth century, global temperatures began, slowly and erratically, to decline.

Through mechanisms that are still poorly understood, global climatic change led to the appearance of agriculture by altering the behavior of humans and the animals and plants that surrounded them. Warmer, wetter climates created regions of great ecological abundance, which encouraged sedentism in regions such as Southwestern Asia. Here there appeared villages of settled or 'affluent' foragers and, eventually, the first surviving evidence of systematic agriculture. Sedentism in communities of affluent foragers may have encouraged population growth, which would eventually have required more intensive exploitation of what had once seemed abundant environments. This is one possible pathway to agriculture. It has also been argued that the unusual stability of post-ice-age climates allowed agriculture while the instability of ice-age climates had ruled it out.[24]

However we explain it, the relatively sudden appearance of agriculture in perhaps seven different regions of the world greatly increased the ecological resources at the disposal of our ancestors.[25] Unlike foragers, agriculturalists systematically and persistently manipulate the plants, animals, and landscapes around them in order to increase the production of those species they find most useful. They remove plants or animals they do not need or find harmful (weeds and pests) and nurture those species they find useful, protecting and watering the soil for plants, and sheltering and feeding animal domesticates. Over time, such intimate symbiotic relations transformed the genetic makeup of domesticated species. Sometimes humans also underwent mild genetic changes. For example, the ability to digest milk has spread widely within populations of pastoralists. But for the most part humans changed culturally as they co-evolved with domesticates that changed genetically. Fire-stick farming was a modest anticipation of this growing capacity for systematic manipulation of landscapes and organisms, but in the agrarian era humans began to manipulate their surroundings on far greater scales and with much greater effect. They began to domesticate the biosphere as a whole; and they also domesticated themselves, creating entirely new types of human communities. The spread of agriculture to new regions, coupled with many small improvements in agricultural techniques allowed human populations to increase and allowed the creation, for the first time, of larger and more densely settled communities. Within these communities there appeared a complex division of labor and new forms of social complexity.

Powerful feedback cycles magnified the impact of agriculture. Increased food production encouraged population growth, which encouraged the spread of agriculture from its heartlands, which in turn stimulated further population growth and further agrarian expansion. Estimates of global populations in this era are obviously speculative, but the widely used estimates of Massimo Livi-Bacci suggest that world populations grew from about six million 10,000 years ago to about fifty million 5,000 years ago and about 250 million 1,000 years ago.[26] Increasing populations and the eventual appearance of towns and cities characterized by new forms of specialization stimulated intellectual exchanges that accelerated the flow of innovations and improvements. These new feedback cycles explain the acceleration in the pace of historical change that is evident wherever agriculture appeared.

Human relations with the environment were transformed. Fire-stick farming apart, towns and cities count as the first predominantly anthropogenic environments, regions whose landscapes, rivers, plants, animals, and even air quality were largely shaped by human activity. Cities also concentrated exchanges of goods, ideas, pollutants (including human and animal wastes), and disease vectors. Indeed, pre-modern cities were so unhealthy that they checked population growth throughout the agrarian era. Outside cities, human impacts were less concentrated, but they could be significant nevertheless on regional scales. Irrigation meant the deliberate re-engineering and redirection of rivers and streams. When practiced too intensively, it could lead to salinization of entire regions. This seems to be the explanation for the sharp falls in population in southern Mesopotamia at the end of the third millennium BCE. Here, the increasing substitution of salt-resistant barleys for wheat is powerful evidence of salinization. Deforestation also transformed landscapes, flora, and fauna over large areas and on an increasing scale.

'If you could watch a time-lapse film showing Earth's surface since agriculture began,' writes William Ruddiman,

> you would see a subtle but important change spread across southern Eurasia during the last several thousand years. In China, India, southern Europe and northernmost Africa, you would see darker shades of green slowly turning a lighter green or a greenish-brown. In these areas, the first villages, towns, and cities were being built, and vast areas of dark-green forest were slowly being cut for agriculture, cooking, and heating, leaving behind the lighter-green hues of pastures or the green-brown of croplands.[27]

The same changes would eventually transform parts of Mesoamerica and the Andes region, parts of the Amazon basin and North America, and many of the islands of the Pacific.

Human environmental impacts in this era may have been much more far-reaching than is commonly recognized. William Ruddiman has argued that it was in this era that humans first began to transform global climates.[28] Levels of atmospheric carbon dioxide began to rise from about 8,000 years ago when, according to the pattern typical during recent interglacials, they should have been falling. Levels of atmospheric methane, which are normally controlled by global levels of solar radiation, began to rise about 5,000 years ago, at a time when they might be expected to have kept falling. Ruddiman argues that the first of these anomalies was a consequence of deforestation, which increased atmospheric carbon dioxide levels by reducing the absorption of carbon dioxide in forests, and (to a lesser extent) by the burning of forests which pumped carbon dioxide into the atmosphere. Rising methane levels can possibly be explained by the spread of wet-rice farming in East and Southeast Asia and, to a smaller extent, by the increasing number of domesticated animals, as pastoralism spread in regions of steppe. If correct, these arguments are immensely significant for without these changes average global temperatures would probably have declined steadily, leading to a renewal of ice-age conditions within the last two millennia. More tentatively, Ruddiman has argued that major pandemics, such as those that decimated populations in the Mediterranean region in the sixth century CE, and those that killed off huge numbers in the most densely settled regions of the Americas in the sixteenth century, may have led to detectable falls in levels of atmospheric carbon dioxide as farms were abandoned and forest returned to formerly cleared lands.[29] If these hypotheses are upheld they imply that human environmental impacts have been global for most of the last 8,000 years. Given the importance of warmer climates for the spread of agriculture, these hypotheses are of immense significance for world environmental history.

THE MODERN ERA

In the last 500 years, trends apparent in the previous two eras have intensified sharply. In the 10,000 years or so of the Agrarian era, human numbers rose from perhaps five or ten million to over 500 million. In the last 500 years they have risen to over six billion. With equal insouciance, our domesticates—our cattle, sheep, cats, and dogs—have multiplied alongside us. Humans have huddled more closely together. In the agrarian era, most humans lived in rural areas; early in the twenty-first century, about half of all humans live in the largely anthropogenic environments of large towns or cities, more than forty of which boast populations of more than five million. Thanks to profligate use of fossil fuels, human energy consumption has risen even more sharply. J. G. Simmons estimates that at the end of the Paleolithic era, each human being consumed, on average, the equivalent of about 5,000 calories a day; by the end of the agrarian era, that figure had risen to about 26,000 calories a day; and today, it has multiplied to about 230,000 calories a day.[30] Combining these estimates for energy consumption and population growth suggests that total human energy consumption may have risen by a factor of 50,000 since the end of the Paleolithic era and by more than 200 in recent centuries. No wonder some scholars estimate that humans may be controlling, consuming, or destroying between 25 and 40 percent of all the carbon fixed by plants and other photosynthesizing organisms on land.[31] John R. McNeill has estimated that between the 1890s and 1990s, the number of humans quadrupled, global economic production increased by fourteen times, human use of energy increased by sixteen times, and total industrial production by forty times, while carbon dioxide emissions increased by seventeen times and water use by nine times.[32]

This huge increase in human control of resources has many sources. One was globalization, the movement of people, crops, diseases, and animals around the world—'ecological imperialism,' as Alfred Crosby called it. These ecological migrations could cause immense suffering: in the sixteenth century the populations of the Americas declined, according to some estimates, by almost 95 percent after the sudden arrival of Eurasian diseases for which they had no immunity. But new domesticates could also raise agricultural productivity, particularly when governments keen to raise populations and revenues supported the settlement of hitherto under-populated regions, a story told superbly by John F. Richards.[33] Machines using fossil fuels, beginning with the steam engine, raised productivity by orders of magnitude; but they were just part of an explosion of technological creativity in recent centuries. Explaining that explosion of innovation remains a fundamental task for world historians, but part of the answer is surely that improved systems of communication and transportation, from the railway to the internet, accelerated exchanges of ideas between regions and individuals throughout the world. Another part of the answer is the growing importance of market forces, which encouraged and rewarded productivity-raising innovations of many different kinds, from legal structures such as patents to new and cheaper forms of transportation such as railways.

From a biospheric perspective, the modern era represents a gigantic takeover of resources by a single species. Not surprisingly, other species have suffered. While domesticated species flourish, other species have felt the pinch, dying out at rates that have been matched only during the five greatest extinction events of the last 600 million years. Humans, too, have felt the pinch. While the number of humans living affluently is greater than ever before, so is the total number of those living in extreme poverty. Increasing consumption has put dangerous pressure on resources such as fisheries and aquifers, and even fossil fuels are not renewable. The burning, in just a few centuries, of fossil fuels whose energy stores had built up over several hundred million years, has returned huge quantities of carbon into the atmosphere so that carbon dioxide levels have risen from about 280 parts per million in 1800 to about 350 in 2000. If, in the agrarian era, deforestation and wet-rice farming may have slowed the return to ice-age conditions, the fossil fuel revolution appears to be turning these trends around entirely.

So fundamental have been the changes in human relations with the biosphere that the optimistic faith in progress of the early twentieth century has slowly given way to fear of ecological catastrophe. In this way, world environmental history leads naturally to discussion of the near future and the ecological challenges that face world society today.[34]

The Centrality of World Environmental History to World History

The story told in the previous sections acquires its full significance only when seen at scales even larger than those of world history. For in the almost four billion years during which life has existed on this planet we know of no other species whose ecological power and impact has increased at such an astonishing rate and in such a brief period (paleontologically speaking). Indeed, there is a sense in which our distinctiveness as a species (and therefore the distinctiveness of human history as a scholarly discipline) is *defined* by our curious and unstable relationship with the natural environment.

Humans, like all other living organisms, extract energy and resources from their environments in order to survive and reproduce. They can do this because they are 'adapted' to their environments. Indeed, as a general rule, we can define species by the distinctive ways in which they extract the energy and resources they need to survive from a particular ecological 'niche.' What makes *Homo sapiens* unique is that in our relatively short tenure as a species (at most 200,000 years), the range of methods we use to exploit our environment has kept expanding, and it has done so at an accelerating rate.

The results of our ecological virtuosity are striking and unprecedented. Vaclav Smil writes: 'The diffusion and complexification of human societies have led to a large array of environmental changes that have transformed this planet during the past 5 ka, and particularly during the past 100 years, more rapidly than any other biogenic process in the planet's history.'[35] It is important to appreciate how remarkable this phenomenon is. Other organisms have transformed the biosphere, as cyanobacteria did when they began pumping oxygen into the atmosphere of the early Earth.[36] But they worked their transformations in teams of thousands of different species, and they took millions or billions of years to do so. Humans have caused even more dramatic changes, but they have done so as a single species and during just a few tens of thousands of years. John R. McNeill makes the point vividly: 'For most of earth's history, microbes played the leading role of all life in shaping the atmosphere. In the twentieth century, humankind stumbled blindly into this role.'[37] It is no exaggeration to say that our species is better at adapting in new ways than any species that has ever existed on Earth. On the other hand, it may be that we are *too* good at adapting, for our activities may now be threatening not just the future of our own species but the health of the biosphere as a whole. We are, perhaps, *hyper*-adaptive.

Our hyperadaptivity is the source of most of the major changes in the course of world history. It explains why, over time, humans have migrated into new environments from the temperate savanna to the arctic tundra, and it explains why human numbers have slowly increased and human societies have become larger and, necessarily, more internally differentiated. In short, our ecological virtuosity explains why human societies, unlike those of chimps or dolphins, have left behind abundant evidence of profound change. It explains why we alone have a 'history.'

What explains our remarkable ecological creativity? Part of the answer is that our species has stumbled upon entirely new ways of adapting to the biosphere. In the animal world, major adaptive changes arise from genetic change over many generations. In contrast, humans have adapted dramatically even without undergoing significant genetic change, and they have done so in what are, from a paleontologist's perspective, very brief periods of time. The mechanism that allows such rapid adaptation is cultural change, change driven by potentially instantaneous exchanges of ideas rather than by the slow exchange and spread of new genes over many generations.[38] Intelligence is part of the explanation, of course, but many species adapt intelligently.

Long-term historical change, such as we see only in the case of our own species, requires more than just changes in the behaviors of intelligent individuals; it requires that such changes be taken up by other members of the same species so that they can accumulate from generation to generation. Human language, uniquely, allows learned information to be shared in such volume and with such precision that knowledge can accumulate within the memory banks of entire communities. As a result, individuals gain access to vast and ramifying wikipedias of knowledge stored in the memories of their communities, and as the information in these encyclopedias accumulates, the ecological (and social and cultural) behaviors of entire communities can change. As A. J. McMichael puts it: 'Each species is an experiment of Nature. Only one such experiment, *Homo sapiens*, has evolved in a way that has enabled its biological adaption to be complemented by a capacity for cumulative cultural adaptation.'[39]

It is this slow but accelerating accumulation of new and ecologically significant information within human cultures (often reversed, but never entirely blocked) that accounts for the astonishing variety of human cultures, the long-term directionality of human history, and indeed for all of the major changes in human history. As Colin Renfrew puts it: 'after the speciation phase, human evolution changed significantly in character. Darwinian evolution in the genetic sense no doubt continued, and underlies the rather superficial differences that are observed between different racial groups today . . . But the newly emerging behavioral differences between the groups were not genetically determined. They were learned, and they depended upon the transmission of culture.'[40]

NOTES

*   My thanks to Jerry H. Bentley and John R. McNeill for their comments on an early draft of this chapter.
1. Cited from J. Donald Hughes, *An Environmental History of the World: Humankind's Changing Role in the Community of Life* (London: Routledge, 2001), 21.
2. Clarence Glacken, *Traces on the Rhodian Shore: Nature and Culture in Western Thought from Ancient Times to the end of the Eighteenth Century* (Berkeley: University of California Press, 1967).
3. Ramachandra Guha, *Environmentalism: A Global History* (New York: Longman, 2000), 3.
4. Hughes, *Environmental History*, 34.
5. Mark Elvin, *The Retreat of the Elephants: An Environmental History of China* (New Haven, Conn.: Yale University Press, 2006), 94.
6. The pioneering work on this topic is Richard H. Grove, *Green Imperialism: Colonial Expansion, Tropical Island Edens and the Origins of Environmentalism: 1600–1869* (Cambridge: Cambridge University Press, 1995).
7. Guha, *Environmentalism*, 6.
8. See Vladimir I. Vernadsky, *The Biosphere*, trans. David B. Langmuir (New York: Copernicus, 1998); for a brief overview of the concept, and a modern and more historical account of the biosphere, see Vaclav Smil, *The Earth's Biosphere: Evolution, Dynamics,*

and Change (Cambridge, Mass.: MIT. Press, 2002). James Lovelock, *Gaia: A New Look at Life on Earth* (Oxford: Oxford University Press, 1979, 1987), describes the biosphere as a single, interconnected entity; Lovelock admitted that when he wrote it, he did not realize his ideas had been anticipated by Vernadsky: see Vernadsky, *The Biosphere*, 32.

9. W. L. Thomas, ed., *Man's Role in Changing the Face of the Earth* (Chicago: University of Chicago Press, 1956); a further update of Marsh's work is B. L. Turner *et al.*, eds., *The Earth as Transformed by Human Action: Global and Regional Changes over the Past 300 Years* (Cambridge: Cambridge University Press, 1990); Rachel Carson, *Silent Spring* (Boston: Houghton Mifflin, 1962).

10. William H. McNeill, *Plagues and Peoples* (New York: Doubleday, 1976).

11. Shepard Krech III, J. R. McNeill, and Carolyn Merchant, in the 'Introduction' to the *Encyclopedia of World Environmental History*, 3 vols. (New York: Routledge, 2004), i. x.

12. David Cannadine, ed., *What is History Now?* (Basingstoke: Palgrave Macmillan, 2002), 153. There are no references to 'environmental history' or 'the environment' in the indices to three important recent surveys of historical scholarship in the English-speaking world: Peter Novick, *That Noble Dream: The 'Objectivity Question' and the American Historical Profession* (Cambridge: Cambridge University Press, 1988); Michael Bentley, ed., *Companion to Historiography* (London: Routledge, 1997); and the companion volume, *Modern Historiography: An Introduction* (London: Routledge, 2000); Joyce Appleby, Lynn Hunt, and Margaret Jacob, *Telling the Truth about History* (New York: Norton, 1994).

13. John R. McNeill, 'Bridges: World Environmental History: The First 100,000 Years,' *Historically Speaking* 8: 6 (July/August 2007), 6–8, cited from p. 6. The 'cashiered mandarin' was Clive Ponting, whose *A Green History of the World: The Environment and the Collapse of Great Civilizations* (London: Penguin, 1991; 2nd edn., 2007) was one of the first and most ambitious of modern texts on world environmental history. For a recent discussion of the field, see 'What is Global Environmental History?,' a forum introduced by Gabriella Corona in *Global Environment: A Journal of History and Natural and Social Sciences* 2 (2008), 229–49.

14. Other examples of the genre include Hughes, *Environmental History*, and I. G. Simmons, *Global Environmental History* (Chicago: University of Chicago Press, 2008), as well as Shepard Krech III, J. R. McNeill, and Carolyn Merchant, eds., *Encyclopedia of World Environmental History*, 3 vols. (New York: Routledge, 2004).

15. Felipe Fernández-Armesto, 'Epilogue: What is History Now?,' in David Cannadine, ed., *What is History Now?* (Basingstoke: Palgrave Macmillan, 2002), 153.

16. McNeill, 'Bridges', 7.

17. Paul Crutzen, 'The Geology of Mankind,' *Nature* 415 (3 January 2002), 23. More recently a group of distinguished geologists has proposed that this idea be taken up formally: Jan Zalasiewicz *et al.*, 'Are We Now Living in the Anthropocene?,' *Geological Society of America* 18: 2 (February 2009), 4–8. There is a good overview of the idea of the Anthropocene in Will Steffen, Paul J. Crutzen, and John R. McNeill, 'The Anthropocene: Are Humans Now Overwhelming the Great Forces of Nature?,' *Ambio* 36: 8 (December 2007), 614–21.

18. Richard Klein with Blake Edgar, *The Dawn of Human Culture* (New York: Wiley, 2002), 7.

19. Klein, *Dawn of Human Culture*, 8.

20. Sally McBrearty and Alison Brooks, 'The Revolution That Wasn't: A New Interpretation of the Origin of Modern Human Behavior' *Journal of Human Evolution* 39 (2000), 453–563; and the summary of this debate in Paul Pettit, 'The Rise of Modern Humans,'

in Chris Scarre, ed., *The Human Past: World Prehistory and the Development of Human Societies* (London: Thames & Hudson, 2005), chapter 4.

21. Pettit, 'The Rise of Modern Humans,' 141–2.

22. Paul S. Martin, 'Prehistoric Overkill: The Global Model,' in P. S. Martin and R. G. Klein, eds., *Quaternary Extinctions: A Prehistoric Revolution* (Tucson: University of Arizona Press, 1984), 354–403, and Flannery, *The Future Eaters: An Ecological History of the Australasian Lands and Peoples* (New York: Braziller, 1995).

23. Flannery, *The Future Eaters,* on Australia, and *The Eternal Frontier: An Ecological History of North America and its Peoples* (New York: Atlantic Monthly Press, 2001) on North America.

24. On the role of population pressure, see Mark Cohen, *The Food Crisis in Prehistory* (New Haven: Yale University Press, 1977); on the possible role of increasing climatic stability, see P. J. Richerson, R. Boyd, and R. I. Bettinger, 'Was Agriculture Impossible during the Pleistocene but Mandatory during the Holocene? A Climate Change Hypothesis,' *American Antiquity* 66 (2001), 387–411. The best general introduction is Peter Bellwood, *First Farmers: The Origins of Agricultural Societies* (Oxford: Blackwell, 2005).

25. The seven likely agricultural heartlands are Southwestern Asia, East Asia, New Guinea, sub-Saharan Africa, Mesoamerica, the Andes region, and regions of eastern North America.

26. Massimo Livi-Bacci, *A Concise History of World Population* (Oxford: Blackwell, 1992), 31.

27. William F. Ruddiman, *Plows, Plagues, and Petroleum: How Humans Took Control of Climate* (Princeton: Princeton University Press, 2005), 4; on deforestation, see also Sing C. Chew, *World Ecological Degradation: Accumulation, Urbanization, and Deforestation: 3000 B.C.–A.D. 2000* (New York: Rowman and Littlefield, 2001).

28. Ruddiman, *Plows, Plagues, and Petroleum,* chapters 8 and 9.

29. Ruddiman, *Plows, Plagues, and Petroleum,* chapters 12 to 14.

30. I. G. Simmons, *Changing the Face of the Earth: Culture, Environment, History,* 2nd edn. (Oxford, Blackwell, 1996), 27.

31. Vaclav Smil, *The Earth's Biosphere: Evolution, Dynamics, and Change* (Cambridge, Mass.: MIT. Press, 2002), 240: strictly speaking, what is being measured is global terrestrial Net Primary Productivity, the amount of carbon fixed by photosynthesizing organisms on land minus the amount they return to the atmosphere through respiration, ibid., 182.

32. John R. McNeill, *Something New Under the Sun: An Environmental History of the Twentieth-Century World* (New York: Norton, 2000), 360.

33. John F. Richards, *The Unending Frontier: An Environmental History of the Early Modern World* (Berkeley: University of California Press, 2003).

34. One of the best discussions of global environmental problems and possible solutions is Lester R. Brown, *Eco-Economy: Building an Economy for the Earth* (New York: Norton, 2001), and later editions.

35. Smil, *The Earth's Biosphere,* 231.

36. McNeill, *Something New Under the Sun,* 265.

37. McNeill, *Something New Under the Sun,* 51; for an important qualification to this argument see the discussion of work by William Ruddiman later in this chapter.

38. Elsewhere, I have described this uniquely human style of adaptation as 'collective learning.' See David Christian, *Maps of Time: An Introduction to Big History* (Berkeley: University of California Press, 2004), particularly chapters 6 and 7.

39. A. J. McMichael, *Planetary Overload: Environmental Change and the Health of the Human Species* (Cambridge: Cambridge University Press, 1993), 33.

40. Colin Renfrew, *Prehistory: Making of the Human Mind* (London: Weidenfeld & Nicolson, 2007), 97.

REFERENCES

In 2007, John R. McNeill lamented that 'There is no single place to go to get a handle on world environmental history' ('Bridges,' 6). This short list of references focuses mainly on synoptic overviews.

CROSBY, ALFRED. *Ecological Imperialism: The Biological Expansion of Europe, 900–1900.* Cambridge: Cambridge University Press, 2004.

BURKE, EDMUND, and KENNETH POMERANZ, eds. *The Environment and World History.* Berkeley: University of California Press, 2009.

DIAMOND, JARED. *Guns, Germs, and Steel: The Fates of Human Societies.* New York: Norton, 1997.

FERNÁNDEZ-ARMESTO, FELIPE. *Civilizations: Culture, Ambition, and the Transformation of Nature.* New York: Simon & Schuster, 2001.

GLACKEN, CLARENCE. *Traces on the Rhodian Shore: Nature and Culture in Western Thought from Ancient Times to the end of the Eighteenth Century.* Berkeley: University of California Press, 1967.

GOUDIE, ANDREW, and HEATHER VILES. *The Earth Transformed: An Introduction to Human Impacts on the Environment.* Oxford: Blackwell, 1997.

GROVE, RICHARD H. *Green Imperialism: Colonial Expansion, Tropical Island Edens and the Origins of Environmentalism: 1600–1869.* Cambridge: Cambridge University Press, 1995.

HUGHES, J. DONALD. *An Environmental History of the World: Humankind's Changing Role in the Community of Life.* London: Routledge, 2001.

——. 'The Greening of World History,' in Marnie Hughes-Warrington, ed., *World Histories.* Basingstoke: Palgrave/Macmillan, 2005, 238–55.

KRECH, SHEPARD, J. R. McNEILL, and CAROLYN MERCHANT, eds. *Encyclopedia of World Environmental History,* 3 vols. New York: Routledge, 2003.

McNEILL, JOHN R. *Something New Under the Sun: An Environmental History of the Twentieth-Century World.* New York: Norton, 2000.

——. 'Bridges: World Environmental History: The First 100,000 Years,' *Historically Speaking,* 8: 6 (July/August 2007), 6–8.

PONTING, CLIVE. *A Green History of the World: The Environment and the Collapse of Great Civilizations.* London: Penguin, 1991; 2nd edn., 2007.

RADKAU, J. *Nature and Power: A Global History of the Environment.* Trans. by Thomas Dunlap. Washington, D.C.: German Historical Institute, 2008.

RICHARDS, JOHN F. *The Unending Frontier: An Environmental History of the Early Modern World.* Berkeley: University of California Press, 2003.

RUDDIMAN, WILLIAM. *Plows, Plagues, and Petroleum: How Humans Took Control of Climate*. Princeton: Princeton University Press, 2005.

SIMMONS, I. G. *Global Environmental History*. Chicago: University of Chicago Press, 2008.

TURNER, B. L., *et al.*, eds. *The Earth as Transformed by Human Action: Global and Regional Changes in the Biosphere over the Past 300 Years*. New York: Cambridge University Press, 1990.

CHAPTER 8

....

AGRICULTURE

....

JOHN A. MEARS

WHEN striving to delineate the contours of the human experience, world historians must highlight the major turning points in the existence of our species. Among the momentous watersheds through which human beings have passed since their appearance over 100,000 years ago, none has been more profound in its consequences than the shift from hunting and gathering to agriculture, a form of subsistence usually defined as different combinations of systematic crop cultivation and livestock raising. Yet the advent of agriculture involved much more than the domestication of plants and animals for the production of food, fiber, and other useful resources. It became the heart of what Islamicist Marshall G. S. Hodgson called a transmutation, that is, an interrelated set of relatively rapid, strikingly radical alterations in social structures and behavior patterns that draws every aspect of human existence into its embrace. For Hodgson, a transmutation is 'constitutive,' giving rise to a much enhanced 'social power' that reorients the flow of historical events and lays the foundation for everything that is subsequently achieved. It thereby brings a more complete fulfillment of human potential.[1]

ORIGINS AND EARLY DEVELOPMENT
....

For countless generations, nearly all humans had lived as hunters and gatherers, dwelling together in small, stable, nomadic bands that operated in close harmony with nature. Then, about 12,000 years ago, a few of them began to transcend the lifeways they derived from their hominid ancestors and create uniquely human modes of subsistence that clearly distinguished them from other animals. Although scattered societies primarily dependent on fishing had preceded any that relied on agriculture alone, they were eventually overshadowed by semi-nomadic peoples who practiced various types of simple horticulture, also known as swidden, slash-and-burn, or shifting agriculture, involving the use of hoes or digging sticks to cultivate small garden plots. The earliest horticultural societies may have emerged around 7000 BCE in the adequately watered and partially wooded grasslands along the Levantine coast, near the headwaters of the Tigris River, and in an area to the west of Anatolia. Within a millennium, cereal horticulture had diffused throughout a broad region encompassing the Balkan Peninsula and Anatolian Plateau in the north to the lower Nile Valley in the south and the foothills of the Zagros Mountains in the east. By 6500 BCE, animal domestications along the fringes of the Fertile Crescent's mountain ranges enabled small bands of hunter-gatherers to become pastoralists, relentlessly moving about as they herded sheep and goats. A few centuries later, widely dispersed village farmers in southern Italy, the Danube basin, the Nile river valley, and the highlands of Pakistan had appropriated herding practices.[2]

Toward the end of the fifth millennium BCE, horticulturalists, having migrated into the Tigris and Euphrates river valleys, began to settle in the hot, arid floodplains at the head of the Persian Gulf. There they learned how to augment their harvests by constructing networks of canals and ditches for irrigation purposes. They further intensified their agricultural systems through a 'Secondary Products Revolution,' exploiting their animals for such commodities as milk and wool, harnessing horses and oxen to scratch plows, spreading manure and cross-tilling fields, and allowing plots to lay fallow at regular intervals.[3] In the early fourth millennium, Anatolian artisans mastered the art of smelting bronze. Within a few more centuries, strong, durable metal tools that augmented agricultural output had become familiar to peoples throughout Southwest Asia. By 3500 BCE the Sumerians were leading humankind into the agrarian era, when the most technologically advanced societies rested on economic foundations provided by intensified agricultural systems.

In making the shift from hunting and foraging to food production, human beings transformed the natural environment to a far greater extent than ever before. Instead of living as their hominid predecessors had lived for millions of years, as integral components of the Earth's ecosystems, farmers and herders manipulated their surroundings to an unprecedented degree, purposefully transforming landscapes with their fields and pastures, often disrupting delicate natural balances as they sought enhanced control over their new modes of subsistence. By deliberately intervening in the life cycles of plants and animals to encourage desirable physical and behavioral characteristics, they initiated what amounted to directed evolution. Human beings ultimately became dependent on their domesticates, just as the plants and animals selected for domestication had to rely on the actions of human beings for their survival. Farming and herding most likely strengthened physical traits and habits of mind decidedly different than those necessary to pursue the old lifeways.

Among the consequences of crop cultivation and animal breeding, the most immediately significant was the ability to generate food surpluses. By raising the carrying capacity of the Earth, agriculture permitted the feeding of rapidly growing human numbers and allowed expanding populations to adopt a permanent sedentary existence. A global total of approximately six million around 7000 BCE had swelled to at least fifty million by 1000 BCE.[4] Moreover, reliable surpluses sustained unprecedented levels of socio-cultural complexity. In Southwest Asia, the Sumerians had organized the first agriculturally based, urban-centered, state-organized civilization on the alluvial lands of the Tigris and Euphrates. Unprecedented hierarchy, specialization, and inequality characterized their social structures.[5]

Although the origins of agriculture and its immediate consequences may have occurred somewhat earlier in Southwest Asia than anywhere else on the planet, it was a world-wide phenomenon involving peoples living on every inhabited continent except Australia. Agricultural lifeways appeared independently and at roughly the same time in widely separated places across the Earth's middle latitudes. Incipient farmers and herders were simultaneously domesticating an impressive array of plants and animals in various locations, using a variety of techniques and practices to augment available food supplies through a series of shared human responses to similar ecological circumstances. Seldom recognizing the long-term significance of their actions, they made few self-conscious breaks with familiar routines, and usually drew on the sophisticated toolkits and extensive knowledge of plant and animal reproduction long familiar to hunter-gatherers. For the first farmers and herders, Upper Paleolithic harvesting and processing skills, burning methods, storage procedures, and private ownership habits served as indispensible pre-adaptations.

Including lands in and around Southwest Asia, five distinct regions emerged as the primary hearths of agriculture. Since 1960, archeologists have uncovered compelling evidence of self-initiated domestication in the flood plains of the Yellow River in north-central China and in the heart of Southeast Asia. In the western hemisphere, investigators have likewise identified core areas of domestication in Mesoamerica as well as in portions of South America reaching across the highlands of the central Andes into the Amazon basin. In addition, there were at least five less significant centers of pristine agricultural development: the extensive river valleys of North America's eastern woodlands, the bend of the Niger River in tropical West Africa, the lowlands of Honshu in central Japan, the Kuk Basin in New Guinea's central highlands, and the forests of the Amazon and the Orinoco Rivers. Sudanic Africa may also have been an independent site of agricultural origin.[6]

Early domestication did take place outside of these hearth lands, in southwestern Europe, Ethiopia, and the highlands at the eastern end of Africa's savanna belt, known as the Sahel. In these regions, however, existing agricultural practices in contiguous areas seem to have stimulated the shift. Isolated instances of significant domestication, likewise influenced by what others had achieved, did appear further afield, notably the taming of the horse in the southern Ukraine roughly 6000 years ago and reindeer in northern Siberia somewhat later.

Ecological factors initially tended to hold farmers and herders within the core areas to which they were so well adapted and ensure that the original core areas remained relatively few in number. Much of the Earth's surface was unfavorable to crop cultivation and animal husbandry. Food production remained virtually impossible in deserts, tropical rainforests, and polar regions. As a result, sparse populations of hunters, fishers, and foragers continued to prevail throughout Australia, Alaska, the southern portions of South America, much of Canada, the western United States, northern Europe, Siberia, and sub-Saharan Africa.

What made agriculture the primary subsistence base for the majority of human beings was its diffusion beyond the original core areas, either by the movement of farmers and herders into adjacent regions or by the spread of ideas, tools, and methods to neighboring foragers. Migrants had already introduced agricultural systems from the Tigris and Euphrates Valleys into Turkey, Greece and the southern Balkans 7000 years ago, while indigenous peoples in the Nile Valley and subsequently in Central Asia appropriated similar Middle Eastern practices essentially unaltered. Two millennia earlier, tiny farming villages, probably built by migrants from Mesopotamia, emerged in the highlands to the west of the Indus Valley. Around 4000 BCE, farmers and pastoralists reached the alluvial plains of the Indus River itself, having augmented the cultivation of wheat, barley, and dates, and the herding of goats and sheep with domesticated cotton and humped zebu cattle. Meanwhile, in South and East Asia, cultivation of domesticated rice had become widespread on the plains of the Ganges River by 4000 BCE, and a thousand years later rice cultivation had reached the coastal areas near modern Shanghai as well as the large islands of Southeast Asia.

Agricultural diffusion in combination with local innovation brought distinctive farming communities into the heart of Europe. Population pressures drove migrants into the river valleys and plains of central Europe, where they contested the ground with native foraging bands. By 3000 BCE, the intruders reached the northern fringes of the continent's deciduous forests. In these less inviting environments, hunter-gatherers began to emulate the newcomers' farming methods. Meanwhile, another flow of colonists spread their domesticated grape vines along with olive and fig trees throughout the Mediterranean basin.

In the separate world of the Americas, indigenous populations domesticated more than a hundred plants, probably commencing over 9000 years ago with bottled gourds. But beyond the llamas and alpacas of the central Andes, domesticated animals never acquired great significance in the western hemisphere until after the arrival of Europeans 500 years ago, primarily because of extensive mammal extinctions in the late Pleistocene. Hence, pastoralism did not emerge as a viable alternative to farming societies in the Americas beyond the Puna, the game-scarce grasslands of Peru's mountain plateaus. As in the eastern hemisphere, however, crop diffusion did occur despite climatic, geographical, and environmental impediments to cross-cultural exchange resulting from the north–south orientation of the hemisphere's two continents. The spread of Mesoamerican maize southward and cotton northward demonstrated that the hemisphere's two primary core areas could be connected at least indirectly from time to time.

Four distinct agricultural complexes evolved in the Americas.[7] As early as 5500 BCE, Mesoamerican farmers were cultivating maize, beans, and squash on an increasingly full-time basis. Their crops could be found in Panama by 3200 BCE, in Argentina and Chile within the next 500 years, and in coastal Ecuador soon thereafter. By then, groups in the southwestern United States had begun to supplement their hunting and gathering with the cultivation of maize, beans, and squash. By 1000 BCE, this crop complex had diffused as far north as Colorado. Over the next 2000 years, it was adopted throughout the eastern woodlands, where increasingly sedentary populations living in the river bottoms of the largest rivers or near the coastlines had already created indigenous components of a second complex by domesticating a variety of seed plants, notably the sunflower, marsh elder, and goosefoot. Around 1500 BCE, an immense region drained by the Amazon and Orinoco river systems sustained a third complex resting on the manioc root and the sweet potato, which ultimately prevailed over much of Central America and the Caribbean. Of greater importance in the long run, a fourth complex built upon a variety of potato species as well as transplanted maize had matured no later than 1000 BCE in the highland basins of the central Andes.

By the beginning of the Common Era, roughly two hundred plants and fifty animals, virtually every species that would become significant for human purposes, had been domesticated. In a complicated process not yet fully completed, perhaps as much as 90 percent of the Earth's population may have been sedentary agriculturalists. The subsistence bases of early civilizations relied primarily on the cultivation of just six high-calorie food plants: wheat, barley, rice, millet, maize, and the potato. With these crops, intensive agricultural systems capable of sustaining dense population concentrations on confined areas of land became and remained a feature shared by nearly all complex societies.

The prominent cereals did spread beyond the civilization centers, but not beyond the world's temperate zone. Wheat, and secondarily barley and millet, prevailed over broad stretches of the eastern hemisphere from Europe and northern Africa through the Middle East to northwestern India, Central Asia, and northern China. Rice cultivation thrived in a great band of lands running from the Ganges River Valley through northern Thailand and Vietnam to coastal China, the Yellow River Valley, Korea, and Japan. Maize thrived in the Americas from Peru to the southeastern United States. Root crops originated in the tropical areas of South America, Africa, and Southeast Asia.

Peoples dependent at least in part on cultigens in the rainforests of Central and South America, West Africa, eastern and central India, the mainland and large islands of Southeast Asia, and southern China continued to utilize slash-and-burn techniques. From the Middle East, nomadic pastoralism had spread westward into the steppes and deserts of Saharan Africa, and the savannas of sub-Saharan Africa, southward into the Arabian Peninsula, and eastward through Central Asia to Manchuria. Foragers quickly disappeared wherever conditions facilitated the spread of agriculture, experiencing the initial stages of a 5,000-year retreat that has now consigned them in tiny, diminishing remnants to such isolated regions as the deserts of southern Africa and western Australia, the rainforests of Southeast Asia and the Amazon and Congo basins, and the fringes of the Arctic. There they continued to survive not by interfering actively with operations of nature in the manner of farmers and herders, but by living in remarkable harmony with their demanding environments.

EXPLAINING AGRICULTURAL ORIGINS

World historians, drawing extensively on the recent scholarship of paleo-archaeologists, have provided ever more comprehensive explanations for the abandonment of hunting and gathering as the dominant mode of human subsistence.[8] Two overriding questions have guided their efforts: why, when myriad combinations of hunting and gathering had been so successful for so long, did post-Pleistocene groups radically transform their familiar lifeways, and how can world-historical perspectives deepen our understanding of this transmutation, given its improbability and the serious complications that accompanied its development?

Although the output potential of intensive agriculture could satisfy the subsistence needs of considerably enlarged human numbers, the transition to farming and herding changed human reproductive habits. It set off a population expansion that fluctuated over the centuries, but continued with only occasional interruptions up to the present day, reaching previously unmanageable rates of growth in the last several hundred years. The relentless if uneven rise in human numbers repeatedly outstripped available supplies of food. Instead of yielding sufficient food reserves to satisfy human requirements on a consistent basis, demographic patterns kept agricultural societies in a Malthusian trap from which none escaped until the nineteenth century. By modern standards, food production remained inefficient until the onset of industrialization. Despite occasional improvement in devices and techniques, technological innovations moved forward at a snail's pace, and never relieved farmers and herders of their dependence on human and animal muscle power. Intensive agriculture sometimes compounded the problem of output limitations by disrupting local ecosystems. Irrigation-induced salination of fields and landscape erosion in the aftermath of deforestation or overgrazing led repeatedly to diminishing returns for heightened efforts. Domesticated plants and animals raised in artificially simplified environments remained highly vulnerable to severe weather, diseases, parasites, and changes in climate.

Even in the best of times, agriculture seldom made the lives of peasant villagers better than the daily routines of hunter-gatherers. The tending of fields proved arduous and restrictive, while the herding of animals seemed less encumbering but equally monotonous. Health and nutrition frequently deteriorated. Especially for farmers, unbalanced diets with little variation probably diminished physical stature, increased infant mortality, shortened life expectancy, and turned such problems as tooth decay, anemia, and rickets into common concerns. Like the deadly famines that invariably followed crop failures, persistent socio-economic and gender inequalities, widespread slavery and other forms of forced labor, state-organized warfare, and destructive attacks by armed raiders accompanied the shift to an agriculturally-based existence. Peasant villages presented problems of sanitation and hygiene unanticipated by foraging bands, and spawned new forms of such bacterial and viral infections as smallpox, influenza, bubonic plague, yellow fever, and cholera. By the end of the fourth millennium BCE, the appearance of crowded cities drove the total regional population of Sumer over half a million, more than enough people in a limited region to make epidemics a persistent dimension of the human experience.[9]

To reflect the physical hardships and psychological strains that accompanied the transition to farming and herding, world historians emphasize alterations in social structures, behavioral patterns, and values systems that took hundreds and sometimes thousands of years to run their course. While the decisions of group leaders may have been crucial at given moments, routine choices made over long periods of time by ordinary individuals were doubtless important too. Those choices underscore the role that unintended consequences can play in the human experience, for participants in the shift to an agricultural existence surely had no sense of being caught up in a larger process. Initially, they saw themselves as doing nothing more than supplementing their subsistence bases. Their incentives must have been strong, involving significant needs rather than dreams of a different future, but the shift to food production could seldom have been a matter of overt intentions.

Why then did food production take hold?[10] The full maturation of anatomically and behaviorally modern humans was certainly a fundamental precondition, for it left our Upper Paleolithic ancestors with the mental abilities to grasp the problems they faced, to formulate viable solutions, and to initiate cooperative responses to their opportunities. The global diaspora of humankind, by compelling widely dispersed populations to manage ever more diverse circumstances, represented another precondition. Wherever they settled down, human beings moving toward a sedentary existence in denser population concentrations readily accumulated the cultural resources that enabled them to realize more of their potential. They had been gradually refining their already elaborate toolkits at a time when the mammal extinctions of the Upper Pleistocene threatened the primary food source of big game hunters. Affected groups understandably intensified their gathering of wild plants, despite the reluctance of those bands facing severe subsistence crises to alter the ways they acquired their food. Instead, bands still operating successfully within their traditional subsistence patterns may have exhibited a greater willingness to strive for the control that accompanied agricultural lifeways. Once they relied on the food reserves made possible by crop cultivation and animal herding, however, they were compelled to recognize that any hope of returning to their old existence had been lost.

Dramatic climate change had previously set the stage for the advent of agriculture. The current interglacial epoch, whose earliest manifestations appeared approximately 18,000 years ago, culminated in a widespread climatic optimum between 6000 and 2500 BCE, when unusually warm and wet weather prevailed in many places. More congenial climates contributed to the domestication process, often by encouraging the diversification of local ecosystems. In the rain-watered regions of Southwest Asia, for example, the range of plant domesticates highly coveted by proto-farmers continued to expand until the fifth millennium BCE, when hybrid wheat and other new plant species appeared in the highlands that bordered the Zagros Mountains. Soon thereafter, as rainfall declined, temperatures rose, and tree cover diminished, some farming groups in the Levant, having already damaged the environment with their long-term grazing and cultivation, had to abandon their villages altogether.[11]

As current interglacial conditions took hold, elevated rates of population growth began to impact Late Pleistocene foraging communities. Human numbers worldwide were approaching the maximum readily sustainable with time-honored traditions. Yet those numbers continued to rise, elevating regional population densities while the rapid melting of glacial ice was leaving broad coastal areas submerged under sea water and the spread of forest cover over once open savannas was threatening long-standing forms of human subsistence. Some foraging bands found themselves confined to smaller homelands. Others moved into marginal or less inviting habitats. In many places, human groups extended their subsistence bases or obtained their food with more specialized methods. They tended to rely less on meat and more on plants. Under favorable conditions, some of them experimented with domestication and cultivation.

And what were those favorable conditions? Examining the primary hearth lands of agriculture from a comparative and global perspective, world historians have identified a number of shared characteristics, starting with ecological diversity. The contrasting zones of climate and terrain within relatively small areas that insured diversity did not always offer a rich natural endowment, but did make the search for a potentially more reliable resource base seem less hazardous. In such inauspicious settings as the Andean highlands, the Mayan lowlands, and the lands of ancient Sumer, foragers could find water supplies and fertile soils as well as some combination of enticing plants and animals prone to domestication. A complicated mosaic of environment zones nurtured cultural differences and yet stimulated interactions between separate groups to satisfy pressing needs. In northern China, the geographical gradients seemed less obvious. Nonetheless, by the third millennium BCE, a traveler going northward might have noticed the intensive agricultural systems covering the Yellow River Valley gradually being replaced by still sedentary herding and rainfall farming, and then by nomadic pastoralism on the arid Mongolian steppes.

The ecology of the primary hearth lands nurtured the broad spectrum of subsistence strategies typical of intensive foragers during the Upper Paleolithic. The earliest farmers readily capitalized upon the pre-adaptations of their predecessors as they imperceptibly enmeshed themselves in a new mode of existence. Increasingly complex forms of social organization contributed to the emergence of food production by hastening the formation of authority structures required to implement decisions, perform rituals, redistribute resources, resolve disagreements, and protect the interests of vulnerable sedentary communities. The shift to agriculture tended to sharpen socio-economic inequalities and status rankings. The availability of sustained food surpluses in turn created new possibilities for the structuring of social life. Farming and herding can thus be viewed in part as an outgrowth of development integral to enhanced cultural complexity at the end of the last ice age.[12]

RECURRING AGRICULTURAL PATTERNS IN THE POST-CLASSIC WORLD

After 7000 BCE, overall population growth became a primary force in altering the conditions of human existence, supporting and being supported by the ongoing spread of simple horticultural societies onto new ground. Most notably, rice cultivation appeared in the Ganges Valley shortly after 1500 BCE, and maize reached the Orinoco Valley after 600 BCE. Sporadic advances in farming techniques brought incremental rises in productivity. In Southeast Asia, for example, the adoption of plowing and double cropping permitted the intensified cultivation of long-stemmed, fast-maturing rice in seasonally flooded paddy fields. The consequent elevation of crop yields set off a growth of population that turned small, isolated settlements into towns and cities by about 700 BCE. Knowledge of iron-working for the manufacture of plowshares and scythes quickly raised agricultural output in the oldest agricultural regions, and during the first millennium BCE, metal axes allowed farmers to exploit the entire Ganges Basin by removing thick forest cover from potentially fertile lands. At the start of the Common Era, worldwide population may have reached 200 million. Thereafter, the growth faltered, and within several centuries human numbers probably declined, not moving upward again until the tenth century. By then, however, nearly 90 percent of all human beings depended directly on food production for their survival.

During the thirteenth century, China under the Song dynasty (960–1279) reached unparalleled levels of agricultural productivity, with India alone coming close to the Chinese achievement. The agricultural surge on the Indian subcontinent can be explained by the spread of cultivation throughout the Ganges plain and the introduction of irrigation techniques to the south of the Deccan Plateau in the early centuries of the Common Era. After the Gupta dynasty (ca. 320–535) established a degree of political unity and peace in northern India, agricultural output increased substantially on the fertile coastal plains, wheat and sugar becoming the dominant crop on the western shores of the subcontinent, rice prevailing on its eastern side. The foundations of Chinese predominance took shape during the age of the Eastern Zhou (771–221 BCE), when artisans mastered the techniques of iron smelting. The availability of iron plows, sickles, and knives and the newly invented wheelbarrow elevated farm output, as did the construction of large-scale dikes and canals systems that improved flood control, field irrigation, and the transport of bulk commodities. Along with the adoption of wet-rice agriculture in the Yangzi basin, other innovations included the collar harness, the use of human waste and animal manure as natural fertilizers, and routine crop rotation with the fallowing of fields. Moreover, the movement of Chinese peasants southward toward the Yangzi River had begun, accelerating after the disintegration of the Han dynasty in the third century of the Common Era.

The process of agricultural expansion driven by the long-term settlement of southern China and portions of Vietnam, the cultivation of new crops over larger areas, the terracing and irrigation of mountain slopes, continuing technological innovation, and the well-planned construction of massive transportation networks maintained its momentum into the era of the Ming (1368–1644). It featured an independent, land-owning peasantry, regional specialization in crops ranging from indigo, sugarcane, cotton, and early-ripening, drought-resistant Champa rice to exotic items such as tea and silk worms. The Chinese economy had become heavily commercialized so that the bulk of the peasantry, by selling their produce for income, found themselves guided by the demands of a nominally free market and the dictates of long-distance trade. While this transformation essentially duplicated principles that had operated for centuries in the economies of Southwest Asia, it made an impact that extended far beyond imperial China, affecting lands as distant as the Mediterranean basin.[13]

Among the societies of the western hemisphere, the most precocious accomplishments took place in Mesoamerica, where a doubling of the length of the corn cob produced a jump in the output of maize during the fourth century BCE. The subsequent adoption of canal irrigation further augmented crop yields, giving a diverse population in the Mayan lowlands the subsistence base required to bring the development of their state-organized society to a climax between 300 and 900 CE. Maya farmers, moving into the lowland forests from the northwest, had to contend with heavy tree cover, torrential downpours, and infertile soils. They lacked metals, beasts of burden, and wheeled carts, and had to import such indispensable resources as salt and stone from afar. Nonetheless, they learned how to cultivate manioc and yams as well as maize on fields elevated above surrounding swamps with sediment captured in their elaborate hillside terraces. They countered heavy rains with intricate canal systems that could also be used as needed for irrigation purposes. Harvesting two or even three crops per year, Maya farmers sustained a dense lowlands population that may have reached almost five million by 300 CE.[14] A broad dissemination of other human groups had furthered the spread of agricultural pursuits by the time the culture of the Maya went into decline. By 4000 BCE, initial waves of Austronesian migrants from Southeast Asia, who integrated farming with hunting and fishing, appeared on the north coast of New Guinea in ocean-going outriggers. They carried with them such food crops as yams, taro, bread-fruit, bananas, and sugarcane along with domesticated dogs, pigs, and chickens. By roughly 1500 BCE, they reached Vanuatu, maintaining their connections with Southeast Asia through expanding networks of kinship ties and trade relations. After settling Tonga and Samoa just before 1000 BCE, they did not advance beyond Melanesia and Micronesia for more than 500 years. When they resumed their colonization, these daring mariners occupied nearly all of the archipelagos of Polynesia by 1300, and apparently acquired the sweet potato from contacts on the coast of South America. Despite mounting diversification, they continued to share a common set of culture traits that relied on an economic base of fishing and gardening.[15]

The feats of Malayo-Polynesian seafarers were meanwhile being matched in sub-Saharan Africa by tribes of Bantu-speakers. Until the first millennium BCE, tropical climates and a host of parasites and diseases had thwarted most attempts to extend crop cultivation and pastoralism south of the Sahel. Archaeologists have uncovered evidence of deliberate crop cultivation in equatorial West Africa almost 10,000 years ago and in the Ethiopian highlands around 500 years later. By 1500 BCE, a farming complex sustained by an incipient Nok culture had begun to develop in the savanna-forest ecotone of northern Nigeria. Local populations there cultivated such plants as yams and rice, tamed guinea fowl, herded livestock, and when necessary continued to supplement their diets with hunting and fishing.

By 500 BCE, people across the Sahel had mastered the techniques of smelting and forging iron, which hastened the spread of agriculture beyond West Africa. Tribes of Bantu-speakers had initially penetrated the equatorial forests of the Zaire Basin before advancing eastward along the southern edges of the Sahel. Acquiring herds of cattle and sheep along the way, they mastered iron-working skills upon reaching the Western Rift Valley, dispersing their understanding of metallurgy along with their farming and herding methods throughout much of the subcontinent during the first millennium of the Common Era. The later stages of their expansion probably involved a spread of their culture as much as a migration of their bands. However it occurred, the Bantus could use their iron weapons to subdue indigenous hunter-gathers. Iron axes and machetes eased the task of clearing forest plots for their gardens. With iron hoes, they cultivated sorghum, millet, oil palms, and a variety of peas and beans, to which they added the coco-yams, plantain, Asian bananas, taro, and sugarcane that either had been native to the Congo-Zambezi River network or had reached the coasts of East Africa on the ships of Austronesian sailors. By the year 1000, they had also supplemented their sheep and cattle herds with the chickens and pigs that had been introduced into the subcontinent by Austronesian settlers.[16]

Two subsequent world-historical phenomena—the sudden rise of Islam in the seventh and eighth centuries and the expansion of Europe from the fifteenth to the eighteenth century—redistributed plants, animals and farming technology on an unprecedented scale.[17] Arab conquests that created the Islamic caliphate eased the journeys of merchants, travelers, and government officials who might carry valuable seeds, animals, and agricultural concepts as far as Spain to the west or Indonesia to the east. Once Arabs reached the Indus River Valley, the Indian subcontinent functioned as a primary center for the diffusion of crops that often originated in Southeast Asia and sometimes ended up at the western end of the Mediterranean basin. In the long run, the most significant of these transplanted crops was sugarcane, which spread to southern China in the first century of the Common Era, and westward to India, later to Iran and Mesopotamia, then to the Levant and Cyprus, and after the tenth century to the East African coast. Other widely dispersed plants included cotton, rice, citrus trees, bananas, spinach, indigo, hard wheat from Ethiopia, and sorghum from Africa.

This diffusion process failed to transform agriculture in any radical fashion. By broadening regional systems, however, it did expand the acreage under cultivation, permit improved crop rotation, and yielded two or three harvests per year. Food production increased slightly, diets became more varied, crop failures diminished in severity, and experiments with new methods of field maintenance happened more frequently.[18] Sugar production became integral to the evolution of a plantation complex whose labor demands provoked the rapid growth of the Atlantic slave trade after about 1550 and led to a dependence on slavery wherever Europeans sought to produce cash crops on a large scale.[19]

What is now described as the 'Columbian exchange,' initiated in 1492, set off by far the greatest diffusion of plants and animals in the whole of human history. It soon affected many societies around the world with consequences larger than those of the first major diffusion. Its global impact continues to reverberate into the twenty-first century. Within a hundred years, every plant and animal vital to European agriculture—wheat, cattle, sheep, horses, pigs, and chickens—had been transmitted to the Americas, and wherever else Europeans were settling in large numbers. Many New World crops such as tomatoes, cacao, and tobacco enriched diets and everyday pleasures, but potatoes, beans, manioc, and especially maize became staples in farming systems around the world. By the eighteenth century, they were contributing to the modern population take-off. The Chinese, having quickly appropriated maize, stood in the forefront of this global demographic surge.[20]

The Industrialization of Modern Agriculture

Until the mid-eighteenth century, over 90 percent of all human beings labored on the land as peasants. Because population and food supplies had never remained in balance, the chronic hardships of peasant existence had still not been overcome, although China under the Song dynasty almost made a critical breakthrough. Not until another great transmutation had spurred the industrialization of society could the technology and techniques of food production be genuinely revolutionized. The sources of industrialization were global in scope, just as the origins of agriculture had been 10,000 years earlier, although the earliest manifestations of the second transmutation associated with farming appeared in northwestern Europe between 1200 and 1800.[21]

Improvements in efficiency and output began with the adoption of a heavy moldboard plow, a three-field system of land use, and the horse collar and horseshoe. Peasants expanded the total area under cultivation and managed to raise yields per acre with better seeding techniques. The sixteenth-century Dutch assumed a leadership role by enclosing open fields, systematically rotating a wider variety of crops, resorting to heavy applications of cow manure, growing turnips for winter feed and clover for nitrogen replacement in fallow ground, expanding tillage by draining swamps, experimenting with stock breeding and the development of hybrid seeds, and inventing such devices as the seed drill. During the eighteenth century, the English took advantage of a moderating European climate to increase the cultivation of potatoes and maize, and raise sheep more intensively to meet an active demand for wool. Drawing on what the Dutch had already accomplished, the English invented various machines to augment productivity and wrote treatises on their latest scientific methods. They joined the Dutch in moving toward a form of modern mixed farming. Large landowners concentrated on commercial crops and livestock for sale in expanding urban markets. They were more inclined to follow rational and capitalistic principles than traditional practices, and managed to double their crop yields over what had been possible 600 years earlier, an improvement replicated by Chinese rice farmers alone.

Not until 1850 did Europe and those parts of the world where Europeans had settled in large numbers begin to transcend the restrictions on human potential typical of agricultural societies. By then, modern industrialization had opened up new possibilities for organizing social structures and augmenting economic productivity. As human numbers sky-rocketed, immense areas, especially in North America and Australia, fell under cultivation for the first time. Industrializing Europe benefited immediately from a sudden growth in agricultural imports made possible by its control over a disproportionate share of the world's resources, and by the development of steamships and railroads. In the United States, where land was abundant and labor often scarce, pace-setting technical invention produced the first mowing, reaping, and harvesting machines. In 1892, gasoline-powered tractors became available. By the end of the century, canning and refrigeration were sufficiently reliable to allow the transport of fruits and vegetables over long distances, and food processing contributed to the growth of large-scale retail enterprises.

Wherever agriculture became commercialized, self-sufficient farming declined and an increasing percentage of the population, migrating to cities, lost their connections with rural life. In those parts of Asia, Africa, and Latin America less affected by global capitalism, much of the population retained peasant lifeways and remained vulnerable to famines or disruptions in world markets. Modern forms of dairy farming emerged in North America, Europe, Australia, and New Zealand. Cattle ranching developed in the Americas, sheep herding in South Africa, Australia, and New Zealand. Large-scale grain production dominated the grasslands of North America, Argentina, and Russia. By World War I, plantations throughout the tropics and subtropics were producing bulk items for export to industrialized countries: rubber, tea, and rice in Southeast Asia, indigo and jute in Bengal, cotton in Egypt, coffee in Brazil, and tobacco in Columbia, along with a host of other commodities ranging from sugar and bananas to cocoa and palm oil.[22]

A far more impressive leap in agricultural productivity occurred in the twentieth century. Worldwide output probably tripled and in the decades following World War II outpaced the rise in population. A larger percentage of people alive today are adequately fed than in 1900. The total acreage under cultivation now amounts to roughly 11 percent of the Earth's land surface, with another 25 percent dedicated to grazing. After 1930, science-driven agricultural technology made greater strides than in all previous centuries combined. In North America, Australia, and Europe, tractors replaced horses. Trucks and grain combines became widely used. Farmers in the industrial world took electric power for granted. Findings in genetic research guided the breeding of more valuable plants and animals. Natural phosphates and artificial fertilizers replaced the use of manures and composts. Herbicides and pesticides were added to the farmer's arsenal.

After World War II, the industrialization of agriculture drew individuals with management talents and investment capital into a corporate network known as agribusiness. Especially in the United States, farmers set up factory systems for the mass production of meat, poultry, milk, eggs, fruits, and vegetables in controlled environments. They often negotiated contracts with suppliers, processors, and distributors. By 1980, the raising of poultry had become the most industrialized sector of modern agriculture.

Beyond the industrialized world, cooperation between economically advanced countries and less developed nations resulted in a 'Green Revolution' in the 1950s and 1960s. It substantially boasted the output of primary cereal grains—wheat, corn, and rice—through the use of genetically engineered hybrid seeds, fertilizers, pesticides, and irrigation water. The first triumphs of the Green Revolution, invariably supported by local initiatives, came in Mexico, followed by India, China, and other countries of East Asia, which ceased to be food importers. India managed to export wheat in years of ample harvests. By contrast, sub-Saharan Africa benefited less from these initiatives, in part because scientists had not bred new varieties of the yams, sorghum, and cassava vital to native farmers. Not only did much of Africa continue to rely on food imports, but terrible famines ravaged Ethiopia and the Sahel as well as Bangladesh even before the Green Revolution lost momentum in the 1970s.

The Green Revolution turned out to be an uneven advance. Difficult climate and terrain, the threats posed by disease to animals as well as humans, and the infertility of the soils explain the failures in tropical Africa. Yet the Green Revolution had deleterious consequences even when it appeared to succeed. Since peasant farmers could seldom muster the investment capital required to participate, the advantages tended to go disproportionately to wealthy landowners, and many peasants lost what little land they possessed. The mixed results of the Green Revolution dramatized the agricultural challenges facing humankind in the twentieth century. The genetic engineering of plants seemed to increase the possibility that an expanding population might be minimally fed in future decades. Between 1950 and 1980 enough food was being produced to achieve that goal. But agricultural commodities remained unevenly distributed, and the gap between rich and poor countries continued to widen. Most people in industrial societies, roughly one-fourth of the world's total, had adequate diets, consuming about half of available food supplies, while at least two billion scattered throughout South Asia, Africa, and South America struggled with chronic malnourishment and had little capacity to rectify the situation through local initiatives alone. An enduring global equilibrium between population and food reserves remained as elusive as ever.

Can agricultural productivity meet human needs in the long run? Since twentieth-century advances, given their costs, do not seem sustainable, further increases in output will not be achieved easily. Global population growth, while showing signs of slowing down, has pushed farmers and herders into areas unsuited to intensive agriculture, accelerating worldwide ecological disruptions. Reserves of arable land

and fresh water have diminished alarmingly. Chemical runoffs have compounded pollution problems. Invasions of natural habitats have hastened species extinction. Desertification has been severe in the last hundred years, especially in the Sahel, North Africa, southern portions of Africa, Australia, northern Mexico, and the American Southwest. Tropical forests have shrunk by one-half since World War II, with agricultural pressures causing three-quarters of that loss. Government intervention produced its share of catastrophes, ranging from a terrible famine in China between 1958 and 1961 that may have killed 30 million people to a vast irrigation project in the Soviet Union that for all practical purposes destroyed the Aral Sea. Taking everything into consideration, we may remain hopeful about humankind's agricultural prospects, but we can scarcely look forward optimistically at the onset of the twenty-first century.[23]

Notes

1. Marshall G. S. Hodgson, *Rethinking World History: Essays on Europe, Islam, and World History*, ed. by Edmund Burke III (Cambridge and New York: Cambridge University Press, 1993), 44–9. Hodgson was discussing the modern transmutation grounded in the industrialization of the West, which exhibited basic similarities when compared to the watershed spawned by the coming of farming and animal husbandry.
2. For straightforward descriptions of different types of human societies, see Gerhard Lenski and Jean Lenski, *Human Societies: An Introduction to Macrosciology*, 5th edn. (New York: McGraw-Hill, 1987), chapter 4.
3. Andrew Sherratt, 'The Secondary Exploitation of Animals in the Old World,' in *Economy and Society in Prehistoric Europe: Changing Perspectives* (Princeton: Princeton University Press, 1997), 199–228.
4. For an introduction to the problem of demographic growth, consult Massimo Livi-Bacci, *A Concise History of World Population*, 3rd edn. (Oxford and Malden, Mass.: Blackwell, 2001), 29–36.
5. Charles Keith Maisels, *The Emergence of Civilization: From Hunting and Gathering to Agriculture, Cities and the State in the Near East* (London and New York: Routledge, 1990) provides extended analysis of the primary themes associated with the coalescence of a complex society in ancient Sumer.
6. A global perspective on most of the areas in which agriculture originated is provided in T. Douglas Price and Anne Birgitte Gebauer, eds., *Last Hunters—First Farmers: New Perspectives on the Prehistoric Transition to Agriculture* (Santa Fe: School of American Research Press, 1995).
7. Stuart J. Fiedel, *Prehistory of the Americas*, 2nd edn. (Cambridge: Cambridge University Press, 1992) provides a systematic overview of developments in the western hemisphere from the spread of Paleo-Indians through the origins of food production to the formation of complex societies. For another convenient reference, see C. Wesley Cowan and Patty Jo Watson, *The Origins of Agriculture: An International Perspective* (Washington and London: Smithsonian Institution Press, 1992), chapters 6–9.

8. Archaeologist Steven Mithen has provided world historians with one model of how this might be done in *After the Ice: A Global Human History 20,000–5000 BC* (Cambridge, Mass.: Harvard University Press, 2003). He sets forth a descriptive overview of developments that took hunter-gatherers from their existence in small bands to their lives in the first complex societies.

9. William H. McNeill, *Plagues and Peoples* (Garden City, New York: Doubleday, 1977), 36–56.

10. For a similar response to this question, but one that presents a somewhat different interpretation than the argument presented here, see David Christian, *Maps of Time: An Introduction to Big History* (Berkeley and Los Angeles: University of California Press, 2005), 207–43.

11. For an extended consideration of climate change and its consequences, see William James Burroughs, *Climate Change in Prehistory: The End of the Reign of Chaos* (Cambridge and New York: Cambridge University Press, 2005), chapter 5.

12. For a multi-authored global approach to these issues, see T. Douglas Price and James A. Brown, eds., *Prehistoric Hunter-Gatherers: The Emergence of Cultural Complexity* (Orlando: Academic Press, 1985).

13. William H. McNeill was among the first scholars to place these developments in a world-historical perspective. See *The Pursuit of Power: Technology, Armed Force, and Society since A.D. 1000* (Chicago: University of Chicago Press, 1982), chapter 2.

14. For world historians, a helpful overview of the Mayan achievement can be found in Stuart J. Fiedel, *Prehistory of the Americas,* 2nd edn. (Cambridge and New York: Cambridge University Press, 1992), 286–302.

15. A compilation of recent research can be found in Patrick V. Kirch, *On the Road of the Winds: An Archaeological History of the Pacific Islands before European Contact* (Berkeley: University of California Press, 2000).

16. Another convenient reference for world historians is Christopher Ehret, *The Civilizations of Africa: A History to 1800* (Charlottesville: University Press of Virginia, 2002), 44–8, 59–64, 75–90, 111–43, 189–200.

17. For a contextualizing of these developments, see Clive Ponting, *World History: A New Perspective* (London: Chatto & Windus, 2000), 351–5, 494–7.

18. The standard reference on this subject is Andrew M. Watson, *Agricultural Innovation in the Early Islamic World: The Diffusion of Crops and Farming Techniques, 700–1100* (Cambridge and New York: Cambridge University Press, 1983).

19. Philip D. Curtin, *The Rise and Fall of the Plantation Complex: Essays in Atlantic History* (Cambridge: Cambridge University Press, 1990), chapters 1–3. For a comprehensive perspective on the plantation system, see D. B. Grigg, *The Agricultural Systems of the World: An Evolutionary Approach* (Cambridge: Cambridge University Press, 1974), chapter 11.

20. The path-breaking scholarship on this problem was presented in Alfred W. Crosby, Jr., *The Columbian Exchange: Biological and Cultural Consequences of 1492* (Westport: Greenwood Press, 1972).

21. For a somewhat different conceptualization of Hodgson's two transmutations, see Carlo M. Cipolla, *The Economic History of World Population,* 7th edn. (New York: Penguin, 1978), chapter 1.

22. Extensive descriptions of main agricultural trends between the twelfth and the nineteenth century can be found in Grigg, *Agricultural Systems,* chapters 9–13.

23. For a positive perspective, consult B. F. Stanton, 'Agriculture: Crops, Livestock, and Farmers,' in Richard W. Bulliet, ed., *The Columbia History of the 20th Century* (New York: Columbia University Press, 1998), chapter 15. Paul Roberts, *The End of Food* (Boston: Houghton Mifflin, 2008) epitomizes the bleak view. Clive Ponting, *A Green History of the World: The Environment and the Collapse of Great Civilizations* (New York: St. Martin's, 1991), chapters 12–16 present an overtly ecological interpretation of recent developments.

References

ADAS, MICHAEL, ed. *Agricultural and Pastoral Societies in Ancient and Classical History.* Philadelphia: Temple University Press, 2001.

BARKER, GRAEME. *The Agricultural Revolution in Prehistory: Why did Foragers become Farmers?* Oxford and New York: Oxford University Press, 2006.

BOSERUP, ESTER. *The Conditions of Agricultural Growth: The Economics and Agrarian Change under Population Pressure.* London: G. Allen & Unwin, 1965.

COCHRANE, WILLARD W. *The Development of American Agriculture: A Historical Analysis.* 2nd edn. Minneapolis and London: University of Minnesota Press, 1993.

CROSBY, ALFRED W. *Ecological Imperialism: The Biological Expansion of Europe 900–1900.* Cambridge: Cambridge University Press, 1986.

GRIGG, DAVID. *The Dynamics of Agricultural Change: The Historical Experience.* New York: St. Martin's, 1982.

McCLELLAND, PETER D. *Sowing Modernity: America's First Agricultural Revolution.* Ithaca and London: Cornell University Press, 1997.

RICHARDS, PAUL. *Indigenous Agricultural Revolution: Ecology and Food Production in West Africa.* London: Hutchinson, 1985.

ROTBERG, ROBERT I. and RABB, THEODORE K., eds. *Hunger and History: The Impact of Changing Food Production and Consumptions Patterns on Society.* Cambridge and New York: Cambridge University Press, 1985.

SMIL, VACLAV. *Feeding the World: A Challenge for the Twenty-First Century.* Cambridge, Mass. and London: MIT Press, 2000.

SCHUSKY, ERNEST L. *Culture and Agriculture: An Ecological Introduction to Traditional and Modern Farming Systems.* New York: Bergen & Garvey, 1989.

TURNER II, B. L. and BRUSH, STEPHEN B., eds. *Comparative Farming Systems.* New York and London: Guilford, 1987.

CHAPTER 9

NOMADIC PASTORALISM

THOMAS J. BARFIELD

DEFINITIONS

NOMADIC pastoralists live in societies in which the husbandry of grazing animals is viewed as an ideal way of making a living and the regular movement of all or part of the society is considered a normal and natural part of life. Although the terms 'nomad' and 'pastoralist' are generally used interchangeably, they are analytically distinct: the former referring to movement and the latter to a type of subsistence. It is an economic specialization that is as much a way of life as a way of making a living.

The variety of animals raised by nomadic pastoralists is surprisingly small: six widely distributed species (sheep, goats, cattle, horses, donkeys, and camels) and three with restricted distribution (yaks at high altitudes in Asia, reindeer at northern sub-arctic latitudes, and dogs that are often kept for protection). Llamas and other cameloid species found in highland South America were raised by alpine farming villagers, not nomads. Pigs are never raised by nomadic pastoralists, so their presence is a negative function particularly useful to archeologists who have only faunal remains to analyze.

Pastoral nomadism is commonly found where climatic conditions produce seasonal pastures but cannot support sustained agriculture. Organized around mobile households rather than individuals, it involves everyone, men, women, and children, in the various aspects of production. This distinguishes nomadic pastoralists from European shepherds or American cowboys who are recruited from the larger sedentary society to which they regularly return. Since people cannot eat grass, exploiting grazing animals effectively taps an otherwise unusable energy source. Using tents or huts to facilitate migration, they rotate their animals among extensive but seasonal pastures. Migration cycles vary in time and length depending on local conditions: few moves where pastures and water are dependable, many more where they are not. While casual observers often assume that nomads simply wander from place to place, in fact they follow predictable routes within a flexible range.

Nomadic pastoral societies in Africa and Eurasia may be divided into six zones, each with its distinctive cultural identity and history.

1. High latitude sub-arctic reindeer herders such as Lapps of Scandinavia are the northernmost nomadic peoples. Living in hide-covered tents, they represent one end of a continuum of reindeer exploitation that ranges from intensive use for milking and traction to raising the animals for meat harvest alone, or to simple hunting.

2. Eurasian steppe nomads such as the Scythians, Turks, Mongols, Kazaks, and Kirghiz inhabited the grasslands immediately south of the Eurasian forest zone. Although they also raise sheep, goats, cattle, and Bactrian camels, horse raising has always been culturally pre-eminent. Using both carts and camels to transport them, steppe nomads lived in distinctive dome-shaped yurts that coped well with the subfreezing temperatures of the Eurasian winter. Historically steppe nomads were famous for their horse-riding skills, archery, and general military talents. Under leaders like Attila the Hun they often terrorized their neighbors through violent raiding, but on the Chinese Great Wall frontier, the Xiongnu and Turks established long-lived empires. Chinggis Qan and the Mongols conquered and ruled the world's largest empire.

3. Sheep and goat pastoralism predominates in the mountain and plateau areas of southwest Asia among people who also raise horses, camels, and donkeys for transport. Pastoralists such as the Bakhtiari, Qashqa'i, Basseri, Lurs, Turkmen, and Pashtuns had a symbiotic relationship with neighboring towns and villages as pastoral specialists, trading meat animals, wool, milk products, and hides for grain and manufactured goods. Nomads in the northern areas retained the Eurasian yurt as a dwelling while in warmer regions the black goat hair tent was more characteristic. Many of the region's sedentary states were ruled by dynasties that had nomadic origins.

4. The camel-raising Bedouin of the Saharan and Arabian deserts were unique in their specialized raising of only one animal, the dromedary camel, for food and transport. Historically they also supplemented their income by selling protection to oasis farmers, providing camels for the caravan trade, and receiving subsidies for military support. A more limited form of pastoralism that added sheep and goats to the herding mix was found near sedentary areas, but since these animals could not survive in the deep desert, their migration range was much more restricted. Both groups used black goat hair tents, which the deep-desert Bedouin acquired by trade.

5. Pastoralists such as the Nuer, Dinka, Turkana, Masai, and Zulu on the grasslands of sub-Saharan Africa so highly prized cattle that anthropologists labeled them a 'cattle complex.' Cattle exchanges among men played such an important role in social relations that other aspects of the economy, including raising sheep and goats or seasonal agriculture done by women, was culturally devalued even when it was economically important. In striking contrast to other pastoral zones there

was no tradition of using tents or large baggage animals for transport. Instead people erected huts at each encampment and used only donkeys for transport. Animals were protected from predators by fencing them in at night.

6. Pastoralism on the high altitude Tibetan plateau relied on a unique form of herding that required few movements. Based on domesticated yaks that could only reproduce at high altitudes, nomads also bred yak/cattle hybrids, high-altitude varieties of sheep, cashmere goats, and a few horses. Because high altitude precluded farming, nomads here had exclusive access to very rich grasslands and abundant water. Tibetan pastoralists traded wool, skins, salt, and milk products to valley villagers for barley which is a mainstay of their diet. They employed tents made of yak hair, often surrounded by rock walls to protect them from high winds.

NOMADS AND THE SEDENTARY WORLD

Ethnographic work has largely discredited the notion of the 'pure nomad' who subsists entirely on pastoral products, free of entanglements with the sedentary world. Nomadic pastoralists have always been tied economically and politically to their sedentary neighbors, links without which they could not easily survive or prosper. More impor-tant from an historical perspective, it was the relationship that nomads established with their sedentary neighbors that had the greatest impact on their political organization. In general the size and complexity of a nomadic society matched the degree of centralization of the sedentary societies it interacted with.

These interactions have not always been happy ones. Sedentary observers con-demned nomads such as the Huns, Mongols, and Bedouin as destructive forces and threats to civilization itself. The fourteenth-century Arab social historian ibn Khaldun was typical in his view that nomads were naturally predatory because

> it is their nature to plunder whatever other people possess. Their sustenance lies wherever the shadow of their lance falls. They recognize no limit in taking the possessions of other people. Whenever their eyes fall upon some property, furnishings or utensils, they take them.[1]

Indeed this view of the violent nomad has long overshadowed the more peaceful relationships that characterized nomadic groups that facilitated long-distance trade or supplied pastoral products to their sedentary neighbors. But perhaps this should not be surprising. Tales of conquerors and their dynasties have always hogged history's stage at the expense of less exciting events. The more significant question is how nomadic societies with low population densities, rudimentary divisions of labor, and simple material cultures ever came to pose such a threat. The answer to this question has less to do with the internal dynamics of nomadic societies than with their external relations.

LEVELS OF SOCIAL AND POLITICAL COMPLEXITY AMONG NOMADS

Although the technology of animal husbandry and the techniques used to conduct it are not radically different from one nomadic zone to another, the degree of social and political organization varies significantly. Across Africa and Eurasia the size of political units and their centralization grows progressively more complex on a northeasterly line from the cattle keepers of East Africa to the mounted horse nomads of Mongolia. The reason for this seems to have less to do with the internal demands of organizing pastoral production than it does with their adaptation to the sedentary world. As Anatoly M. Khazanov best documented, nomadic pastoralists do not live in a vacuum but have always been in constant interaction with their non-nomadic neighbors.[2]

This interaction has produced four distinctive types of social and political organization specific to nomadic pastoralists of (1) sub-Saharan Africa, (2) the desert of Near East and North Africa, (3) the plateau areas of Anatolia, Iran, and Central Asia, and (4) the steppe zones of Eurasia. These coincide with the level of complexity of societies pastoral nomads encountered when dealing with their sedentary neighbors.

1. Acephalous segmentary lineages and age sets in sub-Saharan Africa where nomadic pastoralists encountered few state societies until the colonial era.
2. Lineages with permanent leaders but no supra-tribal organization in North Africa and Arabia where unified tribal groups rarely exceeded ten thousand people and faced regional states with which they had symbiotic relations.
3. Supra-tribal confederations that had populations of a hundred thousand or more people with powerful leaders who were part of a regional political network within large empires in Iran or Anatolia linking tribes to states as conquerors or subjects.
4. Centralized nomadic states ruling over vast distances with populations that could sometimes approach one million on the steppes north of China supported by extractive relationships with neighboring sedentary civilizations.

A closer look shows that each of the larger units incorporates elements of the smaller ones. Descent groups of some type are common to most, but in the larger units they are not autonomous. Similarly, nomadic states that ruled over huge territories were subdivided into smaller supra-tribal component parts.

Most students of nomadic societies see external relations rather than indigenous developments as the source for these differences.[3] They note that nomads were highly dispersed with low population densities, had no significant division of labor, and were hard to tax efficiently. Nor did the mix of animals or herding patterns require substantially higher levels of organization from one region to another. Instead the degree of military and political complexity of a nomadic polity was an adaptation to the threats and opportunities presented by neighboring sedentary societies. Others, however, claim that internal forces could explain these differences if we assume that the nomads ruled over farming populations as elites or if class divisions emerged within a nomadic society.[4]

Understanding Nomadic Social and Political Organizations

Tribe is a term that has long been out of fashion in anthropology and history because of its connotations with the primitive. But if used in a technical sense to describe a society where kinship and descent groups are the basic building blocks, then most of the world's nomadic pastoralists are indeed tribal. Their basic political structures are those that (at least in theory) employ a model of kinship to build corporate groups that act in concert to organize economic production, preserve internal political order, and defend the group against outsiders. Relationships among individuals and groups in such systems are mapped through social space rather than geographic territory. People, therefore, identify themselves as members of a defined social group, not as residents of a particular place. This is a particularly useful way of mapping social space for people who regularly move in physical space.

Although tribes often define themselves on the basis of genealogical principles, 'actual' kinship relations (based on principles of descent and affiliations by marriage or adoption) are empirically evident only within its smaller units: nuclear families, extended households, and local lineages. At higher levels of incorporation clans and tribes often found it necessary to establish relationships that were more politically based because kinship was so problematic as the organizing model for very large groups when the pretense that it was genealogically based could not be maintained. For this reason it is important to distinguish analytically between a tribe, which is the largest unit of incorporation based on a genealogical model, and a tribal confederation, which combines openly unrelated tribes to create a supra-tribal political entity.

For example, in Iran and Mongolia the genealogically based tribe was of far less significance than the tribal confederation. Such confederations swallowed up whole tribes and made local leaders subordinate to the central rule of a khan. They were created by the imposition of political order that was the product of reorganization enforced by division from the top down rather than alliances from the bottom up. Although over time the specific tribes and clans that made up the confederation might change, confederations often had life spans measured in centuries. The creation of such powerful long-lived confederacies with powerful khans on the Iranian plateau and Mongolia was in striking contrast to the fragmented political system of the Bedouin tribes of Arabia and North Africa where supra-tribal confederations were rare and very unstable. After the early Islamic conquest period, Bedouin tribes of Arabian origin played a diminishingly small role in the Middle East and Iran. In this period Turkish nomads from Central Asia came to dominate the political landscape both among the tribes and as rulers of sedentary states. These differences had both cultural and political roots.

There were two very different types of tribal cultural traditions with different styles of polity.[5] The first was the egalitarian segmentary lineage type most closely associated with the Bedouins of Arabia and North Africa or the Nuer of East Africa. The second was the hierarchical tribal model characteristic of the Turco-Mongolian peoples who came into the Iranian and Anatolian plateaus from Central Eurasia. The former had only temporary leaders or weak chieftains (sheikhs), whose authority was limited to their own lineage, clan, or tribe. As a result, the maximum size of their political units rarely surpassed 10,000; and the larger the group, the shorter the time its unity could be maintained. By contrast, Turco-Mongolian leaders (khans) had the ability to command their followers and formed confederations in Iran that commonly ruled over a hundred thousand or more people for many generations. Along the Mongolian border with China, nomads periodically formed empires that organized millions under a centralized administration.

These two types of organization displayed very different political dynamics. Tribes composed of egalitarian lineages had leaders who ruled by means of consensus or mediation. They could unite rival groups only through use of segmentary opposition where cooperation or hostility was determined by the scope of the problem at hand. The numerous petty disputes that ordinarily divided egalitarian lineages would be set aside when they were faced with a common outside threat. But the egalitarian nature of these societies also made them resistant to accepting the permanent authority of any paramount leader who came from a rival kin group. For this reason, as ibn Khaldun first noted, only a leader who stood outside the tribal system, generally in the guise of a religious prophet, could expect to gain the cooperation of enough quarrelling tribes to create a supra-tribal organization:

> Bedouins can acquire royal authority only by making use of religious coloring, such as prophethood or sainthood, or some great religious event in general. The reason is because of their savagery, the Bedouins are the least willing of all nations to subordinate themselves to each other, as they are rude, proud, ambitious and eager to be leaders. Their individual aspirations rarely coincide. But when there is religion (among them) through prophethood or sainthood, then they have some restraining influence upon themselves. The qualities of haughtiness and jealousy leave them. It is easy then to unite (as a social organization) . . . This is illustrated by the Arab dynasty of Islam. Religion cemented their leadership with religious law and its ordinances, which, explicitly and implicitly, are concerned with what is good for civilization.[6]

The classic example of this was the mobilization of the Arab Bedouin tribes during the early days of Islam when religion united them as a single force. In general, however, egalitarian tribes saw little need for supra-tribal organization because they normally confronted only small regional states rather than centralized empires, had a symbiotic relationship with neighboring cities, and often shared a common culture with their region's agricultural and urban populations.

By contrast, the nomads who entered the highland plateaus of Iran and Anatolia after 1000 had a very different concept of political organization. A cursory examination of the history of Southwest Asia during the last millennium reveals an almost unbroken sequence of important empires and dynasties of tribal nomadic (mostly Turkish) origin: Saljuqs, Ghaznavids, Khwarazm Shahs, Mongol Il-Khans, Timurids, Ottomans, Aqquyunlu, Uzbeks, and Qizilbash, to name just some of the more prominent. Largely of Central Eurasian origin, they drew on the cultural tradition of the horse-riding peoples from the steppes of Mongolia. These Turco-Mongolian tribal systems accepted the legitimacy of hierarchical differences in kinship organization that made social distinctions between senior and junior generations, noble and common clans, and between the rulers and the ruled. The acceptance of hierarchy as a normal feature of tribal life made it much easier for their leaders to create supra-tribal confederations by variously incorporating individuals, local lineages, clans, and whole tribes as the building blocks of a political/military organization that could present a united front to the outside world.

These tribal confederacies incorporated hundreds of thousands of people from a variety of tribes, whose political unity was often all they held in common. Religious leaders, if they were important at all, became important only after the nomads had unified politically. The authority of a ruling dynasty, once established, became strictly hereditary and was rarely challenged from below. Their khans possessed the right to command obedience (by using force if necessary), collect taxes, administer justice, and handle all external political relations. Such dynasties often lasted for centuries but needed a substantial flow of revenue to sustain them.

NOMADIC EMPIRES AND CHINA

The largest and most complex nomadic polities arose along China's northern Great Wall frontier largely in response to the unifications of China that created a single imperial government there. Individual nomadic tribes in Mongolia could not hope to effectively confront a unified China to gain access to trade and aid, nor to defend themselves against Chinese aggression. Under the steppe-wide leadership, however, they could organize both an effective defense against the Chinese and, more importantly, create a 'shadow empire' that stood as China's equal on the battlefield or in diplomatic negotiations. Such steppe empires were not autocratic and centralized, but rather imperial confederacies that employed principles of tribal organization and indigenous tribal leaders to rule at the local level while maintaining an imperial state structure with an exclusive monopoly controlling foreign and military affairs.[7]

The stability of such polities depended on extorting vast amounts of wealth from China through pillage, tribute payments, border trade, and international re-export of luxury goods, not by taxing subsistence-oriented steppe nomads. When China was centralized and powerful, under such native Chinese dynasties as the Han

(202 BCE–220 CE), Tang (618–907), and Ming (1368–1644), so too were nomadic empires. When China collapsed into political anarchy and economic depression, so did the unified steppe polities that had prospered by its extortion.

Nomads had a harder time consolidating when north China came under the rule of foreign dynasties such as the Toba Wei (440–557), Jurchen Jin (1115–1234), or Manchu Qing (1644–1912) that chose to engage rather than exclude their nomadic neighbors. They practiced forms of indirect rule that combined policies of alliances with nomadic groups, punitive military campaigns, and open border markets that reduced the incentive of nomads in Mongolia to unify. The success of the Mongols under Chinggis Qan marks one of the few times nomads in Mongolia ever succeeded in displacing a foreign dynasty in China. In doing so they created a superstate that came to dominate most of Eurasia.

The ability of the nomads in Mongolia to face China as a political and military equal is quite remarkable. The number of nomads confronting China was always small, perhaps about a million people overall, and they were trying to extort Chinese dynasties that in Han times ruled over 50 million people, and 100 million in the Tang dynasty. However, as masters of mobile cavalry warfare with an unlimited supply of horses, the steppe nomads could field armies that used their small numbers to great effect. They could concentrate all their strength against a single point, employ a form of mounted archery that was effective at a distance or in retreat, and mobilize a much higher percentage of their population for warfare than their sedentary neighbors. However, again with the exception of the Mongols under Chinggis Qan and his successors, the nomads attacking China could not breach well defended city walls or lay long sieges.

The nomads of Mongolia had to influence decision making at the very highest levels of Chinese government because foreign policy was made at court and not by frontier governors or border officials. To this end the nomads first implemented a terroristic strategy of aggressive raiding to magnify their power. Taking full advantage of the their ability to suddenly strike deep into China and then retreat before the Chinese had time to retaliate, they could threaten the frontier at any time. Such violence and the disruption it caused encouraged the Chinese to negotiate agreements favorable to the nomads. Military action against the nomads proved generally ineffective because they could always retreat, and their land could not be permanently occupied by the Chinese, as it was unsuitable for agriculture.

A striking element of the nomad strategy was the deliberate refusal to occupy Chinese land that they would then have to defend. They knew that they could never hope to defeat China's vast armies if they had to hold a fixed point. They also lacked the administrative skills to govern sedentary conquests effectively. The nomad strategy was one of extortion that let the Chinese administer, tax, and defend their own territory, territory which could then be put at risk by nomad attacks. In return for not bothering China the nomads expected to be paid handsomely. The alternatives to paying off the nomads were few. Military campaigns against the nomads could be temporarily effective but generally cost vastly more than peace treaties and disrupted

China's economy. Indeed, no native Chinese dynasty ever maintained an offensive war policy against the nomads for longer than the reign of a single emperor. But ignoring the nomads was not an option either, as this would provoke raids all along the frontier in which the nomads seized loot directly and did great damage to frontier areas.

The pattern of relations between the nomads and Chinese native dynasties followed a regular course. At first new nomad empires would engage in violent raiding to terrify the Chinese court. They would then seek treaties that guaranteed peace along the frontier in exchange for direct subsidies and trade privileges. Threats of war, or war itself, would be used periodically to increase the size of these grants and improve the terms of trade in border markets. Although the treaties created long periods of peace, the threat of violence always lurked beneath the surface. Zhonghang Yue, a Chinese defector working for the Xiongnu nomads in the first century BCE, once warned some Han Chinese envoys of the danger they faced in very simple terms:

> Just make sure that the silks and grain stuffs you bring the Xiongnu are the right measure and quality, that's all. What's the need for talking? If the goods you deliver are up to measure and good quality, all right. But if there is any deficiency or the quality is no good, then when the autumn harvest comes we will take our horses and trample all over your crops![8]

China first disguised the true nature of its appeasement policy by devising an elaborate 'tributary system' in which large payments to the nomads were described as gifts given to loyal subordinates who were in theory coming to pay homage to the emperor. The cost of this system was very high. For example, between 50 and 100 CE, when the system was first regularized during the Later Han dynasty, records show that the estimated annual cost of direct subsidies to China's frontier peoples amounted to one-third of the Han government payroll or 7 percent of all the empire's revenue, goods that would have the value of around $500 million in modern terms.[9] The Tang dynasty made similarly large payments to the steppe nomads during the mid-ninth century when the Uighurs collected 500,000 rolls of silk a year in subsidies of China disguised as payment for tributary horses.[10] The Ming dynasty had a similar arrangement with the Mongol tribes in the sixteenth century that included a system of extensive subsidy payments and lucrative trade deals involving horses and tea.[11]

As interactions became more frequent and profitable, the nomads found that they no longer needed to threaten China, and the politics of naked extortion developed into a more symbiotic relationship. Over time they saw that it was in their own best interest to preserve the dynasties that paid them so handsomely, so the nomadic empires began to provide weak Chinese dynasties with critical military aid in periods of decline. This aid included auxiliary troops to guard the frontier against other non-Chinese enemies or troops from the steppe that helped put down rebellions in China itself. In the later Han dynasty (25–220) nomadic troops became essential to maintaining frontier security, and the Uighurs saved the Tang dynasty from extinction by putting down the An Lushan Rebellion in the mid-eighth century.

The impact of nomadic steppe empires on China had worldwide implications as well because it was the catalyst for long-distance foreign trade. Payments from China that funded nomadic states with luxury goods attracted international merchants from the west who often used the nomads' political influence to establish their own profitable relations with China. Attempts to undercut steppe nomadic power by denying them access to the resources of the oases of eastern Turkestan also drew China into the so-called 'Western Regions,' which served as the main east–west overland transit route for Central Eurasia. Indeed one may say that without nomad pressure that there would have never been a 'silk route,' given the traditional negative Confucian attitudes about foreign trade.

The politics of the Chinese frontier had a wider Eurasian impact as well. During periods of time when Mongolia was being united, weaker tribes often used their mobility to escape domination by moving west. In the process they displaced resident nomads who themselves pushed others before them. The relationship between such political upheavals on the Mongolian steppe and their consequences further west have long attracted the attention of historians of Eurasia, but there are similar patterns elsewhere such as the rise of the Zulu in southern Africa in the nineteenth century.[12] In response to European expansion, a formerly decentralized age-set system among a cattle-keeping people led to the rapid transformation of the Zulus into a centralized state in a manner strikingly similar to that seen on the Chinese–Mongolian frontier two millennia earlier. The consequences of Zulu expansion to surrounding groups were equally as disruptive.[13]

LONG-DISTANCE TRADE

While the history of nomadic raids and conquests captures most attention, the role of Eurasian nomadic pastoralists in facilitating overland trade has received far less attention. Without their cooperation the famous 'silk route' that linked China and the West would have never come into existence. They both guaranteed the protection of the routes and used their military strength to open Chinese markets. Indeed, while it is conventionally assumed that China favored such trade, in fact Confucian bureaucrats did their best to restrict exports from China because they believed it weakened the state and undermined the economy. Such attitudes stood in sharp contrast to those of the nomad elites in Mongolia. They actively encouraged trade and attempted to attract merchants into their territories because the pastoral economy was not self sufficient except in terms of sheep or horses.

While animal husbandry produced regular surpluses of live animals, skins, milk products, wool, and hair, only by exchanging them with sedentary areas could the nomads acquire the commodities they did not produce themselves. This often required the overland movement of goods across long distances since most steppe tribes specialized in the same type of animal production. The most important products they sought were grain, metals (iron, copper, and bronze in raw or finished form), and hemp or cotton cloth. Sedentary areas were also the source of coveted luxury items such as silk, satin, wine, precious metals, bronze mirrors, and even musical instruments. Far from viewing export trade as a drain on national wealth, nomads saw it as a source of prosperity and stability because it diversified the economy and provided access to both necessities and luxuries the steppe itself could not provide.

The demand for trade and the extortion of luxury items increased exponentially with the unification of the steppe. The imperial nomad leader, such as the Xiongnu *Shanyu* or Turkish *khaghan*, was a large-scale redistributive chieftain whose power was secured in large part by his ability to generate revenue from China and secure trading privileges there. But the nomads' increasing demands for luxury goods, particularly silk, was not simply for their own use. Once they had acquired a surplus of these valuable commodities, the nomads in Mongolia became the center of an international re-export trade which attracted traders, especially from the oases of central Asia, who became wealthy middlemen linking the economies of China and the West.

Even more striking was the emergence of trading cities in Mongolia in the Tang dynasty such as Uighur capital Karabalghasun that was established soon after the empire was founded in the eighth century. Although rulers of a nomadic people, the Uighur elite also acted as middlemen in the lucrative re-export of silk that they extracted from China. To handle the volume, they needed an urban center on the steppe as a place to store and protect the silk, and to receive traders who flocked to Mongolia to buy it. The Arab traveler Tamim ibn Bahr, who saw Karabalghasun in the 830s, described it as a large town surrounded by intensive cultivation with twelve iron gates enclosing a castle that was populous and thickly crowded with markets and various trades.

Thus, although Mongolia was never a center of production, as a center of extraction the nomad empires acted as a trade pump, drawing surplus goods from China and redirecting them into international markets. While it has often been noted that the political unity of the steppe facilitated long-distance overland trade by securing the routes for peaceful passage, it may be equally true that the nomads themselves (and not the Chinese) were the source of much of what was traded along the silk route. This is particularly true if, in addition to the goods the nomads themselves resold, we take into account the number of foreign merchants who were incorporated into official tributary visits to China or who traveled under the protection of nomadic states in order to participate in border markets. The latter may have been particularly important since rich foreign merchants were less vulnerable to exploitation by Chinese officials when under the diplomatic protection of a powerful nomad empire.

Perhaps the best example of this is the relation between the merchant Sogdians from western Turkestan and the Turks and Uighurs in the Tang dynasty. Sogdian merchants had been known in China since the end of the Han dynasty, but beginning in the sixth century they allied with a series of Turkish empires that ruled over Mongolia until 840. Much to the annoyance of the Chinese, the nomads often let Sogdian merchants travel under their diplomatic protection to trade during tributary visits. They also received protection in the Chinese capital where they had extraterritorial status and became the most prosperous group of foreign moneylenders in China. Sogdian success was due in small part to their close alliance with the Turks and Uighurs whom Tang Chinese officials feared offending.

While the overland silk trade, and trade in other luxury goods for that matter, began well before the rise of powerful steppe nomadic tribes in Mongolia, it is clear that the centralization of power there acted as a stimulus to its expansion. The nomads themselves were not the great long-distance traders, but they acted as patrons for sedentary Central Asians who were. It was during these periods of nomad political power in the Han and Tang periods that the silk route took on its greatest importance. Perhaps most important, the large-scale extraction of silk from China in tributary payments generated more than just wealth, it created a form of international currency measured in bolts of silk that had unquestioned value everywhere. This meant that it could be used to buy anything the nomads wanted and attracted merchants trading imported goods into Mongolia and Central Asia. The profits available to these merchants were immense, not only because silk in the West was worth its weight in gold, but because to the nomads it was an essentially free good. They did not have to bear the cost of producing the silk itself or having it dyed and woven. Their only cost was transport and storage.

The workings of this network can be seen most clearly in the Mongol Empire when both China and the steppe fell under a dynasty of steppe nomadic origin beginning in 1234.[14] Unlike native Chinese dynasties that attempted to restrict and control foreign trade, the Mongols actually created quasi-governmental trading corporations (*ortaq*) in partnership with international merchants who had access to government finance. Initially they had special access to the Mongol horse relay system and were treated as a privileged class that was exempt from most state obligations. While they lost many of these privileges during the reign of the Grand Khan Möngke, international trade remained a priority throughout the dynasty and included such innovations as paper money. They also gave high priority to securing the safety of overland trade routes. But while this direct control of China by steppe nomads was a rarity, the steppe nomad interest in trade was not. Although it may have been the movement of Chinese products that gave the silk route its importance, it was the nomads who kept the goods moving at a rate that China, if it had had a choice, would have never permitted on its own. The nomads were, if you will, the godfathers of international overland trade in Eurasia, making peoples all along the route offers they could not refuse.

NOMADIC DYNASTIES

Paradoxically, pastoralists had the greatest historical impact on sedentary peoples when they abandoned their nomadic life for a sedentary one as a ruling elite. Indeed, most of what could be considered 'nomad influence' on sedentary societies historically involved the imposition of a certain number of the nomadic elite's values, tastes, and styles of political organization on sedentary populations that then permeated the larger society.

This was particularly evident in North Africa, the Near East, and Central Asia, where the list of the regions' important dynasties often seems to be a roll call of nomadic tribes turned imperial conquerors. The medieval Arab historian ibn Khaldun even proposed a general model of dynastic replacement for Islamic North Africa in which weak dynasties in sedentary states were replaced by desert nomads who possessed superior military ability and 'group feeling,' a process that he argued took place every three or four generations. While this process was nowhere near as regular in Eurasia, most of the dynasties that ruled the Iranian plateau in ancient and medieval times, and Anatolia in the Islamic period, were nomadic in origin. Similarly China's dynastic history had many periods of foreign rule by people from steppe nomadic origin, particularly immediately after the end of the Later Han dynasty from the third to sixth centuries, in the tenth and eleventh centuries following the destruction of the Tang dynasty, and most famously after the Mongol conquest under the successors of Chinggis Qan in the thirteenth and fourteenth centuries.

By contrast, nomads who stayed nomads generally had far less influence. They had small populations when compared to those in urbanized agricultural societies, and as nomads they were more mobile and more widely dispersed. Nomadic pastoral economies were undiversified and often surprisingly dependent on economic ties to urban areas that provided items like metal, cloth, and foodstuffs, as well as a market to sell their animals. In spite of their highly vaunted political independence from sedentary states, nomads such as the Bedouin were vulnerable to exploitation because of their reliance on sedentary areas for necessities such as tools and weapons.

This was true even when sedentary areas were ruled by dynasties of nomadic origin. While one might assume that nomads would benefit more from a situation in which it was their people who held the reins of power, such was not the case. Conquest dynasties always attempted to use their newly acquired power to crush the autonomy of their more nomadic cousins by refusing to share revenue or political power.

THE DECLINE OF NOMADS IN HISTORY

The importance of nomadic peoples in history declined significantly after the 'gunpowder revolution' reduced the military advantages of mounted horse archery that had given the steppe nomads a political edge for two millennia. By the mid-eighteenth century the expanding empires of China and Russia had destroyed the last of the independent nomad states in Asia. Nomads there moved from the status of political equals to colonial subjects. European colonial expansion in Africa eliminated the political dominance that the cattle-keeping people there had over their neighbors by the end of the nineteenth century. Nomads in Arabia and North Africa lost their autonomy in the early twentieth century with the appearance of motorized vehicles and airplanes. They could no longer avoid domination simply by disappearing into the deep deserts where no one could follow them.

In spite of this decline the legacy of nomadic peoples retains an unshakable hold on the historical imagination. China uses the Great Wall as a symbol of that country's greatness, although it was built at great expense because the Chinese so feared the nomads to their north. The urbane resident of Cairo or Damascus finds it impossible to shake off the Western use of the camel as the cartoon symbol for the entire Middle East. The haughty Maasai warrior leaning on his spear remains a popular poster icon for Kenyan tourism. And in popular fiction the horsemen of Chinggis Qan still regularly overrun Eurasia. But perhaps the most lasting legacy of a nomadic people is one never much commented: the replacement of the flowing robes, togas, and gowns worn by men in so much of the ancient world with tailored clothing better suited to people who rode animals.

NOTES

1. Ibn Khaldun, *The Muqaddimah*, trans. F. Rosenthal (Princeton: Princeton University Press, 1967), 118.
2. Anatoly M. Khazanov, *Nomads and the Outside World* (Cambridge: Cambridge University Press, 1994).
3. William G. Irons, 'Political Stratification among Pastoral Nomads,' in L'Équipe Écologie, ed., *Pastoral Production and Society* (Cambridge: Cambridge University Press, 1979); Thomas J. Barfield, 'The Hsiung-nu Imperial Confederacy and Foreign Policy,' *Journal of Asian Studies* 41 (1981), 45–61.
4. Nicola di Cosmo, *Ancient China and Its Enemies: The Rise of Nomadic Power in East Asian History* (Cambridge: Cambridge University Press, 2002); David Sneath, *The Headless State: Aristocratic Orders, Kinship Society, and the Misrepresentation of Nomadic Inner Asia* (New York: Columbia University Press, 2007); Boris I. Vladimirtsov, *Le régime social des Mongols: Le féodalisme nomade* (Paris: Adrien Maisonneuve, 1948).
5. Charles Lindholm, 'Kinship Structure and Political Authority: The Middle East and Central Asia,' *Comparative Studies in Society and History* 28 (1981), 334–55; Thomas J. Barfield, *The Perilous Frontier: Nomadic Empires and China* (Oxford: Blackwell, 1991).
6. Ibn Khaldun, *The Muqaddimah*, trans. F. Rosenthal (Princeton: Princeton University Press, 1967), 121.
7. Barfield, 'The Hsiung-nu Imperial Confederacy and Foreign Policy,' *Journal of Asian Studies* (1981) 41: 45–61.
8. Burton Watson, trans., *Records of the Grand Historian of China* (New York: Columbia University Press, 1993), 2: 144–5.
9. Ying-shih Yü, *Trade and Expansion in Han China: A Study in the Structure of Sino-Barbarian Economic Relations* (Berkeley: University of California Press, 1967), 61–4.
10. Colin T. Mackerras, *The Uighur Empire (744–840) According to the T'ang Dynasty Histories* (Columbia, S.C.: University of South Carolina Press, 1972).

11. Morris Rossabi, 'The Tea and Horse Trade with Inner Asia during the Ming,' *Journal of Asian History* 4: 2 (1970), 136–68.
12. Frederick J. Teggart, *Rome and China: A Study of Correlations in Historical Events* (Berkeley: University of California Press, 1939); Andre Gunder Frank, 'The Centrality of Central Asia,' *Studies in History* n.s. 8: 1 (1992), 101–6.
13. Leonard Thompson, 'Conflict and Cooperation: The Zulu Kingdom and Natal,' in Monica Wilson and Leonard Thompson, eds., *The Oxford History of South Africa* (Oxford: Oxford University Press, 1969); Monica Wilson, 'The Nguni People,' in Monica Wilson and Leonard Thompson, eds., *The Oxford History of South Africa* (Oxford: Oxford University Press, 1969).
14. Thomas T. Allsen, *Mongol Imperialism: The Policies of the Grand Qan Mögke in China, Russia, and the Islamic Lands, 1251–1259* (Berkeley: University of California Press, 1987) and *Culture and Conquest in Mongol Eurasia* (Cambridge: Cambridge University Press, 2001).

References

ALLSEN, THOMAS T. *Mongol Imperialism: The Policies of the Grand Qan Möngke in China, Russia, and the Islamic Lands, 1251–1259.* Berkeley: University of California Press, 1987.
——. *Culture and Conquest in Mongol Eurasia.* Cambridge: Cambridge University Press, 2001.
BARFIELD, THOMAS J. 'The Hsiung-nu Imperial Confederacy: Organization and Foreign Policy,' *Journal of Asian Studies* 41 (1981), 45–61.
——. *The Perilous Frontier: Nomadic Empires and China.* Oxford: Blackwell, 1989.
——. 'Tribe and State Relations: The Inner Asian Perspective,' in Philip Khoury and Joseph Kostiner, eds. *Tribes and State Formation in the Middle East.* Berkeley: University of California Press, 1991, 153–85.
——. *The Nomadic Alternative.* Englewood Cliffs, N.J.: Prentice-Hall, 1993.
DI COSMO, NICOLA. *Ancient China and its Enemies: The Rise of Nomadic Power in East Asian History.* Cambridge: Cambridge University Press, 2002.
FRANK, ANDRE GUNDER. 'The Centrality of Central Asia,' *Studies in History* n.s. 8: 1 (1992), 101–6.
KHALDUN, IBN. *The Muqaddimah*, trans. Frans Rosenthal. Princeton: Princeton University Press, 1967.
KHAZANOV, ANATOLY M. *Nomads and the Outside World.* Cambridge: Cambridge University Press, 1994.
LINDHOLM, CHARLES. 'Kinship Structure and Political Authority: The Middle East and Central Asia,' *Comparative Studies in Society and History* 28 (1986), 334–55.
MACKERRAS, COLIN. *The Uighur Empire (744–840) According to the T'ang Dynastic Histories.* Columbia, S.C.: University of South Carolina Press, 1972.
ROSSABI, MORRIS. 'The tea and horse trade with Inner Asia during the Ming,' *Journal of Asian History* 4: 2 (1970), 136–68.
SNEATH, DAVID. *The Headless State: Aristocratic Orders, Kinship Society, and the Misrepresentation of Nomadic Inner Asia.* New York: Columbia University Press, 2007.

TEGGART, FREDERICK J. *Rome and China: A Study of Correlations in Historical Events.* Berkeley: University of California Press, 1939.

THOMPSON, LEONARD. 'Conflict and Cooperation: The Zulu Kingdom and Natal,' in Monica Wilson and Leonard Thompson, eds. *The Oxford History of South Africa.* Oxford: Oxford University Press, 1969.

VLADIMIRTSOV, BORIS I. *Le régime social des Mongols: Le féodalisme nomade.* Paris: Adrien Maisonneuve, 1948.

WILSON, MONICA. 'The Nguni People,' in Monica Wilson and Leonard Thompson, eds. *The Oxford History of South Africa.* Oxford: Oxford University Press, 1969.

YÜ, YING-SHIH. *Trade and Expansion in Han China: A Study in the Structure of Sino-Barbarian Economic Relations.* Berkeley: University of California Press, 1967.

CHAPTER 10

··

STATES, STATE
TRANSFORMATION,
AND WAR

··

CHARLES TILLY†

MIDDLE Eastern kings of three millennia ago wasted few words on false modesty. They claimed protection of the gods or even claimed to be gods. They exulted in the vigor with which they visited violence on their enemies. They had their scribes produce boastful accounts of their accomplishments for inscription on clay tablets, stone pillars, or audacious monuments. The annals of Tiglath-pileser I, ruler of Assyria 1114–1076 BCE, included this set of claims:

> Tiglath-pileser, strong king, king of the universe without rival, king of the four quarters, king of all rulers, lord of lords, herdsman, king of kings, pious purification priest, to whom was given the pure scepter at the command of Shamash and who was given complete control over the people, subjects of Enlil, steadfast shepherd, whose name was called over the rulers, exalted high-priest, whose weapons Assur has sharpened and whose name he has called forever for the ruling of the four quarters, who captures distant regions with borders above and below, brilliant day whose shine overwhelms the quarters, splendid flame that covers the enemy land like a rain storm, who by the command of Enlil has no rival (and) defeats the enemy of Assur.[1]

Tiglath-pileser claimed protection of the great god Enlil, and subjected his conquered territories to Enlil. He built a large empire centering on his capital Assur. His empire reached the Zagros Mountains, Babylon, the Mediterranean, and Lake Van. He drew his revenues from trade networks that extended even farther into the Mediterranean, North Africa, Persia, the Indian Ocean, and Central Asia.

Tiglath-pileser built one sort of state, a composite empire connecting heterogeneous tribute-paying units to a single ruler and his staff. This chapter places Middle Eastern empires in a much wider range of states across the entire world from the state's first emergence toward 3000 BCE to the present. It links the history of states closely to the evolution of war. It shows that war strongly affected the organization and the very survival of states. But it also shows that the prevailing character of states in each period and region shaped the sorts of wars that occurred then and there.

By the time Tiglath-pileser was creating his empire, states had already thrived—and warred—in the Middle East for 2,000 years. A state is a structure of power involving four distinctive elements: (1) major concentrated means of coercion, especially an army, (2) organization that is at least partly independent of kinship and religious relations, (3) a defined area of jurisdiction, and (4) priority in some regards over all other organizations operating within that area. No states existed anywhere in the world before 4000 BCE. Although the four elements had existed separately for some time, no one put all four of them together before then. Over the next millennium, states became permanent fixtures in Eurasia.

To simplify a complex set of connections, this chapter will usually employ a stripped-down model of a state: a ruler (even if that ruler is a legislature or a vast aristocracy), an apparatus of rule (even if the apparatus has many and/or conflicting segments), a subject population (even if that population divides among multiple territories, interests, or factions), and external interactions of various sorts, from trade, diplomacy, and mass migration to war. The simplification will make it easier to identify common properties and systematic variations among states, including their involvement in war.

If by war we mean armed struggle between well defined separate populations, war certainly existed before states came into being.[2] The emergence of states, however, significantly increased war's scale. Anthropologist Robert Carneiro sees the crucial transition as occurring during the late Stone Age. 'As waged until late in the Neolithic,' comments Carneiro,

> the effect of warfare on a defeated enemy was generally no more than to drive him away. Thus, warfare of this type served to keep villages separate and independent. With the coming of agriculture, though, human numbers increased until arable land came into short supply. And then something novel and transcendental occurred. Warfare began to lead, not to the dispersal of defeated villages, but to their subjection and incorporation. Village was added to village, and polities grew in size and structure. For the first time in human history, multi-village units—chiefdoms—came into being.[3]

The 'coming of agriculture' means a shift to full-fledged, durable domestication of plants and animals as a way of life. So far as the archaeological record can tell us, that happened first in Southwest Asia, by around 8500 BCE. Central Mexico followed by 7000 BCE, South China by 6500 BCE, the Indus Valley (most likely through diffusion from Southwest Asia) by 6000 BCE, New Guinea (most likely through independent invention) likewise by 6000 BCE, then Egypt and Western Europe (diffusion!) after 6000 BCE.[4] Agricultural villages compounded into larger and more differentiated political units. The aggregative process proceeded rapidly, according to Carneiro;

full-fledged states soon emerged. In the presence of agriculture and trade, war made states. It happened first in the Middle East, but the rest of Eurasia and the Mediterranean did not lag far behind.

Cities first appeared in the same periods and regions as states. Like states, cities can only exist in symbiosis with agriculture that is sufficiently productive to support significant non-agricultural populations. Cities differ from strictly agricultural settlements, furthermore, by virtue of substantial populations, differentiated and specialized activities, and location as nodes in far-reaching networks of trade and political coordination. Cities and states maintain ambivalent relations: urban merchants and intellectuals seek the protection that states can provide, but resist the extraction and control that rulers impose on them. Rulers, on their side, commonly try to combat urbanites' independence, but also to benefit from concentrations of resources in cities as well as from the relative defensibility of compact cities as compared with scattered rural populations.

Accordingly, states vary significantly in their relations to cities within their territories. At one extreme we find the city-state, in which urban oligarchs control the state. At the other extreme lie nomadic empires, which typically build administrative capitals, but which frequently feed themselves by seizing, sacking, or exacting tribute from cities outside of their own territories. In such regions as Egypt and Central Asia, it remains unclear whether early states flourished without substantial cities or archaeologists' searches have simply failed so far to locate the remains of those states' concentrated settlements. Elsewhere, cities and states grew up together.

Soon after the development of settled agriculture, states were multiplying not only in the Middle East, but also in Egypt, the Mediterranean, the Indus Valley, and China. Almost everywhere that large-scale farming of plants and domesticated animals developed, states followed within a few thousand years. Farming (unlike herding, hunting, and gathering) favored the formation of states by generating a material surplus, encouraging trade, and settling populations into stable communities. All three made it much easier for rulers to exercise enduring control over substantial populations. The three together promoted the emergence of full-time specialists: merchants, priests, officials, soldiers, and, of course, farmers.[5]

After all, it takes substantial resources to support a state. Even a lightweight state maintains a ruler, a central staff, an armed force, and agents that enforce its priority within the delimited territory. Most rulers also distribute resources to clients who are not state officials, but extend the state's influence into their own zones of power. All of these activities require a surplus large enough to support a significant non-farming population. Typical state-supporting resources include labor power, food, animals, precious goods, information, and money. Across history, rulers have used multiple means of acquiring the essential resources: seizing them from external victims, producing them in state-run enterprises, bartering or selling other goods to acquire them, or extracting them from the state's subject population. Tiglath-pileser and his fellow Middle Eastern monarchs concentrated on the first and the last: seizure and extraction.

Seizing resources from external victims—banditry and piracy on the large scale—sometimes works for highly mobile, well armed predatory states. Yet it produces great instability in state support unless it turns into regularized tribute. Production in state enterprises has sometimes provided substantial support for rulers (including socialist rulers) who were also great landlords, but it typically sets strict limits on state activity and depends on well-managed cooperation from underlings. Bartering or selling other goods such as minerals in exchange for armed force and other state requisites sustains states so long as demand for the goods and state monopolies over their supply persist. Failure of either condition, however, makes a bartering or selling state vulnerable to resource shortages. If alternative energy supplies become abundant, energy prices drop precipitously, or state monopolies collapse, such prosperous energy-exporting states as today's Algeria, Russia, Burma, and Venezuela will have trouble maintaining their styles of rule. Over the long run, the last alternative—extracting resources from the subject population in the form of taxes, military conscription, labor service, and similar devices—has most often kept viable states going.

Over that long historical run, struggles and bargains over the resources to sustain states have played a central causal role in the creation of different sorts of states, from tyrannical empires to constitutional democracies. Should we speak of state formation? Years ago, I made one of my larger conceptual mistakes in a long career as an analyst of state-related processes: I introduced the term 'state formation' into the scholarly discussion of European states.[6] I meant to displace two other terms that scholars then commonly used to describe the emergence of strong, independent states: state-building and political development. I also meant to discourage the widespread idea that strong Western states provided models of development non-Western states could and should emulate. I thought mistakenly that 'formation' avoided both the engineering implications of 'building' and the strong analogy with deliberately induced economic growth suggested by 'development.' I supposed that the idea of state formation would help historical analysts escape intentionality and teleology.

Alas, the term 'state formation' caught on fast, but with a teleological twist, the idea that fully formed states followed their destiny as oaks follow acorns. Analysts frequently took state formation to identify a standard process by which weak, dependent states (including former colonies) became strong and independent on the model of Western capitalist states.[7] Scholars began to wonder out loud why states in their regions had failed to 'form' properly, and undertook comparisons with European models.[8] In order to avoid that teleology, let us speak of state *transformation*, recognizing it as a bundle of processes that produce multiple varieties of states, and continue indefinitely. Perhaps the term transformation will help shield analysts of those processes from the assumption of predestined direction. State transformation, then, centers on struggles and bargains between rulers and ruled over the means and conditions of rule. Those struggles became more intense and consequential in preparations for war.

The rest of this chapter will proceed through four stages: an analysis of how states maintain themselves, a closer look at war's place in state transformation, a comparison among major types of state, and reflections on states and war in recent world history.

By the end, the historical interdependence of states and war should become clear. Whether states of our own time will break that interdependence is one of our day's most pressing political questions.

COERCION, CAPITAL, AND COMMITMENT

War has always mattered in the past for two reasons: because military buildup, on average, demanded far more resources than any other activity states undertook, and because war arrived in bursts rather than allowing incremental accumulation of resources. It engaged rulers in strenuous resource extraction. How do rulers wrest essential resources from their domains? They extract resources and maintain control over their subject populations via three broad sets of connections: coercion, capital, and commitment.[9] *Coercion* includes all concerted means of action that commonly cause loss or damage to the persons, possessions, or sustaining social relations of social actors. It features means such as weapons, armed forces, prisons, damaging information, and organized routines for imposing sanctions. Tiglath-pileser boasted of his coercive might. Coercion's organization helps define the nature of regimes. With low accumulations of coercion, all regimes are insubstantial, while with high levels of coercive accumulation and concentration all regimes are formidable.

Capital refers to certain kinds of resources: transferable goods that with effort produce increases in use value, plus enforceable claims on such resources. State-relevant resources include human capital, animal power, food, raw materials for manufacturing, inanimate energy, and the means of buying them. Regimes that command substantial capital—for example, from rulers' direct control of natural resources, itself often backed by coercion—to some extent substitute purchase of other resources and compliance for direct coercion of their subject populations. Tiglath-pileser's self-description downplayed capital, but his regime would not have lasted a year without tribute and taxes.

Commitment means relations among social sites (persons, groups, structures, or positions) that promote their taking account of each other. Shared language, for instance, powerfully links social sites without any necessary deployment of coercion or capital. Commitment's local organization varies as dramatically as do structures of coercion and capital. Commitments can take the form of shared religion or ethnicity, trading ties, work-generated solidarities, communities of taste, and much more. Tiglath-pileser claimed to have the great god Enlil's protection, indeed to rule in Enlil's name. To the extent that commitments of these sorts connect rulers and ruled, they substitute partially for coercion and capital. Once rulers have acquired power by means of coercion and capital, furthermore, they commonly seek to facilitate and consolidate their rule by building up commitment; they give preference to their own languages, assign privileges to their own and their clients' lineages, favor certain religious cults, and foster myths of national origin.

Enduring states face two challenges: production and reproduction. If rulers fail to reward their followers, manage their armed forces, and provide some minimum of protection to their subject populations, they lose power. To sustain that power, however, they must reproduce their combination of coercion, capital, and commitment by acquiring new resources year after year. Natural disasters, military conquests, and popular resistance threaten both production and reproduction of state power. Even mighty Napoleon lost power in military defeat.

States vary greatly in their relative emphasis on coercion, capital, and commitment. A hit-and-run predatory state like that of the Mongols relies chiefly on coercion. Capital-centered states such as the mercantile cities of Renaissance Italy mark a very different extreme, with merchants holding great power even in the presence of hereditary rulers. Commitment-centered theocracies such as contemporary Iran draw on coercion and capital to sustain themselves, but bestow far more power on clergy and cultural entrepreneurs than other states do.

The earliest states for which coherent records exist differed dramatically in their relative reliance on coercion, capital, and commitment. As the case of Tiglath-pileser's Assyria suggests, early Middle Eastern states expanded through military conquest, but their kings commonly also served as high priests or even claimed to be gods. In Egypt, a unified state with substantial coercive power controlled the Nile valley from its delta to a thousand kilometers south by 3000 BCE. Its vast religious-dynastic monuments, such as sphinxes and pyramids, reveal a strong claim of its rulers to close connections with the gods. In fact, the Old Kingdom's so-called Palermo Stone (Old Kingdom: 2686–2125 BCE), describes the god Horus as giving the Egyptian throne to King Menes, the first great unifier, sometime between 3100 and 3000 BCE. Although Egyptian states engaged in trade extending at least to Palestine, capital seems to have played a secondary role to coercion and commitment in Egypt.

That was not true everywhere. In South Asia's Indus Valley (where a rich civilization thrived from about 2500 to 1900 BCE and maintained extensive connections with the Middle East), the archaeological evidence reflects extensive trade, but includes neither great religious monuments nor traces of large armies. The Indus Valley seems to have created a set of capital-intensive states. For China, meanwhile, literary texts and archaeological remains point in different directions, with literary tradition identifying imperial dynasties from about 2200 BCE onward, but physical remains suggesting the flourishing of warring city-states from around 1650. In any case, coercion and capital long intersected in early Chinese states, while commitment-based institutions such as ancestor cults seem to have figured less prominently in Chinese state control than in the Middle East or Egypt. As we will soon see, however, once a unitary Chinese state appeared under the Qin and Han dynasties (respectively 221–206 BCE and 202 BCE–220 CE, with interruptions), China built up an elaborate structure of commitment-maintaining institutions centered on the emperor and the Mandate of Heaven.

In the Americas, sedentary agriculture did not develop until between 2000 and 1500 BCE, some five millennia later than in the Middle East. Very quickly thereafter, such complex cultures as the Olmec and the Chavin grew up, respectively, along the

Caribbean coast and in the Andes. By 600 BCE, Mesoamerican, Andean, and Pacific city-states were both trading and battling with each other, creating religious symbols and monuments that suggest a relatively even balance among coercion, capital, and commitment. Empires such as the Maya (roughly 600 BCE to 900 CE, with their Yucatán branch surviving until the sixteenth-century Spanish conquest) were soon to come.

Africa's distributions of climate and vegetation hindered the development of agriculture dense and widespread enough to support the more crowded populations that favor cities and states.[10] Except for Egypt and its sometime colony Nubia, Africa, therefore, produced recognizable states somewhat later than Eurasia and the Americas. The Nile and its parallel trade routes led from Ethiopia through Nubia to Egypt; the entire region waxed and waned together. The first solid evidence of Egyptian and Nubian states dates from around 3000 BCE. Around the eighth century BCE, the D'mt kingdom formed in Ethiopia. From that time, states have existed more or less continuously in the region between the Nile delta and the Horn of Africa.

Elsewhere in Africa, however, recognizable states took another thousand years or so to emerge. The West African kingdom of Ghana, for example, brought together salt- and gold-trading towns into a state around 700 CE, and remained independent until it fell to Islamic forces in 1076 CE. In southern Africa, the Mapungubwe state (in the vicinity of today's Botswana) became visible between 900 and 1000 CE. Its merchants engaged in active trade with city-states along Africa's Indian Ocean coast. Early states

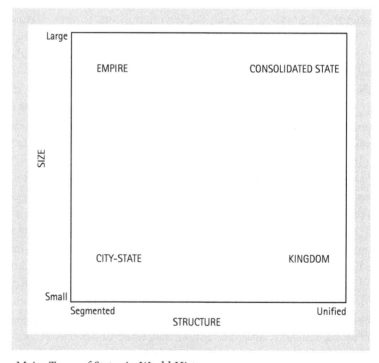

FIGURE 10.1 Major Types of States in World History

of the Middle East, Egypt, the Indus Valley, China, the Americas, and Africa varied enormously in scale and organization. So did later states, up to our own time. In order to follow states through the millennia since their first formation, we need a rough classification by size and structure. Figure 10.1 provides one classification, with its four corners representing extreme types: the small, segmented *city-state*, which sometimes had a single ruler, but always divided into factions by lineage, locality, and/or trade; the unified and compact *kingdom*, with a well defined ruler (who might well be a duke or a religious authority rather than a king) whose jurisdiction extended to the state's boundaries; the *empire*, likewise typically having a single well defined ruler, but large in territory and divided into segments each of which maintained a somewhat different relationship to the center; and the much rarer *consolidated state*, with both a unitary ruler and a fairly uniform system of rule throughout a large territory.

All historical states have, of course, fallen somewhere between the extremes of Figure 10.1's four corners. Nevertheless, the diagram makes two things clear: first, that states have taken a wide variety of forms; second, that in general a tradeoff exists between size and segmentation. The exceptional consolidated state notwithstanding, states have generally grown large by adding heterogeneous units, and have rarely succeeded in subjecting them all to a uniform system of rule. In fact, most large states have managed through indirect rule, in which powerful intermediaries such as warlords, lineage heads, and landlords governed the state's segments on behalf of the center, and enjoyed considerable autonomy as they did so. Direct rule and uniform, centralized field administration have only appeared in most of the world during the last few hundred years. The main exception is consolidated state China, where one central power or another has maintained fairly direct and uniform field administration over a vast population—typically about a sixth of the world's total—for most of the last 2,000 years.

WAR AND STATE TRANSFORMATION

Even in China, war has played a prominent part in shaping the sort of state that has prevailed. War consists of sustained campaigns by two or more organized armed forces that use reciprocal violence to check or destroy each other. Since states emerged, war has varied along a continuum from strictly interstate (pitting two or more states against each other) to strictly civil (two or more armed forces battling within the territory of a state's jurisdiction, typically with at least one of them claiming rights to control the state). The effects of war on states range from utter destruction to strengthening of central state power. On the whole, civil wars occur in relatively weak states, and weaken them further.[11] The American Civil War offers an exception to that rule: as it mobilized for war and then imposed its power on the defeated Confederacy, the victorious North built up a state of unprecedented strength.[12]

In Latin America, matters went differently: the nineteenth century's frequent civil wars and border skirmishes fostered relatively weak states that remained vulnerable to military takeover.[13] In the situation of segmented sovereignty that emerged in Europe after the Roman Empire's disintegration and a long interval of raiding and feuding, interstate wars eventually built up the central power of victorious states.[14] The fundamental principle, therefore, runs like this: to the extent that making war weakened a ruler's opponents and consolidated the ruler's control over the state's armed forces, it strengthened the central state; to the extent that it strengthened opponents and/or loosened the ruler's control over armed forces, it weakened the central state.

Analysts of war hesitate between technological determinism and stress on national culture.[15] While the Chinese invention of gunpowder did not much affect Asian warfare in the short run, for example, its introduction to Europe during the 1330s soon made artillery far more central to European wars, and rendered those wars far more destructive. From World War I, aerial reconnaissance and bombing likewise greatly increased war's lethality across the earth. Such episodes highlight new technologies.

Yet the capacity to use weapons effectively clearly depends on well managed social organization and the exercise of political will. The development of the atomic bomb during World War II certainly helped shift the technical balance between the Axis and the Allies. Nevertheless, it depended on close collaboration between the American and British military establishments. US President Harry Truman's decision to drop the bomb on Hiroshima and Nagasaki in August 1946 surely hastened Japan's surrender, but so did the Soviet Union's invasion of Manchuria between the two bombs. No simple technological account of warfare captures the interplay of military invention, strategy, and social organization.

Still, one technology of war has profound effects on states: logistics. Beyond the level of self-equipped soldiers who either carry their own supplies or live off the land, every warring state invests substantial resources and organization in providing daily support for its military organizations. Alexander the Great's army pursued conquest almost continually from Alexander's succession to the Macedonian throne in 336 BCE to his death (at age 33) in 323. At its peak, that army consumed an estimated 225,000 kilos of grain and 720,000 liters of water every single day.[16] A second army of men and draft animals supplied Alexander's warriors with grain, water, and other life support.

In his close study of the Ottoman Empire's military forces between 1500 and 1700, Rhoads Murphey concludes that:

> No single concern was more critical to the troops' performance in battle than the adequacy of food supply for themselves and their mounts. The elaborateness (as well as generosity) of Ottoman arrangements for grain provision shows their appreciation of the fact that in warfare of the pre-modern era logistics played a more decisive role than tactics. Any disruption of regular supplies organized through central planning and distribution put immediate and severe restraints on the scope and reach of army operations in the field. The critical importance of the bureaucratic structure which intervened to meet supply demands even before they

were sensed or even foreseen by forces in the field was critical to the success of the Ottoman military enterprise.[17]

In its time, the Ottoman war machine was arguably the world's most formidable. In every war, logistics sets strong limits on military action, but it also recasts states by drawing down their available resources.[18]

War shapes states because it simultaneously affects all four defining elements of the state: means of coercion, autonomous organization, area of jurisdiction, and priority over other organizations. A lost war, for example, commonly diminishes a state's armed forces, batters its organizational structure, shrinks its area of jurisdiction, and shakes its priority over other organizations within the remaining area, including rival claimants to state power. At the extreme, the losing state disappears. Military triumph, in contrast, commonly expands the state's armed forces, reinforces the state's autonomous organizational structure, extends its territory, and bolsters its priority over competing organizations within the territory. States wax and wane for other reasons, such as swings in their economies, mass migrations, and fluctuations in lethal diseases. But over the five-plus millennia of state history, won and lost wars have made the largest differences to their fates.

Conversely, the history of war since 4000 BCE clings closely to the history of states. Martin van Creveld's technology-tinged chronology of war also marks broad distinctions among eras of states: the Age of Tools (from 2000 BCE to 1500 CE), the Age of Machines (1500–1830), the Age of Systems (1830–1945), and the Age of Automation (1945 onward).[19] For several millennia, van Creveld's tool-using armed forces relied on relatively simple hand-held weapons and hand-launched projectiles: lances, swords, staves, arrows, stones, and more. For militaries of this sort, the state's organizational problem centered on bringing weapon-equipped men into contact with an enemy and sustaining their efforts to destroy or disperse the enemy. The Age of Machines complicated a state's war work, since the shift to weapons powered by inanimate sources, such as cannon, also entailed a shift from individual prowess in battle toward trained and collective professional skill.

In van Creveld's Age of Systems, long-distance communication and large-scale coordination pivoted armies' and navies' effectiveness on command and control; even more so than in the machine age, the systems age also depended on a vast civilian support apparatus, with both military force and civilian support most often ultimately responsible to civilian rulers. Except for show—think of kings who still attend ceremonies in military uniform—the warrior-king finally began to disappear. Finally, the Age of Automation incorporated science, information processing, and civilian technology into warfare as never before. During the periods of systems and automation, large capitalist states increasingly dominated the world of interstate war, with two qualifications: first, that for a while state socialist regimes gave the capitalists a military run for their money, second that after 1940 genocides and civil wars began to displace interstate wars as the world's primary sites of mass killing.[20]

CHINA OVER THE LONG RUN

In order to clarify differences in major types of state transformations and to see their connections with war, let us make an outrageous comparison: China on one side, Venice on the other. The cases are obviously unequal. Chinese states, as we have seen, entered the historical record about three thousand years ago, and have dominated their corner of the world most of the time since then. The Venetian state barely existed a thousand years ago, and disappeared into unified Italy during the nineteenth century. Properly pursued, nevertheless, the comparison becomes illuminating.

Over the long run, China moved around all four corners of Figure 10.1's state typology. The subcontinent's major trajectory over three thousand years, goes from warring city-states to more substantial but still warring kingdoms to a great empire to the world's most durable approximation of a large consolidated state. More recently, for a century or so European colonies such as Hong Kong and Macao greatly resembled merchant-dominated city-states, with their extensive trade connections, internal factions, and compact central territories.

Box 10.1 presents a chronology of Chinese rule since 770 BCE, dividing regimes into segmented and (relatively) unified. Clearly the Chinese regime passed most of its first 2,000 years of well documented political history in divided control over its vast territory. Yet Victoria Tin-Bor Hui argues cogently that the country's initial unification under the

---

Box 10.1 Periods of Segmented and Unified Rule in China, 770 BCE–2007 CE[21]

Segmented	Unified
770–453 BCE: Spring and Autumn	
453–221 BCE: Warring States	
	221–206 BCE: Qin
	206 BCE–220 CE: Han
220–280 CE: Three Kingdoms	
265–420 CE: Jin	
386–589 CE: Northern and Southern	
	589–618 CE: Sui
	618–907 CE: Tang
907–979 CE: Ten Kingdoms	
960–1279 CE: Song	
	1271–1368 CE: Yuan (Mongol)
	1368–1644 CE: Ming
	1644–1911 CE: Qing (Manchu)
	1912–1949 CE: Republic
	1949–2007 CE: People's Republic (except Taiwan)

Qin in 221 BCE set it permanently on a different trajectory from segmented Europe.[22] In her analysis, Chinese politics before the crucial transition centered on war among rival states—first city-states, then larger aggregations. They engaged in balance of power politics, uniting against larger states if they became too expansive. But during the more than two centuries of the Warring States period the Qin, once one of the weaker states, astutely played not balance of power but divide and conquer, breaking hostile alliances with well timed combinations of concessions and attacks. During their advance, the Qin backed up their military power by building two huge irrigation systems to transport food, and by exploiting iron-working centers they captured along their way.[23]

The Qin unification, in Hui's account, installed in China as a whole centralizing organizational structures that the Qin had developed within their own territories a century earlier:

> It was Qin under Shang Yang that made the final leap toward universal conscription and direct rule, thus generating another 'punctuation' in the mid-fourth century BCE. When Shang Yang introduced military service, he also perfected the linked institutions of hierarchical administration, small-scale farming, household registration, collective responsibility, standardized weights and measures, systematic ranking of the population, and rigorous rewards and punishments.[24]

Once the Qin had conquered the whole of China, they imposed that centralized system on the entire Chinese population. Even during later periods of segmented sovereignty, rulers of China's fragments continued the same system of top-down control.

In his own far-reaching comparison of Chinese and European trajectories, R. Bin Wong makes four additional points about China's distinctiveness.

- As centuries wore on, China created a set of institutions (such as state granaries held in reserve for periods of famine and a classical educational system for gentry officials and allies of the state) that gave large segments of the population an interest in the state's survival.
- Even external conquerors such as the Mongols and the Manchus tended to retain or fortify the Chinese administrative system instead of substituting their own forms of government.
- The military threats of nomadic peoples from the steppe to China's north and of internal rebellions by subjugated minorities kept China's emperors alert to the necessity of substantial armed force even in times of relative domestic peace.[25]
- When external military threats grew strong, Chinese rulers recurrently used tribute and diplomacy to buy off potential enemies instead of going to outright war.[26]

Indeed, Thomas Barfield establishes that diplomatic exchanges with steppe nomads ostensibly ritualizing Chinese superiority regularly involved substantial net payments to the nomads.[27] Those experiences of the Chinese state transformed it into the world's largest consolidated state. In more ways than one, war and the threat of war shaped the long, surprising trajectory of Chinese states.

VENETIAN TRADE AND WAR

The Venetian state came into existence millennia after China's, and never rivaled China's power. Nevertheless, within its own zone it enjoyed a dominant position for several centuries. In contrast to China, its trajectory illustrates the power of capital to propel a state. Moreover, it underlines the interdependence between Asian and European prosperity before the last few centuries.

Venice became rich and powerful as a hinge between Asia and the rest of Europe. The Lombard invasion of Italy in 568 had sent refugees to the Venetian islands. The islands long remained part of the Byzantine empire while Lombards and Franks successively occupied nearby mainland territory. Venice then served as a transfer station for goods shipped north from the Byzantine trading system. Eventually Venice became an independent power. Venetians traded Asian goods, salt, fish, slaves, and lumber to the rest of Europe, established colonies around the Adriatic, and managed much of Byzantium's own long-distance commerce. Venice profitably mixed trade, piracy, conquest, and participation in Crusades against Muslim lords of the Near East.

During its early years of expansion, Venice manned its sleek galleys with citizens who shared in maritime profits and spoils. The fleet relied on widely spaced supply stations where galleys could put in for water, food, supplies, and trade. The Doge (or duke, occupant of an office that had its origin in service to the Byzantines) headed an oligarchy represented by a powerful hierarchy of councils in which the general assembly of inhabitants occupied the lowest and least influential rank. They led a predatory trading state that served their commercial interests as it balanced among conquest, paid services to Crusaders and their Muslim enemies, and extensive trade around the eastern Mediterranean. In 1203 and 1204, it collected on debts from services to Crusaders by conquering and pillaging Constantinople, then capital of a threatened Byzantine empire; the bronze horses of San Marco came to Venice as part of the booty.

Venice faced intense rivalry from another great maritime city-state, Genoa. The two titanic cities competed throughout the Mediterranean, especially around its eastern end. Up to the thirteenth century Genoa controlled trade on the Black Sea, which blocked easy Venetian access to Central and East Asia. Genoese influence in Trebizond gave Genoa privileged connections to the Mongols and, therefore, to China. After Venice signed a treaty with the rising Mamluk power in the eastern Mediterranean during the 1290s, Genoa and Venice fought for control of the sea lanes, and Genoa defeated Venice in 1299. Not until 1380, when Venetian galleys returned the Genoese favor of 1299 by smashing the Genoese fleet definitively, did Venice become supreme in the eastern Mediterranean.

After that, Venice maintained a major island and port empire (including, for example, Cyprus and Crete) until Ottoman expansion finally squeezed it out of the Aegean during the fifteenth and sixteenth centuries. Ottoman conquest of Constantinople (1453) started the Venetian contraction. The victory of Ottoman forces over

Venetian mariners drove Venice from its chief Aegean base in 1470. Another Venetian–Turkish war in 1499–1503 took a number of Mediterranean, Greek, and Albanian cities away from Venice. Ottoman expansion turned Venice from an East–West conduit into an Italian and European power.

As Venice grew richer and its involvement in European political struggles more extensive, the city shifted from voluntary citizen service in its military forces to conscription of Venetian workers, and then to forced labor by convicts and captives. As for the Adriatic and the Mediterranean, its policy remained more or less constant: stay out of wars when possible, but fight them by any means available when they became inevitable.

Throughout the period 1000–1500, however, Venice thrived on its connections with Asia. Even today, Venice overflows with reminders of the city's Eastern orientation. In the splendid cathedral of San Marco, for example, the mosaics contain numerous Egyptian scenes, and the great domes echo designs from the Muslim world. But by 1600 the Ottoman war machine had made those monuments relics of the past. That past overflowed with war and state transformation.

The far-fetched comparison of China with Venice yields two important results. First, it establishes that both, in the huge space of the Chinese empire and the relatively restricted scope of Venice external relations, including relations of war, strongly affected state policy and form. Second, it qualifies the simple impressions of China as a coercion-centered state and of Venice as a capital-centered state by underlining the complementary importance of coercion, capital, and commitment. Yes, the initial imposition of militarily-backed centralized institutions by China's unifying Qin permanently marked the Chinese regime. Yes, trade remained Venice's lifeblood for almost a thousand years. Yet each regime created a distinctive synthesis of coercion, capital, and commitment as means of assuring that subjects would accept their rulers' demands. Today's Chinese Communist rulers are certainly discovering that coercion does not suffice alone.[28]

STATES AND WAR IN THE HEYDAY OF CAPITALISM

Ninety-five percent of states' history passed before 1750. But the years from 1750 onward packed a millennium's worth of change in war and states into fewer than 300 years. The two centuries from 1750 to 1950 disrupted the relationship between China and Europe. It did so in an abstract sense: after centuries during which the Chinese economy surpassed or equaled the prosperity of European economies, Europe surged ahead economically. Following centuries in which China had operated the world's most powerful state, European states became dominant in much of the world. The period 1750–1950 also disrupted the Asia–Europe relationship in a concrete sense: whereas for centuries the net flow of wealth ran from Europe to China, Europe began extracting wealth from China and the rest of Asia, and European states began serious incursions into the Chinese mainland. It was not simply that Europe surged ahead.[29] A great reversal in the China–Europe connection occurred. For a while, East Asia lost its place as the world's dynamic center.

That happened in part because the relations of European states to each other and the rest of the world were changing. The changes had a historical background. As Venice was turning toward Europe after 1500, a distinctive and increasingly connected European system of states was forming.[30] Although war, commercial competition, and religious faith often divided pairs of European states, they paradoxically knit the whole system together; shifting alliances created far-reaching connections across the continent. European states including Portugal, Spain, the Netherlands, Great Britain, and France were creating competitive overseas empires; furthermore, the European state system became the center of a worldwide network of states.

In Kalevi J. Holsti's comprehensive catalog of 177 major wars across the world from 1648 to 1989, only forty-four wars did *not* involve at least one European power as a major participant, and only five of those occurred before 1918.[31] For the shorter period 1816–1976, Daniel Geller and David Singer similarly detect European preponderance in war, especially before 1945.[32] Of course we might suspect Holsti, Geller, Singer, or their sources of Eurocentrism. But surely when it came to large-scale warfare in the heyday of capitalism, European states participated in disproportionate numbers. Only late in the heyday of capitalism did the United States become a military giant and a major participant in interstate wars.

Ironically, the sheer growth of Western military establishments civilianized governments. Reliance on heavy taxation, to take the most obvious point, empowered both the civilian bureaucrats who assessed or collected taxes and the civilian legislatures (however aristocratic) that authorized assessment and collection. Mobilizing production and supply for greatly enlarged military forces demanded the efforts of civilian administrators. Increasingly the military depended for their maintenance on civilian officials. As a consequence, rulers themselves became civilian officials, and armies answered to civilian officials.

Nevertheless, to a degree rarely seen in history, accumulations of coercion and of capital reinforced each other during the capitalist centuries 1500–1900.[33] States used their coercive means to protect capital in three very different ways: by forcefully acquiring colonies and opening markets; by providing security from foreign predators, including military rivals; and by regulating domestic relations among capital, labor, and suppliers of raw materials. Yet states also moved willy-nilly into the provision of public goods for their citizens. Extraction of resources by means of taxation and conscription involved rulers in collecting information about their populations, responding to dearth or natural disaster, offering benefits to military veterans, and even listening to citizen complaints about public administration. Rulers facilitated the work of coercion and capital by building communications infrastructure in the form of roads, canals, schools, postal services, and (later) telegraph lines. Willed or not, improved infrastructure then made it easier for citizens to communicate, organize, and make demands.

From the eighteenth century onward, Western states even began to create welfare systems that sustained households in times of hardship. Peter Lindert has documented that change and traced its wide-reaching consequences. Looking at a large number of countries, he has established how regularly economic expansion has led to formation of redistributive systems of social spending, especially as ordinary workers acquired political voice. 'Since the eighteenth century,' he remarks,

> the rise of tax-based social spending has been at the heart of government growth. It was social spending, not national defense, public transportation, or government enterprises, that accounted for most of the rise in governments' taxing and spending as a share of GDP over the last two centuries.[34]

But wage-labor became more central to economies, first in the West and then across the world. As it did so, redistributive social spending skyrocketed. Most of that increase has occurred recently. Social spending never sufficed to maintain poor people in idleness, much less to entice them away from viable employment. Conservative critics to the contrary notwithstanding, Lindert challenges the view that welfare benefits sap initiative.

Lindert concludes that social spending stabilized the labor force and increased its productive capacity. Because it did so, even very high levels of expenditure occurred at little or no net cost to the whole economy. But capitalists and public authorities did not simply drift in an irresistible river. Which policies governments adopted, Lindert continues, depended closely on the organization of public politics. Great Britain led Europe in poor relief between the 1780s and 1834 because its great landlords invested in retaining their agricultural labor force. But when the Reform Act of 1832 gave industrial capitalists new voice, a dramatic cutback in benefits occurred.[35]

Nevertheless, a rapidly urbanizing and industrializing Great Britain also raised its levels of social spending during the later nineteenth century, and became a world leader in redistributive programs during the twentieth century. Where the Roman Catholic Church wielded great political influence, to take another case in point, its opposition to public programs slowed their expansion until after World War II. Then an increasingly anti-communist church began to support social spending as it fashioned Christian democracy into a competitive political strategy.[36]

Note a profound implication: after millennia during which war or preparation for war provided the central rationale and activity for states across the world, support and regulation of civilian activities came to preoccupy rulers. War lost its centrality. When war did come, to be sure, it still engaged and transformed state power. But from the later twentieth century onward, the overall frequency of interstate war in the world began to decline.[37] For a time after 1945, civil war displaced interstate war as a major context for killing. But during the later 1990s, even civil war became less frequent.[38] We face the prospect of a new world of states, still relying on coercion, capital, and commitment to accomplish their coordinated work, but no longer so tightly yoked to war.

NOTES

1. Marc Van de Mieroop, *Cuneiform Texts and the Writing of History* (London: Routledge, 1999), 49.
2. H. Keeley, *War before Civilization. The Myth of the Peaceful Savage* (New York: Oxford University Press, 1996).
3. Robert L. Carneiro, 'War and Peace: Alternating Realities in Human History' in S. P. Reyna and R. E. Downs, eds., *Studying War: Anthropological Perspectives* (Langhorne, Penn.: Gordon and Breach, 1994), 14.
4. Jared Diamond, *Guns, Germs, and Steel: The Fates of Human Societies* (New York: Norton, 1998), 100. Bruce D. Smith, *The Emergence of Agriculture* (New York: Scientific American Library, 1995), 13.
5. Diamond, 88–90.
6. Charles Tilly, ed., *The Formation of National States in Western Europe* (Princeton, N. J.: Princeton University Press, 1975).
7. Charles Tilly, 'Why and How History Matters,' in Robert E. Goodin and Charles Tilly, eds., *The Oxford Handbook of Contextual Political Analysis* (Oxford: Oxford University Press, 2006).
8. Miguel Centeno, *Blood and Debt: War and the Nation-State in Latin America* (University Park, Penn.: Penn State University Press, 2002).
9. Charles Tilly, *Trust and Rule* (Cambridge: Cambridge University Press, 2005).
10. Christopher Ehret, *The Civilizations of Africa. A History to 1800* (Charlottesville, Va.: University of Virginia Press, 2002), chapter 4.
11. Stathis Kalyvas, 'Civil Wars,' in Carles Boix and Susan C. Stokes, eds., *The Oxford Handbook of Comparative Politics* (Oxford: Oxford University Press, 2007).
12. Richard Bensel, *Yankee Leviathan: The Origins of Central State Authority in America, 1859–1877* (Cambridge: Cambridge University Press, 1990).
13. Centeno, *Blood and Debt.*
14. Victoria Tin-Bor Hui, *War and State Formation in Ancient China and Early Modern Europe* (Cambridge: Cambridge University Press, 2005). Hendrik Spruyt, 'War, Trade, and State Formation' in Carles Boix and Susan C. Stokes, eds., *The Oxford Handbook of Comparative Politics* (Oxford: Oxford University Press, 2007).
15. Leonard M. Dudley, *The Word and the Sword. How Techniques of Information and Violence Have Shaped the World* (Oxford: Blackwell, 1991). John Lynn, *Battle. A History of Combat and Culture* (Boulder, Colo.: Westview, 2003).
16. Giorgio Chittolini, ed., *Two Thousand Years of Warfare* (Danbury, Conn. Grolier Educational Corporation, 1994), 137.

17. Rhoads Murphey, *Ottoman Warfare, 1500–1700* (New Brunswick, N.J.: Rutgers University Press, 1999), 93.
18. John Lynn, ed., *Feeding Mars: Logistics in Western Warfare from the Middle Ages to the Present* (Boulder, Colo.: Westview, 1993).
19. Martin van Creveld, *Technology and War: From 2000 B.C. to the Present* (New York: Free Press, 1989).
20. Charles Tilly, *Regimes and Repertoires* (Chicago: University of Chicago Press, 2006), chapter 6.
21. Source: adapted from Hui, *War and State Formation*, 257–8.
22. Hui, *War and State Formation*.
23. Caroline Blunden and Mark Elvin, *Cultural Atlas of China* (New York: Facts on File, 1984).
24. Hui, *War and State Formation*, 180.
25. See also Pamela Kyle Crossley, *The Manchus* (Oxford: Blackwell, 1997), David Morgan, *The Mongols* (Oxford: Blackwell, 1986).
26. R. Bin Wong, *China Transformed. Historical Change and the Limits of European Experience* (Ithaca, N.Y. Cornell University Press, 1997).
27. Thomas J. Barfield, *The Perilous Frontier. Nomadic Empires and China, 221 BC to AD 1757* (Oxford: Blackwell, 1989). Barfield, 'The Devil's Horsemen: Steppe Nomadic Warfare in Historical Perspective,' in S. P. Reyna and R. E. Downs, eds., *Studying War.: Anthropological Perspectives* (Langhorne, Penn.: Gordon and Breach, 1994).
28. Thomas P. Bernstein and Xiaobo Lü, *Taxation without Representation in Contemporary Rural China* (Cambridge: Cambridge University Press, 2002). Kevin J. O'Brien and Lianjiang Li, *Rightful Resistance in Rural China* (Cambridge: Cambridge University Press, 2006).
29. Kenneth Pomeranz, *The Great Divergence: Europe, China, and the Making of the Modern World Economy* (Princeton, N.J.: Princeton University Press, 2000).
30. Charles Tilly, *Coercion, Capital, and European States, AD 990–1992* (Oxford: Blackwell, 1992, rev. edn.), chapter 6.
31. Kalevi J. Holsti, *Peace and War: Armed Conflicts and International Order, 1648–1989* (Cambridge: Cambridge University Press, 1991).
32. Daniel S. Geller and J. David Singer, *Nations at War: A Scientific Study of International Conflict* (Cambridge: Cambridge University Press, 1998).
33. S. P. Reyna, 'The Force of Two Logics: Predatory and Capital Accumulation in the Making of the Great Leviathan, 1415–1763' in S. P. Reyna and R. E. Downs, eds., *Deadly Developments: Capitalism, States and War* (Amsterdam: Gordon and Breach, 1999).
34. Peter H. Lindert, *Growing Public: Social Spending and Economic Growth Since the Eighteenth Century* (Cambridge: Cambridge University Press, 2004), I, 20.
35. Lindert, I, 67–86.
36. Lindert, I, 216–17.
37. John Mueller, *The Remnants of War* (Ithaca, N.Y.: Cornell University Press, 2004).
38. Tilly, *Regimes and Repertoires*, chapter 6.

REFERENCES

BARFIELD, THOMAS J. *The Perilous Frontier: Nomadic Empires and China, 221 BC to AD 1757.* Oxford: Blackwell, 1989.

CHITTOLINI, GIORGIO, ed. *Two Thousand Years of Warfare.* Danbury, Conn.: Grolier, 1994.

DUDLEY, LEONARD M. *The Word and the Sword: How Techniques of Information and Violence Have Shaped the World.* Oxford: Blackwell, 1991.

GAT, AZAR. *War in Human Civilization.* Oxford: Oxford University Press, 2006.

GELLER, DANIEL S. and J. DAVID SINGER. *Nations at War: A Scientific Study of International Conflict.* Cambridge: Cambridge University Press, 1998.

HOLSTI, KALEVI J. *Peace and War: Armed Conflicts and International Order, 1648–1989.* Cambridge: Cambridge University Press, 1991.

LINDERT, PETER H. *Growing Public: Social Spending and Economic Growth since the Eighteenth Century.* Cambridge: Cambridge University Press, 2004.

LYNN, JOHN. *Battle: A History of Combat and Culture.* Boulder, Colo.: Westview, 2003.

TILLY, CHARLES, ed. *The Formation of National States in Western Europe.* Princeton, N.J.: Princeton University Press, 1975.

——. *Coercion, Capital, and European States, AD 990–1992,* rev. edn. Oxford: Blackwell, 1992.

——. *Regimes and Repertoires.* Chicago: University of Chicago Press, 2006.

VAN CREVELD, MARTIN. *Technology and War from 2000 B.C. to the Present.* New York: Free Press, 1989.

WONG, R. BIN. *China Transformed: Historical Change and the Limits of European Experience.* Ithaca, N.Y.: Cornell University Press, 1997.

CHAPTER 11

....

GENDERS

....

MARNIE HUGHES-WARRINGTON

GENDER is commonly held to be a neglected topic in world historical scholarship. In response, one could point to the large and ever-growing body of scholarship that has outlined how gender—the 'social organization of the sexes' as Joan Wallach Scott defines it—is implicated in the full range of human activities, from the construction of communities to the delegation of economic activities, from the transmission of knowledge to forms of representation. Gender, writers like Merry Wiesner-Hanks, Judith Zinsser, Peg Strobel, Ida Blom, and Peter Stearns have argued, is not an optional part of world-history making; world historians do not work above gender. Rather, the relations that bind men and women, men and men, and women and women together in social, political, economic, and cultural activities are so fundamental a part of human experience that they cannot be glossed over, passed by or passed on as the province of specialist historians.

And yet the perception of gender as a neglected topic in world history persists, as does the assumption that it is best or only done by specialist historians, and more particularly women historians of a feminist inclination. In part, this perception stems from the histories that world historians commonly tell about their own field, which claim that writing about gender only emerged after the second wave of feminism in the 1960s. There is no doubt that since the 1960s the volume of writing on gender in world history—taking in everything from introductory textbooks to specialized monographs—has increased dramatically, and it seems like the experiences of men and women from all parts of the globe are finally being addressed. But this vision of world history reflects both a particular view of 'history' and an all too short timeframe. Rather than outlining current understandings of how gender has played a role in men's and women's activities from the earliest human communities to the present—an account of gender *in* world history that could fill many volumes—this chapter instead explores the gender *of* world history; that is, how world historians have shown an interest in gender since ancient times. This is a history that is potentially as large as that of gender *in* world history, but in order to realize that potential, we need to cast our definition of 'world history' wider to take in collective biographies, historical fiction, genealogy, travel writing or folklore, and to look to the writings of women and men. Further, we have to reconsider the view that early approaches are 'worthy' but limited. When we do so, we will see that gender has been of concern to historians for far longer than fifty years, of interest to male and female writers from diverse walks of life, and connected with an imperative to outline actual and desired world orders.[1] In this way, gender functions as a useful lens for considering the normative purpose of world histories.

The *Histories* of arguably the first world historian, Herodotus (ca. 430–424 BCE), for example, do not lack comment on gender relations. Depending on whom you read, Herodotus either presents women as they were, unconstrained by the strictures of genre and moral world order, or as generic constructions of otherness, particularly barbarian otherness.[2] There is no single formula or program of the role of women in the *Histories*. It would also be a mistake, however, to deny the presence of typologies of women *and* men in his work. Importantly, men are not consistent champions or women perennial transgressors of moral custom. Both function as symbols of the health of the *polis* and agents of social order, and as indicators of the despotic transgression of moral order in barbaric otherness.[3]

While few of the historians who followed Herodotus held to his flexible assignment of typologies, they shared his understanding of history as a source of orientation towards the world and as a guide to action. Further, early and persistently, the relations between men and women came to be used as a historiographical device to signal the maintenance of—or more commonly threats to—world order. Most ancient historical writing on individual women and men belongs to the biographical catalogue genre. Originating from catalogue verse, this broad group of writings has in common the production of a list organized around a single theme. There are, for instance, ancient catalogues of priestesses, queens, women responsible for causing wars and ruining or joining family houses, and prostitutes, as there are catalogues of virtuous and wicked men.[4] Ancient biographical catalogues are further characterized by the apparently random order of their entries (e.g., non-chronological or non-alphabetical), the use of male relatives to place or identify female figures and the judgment of women according to their physical appearance and sexual passion. Some of these works range far over known space and time, and deserve recognition as universal histories because their authors were evidently interested in drawing together historical events to lay bare universal moral truths.[5]

Across ancient biographical catalogue works of a large spatio-historical scale, a continuum of opinion on women and men and their interaction is discernible, from sympathetic treatments to misogynistic accounts brimming with vitriol. A notable example of the former is the anonymous *Tractatus de mulieribus claris in bello* (*Women Intelligent and Courageous in Warfare*, ca. 200 BCE), which celebrates the achievements of Greek and barbarian queens without passing comment on their physical appearance or sexuality.[6] Such is the sympathetic stance towards women in this text that recent commentators have wondered whether the author might have been a woman. The most important of the sympathetic catalogues is undoubtedly Plutarch's

Mulierum virtutes (*Virtues of Women*, ca. 75 CE). In *Virtues of Women*, Plutarch signals his departure from Thucydides' declaration that the best woman 'is she about whom there is the least talk among persons outside regarding either censure or commendation' and alignment with the Roman custom of commemorating the dead.[7] In twenty-seven sketches, he identifies virtues and vices that are common to both men and women and peculiar to the latter like chastity, fidelity, and a lack of ambition. Far less sympathetic is the parallel satiric tradition of catalogue writing, in which we are warned of the potential sexual impropriety, idleness, and disobedience of women. Drawing on sources like Semonides of Amorgo's *Females of the Species* (ca. 550 BCE) in which evil—and possibly all—women are classified by animal type, writers like Juvenal connected the idleness, moral, and sexual depravity of women with the decline of the Roman state.[8] This connection of the actions of women with domestic *and* social order became an important feature of ancient histories. It is tempting to conclude that Greek and Roman society was at base misogynistic, but as Vidén has argued, misogyny was symptomatic of a more fundamental fear of the disintegration of the traditional standards of their world.[9] To Juvenal, as for other writers like Seneca and Tacitus, individuals were assigned roles according to gender and nobility. When women *and* men acted contrary to those roles, the foundations of the state and, thus, the world were undermined.[10]

Fear of the social and intellectual impact of male and female actions upon world order also inspired patristic and medieval works like Jerome's *Adversus Jovinianum* (*Against Jovinian*, ca. 392 CE) and Walter Map's *Dissuasio Valerii ad Rufinum* (*Valerie's Dissuasion to Rufinus against Taking a Wife*, ca. 1181–2). In these, historical events were used to argue for chastity being the sole measure of female conduct and women being the cause of the 'downhill tumble' of men. This view—and the New Testament prohibition of women teaching—made it difficult for women to position themselves as pedagogical writers or authorities. In some cases, like that of Hildegarde of Bingen (*Liber divinorum operum*, *Book of Divine Works*, 1163–73) and Herrad of Hohenbourg (*Hortus deliciarum*, *Garden of Delights*, ca. 1176–91), expression was possible through the use of writing forms in which they positioned themselves as observers of phenomena and the servants of readers.[11]

Probably the best-known gender history of the medieval period is Boccaccio's *De mulieribus claris* (*Famous Women*, 1361–75). It is not easy to decipher Boccaccio's attitude to the women he writes about. At first sight, his appraisal is not encouraging: women are apparently inferior to men in both mind and body. They are prone to be idle, fickle, cunning, avaricious, lascivious, suspicious, timid, stingy, obstinate, and proud.[12] And when women are praised unreservedly, they are so upon the grounds of being 'man-like,' or as if by some mistake they had been given the wrong sex.[13] Commentators like Jordan thus characterize the work as equivocal: while Boccaccio declares that he will subject women to the same judgments of virtue as men, he undercuts such an aim by noting that even the most virtuous of women often meet unfortunate ends. It is as if 'the concept of a truly genderless *virtus* will undermine the social order.'[14] In Boccaccio's defense, Brown notes that Boccaccio is more expansive than his sources on occasion in praising women's abilities or accomplishments.[15]

Whatever Boccaccio's intentions, his work became the foundation for more positive world histories, including the fifteenth-century writer, Christine de Pizan's *Mutacion*, *Livre de la cité des dames* and *Livre des trios vertus*. In de Pizan's case, trespass into the male domain of universal-history writing was made possible by her use of fictional allegory, the transformation of her voice and body into a male one by Fortune (*Le Livre de la mutacion de fortune*, §1350) and her presentation of herself as a witness participant and messenger to the world.

In *Livre de la cité des dames* (*The Book of the City of Ladies*, 1405) and its sequel *Livre des trios vertus* (*The Book of the Three Virtues*) de Pizan looks to the genre of universal history—which in that context meant discerning God's plan in different events—and to her female form to narrate the fortunes of women and men. *The Book of the City of Ladies* is a reworking of the conceptual and structural norms of earlier universal and biographical catalogue writings by male authors such as St Augustine and Boccaccio. The *City* in de Pizan's title, for instance, is evocative of Augustine's *City of God*, and both texts are united in their interest in the deeds of people 'who deserved to reign with God.' Like Augustine's work, de Pizan's *City* is structured according to a hierarchy of virtue that sees saintly women ranked above good wives and female warriors. In distinction from Augustine, though, de Pizan stresses woman's common humanity with man in spiritual and mental terms and ability to be man's companion in society.

De Pizan's positioning of herself in the text is worthy of note. Through the use of the narrative frame of a dream vision, she places herself in history and shows her readers that they, like her, can emulate the deeds of virtuous ladies. As Brown-Grant has argued, de Pizan's 'readers can choose to copy her lead and so "write" themselves, metaphorically, into the *Cité*.'[16] Following her lead, we see the divergence of men and women along different paths through time. When discussing the role of men in the history of civilization, for instance, de Pizan looks to contemporary events and echoes the late medieval view of society's decline and decadence. When discussing the contributions of women, however, she looks to events over the long term and observes progress. Women are credited with the invention of the letters of the alphabet, arms and agriculture, and the development of cities and education. They are capable of bringing good into the world if they are educated and treated with respect. Their virtue is not, as Boccaccio had suggested, a 'manly quality,' but something exercised in the home, marriage, and society. Women are also expected to make valuable contributions to society in future, mostly through their companionship with men. Men, on the other hand, are portrayed as increasingly willing to slander women and as connected with the decadent institutions of church and state. Despite her belief in a common human rationality and virtue, therefore, de Pizan's view is thus characterized by two gendered narratives of differing time scales and plot structures.

Later writers rarely embraced de Pizan's reworking of the biographical catalogue genre into universal history, but she clearly anticipated some of the key developments in renaissance and reformation world history writing. Topical issues also continued to be important, particularly those in politics and religion. Both came together in the *querelle des femmes* or literary debate about women from the sixteenth to the seventeenth centuries, a debate that affirmed the orientation of universal histories towards the present. Generally, *querelle des femmes* works are characterized by theological, philosophical, and legal arguments, but many also included biographical catalogues. For example, Joseph Swetnam's *The Arraignment of lewd, idle and froward women* (1615), as well as defenses of women by Moderata Fonte (*Dei meriti delle donne, The Worth of Women,* 1600), Ester Sowernam (most likely a pseudonym) and Joane Sharp (*Ester Hath Hang'd Haman,* 1617), Rachel Speght (*Mortalites Memorandum,* 1621), Mary Fage (*Fames Roule,* 1637), and Bathsua Makin (*Essay on the Antient Education of Gentlewomen,* 1673) employ catalogues to advance their arguments. Of particular interest to these writers was whether women were morally, socially, and intellectually complementary to men, rather than subordinate to them, and capable of being citizens and even sovereigns. L. Woodbridge, and F. Teague and R. de Haas have argued that defenses outnumbered attacks by a ratio of four to one, and that the number of works by women or purportedly by women increased steadily up to the nineteenth century. Women, they note, might have felt more confident to defend themselves, but the connection of defenses to women writers might have also enhanced the bifurcation of gender roles.[17]

By the seventeenth century, history writing moved away from theology and towards science and philosophy. Historians continued in universal fashion, however, to search for the fundamental principles that shape the behavior of individuals and societies. Further, they often sought confirmation of the leading role Western Europe held in progress towards intellectual, moral, aesthetic, technological, and social perfection. In histories of 'civilization,' race and gender often elided, producing modernization narratives of the rise of the (masculine) West that were not challenged until the twentieth century. Modes of subsistence were cited as evidence, but so too were manners.[18] A number of histories, including John Millar's *Observations Concerning the Distinction of Ranks in Society* (1771), William Russell's *Essay on Character, Manner and Genius of Women* (1773), Lord Kames' *Sketches of the History of Man* (1778), John Adams' *Woman: Sketches of the History, Genius, Disposition, Accomplishments, Employments, Customs and Importance of the Fair Sex in all Parts of the World* (1790), the Marquis de Condorçet's *Sketch for a Historical Picture of the Progress of the Human Mind* (1793), and William Alexander's *The History of Women, from the Earliest Antiquity, to the Present Time* (1796) dedicated a great deal of attention to the liberation of women. In their eyes, 'the rank . . . and condition in which we find women in any country, mark out to us with the greatest precision the exact point in the scale of civil society, to which the people of such country have arrived.'[19] With the exception of works like Christoph Meiners' *Geschichte des weiblichen Geschlechts* (1788–1800)[20] and Samuel Goodrich's *Lives of Celebrated Women* (1844), 'civilization' saw the transformation of Western women from 'slaves' and 'sexual idols' into 'friends and companions' in the private sphere of the home.[21] Further, women remained a product of what men made of them.

Historical writing on gender proliferated in the nineteenth century, with approximately 300 volumes produced during that period. Miriam Burstein has noted that at least half of those volumes were produced by men, and that the demands of readers, reviewers, and publishers for morally edifying works quashed methodological innovation, leading authors to produce didactic and 'encyclopedic texts characterised by instances of déjà vu, plagiarism and mutual raiding of sources.'[22] As Sarah Strickley Ellis, the author of *The Mothers of Great Men* (1859) realized, the moral needs of readers dictated that historical order be subordinated to moral order. The primacy of moral order meant, for instance, that 'world-noted women,' as Mary Cowden Clarke called them, were not so much individuals as exemplars or 'types of particular womanly attributes' such as chastity, modesty, and steadfastness.[23]

The valuation of biographies for their perceived potential to bring about moral change reinforced the longstanding affiliation of world history writing with the biographical catalogue genre. Women's lives were thought to be particularly edifying, for as Sarah Josepha Hale argued in *Woman's Record; or, Sketches of All Distinguished Women, from 'The Beginning' until A.D. 1850* (1853), 'woman is God's appointed agent of morality' and the mainspring of human progress towards 'millennial peace' because she was created last in an ascending scale from matter to man. Mary Hay's *Female Biography, or Memoirs of Illustrious and Celebrated Women, of all Ages and Countries* (1803), Lucy Aikin's poetic *Epistles on Women, Exemplifying their Character and Condition in Various Ages and Nations with Miscellaneous Poems* (1810), and Clara Balfour's *Women Worth Emulating* (1877) are just some of the many nineteenth-century world histories of women that took the form of biographical surveys.

A notable exception to this trend was Lydia Maria Child's *The History of the Condition of Women, in Various Ages and Nations* (1835), which arranged materials spatially. Reflecting contemporary stereotypes and lacunae in evidence, Child's work diachronically relates European history and synchronically relates contemporary contexts and customary activities in non-European locations. Unlike many of her peers, though, she steadfastly refused to deduce overt philosophical or universal explanations from the many and varied facts she assembled. This was noted by Sarah Josepha Hale, who in her review of the work complained that 'from her we did anticipate somewhat more of the philosophy of history.... In the few general remarks she has ventured, there is so much good sense, that we only regret in these volumes she should have transcribed so much, and written so little.'[24] The Preface Child added to the 1845 edition confirmed that she did not want her work to be read as a philosophical or universal text:

> This volume is not an essay upon women's rights, or a philosophical investigation of what is or what ought to be the relation of the sexes. If any theories on this subject are contained in it, they are merely incidentally implied by the manner of stating historical facts. I have simply endeavoured to give an accurate history of the condition of women, in language sufficiently concise for popular use.[25]

Many of Child's other writings are concerned with liberation from slavery, and it is true that her interest in that cause influenced her choice and presentation of materials in *The History*. As a theme, however, it does not loom large enough to draw all of the narrated details together. Above all, the basic message of the *History* is that there is no single narrative that can be used to celebrate or condemn women.

It is ironic that female authors of world histories argued for the domesticity of women at the same time that they enlarged their own sphere of influence by becoming publicly known figures with opinions on the experiences of women in far-flung parts of the globe. Furthermore, women's world histories, as Hobbs has argued, were double-edged because while on the one hand they provided reading material designed to reinforce prevailing norms regarding girl and womanhood, they also contributed to and thus promoted the literacy and education of women.[26] Many nineteenth-century women's world histories were conduits for feminist thought, demonstrating that women were not lesser instantiations of humanity than men, but their complementary companions, enhancing their abilities and turning them away from iniquity. Moreover, they were conduits for more or less oblique political comment, ranging from Balfour's comments on the damaging effects of making girls wear restrictive clothing and Clarke's observation that men were quick to misrepresent intelligent women as full of vice, to Hale's careful selection of figures to suggest the power of women to realize social transformation.

Few nineteenth-century universal histories are mentioned in historiographical surveys today, but the neglect of women contributors to the field is glaringly apparent. As some commentators have noted, this is likely due to their exclusion from academic discussions and privileges and even library facilities: few women could hope to produce the archival research that was increasingly valued.[27] It is also worth noting, however, that the biographical, ethnographic, and narrative methods that they used to either compensate for or react against their exclusion meant their easy assimilation into the gendered diminutives of 'travel writing' and 'biography' and thus movement out of an increasingly professionalized 'history.'[28] Stigmatized as well intentioned but amateurish, 'women's worthies' remain today on the margins of professional world historical writing, with production limited almost exclusively to the growing market of eight- to twelve-year-old girls.

While the professionalization of history also brought to an end the dominance of universal approaches to the writing of history, the variety of twentieth-century 'world histories' is still remarkably rich. Early in the twentieth century, writers like Arnold Toynbee looked for patterns in the past for an indication of health of Western civilization. While best known for his *A Study of History*—a work in which women are rarely mentioned—in the 1960s he penned a response to the question 'When was the best time in history for women to live?' His conclusion, that 'it was a black day for woman when man...[wrenched] the hoe out of women's hands and [transformed] it into a plough,' was an early contribution to the continuing debate about whether there was a particular point in world history that ushered in gender inequalities.[29] Toynbee's identification of agriculture as a turning point in world history brings him into rough agreement with Friedrich Engels (*The Origin of the Family, Private Property and the State*, 1884), Marija Gimbutas (*Civilization of the Goddess*, 1991), Margaret Ehrenberg (*Women in Prehistory*, 1989), Rosalind Miles (*The Women's History of the World*, 1989), and Paul V. Adams *et al.* (*Experiencing World History*, 2000).[30] It may also be compared to the claims of Gerda Lerner (*The Creation of Patriarchy*, 1986), and Jared Diamond (*The Rise and Fall of the Third Chimpanzee*, 1991) that inequalities were present earlier or even always present in hominid history.[31] Other writers, like Sarah Hughes and Brady Hughes have argued for recognition of variations in the experiences of women in ancient civilizations.[32] Kevin Reilly has argued that more attention needs to be given to the critical discussion of the origins of inequalities.[33] In dissent, though, have been writers like Mary Ritter Beard, who have worked to shift the emphasis of world history discourse away from 'subjection' and towards an appreciation that 'women have been a force in making all the history that has been made.'[34] Despite her efforts, gender in world history today rarely means anything other than a consideration of the origins of inequality in the agrarian era.

A related area of discussion examined the impact of industrialization in world history. In the mid-twentieth century, modernization analysis dominated world history research and writing. Of interest to modernization theorists were the paths of development in the West that might be used to study and foster development in the 'developing' world. Writers like Esther Boserup (*Women's Role in Economic Development*, 1970) considered development and female empowerment to be complementary. A disparate group of neo-Marxist theorists disagreed, noting the inadequacy of modernization theory for an explanation of Latin American development and the marginalization and exploitation of women, and suggested an alternative in the form of world(-) systems and dependency theory.[35] Whereas modernization theorists had favored the study of the internal characteristics of particular civilizations, world(-)systems and dependency theorists stressed the need to study networks of economic and political relations between societies and more particularly inequalities in the distribution of roles, functions, and power that fostered states of underdevelopment or dependency.[36] Writers like E. Baron and Joya Misra have noted the possibilities for historically oriented world(-)systems studies of gender, but as yet few have emerged.[37] The paucity of these kinds of studies is probably due in part to the popularly perceived disjunction between feminism and Marxism.

An additional reason is the growing preference for identification under the rubric of 'postcolonial studies.' World(-)systems and dependency theory overlap with but do not entirely coincide with the postcolonial perspectives that emerged in world history research in the second half of the twentieth century. First brought to the attention of world historians with the publication of Edward Said's *Orientalism* (1978), postcolonial theorists enhance political and economic criticisms of colonialism with cultural analyses. For example, representation and language are crucial for the construction of an 'Other', as works by Joanna De Groot have demonstrated.[38] Conversely, postcolonial scholars have also highlighted the agency of the colonized, as with Evelyn Brooks Higginbottom's argument that African matrifocal family structures were revitalized in

New World slave societies.[39] Postcolonial scholars have been tugged by opposing aims: to establish the alignment of the experiences of women and colonized subjects and to recognize the specificities of race, class, nationality, religion, sexuality, epistemic, social, political, and economic hierarchies and gender relations. Some have managed to strike a balance, as with Michael Adas' investigation of the ways in which gender representations shaped Western colonization or expansion in Africa, Nupur Chaudhuri and Margaret Strobel's study of the varying impacts of European women's activities on men and women in colonial societies, and Louise Tilly's recognition that industrialization did not lead to the marginalization of all women.[40] Similarly, Cheryl Johnson-Odim and Margaret Strobel have stressed the complexities of the impact of colonialism, writing:

> As with any major societal upheaval resulting in challenges to existing authority, colonialism both created opportunities and oppressed women. In the final analysis, however, the vast majority of women have opted to work for the independence of their societies.[41]

However, the tug between universality and particularity can, as Judith Tucker has argued, result in a loss of confidence in one's methods and ability to write the experiences of others, a result that makes writing world history appear difficult or even unethical.[42]

Postcolonial theorists encouraged a shift to relational studies and particularity, but so too did the 'new' world historians of the second half of the twentieth century. With the exception of sociological macro-histories, new global histories and neo-universal 'big' histories, new world histories are smaller in scale and more cross-cultural and comparative in approach than earlier works. This shift is mirrored in new world historical writing on women: for example, recent women's world histories by Bonnie Anderson and Judith Zinnser, Bonnie Smith, and Pauline Pantel are restricted to Europe or the West.[43] Further, Sarah Hughes and Brady Hughes' *Women in World History* (1995), the American Historical Association's 'Women's and Gender History in Global Perspective' series, and Ruth Roach Pierson, Nupur Chaudhuri, and Beth McAuley's *Nation, Empire, Colony* suggest large-scale perspectives through the combination of specialist and small-scale analyses.[44] Postcolonial and world(-)systems studies may be credited for this shift, as may concerns about the practicalities of world history education, postmodernism, and the rise of gender history.[45]

First popularized with the publication of Joan Scott's *Gender and the Politics of History* (1988), gender historians sought to move away from the 'add women and stir' approach of women's history and towards a consideration of varying relations between constructed gender categories. Their interest was in exploring how gender—like race, religion, and class—shaped and constrained power relations. The potential impact of a gender studies approach to world history research and writing is enormous, though the number of writers cognizant of it is few. For example, Michel Foucault has noted the shifting shape of 'sexuality' across ancient and modern history, Ashis Nandy and Lewis Wurgaft have illuminated the role of binary definitions of gender in destructive conflicts, Judith Zinnser has explored the intersection between gender and technology, and Ida Blom and Sarah Hughes have argued that the world—and thus the writing of world history—is structured through a 'gendered order' or 'system.'[46] Blom has demonstrated this through an analysis of how varying gender systems shaped understandings of the nation-state, and Sarah Hughes has located gender relations at the base of different forms of society. Hughes has argued for gender to be brought to the forefront of world history education, and Marilyn Morris's survey of world history textbooks has further illuminated unconscious biases against homosexuality and its conflation with the East.[47]

The extent to which gender might reorder our understanding of world history is demonstrated not so much through chronological works that feature gender as a theme, but through works that use gender to order chronology. A good case in point is Merry Wiesner-Hank's *Gender in History* (2001), which disturbs the conventional association between the movement from agriculture to industrialization and then post-industrialization with social progress. It encourages us to see the chronologies of most world histories as acts of organization that serve to highlight the achievements of some people and to render invisible the acts of others. *Gender and History* also intimates that it is fruitful to think of genders in world history. That is, as Ruth Roach Pierson has argued, gender is not a fixed bipolar relationship; rather the past and the present suggest a 'plurality of genders,' a complex web of interrelations between masculinities and femininities, lesbian, gay, and transgendered identities.[48]

Deborah Smith Johnston has wondered whether the overlaps that result when we disentangle gender from demography, work, politics, and culture mean that gender is an approach rather than a theme of world history.[49] We might ask in response whether the persistent connections between gender and these topics mean that gender should not be separated out, but rather treated as integral in world history research and teaching. There is no shortage of writing on gender in world history, even though the number of articles explicitly on that topic in the *Journal of World History* and the *Journal of Global History* is very low. What is still lacking, however, is widespread awareness of the extent to which gender shapes world historical research, writing, and teaching, particularly works in which women are not mentioned. It is time for studies of gender *in* world history to be joined by those of the gender *of* world history writing.

NOTES

1. Ross E. Dunn, 'Gender in World History,' in Ross E. Dunn, ed., *The New World History: A Teacher's Companion* (Boston: Bedford St. Martin's, 2000), 441–2; Judith Zinnser, 'And Now for Something Completely Different: Gendering the World History Survey,' *Perspectives* 34 (May/June 1996), 11; Jerry H. Bentley, *Shapes of World History in Twentieth-Century Scholarship* (Washington, D.C.: American Historical Association, 1996), 25; Patrick Manning, *Navigating World History: Historians Create a Global Past* (New

York: Palgrave Macmillan, 2003), 209; Philip Pomper, R. H. Elphick, and Richard T. Vann, eds., *World History: Ideologies, Structures, and Identities* (Oxford: Blackwell, 1998); Benedikt Stuchtey and Eckhardt Fuchs, eds., *Writing World History, 1800–2000* (Oxford: Oxford University Press, 2003); and Merry Wiesner-Hanks, 'World History and the History of Women, Gender, and Sexuality,' *Journal of World History* 18, no. 1 (March 2007), 53–67.

2. See for example C. Dewald, 'Women and Culture in Herodotus' *Histories*', in H. Foley, ed., *Reflections on Women in Antiquity* (New York: Gordon and Breach Science, 1981); and S. Flory, *The Archaic Smile of Herodotus* (Detroit, Mich.: Wayne State University Press, 1987).

3. V. Gray, 'Herodotus and the Rhetoric of Otherness,' *American Journal of Philology* 116, no. 2 (1995), 185–212.

4. See for example John the Lydian's report of Suetonius' *On Famous Courtesans*: John the Lydian, *On the Magistracies of the Roman Constitution*, trans. T. F. Carney (Sydney: Wentworth Press, 1965), 107.

5. R. Mortley, *The Idea of Universal History from Hellenistic Philosophy to Early Christian Historiography* (Lewiston, N.Y.: Edwin Mellen, 1996), 197.

6. D. Gera, *Warrior Women: The Anonymous Tractatus de Mulieribus* (Leiden: Brill, 1997).

7. Plutarch, *Mulierum Virtutes*, in *Moralia* (London: Heinemann, 1927–76), vol. 3, 242e–f. See Thucydides, *History of the Peloponnesian War* 2.45.2.

8. Semonides of Amorgos, *Females of the Species: Semonides on Women*, ed. and trans. by H. Lloyd-Jones and M. Quinton (Park Ridge, N.J.: Noyes Press, 1975); and Juvenal, 'Satire Six,' *Juvenal and Perseus*, ed. G. G. Ramsay (Cambridge, Mass.: Harvard University Press, 1956), 82–135.

9. G. Vidén, *Women in Roman Literature: Attitudes of Authors under the Early Empire* (Gothenberg: Acta Universitatis Gothoburgensis, 1993), 178–9. See also C. Edwards, *The Politics of Immorality in Ancient Rome* (Cambridge: Cambridge University Press, 1993).

10. Juvenal, *Juvenal and Persius*, trans. G. G. Ramsay (London: W. Heinemann, 1961), esp. 6th satire; Seneca, *Dialogues* (Paris: Société d'Edition 'Les Belles Lettres,' 1927); and Tacitus, *Tacitus: Annals, Agricola, Germania, Diologus, Histories, Annals*, trans. C. H. Moore, J. Jackson, H. Hutton, R. M. Ogilvie, E. H. Warmington, W. Peterson, and M. Winterbottom (London: Heinemann, 1967–70), esp. *Annals*.

11. Hildegard of Bingen, *Hildegard of Bingen's Book of Dvine Works with Letters and Songs*, ed. M. Fox (Sante Fe, N.M.: Bear, 1987); and Herrad of Hohenbourg, *Hortus deliciarum*, eds. R. Green, M. Evans, C. Bischoff, and M. Curschmann (London: Warburg Institute, 1979), 4.

12. Boccaccio, *Famous Women*, trans. V. Brown (Cambridge, Mass.: Harvard University Press, 2001), 1.6, 2.4, 3.2, 15.6, 23.8, 69.6, 74.4, 76.6, 86.3, 95.2, 96.4, 97.10, 103.8, and 105.32.

13. Ibid., 57.21. See also 2.13, 62.4, 66.2, 69.3, 76.4 and 86.4.

14. C. Jordan, 'Boccaccio's In-Famous Women: Gender and Civic Virtue in the *De mulieribus claris*,' in C. Levin and J. Watson, eds., *Ambiguous Realities: Women in the Middle Ages and Renaissance* (Detroit, Mich.: Wayne State University Press, 1987), 26.

15. V. Brown, 'Introduction,' in Boccaccio, *Famous Women*, p. xix. See also 6.4, 27.1, 43.2, 97.4, and 106.2.

16. R. Brown-Grant, *Christine de Pizan and the Moral Defence of Women: Reading Beyond Gender* (Cambridge: Cambridge University Press, 1999), 154.

17. L. Woodbridge, *Women and the English Renaisssance: Literature and the Nature of Womankind, 1540–1620* (Urbana, Ill.: University of Illinois Press, 1984), 44; F. Teague and R. de Haas, 'Defences of Women,' *A Companion to Early Modern Women's Writing*, ed. A. Pacheco (Oxford: Blackwell, 2002), 248–63.

18. Mark Salber Phillips, *Society and Sentiment: Genres of Historical Writing in Britain, 1740–1820* (Princeton, N.J.; Princeton University Press, 2000), chapters 6 and 7.

19. John Millar, *Origin of the Distinction of Ranks*, ed. J. V. Price (Bristol: Thoemmes, 1990); W. Russell, *Essay on the Character, Manners, and Genius of Women in Different Ages. Enlarged from the French of M. Thomas, by Mr. Russell*, 2 vols. (Edinburgh, 1773); H. H. Kames, *Sketches of the History of Man*, 4 vols. (Hildesheim: Olms, 1968); J. Adams, *Women. Sketches of the History, Genius, Disposition, Accomplishments, Employments, Customs and Importance of the Fair Sex, in All Parts of the World* (London: 1790); M. de Condorçet, *Sketch for a Historical Picture of the Progress of the Human Mind* (New York, N.Y.: Greenwood, 1979); W. Alexander, *The History of Women, from the Earliest Antiquity, to the Present Time, Giving Some Account of Almost Everything Every Interesting Particular Concerning that Sex Among All Nations* (Bath: Thoemmes, 1779 [1994]), vol. 1, 151.

20. M. Harbsmeier, 'World Histories Before Domestication: The Writing of Universal Histories, Histories of Mankind and World Histories in Late Eighteenth Century Germany', *Culture and History* (Copenhagen: Akademisk forlag, 1989), 93–131.

21. John Millar, as quoted in P. Bowles, 'John Millar, the Four Stages Theory, and Women's Position in Society,' *History of Political Economy* 16, no. 4 (1989), 619–38.

22. Miriam Burstein, ' "From Good Looks to Good Thoughts": Popular Women's History and the Invention of Modernity, c. 1830–c. 1870,' *Modern Philology* 97 (1999), 46–75.

23. M. C. Clarke, *World-Noted Women; or, Types of Womanly Attributes of All Lands and Ages* (New York: D. Appleton and Company, 1858), 3.

24. S. J. Hale, 'The History of the Condition of Women, in Various Ages and Nations. By Mrs. D. L. Child,' *American Ladies' Magazine* 8 (1835), 588; as quoted in C. L. Karcher, *The First Woman in the Republic: A Cultural Biography of Lydia Maria Child* (Durham, N.C.: Duke University Press, 1994), 224.

25. L. M. Child, *History of the Condition of Women in Various Ages and Naions* (Boston, Mass.: John Allen, 1845), vol. 1, Preface.

26. C. Hobbs, ed., *Nineteenth-Century Women Learn to Write* (Charlottesville, Va.: University Press of Virginia, 1995), 10.

27. C. L. Karcher, *The First Woman in the Republic: A Cultural Biography of Lydia Maria Child* (Durham: Duke University Press, 1998).

28. Bonnie Smith, *The Gender of History*, pp. 37–69; see also M. Spongberg, *Women Writing History Since the Renaissance*, introduction.

29. A. J. Toynbee, 'A Woman's Life in Other Ages,' eds. P. J. Corfield and P. Ferrari, *Historical Research* 74 (183) (2001) 1–16.

30. Friedrich Engels, *The Origin of the Family, Private Property and the State* (New York: Pathfinder, [1844] 1972); M. Gimbutas, *The Civilization of the Goddess* (San Francisco: Harper, 1991); M. Ehrenberg, *Women in Prehistory* (Norman, Okla.: Oklahoma University Press, 1989); and Paul V. Adams, E. D. Langer, L. Hwa, Peter N. Stearns, and Merry Wiesner-Hanks, *Experiencing World History* (New York: New York University Press, 2000).

31. Gerda Lerner, *The Creation of Patriarchy* (Oxford: Oxford University Press, 1986); R. Miles, *The Women's History of the World* (New York: Crown, 1989, reissued as *Who Cooked the Last Supper* in 2001), 64–6; and L. Shlain, *The Alphabet versus the Goddess: The Conflict Between Word and Image* (New York: Viking Penguin, 1999).

32. Sarah S. Hughes and Brady Hughes, *Women in Ancient Civilizations* (Washington, D.C.: American Historical Association, 1998).

33. Kevin Reilly, 'Women and World History,' *World History Bulletin* 4, no. 3 (1987), 1–6.

34. M. R. Beard, *Woman as Force in History: A Study in Traditions and Realities* (New York: Persea Books, 1946), vi.

35. The use of a hyphen in parentheses here (and throughout the chapter) marks the continuing debate about whether there was one world system or many.

36. E. Baron, 'Romancing the Field: The Marriage of Feminism and Historical Sociology,' *Social Politics* 5 (1998), 17–37.

37. J. Misra, 'Gender and the World-System: Engaging the Feminist Literature,' in Thomas D. Hall, ed., *A World Systems Reader: New Perspectives on Gender, Urbanism, Cultures, Indigenous Peoples and Ecology* (New York: Rowman and Littlefield, 2000), 105–29.

38. J. De Groot, '"Sex" and "Race": The Construction of Language and Image in the Nineteenth Century,' in *Sexuality and Subordination: Interdisciplinary Studies of Gender in the Nineteenth Century* (London: Routledge, 1989), 89–128; and 'Conceptions and Misconceptions: The Historical and Cultural Context of Discussion on Women and Development,' in H. Ashfar, ed., *Women, Development and Survival in the Third World* (London: Longman, 1991), 107–35.

39. E. B. Higginbottom, 'Beyond the Sound of Silence: Afro-American Women in History,' *Gender and History* 1, no. 1 (1989), 50–67.

40. Michael Adas, 'Bringing Ideas and Agency Back In: Representation and the Comparative Approach to World History,' in Philip Pomper, R. H. Elphick, and Richard T. Vann, eds., *World History: Ideologies, Structures, and Identities* (Oxford: Blackwell, 1998), 100–1; Nupur Chaudhuri and Margaret Strobel, eds., *Western Women and Imperialism: Complicity and Resistance* (Bloomington, Ind.: Indiana University Press, 1992); and Louise A. Tilly, 'Industrialization and Gender Inequality,' in Michael Adas, ed., *Islamic and European Expansion: The Forging of a Global Order* (Philadelphia: Temple University Press, 1993), 243–310. See also Margaret Strobel, *Gender, Sex, and Empire* (Washington, D.C.: American Historical Association, 1993).

41. C. Johnson-Odim and Margaret Strobel, eds., *Restoring Women to History: Women in the History of Africa, Asia, Latin America, and the Middle East* (Bloomington, Ind.: University of Indiana Press, 2nd edn. 1999), xli–xlii.

42. J. Tucker, 'Gender and Islamic History,' in Michael Adas, ed., *Islamic and European Expansion: The Forging of a Global Order* (Philadelphia: Temple University Press, 1993), pp. 37–74. See also Roxann Prazniak, 'Is World History Possible?,' in Arif Dirlik, V. Bahl, and Peter Gran, eds., *History after the Three Worlds: Post-Eurocentric Historiography* (Lanham, Md.: Rowman and Littlefield 2000).

43. Judith P. Zinsser and Bonnie S. Anderson, *Women in Early Modern and Modern Europe*, rev. edn, 2 vols. (Oxford: Oxford University Press, 2000);. Bonnie G. Smith, *Changing Lives: Women in European History Since 1700* (Toronto: D. C. Heath, 1989); and P. S. Pantel, ed., *A History of Women in the West*, 5 vols. (Cambridge, Mass.: Harvard University Press, 1992).

44. Sarah S. Hughes and Brady Hughes, eds., *Women in World History*, 2 vols. (Armonk, N.Y.: M. E. Sharpe, 1995); and B. A. Engel, *Women in Imperial, Soviet, and Post-Soviet Russia* (1999); *East Asia (China, Japan, Korea)* (1999); *Medieval Women in Modern Perspective* (2000); and *United States After 1865* (2000), all published by the American Historical Association; and Ruth Roach Pierson, Nupur Chaudhuri, and B. McAuley, eds., *Nation, Empire, Colony: Historicizing Gender and Race* (Bloomington, Ind.: Indiana University Press, 1998).
45. Merry Wiesner-Hanks, 'World History and Women's History.'
46. Michel Foucault, *The History of Sexuality*, 3 vols., trans. R. Hurley (Harmondsworth: Penguin, 1976–84); Ashis Nandy, 'History's Forgotten Doubles,' and Lewis D. Wurgaft, 'Identity in World History: A Postmodern Perspective,' both in Philip Pomper, R. H. Elphick, and Richard T. Vann, eds., *World History*, 159–96; Judith Zinsser, 'Technology and History: The Women's Perspective: A Case Study in Gendered Definitions,' *World History Bulletin* 12 (1996), 2, 6–9; Ida Blom, 'World History as Gender History: The Case of the Nation-State,' in Stein Tønnesson, J. Koponen, Niels Steensgard and Thommy Svensson, eds., *Between National Histories and Global History* (Helsinki: Finnish Historical Society, 1997), 71–91; and Sarah S. Hughes, 'Gender at the Base of World History,' *The History Teacher* 27 (1994), 417–23; all reproduced in Ross E. Dunn, ed., *The New World History: A Teacher's Companion* (Boston, Mass.: Bedford St. Martin's, 2000), 446–76.
47. M. Morris, 'Sexing the Survey: The Issue of Sexuality in World History Since 1500,' *World History Bulletin* 14 (1998), 11–20. See also Peter N. Stearns, 'Social History and World History: Prospects for Collaboration,' *Journal of World History* 18, no. 1 (2007), 45.
48. Ruth Roach Pierson, 'Introduction,' in Ruth Roach Pierson, Nupur Chaudhuri, and B. McAuley, eds., *Nation, Empire, Colony*, 2.
49. Deborah Smith Johnston, Review of *Experiencing World History*, *Journal of World History* 14, no. 1 (2003), 89.

REFERENCES

BENTLEY, JERRY H. *Shapes of World History in Twentieth-Century Scholarship*. Washington, D.C.: American Historical Association, 1996.
DUNN, ROSS E. 'Gender in World History,' in Ross E. Dunn, ed., *The New World History: A Teacher's Companion*. Boston: Bedford St. Martin's, 2000, 441–2.
HOBBS, C., ed. *Nineteenth-Century Women Learn to Write*. Charlottesville, Va.: University Press of Virginia, 1995.
HUGHES-WARRINGTON, MARNIE. 'World History,' in M. Spongberg, B. Caine, and A. Curthoys, *Companion to Women's Historical Writing*. Basingstoke: Palgrave Macmillan, 2005, 611–17.
MANNING, PATRICK. *Navigating World History: Historians Create a Global Past*. New York: Palgrave Macmillan, 2003.
POMPER, PHILIP, R. H. ELPHICK, and RICHARD T. VANN, eds. *World History: Ideologies, Structures, and Identities*. Oxford: Blackwell, 1998.
SMITH, BONNIE. *The Gender of History: Men, Women, and Historical Practice*. Cambridge, Mass.: Harvard University Press, 1998.

SPONGBERG, M. *Writing Women's History since the Renaissance*. London: Palgrave Macmillan, 2002.

STUCHTEY, BENEDIKT, and ECKHARDT FUCHS, eds. *Writing World History, 1800–2000*. Oxford: Oxford University Press, 2003.

TEAGUE, F., and R. DE HAAS. 'Defences of Women,' in *A Companion to Early Modern Women's Writing* (ed. A. Pacheco). Oxford: Blackwell, 2002, 248–63.

WIESNER-HANKS, MERRY, *Gender and History*. Oxford: Blackwell, 2001.

——. 'World History and the History of Women, Gender, and Sexuality,' *Journal of World History* 18, no. 1 (2007), 53–67.

WOODBRIDGE, L. *Women and the English Renaisssance: Literature and the Nature of Womankind, 1540–1620*. Urbana, Ill.: University of Illinois Press, 1984.

ZINSSER, JUDITH. 'And Now for Something Completely Different: Gendering the World History Survey', *Perspectives* 34 (May/June 1996), p. 11.

——. 'Gender', in *Palgrave Advances in World Histories* (ed. Marnie Hughes-Warrington). Basingstoke: Palgrave Macmillan, 2005, 189–204.

CHAPTER 12

RELIGIONS AND WORLD HISTORY

ZVI BEN-DOR BENITE

WHEN Samuel Purchas (1575?–1626) embarked on the monumental project of writing the world's history and geography, he named it 'Pilgrimages': *Purchas, his Pilgrimage; or, Relations of the World and the Religions observed in all Ages* (1613).[1] Purchas's initial approach to world history was simply 'observing' all the world's religions. The project grew to encompass much more, but the idea of 'pilgrimage' remained prominent. Perhaps the most systematic early modern writer of global history, Purchas saw world history and religion as inseparable. First, world history—both as a history of the globe and as the history of humankind—was at heart the history of its religions. Second, the writing of world history itself appeared to Purchas as a religious act of sorts, a form of 'pilgrimage.' Purchas's word, 'observing,' serves also as reminder of one of the hard truths about modern discussions of religions: many of the world's religions came to be defined as such through the ongoing process of Western observation of them over the past centuries. That process began just a few decades before Purchas's time. We should also remember that for the average early modern Christian European, having a religion was the quintessential mark of humanity. The 'savages' in the Americas, for instance, first appeared to Europeans as not 'fully human' partly because they seemed to lack 'religion.' Indeed, one of the first questions that Europeans asked upon encountering a 'new' group of people was what their religion was—both in terms of beliefs and in terms of ceremonies and rites (the latter an interest that has left a lasting mark on Western anthropology to this day).

Classifying and identifying religions, and classifying and identifying humans mainly through their religious identity, is an ancient practice. Religious texts and institutions often identify 'Others' through classification of their religions; 'secular' institutions do so, too. The Greek historian Herodotus detailed the religious practices of the peoples whose histories he narrated. Indeed, it was their religions that in large part defined them as identifiably different peoples. In the ancient world, there was a strong correlation between locale and religious practices. The Bible tells us that when the

Assyrians exiled people to the land of Israel after conquering it, they had trouble maintaining social stability because the newcomers' religious practices did not 'agree' with the local deity (YHWH). The Assyrians had to bring back one of the Israelite priests, whom they had exiled elsewhere, to teach the newcomers how to practice the new religion of their new land.[2] The ancient Persians managed their large and diverse empire by encouraging its different groups to practice their own religions freely—a system that entailed classifying people according to religious practices. Famously, as part of this effort, in the late sixth century BCE the Persians ordered the restoration of the Jewish temple in Jerusalem. The Romans had a sophisticated way of 'ranking' the numerous religions and practices they encountered in their empire. Early Christians suffered persecution because their religion was considered suspect by the Romans because it was 'new' and unknown to them.[3] The Talmudic tractate *Avodah Zarah* (Hebrew for 'foreign worship'), of late antiquity, begins with a detailed description of various peoples and their religious practices and holidays. In sum, one of the most important ways in which humans were identified and classified by one another was through religion and religious practice. In this regard, among others, inasmuch as world history is also human history, one of its most important and constant factors is religion.

Religions are often presented as a universal human experience, yet there is in fact no universal definition of religion. In some cultures a religion is more a system of faith or of thought or philosophy; in others a set of practices; in yet others a combination of all these elements. One critic of the study of religion is right in declaring, 'there cannot be a universal definition of religion, not only because its constituent elements and relationships are historically specific, but because that definition is itself the historical product' of processes involving the observation and study of religions.[4] The subject and frame of inquiry alike are creations of a specific set of historical circumstances. And we are constantly reminded that the very concept of 'religion' comes from the eighteenth-century Enlightenment. The first 'religion' was Christianity—St Augustine was probably the first to define it as such. If one binding definition of 'religion' is possible (this author thinks not), then it applies only, maybe, to Christianity, the 'world religion' that came into existence at the same time as the very term. This implies that everything else that in varied contexts we call 'religion' is not, and cannot be, a religion in the strict sense of the word. Such quibbles and debates about what religion is are endless, and in fact have become part of the history of study of religion over the last century.[5]

There is also sharp contrast between the ease with which one talks about, say, Islam (or any other 'faith') or 'religious people' (those who in some way are linked to that faith) and the difficulty in defining these terms.[6] Disputes about the exact definition of each religion are even more persistent, and involve outsider observers and insider practitioners alike. Debates about, for instance, what Hinduism is, or who is a 'true' Muslim are an integral part of these traditions as well as the scholarly discussion about them. In the process of defining itself, any religion must also define what it *is not*. Finally, in most cases religions do not usually refer to themselves as 'religions.' For instance, you will find the word 'Judaism,'—commonly thought to be the name of the

'Jewish religion'—far more frequently in discussions *about* this religion than in Jewish religious texts (particularly pre-modern ones). One could make a similar statement about many other religions as well. The act of identifying and assembling doctrinal texts, beliefs, practices, and rituals and labeling them religion or assigning the suffix 'ism' to them, is more often than not the act of an outsider—a modern scholar in many cases. It is, therefore, more useful to discuss the role in history of various forms of human organization, practices, and ideas that we associate with religions than it is to talk about religions *per se*.

Experienced world historians have learned to be prudent about making such generalizations. But, at the very least, we can talk in many cases about 'widely prevalent patterns' associated with religions spread across many areas in the world.[7] This perspective is important for the world historian: not because world historians write about the history of the 'whole world' (which they do not) should they look at 'universal phenomena.' This perspective is important because the world historian is, by definition, above all interested in identifying connections across borders of various sorts. Religions in world history are one of the most significant phenomena testifying to interactions and connections—military, commercial, cultural, political, and other—between regions, civilizations, empires, tribes, and other collectivities.

All that said, it is impossible to narrate—to 'observe'—every religion in the world. For that, one would need an encyclopedia such as Purchas's, or perhaps the *Dictionary of all Religions* which appeared as early as 1704, brought out by none other than Daniel Defoe—himself careful to note that religions have history: 'There has been no religion (that I know of) upon Earth . . . which hath not been subjected to alterations, Division, Sects and Heresies.'[8] Aside from *having* histories, religions have *shaped* world history in significant ways, both in terms of 'what happened' and in terms of the ways that history was conceived and written. Religions have had a decisive and everlasting impact on the way in which the 'world' and 'worldly time'—the two most basic building blocks of any continuum assumed for world-historical writing—are understood and conceived. That is why this chapter speaks of religions *and* world history. Without the concept of religion, world history is impossible. Religion, writ large, enables, charges, and challenges the writing of world history. Likewise, the history of the world is not complete if a significant component is not dedicated to religions.

For the past millennia, more often than not, humans all over the globe were grouped together and identified as members of a specific religion. Religions played a key role in defining other entities of world-historical significance: civilizations and even nations have been framed largely by religion. Religious encounters have reshaped world history numerous times. The current geography of Europe owes much to the Reformation wars of the early modern period. If one is to follow Pope Benedict XVI on the matter, Europe owes much, if not everything, of its identity and place in history to Christianity. The contemporary political and cultural geography of Africa was largely determined by its religious history[9]—the creation of the first Christian polity in history in Ethiopia, the Islamization of North Africa, the conversion to Islam and Christianity of major portions of the population in sub-Saharan Africa (the legacy of which can be seen in many of the civil wars raging in Africa today). The image of Asia owes much to the Islamic conquests and expansion from the seventh century CE, of which the complicated position of Turkey vis-à-vis Europe and the European Union is a constant reminder. Similarly, Buddhist expansion shaped regions such as East Asia and Southeast Asia. Indo-China as both Indian and Chinese is due not only to the borders of these two countries, but also the history of Buddhism in the peninsula as observed by the French. Hinduism played a key role in defining India and the subcontinent. Indeed, religion and its close associate 'spirituality' are what often define India in Western eyes.

Religions not only define real territories but shape the histories and geographies of languages. Languages developed and migrated in some significant cases through religious activity. Most of the surviving documents of the ancient languages are religious texts. Most, if not all, literate people in human history until very recently were clergy of sorts; literacy was closely connected to religious education. Many ancient texts survived because they were considered 'sacred.' Almost all the ancient literature of India is religious text of one sort or another. The earliest Chinese writings are found on divination tools. Sanskrit is used today mainly in religious contexts. The chronicles of the kingdom of ancient Israel, which were no doubt written, did not survive. We know they existed, however, because the scribes of the temple in Jerusalem incorporated portions of them into the biblical narrative they produced for religious purposes. Much later, Latin was granted new life after the fall of the Roman Empire when Roman Catholicism made it its main religious language. It is used today almost exclusively in religious context. Hebrew existed in the pre-modern world mostly in religious text. Arabic was never written before the Qur'an and it spread beyond the Arabic world only because it is the holy language of Islam. Islamic cultures that resisted Arabic as their language, such as the Persians or the Turks, still adopted the Arabic script. The person who, according to tradition, introduced writing to Russia was a Greek monk who also introduced Christianity. Oftentimes the very first printed text in a given language is a translation of the Bible, undertaken by missionaries. There are countless world-historical linkages between languages and religions.

One of the most enduring outcomes of encounters or clashes between polities, civilizations, and cultures, is religion. The long process of exchange, war, and trade between ancient Egypt and Mesopotamia produced biblical monotheism—perhaps the most potent religious idea in world history. The Bible is explicit that the first monotheists, embodied by the image of Abraham, were nomads travelling between Mesopotamia and Egypt. These great ancient civilizations no longer exist, but more than half of humanity today defines itself, one way or another, as the 'children of Abraham.' This came to be through numerous encounters between biblical monotheism and, among others, Hellenism and Greek culture, Persian and Central Asian cultures and religions, pre-Christian European religions, and pre-Islamic Arabian religions. Similarly, the long transformation of Buddhism from a Sanskrit Indian religion to an East Asian religion owes much to the long-lived trade and communication routes between India and China and the peoples—most notably Tibetans—who inhabited them. It is not incidental that one of China's most important travel epics, *The Journey to the West*, is framed around a Chinese monk going to the West to bring Buddhism.[10] The 'Buddhist assimilation of China,' as one scholar once called this process, produced numerous new variations and inflections, and entirely new religions. The famous Zen/Chan Buddhism, an amalgamation or syncretism of Daoism and Buddhism, is one example. Nichiren Buddhism, a specifically Japanese version of the religion, is another.[11] Later on, encounters, migration, and trade played a decisive role in the spread of Islam in Asia, the Indian Ocean, and Africa after the initial conquests. Within Islam, Sufism and Sufi culture benefited a great deal from the encounter between Western Islamic and Eastern Indian tradition and practices. Sikhism is in part the product of the encounter between Islam and Hinduism in early modern India. Much later on, the (unhappy) encounter between West Africans, Europeans, and Native Americans in the Caribbean basin and South America produced a whole range of new religions such as Voodoo and what can be classified broadly as Afro-Brazilian religions. In North America, Christianity and African slave culture gave rise to a whole range of new black denominations and theologies. Attempts to 'recover' African religious memory gave rise in the twentieth century to a distinct version of African-American Islam, or to groups such as the Black Hebrews. The encounter between Europeans and Native Americans was crucial in the rise of Mormonism. And 'recovered' Native American religions now enjoy great popularity among White Americans.

It is safe to say that as long as human encounters continue, new religions will keep emerging, and old religions will keep changing.

THE UNIVERSALITY OF RELIGIONS

It would probably be wrong to assume that cultural and social phenomena related to what we call religion have always existed in every corner of the world. Yet religion seems to be a universal phenomenon. More precisely, discussion about religions since early Western modernity tends to speak of them in universal, 'all-over-the-world' terms; Defoe's views are just one example. Contemporary scholarship on religions, more sophisticated and cautious about applying Western categorizations to global human phenomena, seems nevertheless in several regards to be in agreement with the notion of universality.[12] Karl Jaspers coined the term 'Axial Age' to describe a supposedly all-encompassing development in thought, the world over, between the years 900–200 BCE. Most, if not all, of its features could be associated with religions that shape the world to this day.[13]

Up-to-date thinking about religions often invokes their relationship to world history in ways that resemble Purchas's original approach. The recent *Cambridge Illustrated History of Religions*, edited by an eminent scholar, begins: 'There is no known society in which religion has not played a part, and frequently a controlling and creative part. This seems to have been true of the earliest societies.'[14] Another recent encyclopedia of world religions, this time a product of a large team, makes the same argument in the reverse order. Moving from the plural 'world religions' found in the title to the unifying one universal, it opens: 'Religion has been one of the great uplifting and unifying forces of human history.'[15] It is interesting to compare these statements to one of the earliest encyclopedic projects dealing with religions, the famous *Dictionary of All Religions and Religious Denominations: Jewish, Heathen, Mahometan, Christian, Ancient and Modern*, published in 1817. From the title, we learn that in the view of the nineteenth-century West, there were only four religions—Christianity, Islam, Judaism, and 'heathen' (what might today be termed 'paganism'). Today, almost 200 years on, we have many others—a string of 'isms' from A to Z. Not only are new religions born every day in different parts of world, the process of *identifying* and classifying certain practices, ideas, and beliefs as religions is expanding as well. The category of religion itself becomes more and more flexible over time. What in the early nineteenth century were grouped together as 'heathen' religions, now receive a more respectful treatment, classified separately as, say, 'indigenous Religions,' and so on. This process is of course not smooth. Take for instance the endless debates as to whether Confucianism is a textual classical tradition, a religion, or a system of faith. The history of this debate dates back to the first encounter between Western observers—sixteenth-century Jesuits, who were, as it were, quite religious—and the Chinese Confucian Mandarins.

But whatever the precise definition, religions, writ large, cover the inhabited earth. That alone makes them crucially important for the study and writing of world history.

RELIGIONS AND THE POSSIBILITIES OF WORLD HISTORY: TIME, SPACE, PEOPLE

When Rashīd al-Dīn (1247–1318) began writing his *Universal History*, one of the greatest early world history projects, he started 'small.' This Jewish polymath who converted to Islam first set out to write the history of the Mongol ruling dynasty up to his time. He ended up endeavoring to write the history of the world since Adam,[16] significantly, setting his starting point on a single father of humanity. A single human parent, or 'first human,' most often a very basic cornerstone in religions, is not exclusive to monotheist religions. Australian mythology speaks of the first couple Wurugag and Waramurungundi. Chinese tradition holds that Pangu emerged out of the 'cosmic egg' formed after the initial stage of chaos that characterized the universe. The goddess Nuwa made humans by mixing Pangu's sweat with mud. The Hindu Mahabharata tells of Manu, out of whose 'race have been born all human beings.' Shinto religion focuses on Jimmu Tenno, the first direct descendant of the sun goddess Amaterasu. These first humans serve as the starting point in the numerous histories of humanity that have been produced over the past millennia. They still resonate, even if at some stage in history's progression they have been invalidated or replaced.

So religions have shaped the writing of world history in three related keys: they have enabled world history, shaped global (or cosmic) times, and drawn and redrawn global maps. Each of these processes has occurred too many times to count and certainly more times than human records contain—many were never written in the first place, or were, but were subsequently destroyed or forgotten. The very possibility of world history is intimately connected to sets of ideas associated with religion—most prominent among them are what we call cosmologies, stories that explain the origins of the world and historical time. The earliest and most potent definitions of time first appeared as integral to religious thinking. Whether linear as in the Judeo-Christian-Islamic tradition, or cyclical as in many Asian, African, and Native-American traditions, religious conceptions of time have had an everlasting effect on the way in which history, including world history, has been conceived, conceptualized, and written. As is well-known, even modern-day 'secular' understandings of world history owe their structure to religious conceptions. Think for instance of the famous notion of the 'end-of-history,' which is in fact a secularized version of the religious notion of the 'end-of-time.'[17]

More importantly, cosmologies, particularly those that center on the creation of the world, define the very basic box, or vessel, within which world history occurs. The range of definitions for that vessel stretches from the big piece of cheese for which Carlo Ginzburg's famous sixteenth-century miller, Menocchio, got into a world of trouble, to Bruce Mazlish's 'Space-ship Earth.'[18] Most religions, certainly those that have had a strong impact on world history over the past few millennia, rest on cosmologies that define the world and its time.

Texts and ideas that we call today religious or sacred identify the origins of the world and the beginning (and sometimes also the end) of time. In many respects 'big ideas' about the world and time tend to be become sacred even if in origin those ideas are secular. These ideas set and define the space and time that constitute the world, and oftentimes charge them—and human existence—with meaning and a sense of purpose. Indeed, they are themselves a form of world history.

The most ubiquitous example is, of course, the biblical cosmology, most notably the first chapters of the book of Genesis. Far from being only Jewish or Christian or Islamic or Monotheistic, Genesis is best viewed as documenting numerous converging ideas and stories from various ancient sources, many of them unknown. It provides us with an all-encompassing narrative of world history in its various manifestations. Genesis presents a world history as 'big history'—that is, the writing of history within large-scale periods, using the broadest approach possible concerning the question of what constitutes an historical event. Big history brings the natural and environmental strongly into the fold of world history. Genesis explains how the universe itself came to be, fixing its beginning in one single point in time and telling how our solar system was created. It proceeds to tell how the earth was covered with waters, lands, plants, animals, and, finally, human beings. Its author(s) also explain(s) the beginning of human civilization—the eating of the fruit of the tree of knowledge and the expulsion from paradise; the making of tools; man being cursed with work—and the agricultural revolution and origins of urbanization. We learn about these axial moments in human history through Genesis' presentation of the drama of Cain and Abel. We also learn about the origin of language, and why there are different languages (as in the story of the Tower of Babel). Finally, we learn about the creation of nations all over the world, and of human migrations between then.

The intimate connection between this narrative and contemporary big history is evident. Consider recent world history titles such as Jared Diamond's big books on human civilizations, which cover no less than the past 20,000 years.[19] Modern, scientific, and secular, these books are of course quite different from the story of Genesis, but they are written in a dialogue with the ancient narrative and take up its great themes: the beginning of human history, the birth of civilizations, and the agricultural and other revolutions that made them possible. In the introduction to his book, David Christian, one of the world historians most engaged with big history, readily acknowledges the connection between creation myths such as the one contained in Genesis and his field:

> creation myths provide universal coordinates within which people can imagine their own existence and find a role in the larger scheme of things . . . as the Genesis story is within the Judeo-Christian-Islamic tradition . . . *Maps of Time* attempts to assemble a coherent and accessible account of origins, a modern creation myth.[20]

In other words, though modern, scientific, and secular, global histories take their inspiration from ancient narratives such as Genesis, at least in their aspiration to the tell a 'big story' about the world.

Genesis stresses the relationship between work and key initial moments in the development of human civilization on earth. All contemporary world historians consider the beginning of work, the use of tools and fire, as crucial moments in human history. Indeed, if there is a real distinction between history and prehistory it is probably located in between such key moments.[21] Interestingly, as humans observe the multiple sets of environmental woes threatening our planet, old tropes such as the hostility and suspicion expressed in Genesis towards human civilization resonate in big history studies today. Recall that in Genesis, knowledge and work come to the world in the context of sin and punishment. The first farmer, Cain, murders his brother after God rejects his offering, produced by tilling the land. After the murder and the punishment that follows, Cain builds the first city.

The *Dao De Jing*, a founding text in Daoism that preaches extreme avoidance of interfering with the Cosmic Dao and with nature, says that the smart ruler keeps his subject ignorant and inactive: 'When there is this abstinence from action, good order is universal.'[22] Hesiod taught already in the eighth century BCE that human work displeased the gods. Prometheus was punished by Zeus for stealing fire and giving it to mortals.

He is not the only one who steals fire from the gods and, thus, ignites human history. A large number of African, Polynesian, and Native American religions have similar myths in their arsenal.[23] Also in this way—suspicion of the impact of civilization on the once-pristine world—religious thinking about the world oftentimes intersects with contemporary world history. In short, the old sacred stories are, in many respects, world histories.

But the intersections between sacred texts and ideas and contemporary world history are not always evident. Consider a cosmology that did not come to dominate the world, yet is closely connected to world-historical debates today. Many Native American 'emergence myths' hold that humans are 'Earth-Surface-People' that emerged from the 'underworld' to the earth's surface.[24] This cosmology suggests that humans, thus, did not come to the Americas 10,000–35,000 years ago through the Bering Strait. This interesting conflict made its way to the front page of the *New York Times* when the Zuni openly challenged the view that humans migrated to the Americas. 'Even though no human burial [ground]s' were involved, the 'Indians' viewed archeological research seeking to find more evidence of that migration as 'sacrilegious.'[25] In a similar vein are debates between creationists, advocates of 'intelligent design,' and proponents of evolutionary theory as to which of these big history narratives ought to be taught in schools.

The point here is not to adjudicate between conflicting ideas and theories, but to show how religious narratives and world history are intertwined despite, like other historiographies, being secular in nature. Ironically, Western debates about the origins of Native Americans were themselves for centuries dominated by religious (biblical) thinking. The encounter with peoples not 'accounted for' by the sacred text posed major theological problems for Europeans, and gave rise to a vast new edifice of religious thinking and even to a new religion—Mormonism.[26] One of the fastest-growing religions worldwide, Mormonism is based on a theology stemming from one of the most quintessential and debated world-historical questions: how did humans come to America? It does so by using one of the most potent utensils in the religious toolkit—revelation. Modern science and history provide a scientific solution to the question of the inhabitation of the Americas; Mormonism presents scripture of angelic source to do the same.

RELIGIONS AND THE INTERPRETATION OF WORLD-HISTORICAL EVENTS

Revelation, the supernatural disclosure of the hidden reasons behind worldly phenomena, is often invoked in the context of world-historical events of political significance. Rulers have been particularly fond of the use of revelation for establishing their own legitimacy—the claim that, as George W. Bush succinctly put it, 'God is on our side.' Chinese rulers beginning with the early Shang Dynasty (seventeenth to eleventh centuries BCE) based their rule in part on a mysterious connection to Shang Di, or 'Lord on High.' Their successors, the Zhou Dynasty (eleventh to third centuries BCE), introduced Tian (Heaven), and designated the emperor Tianzi, or 'Son of Heaven,' a title held by all subsequent rulers until the collapse of the empire in 1911. Similarly, the idea of the Mandate of Heaven was used in China in order to justify, or delegitimize, a ruler or a whole dynasty. The mere fact that someone had ascended to power was a sign of divine approval. When heaven did not approve of a certain ruler's actions, it sent signs: social unrest and natural phenomena such as floods and earthquakes were interpreted as signs of Heavenly approval or disapproval of imperial policy.

In the West, Assyrian rulers of the ancient Near East insisted that their empire (tenth to seventh centuries BCE) was enabled, expanded and guided by divine forces. Many of the titles held by Assyrian rulers—'King of Kings,' for instance—became titles of the central biblical divinity. When the great Persian ruler Cyrus (559–530 BCE) conquered much of Western Asia and the Near East, he proclaimed that the deity Marduk, King of Gods, had declared him 'ruler of the world' after 'scanning all countries' in search of a righteous leader. In the Biblical book of Ezra, it is the God YHWH, not Marduk, who gives the world for Cyrus to rule. Intensive imperial activity in the ancient Near East helped convince the local rulers of a small kingdom in southern Palestine, Judea, that they were the Messiahs. Many in the world to this day await the return of the progeny of the Davidic dynasty to his capital, Jerusalem. The messianic idea has become a code for the desire to see a major transformation sweep the world. Later rulers—from Alexander the Great to Augustus and many others—were deified or depicted as messengers of God(s). Their political careers were not only framed and interpreted by the relevant religious concepts of time, they also became crucial moments in the development of new religions. The ascendency of Constantine the Great (272–337 CE) in the Roman Empire is probably one of best examples world history can provide. Christianity, until then a persecuted and suspect Mediterranean religion, was presented as the reason behind Constantine's military success—and benefited a great deal from it. Similarly, the institutionalization and expansion of Buddhism was immensely enabled by the great Indian emperor Asoka (304–232 BCE), who embraced it after creating his huge empire.

This relationship between religion and world empires was again transformed with the appearance of Islamic imperial rule in the seventh and eighth centuries. Early Islamic successes in the battlefield were interpreted as signs of divine approval for the mission to spread Islamic rule and justice (though not necessarily Islam *per se*) through the world.

The list of world-leaders, or aspirants, who have assigned religious significance to their careers continues down to twentieth-century dictators and perhaps even to certain twenty-first-century democracies.[27]

It is important to emphasize the shared or 'symbiotic' nature of religious interpretations of events of world-historical significance. Different religions converge in the view that a given event has great significance, even if their precise interpretation of it differs. Cyrus's proclamation is one example. The Mongol claim that Sky God gave them the earth to rule was accepted and corroborated by subordinated Daoist monks, Muslim clerics, Nestorian Christian merchants, and even Jewish rabbis. These people interpreted Mongol success in the thirteenth century as affirmation of their own sacred texts, which predicted the coming of a world conqueror such as Genghis Khan, even at the same time that the Mongols viewed his successes as confirming their *own* religio-political views. Depending on the worldview of the beholder, then, the Great Khan was seen either as a positive messianic figure, or as the 'Rod of God' coming to punish the wayward believers for their sins.

World-historical events of great magnitude tend to be interpreted as revelatory moments of profound religious significance—from multiple points of view, by multiple different groups—and the histories of those events are oftentimes written and understood within a framework that we can call religious. This is true even in the case of secular (and utterly ungodly) entities such as the Nazi Third Reich. The religious aspirations behind the notion of the '1000-years Reich' are relatively well known. And historian Saul Friedlander has recently advanced the theory of 'Redemptive anti-Semitism,' which he argues characterized the specific strand of German anti-Semitism heralded by the Nazis. By his argument, Nazi anti-Semitism became a religion in and of itself in the sense that it advanced the idea that the redemption of the German people (and of humanity) entailed the annihilation of the Jews.[28] Of course, the holocaust—the word itself means a 'sacrifice that is completely burned on the altar'—brought in its wake major theological transformations in many parts of the world.

So too other events of world-historical significance. Historians today recognize that Columbus assigned great religious significance to his discoveries, and that the voyages that became a hallmark of the beginning of modernity were, to a certain extent, driven by religious motivations. The discovery of the Americas itself was interpreted by many in his day (and after) as a religious event, most notably by Jews and Christians in Europe.

However, the coming of the white man to the Americas was interpreted as religious not only by Europeans. Famously, in some cases Native Americans viewed the appearance of white men at their shores as a divine or supernatural sign according to their own religious beliefs. Hernán Cortés was identified as the returning god Quetzalcoatl upon his arrival in Mexico. Captain James Cook (1728–79), who during an earlier visit to Hawai`i was treated nicely by the Hawaiians, was upon his return murdered for no apparent reason. This mystery gave rise to a heated debate among scholars during the 1990s. According to one interpretation, the British explorer was killed because of religious reasons having to do with his identification by the Hawaiians as the god Lono. According to anthropologist Marshall Sahlins, this identification was fatal, since it brought Cook into the ritual cycle of Hawaiians: after Cook left the island, he was not supposed to return at the time that he did. As Lono, his life had to proceed according to ritual. According to a different interpretation presented by anthropologist Ganaanth Obeyese-kere, Cook did indeed become a god: but his apotheosis was the result of Western mythical thinking and not any thinking on the part of Hawaiians.[29] The reader may choose either side in this heated debate that has divided historians and anthropologists for over a decade now. But either way, religion seems to be highly important if we wish to understand one of the most interesting episodes of the 'age of sail.'

To this day, religions supply an important, and very potent, tool for the interpretation of historical events. When Mao Zedong died in 1976, many in China linked it to a great earthquake that had occurred only months before. The earthquake, so it was thought, signaled that the 'Mandate of Heaven' had been taken from Mao.

Of course, religious interpretation of history is not detached from history itself. In many respects, religious interpretations of history *make* history; they frame it. When today we talk of 'holy wars,' or a 'Shiite Bomb' that could cover the face of the earth, it is not difficult to understand how our very own, present, lived history is being shaped as religious and by religions, often without our even noticing.

RELIGIONS AND GLOBAL KNOWLEDGE

Millennia after it was conjured into existence in Zhou China, the mysterious deity Tian stood as one of the most important bones of contention within the Catholic Church. What was the most 'theologically sound' way to convert the peoples of the East and South East Asia with whom Europeans had recently made contact? This Chinese version of this debate, known as the 'Chinese Rites Controversy,' is the best known. At its heart stood the Jesuit strategic claim that the Chinese rites were not in conflict with Christianity since they were not a form of idolatry. The Chinese, so the argument ran, were simply following a tradition that was 'natural' or civic, and, therefore, should be allowed to continue their practices even after conversion to Christianity. These Jesuits argued that the Chinese terms Tian and Shang Di could be used for the Christian god since they were philosophical concepts (hence the Jesuit insistence that Confucius was a 'philosopher'). The counterargument, marshaled mostly by Dominicans, insisted that the Chinese rites *were* religious in nature and that Tian and Shang Di were deities in and of themselves and the conversion of a Chinese person to Christianity should entail a total desertion of traditional practices and beliefs. The difference in positions stemmed not only from different theological approaches to Christianity among Jesuits and Dominicans, but also from their experiences in China. The Jesuits engaged mostly the 'cerebral' Confucian elite, while the Dominicans (and the Franciscans) worked mostly among the commoners who practiced Buddhism, Daoism, and a host of local Chinese religions. The very field of 'sinology,' as a branch of Western knowledge concerned with China, was born in the context of this debate— which produced thousands of pages of documentation. Neither 'side' really won, and the grand project of 'converting China' did not succeed.[30] Nevertheless, the Chinese Rites Controversy has immense world-historical significance, most notably in the accumulation of knowledge about the world that it spurred.

At the time of the Chinese Rites Controversy, missionaries were engaged in a major global effort to convert to Catholicism numerous newly 'discovered' peoples, from South America to Japan. This effort went hand in hand with the rise to global significance of the Portuguese and Spanish empires. Missionary efforts also accompanied the rise of later empires such as those of the French and British. The rise of the United States, too, was marked by the global expansion of missionary efforts. Whether or not these (often tragic) efforts were successful, they yielded immense knowledge about the world and its peoples. Virtually the entire scholarly literature about the civilizations and nature that Europeans encountered in the Americas, China, India, Japan, and parts of Africa was produced by missionaries.[31] A few examples are the great *Natural and Moral History* of the Americas by the Jesuit José de Acosta (1539–1600) and the *General History of the Things of New Spain*, by Bernardino de Sahagun (1499–1590), a Franciscan.[32] The great explorer, ethnographer, and cartographer of Central Africa, David Livingstone (1813–73), was a missionary as well.[33] Also in the nineteenth century, British and American missionaries laid the second layer of Western Sinology, producing an invaluable body of scholarship on China and Japan. The translations of Chinese Classics made by the Scottish missionary James Legge (1815–1897), for example, are still in use today. The foundations of many of the academic fields we call today 'area studies' were first laid by missionary scholars and travelers. As Jerry H. Bentley argues, knowledge production in the context of 'area studies' is closely connected to global history, and it is a major chapter in the history of globalization.[34]

The relationship between religious encounter and global knowledge is certainly most dominant in the Western tradition. However, before European hegemony, Islamic scholarship also showed a close link between religious motivations and global knowledge. As in the case of Christian missionary knowledge, Islamic learning of the world came in the context of empire. In a manner not dissimilar to the early Catholics in China after them, Muslim leaders needed to classify the religions they encountered in the course of conquest, in order to set policies and attitudes towards them. They needed to know who was a 'pagan,' and therefore had to convert to Islam, and who qualified as 'people of the book,' considered to have knowledge of god and thus not to be forcibly converted. Initially only Jews and Christians were so classified, but later some Islamic scholars agreed that adherents of Zoroastrianism could also be. Furthermore, the designation of Muhammad as the last and the greatest of the prophets created a field of study concerned with previous prophets and their societies. And the sharp distinction between the House of Islam and the world outside drove Muslims to study the history of their world and that of the Other, producing a vast body of knowledge about the world and its peoples, preserved later in such tomes as Rashid al-Din's world history. Indeed, the first systematic attempt to assess the world's civilizations was carried out by a Muslim scholar and jurist, ibn Khaldun (1332–1406). In his *Muqaddimah*—the prolegomena to his world (or Universal) history—he writes that history's 'goal is distinguished,' for it

> makes us acquainted with the conditions of past nations as they are reflected in their (national) character. It makes us acquainted with the biographies of the prophets and with the dynasties and policies of rulers. Whoever so desires may thus achieve the useful result of being able to imitate historical examples in religious and worldly matters.[35]

In other words, world history is an important tool in the hands of the religious scholar. Further important religious motivations behind studying the history and the geography of the world were the Islamic religious obligations of the Hajj (pilgrimage to Mecca) and prayer (which must be oriented towards Mecca). The creation of a huge empire outside the Arabian Peninsula made the question 'where is Mecca?' critical, and it emerged as an impetus for the study of world geography. In this regard, geography (and history, since the terms were in effect synonymous) became an Islamic intellectual tradition—part of the religious curriculum of learned men. Here figures such as the Persian polymath al-Biruni (973–1048) or the Baghdadi al-Masudi (896–956), known as the 'Herodotus of the Muslims', come to mind.[36] It is no wonder that the *Tabula Rogeriana*, perhaps the most advanced among the early world maps, was produced by the Muslim polymath al-Idrisi (in 1154).

A final example of this interplay between religion and global knowledge is the famous Islamic dictum of 'Seeking Knowledge' (Talab al-'ilm), best embodied by the proverb (probably erroneously) attributed to the prophet Muhammad: 'Seek Knowledge even unto China.' It is clear that from early on, Muslims held to the idea of travel in order to seek knowledge as constituting a religious duty.[37] Travel literature, or, in Arabic, *rihla*, became an important genre, with a wide readership across the Muslim world. It has even been suggested recently that this Islamic literature had some influence on Christian medieval travel writing as well.[38] A significant example of the genre are the works of ibn Jubayr (1145–1217), a Spanish Muslim who not only went on the Hajj, but also wrote about Baghdad and Palestine under the crusades.[39] Another is the famous *rihla* of ibn Batuta (1304–1369), a jurist from Tangiers, North Africa, who travelled from the westernmost place in Africa to the easternmost point in Asia, without which no world history course is complete.[40]

BY WAY OF CONCLUSION: PILGRIMAGE

In 1968, the Virgin Mary appeared atop of a church in Cairo. The amazing spectacle drew the attention of many in the city and the rest of the world; the image reappeared for a long while (and can still be seen on Youtube.)[41] At the time, it was speculated that the appearance had something to do with the Egyptian defeat in the 1967 war. Later on, when the great Egyptian Nasser, a Muslim, died in 1970, people said that Mary had been signaling his coming death. Here we have yet another example of how religion shapes the way one understands history. But more relevant here is the way in which the site of the appearance was transformed. Simply put, it became holy. In this regard it joined countless other sites all over the world where Mary had been seen. The Earth is dotted with them and they attract annual and frequent visitors from all over the world.

Mircea Eliade writes that for the 'religious man, space is not homogeneous; he experiences interruptions, breaks in it; some parts of it are qualitatively different from others.'[42] The Virgin Mary of al-Zaytoon marks one such interruption, one that seemed to ignore the fact that Egypt had been ruled by Muslims for 1,300 years. The face of the earth is in no way religiously homogenous. Religions have dotted it with countless sites charged with meaning and significance well before humans began interrupting it with political borders of all sorts—from the smallest African village shrine to the largest possible statue of the Buddha; from the smallest tomb of a local saint, to the largest pyramid.

Such sites are important to world history. First, they 'govern,' or even cause, human movement—of believers and in modern times tourists as well—across the world, and have done so for millennia.[43] Not only is the Earth covered with religiously significant sites, it is also covered with the roads leading to them. The sacred itineraries they trace are regional or global, depending on the significance of the holy site in question and the spread, globally, of the believers it attracts. With the intensification and diversification of migration, the sacred itineraries of the world will only become further-flung.

Moreover, these sites have a long history as do the roads leading to them. The history of holy sites and their sacred itineraries is a world history. One could tell a world history through focusing on just one. The Black Stone in Mecca has attracted pilgrims since well before the appearance of Islam. Today, the Hajj brings together people from virtually every nationality in the world. The Yonggang Grottoes that house 51,000 Buddha statues and statuettes near Datong, China, are situated near a strategic roadway linking China with Mongolia and Central Asia. In 2001, they were declared a UNESCO World Heritage Site, in part to protect the 252 caves from the effects of air pollution.[44] If one were to set about writing a history of the pilgrimage to Datong or to Mecca, one would be writing a world history—one stressing connections and interactions, trade and commerce, migration, and the environment.

I bring this chapter to a close with one specific illustration of how religions change locations on the face of the earth, charging them with meaning to create a world history of sorts, and shaping the history of the world.

The very local holy site of Mt Moriah, or the Temple Mount, in Jerusalem began thousands of years ago simply as a holy rock. We have a faint reference to its local ruler in Genesis (14:18): 'Melchizedek king of Salem . . . he was priest of God the Most High'—suggesting that some sort of a local cult existed in the mountain. Soon after, however, the Bible declares the place holy as the site of the binding of Isaac. Later on, a temple was built on the rock, and the rock itself was declared the foundation stone and the 'Navel of the World.' The designation of a certain location as the center of the world and its starting point is not unique, of course;[45] but the Rock of Jerusalem has had the greatest global impact. Over the years, it accumulated layer upon layer of holiness, significant to Jews, Christians, and Muslims; and it became the site of numerous churches, mosques and synagogues, each holy in its own right. It was where Jesus drove out the money changers, and from whence Muhammad ascended into heaven. This center of the world was the prime target of several major European military campaigns during the Middle Ages, was in Muslim hands, and then later fell back into Christian ones courtesy of the British Empire which ruled it for thirty years. After a short period under Jordanian Muslim rule, it passed to the hands of a Jewish government. Throughout the ages, it was depicted in numerous world maps as the real center of the world. It attracted countless pilgrims of all religions from the world over. Contemporary conversations about global politics identify the Temple Mount as one of the most important locations on Earth that could change world history. This 'navel' is a site of conflict about which millions, if not billions, of people feel very strongly. It could start a world war or, as the biblical prophets say, usher in an era of global peace.[46] This site, one rock, is the place where many of the aspects of the relationships between religions and world history outlined here converge and intersect. It is perhaps the most potent—if most worrisome—ongoing illustration of how and why religions matter in world history.

NOTES

1. Samuel Purchas, *Purchas his Pilgrimage: Or, Relations of the World and the Religions Observed in all Ages* (London, 1613).
2. Zvi Ben-Dor Benite, *The Ten Lost Tribes: A World History* (Oxford: Oxford University Press, 2009), 31–56.
3. J. B. Rives, *Religion in the Roman Empire* (Malden, Mass.: Blackwell, 2007).
4. Talal Asad, *Genealogies of Religion: Discipline and Reasons of Power in Christianity and Islam* (Baltimore, Md.: Johns Hopkins University Press, 1993), 29.
5. Jonathan Z. Smith, *Map Is Not Territory: Studies in the History of Religions* (Leiden: Brill, 1978); *Relating Religion: Essays in the Study of Religion* (Chicago: University of Chicago Press, 2004).
6. John C. Super and Briane K. Turley, *Religion in World History: The Persistence of Imperial Communion* (New York: Routledge, 2006), 1–16.
7. Wendy Doniger, 'Foreword' in Mircea Eliade, *Shamanism* (Princeton: Princeton University Press, 1972), xii.
8. Tomoko Masuzawa, *The Invention of World Religions, or, How European Universalism Was Preserved in the Language of Pluralism* (Chicago: University of Chicago Press, 2005), 52.
9. See for example Adrian Hastings, *The Church in Africa, 1450–1950* (Oxford: Oxford University Press, 1994); Nehemia Levtzion and Randall Lee Pouwels, *The History of Islam in Africa* (Athens, Oh.: Ohio University Press, 2000); Elizabeth Allo Isichei, *The Religious Traditions of Africa: A History* (Westport, Conn.: Praeger, 2004).
10. Wu Chenen, *Journey to the West* (Beijing, 2007).
11. Matthew Kapstein, *The Tibetan Assimilation of Buddhism: Conversion, Contestation, and Memory* (Oxford: Oxford University Press, 2000).
12. See, for example, Mircea Eliade, particularly his *Cosmos and History: The Myth of the Eternal Return* (New York: Harper, 1959); *Patterns in Comparative Religion* (New York: Harper, 1958); and *A History of Religious Ideas* (Chicago: University of Chicago Press, 1978).
13. Karl Jaspers, *The Origin and Goal of History* (New Haven, Conn.: Yale University Press, 1953); *The Great Transformation: The Beginning of Our Religious Traditions* (New York: Knopf, 2006).

14. John Bowker, *The Cambridge Illustrated History of Religions* (Cambridge: Cambridge University Press, 2002), 10; *The Oxford Dictionary of World Religions* (Oxford: Oxford University Press, 1997); *God: A Brief History* (London: DK, 2002).

15. Wendy Doniger, ed., *Britannica Encyclopedia of World Religions* (Chicago: University of Chicago Press, 2006), viii.

16. Rashid al-Din Tabib, *The Illustrations to the World History of Rashīd al-Dīn*. (Edinburgh: Edinburgh University Press, 1976).

17. Jonathan Kirsch, *A History of the End of the World* (San Francisco: HarperSanFrancisco, 2006).

18. Carlo Ginzburg, *The Cheese and the Worms: The Cosmos of a Sixteenth-Century Miller* (Baltimore: Johns Hopkins University Press, 1980). Bruce Mazlish, 'Introduction,' in Bruce Mazlish and Ralph Buultjens, eds., *Conceptualizing Global History* (Boulder, Colo.: Westview, 1993); and Bruce Mazlish, *The Idea of Humanity in a Global Era* (New York: Palgrave Macmillan, 2008), 20.

19. On scale in world history, see Patrick Manning, *Navigating World History: Historians Create a Global Past* (New York: Palgrave Macmillan, 2003), 265–73. Also see Jared Diamond, *Collapse: How Societies Choose to Fail or Succeed* (New York: Viking, 2005); *Guns, Germs, and Steel: The Fates of Human Societies* (London: Cape, 1997). Richard Manning, *Against the Grain: How Agriculture Has Hijacked Civilization* (New York: North Poing, 2004); David Christian, *Maps of Time: An Introduction to Big History* (Berkeley: University of California Press, 2004); Fred Spier, *The Structure of Big History from the Big Bang Until Today* (Amsterdam: Amsterdam University Press, 1996); Cynthia Brown, *Big History: From the Big Bang to the Present* (New York: New Press, 2007).

20. Christian, *Maps of Time*, 2.

21. Prehistory, a crucial term for both religion and world history, is itself a recent invention. See Alice B. Kehoe, 'The Invention of Prehistory,' *Current Anthropology*, 32: 4 (1991), 467–76; Peter Rowley-Conwy, 'The Concept of Prehistory and the Invention of the Terms "Prehistoric" and "Prehistorian": The Scandinavian Origin, 1833–1850,' *European Journal of Archaeology*, 9: 1 (2006), 103–30; Donald Kelley, 'The Rise of Prehistory,' *Journal of World History,*' 14: 1 (March 2003), 17–36.

22. *Dao De Jing*, trans. By James Legge, 3.3.

23. See Hartley Burr Alexander, *The Mythology of All Races 10. North American* (Boston: Marshall Jones, 1916), 310; W. D. Westervelt, *Legends of Maui—a Demigod of Polynesia and of His Mother Hina* (Honolulu: Hawaiian Gazette, 1910), 56–77; Katherine Judson, *Myths and Legends of the Pacific Northwest* (Gardners Books, 2007), 44–6.

24. Dawn E. Bastian and Judy K. Mitchell, *Handbook of Native American Mythology* (New York: Oxford University Press, 2004).

25. George Johnson, 'Indian Tribes' Creationists Thwart Archeologists,' *New York Times,* 22 October 1996, (section A, 1).

26. See for example Colin Kidd, *The Forging of Races: Race and Scripture in the Protestant Atlantic World, 1600-2000* (Cambridge: Cambridge University Press, 2006); Richard L. Bushman, *Mormonism: A Very Short Introduction* (New York: Oxford University Press, 2008); and also Ben-Dor Benite, *The Ten Lost Tribes*, 184–7.

27. See for instance, Randall Herbert Balmer, *God in the White House: A History: How Faith Shaped the Presidency from John F. Kennedy to George W. Bush* (New York: HarperOne,

2008); and Paul Kengor, *God and George W. Bush: A Spiritual Life* (New York: Harper Perennial, 2004).

28. Saul Friedlander, *Nazi Germany and the Jews,* Vol. I: *The Years of Persecution, 1933–1939* (New York: Harper Perennial, 1997), 3–112, particularly 86–7.

29. See Victor Li, 'Marshall Sahlins and the Apotheosis of Culture,' *CR: The New Centennial Review* 1: 3 (2001), 201–87.

30. For a recent study see Matthew Liam Brockey, *Journey to the East: The Jesuit Mission to China, 1579-1724* (Cambridge, Mass.: Harvard University Press, 2007).

31. David F. Lindenfeld, 'Indigenous Encounters with Christian Missionaries in China and West Africa, 1800–1920: A Comparative Study,' *Journal of World History* 16: 3 (2005), 327–69.

32. On Sahagún see Miguel León Portilla, *Bernardino de Sahagun, First Anthropologist* (Norman: University of Oklahoma Press, 2002); on Acosta see Claudio M. Burgaleta, *José De Acosta, S.J., 1540-1600: His Life and Thought* (Chicago, Ill.: Jesuit Way, 1999).

33. See Andrew Ross, *David Livingstone: Mission and Empire* (London: Hambledon and London, 2002).

34. Jerry H. Bentley, 'Globalizing History and Historicizing Globalization,' *Globalizations* 1: 1 (2004), 69–81.

35. Ibn Khaldun, trans. Franz Rosenthal, *The Muqaddimah; An Introduction to History* (Princeton: Princeton University Press, 1958), 11. On Islamic universalism and global knowledge see also Amira Bennison, 'Muslim Universalism and Western Globalization,' in A. G. Hopkins, ed., *Globalization in World History* (New York: Norton, 2002), 73–98.

36. George Saliba, *Islamic Science and the Making of the European Renaissance* (Cambridge, Mass.: Harvard University Press, 2007).

37. Richard Netton, *Seek Knowledge: Thought and Travel in the House of Islam* (Richmond: RoutlegeCurzon, 1996).

38. Ana Pinto, *Mandeville's Travels: A Rihla in Disguise* (Madrid, 2005).

39. Ian Richard Netton, ed., *The Travels of Ibn Jubayr: Islamic and Middle Eastern Geographers and Travellers: Critical Concepts in Islamic Thought* (Vol. 2. London: Routledge, 2008).

40. Ross Dunn, *The Adventures of Ibn Battuta, A Muslim Traveler of the Fourteenth Century* (Berkeley: University of California Press, 1986).

41. Youtube has about 300 different clips about the sighting. See for example <http://www.youtube.com/watch?v=dVXEh4Jzs2s>; and <http://www.youtube.com/watch?v=S_X8l9OcEDI&NR=1>.

42. Mircea Eliade, *The Sacred and the Profane; The Nature of Religion* (New York: Harcourt, 1959), 20.

43. For a recent study see P. J. Margry, *Shrines and Pilgrimage in the Modern World: New Itineraries into the Sacred* (Amsterdam: Amsterdam University Press, 2008).

44. See that at <http://whc.unesco.org/en/list/1039>.

45. Baldwin Spencer and F. J. Gillen. *The Arunta: A Study of a Stone Age People* (Oosterhout, 1969).

46. Oleg Grabar, *The Dome of the Rock* (Cambridge, Mass.: Harvard University Press, 2006).

REFERENCES

ARMSTRONG, KAREN. *The Great Transformation: The Beginning of Our Religious Traditions.* New York: Knopf, 2006.

BRAGUE, RÉMI. *The Wisdom of the World: The Human Experience of the Universe in Western Thought.* Chicago: University of Chicago Press, 2003.

CLARKE, PETER B. *New Religions in Global Perspective: A Study of Religious Change in the Modern World.* London: Routledge, 2006.

COWARD, HAROLD G. *Sacred Word and Sacred Text: Scripture in World Religions.* Maryknoll, N.Y.: Orbis Books, 1988.

ELIADE, MIRCEA. *A History of Religious Ideas.* Chicago: University of Chicago Press, 1978.

FUNKENSTEIN, AMOS. *Theology and the Scientific Imagination from the Middle Ages to the Seventeenth Century.* Princeton: Princeton University Press, 1986.

HUGHES-WARRINGTON, MARNIE. *Palgrave Advances in World Histories.* Houndmills, Basingstoke: Palgrave Macmillan, 2005.

JOHNSON, DONALD, and JEAN JOHNSON. *Universal Religions in World History: The Spread of Buddhism, Christianity, and Islam to 1500.* Boston: McGraw-Hill, 2007.

KIRSCH, JONATHAN. *A History of the End of the World: How the Most Controversial Book in the Bible Changed the Course of Western Civilization.* San Francisco: HarperSanFrancisco, 2006.

MARGRY, P. J. *Shrines and Pilgrimage in the Modern World: New Itineraries into the Sacred.* Amsterdam: Amsterdam University Press, 2008.

MASUZAWA, TOMOKO. *The Invention of World Religions, or, How European Universalism Was Preserved in the Language of Pluralism.* Chicago: University of Chicago Press, 2005.

SUPER, JOHN C., and BRIANE K. TURLEY. *Religion in World History: The Persistence of Imperial Communion.* New York: Routledge, 2006.

....

CHAPTER 13

TECHNOLOGY, ENGINEERING, AND SCIENCE

....

DANIEL R. HEADRICK

By technology, we mean the tools, artifacts, skills, and processes that humans have devised to use nature for practical purposes—from the most primitive hand-axe to the Internet. Technology has existed since the first ancestors of humans picked up the first sticks and stones. Large-scale projects requiring the cooperation and labor of many people are a relatively recent phenomenon. Megalithic structures—huge stones weighing many tons—date back 5,000 years. Creating such monuments involved a complex form of technology we will call engineering.

Technology and engineering require practical, hands-on knowledge of nature. Yet human beings have also been curious about the underlying causes of natural phenomena. For most of history, they have explained life and death or the vagaries of the weather by supernatural forces or divinities. Discovering natural explanations for physical phenomena—what we call science—began long after the first great engineering projects.

Technology, engineering, and science are intimately related. Simple technologies—for example breaking a stone to form a sharp edge or weaving a basket out of reeds—were learned by trial and error and passed on by apprenticeship. However, the engineering involved in building megalithic monuments required experience, foresight, and calculations, in other words expertise. With few exceptions, engineering has been the hallmark of complex societies ruled by governments powerful enough to conscript labor and collect taxes to pay for massive projects. Societies like ancient Egypt demonstrated their engineering skills by building pyramids, cities, temples, and palaces. The technologies at their disposal were far more varied than in earlier times, from domestic crafts like cooking and weaving to metallurgy, shipbuilding, and architecture. Since their day, technology and engineering have sometimes advanced rapidly and sometimes slowly, but have never reversed. The world we live in today is built upon millennia of experimentation and innovations.

Today's technology has moved far beyond trial and error and demands a deeper knowledge of nature than what our senses perceive. It requires science and often mathematics. If today's technology is heavily indebted to science, the obverse is also true. Science is not built on logic and mathematics alone, but requires complex and costly instruments like cyclotrons, space probes, and supercomputers. The symbiotic relationships between technology, engineering, and science are the hallmarks of the modern world.

STONE AGE TECHNOLOGIES

Between 4 and 2.5 million years ago, *Australopithecines*, hominids living in the grasslands of Eastern and Southern Africa, carried fist-size cobbles miles from the river beds where they were found, thereby demonstrating foresight as well as tool use. *Homo habilis*, who lived between 2.5 and 1.8 million years ago, learned to break pieces off stones to create choppers. With these (and other tools made of wood, bone, or animal skins that have long since deteriorated), *Homo habilis* became the first creature whose survival depended on technology. Their descendants, called *Homo erectus*, whose brains were two-thirds the size of modern humans', created more complex toolkits of hand-axes, cleavers, and bifaces, and learned to make and control fire. With these technologies they became big-game hunters and spread out from Africa to the colder climates of Europe and Asia.

None of these technologies can compare with what *Homo sapiens* (modern humans) have accomplished. *Homo sapiens* appeared in East Africa between 150,000 and 100,000 years ago. Approximately 70,000 year ago, humans entered a new era, one defined not by physical changes—the result of slow biological evolution—but by cultural changes associated with the development of language. Where the tool kits of earlier hominids had remained unchanged for hundreds of thousands of years, *Homo sapiens* created an astonishing variety of tools out of stone, bone, ivory, wood, animal skins, and other materials. Alongside objects of practical use, they also painted pictures on cave walls and made decorative objects like bead necklaces and stone carvings.

Humans spread rapidly throughout the Eastern hemisphere. They reached Australia between 55,000 and 35,000 years ago, despite the sixty-two miles of ocean separating that continent from New Guinea, the nearest land mass. We do not know what kinds of boats they used, but we know they had the skills and courage to take to the sea.

Humans also learned to survive in far colder climates than their hominid ancestors. Approximately 3300 BCE, a man, nicknamed 'Ötsi the Ice Man' by the scientists who studied his remains, died high in the Alps between Austria and Italy. We know a lot about him because the freezing temperatures preserved his body and equipment almost intact. He wore a cloak of woven grass, leather leggings, and boots stuffed with grass to protect him from the cold. He also carried a copper axe and a flint knife, a bow and arrows, a basket, and tinder to start fires.

Sewn clothing of the kind the Ice Man wore also allowed people to live in northern Europe and Siberia. From Siberia, the ancestors of Native Americans crossed a land bridge to Alaska at least 11,000 years ago. Another group of Siberians, ancestors of the Inuit or Eskimo, learned to live in the high Arctic beyond the tree line. They survived thanks to their clothing made of animal furs, their animal-skin kayaks, harpoons, and bows and arrows, and their sleds pulled by dogs. Theirs was probably the most sophisticated technology ever created by humans that relied entirely on local materials.

All of the peoples mentioned above were foragers who consumed the wild plants they gathered and the animals they killed or scavenged. To survive, Stone Age foragers had to know more about their environments, the terrain, the weather, and the local plants and animals than the most highly educated naturalist living today. They knew which plants were edible, which had medicinal properties, and which were poisonous. They knew where these plants grew, when they ripened, and how much sun and water they needed.

Some 12,000 years ago people living in the Middle East began to sow the seeds of desirable plants in favorable locations and help them grow by watering them and weeding out undesirable plants. Such gardening was probably the work of women, for most of the vegetable matter that foragers ate was gathered by women. Gradually, as the climate became drier and wild crops and animals harder to find, the inhabitants of that region relied more and more on wheat and barley, and then on lentils and peas. Similar changes took place independently in several other places in the world, such as Southeast Asia, New Guinea, West Africa, Central America, and the Andes.

Meanwhile hunters began to capture animals rather than killing and eating them on the spot. Young herd animals like goats and sheep were the easiest to capture. Their captors slaughtered the more aggressive ones but kept the tamer ones to breed. As these species slowly became domesticated, their keepers turned increasingly from hunting to herding. Later, pigs, donkeys, cattle, and horses were added to the list. Camels were the last animals to be domesticated, about 3,000 years ago.

Once humans came to rely on domesticated plants and animals for most of their food, their lives and their technologies changed dramatically. They were able to settle down and build permanent dwellings. They could create things, such as pottery and looms, that could not easily be carried from place to place. They made stone tools, but in a different way; instead of chipping stones, they polished them. We call this culture the Neolithic or 'New Stone' Age.

The Neolithic Age also saw the first megalithic monuments. To build them required not only the labor of hundreds of people over many years, but careful planning and design. The great monument at Stonehenge in England, built in the third millennium BCE, is thought to have been used as an astronomical observatory with the stones lined up with the rising sun on the solstices. Such constructions were the first works of engineering.

ANCIENT TECHNOLOGIES

The first complex societies arose in the fifth and fourth millennia BCE in Mesopotamia, Egypt, and the Indus Valley, hot dry regions along rivers where irrigation produced far greater yields than on rain-watered land. To bring water to the land required massive labor under expert supervision. Hydraulic engineers directed teams of workers to dig canals and drainage ditches and to build reservoirs, dikes, and embankments. They also devised machines to lift water, such as well sweeps (long poles with a bucket at one end and a weight at the other) and chains of buckets powered by men or animals.

Chinese civilization began in northern China and later spread to the Yangzi Valley and southern China. Along the Yellow River massive effort was required to build dikes to protect the land from periodic devastating floods. In central and southern China, mountainous regions with abundant rainfall, the challenge was to drain marshes and to build terraces on hillsides to provide more arable land. The natives of the Andes built canals to bring water from the mountains to the dry coastal plains. In the Valley of Mexico, Indians dug up mud from the bottom of shallow lakes to form raised fields; these artificial islands were so fertile that farmers could grow up to seven crops a year.

In these newly settled regions, farmers grew crops that have been staples ever since: wheat, barley, lentils, and peas in the Middle East; wheat and millet in northern China; rice in southern China and Southeast Asia; and maize, beans, potatoes, and cotton in the Americas. They also raised domesticated animals: sheep, goats, pigs, donkeys, and cattle in Eurasia; dogs and turkeys in Mesoamerica; and llamas and alpacas in South America. The result was a surplus of crops and animals that could support not only the farmers but also large numbers of rulers and priests, as well as merchants, servants, and craftsmen of all sorts. These people congregated in towns and cities. The elites used their power to undertake construction projects, such as pyramids, temples, and cere-monial centers. Some cities were carefully planned, with great palaces, rectangular blocks, aqueducts to supply water, or massive walls and gates.

Crafts flourished in farm villages and urban centers. Spinning and weaving were almost everywhere the work of women. Egyptians made linen out of flax. Mesopota-mians used the wool of sheep, while people of the Andes used that of alpacas. The Chinese learned to raise silkworms on mulberry bushes and to weave silk that could be dyed in bright colors. Cotton originated independently in India, West Africa, and the Americas. Pottery was also universal among peoples who did not need to move around. Like textiles, pottery making was mostly the work of women. Earthenware pots were used to store food and to cook.

Metallurgy had enormous political as well as technological and economic conse-quences. Copper and gold were occasionally found in nature as pure metals; the Ice Man's axe blade was of native copper. Making copper in quantity began at the same time as the first cities arose, for smelting ores required large furnaces and much fuel. In the third millennium BCE, smiths learned to mix copper with tin to make bronze, an alloy that was stronger and more resistant than either of its constituents. With bronze, they were able to make tools and weapons that were far superior to stone. Though known in many places, bronze items were so costly that only the elites could afford them.

Smelting iron requires a much higher temperature than copper or tin. In 1500 BCE, the Hittites, a people living in Anatolia, learned to make tools and weapons of iron. Once the skill of smelting was mastered, iron became cheap enough to make axe and hoe blades, plowshares, even pots and pans, for iron ores are found almost everywhere. People wielding iron axes cut down forests in India, Africa, and Europe, permitting the migration of agricultural peoples into territories originally inhabited by hunter-gatherers. Armies could be equipped with iron swords and arrow and spear heads.

The first horses to be domesticated in the third millennium BCE were too small to ride. The original harness, a strap around the horse's neck, choked the animal if the load were too heavy; hence horses were only used to pull light-weight war chariots. In the second millennium BCE, when horses were bred large enough to carry a man, cavalry replaced charioteers. Armed with iron weapons, nomadic herdsmen on horseback could attack settled agricultural peoples. Warfare between the inhabitants of complex urbanized societies and peoples they called 'barbarians' raged throughout Eurasia for almost 3,000 years.

CLASSICAL AND MEDIEVAL EUROPE

All civilizations used some form of science to aid their technology. Hydraulic engineers and architects needed geometry. Astronomy helped ancient river civilizations predict floods. Such sciences were based on observation and had a practical purpose. The Greeks, however, speculated about the causes of natural phenomena. Their male citizens had the leisure to meet in the marketplaces and debate political and philosophical ideas. Unlike other peoples, the Greeks drew a clear separation between the natural world around them and the supernatural world of the gods. They were the first to think of nature as open to human investigation and of logic and mathematics as forms of thinking.

As early as the sixth century BCE, several Greek thinkers began offering explanations for the natural world that did not involve gods and spirits. Thales was the first to suggest that the world consisted entirely of material objects and forces, hence open to human inquiry. His disciple Anaximander conceived of the world as made up of fire, water, air, and earth, and suggested that living beings arose spontaneously out of inanimate elements and evolved into the familiar species. Nature, to the early Greek thinkers, was made up of discrete parts they called atoms. Another thinker, Pythagoras, described the world in mathematical terms. His followers concentrated on the geometry of the universe, describing the heavens as composed of a terrestrial sphere, the cosmos or realm of the sun, stars, and planets, and Olympus, abode of the gods.

Not all Greek philosophers were interested in the natural world. The two most famous, Socrates and Plato, were much more interested in ideal attributes, such as truth and beauty, than in the flawed reality of the world around them. Plato's pupil Aristotle, however, bridged the gap between ideal and reality. Building upon a system of logic and a few axioms, he constructed a system of classification of natural objects and sought the causes of natural phenomena.

After Alexander the Great, the center of Greek learning shifted to Alexandria in Egypt, whose Greek rulers built a cultural center with the most complete library in the world. There, several outstanding thinkers contributed to the development of science, especially mathematics. The foremost among them was Euclid, whose book *Elements* offered proofs of problems in geometry and number theory. His follower Archimedes continued his research into numbers, defining the number *pi* and investigating the physics of fluids.

Unlike the Greeks, the Romans showed little interest in the speculative side of science, but only in its practical applications. Their civil engineers erected large buildings with arches, vaults, and domes, their stones held together with cement. They built canals and aqueducts to supply their cities with water, and they created a superb network of stone roads upon which their legions could rapidly reach any part of their empire.

Yet under the Romans, three sciences—astronomy, geography, and medicine—made significant advances. Ptolemy applied Euclid's geometry to the study of the heavens. In a book known by its Arabic title, *Almagest*, he proposed a model of the universe in which the sun and the stars rotated around the Earth. Though later proven wrong, this theory was useful to navigators and remained influential for over a thousand years. In his other major work, *Geographia*, he applied geometry to the Earth in the form of a grid of longitude and latitude, a system that is still used today.

The other major scientist of the Roman world was the physician Galen. By treating wounded gladiators, he learned about human anatomy and the functions of the organs, especially the lungs and arteries. His fame reached Rome itself, where he was appointed personal physician to four emperors. Like Aristotle's and Ptolemy's, Galen's teachings formed the foundation of learning for centuries.

When the Roman Empire broke up in the fifth century, the western half disintegrated. Many of the technologies that the Romans were famous for were lost, as was the scientific knowledge of the Greeks. The eastern half, centered on Constantinople, survived for another thousand years, but most of its lands and peoples, including the entire Middle East and North Africa, were taken over by the Arabs.

The fall of Rome may have marked a step backward in science and the humanities, but it led to several important advances in technology. Between the fifth and fifteenth centuries, innovations transformed Western European agriculture. The moldboard plow turned over the wet heavy soils of Northern and Western Europe that the Romans had never mastered. The horse-collar, a Chinese invention, made it possible to harness a horse to a plow or a heavy cart. The iron horseshoe prevented horses' hooves from wearing out on wet ground. And under the three-field rotation system, a field was planted in wheat or oats one year, in peas or other legumes the next, and left fallow the third, causing a 50 percent increase in yields. With the introduction of the stirrup and the breeding of bigger horses, European knights wearing suits of armor dominated the battlefields.

Western Europeans also built water wheels (a Mesopotamian invention) and introduced windmills (invented in Persia) to grind grain, pump water, and saw lumber. By the thirteenth century, they equipped their churches with mechanical clocks that could tell the hour even at night (when sundials were useless) or in the winter (when water-clocks froze). European technologies relied less on human labor, and more on animals and the energy of wind and water than any other culture.

ISLAMIC SCIENCE AND TECHNOLOGY

The fall of the western Roman Empire interrupted the scientific study of nature in Europe for a thousand years. It was Arabs, not Europeans, who were the true successors to the Greeks in the realm of science. The dramatic successes of their armies in the seventh and eighth centuries created an empire that absorbed the Greek-speaking world. Their conquest of Persia and the Indus Valley, though short-lived, gave them access to other sources of knowledge about nature.

The victorious Arabs encouraged the sciences, both practical and theoretical. In the early ninth century, the Abbasid caliph al-Mamun founded the *Bait al-Hikmah* or House of Wisdom in Baghdad, where scientists translated the works of the Greeks into Arabic. There, they studied astronomy and mathematics and performed experiments in chemistry and medicine. Other rulers built observatories, libraries, schools, and hospitals. Among the most famous scientists of the Arab empire were the physicians ibn Sina (known to the West as Avicenna) and ibn Rushd (or Averroes). Ibn al-Haytham (or Alhazen), called 'the father of modern optics,' was the first to write about the diseases of the eye. The origins of chemistry can be traced to experiments in *alchemy*, another word derived from Arabic. Arab mathematicians transmitted our 'Arabic' numerals and the concept of zero from India to the Middle East and from there to Europe. Our word *algorithm* is named after the mathematician and astronomer Al-Khwarizmi, whose book *Kitab al-Jabr* gave us the word *algebra* as well as the basic concepts of trigonometry.

The prosperity of the Arab empire at its height was due to their encouragement of the practical sciences. Under their tutelage, the much neglected irrigation works in Persia, Egypt, and Mesopotamia were rebuilt and extended. They introduced new crops, such as citrus fruits and cotton, from South and East Asia. Their artisans perfected the arts of ceramics and glass-making, and their metallurgists produced the world's finest steel blades. The efflorescence of Islamic science ended in the thirteenth century. Thereafter, conservative clerics and religious mystics opposed the tolerance of unusual ideas and curiosity about nature that had advanced science and technology in earlier times.

CHINESE TECHNOLOGY AND SCIENCE

Technologically, China was the world's most advanced civilization before modern times. Because the population of China was larger and denser than any other, the need to prevent floods, irrigate land, and drain wetlands led them to master hydraulic engineering from early on. Many crafts and industries flourished under the auspices of a centralized and autocratic government, especially during the Song dynasty (960–1279), the golden age of classical China. The Song introduced varieties of rice that increased the food supply, bringing prosperity to the nation. Under the Ming dynasty (1368–1644), engineers completed the Grand Canal, the world's longest, linking southern China with the capital at Beijing.

Several centuries before Europe, Chinese foundries used bellows and burned coke to produce cast iron in large quantities for the manufacture of weapons, bells, and tools. The manufacture of silk, salt, and paper, all government-controlled, reached levels of quality and quantity unknown anywhere else. Chinese potters discovered glazes that could be painted; once fired, glazed pottery was waterproof. Chinese porcelain, thin, translucent, and colorful, reached perfection under the Ming and was the envy of other civilizations. Likewise, the Chinese invented gunpowder and the magnetic compass, though they made less use of them than Arabs or Europeans.

Despite these 'firsts,' Chinese technology played a peripheral role in Chinese society and culture. Since the Han dynasty (206 BCE–220 CE), the Chinese government had created a large and complex bureaucracy recruited by examination. The examination system emphasized the study of the Confucian classics, poetry, and calligraphy and neglected engineering and science. Technicians and engineers were neither free from government control nor well respected.

Science also played a peripheral role in Chinese society and culture. The bureaucracy excelled at creating compilations of useful knowledge in cartography, seismology, meteorology, medicine, and other fields. Astronomy was a state monopoly, for it served to create calendars that set the dates for imperial ceremonies; unusual events such as comets, eclipses, and earthquakes were considered dangerous omens and descriptions of them were state secrets. Chinese mathematicians developed sophisticated arithmetic and algebra, but neglected geometry and ignored the works of Greek mathematicians that Muslims brought to their attention. The immense quantities of data Chinese scientists collected never led to speculation about nature, nor was any research done for the sake of pure knowledge. Science was neither taught in schools and academies nor included in the examinations. Like technology, Chinese science reached its peak under the Song and stagnated during the later Ming dynasty.

THE SCIENTIFIC REVOLUTION

The Scientific Revolution was not merely another advance in human knowledge, but a dramatic change in the way humans studied nature. Beginning in Western Europe in the sixteenth century, that movement brought together trends that had their origin elsewhere long before. One was the Greeks' eagerness to speculate about natural phenomena. Another was the tradition of careful observation of natural phenomena inherited from the Arabs and Persians. A third was the mathematics inherited from the Greeks and Arabs. The result was a new kind of inquiry into the causes of natural phenomena combining logical speculation, careful observations or experimentation, and the use of mathematics. We call this modern science. Many have asked why modern science originated in Western Europe, rather than in China or the Middle East, civilizations with long-standing interests in nature and in technology. Most historians attribute it to the peculiar nature of European society in the late Middle Ages. Europe was divided into many competing states, none of which had absolute power over its own people, let alone its neighbors. The Roman Catholic Church competed with the authority of kings, princes, and towns; once the Reformation began in the early sixteenth century, the Church faced religious as well as secular challenges. Scientists still faced risks, but their inquiries into the mysteries of nature were not as beholden to political or ecclesiastical authorities as in other societies. Furthermore, new ideas were widely disseminated thanks to Johannes Gutenberg's invention of printing with movable type in 1439. In contrast, scientists in the Middle East and China worked for the state or under state supervision. In neither civilization were there cities, guilds, corporations, or universities independent of governments. During certain periods like the Abbasid or Song dynasties, engineering and the applied sciences flourished under government auspices. At other times, they stagnated. In few places did governments tolerate pure speculation that might challenge the official philosophy or religious doctrine. Even in Western Europe, such tolerance was sporadic and unpredictable before the eighteenth century.

Philosophical and religious explanations have also been offered for the peculiar nature of European science. Unlike the Chinese, who thought of nature as an organic whole, Europeans inherited the Greek idea of nature as consisting of many different parts. And unlike Muslims, for whom all truth was revealed in the Qur'an and the *hadith* or sayings of Muhammad and all law derived from the Shari'a or sacred law, Christian Europeans were used to the separate spheres of church and state, hence more willing to tolerate new ideas.

Such explanations, however, neglect the importance of historical events. Chinese technology was very creative until the Song and began to stagnate during the Ming dynasty when Chinese thought turned to a revival of Confucianism. Arab-Islamic science likewise stagnated after the thirteenth century. Both developments were conservative reactions to the shock of defeat at the hands of Mongols (in China and Persia) and Christians (in Spain).

The beginning of the Scientific Revolution can be traced to the Polish priest Nicolas Copernicus. In his book *On the Revolutions of the Celestial Spheres*, he suggested that the Earth rotated around the Sun, a theory (called heliocentric) at odds with the works of Ptolemy and with the doctrine of the Catholic Church, for which the Earth, home of Christ, was the center of the Universe. After Copernicus, astronomers like Tycho Brahe and Johannes Kepler debated how the new ideas fit with celestial observations and how they could be formulated mathematically.

It was the Italian Galileo Galilei, court mathematician and philosopher to the duke of Florence, who made the heliocentric theory famous. Using a telescope invented in 1608 by the Dutch lens maker Hans Lippershey, Galileo was the first to observe the moons of Jupiter, the craters of the Moon, and the Milky Way. When he defended the heliocentric theory in this *Dialogue on the Two Chief World Systems* (1632), his work was condemned by the Inquisition, he was forced to abjure his dangerous ideas, and he was placed under house arrest.

Yet the heliocentric theory could not be suppressed. What finally convinced other astronomers was the work of the English mathematician Isaac Newton. The calculus which he invented allowed him to formulate the laws governing the motions of bodies in space and calculate the orbits of the planets. His *Philosophiae Naturalis Principia Mathematica* (commonly known as *Principia*), published in 1687, established not only the new astronomy, but the very idea that science could advance by relating theory to data and expressing the results mathematically.

In the course of the sixteenth and seventeenth centuries, educated Europeans began to see science as a source of useful knowledge that would contribute to the public good. This attitude toward science was enshrined in the founding of state-funded scientific societies, such as the Royal Society of London for Improving Natural Knowledge in 1662 and the Paris Academy of Sciences in 1666. Scientists gave learned papers, corresponded with one another, and published periodicals. Research took place in fields that could be investigated through experimentation as well as observation. William Harvey discovered the circulation of the blood and Antonie Philips van Leewenhoek used a microscope to investigate bacteria, spermatozoa, and muscle fibers.

By the eighteenth century, natural science, and Newton in particular, had become the darling of Enlightenment philosophers who used its findings in their attacks on religion and tradition. The governments of France and Britain built observatories and funded expeditions around the world, such as the French expeditions to Lapland and South America in the 1730s and 1740s, and the Pacific voyages of the Englishman James Cook (1768 to 1779) and of the Frenchman Louis Antoine de Bougainville (1766 to 1769). They established botanical gardens for the collection, study, and dissemination of useful plants; the Royal Botanic Gardens at Kew near London and the Jardin des Plantes in Paris exchanged seeds, plants, and botanical information with gardens and scientists around the world.

For centuries, mariners had known how to estimate their latitude, or distance from the poles, while out of sight of land. But their longitude, or east–west position, remained a mystery, causing several disastrous shipwrecks. In response to the British government's offer of a prize of £20,000 (over ten million dollars in today's money) for a way to calculate a ship's longitude at sea, astronomers devised a method called 'lunar distances' from the angle of the moon with another celestial body; equipped with a table of lunar distances, a trained mariner could determine the difference in time between the ship and a known place on land, and hence calculate the difference in degrees of longitude. This method was difficult to carry out and was overshadowed by the invention of an accurate marine chronometer by the clockmaker John Harrison. Though costly to make, chronometers allowed mariners to determine their longitude easily and precisely.

The Scientific Revolution led to a number of other useful technologies. Newton's calculus and his mathematical expression of the force of gravity allowed artillery officers to calculate the trajectories of cannonballs. Triangulation and trigonometry had applications in surveying and in drawing accurate maps of entire countries. Scientific experiments led to improvements in mirrors, telescopes, thermometers, and surveying instruments.

THE FIRST INDUSTRIAL REVOLUTION
(CA. 1750–1869)

The late eighteenth and early nineteenth centuries witnessed the beginnings of a new era in world history: the Industrial Revolution. Work, especially in manufacturing, was divided into distinct and simple tasks. New machines were introduced into manufacturing, transportation, and communication. Goods were increasingly pro-duced in large volume. New methods made iron cheap enough to replace wood and stone. And coal became the main source of energy.

The Industrial Revolution began in Great Britain, a nation with a large proportion of its people engaged in commerce, shipping, and finance and interested in questions of science and technology. Its government respected individual enterprise, and its patent system encouraged innovators. While Britain took part in several wars between 1776 and 1815, none were fought on British soil. Finally, Britain's indented coastline and navigable rivers made transportation cheaper than elsewhere, and its abundant coal and iron and other ores were near the surface and easy to extract.

British industrialization began with the cloth trade. Britain had long been a major producer of woolens, but cotton, a more comfortable textile, was imported from India. Import restrictions on Indian cloth but not on fiber provided an incentive to devise ways of spinning yarn. James Hargreaves's spinning jenny (patented in 1764) and

Richard Arkwright's water frame (1769) allowed one worker to supervise many spindles at once. As the cost of yarn dropped sharply, inventors devised other machines to weave, bleach, and print the finished cloth. As Britain's cotton industry expanded, it imported increasing amounts of fiber produced by slaves in America. Mechanization transformed other industries. Until the eighteenth century, ceramics, ranging from simple earthenware to fine china, were hand-made by skilled potters. In the 1760s, Josiah Wedgwood broke down the manufacturing process into simple repetitive tasks that required little training and introduced machines to stamp out identical plates, cups, and other pieces. The result was a higher quality product at a lower price than had ever been made before. Similar methods of dividing and mechanizing labor appeared in other industries, such as brewing beer, casting cannon, and milling wood.

In the early eighteenth century, Abraham Darby and his son Abraham II found a way to smelt iron with coke in place of the increasingly expensive charcoal. In 1783 Henry Cort introduced a method of puddling (i.e., mixing) molten iron to produce high-quality wrought iron at very low cost.

The most celebrated invention of the Industrial Revolution was the steam engine. In 1712, Thomas Newcomen devised the first practical machine to extract work from fire. Newcomen engines were adopted in mines throughout Britain, replacing the horses that powered chains of buckets. The Newcomen engine would have remained limited to mines, but for the insight of James Watt, a Scottish instrument maker. While working on the University of Glasgow's model of a Newcomen engine, he realized that much energy was wasted by alternately heating and cooling the cylinder. By using a separate condenser, Watt's engine consumed 75 percent less fuel than Newcomen's. With the iron manufacturer Matthew Boulton, Watt founded a firm to build steam engines. When their patent expired, inventors experimented with high-pressure engines that could be used to propel a vehicle. The American Robert Fulton was the first to build a commercially successful steam-powered boat, the *North River* (or *Clermont*) in 1807. After 1830, a railroad boom swept Britain, the United States, and continental Europe.

For centuries, people had been interested in communicating quickly over long distances. In 1794, the Frenchman Claude Chappe began building a network of telegraph towers topped with wooden beams that could signal to one another over great distances. But such networks were costly and only worked on clear days. The idea of sending a message by electricity occurred to several inventors, but the first commercially successful telegraph was the one patented by the Englishmen William Cooke and Charles Wheatstone in 1837. Though it worked well, it was soon overshadowed by the American Samuel Morse's telegraph code (patented in 1837), which required only one wire. By the mid-nineteenth century, telegraph lines crisscrossed Europe and eastern North America.

THE ACCELERATION OF CHANGE (1869–1939)

In the late nineteenth century, industrialization spread from Britain to continental Europe and North America. Its impact was felt even in the most remote corners of the world. Western nations were quick to see the commercial and military advantages that industrialization gave Britain. France and Belgium were the first to industrialize. After 1871, a newly united Germany industrialized rapidly and soon surpassed Great Britain in railroads and steel, and led the world in industrial chemicals, especially organic dyes. The United States benefited from the British experience by attracting workers and engineers from Britain. Their skills, combined with America's abundance of raw materials and voracious demand for goods of all sorts, made cotton mills, iron foundries, railroads, and machine shops profitable ventures. Russia lagged behind until the twentieth century, but after 1929, its massive manpower, abundant raw materials, and Stalin's brutal regime quickly overcame its backwardness.

Outside of Europe and North America, the results were less positive. Britain used its colonial rule over India to impede the rise of modern industries, and its steamships and modern weapons to defeat China, Egypt, and many other societies. By offering industrial products such as cotton cloth and metal goods at low prices in exchange for raw materials and tropical products like coffee, tea, and tobacco, the industrialized nations were able to delay the industrialization of Latin America and Asia by several decades. The exception was Japan, which began founding its industries soon after it ended its isolation in the 1860s and 1870s; by the 1890s, it was building its own railways, shipyards, and modern weapons.

As entrepreneurs learned to make use of the latest scientific advances, they quickly developed new technologies. In 1876, the American Thomas Alva Edison established a research laboratory in Menlo Park, New Jersey. There he hired technicians and scientists. Edison's researchers were able to apply the discoveries of physicists like Hans Christian Oersted and Michael Faraday on the nature of electricity and magnetism. The result was a spate of inventions, the best known being the phonograph in 1877 and the electric lighting system in 1879–1880.

Edison's was only one of many new industries that resulted from the close interactions between engineering, science, and business. In the 1860s and 1870s, metallurgists discovered several ways to make steel so cheaply that it soon replaced iron in the manufacture of rails and machinery of all sorts, and was even used for bridges and the framework of large buildings. Chemists unraveled the mysteries of organic chemicals to produce dyes, fibers, and pharmaceutical products from coal, and fertilizers and explosives from atmospheric nitrogen.

Science-based technologies rapidly transformed the lives of inhabitants in industrial countries. Several late-nineteenth-century inventions revolutionized communications. One was the submarine telegraph cable that transmitted coded messages to all parts of the world in a matter of hours. Another was the telephone, invented in 1876 by the

American Alexander Graham Bell. In 1895, the Italian Guglielmo Marconi demonstrated the transmission of messages by electro-magnetic waves, based on the discoveries of physicists James Clerk Maxwell and Heinrich Hertz. Soon, wireless telegraphy turned into radio able to transmit voice and music as well as dots and dashes.

Another innovation that was to change the world appeared at the turn of the nineteenth century: the automobile. Inventors had long sought to propel a vehicle by mechanical means. Steam engines were too heavy for road use. The solution was to build a carriage powered by an internal combustion engine burning gasoline. The first to build such a machine in 1885 was the German engineer Karl Benz. In 1908 the American Henry Ford introduced the Model T, the first car to be mass produced on an assembly line. The price of this simple but durable vehicle dropped every year, reaching $300 in the 1920s, a price so low that even farmers and industrial workers could afford one.

Most astonishing and eagerly awaited of all was human flight in a heavier-than-air machine. This was the achievement of the brothers Wilbur and Orville Wright. Their first powered flight in December 1903 was soon followed by other flights by the Wright brothers and their many imitators.

By the end of the first decade of the twentieth century, these and other advances in technology seemed to promise a bright and exciting future for the inhabitants of the wealthier industrial countries of the world, and even hope for the rest of humankind. Yet technology's dark side became clear in 1914, when World War I broke out. Industrialization allowed the mass production of rifles, machine guns, and heavy artillery against which soldiers had few defenses. Most horrifying were the poison gases that blinded or killed hundreds of thousands of soldiers.

POST-INDUSTRIAL TECHNOLOGY (SINCE 1939)

In the 1930s, as war approached, the major powers recruited scientists and engineers to help devise new and more powerful weapons. The results of their efforts have been felt ever since.

Since the 1920s, engineers knew that radio waves are reflected off hard surfaces and can be captured and analyzed. When World War II began in September 1939, scientists in Germany and Britain accelerated their research into this phenomenon. The resulting technology, radar, was instrumental in helping the Royal Air Force detect incoming German bombers in the summer of 1940. Radar was later used by Germany against Allied bombers and by Britain and the United States against German submarines. It has since become indispensable for airplanes and ships, and is even used in law enforcement.

In the 1930s, two engineers, Frank Whittle in Britain and Hans von Ohain in Germany, worked on the application of turbines—long used in hydroelectric power plants and steam engines—to propel airplanes. Germany was the first nation to use jet planes in combat. After the war, all the major aircraft manufacturers adopted the jet engine, not only to achieve greater speed, but also because it produced more power at lower cost than propeller engines. From the 1950s on, jets replaced piston-engine passenger planes.

To fly beyond the Earth's atmosphere, where neither piston nor jet engines could operate, required a rocket that carried both fuel and oxidizer. The idea of using rocket propulsion for travel to outer space was publicized independently by three visionary scientists: the Russian mathematician Konstantin Tsiolkovsky, the American physicist Robert Goddard, and the German physicist Hermann Oberth. During the war, the German army launched a crash program in rocket development under Wernher von Braun that built the first long-range ballistic missile, the V-2. After the war, the United States and the Soviet Union recruited German physicists to develop long-range missiles. In 1957, the Soviets placed a satellite, called Sputnik, into orbit. After that, both nations engaged in an arms race of intercontinental ballistic missiles. Since the 1960s, many nations have launched Earth-orbiting satellites, some for military purposes, others for communications, navigation, or scientific research.

Of all the technologies that emerged from World War II, none evoked as much astonishment and fear as nuclear power. Before World War I, physicists like Ernest Rutherford and Pierre and Marie Curie had been investigating the structure of the atom. In the 1930s, scientists in Europe and the United States had become aware of the power of nuclear fission. As war approached, Albert Einstein, Leo Szilard, Enrico Fermi, and other European scientists immigrated to the United States. In 1942, the United States government undertook the Manhattan Project to build atomic bombs. The first two such bombs were dropped on Japan in August 1945, ending the war. The Soviet Union exploded its first nuclear device in 1949, followed by American and Soviet hydrogen bombs three years later. The nuclear missile race did not end until the collapse of the Soviet Union in 1991.

Many countries built nuclear reactors to generate electricity. Though such plants cost billions of dollars and take years to build, they burn no fossil fuels and, when operating properly, emit no pollutants. Malfunctions, though rare, are catastrophic, as in the eruption of the reactor at Chernobyl in Ukraine in 1986. Furthermore, the uranium they consume and the plutonium some plants produce can be used to make nuclear bombs.

Overshadowing even aviation and nuclear power is a technology that has become all-pervasive: computers. During World War II, engineers in Germany, Britain, and the United States built primitive electronic computers to calculate artillery trajectories or to break enemy codes. After the war, the American IBM Corporation took the lead in building large mainframe computers for military and commercial applications. The invention of the transistor by the Americans John Bardeen and Walter Brattain of Bell Laboratories in 1947 allowed the design of much smaller but more powerful computers than the switches and tubes formerly used. By the 1970s, IBM effectively dominated the world computer market.

The introduction in the 1960s of the micro-processor (or chip) that contained hundreds (later millions) of transistors allowed the creation of personal computers. One of the most effective incentives to the spread of computers was the Internet that began functioning in the 1980s. In 1989 the Englishman Tim Berners-Lee devised the World Wide Web, making the Internet useful for research, business, and entertainment. Interconnecting computer networks across the world was facilitated by the introduction of fiber-optic cables, lowering the cost of communicating data around the world almost to zero.

One more science-based technology holds promise for the future, namely biotechnology. The scientific study of living beings began to produce important results in the late nineteenth century with the germ theory of disease. Penicillin, introduced in World War II, saved the lives of countless soldiers. The development of other antibiotics after the war helped combat bacterial infections and reduced death rates throughout the world. The introduction in the 1960s of the contraceptive pill separated sex from the risk of pregnancy and helped lower the birth rate.

More recently, advances in biotechnology have relied increasingly on discoveries in genetics. Genetics dates back to the work of the Austrian scientist and monk Gregor Mendel, who derived the laws of inheritance from his research on the transmission of genetic traits in peas. In the 1950s, Francis Crick and James Watson discovered the double-helix model of deoxyribonucleic acid, or DNA, a substance that exists in all living cells and determines how that organism is formed and reproduces. Laboratory equipment that can replicate millions of copies of DNA in a few hours permitted the creation of new varieties, even new species, of plants. Genetic engineers are now able to create crops resistant to insects, diseases, and frost. Genetically-modified crops and animals cause a great deal of anxiety, as the reproduction of living beings is certain to have unexpected consequences, possibly even ones that could endanger humans or the natural environment.

Almost all the innovations since the Industrial Revolution originated in Europe and the United States. Other parts of the world were the beneficiaries or victims of Western innovations. Before World War II, only Japan among the non-Western nations succeeded in industrializing. After the war, Japan's engineers and technicians turned toward civilian consumer industries. Within two decades, Japanese firms were surpassing their Western competitors in the quality and sophistication of their products. While discoveries and inventions continued to originate in the West, the Japanese excelled at making these innovations appealing to consumers and, thereby, captured a large part of the global market.

Recently, other East Asian countries have caught up with the West in most technologies and joined the ranks of the industrial nations. China has undertaken the world's largest engineering project, the Three Gorges Dam on the Yangzi River. India is becoming a major producer of computer software. Industrial and post-industrial technologies can spread quickly to other cultures when conditions are right. Yet, the rest of the world still lags behind. Latin America, the Middle East, the rest of Asia, and sub-Saharan Africa remain in the same position of dependency today as they were a century ago. Science and technology do not have a life of their own, but are subject to politics, economics, and cultural values.

CONCLUSION

The story of science and technology tells of humans' increasing power over nature, our ability to live healthier and more comfortable lives, to travel and communicate faster, and to transform the world. Is this a story of triumph, or 'taming the wilderness,' as nineteenth-century thinkers believed? Or are there are clouds behind the silver lining?

One risk is humans' ability to kill and destroy with increasing efficiency. Wars have been fought since the dawn of civilization, but only in the past half-century have nations possessed the power to extinguish life on Earth, and there is no guarantee that they will never use it. The other effect of technology—this one not a risk but a reality— is the destruction of the natural environment. While humans have long transformed their local environments, only since the Industrial Revolution have the effects of our technologies become global. Fossil fuels provide most of the energy to make modern civilization possible, but at the expense of the planet's climate. Today, the world faces a challenge: will we find a way to generate the energy our civilization demands without polluting the environment? Or will we damage the Planet Earth irreversibly in our pursuit of ever more advanced, and ever more damaging, technologies?

REFERENCES

BARBER, ELIZABETH W. Women's Work: The First 20,000 Years. New York: Norton, 1994.

CARDWELL, DONALD. Wheels, Clocks, and Rockets: A History of Technology. New York: Norton, 1995.

EDE, ANDREW, and LESLEY B. CORMACK. A History of Science in Society: From Philosophy to Utility. Peterborough, Ontario: Broadview, 2004.

HEADRICK, DANIEL R., Technology: A World History. New York: Oxford University Press, 2009.

HUFF, TOBY. Rise of Early Modern Science: Islam, China, and the West. Cambridge: Cambridge University Press, 1993.

MCCLELLAND, JAMES E., and HAROLD DORN. Science and Technology in World History. Baltimore, Md.: The Johns Hopkins University Press, 1999.

MOKYR, JOEL. The Lever of Riches: Technological Creativity and Economic Progress. New York: Oxford University Press, 1990.

NEEDHAM, JOSEPH. Science and Civilisation in China, 7 vols. Cambridge: Cambridge University Press, 1959–2008.

PACEY, ARNOLD. Technology in World Civilization. Cambridge, Mass.: MIT Press, 1990.

STEARNS, PETER N. The Industrial Revolution in World History. Boulder, Colo.: Westview, 1993.

WHITE, LYNN, JR. Medieval Technology and Social Change. Oxford: Oxford University Press, 1962.

CHAPTER 14

....

ADVANCED AGRICULTURE

....

KENNETH POMERANZ

'ADVANCED' agriculture must be advanced relative to something and by some criteria. There is no consensus on what those criteria are—though certainly high yields per acre, and perhaps per labor hour, would be likely choices. Meanwhile, caution about this label is not just an intellectual issue: attempts to change or remove supposedly 'backward' farmers have recurred over the last few centuries, sometimes causing catastrophes.

We might also define 'advanced' agriculture retrospectively—as whatever is more like the farming that accounts for most of today's acreage and output. Using that approach, we can list traits that are now very common, but were rare or non-existent until the last century or two. They include unprecedented yields per acre; heavy use of fertilizers, pesticides, and other inputs purchased from manufacturers; the sale of most of the farm's output (either by the cultivator or some other claimant to the farmer's output); concentration of each farm on a relatively small number of crops and crop varieties; and, in most though not all cases, much higher productivity per labor day than was common for earlier farmers. One other recent trend initially seems surprising: much lower energy efficiency than older farming methods. Some earlier farmers produced as many as ninety food calories for every calorie of energy they put in (not counting the energy of the sun); today, ratios of 2:1 or 3:1 are more common, and some very high-input kinds of agriculture in wealthy countries actually have ratios below 1:1.[1]

Some of these trends have been found around the world for many centuries (though not without reversals). Others were unusual until very recently; indeed in many regions the predominant trends were *opposite* to several of those listed above until at least 1800, or even 1950. Thus, a long-range, global perspective plays havoc with any neat teleological scheme, though a *very* long-range view—one which contrasts advanced farming to early Neolithic agriculture—might abstract away from enough history to restore such a schema.

Consequently, this chapter will distinguish between 'advanced organic agriculture'— which was commercialized, often specialized, intensive in its use of labor and/or capital, and relatively high-yielding per acre (though often not per labor day), but was not a big user of machinery or products of modern chemical industries—and 'energy-intensive agriculture,' which appeared in a few places in the 1800s, but reached most of the world only after 1945. This roughly follows E. A. Wrigley's influential, though controversial, distinction among 'organic,' 'advanced organic,' and 'mineral-based' economies.[2]

POPULATION, TECHNOLOGY, AND AGRICULTURAL CHANGE, CA. 800–1800

Agriculture was far from stagnant during the millennia before 800 CE. Some times and places achieved yields roughly matching early modern levels: some Roman treatises cite yields so high that some Renaissance Europeans doubted their accuracy, while many others preferred them to any contemporaries as guides to best agricultural practices.[3] Irrigation systems were built in numerous places. And while agricultural change is often profoundly local, there were also important transregional developments. The so-called 'Islamic Green Revolution,' beginning in the seventh century, in which Islamic expansion helped diffuse numerous crops across a vast region from South Asia to North Africa and Spain, is perhaps the outstanding example: the cultivars in question include oranges, cotton, eggplant, spinach, sugar cane, wheat, rice, sorghum, and bananas.[4] But the vast majority of agricultural growth in this period was 'extensive': it came from using additional labor to bring new land under cultivation.

Beginning around 800 CE, one sees more signs of intensification—raising output per acre, and sometimes per labor hour—at least at the ends of Eurasia. Europe began a long, slow transition from the two-field to the three-field system, reducing the amount of land being fallowed in any given year from one-half to one-third. (This shift was, however, very gradual: in parts of Eastern Europe, it was not complete until the nineteenth century.)[5] Meanwhile, Han Chinese were moving in much larger numbers into the Yangzi Valley and points further south. Sometime in the ninth century, lower Yangzi settlers became familiar with early-ripening rice varieties from Southeast Asia; this allowed them to use southern China's plentiful water and sunshine to plant more than one crop in a year on the same plot. (Abundant manure from a dense population, nutrients carried in the irrigation water for wet-rice agriculture, and other factors made fallowing largely unnecessary here.)[6] These were relatively straightforward examples of the complex relationships between population growth and more 'advanced' agriculture that would be central features of the next millennium, and remain crucial—and controversial—today.[7]

It is important not to be overly teleological. Very few places were truly short of land before 1800. (Moreover, there is no magic density at which land becomes scarce—the available crops and technology, the numbers of other large animals, the distribution of property, and other factors are all influential.) Even many places now famous for population pressure—Bengal and Java, for instance—still had abundant reclaimable land well into the 1800s; in others, especially in Africa, extensive growth remained perfectly viable until the last few decades. And it was not until the 1400s (the 1600s in the Americas, and perhaps the 1800s in Africa) that world population began centuries of sustained and unprecedented growth: it roughly doubled between 1400 and 1800, grew perhaps 60 percent from 1800 to 1900, and then almost quadrupled in the twentieth century. Still, ca. 800 CE is as good a date as any to begin the slow spread of advanced organic agriculture.

Pockets of high-yielding intensive agriculture appeared quickly, but they remained very exceptional. Some farms in Eastern Norwich—probably not coincidentally, one of the most densely populated areas of medieval England and one where an unusually large percentage of the population became free early—had attained 'late eighteenth-century levels of productivity' and greatly reduced fallowing by the 1300s;[8] their yields were more than double those elsewhere in England. Similarly, a few farms in China's lower Yangzi region already showed rice yields ca. 1200 that were not clearly surpassed until the twentieth century.[9] In both areas, agricultural progress over the next several centuries mostly involved other farms gradually approaching the yields that these farms had already attained; the average gains were crucial for early modern societies, but paltry by post-1800 standards. Yields per acre in English agriculture as a whole probably rose about 40 percent between 1300 and 1800; considerably more fragmentary data for the lower Yangzi suggest a similar gain for the rice crop (and thus somewhat more when we also consider increased double-cropping) between 1200 and 1800.[10]

Increasing yields was difficult, even with successful examples nearby. Even adjacent plots of land are irreducibly heterogeneous in ways that looms, grindstones, and so on are not; small differences in drainage, insolation, microbes, and soil chemistry can be crucial. Consequently, best practices on one plot do not automatically transfer to another and, particularly without modern chemistry, guessing what adjustments might be needed is very difficult. Weather fluctuations further complicate the learning process. Second, the rusts, insects, weeds, and other species that reduce crop yields are constantly evolving, so farmers must adapt just to avoid declining yields. Third, since few pre-modern cultivators were educated, spreading new technical knowledge could be difficult. Finally, cultivators often lacked strong incentives to increase output. Many were unfree in one way or another, and might not benefit from greater output; the elites who would benefit often lacked the capacity and/or desire to supervise farmers closely enough to impose yield-maximizing practices. (There were, of course, many efforts to give people farming for others the 'right' incentives, but such arrangements were neither fool-proof nor costless.)

Even cultivators who could keep their output might not seek to maximize it. Many had little to fall back on if their crops failed, and, therefore, focused on minimizing risk.[11] Thus, they might plant a high-yielding but drought-sensitive crop on just a small portion of their land or not at all; prefer scattered 'inefficient' plots with different characteristics to consolidated ones; prefer a crop for which their family's labor was adequate rather than one that might require using scarce cash to hire peak-season laborers; and so on. Moreover, grains in particular are not very valuable per unit of weight or volume; for people not living near navigable waterways, this meant that surpluses could only be marketed locally. For centuries, then, most high-yielding agriculture was found near cities: the lower Yangzi, the irrigated lands around Delhi and (probably) Tenochtitlan, Japan's Kinai, southern England, the Paris basin, and so on. The causation was generally reciprocal. On one hand, urban growth required agricultural surpluses, unless grain that farmers also needed could be taken by force. But urban markets also encouraged nearby farmers to increase yields per acre: further away from concentrated demand, farmers might instead devote time to non-farming pursuits and/or use land to graze livestock—which yield less than crops per acre, but require less work and can walk themselves to distant markets. Urban centers often also stimulated high per-acre yields by providing plentiful manure and other inputs; in many semi-arid parts of the Islamic world, for instance, charitable endowments created by wealthy urbanites financed well-digging nearby, making peri-urban farms more productive. But through most of our period, most farms lacked strong relationships to nearby cities.

Working land more intensively required using more of other factors of production. Capital inputs per acre certainly increased, though this is hard to measure: better plows, more wells, sluices, water pumps, and so on. More significantly, more intensive cropping regimes—whether achieved through reducing fallowing or by introducing multi-cropping—necessarily meant that each plot needed more days of labor per year. Other ways of increasing yields—more manuring, more careful weeding, and so on— also meant more work per acre. Some innovations (such as multi-cropping, stall-feeding animals rather than pasturing them, or creating irrigation works that then needed maintenance) made farmers' work years longer. This tendency may have gone farthest in England (despite its far-from-tropical climate): by ca. 1700, agriculturalists there often worked 300 days a year, and one study concludes that the average agricultural year peaked ca. 1800 at an astonishing 4,171 hours per worker.[12]

Other tasks, such as gathering enlarged harvests, had to be done when nature demanded, and could not be spread over more days. So unless tools improved, or people simply worked harder (which is hard to prove, but probably did happen in some situations),[13] more family members, neighbors, and/or hired hands would have to be mobilized. Thus, advanced organic agriculture not only meant more work, but often intensified the problem of seasonality: that is, it required huge amounts of workers at peak seasons, but needed few of them during most of the year. Some had other occupations in other seasons: as late as World War I, many French factories closed at harvest to release workers, and school schedules in most countries still reflect the days when young people worked on farms in summer. But these solutions were imperfect, leaving many people struggling to subsist year-round on income from short work stints, while various non-farmers—from early modern moralists decrying 'idleness' to twentieth-century development economists hoping to eliminate 'surplus labor'—decried this situation.

Overall, labor demand increased enough that even quite impressive output increases may not have raised farmers' earnings per day. In England, income per day probably fell between 1500 and 1800, though a lengthening work year increased farmers' annual incomes.[14] Shaky data for the Yangzi delta suggest a slightly different, equally ambiguous situation. Labor time per acre increased (especially for double-cropping), but the average size of a family's farm shrank by a comparable amount, so both agricultural income and agricultural labor days per family probably grew only slightly. Meanwhile wives—needed less often on smaller farms—switched their labor into other activities, especially textiles; their daily earnings probably increased slightly, while total family labor and income per year clearly rose.[15] The returns to owning land rose in many places as it became more productive, benefiting some farmers; and at least for some parts of Western Europe—the only places for which we have calculations—output rose faster than the weighted average of land, labor, and capital inputs, indicating a slow but noticeable growth in efficiency from roughly 1450 to 1815.[16] (The huge disruptions caused by fourteenth-century plague make longer term comparisons extremely hazardous.) But returns to each unit of labor time probably did not rise.

So far, we have emphasized how cultivation became more intensive on land that was already being farmed. But that should not imply that bringing additional acres under cultivation—which occurred on an enormous scale—was trivial, or merely replicated old practices on new land. Global croplands probably doubled just from 1700 to 1850, with the biggest gains in China, Russia, Europe, and North America.[17]

Much of this involved displacing people who did not farm, or who farmed less intensively (using slash and burn techniques, for instance), and planting well-known crops; in these cases the new technologies applied were as likely to be coercive or cartographic as agricultural. In other cases, however, agricultural acreage was expanded by using new crops that were particularly well-suited to some area. The most famous cases involved the 'Colombian exchange'—the movement of American plants (as well as animals and diseases) to Afro-Eurasia, and vice versa, after 1492. Even if we restrict ourselves to plants, the list of transplants is staggering. Wheat, rice, barley, sorghum, sugar, oranges, grapes, coffee, olives, and so on came to the Americas; potatoes, sweet potatoes, corn, various peppers, tomatoes, squash, peanuts, and more reached Afro-Eurasia.[18]

Often these new crops made far more intensive farming possible. In many places in East and Southeast Asia, the potato, sweet potato, and maize helped sustain sedentary populations in highland areas that had previously not supported settled agriculture. (Parts of China later paid dearly for these additional acres: as annual crops replaced trees on many hillsides, erosion and downstream flooding increased markedly.) Many shifting cultivators also innovated with American crops. In particular tubers, which need not be harvested on a precise schedule, were attractive to mobile people who often preferred avoiding would-be landlords and officials. American crops had less impact in Asian lowlands, being unable to displace high-yielding rice, but they sometimes became valued second crops. Farmers in China's Pearl River delta, for instance, became more willing to put some of their acreage into high-yield, high-risk, labor-intensive sugar once they could put the rest of it (or nearby hills not previously farmed) into sweet potatoes: the latter were a much less desired food than rice, but they were nutritious, yielded many calories per acre, and required relatively little labor.[19] Meanwhile in Europe, where the pre-existing lowland crops yielded much less per acre, potatoes spread rapidly in some densely populated areas, such as Flanders and Ireland. Simultaneously, maize spread through various parts of Africa. It offered far more nutrition per acre than African millets and sorghum with similar cultivation techniques and it matured earlier, so it could feed farmers waiting to for sorghum to ripen. But most Africans did not yet face intense pressures to increase per-acre yields, and there is much we do not know about how far and how fast American crops spread prior to the twentieth century—which is when maize monocultures began to displace other crops on a large scale, rather than complementing them. (Maize does seem to have spread quickly where provisioning slave ships offered a market to those producing surpluses of a cheap, easily stored food—a grim example of concentrated demand encouraging agricultural intensification.)[20]

   To sum up, then, agriculture intensified slowly from 800 to 1800. Fallowing decreased, and multi-cropping increased, especially near cities and/or when new, complementary, crops became available. Elsewhere—usually further from major cities— vast areas once farmed by shifting cultivators, used by pastoralists, or (in the case of marshes and forests) exploited in other ways were turned over to annual crops, especially after 1500. Some new tools were developed, though the gradual spread and adaptation of already-known 'best practices' was more important than truly new techniques. Various forms of physical capital, such as barns, wells, and plows, accumulated, and efficiency increased where improved transportation and new markets allowed for greater specialization. But the biggest gains in output came from increased inputs of land and above all, labor. Even in relatively 'advanced' areas, agriculture remained dominant: Europe was about 13 percent urban in 1800, and China's 'advanced' lower Yangzi only about 9 percent urban (though the latter, in particular, had huge numbers of rural people making handicrafts).[21] (By comparison, the contemporary United States has between 1 and 2 percent of its workforce in agriculture, and is a net food exporter.) Crop production per farmer did rise (allowing other population groups to grow), but farmers generally worked more hours per year to achieve those gains in output (and, for some of them, in income). Labor-saving innovations were not unknown, even where labor was plentiful; but everywhere, labor-absorbing innovations were predominant.

   Finally, the major developments in agriculture during this period were largely generated from *within* agriculture. Other parts of society mattered, of course. Governments and other armed groups decided among claimants to land, and removed the losers, often brutally; artisans gradually made iron plows cheaper and more common; urban consumers, purveyors of new goods, and tax collectors all, in different ways, prodded farmers to raise their output; and the building of roads, piers, and so on, intensified those influences. But ca. 1800, almost all the inputs into agricultural production came from farms (sometimes from other farms, which might specialize in raising draft animals, high-quality seed, or soybean that was crushed into fertilizer), as did most knowledge about how to use those inputs. Post-1800 developments were very different.

Agriculture in an Industrial(izing) World

Rigidly-defined eras are always misleading, and much agricultural change after 1800 still resembled trends from earlier periods. This is especially true outside of Europe and the so-called 'neo-Europes': temperate zone areas such as North America, Argentina, and Australia which were colonized by Europeans, adopted many crops of European origin, and became the epicenters of a new mechanized agriculture. Even in these areas, technified agriculture did not triumph quickly. Several machines for doing fieldwork were *invented* in the nineteenth century, but only one—the McCormick reaper (invented 1831, first mass produced 1847)—entered widespread use before 1920. With this one exception, the major *mechanical* innovations in pre-World War I agriculture were all in post-harvest processing: cotton ginning, wheat threshing, sugar cane crushing, and so on.[22] In only three countries—Belgium, the United Kingdom, and France—did the number of farmers decline prior to 1910, though farmers were a gradually declining *percentage* of workers in most countries.[23] In China, the number of farmers kept increasing until the late 1990s, and in India until around 2000.[24] Worldwide, most agricultural output growth was probably driven by increases in inputs until the 1930s; only after World War II did increases in total factor productivity (i.e. increased technical and organizational efficiency) become more important.[25]

Indeed, the growth of cultivated acreage accelerated greatly after 1800, though it had reached its end in China proper (excluding Manchuria, Mongolia, etc.) and Western Europe.[26] The greatest displacement of indigenes by (mostly) farmers of European descent in Brazil, Argentina, Chile, Canada, the United States, Australia, and elsewhere came between roughly 1830 and 1920.[27] (Expansion of white settler agriculture was less successful in various parts of Africa.)Though fewer Westerners settled in Asia, there was nonetheless considerable displacement of other lifeways by sedentary agriculture, often in order to grow export crops and often with the aid of colonial legislation, such as the British 'Criminal Tribes Act,' which essentially criminalized nomadism. Examples include the creation of tea plantations in Assam, coffee estates in Kenya, and tobacco and rubber plantations in Sumatra. Other land was 'opened' with little or no European involvement: thus, while the Qing had kept Manchuria mostly forest until about 1850, their grip loosened thereafter, and they began to encourage Chinese immigration after 1895 (to avoid losing the region to Russia or Japan); roughly eight million permanent migrants and seventeen million temporary ones, mostly farmers, had arrived by 1937, and today the region is one of China's breadbaskets.[28] In Southeast Asia's Mekong, Chaophraya, and Irrawaddy deltas, colonial regimes (and the British-influenced Thai monarchy) drained the swamps and enforced the property claims, but it was mostly local people, plus some Indians and Chinese, who created enormous, mono-cultural rice export zones, in many ways paralleling the creation of wheat monocultures in neo-Europes. Worldwide, cropland rose about 75 percent from 1850 to 1920; Russia[29] and North America accounted for over half of that, but the biggest *percentage* increases were in Latin America, Oceania, and Southeast Asia.[30]

This round of land clearance was also qualitatively different from earlier ones, largely thanks to new non-agricultural technologies. Ocean freight rates had begun falling well before the advent of steamships, but they fell faster thereafter. Shipping wheat from New York to Liverpool cost 79 percent less in 1902 than in 1868; sending sugar from Java to Amsterdam in 1913 cost less than half of 1870 rates.[31] Overland freight rates also plunged as railroads improved: sending wheat from Chicago to New York was 71 percent cheaper in 1902 than in 1868.[32] The differences between motorized and non-motorized land transport were even larger. Bringing wheat to land-locked and famine-stricken Shanxi, China in 1928 cost $0.79 per ton-mile; tractors could have moved it for $0.13, and a railway, had it existed, for $0.02.[33] Cheaper freight made cultivating far more remote areas economically viable.[34]

Modern technologies also changed how farms engaged with the market. Consider the grain elevator, introduced in Chicago circa 1840 to solve a pressing new problem. Shutting down a locomotive to load it was enormously expensive; so was keeping it waiting under a full head of steam. Thus, releasing a flood of grain from above became vastly preferable to loading hundreds of sacks. This had profound implications. With sacks, each farmer's wheat arrived in New York packed separately, and could be graded and priced accordingly. Now they were indistinguishable; it became necessary to grade and price the entire shipment together. Thus were born abstractions such as '#2 spring wheat'—categories within which the grain was interchangeable. Once such standardized commodities existed, the right to receive a certain amount at a certain time and place could be traded easily, on a huge scale, and even before the grain existed. The resulting growth of futures markets transformed relationships among farmers, consumers, and middlemen.[35]

This standardization of agricultural products helped reverse one significant trend of early modern agriculture. Botanists and others were often astounded by how many crop varieties 'traditional' farmers used; the Economic Museum in 1920s Calcutta held over 4,000 rice varieties from Bengal alone.[36] These were not simply the residue of natural variety; farmers in many societies consciously created, saved, and exchanged a huge variety of seeds with tiny (to our eyes) differences, which they deemed suitable for subtly different plots of land, expected weather, and desired plant characteristics. This represented an enormous reservoir of local knowledge generated (in most cases) by farmers themselves (including swidden cultivators).[37] But in the last 150 years, this trend has been sharply reversed, with crop varieties increasingly standardized by large-scale markets, large seed companies, laboratory-based scientists, and development experts.

Cheaper transport also made farmers thousands of miles apart into competitors— often unequal competitors. Cheap American, Australian, and Ukrainian grain was as devastating to many European farmers as it was welcome to urbanites: and many farms were too small to adopt similar cost-saving technologies. Hungarian farms, for instance, used only 168 steam engines in 1863, and 3,000 by 1871; but they made sense only on larger farms, which could then outcompete and gobble up their neighbors. Hungarian exports soared, while the percentage of farms large enough to support a family fell to 30 percent; in Galicia (Poland), it fell to 19 percent.[38] Near large cities, many farmers switched to vegetable-growing or dairying, in which proximity to the market was still vital and large farms unnecessary; they could even benefit from cheap grain, feeding it to animals. Others became city-dwellers themselves. Others still moved overseas, often helping to expand the farms which drove even more of their erstwhile neighbors out of farming. Similar, though smaller, feedback loops operated elsewhere. New rice bowls in Southeast Asia out-competed Chinese and Indian farmers for markets in Shanghai, Hong Kong, Calcutta, and Bombay, increasing emigration from those countries; much more recently, post-NAFTA corn imports from the United States made many Mexican farmers uncompetitive, with some becoming farm workers in the United States.

New technologies on the farms themselves wrought even greater transformations. Besides new machines, the other important new technologies were chemical and biological; many originated in land-scarce Europe, and most raised yields per acre (while mechanical inventions, often invented in the land-rich, labor-scarce United States, mostly raised yields per labor hour).[39]

Probably the most important innovation was chemical fertilizer: non-biological substances (unlike manure, grass, algae, or soybean cake) which could replace some of the nitrogen, phosphorus, or potassium that crops took from the soil. Early examples, from the 1840s, were generally mined and processed only slightly. Bones and certain rocks, treated with acid, supplied large amounts of phosphorus and potassium. Guano (dried seagull excrement) found in huge quantities in Peru and Chile, and in lesser quantities in some other places, provided nitrates. Chilean nitrate exports, which began ca. 1840, reached 100,000 tons by 1860, and 3,000,000 by 1913.[40]

Manufactured nitrates, developed by German chemists in 1909, were even more important. Producing them required lots of electricity but no rare raw materials; thus, anyone with enough cheap energy could now fertilize far more intensively than ever before, raising yields enormously. (Artificial fertilizers cannot, however, replace all biological inputs. Without some manure, soils lose essential organic matter and micronutrients.) This eventually allowed certain crowded regions (such as Western and Central Europe) to regain net self-sufficiency in food; and it allowed the world to support vastly more people. Without synthetic fertilizers, Earth's maximum carrying capacity is probably about 3.6 billion people;[41] and though some of today's 6.7 billion people do go hungry, this stems from problems of distribution, not inadequate production. Looked at another way, synthetic fertilizers turn fossil fuels into crops, tapping millions of years of stored-up solar energy.

Chemical fertilizers did not immediately spread worldwide, however; some farmers could not afford them and others, with plentiful land, saw little need for them. As we shall see, their *global* heyday came after 1950. Nonetheless, they may be the twentieth century's most important invention. The synthetic nitrogen used today is (very roughly) five times what could be garnered by recycling every last gram of liquid and solid human waste; it makes possible perhaps 40 percent of human protein intake.[42]

Three more inter-connected, transformative, non-farm inputs began in the nineteenth century but blossomed in the twentieth: chemical pesticides (many of them based on coal tars or petrochemicals), hybrid seeds, and irrigation projects using modern construction materials and energy sources. It is easiest to begin with pesticides.

Farmers have always struggled against bugs, weeds, and fungi that competed with, ruined, or ate their crops. The most common methods, acquired through generations of trial and error, involved crop rotation (depriving pests linked to one particular plant of a host), destruction of crop residues (for similar reasons), and so on. Off-farm ingredients existed—Chinese gardeners used arsenic on pests in the tenth century[43]— but they were a minor weapon in farmers' arsenals. Several nineteenth-century trends converged to change this.

First, booming long-distance trade carried with it many unwanted organisms, sometimes to areas where they had no natural enemies. The blight behind the 1840s Irish potato famine almost certainly came from the Americas; it may, ironically, have come on a ship bringing Peruvian guano.[44] Since the transportation revolution also encouraged specialization, large concentrations of one crop, often in only one variety, became more common: this facilitated the rapid spread of pests, while ruling out certain traditional pest-control methods. (The problem resembles that which requires animals kept close together in today's Concentrated Animal Feeding Operations to be heavily dosed with antibiotics—though CAFOs also have the problem of huge concentrations of potentially infectious excrement.) The California fruit industry—a creature of rail transport and large-scale irrigation, which in many ways epitomizes modern farming, and was inconceivable without railroads—provides a perfect example.[45]

Pests can be particularly devastating for orchard or vineyard keepers. Destroying a diseased wheat crop, thus losing one year's income, was bad enough; destroying trees could mean sacrificing several years' income. That might still be bearable if the trees represented a small part of a diversified farm, as they generally had in the past; it became unbearable if pears, oranges, or whatever were the farm's only crop. Furthermore, most California orchards grew non-native species—hundreds of new tree and vine varieties were imported, each one of which could bring new pests with it. In the 1870s and 1880s, California farmers suffered repeated infestations, and sought help from chemical companies and the University of California. Various new insecticides, mostly based on lead and arsenic, followed. These sprays were cheap and easy to apply, but nobody was sure what the necessary dose was: many growers preferred spraying too much to risking their investment by spraying too little. Though complaints from consumers, doctors, and public health authorities mounted during the 1920s and 1930s, and some agronomists feared damage to the soil, farmers generally increased their spraying—and consumers their buying. The average California farm acre cost 350 percent more in 1925 than in 1900, and so was that much more worth protecting; there was no turning back. When more effective and seemingly safer insecticides

Table 14.1 The cost of non-farm inputs as a percentage of the value of United States farm output

Year	Percentage
1800	2
1870/72	8
1911/13	13
1936/8	17
1985	53
1998/2000	64

Source: Federico (2005), p. 53.

became available after World War II, far more farmers came to use them, in even greater quantities.

Whether increasingly heavy use of these pesticides was indeed safe became controversial after Rachel Carson published *Silent Spring* in 1962. Global pesticide consumption peaked around 1980 and has declined since then. However, it continues to rise in many poor countries, where it is particularly urgent to increase yields—but the danger that health and environmental hazards will be ignored is also greater.

Together, these mechanical, biological, and chemical inputs made twentieth-century advanced agriculture fundamentally different from any before. Output grew at unprecedented rates—per acre and especially per labor hour. (The latter, as we have seen, constituted a much more radical break with advanced organic agriculture.) A United States corn farmer ca. 1970 produced between 100 and 1,000 times as much food energy per labor hour as pre-industrial farmers.[46] Capital- and energy-intensive farming thus meant that for the first time, feeding more people might not require more drudgery.

These changes also made farms increasingly dependent on inputs purchased from other sectors, like other modern industries. The figures in Table 14.1 estimate the cost of non-farm inputs as a percentage of the value of United States farm output. Trends for other wealthy countries look broadly similar; however, the equivalent estimate for Africa in 1960 was 2 percent, like the United States in 1800.[47]

This helps explain why, though farmers have become vastly more productive in the twentieth century, they have not necessarily become much richer. (Other reasons are discussed below.) It also helps explain why credit has become ever more important to ever more farmers, giving some larger farmers with more collateral competitive advantages even when they are not more efficient in physical terms.

The environmental contrast between advanced organic farming and twentieth-century energy-intensive farming is equally stark. Table 14.2 compares the food energy farmers of different kinds produce to the energy they use in producing food.

As we have seen, this technification of agriculture was still incipient in the early 1900s, even in many wealthy countries. Though that process continues everywhere, the biggest story since World War II has been the spread of high-input agriculture to poorer

Table 14.2 Food energy compared to the energy used in producing food (%)

Subsistence, cassava crop	60–65
Chinese peasants	41
Tropical crops, subsistence	13–38
Tropical crops: some fertilizer, machinery	5–10
Sugar beet, UK	4.2
Wheat, UK	3.35
Maize, USA	2.6
Barley, UK	2.4
Potatoes, UK	1.6
Rice, USA	1.3
Peas, UK	0.95
Milk, UK	0.37
All agriculture, UK 1968	0.34
All food supply, UK	0.2

Note: Data (mostly from the late 1960s) from Grigg (1982), p. 79.

countries. One crucial part of this has been an enormous irrigation boom; the other a set of biological and chemical changes which are epitomized by (though broader than) the 1960s–1970s 'Green Revolution.' Let us begin with water.

Most of Europe and eastern North America gets moderate amounts of rainfall distributed relatively evenly throughout the year; many other places are less fortunate. A huge arid and semi-arid zone runs across North Africa and parts of Asia, from Morocco to northwestern China; in most of it, agriculture requires digging wells, diverting rivers (often fed by high-altitude snow-melt and thus highly seasonal), or both. Other huge areas of Asia and East Africa get adequate or even excessive rainfall, but mostly in brief, monsoon-driven concentrations, not necessarily coinciding with farmers' needs, and varying significantly from year to year. Large regions in the Americas, Australia, and sub-Saharan Africa also have limited or highly seasonal rainfall; farming them reliably requires massive transport and/or storage of water.

In some of these places, irrigation goes back millennia, but the last hundred-plus years have witnessed an enormous expansion. Structural steel, concrete, and other new materials made much bigger dams possible; gas-powered or electric pumps could move more water greater distances; and stronger states with growing populations found it possible and desirable to make some lands more fertile by submerging others. Electricity sales from dams with turbines often subsidized farmers' water.[48] The western United States, Australia, Punjab, and Egypt—all low-rainfall regions—were early sites of modern irrigation projects. Yet these were not yet a major global phenomenon. Giovanni Federico estimates global irrigated acreage at 40,000,000 hectares ca. 1900; China alone had 23,000,000 hectares, all using traditional methods, materials, and power sources.[49]

By 2000, however, 280,000,000 hectares were irrigated. Half of the growth came after 1960, with the Soviet Union, China, and India accounting for half of that.[50] Multipurpose dams, providing power, water, and (sometimes) flood protection appealed to many constituencies. By making new lands cultivable, irrigation often provided far greater returns than incremental improvements to existing farmlands—though in the longer run, unanticipated environmental damage, especially where drainage is inadequate, has often reduced these gains.[51] Dams also made wonderful symbols of technological mastery for newly-sovereign nations and Cold War aid donors. Elsewhere, gas- or electric-powered pumps made it economical to tap aquifers far underground, turning formerly drought-prone areas into breadbaskets. This yielded spectacular results after 1960 in north China and northwest India/Pakistan, and after 1950 on the American Great Plains; now, however, all of these aquifers are becoming dangerously depleted. Other very ambitious schemes were not for food production, but to provide domestic supplies of cotton, a very thirsty crop: this included one of the world's biggest irrigation disasters, in Soviet Central Asia.[52] Still, irrigation has been essential to feeding the world's burgeoning post-1945 population, both raising yields and expanding acreage. Arable land grew at the same percentage rate in the period 1920–1980 as in 1850–1920, and thus faster than ever in absolute terms. Over 70 percent of newly irrigated land was in Africa, South and Southwest Asia, and Latin America.[53] The largest remaining potential for further irrigation today probably lies in sub-Saharan Africa, where only 7 percent of farmland is irrigated (vs. 40 percent in South Asia).[54] However, many places that already make heavy use of modern irrigation techniques (notably India, Pakistan, north China, Australia, and parts of the western United States) now face increasingly serious problems with pollution, salination, water-logging, groundwater depletion, and decaying infrastructure.[55]

Chemical and biological transformations of 'third-world' agriculture, occurring mostly after 1960, have been equally important. Political changes were crucial here, because governments played critical roles in both inventing and disseminating new agricultural technologies. Even where land ownership is exceptionally unequal, agriculture is never as concentrated as many modern industries—even the largest farms have a minuscule percentage of the overall market for any crop. Consequently widely available new technologies increase many farms' output, pushing prices down (unless the state intervenes); most of the gains go to consumers, and no single farmer gains enough to justify investing heavily in research. Therefore, systematic agricultural research tends to be financed by governments; by corporations that can patent the improvement (which, until 1960, was possible for agricultural chemicals, but not for biological innovations such as seeds[56]); or by associations of large, easily-organized processors (e.g. textile or flour mills, rather than ordinary buyers of bread or cotton clothing).

Thus, agricultural research and development was heavily concentrated in richer, more industrialized countries, and emphasized their concerns; in the many parts of the world that were colonies until the 1950s or 1960s, what little was spent on agricultural research usually targeted export crops rather than locally consumed ones.[57] But decolonization created governments and universities at least potentially more responsive to local interests. Meanwhile, rapid population growth intensified various Western worries—about peasant revolutions, massive emigration, and human suffering—and led to much greater funding for research relevant to agriculture in poorer countries. The results included high-yielding hybrid seeds for wheat, rice, and other basic crops. Much of the most important work was promoted by the United Nations' Food and Agriculture Organization (FAO) and the Rockefeller Foundation, but scientists outside this network also made breakthroughs: China developed its own hybrid rice, wheat, and sorghum, and Southern Rhodesia (now Zimbabwe) developed improved maize that quadrupled yields.[58]

The results were spectacular. From 1961 to 2000, global agricultural output increased 145 percent, with the biggest gains in poorer countries: 216 percent in South America, and 302 percent in Asia.[59] Moreover, almost all these gains stemmed from increased capital inputs and improved total factor productivity. Green Revolution innovations did not bring that much more land under cultivation and usually did not require much more labor (except to gather and process larger harvests). Sometimes the new varieties actually required less labor, which was a mixed blessing in countries already facing massive unemployment and under-employment.

Hybrid seeds did not raise yields by themselves; they were bred, among other things, to respond to (and require) large amounts of fertilizer. And indeed, global consumption of chemical fertilizers rose 900 percent between 1950 and 1988. Since then it has declined by about one-quarter in the wealthier countries, but has continued to rise elsewhere; "third-world" fertilizer consumption is up more than 2,500 percent since 1960.[60] So far, sub-Saharan Africa has been least affected by this trend: farmers there used 9 kilograms per hectare in 2004, versus 73 in Latin America, 100 in South Asia, 135 in developing countries of East and Southeast Asia, and 206 in the industrialized countries.[61]

Applying so much fertilizer can seriously damage the soil if it is not properly diluted. Thus, farmers using these seeds need greater and more reliable water supplies; the gains from biological, chemical, and hydraulic innovations are strongly inter-dependent. And since the hybrid seeds themselves degenerate quickly, farmers must buy new supplies each year, rather than saving seeds from this year's crop.

Therefore, most third-world farmers, like those in richer countries, have become more productive by using more purchased inputs. But in many poor countries, agricultural credit is scarce and expensive, political disturbances may interrupt deliveries, irrigation infrastructure may be poorly maintained, and so on—magnifying the social risks accompanying this kind of development. They are greatest for poorer farmers who can be driven to bankruptcy by one bad season; yet such farmers cannot avoid competing with their richer neighbors, who can use new inputs more easily. Hence, the Green Revolution, for all its benefits, has also often increased inequality, with richer farmers buying up the land of those who had too little land or money to follow the technified path, or encountered problems with credit costs, interruptions of key inputs, or other misfortunes. And as some farms grow larger, they increasingly find it useful to buy labor-saving machinery, deepening the plight of those who need wage labor opportunities.[62] Thus, even more than earlier booms in the West, the technological transformation of third-world farming has been great for agricultural productivity, and a life-saver for many food-buyers, but painful for many of the farmers.

Another reason why farmers have not necessarily prospered as they became more productive is unfavorable twentieth-century price trends for farm products relative to other goods. This has been especially pronounced for growers of tropical crops (mostly in poor countries), which are cheaper today even in absolute terms than before World War I.[63] But even for temperate zone farmers, relative prices have generally stagnated or declined since 1850—in part because output has soared.[64] The predominant trend under advanced organic agriculture was quite different: while there are many exceptions (and even more data problems), relative prices for farm products seem to have risen more than they fell over those centuries, as cropland/labor ratios gradually worsened.[65]

Heavy state extraction in most poor countries has also helped perpetuate agricultural poverty amidst impressive agricultural growth. The policy instruments have varied across times and places—fixing artificially low grain prices, directing state investment disproportionately toward industry, tariff protection for inefficient producers of agricultural inputs, collectivization on unfavorable terms, and so on—but the pattern recurs across governments with vast ideological differences. With strikingly few exceptions, states in less-industrialized societies have taken more from agriculture than they have given to it, often asserting that this was necessary to financing industrial growth.[66] (Ironically, once common scholarly views linking early industrialization to increased surplus extraction in agriculture now look decidedly dubious.[67])

Meanwhile, rich countries have moved in the opposite direction, heavily subsidizing relatively small numbers of farmers. In recent years rich countries' farm subsidies have exceeded five times the value of all development aid they have given.[68] This often makes it impossible for farmers in poorer countries (or non-subsidized farmers in rich ones) to compete for markets. Removing these subsidies would thus help many poor farmers, though the net effects on 'the poor' in general are harder to calculate: millions of the very poorest people are wage earners, unemployed people or others who benefit when subsidies push down prices for globally traded foodstuffs.

These subsidies go mostly to a relatively small number of bulk crops (in the USA, corn, soybeans, cotton, and sugar) which, once made exceptionally cheap, have become even more prevalent; the increased use of high-fructose corn syrup and maltodextrin in many processed foods, and of corn as animal feed (for cows that evolved eating grass, and sometimes even for farmed fish) are prominent examples. (Only in Africa is more than half of corn production consumed directly by humans.[69]) Meanwhile food consumers buy increasing amounts of processed foods marketed under heavily-promoted brand names by manufacturers who buy a large share of a given crop. In such cases, farmers become providers of interchangeable bulk inputs to intermediaries with much greater market power, often receiving relatively little of the final selling price. (This is also true with some brand-name foods that are not much more processed than a generation ago: only 10–15 percent of the United States' supermarket price of coffee goes to growers, versus almost 30 percent in the mid-1970s.[70])

Incipient developments seem likely to recapitulate both positive and negative features of post-1950 agricultural development. Biological and chemical research—now increasingly organized by for-profit corporations[71]—has developed various genetically modified crops, which have the potential to raise per-acre yields significantly: a goal that remains attractive with populations still growing and increasing acreage likely to be devoted to 'bio-fuel' substitutes for planet-warming coal and oil. In many cases, these new varieties are engineered to succeed only in combination with very-specific off-farm inputs. (For example, Monsanto's 'Round-up ready' crops are designed to tolerate heavy doses of the company's 'Round-up' weed-killer.) Thus, the technological 'package' often requires that the farmer keeps the fields clear of any other crops or crop varieties. (This also reduces the risk of transferring the gene conferring pesticide resistance to the pests themselves.) Moreover, the patented seeds themselves need to be repurchased for each year's crops: not only can they degenerate biologically, but farmers re-using them may face patent-infringement suits.

Claims about possible environmental and health risks of these new crops are hotly contested. What is certain is that this further technification of agriculture will deepen the dependence of farmers on off-farm inputs and mono-cultural production strategies—which, as we have seen, have been persistent trends since the mid-nineteenth century, and especially since the mid-twentieth. If these crops succeed, they will also intensify the recent patterns of yield increases based largely on increased capital inputs and gains in total factor productivity, rather than the output increases based on using more land and labor that predominated in advanced organic agriculture. Whether these changes will again benefit larger farmers more than smaller ones is hard to predict: it depends on factors ranging from how large a sterile zone is needed to prevent unwanted cross-pollination of other plants, to how the genetically modified crops affect farmers' need for timely applications of purchased fertilizers and pesticides, to what sorts of non-farm jobs will be available for those displaced from farming.

Some agronomists and development experts advocate a different approach, more continuous with earlier kinds of growth: arguing, for instance, that labor-intensive agriculture using complex inter-cropping schemes can provide the per-acre yields needed for food security with much less environmental risk and without making farmers more dependent on credit and purchased inputs.[72] Such arguments are hard to evaluate—reliable yield data for complexly inter-cropped land are particularly hard to come by,[73] and the risk of environmental disaster very hard to estimate. Faced with an immense gamble either way, most policy makers seem to be betting on further technification. Thus, the recent past of advanced agriculture will probably be the most relevant to our future. It is important, however, to see how these trends both build upon and reverse key features of a longer history including advanced organic agriculture.

NOTES

1. David Grigg, *The Dynamics of Agricultural Change* (London: Hutchinson, 1982), 78–80.
2. E. A. Wrigley, *Continuity, Chance and Change: The Character of the Industrial Revolution in England* (Cambridge: Cambridge University Press, 1988), especially 17–30.

3. Mauro Ambrosoli, *The Wild and the Sown* (Cambridge: Cambridge University Press, 1997).

4. Andrew Watson, *Agricultural Innovation in the Early Islamic World* (Cambridge: Cambridge University Press, 1983).

5. For the system's slow spread through medieval Western Europe, see David Grigg, *Population Growth and Agrarian Change: An Historical Perspective* (Cambridge: Cambridge University Press, 1980), 73; for Eastern Europe, see Peter Gunst, 'Agrarian Systems of Central and Eastern Europe,' in Daniel Chirot, ed., *The Origins of Backwardness in Eastern Europe* (Berkeley: University of California Press, 1989), 76–7.

6. Mark Elvin, *The Pattern of the Chinese Past* (Stanford: Stanford University Press, 1973), 121–4; Francesca Bray, *The Rice Economies* (Berkeley: University of California Press, 1986), 15–16, 119, 203 (giving a later date for early-ripening rice than Elvin).

7. Much of this debate was touched off by Ester Boserup's 1965 book, *The Conditions of Agricultural Growth: The Economics of Agrarian Change Under Population Pressure* (New Brunswick, N.J.: Aldine Transactions, 2005), which argued that population growth often stimulated agricultural development, thus undermining Malthusian claims. A separate strand, focused on the stimulatory effect of cities on agriculture, has been particularly important in the literature on medieval and early modern Europe. See Philip Hoffmann, *Growth in a Traditional Economy: The French Countryside, 1450–1815* (Princeton: Princeton University Press, 1996). For a contrary view see Robert Brenner, 'The Agrarian Roots of European Capitalism,' in T. H. Aston and C. H. Philpin, eds., *The Brenner Debate* (Cambridge: Cambridge University Press), 213–327.

8. Bruce Campbell, 'Agricultural Progress in Medieval England: Some Evidence from Eastern Norfolk,' *Economic History Review*, n.s. 36: 1 (February, 1983), 30–1. See also Robert Allen, 'The Two English Agricultural Revolutions, 1450–1800,' in Bruce Campbell and Mark Overton, eds., *Land, Labour and Livestock: Historical Studies in European Agricultural Productivity* (Manchester: Manchester University Press, 1991), 239; Mark Overton, *Agricultural Revolution in England: The Transformation of the Agrarian Economy 1500–1850* (Cambridge: Cambridge University Press, 1996), 77.

9. E. C. Ellis and S. M. Wang, 'Sustainable Traditional Agriculture in the Tai Lake Region of China,' *Agriculture, Ecosystems and Environment* 61 (1997), 185; Kenneth Pomeranz, 'Beyond the East–West Binary: Rethinking Development Paths in the Eighteenth Century,' *Journal of Asian Studies* 61: 2 (May, 2002), 555, 582.

10. Pomeranz, 'Beyond the East–West Binary,' 554–5 and accompanying notes.

11. See James Scott, *The Moral Economy of the Peasant* (New Haven: Yale University Press, 1976).

12. Gregory Clark and Yves Van der Werff, 'Work in Progress? The Industrious Revolution,' *Journal of Economic History* 58: 3 (September, 1998), 837, 841; Hans-Joachim Voth, *Work and Time in England 1750–1830* (Oxford: Oxford University Press, 2000), 129. The 1800 figure may be slightly inflated by wartime pressures, but Voth's 1830 figure is still 3,716 hours per year.

13. Gregory Clark, 'Productivity Growth without Technical Change in European Agriculture before 1850,' *Journal of Economic History* 47: 2 (June, 1987), 419–32.

14. Stitching together an index of labor time per year from the sources cited in note 12, and combining it with Robert Allen's figures for agricultural output per laborer ('Economic Structure and Agricultural Productivity in Europe, 1300–1800,' *European Review of Economic History* 4: 1 (2000), 20) yields a 14 percent *decline* in output per hour between

1500 and 1800—which may be understated since most scholars think that the work year in 1500 was not yet as long as Clark and Van der Werff say it was.

15. Li Bozhong, *Agricultural Development in Jiangnan, 1620–1850* (New York: St. Martin's, 1998), 81–97, 119–55.

16. Hoffmann, *Growth in a Traditional Economy*, 102–31.

17. John Richards, 'Land Transformation,' in B. L. Turner *et al.*, *The Earth as Transformed by Human Action* (Cambridge: Cambridge University Press, 1990), 165.

18. Alfred Crosby, *The Columbian Exchange: Biological and Cultural Consequences of 1492* (Westport, Conn.: Greenwood Press, 1972).

19. Sucheta Mazumdar, *Sugar and Society in China: Peasants, Technology, and the World Market* (Cambridge, Mass.: Harvard University Asia Center, 1998), 258–9.

20. On the early spread of maize in Africa see James McCann, *Maize and Grace: Africa's Encounter with a New World Crop, 1500–2000* (Cambridge, Mass.: Harvard University Press, 2005), 39–58. On the link to provisioning slaves and coastal garrisons, see McCann, 30, 46, and Marvin Miracle, 'The introduction and Spread of Maize in Africa,' *Journal of African History* 6: 1 (1966), 38–55.

21. Jan de Vries, *European Urbanization, 1500–1800* (Cambridge, Mass.: Harvard University Press, 1984), 74; G. William Skinner, 'Regional Urbanization in Nineteenth Century China,' in G. William Skinner, ed., *The City in Late Imperial China* (Stanford: Stanford University Press 1977), 226, adjusted for G. William Skinner, 'Sichuan's Population in the 19th Century: Lessons From Disaggregated Data,' *Late Imperial China* 8: 1 (June 1987), 72–9.

22. Giovanni Federico, *Feeding the World: An Economic History of Agriculture, 1800–2000* (Princeton: Princeton University Press, 2005), 90–1.

23. Federico, *Feeding the World*, 56.

24. See data from 1998 *China Statistical Yearbook* displayed by the International Institute for Applied Systems Analysis at <http://www.iiasa.ac.at/Research/LUC/ChinaFood/data/urban/urban_5.htm>. For India, Amrita Sharma, 'The Changing Agrarian Demography of India: Evidence from a Rural Youth Perception Survey,' *International Journal of Rural Management* 3: 1 (2007), 28 says 'several parts' of the country first recorded declines in 1999–2000; Indian Ministry of Agriculture and Cooperation, Institute of Economics and Statistics, 'Agricultural Statistics at a Glance 2008' <http://dacnet.nic.in/eands/At_Glance_2008/ch_2tb2.2u.xls> shows decade-by-decade increases continuing through 2001 (the last data provided).

25. Federico, *Feeding the World*, 2.

26. Federico, *Feeding the World*, 35.

27. Alfred Crosby, *Ecological Imperialism: The Biological Expansion of Europe, 900–1900* (Cambridge: Cambridge University, 1986).

28. Thomas Gottschang and Diana Lary, *Swallows and Settlers: The Great Migration from North China to Manchuria* (Ann Arbor: Center for Chinese Studies, University of Michigan, 2000), 2.

29. Data compiled prior to 1991 often uses the USSR as the unit; I have substituted 'Russia' for convenience, though this leads to some exaggeration.

30. Richards, 'Land Transformation,' 165.

31. See Kevin O'Rourke and Jeffrey Williamson, *Globalization and History* (Cambridge, Mass.: MIT Press, 1999), 41 (wheat) and 53 (sugar).

32. Ibid., 41.

33. R.H. Tawney, *Land and Labor in China* (Armonk, N.Y.: M. E. Sharpe, 1966), 87.

34. If frontier farmers had instead sought self-sufficiency (and eschewed credit), there would have been far fewer of them: circa 1860, starting a new farm in the United States cost seven–ten years of an average yeoman's earnings (plus the costs of migration). Federico, *Feeding the World*, 43.
35. William Cronon, *Nature's Metropolis* (New York: Norton, 1991), 109–47.
36. Frank Perlin, 'The Other Species World,' in Frank Perlin, *Unbroken Landscape. Commodity, Category, Sign and Identity: Their Production as Myth and Knowledge from 1500* (Aldershot, Ver.: Variorum, 1994), 206.
37. Ibid., 206–11.
38. John Bodnar, *The Transplanted: A History of Immigrants in Urban America* (Bloomington, Ind.: Indiana University Press, 1985), 25.
39. Federico, *Feeding the World*, 94. For a contrary view, see Alan Olmstead and Paul Rhode, *Creating Abundance: Biological Innovation and American Agricultural Development* (New York: Cambridge University Press, 2008).
40. José Ignacio Martínez Ruiz, 'Nitrates' in John McCusker, Lewis Cain, Stanley Engerman, David Hancock, and Kenneth Pomeranz, eds., *The History of World Trade Since 1450* (New York: Thomson Gale, 2006), 536–7.
41. Vaclav Smil, *Enriching the Earth: Fritz Haber, Carl Bosch, and the Transformation of World Food Production* (Cambridge, Mass.: MIT Press, 2001), xv.
42. Protein figure from Smil, *Enriching the Earth*, 157; comparison with human waste calculated using ibid., 27 and 142.
43. 'Pesticides' <http://www.pollutionissues.com/Na-Ph/Pesticides.html>.
44. James S. Donnelly, Jr., *The Great Irish Potato Famine* (Thrupp, U.K.: Sutton Publishing, 2005), 41.
45. The following account is drawn from Steven Stoll, *The Fruits of Natural Advantage: Making the Industrial Countryside in California* (Berkeley: University of California Press, 1998), 94–123.
46. Grigg, *Dynamics of Agricultural Change*, 78.
47. Federico, *Feeding the World*, 52–3.
48. Marc Reisner, *Cadillac Desert: The American West and its Disappearing Water* (New York: Penguin), 134.
49. Federico, *Feeding the World*, 45; Dwight Perkins, *Agricultural Development in China, 1368–1968* (Chicago: Aldine, 1969), 64.
50. Federico, *Feeding the World*, 45.
51. Overviews include Sandra Postel, *Pillar of Sand: Can the Irrigation Miracle Last?* (New York: Norton, 1999), and Fred Pearce, *When the Rivers Run Dry* (Boston: Beacon, 2006).
52. Pearce, *When the Rivers Run Dry*, 201–16.
53. Calculated from Richards, 'Land Transformation,' 165.
54. Ernest Harsch, 'Agriculture: Africa's "Engine for Growth,"' *African Recovery* 17: 4 (January 2004), accessed at <http://www.un.org/ecosocdev/geninfo/afrec/vol17no4/174ag.htm>.
55. Postel, *Pillar of Sand*; Kenneth Pomeranz, 'The Great Himalayan Watershed: Agrarian Crisis, Mega-Dams and the Environment,' *New Left Review* 58 (July/August 2009), 5–39; Reisner, *Cadillac Desert*; Pearce, *When the Rivers Run Dry*.
56. Federico, *Feeding the World*, 102. Several wealthy countries have aggressively promoted international patents for seeds; most of the poorer countries are opposed.
57. Federico, *Feeding the World*, 106.

58. Benedict Stavis, *Making Green Revolution* (Ithaca, N.Y.: Cornell University Center for International Studies Rural Development Committee, 1974), 26–40; McCann, *Maize and Grace*, 140–1.

59. Calculated from FAO data reported in Federico, *Feeding the World*, 20.

60. Federico, *Feeding the World*, 54, Smil, *Enriching the Earth*, 246. Since chemical fertilizer use in poor countries was minuscule in 1950, using that as a base year would produce even more astronomical increases.

61. Harsch, 'Agriculture: Africa's "Engine for Growth."'

62. Francine Frankel, *India's Green Revolution: Economic Gains and Political Costs* (Princeton: Princeton University Press, 1971), 35–40, 70–4, 105–9, 134–6, 175–7 shows a variety of outcomes across India; on Mexico, Joseph Cotter, *Troubled Harvest: Agronomy and Revolution in Mexico, 1880–2002* (Westport, Conn.: Praeger, 2003) 233–320, documents many of the major claims made about the impact of the Green Revolution, though often without judging the controversies.

63. Federico, *Feeding the World*, 193.

64. Federico, *Feeding the World*, 221.

65. Wilhlem Abel, *Agricultural Fluctuations in Europe From the Thirteenth to the Twentieth Centuries* (London: Methuen, 1989), esp. 1–5; Zhao Gang, *Man and Land in Chinese History: An Economic Analysis* (Stanford: Stanford University Press, 1986) and 'Zhongguo lishishang gongzi shuiping de bianqian,' *Zhongguo wenhua fuxing yuekan* 16: 9 (September, 1983), 52–7 make this case for Europe and China (which have better than average long run price data) respectively.

66. Federico, *Feeding the World*, 201–20.

67. Robert Allen, *Enclosure and the Yeoman* (Oxford: Clarendon Press, 1992), especially 235–65; Hoffmann, *Growth in a Traditional Society*, 16–20, 201–5; Federico, *Feeding the World*, 226–31; Penelope Francks, 'Rural Industry, Growth Linkages, and Economic Development in Nineteenth Century Japan,' *Journal of Asian Studies* 61: 1 (February 2002), 33–55; Harry Oshima, 'The Transition from an Agricultural to an Industrial Economy in East Asia,' *Economic Development and Cultural Change* 34: 4 (July 1986), 783–809. Pomeranz, 'Beyond the East–West Binary,' 550–5, 572–82.

68. 'Agricultural Subsidies: Facts and Figures,' Center for Trade and Development, <www.centad.org/relatedinfo9.asp>. These subsidies also far exceed those that European farmers received 1870–1914, when they were losing markets rapidly, Federico, *Feeding the World*, 190, 199–200.

69. McCann, *Maize and Grace*, 1.

70. John Talbot, *Grounds for Agreement: The Political Economy of the Coffee Commodity Chain* (Lanham, Md.: Rowman and Littlefield, 2004), 167–9. Ethiopian growers involved in contentious discussions with Starbuck's claim that they get only 5 percent of the retail price for their high-end coffee: see Kim Fellner, *Wrestling with Starbucks: Conscience, Capital, Cappuccino* (New Brunswick, N.J.: Rutgers University Press, 2008), 163–4, 180.

71. In the United States, private research and development spending for agriculture surpassed public spending in the 1980s: Federico, *Feeding the World*, 111.

72. Arega D. Alene, Victor M. Manyon, and James Gockowski, 'The Production Efficiency of Intercropping Annual and Perennial Crops in Southern Ethiopia: A Comparison of Distance Functions and Production Frontiers,' *Agricultural Systems* 91 (2006), 51–70; Special issue of *Agricultural Economics* 34: 2 (March 2006).

73. Paul Richards, *Indigenous Agricultural Revolution: Ecology and Food Production in West Africa* (London: Hutchinson, 1985), 66, 70–2, has some data, suggesting that inter-cropping compares particularly well with technified single-crop agriculture on less fertile soils; Gene Wilken, *Good Farmers: Traditional Agricultural Resource Management in Mexico and Central America* (Berkeley: University of California Press, 1987), 265–6, describes some of the problems in making quantitative comparisons.

References

ABEL, WILHELM. *Agrarian Fluctuations in Europe From the 13th to the 20th Centuries.* New York: St. Martin's, 1980.

ALLEN, ROBERT. *Enclosure and the Yeoman: The Agricultural Development of the South Midlands, 1450–1850.* New York: Oxford University Press, 1992.

BRAY, FRANCESCA. *The Rice Economies: Technology and Development in Asian Societies.* New York: Oxford University Press, 1985.

CAMPBELL, BRUCE. *English Seigniorial Agriculture, 1250–1450.* Cambridge: Cambridge University Press, 2000.

FEDERICO, GIOVANNI. *Feeding the World: An Economic History of Agriculture, 1800–2000.* Princeton: Princeton University Press, 2005.

GRIGG, DAVID. *The Dynamics of Agricultural Change.* London: Hutchinson, 1982.

HOFFMAN, PHILIP. *Growth in a Traditional Economy: The French Countryside, 1450–1815.* Princeton: Princeton University Press, 1996.

HURT, R. DOUGLAS. *American Agriculture: A Brief History.* West Lafayette, Ind.: Purdue University Press, 2002.

LUDDEN, DAVID. *Peasant History in South India.* Princeton: Princeton University Press, 1985.

MCCANN, JAMES. *Maize and Grace: Africa's Encounter with a New World Crop, 1500–2000.* Cambridge, Mass.: Harvard University Press, 2005.

MOON, DAVID. *The Russian Peasantry 1600–1930: The World the Peasants Made.* London: Addison Wesley Longman, 1999.

PERKINS, DWIGHT. *Agricultural Development in China, 1368–1968.* Chicago: Aldine, 1969.

SCHWARTZ, STUART B. *Sugar Plantations and the Formation of Brazilian Society.* Cambridge: Cambridge University Press, 1985.

SMITH, THOMAS. *The Agrarian Origins of Modern Japan.* Stanford: Stanford University Press, 1958.

WATSON, ANDREW. *Agricultural Innovation in the Early Islamic World.* Cambridge: Cambridge University Press, 1983.

PART III

PROCESSES

CHAPTER 15

....

MIGRATIONS

....

DIRK HOERDER

MIGRATIONS have long been studied under a nation-state paradigm as emigrants and immigrants—although these were the same men and women viewed under a constraining ideology of national identities from opposing viewpoints. Many early 'people's migrations'—the Mongols, the Huns, the Vikings—were conceived of as destructive; moving peoples were considered threatening by many resident peoples and administrators who made 'settlement' the norm. Most older research employed an interest-driven, color-of-skin hierarchy to buttress the dominance of colonizer migrants of the 'white races' over the 'colored races'—as if white is no color. Since the 1970s, the late nineteenth-century 'scientific racism' has been critiqued by 'Whiteness Studies' (Fredrickson) and 'Subaltern Studies' (Guha), and 'race' has been recognized as a social construction. New approaches, at first in Europe and North America, then in most societies of the world, consider migrating men and women as agents or even 'entrepreneurs' of their own lives who plan to invest their human and social capital under better if, usually, still (severely) constraining conditions.

While no accepted theory of migrations had been developed, a 'systems approach' and a global–local relationship are now widely accepted. The systems approach connects migration decisions and patterns (1) in the society of departure in local, regional, state-wide, and global frames; via (2) actual movement across distance given an era's means of transportation and communication; to (3) the society or, in the case of intermediate sojourns, societies of destination again in micro-, meso-, and macro-regional perspectives; and (4) linkages between the communities in which migrants spent or spend part of their lives (transcultural or diasporic). Interdisciplinary Transcultural Societal Studies (Hoerder) permit comprehensive analyses of the structures, institutions, and discursive frames of both the societies of origin and of arrival in particular local or regional variants—including industrialization, urbanization, social stratification, gender roles and family economies, demographic characteristics, political situation and developments, educational institutions, religious or other belief systems, ethno-cultural composition, and traditions of short- and long-distance migrations.

The systems approach analyzes the impact of out-migration onto families and societies of departure and of in-migration onto communities and receiving societies. What was the impact of the forced departure of millions of enslaved Africans or of hundreds of thousands of women from Philippine society today on each and every family involved (micro-history), on the region of departure (meso-level), and on whole societies and macro-regions? Could plantation societies have developed without forced, imported workers or European and American industrialization without the proletarian migrants from Europe's rural peripheries? How did migrating men and women negotiate cultural changes and necessary adjustments? The traditional interpretation of *im*migrant assimilation has been discarded (or reframed) since migrants come as fully socialized individuals. They *insert* themselves into economic niches, *accommodate* and *adjust* to particular sectors of the economy, society, and polity that are important and accessible to migrants. Over time, they complete a process of acculturation that fuses elements from the society of origin with those of the receiving society. This process, including partnership or marriage across cultural (formerly 'racial') lines has been called *métissage* or *mestizaje* or, in a 1930s and 1940s conceptualization in Latin American research, transculturation.

The systems approach, based on migrant agency within structural constraints, needs to be modified for involuntary migrants like forced, indentured, or enslaved workers, as well as refugees. These are deprived of agency at the time of departure. Their postmigration survival and insertion, however, depends on choices if under severe constraints.

Acculturation, that is, migrant agency, involves a continuous negotiation between different society-mandated demands or constraints and individual and family goals. The recent term 'transnationalism' overemphasizes nations, states, and political borders. Yet migrants connect their families, communities, and regions of origin with those of their destination (i.e. the 'local') across the globe. Thus, such connectivity has been called 'glocal.'[1]

The history of humanity is a history of migration rather than an early nomadic 'prehistory' and a subsequent 'history' of settled peoples. Migration periodization differs between macro-regions but the following eras may be discerned:

- after 200,000 BP: early spread of *Homo sapiens* out of East Africa across the world;
- 15,000 to 5000 BCE: early sedentary agriculture;
- 5000 to 500 BCE: differentiation during urbanization from Mesopotamia to Indic societies and the Egyptian-Phoenician world;
- 500 BCE–1500 CE: migrations in a settled world;
- 1400–1600: intercultural contact and trade circuits;
- 1600–1800: colonizer and colonized societies;
- 1800–1914: global systems;
- post-1914 refugee and labor movements with a caesura about 1950.

Migrations involve intercultural exchange as well as conflict; a human-agency approach emphasizes that even forced migrants leave their mark, if under severely constrained conditions.

For heuristic purposes the multiplicity of early migrations may be simplified into types by variables including reasons for departure, establishment of new communities in unsettled areas or after establishing rule over settled peoples, duration of stay, and degree of mobility.

- Migration *within a cultural group* over different geographic locations involved hunting-and-gathering as well as matrilineal or patrilineal marriage migration.
- *Outbound branching* or *filiation migration* of segments of a cultural group into new, unsettled areas.
- *Colonization migrations* into settled areas involve establishing rule over peoples already present with *conquest* that may involve violence, exploitation, and oppression.
- When a group's survival is threatened or new living spaces are sought *whole-community migration* or *migration of peoples* to unsettled or settled regions involving conquest or cohabitation.
- *Cross-community migration* denoting (a) peaceful permanent moves into, or (b) temporary 'sojourning' within another group's social space, or (c) involuntary transport of captives for forced labor in another community.
- Itinerant or nomadic ways of life, all involving both men and women, and sometimes also children and the elderly.

Dispersion of humans involves spatial separation and distinct cultural evolutions. Migrations impact the group of origin since those departing take their knowledge and skills, their emotions and spirituality with them: 'funds of knowledge' as resources to reestablish societies under different, often difficult conditions at the destination where fusion of capabilities, spirituality, and emotions may be innovative. But newcomers may also spread diseases or destroy local belief systems. Peoples decimated by epidemics or warfare may have to migrate to reconstitute viable communities or flee further oppression. Instead of peaceful resolution or prolonged warfare, competition over spaces may involve asymmetrical, interest-driven, and power-mediated ways of interaction.

Homo Sapiens' Migrations and the 'Agricultural Revolution'

About 150,000–200,000 years ago, *Homo sapiens*, knowledgeable men and women, evolved in East Africa and perhaps also in Asia. They spread across the world in three major phases, beginning with settlement of the African-Eurasian tropics before 60,000 BP. A second phase expanded human habitation from the Nile Valley and Red Sea to South

Asia relying on water's-edge technology; and, when the 'ice age' before 20,000 BP lowered sea levels, peoples moved to a subcontinent Sunda, now the Southeast Asian islands, and with new seafaring techniques, to Sahul, now the islands from New Guinea to Australia.

In a third phase, 40,000–30,000 BP, humans moved toward cooler and drier climates along three major routes: northward from Southeast Asia to Korea, the Japanese islands, and into the Amur River Valley; westward from the Sino-Tibetan region through the steppes to Europe; and from the Nile Valley-Fertile Crescent-Black Sea region northward and westward. In addition, small groups crossed the then-dry Bering Strait into the Americas. In *Homo sapiens'* differentiation in 'deep time,' women's genes and their child-bearing capability played a particularly important role as modeling in linguistics, genetics, and archaeology indicates. Early human beings are defined by language, by genetic variation, and by tools and pottery, but not by ethnic or national culture. Cultural exchange required translators, and new ecological environments demanded adjustment strategies.

By the beginning of the 'Agricultural Revolution,' 15,000 to 5000 BP, the locations of the twelve major language groups had been established, and humans achieved an understanding of plant and animal evolution: 'domestication' permitted the transition from *natural* to agri- and horti-*cultural* foods. In a first phase humans experimented with intensive harvesting and new fishing techniques, and migrants spread the knowledges outward from the Fertile Crescent (Anatolia to the Nile), Southeast Asia, Yunnan, New Guinea, West Africa, and Mesoamerica. The productivity stimulated demand for storage facilities and craft products, permitted sedentary ways of life, and resulted in higher population growth rates. Uneven population growth set in motion new social dynamics and migrations. The second phase involved a re-peopling of settled regions through cross-cultural or colonizer contact. In this period, Africa stopped holding the majority of the world's population.[2]

CITIES, CIVILIZATIONS, AND SEABORNE MIGRATIONS TO 500 CE

Intensification of food production, especially of grains and tubers, domestication of pack and draft animals, the invention of the wheel, and new shipbuilding technologies and navigational supports enlarged the distances humans could traverse. Mariners decoded the seasonal monsoons in the first millennium BCE and thus 'domesticated' the Indian Ocean. Migrating people further differentiated themselves.

Freed from foraging, labor could be devoted to handicrafts and improved abodes; exchange required places of meeting. Around 8000–6000 BCE the first towns emerged in Palestine and Egypt. By 2000 BCE Mesopotamian cities accommodated 50,000 or more; around 250 BCE Patna and Chang'an became the world's largest cities. Urban concentration involved high mobility and specialization. Men and women moved in and out depending on a city's relative position in trading systems, inter-dynastic warfare, or relocation of capital and capitals. Cities' needs for provisions required belts of intensive agriculture, which attracted rural families and laborers. Denser populations were more vulnerable to natural as well as man-made disruptions.

Rural–urban exchanges intensified, commercial networks expanded, and ruling families or groups extended their realms. Coastal shipping and land routes (later known as the 'silk roads') linked the eastern Mediterranean and Sumerian worlds with the Southeast Asian islands and south China. A trans-Mediterranean Eurasian–North African trading sphere also emerged. Along their routes migrants relied on mobile carters or sailors, translators or moneychangers. Men and women formed intercultural unions; their children might be ostracized as 'bastards,' become part of a sedentary mother's community, or emerge as a new people ('ethnogenesis'). In-migrating men might marry local women to gain access to social relations and practices. In addition, scholars moved between patronage-providing courts, and translators mediated between cultural significations. Walled cities distinguished insiders from outsiders and forced migrants and merchants to ask permission to enter. 'Citizenship' as a membership category established formal hurdles, while ascriptions based on language established informal hurdles. The Greek term 'barbarian,' originally designating those out-siders not speaking Greek, came to imply uncouth and inferior outsiders.

Rulers' destructive expansionist and inter-imperial warfare commanded armed men to move and sparked civilians' temporary or long-term refugee migrations. To satisfy demand for labor, powerful states bound workers temporarily or enslaved them for life in both involuntary forced mobility and subsequent immobility at destination. The building of ceremonial places, such as pyramids, the construction of canals in China or roads in Rome, the erection of fortifications as in Cuzco required multi-annual mobilization of tens of thousands of laborers and service personnel.

The urban and imperial civilizations provided long-distance connective structures. Inter-faith contact could result in religio-cultural conversion processes and new cultures. New belief systems about societal and spiritual realms emerged from migrant philosophers and prophets; some religions encouraged contemplative pilgrimages; the Hebrews remem-ber their forced migration into bound labor; missionaries migrated as humble servants of their God, as warrior preachers, or as faith-propagating merchants. Codification and homogenization of belief systems also generated dissent and schisms which could result in out-migration or, in the case of so-called holy wars, refugee migrations. Whole religious-social groups, like the Jews and the Zoroastrians, (were) dispersed. The change from agrarian to urban spiritual practices replaced fertility goddesses with male gods in the religions of the book and the Sino-Tibetan system of transcendental thought. As new societal norms, such beliefs restricted women's migrations over the next millennia.

MIGRATIONS AND SOCIETIES, 500 BCE–1500 CE

In Africa, Nile Valley peoples connected to the Mediterranean seafaring cultures, the sub-Saharan Khoi and Bantu speakers moved westward and southward, and the savannah peoples migrated westward. In the first millennium CE, West African societies stabilized and connected through trans-Saharan caravan trading to the Mediterranean. Under rights-in-persons slavery, men admitted mobile poor relatives and debtors to their households. Since women's labor was highly valued, their involuntary migrations often remained within the region. Male war captives were sold over longer distances and across the Indian Ocean. Swahili-speaking merchants provided inland connections, Arab speakers the trans-oceanic ones. Ocean-borne eastbound connectivity was high.

Peoples in the eastern Mediterranean world experienced mobility and realignments of cultures with the spread of the Greek-Persian 'Hellenistic' culture and brief expansion of Macedonian rule to the Indus River. Subsequently, the Roman empire's politics of conquest and incorporation involved Greek artisans' migrations, forced migration of slaves, recruitment of soldiers from sub-Saharan and northern Africa, and the dispersal of the Jewish population. Expansion involved intermarriage and cultural *métissage*.

From the fifth century BCE, central European Celtic and Germanic peoples migrated eastward to Asia Minor, northward to Scandinavia, westward to the British Isles, and south-westward to Iberia. Around 800 CE peasants became sedentary, but secular and religious administrators moved in circuits of rule. In the central European empire, which temporarily extended from Sicily to Scandinavia, emperors spoke Arabic, empresses came from Byzantium, African personnel migrated to northern courts. Peasants, seemingly immobile as serfs, escaped to cities or were sent off by their owners. From the eighth century, northern peoples with little land for farming and much seafaring experience reached North America via Iceland and Greenland, migrated across the Baltic Sea, established rule over local peoples along the Dnieper River, and sailed out to occupy England, settle Normandy, and establish a state in Sicily. Medieval European societies were mobile.

Migrants and armies of the new Islamic faith moved via North Africa to Iberia where they settled as cultivators or craftsmen. A tri-cultural, inter-religious Muslim-Jewish-Christian society and center of learning emerged. Its capital, Córdoba, housed a population of perhaps 500,000 by the tenth century. Migrations reversed direction when Frankish Christian armies conquered this multicultural society.

Across the Eurasian steppes, mobile horse-borne men and women established aggressive realms of rule. From their intrusion into northern India, the Vedic culture emerged after 1500 BCE, and in the first millennium CE, they conquered Chinese peasant societies. This war-faring mobility disrupted the silk road trade and thus intensified the Arab and Gujarati Indian Ocean exchanges until the trans-Asian *pax mongolorum* reopened connections.[3]

In East Asia, people realigned themselves from mid-eighth century. By the eleventh century, Chinese seafarers, having invented the compass, established diasporic communities. The empire's cosmopolitan urban populations included migrants of many faiths from as far as the Caucasus and the British Isles. Internally, artisans migrated to centers of demand, urban men and women moved to distant towns, and administrators circulated. Peasants moved to more thinly settled lands. Recurring natural calamities caused short-term and long-term population displacement. Reliance on human porters implied high mobility, and large canal construction projects required workers from afar.

In the Americas, migrating Mesoamerican peoples carried maize, the yields of which permitted peoples to become sedentary, to the Adena and Hopewell mound-builders of the Mississippi Valley (ca. 700 BCE–400 CE). A succession of cultural encounters, state-building, and warfare mobilized peoples. The Mayan cities in the Yucatan peninsula attracted migrants from 1800 BCE but were abandoned in the tenth century CE. The agricultural and scholarly achievements of in-migrating peoples provided the base for the fourteenth-century Mexica (Aztec) culture. In the Inca empire, mandatory labor, involuntary resettlement of rebellious populations, and voluntary rural–urban moves were integral to life.

In these interactions over great distances contemporaries recognized a many-cultured Eurasian-African 'ecumene.' When the mid-fourteenth century plagues killed about one-third of the people in the regions touched, migrations of resettlement had to reestablish viable population centers.

Two Worlds into One, 1400–1600

Two unrelated developments at the eastern and western rim of the ecumene changed global power relations after 1400. The Chinese empire's outward contacts, during their apogee (1405–35), extended to India, Ceylon, Aden, and perhaps beyond. Hundreds of thousands moved. Then the imperial authorities abruptly ended outreach, and only the southern provinces' merchants and migrants continued to connect to the diasporic communities in Southeast Asia without government support, arms, or other defenses. At the same time, the Crown of tiny Portugal sent armed trader-warriors southward along the African coasts for direct gold trading and access to bound, exploitable human labor.

The rise of Europe's Atlantic littoral induced seafarers from declining Mediterranean economies to migrate to the new opportunities, among them Christopher Columbus, whose tiny vessels, one-eighth the size of Chinese junks, reached the 'West Indies.' Along a circum-African route Vasco da Gama reached India's ports, using his guns to force East African cities to re-provision his ships and provide him with pilots. The armed Iberian migrants connected the Americas into the worldwide migration patterns, destroyed the Indian Ocean's trade protocols and—in the long run—established the Euro-Atlantic world's predominance.

The Iberian Catholic rulers, by expelling the Jewish and Muslim communities, deprived themselves of long-distance trading expertise and artisanal producers. The Protestant urban Netherlands, the Ottoman empire, and North African societies welcomed these refugees with their funds of knowledge. These fifteenth- and sixteenth-century global power structures are the origins of post-colonial migrations since the mid-twentieth century.

In the Americas, where exchange and migration networks had connected complex and simple cultures, the conquistadores' wars, brutal exploitation, and even more so their unwitting introduction of Euroasian pathogens caused population collapse. Their in-migration became genocidal in the Caribbean, near-genocidal in Mesoamerica, and destructive to the dispersed North and eastern South American peoples. The forced migrations of African slaves and forced relocation of native peoples created a labor force for the Spanish and Portuguese newcomers. A trans-Pacific exchange from New Spain to Spanish Manila, the first phase of the Pacific migration system, brought enslaved and free Asian migrants as well as diasporic Chinese to American colonies.

The subsequent 'peopling of the Americas' by Europeans—one-half to two-thirds of whom came as indentured laborers[4]—was a re-peopling. The 'white Atlantic's' numerically small migrations and its new power relations brought forth a 'black Atlantic': to the 1830s more Africans than Europeans would reach the Americas. Societies and economies in the Americas were built by migrating men and women, free and unfree. The 'Columbian exchange' introduced domesticated animals into the Americas and some native peoples developed horse-borne mobility. To Europe it introduced food plants and stimulants. Potatoes, corn, and beans provided new food resources that sustained population growth which, by the nineteenth century, compelled millions to depart for the Americas.

Two approaches—one cultural, one economic—help to conceptualize this early globalization. According to Jerry H. Bentley inter-civilizational and cross-cultural exchange involved conversion through voluntary association, political-social-economic pressures, or assimilation. Immanuel Wallerstein's world-systems analysis, which emphasized economic factors to explain Europe's post-1500 predominance, was decentered by Janet L. Abu-Lughod, who synthesized the multiple pre-1500s circuits of trading and mobility with their respective independent accumulation processes. Eric Wolf discussed the subsequent connecting migration across the tropical and subtropical plantation belt.[5]

People on the Move in Colonizer, Self-ruled, and Colonized Societies to 1800

In the first century of trans-Atlantic, circum-African, and trans-Indian Ocean sailings, the state-supported armed merchants of Europe established fortified places of exchange in much of West Africa and Asia, which at first required little in-migration, scarcely impacting local migrations and societies inland, but would later force tens of millions into long-distance slave migrations.

Slaves first came to the Iberian peninsula as servants and laborers. Then the often deadly regime of chattel slavery was instituted in the plantation economies and some 12.4 million men and women were force-migrated towards the Americas in this age of gunpowder empires—misnamed by Europeans the 'age of exploration.' Of those enslaved, some two million did not survive the Middle Passage. Within Africa, population loss was higher still due to deaths through raids and the march to coastal or desert-edge depots. In the Americas, the enslaved recreated specific ethno-cultures, especially in societies like Brazil with a high percentage of manumitted and free Africans as well as 'mulattos' (offspring of white–black unions and rape). In other societies (the United States, for example) generic slave cultures emerged because of intermediate sojourns on Caribbean plantations and small numbers of people from each specific culture of origin.

Asia's macro-regions, the land-centered Chinese empire, the Japanese islands, the Southeast Asian societies, and the peoples of South Asia developed widely differing patterns of migration. China's southern provinces became regions of emigration; people further north migrated within the empire. In India people migrated to territories depopulated by warfare, more thinly settled, or more difficult to till. Regardless of culture, each peasant family with more than two surviving children needed additional land, or the next generation had to resort to migration to feed itself. Social ecologies framed migration strategies: whole families departed if means permitted. More often, some children migrated to marginal regions nearby, to distant quality land, or to urban labor markets whether in a nearby town or across an ocean. Their remittances sustained kin at a 'home' that did not sustain a family.

Parallel to China's inward and Portugal's outward turn, a third change of global impact in the 'hinge region' between the Indian Ocean migration and trade routes and the Mediterranean world involved the rise of the Muslim Ottoman Empire. To develop under-populated regions, its authorities resettled families involuntarily but offered incentives to induce kin and friends from the region of origin to follow voluntarily. Its innovative 'neutral' imperial state governed peoples defined by religious and ethno-cultural groups which administered themselves. To avoid ethnocratic rule (which became the principle of nineteenth-century nation-states), the imperial administration used an artificial *lingua nullius*, the imperial court's women were chosen from in-migrating educated Central Asian or African slaves, the core army consisted of bound soldiers recruited from afar. The Empire attracted refugees with human and social capital. From 1300 to 1600 it provided a model of a state that permitted structural accommodation for residents and migrants of many cultures and religions.

When sixteenth-century Christian Europe divided itself into Catholics, Protestants, and smaller 'sects,' religious strife generated refugees. The Thirty Years' or First European War (1618–48) left one-third of the population dead, and whole regions needed in-migrants to regain socio-economic viability. The Huguenots from Catholic France carried their capabilities to other Protestant societies; the English Puritans fled to the Netherlands and migrated on to North America. Intra-European migrations remained far more voluminous than long-distance ones, and three migration regions emerged at mid-seventeenth century: the North Sea system centered on the urbanized Netherlands, the circum-Baltic economies attracted migrants, and central Spain received laboring men from south-central France who usually married locally.[6]

In the post-contact Americas, the decimated native peoples still formed majorities; enslaved and a few free Africans the second-largest group, and Europeans the smallest but heavily armed and, thus, most powerful group. From the migrations new societies emerged in the Caribbean, New Spain, and Portuguese Brazil. In North America, migrants from New Spain, Catholic French migrants, and, last, Anglophone Puritans arrived.

While in all societies of the globe traditional patterns of migrations persisted, many of the migrations became interrelated: ascendant Europe's colonizer migrants, upon arrival, set in motion local producer and trader migrations; migrant imperial personnel moved colonized people; investor migrants imposed slave and indentured migrations. By the eighteenth century, a plantation belt circled the world. Most of the colonizer migrants were men without families. They hired 'boys' and servant women to do their work and provide local food. The administrators of the gunpowder empires lacked intercultural capabilities and had to rely on the transcultural skills and initiative of Chinese, Jewish, Armenian, Arab, or other migrants to obtain goods from local producers. The dialectic of Europe's regime of forced labor involved involuntary mobilization of men and women in less well-armed societies as well as immobilization through bondage after transport. Europe's emigrant peasant families expelled hunting as well as settled farming populations in the Americas, Australia, South Africa, and elsewhere. Across the globe, region-specific migrations continued regardless of long-distance and colonizer out- or in-migration.

In regions of farming and home production—Indian villages, Swiss mountain valleys, New England's hills—where women and men produced cloth or labor-intensive goods in winter, the introduction of large 'manufactures' (centers of hand produc-tion) in towns and cities dislocated people. They had to migrate to jobs, and out of such 'proto-industrial' mobility the nineteenth-century proletarian mass migrations would develop.

NINETEENTH-CENTURY GLOBAL MIGRATION SYSTEMS

Four major migrations systems operated from 1815 to 1914:

- the Afro-Atlantic slave migration and forced labor system to the 1870s;
- in and from Asia, a regime of migration under indenture, by credit-ticket, and free migration under economic constraints from the 1830s to the 1920s–1930s;
- from Europe outward, after 1815, the Atlantic migration system, which stagnated from the 1930s; and
- a continental system stretching from European to Siberian Russia after the 1820s, changing in the 1930s, and ending in the 1950s.

The vast majority of migrating men and women were laborers.

Trans-Atlantic moves involved some 50–55 million from the 1820s to the 1930s. In the Russo-Siberian system, including the trans-Caspian region, some 10–20 million moved in the century before 1914. The Asian systems involved approximately 48–52 million Indians and southern Chinese. Toward the end of the nineteenth century, a Northeastern Asian and Russian system began, that would involve around 46–51 million. Only about one million Asian migrants bound for the Americas accounted for the Pacific migration system's second phase.[7]

In Europe, the revolutionary, anti-revolutionary, and Napoleonic-imperial warfare after 1792 mobilized more than a million soldiers, uprooted millions of men, women, and children as refugees, and discarded wounded and exhausted soldiers far from their places of origin. From the 1820s German-language peasant families resumed migrations. Since Tsarist authorities came to prefer Slavic migrants for the south Russian plains, they turned westward to the Atlantic and, over the century, this route became the common choice in western, then northern, and finally in eastern and southern Europe. Other migrants targeted colonized lands of non-white peoples for agricultural settlement—Algeria, South Africa, Kenya, Australia—or, in small numbers, colonies of exploitation in the Caribbean, South Asia, the Southeast Asian islands, or elsewhere. In the nineteenth century, Europe's population growth was the highest in the world; in the twentieth century, other macro-regions would send out emigrants for this very reason.

In mid-nineteenth century, one-third of the North America-bound migrants went into agriculture, but by the 1890s the 'proletarian mass migration' targeted jobs in industry. The combination of rural immigrants, in a gender ratio of 60 men to 40 women, and mechanization permitted the transition to urban-industrial production. From the Iberian and Italian peninsulas most migrants selected South America as a destination whose frontier societies seemed attractive, but most had to become rural or urban wage workers. About one-third of the so-called immigrants returned to Europe; they had come as sojourners or 'guest-workers.' Racism in North America led to exclusion of migrants from Asia since the early 1880s and of 'olive' or 'dark' South and East Europeans after 1921. Canada admitted migrants through the 1920s.[8]

The forced migrations of the 'black Atlantic' seemed about to end when slaves in Haiti, in the Afro-Caribbean phase of the age of revolution, freed themselves and when the slave trade was prohibited in 1807/08 and 1815. Immigrant white plantation investors experimented with replacement labor—impoverished European (white) workers or Asian (yellow or brown) workers—but they also purchased a further two million force-migrated Africans. Abolition of slavery, in the 1830s in British colonies and in 1863–65 in the United States, came in Brazil and Cuba only in the 1880s. Few free and freed African-origin Americans returned to Africa, especially Liberia and Sierra Leone. In Brazilian and Cuban Afro-European-Amerindian mixed societies, transculturation processes differed from those in the segregated Protestant United States. Freed African-origin people in South America and the Caribbean migrated inter-regionally, but in the United States, racist control mechanisms delayed out-migration from the southern states until the early 1900s.[9]

The rising consumption of tropical foods in the white Atlantic world kept the demand for bound colonial labor high. Parallel to the end of slavery, the British empire introduced indentured servitude to India in the 1830s and, forcing the opium trade on Chinese society in the 1840s, increased poverty- and debt-related indentured migration. In Japan, the new elites' program of industrial modernization, funded through heavy taxation of the peasantry, forced young rural people into emigration from the 1870s. In the European-owned plantation belt from Burma and Mauritius via Natal to the Caribbean, the indentured 'coolies' and, in far larger numbers, credit-ticket migrants faced brutal exploitation. One-third of the bound laborers from India were women; Chinese gender relations almost excluded women; from Japan, men and women migrated. Parallel free 'passenger' migrant families set up business and established communities. In World War I, hundreds of thousands of indentured workers labored as 'colonial auxiliaries' in Britain and France. India's pro-independence politicians then negotiated the abolition of the system sometimes called 'second slavery.'[10]

Both workers and peasants created the fourth, Russo-Siberian migration system. The Siberia-bound migrants interacted with deported criminals and political dissidents. Though the communal character of villages in European Russia made individual out-migration difficult, ever more peasants migrated temporarily to industrializing cities and the Donbass and Urals mining region, thirteen million in the decade after emancipation in 1861. Small numbers of West and Central European experts and skilled craftsmen crossed the divide between this and the Atlantic migration system eastbound and, from the 1880s, economic and ethnic oppression resulted in emigration of Jews, Ukrainians, and German-speaking former immigrant peasants to Western Europe and North America.

At the end of the nineteenth century, specific consequences of these mass migrations accelerated the rate of departures: settlement of grain-producing plains in North America, South Russia, Argentina, and Australia, together with mechanization of harvesting, caused a collapse of world market prices. Europe's marginal farming families, unable to compete, had to send sons and daughters to distant wage work to support by remittances the deficit-producing 'home'—a process that would be repeated in the southern hemisphere in the second half of the twentieth century. At the same time, eastward city-bound migrations of farming family's children to industrial jobs and urban amenities in the United States surpassed in volume the mythologized westward migrations.

Rather than expect 'unlimited opportunities,' an image carefully developed by some receiving societies, migrants moved to 'bread' and hard work. Asian-origin plantation laborers in Hawai`i, European-origin workers in Brazil's coffee plantations or North America's industries, and African-origin Caribbean laborers built the urban and industrialized societies of the early twentieth century. Nineteenth-century bound and free migrants in the (sub)-tropical global plantation belt—factories in the fields— produced food for the industrializing societies as well as for other labor migrants.[11]

REFUGEE-GENERATION, UNMIXING OF PEOPLES, AND FORCED LABOR MIGRATIONS TO THE 1950S

In Asia, mobility accelerated from northern China to Manchuria. Japan's elites—pursuing both Western concepts of 'modernization' and an anti-(Western)-imperialist rhetoric—undertook aggressive expansion. Dislocated colonized Koreans had to labor for the occupier. Millions of migrant Indian laborers produce rice in British Burma.

In the Atlantic world, the decades from the 1880s to the 1920s have been called the apogee of nation-states as well as—in a certain contradiction—of imperialism. However, Europe's Habsburg, Hohenzollern, Romanov, and Ottoman dynasties ruled over many peoples; the Windsor dynasty as well as republican France ruled over colonized peoples across the world; and the United States established hegemony over peoples in Spain's former possessions—Cuba, Puerto Rico, and the Philippines. Multicultural polities with intercultural power hierarchies were the rule, and they forced disadvantaged and/or oppressed ethno-cultural groups into migration. Empire-wide transport and communication connections were usually not intended for migrations but did facilitate them.

From the 1880s, Europe's imperial bureaucrats began to impose one nation's dominance over 'lesser' peoples and, to escape de-culturalization, Jews emigrated from Russia, Slovaks from Habsburg lands; others fled decimation, for example the Armenians. The nation-states' late-nineteenth-century introduction of passport legislation made entry regulation far more restrictive while demands for loyalty and military service increased. To belong, migrants and resident minorities in a kind of unconditional surrender of culture had to 'assimilate' to the newly constructed nation's ways of life. If migrants' supposed inferiority was alleged to be genetic, they became unassimilable 'races.'

Europe's empires' refusal to grant equality to minority peoples resulted in the Balkan War and World War I and generated millions of refugees. New post-war nation-states, driven by the ideology of national homogeneity, initiated programs of 'unmixing' of peoples or 'ethnic cleansing.' For half a century, Europe became the world's major refugee-generating region.[12]

By the 1920s and in particular during the Great Depression, most states in the North Atlantic world no longer required migrant workers. Exceptions were France and Canada (as well as Australia in Asia). In North America, macro-regional disparities and American economic growth led to African-Americans' and Mexicans' northbound mass migrations. In the Soviet Union, the 1930s reconstruction of cities and industries after war and civil war resulted in harsh, Stalinist labor regimentation and forced migrations. Peasant families fled collectivization, and consequent production collapse led to famine-induced mass migrations, especially in Ukraine.

In their warfare, the European and Japanese imperial powers had to rely on colonized, auxiliary laborers and soldiers. By the late 1930s, millions of workers had to labor where the Japanese needed them, and 100 million Chinese were fleeing the advancing armies. Nazi Germany, from the occupation of Poland in 1939, deported some eleven million men, women, and—sometimes—children to labor camps. After the war, mass refugee movements, repatriation of prisoners of war and Japanese soldiers, migrations from and to destroyed cities, emigration of displaced persons, and flight from new communist regimes in East Central Europe kept mobility high. The fascist German state had deported Germans of Jewish faith as well as others. Fleeing Jews often went to Palestine where their arrival and Arab states' warfare, in turn, created a Palestinian Muslim refugee population. At this time, white-ruled South Africa imposed forced labor migration and rigorous apartheid on its Black African population.

In the interwar years, from among colonized peoples Indian students migrated to Great Britain, while West African and Caribbean students went to France. Invited to absorb colonizer cultures, the students experienced discrimination and racism. These bicultural migrants developed a new intercultural dialectic. Recognizing the equal value of European and African, white and black cultures, students from Senegal and Martinique called for cultural fusion, 'négritude.' At this time, the first colonial African laborers settled in southern France, Indian sailors lived in London, Chinese sailors in port cities across the world. The white societies uneasily tolerated such marginal enclaves.

DECOLONIZATION AND NEW GLOBAL PATTERNS
OF MIGRATION SINCE THE 1950S

The imperialist states did not use the post-1945 rearrangement of power for a negotiated end to colonialism. (Re)-colonized peoples thus had to resort to wars of liberation. From decolonization three major types of migration ensued, 'reverse,' 'displacement,' and income-generating migrations. The 'Western' countries, which had sent migrants—often armed—to all parts of the world, became the destination of unarmed, often desperately poor migrants who defied controls if barred from entry.

Decolonization ended, first, the temporary presence of administrators and soldiers in colonies of exploitation, and, second, the privileged position of long-term settler families in food- and stimulant-producing colonies. Many left in 'reverse migration,' whether in immediate flight or over time. Such colony-born 'Creoles' had never known the colonizer society of origin, and thus their flight was not 'return' migration. Third, colonial auxiliaries of the empires, often used to police their co-ethnics, had to leave— whether they were locally recruited as in French Algeria, transported across the British empire as the Sikhs, or pitted as minority against majority as in the case of the Hmong support for the United States in Indochina. Fourth, people of mixed ancestry and elites with cultural affinity to a colonizer core found themselves in a precarious position.

The former colonizer states, however, refused to admit their erstwhile allies as immigrants but reluctantly accepted some 5.5–8.5 million Italian, French, British, Belgian, Dutch, and other white colonial Creoles before 1975. In the 'mother country' mixed-origin families faced racism; 'colored' auxiliaries ended up in camps or substandard housing.

Displacement migrations began when, first, the departure of colonizer elites with their capital, skills, and knowledge, created havoc in the economies of the new nations. Second, some newly independent states 'unmixed' peoples by ethnic or religious affiliation: the division of British India into a predominantly Hindu India and a predominantly Muslim Pakistan in 1947 generated four million refugees. Third, dominant majorities or ruling elites might displace immigrant minorities perceived as a threat to the new states' 'national' homogeneity: South Asians were expelled from Kenya and Uganda, Tamils from Sri Lanka. A fourth issue involved status or class as when in China and Vietnam landowners were deported. Such policy-induced mass departures resulted in further disruptions of socio-economic structures. Dysfunctional systems lost their educated and economically active members as Europe's reactionary dynastic states in the nineteenth century. Internally, new (male) elites often did not achieve stability: single-party rule by the former forces of national liberation, by clans or dictators, war between ethno-cultural and ethno-religious segments of a population, warlord self-enrichment, and religious or ideological fundamentalism generated refugees from lives without prospects, comparable to post-1945 European displaced persons. Many post-colonial migrants decide to move to the wealthy former colonizer countries with which, after generations of rule, they shared language and at least some practices, but far more moved among developing countries.[13]

In addition, migration-inducing disruption resulted from the post-colonial North–South divide institutionalized by re-colonizing unequal terms of trade that favored the industrialized and powerful world north of the Mediterranean and the Caribbean and, thus, pitted one-sixth to one-quarter of the global population (living in the European Union, the Soviet Union, and North America) against the rest of the world. According to United Nations as well as World Bank reports, in the mid-1990s the richest 20 percent of the world's populations are almost sixty times as wealthy as the poorest 20 percent. This gap doubled since decolonization and continues to grow. Under this regime of economic 'global apartheid,' the average annual per capita Gross National Product amounted to $380 in low-income countries as compared to $23,090 in high-income economies. Ever more people attempt to reach job-providing societies and economies with or without official documents. Similar migrations connected China's investment-deprived countryside to the metropoles and industrializing towns. By 2000, some 160 million Chinese men and women were on the move, and similar migration took place in India, Russia, and Brazil.

Across the globe, eight macro-regional overlapping migration systems emerged in the latter twentieth century. Two south–north systems replaced the transatlantic one.

(1) Western Europe's population, depleted by warfare, grew by millions of eastern German-origin refugees and expellees, displaced persons, and reverse colonial migrants. Post-war economic growth brought demand for additional labor, and in the mid-1950s South European and, from the 1960s, North African 'guest workers' moved north. Expected to return, they pursued their own strategies. They settled, called for their families, and by 2000 accounted for approximately 8–10 percent of the receiving societies' populations.

(2) A parallel south–north system developed in the Americas. From the 1880s, but especially from the 1940s, migrants from Mexico and, since the 1920s, migrants from the Caribbean went to the United States and, from the mid-1950s, to Canada. They often departed in connection with disruptive or mobilizing penetration of American capital into their societies. When in the 1960s Canada and the United States replaced race-based admission criteria by merit systems, migrants arrived from some 180 cultures.

(3) The dependent position of Latin American economies in the global system of inequalities as well as the limited investment strategies of these societies' elites explain the gap between labor supply and job availability. Within the region Caribbean, Central, and South American peoples moved to faster-developing countries. The 1970s and 1980s right-wing dictatorships, supported by some United States administrations, generated refugees who created a North American–European diaspora. Recently, Brazil, Argentina, and Venezuela have become centers of attraction.

(4) South Korea, Singapore, and Malaysia attracted Asian migrants inter-regionally to sustain their economic growth. The historic Chinese diaspora, under pressure from increasingly nationalist host societies, often had to depart or flee. Japan, for racist reasons, did not admit migrants and continues to discriminate against its Korean laboring population.

(5) The intra-Asian migrations were supplemented by the third phase of the Pacific migration system that emerged from the late 1960s. Men and women from the three Chinas, India, the Philippines, and Southeast Asia moved to the United States and Canada and, in smaller numbers, to those European societies to which colonial ties had existed.

(6) The booming oil-extracting economies of the Persian Gulf region attracted experts from the West, male workers from the societies of West Asia, North Africa, and the Indian Ocean rim as well as the Philippines; and women in distinct migration circuits for domestic labor. These states do not grant resident status but rely on labor force rotation. The exclusion of women, one-half of the population, from education and waged labor outside the home generates part of the permanent need for foreign temporary workers. In the United Arab Emirates they account for 80 percent of the population.

(7) In sub-Saharan Africa, expanding economies, like those of Somalia and Kenya at some periods of time and, since the end of apartheid, South Africa, attracted workers. In some countries, dysfunctional elites (at first still colonizer-trained or

colonizer-supported) and equally disruptive World Bank-imposed cuts in social services exacerbated poverty and joblessness. Large-volume internal rural–urban moves
and out-migration to former colonizer countries (which often refused to grant admission papers) have been the consequence.

(8) Before 1989, the socialist East European countries' social-human right to
work seemed to preclude the need for labor migration to distant jobs. However,
collectivization, uneven rural–urban development, economic growth in Hungary and
Yugoslavia and in sections of the USSR, and investments in southern Siberia, did result
in high levels of inter-regional and inter-state mobility. Prohibition of emigration
separated this macro-region from all other migration regions. Since 1989, new East–
West migrations took shape and centers like Moscow or Prague attracted internal,
Chinese, and Western migrants.

Migrations at the turn of the twenty-first century evidenced two new global phenomena: feminization and de-/re-racialization. In present-day refugee-generation, the vast
majority of the displaced are women, since warfare remains a male undertaking. In
addition, unaccompanied children have to flee on their own. In the labor-importing
segments of the world, women account for the majority of in-migrants due to the rise
of electronics and 'light' manufacturing as well as to the growth of the service sector. In
societies where resident women have achieved some measure of job parity but men do
not share the household labor, the need for domestic help has evolved from cleaning
jobs to care-giving skills. Infants and small children are raised and the elderly cared for
by in-migrating women of different cultural background. Their presence implies early
childhood multicultural socialization; their remittances support families 'at home' and
whole economies of their state of birth, for example in the Philippines, Bangladesh,
and Latin American countries.

The differentiation of people by race, that is, assumed genetic difference and
phenotypical markers like skin color, led to the construction of a white-v.-black/
colored dichotomy since the period of Europe's expansion. The post-colonial reverse
migrations and the abolition of racist immigration criteria have made 'white' societies
as many-colored as 'black' or 'brown' societies had become through colonizer migrations. The post-colonial de-racialization of admission procedures in the white world is
countered, however, by re-racializing assignments of migrants of colors other than
white or of ethno-cultural difference to poorly paid service jobs in the developed
and the developing worlds.

Currently young people in many societies grow up in intercultural and many-
colored educational institutions. A non-race-based global frame for the regulation of
migration and intercultural contact is being discussed, but global restructuring
of production and service migration has led to new forms of xenophobia—whether
anti-Mexican racism in the United States, South African anti-immigrant violence, or
'fortress Europe' policies. While some societies debate inclusion, many still practice
exclusion.

NOTES

1. Christiane Harzig and Dirk Hoerder with Donna Gabaccia, *What Is Migration History?* (Cambridge: Polity Press, 2009), provide a summary of traditional and recent approaches to migration history in chapters 3 and 4. Hoerder, *'To Know Our Many Selves': From the Study of Canada to Canadian Studies* (Edmonton: Athabasca University Press, 2010), chapter 14; James H. Jackson, Jr., and Leslie Page Moch, 'Migration and the Social History of Modern Europe,' *Historical Methods* 22 (1989), 27–36, reprinted in Dirk Hoerder and Leslie Page Moch, eds., *European Migrants: Global and Local Perspectives* (Boston: Northeastern University Press, 1996), 52–69; George M. Fredrickson, *The Black Image in the White Mind: The Debate on Afro-American Character and Destiny, 1817–1914* (New York: Harper, 1971); Ranajit Guha and Gayatri Chakravorty Spivak, eds., *Selected Subaltern Studies* (New York: Oxford University Press, 1988).
2. Patrick Manning, *Migration in World History* (New York: Routledge, 2005).
3. George F. Hourani, *Arab Seafaring* (Princeton: Princeton University Press, 1995); Thomas T. Allsen, *Culture and Conquest in Mongol Eurasia* (Cambridge: Cambridge University Press, 2001); UNESCO, *The Silk Roads: Highways of Culture and Commerce*, introduction by Vadime Elisseeff and Doudou Diène (Oxford: Berghahn, 1999).
4. Europe's poor who could not afford the cost of the transatlantic voyage sold their labor for three to seven years.
5. Jerry H. Bentley, *Old World Encounters: Cross-Cultural Contacts and Exchanges in Pre-Modern Times* (New York: Oxford University Press, 1993); Immanuel M. Wallerstein, *The Modern World-System*, 3 vols. (New York: Academic Press, 1974–88); Janet L. Abu-Lughod, *Before European Hegemony: The World System, A.D. 1250–1350* (New York: Oxford University Press, 1989), 3–40; Eric R. Wolf, *Europe and the People without History* (Berkeley: University of California Press, 1982).
6. Simonetta Cavaciocchi, ed., *Le migrazioni in Europa secc. XIII–XVIII* (Florence: Monnier, 1994).
7. Adam McKeown, 'Global Migration, 1846–1940,' *Journal of World History*, 15: 2 (2004), 155–89.
8. Shula Marks and Peter Richardson, eds., *International Labour Migration: Historical Perspectives* (London, 1984); Dirk Hoerder, ed., *Labor Migration in the Atlantic Economies: The European and North American Working Classes during the Period of Industrialization* (Westport, Conn.: Greenwood, 1985).
9. John K. Thornton, *Africa and the Africans in the Making of the Atlantic World, 1400–1800*, rev. ed. (New York: Cambridge University Press, 1998); José C. Curto and Renée Soulodre-La France, eds., *Africa and the Americas: Interconnections during the Slave Trade* (Trenton, N.J.: Africa World Press, 2005).
10. David Northrup, *Indentured Labor in the Age of Imperialism, 1834–1922* (Cambridge: Cambridge University Press, 1995).
11. Wolf, *Europe and the People without History*; Carey McWilliams, *Factories in the Field: The Story of Migratory Farm Labor in California* (Boston: Little, Brown, 1939).
12. John Torpey, *The Invention of the Passport: Surveillance, Citizenship and the State* (Cambridge: Cambridge University Press, 2000); Michael R. Marrus, *The Unwanted: European Refugees in the Twentieth Century* (Oxford: Oxford University Press, 1985).

13. Mike Parnwell, *Population Movements and the Third World* (London: Routledge, 1993); Ronald Skeldon, *Population Mobility in Developing Countries: A Reinterpretation* (New York: Belhaven, 1990).

REFERENCES

APPLEYARD, REGINALD T., ed. *International Migration Today*, 2 vols. Paris: Unesco, 1988.

BADE, KLAUS J., PIETER C. EMMER, LEO LUCASSEN, and JOCHEN OLTMER, eds. *Migration—Integration—Minorities since the 17th Century: A European Encyclopaedia*. Cambridge: Cambridge University Press, 2011.

COHEN, ROBIN, ed. *The Cambridge Survey of World Migration*. Cambridge: Cambridge University Press, 1995.

DUPEUX, GEORGES, ed. *Les Migrations internationales de la fin du XVIIIe siècle à nos jours*. Paris: CNRS, 1980.

ELTIS, DAVID, ed. *Coerced and Free Migration: Global Perspectives*. Stanford: Stanford University Press, 2002.

GUNGWU, WANG, ed. *Global History and Migrations*. Boulder: Westview, 1997.

HARZIG, CHRISTIANE, and DIRK HOERDER, with DONNA GABACCIA. *What Is Migration History?* Cambridge: Polity, 2009.

HOERDER, DIRK. *Cultures in Contact: World Migrations in the Second Millennium*. Durham, N.C.: Duke University Press, 2002.

KRITZ, MARY M., LIN L. LIM, and HANIA ZLOTNIK, eds. *International Migration Systems: A Global Approach*. Oxford: Oxford University Press, 1992.

PAN, LYNN, ed. *The Encyclopedia of the Chinese Overseas*. Richmond: Curzon, 1999.

SIMON, RITA J., and CAROLINE B. BRETTELL. *International Migration: The Female Experience*. Totowa, N.J.: Rowman & Allanheld, 1986.

CHAPTER 16

···

TRADE ACROSS EURASIA
TO ABOUT 1750*

···

JAMES D. TRACY

In a Kenyan cave 40,000 years ago, people made beads from bits of ostrich-egg shells, drilling holes in the fragments and rounding them. From the amount of debris, it seems they made enough beads to pass some on.[1] At ceremonial sites in Upper Paleolithic Europe, human bands left behind sea shells and other objects transported from a distance, evidently for purposes of exchange: at Isturitz in the Pyrenees, a cavern with painted caves and a river running through; and at Göbekli Tepe in southeastern Anatolia, circles of limestone pillars carved and set in place by hunter-gatherers.[2] Obsidian turns up at human sites from about 14,000 years ago. In Asia Minor, distribution clusters near the source-points, then fall off in proportion to distance; obsidian was thus passed 'down-the-line' from one group to the next. But, from about 7,000 years ago, major settlements have large amounts, small ones often none at all.[3] That obsidian was carried from point to point by professional merchants or peddlers seems unlikely. What is clear is that the habit of exchange extends far back into the human past.

A consideration of trade in world history should privilege the time dimension, which means narrowing the focus in other respects: this chapter deals only with long-distance traffic in luxury goods, and only for Eurasia and parts of Africa. Entrepôts were redistribution centers for a vast array of goods, not just high-value 'staples,' but the traffic that helped link distant regions was in luxuries. And while evidence of ancient trade is not lacking elsewhere, it is only for Eurasia that one can track the local connections that would eventually be knitted into a global framework. Here the discussion starts with the beginnings of a distinctively urban civilization (ca. 3500 BCE),[4] and concludes ca. 1750 when the vast and polyglot network of trade in the Indian Ocean had come to be dominated by the English East India Company. From about 3500 BCE, commercial institutions slowly radiated outwards from southern Mesopotamia. Though policy was dictated by kings, some kingdoms had grand mercantile ambitions, notably the Phoenicians and their Carthaginian heirs. From

560 BCE much of Eurasia was ruled by great empires. A city that provoked an emperor's wrath could be erased from the map, but empires also built roads, improved harbors, and made life difficult for bandits and pirates. From ca. 589 CE, China experienced an economic boom, with greater production of silks and other goods coveted elsewhere, and greater demand for imports—just as the rise of Islam created a trading *ecumene* that facilitated the movement of goods by land and sea. Mongol imperialism initially disrupted overland commerce, but it also brought a vast swath of Eurasia under the same law. From the time of Crusades, Italy's maritime towns fought to control distribution of Asian goods. Venice eventually bested its rivals, only to see Portugal project its power into the Indian Ocean, followed by the Dutch Republic and England. The Atlantic nations all had the idea of trying to convert a pre-existing trading *ecumene* into a trading empire. In sum, the commercial institutions familiar from the last two centuries represent, as it were, the top stories of an edifice whose foundations lie deep in the past, buried with peoples whose cities are still being unearthed.

MERCHANTS, TOWNS, AND MERCANTILE STRATEGY, CA. 3500–143 BCE

Uruk (ca. 3500–3000 BCE) was enriched by its irrigated fields. The great temple of Anu controlled granaries and herds of sheep raised for their wool. To obtain silver, and copper and tin for bronze, donkey caravans carried packs of textiles up the Euphrates valley to Anatolia's mining districts; the men in charge traveled as agents of the temple, but also traded on their own account.[5] On the Persian Gulf, artifacts from Uruk are found as far south as Bahrain, a meeting point for traffic coming from Oman, Elam (southwest Iran), and the Indus delta. Uruk had merchant colonies in northern Syria, whence ships sailed to Egypt, for gold coming down the Nile from Nubia. One commodity sent to Egypt was lapis lazuli, brought from northern Afghanistan,[6] by way of Transoxonia and the Iranian plateau.[7] Tepe Yahya in southeastern Iran housed a distribution center for goods from Mesopotamia. Rather suddenly, from about 2750, local craftsmen working with chlorite started producing stone bowls of a distinctive style, marketed up and down Mesopotamia's trade routes for a century. One might speak here of 'economic imperialism,' an exploitation of the Iranian plateau by Mesopotamians,[8] or a case of feed-back or secondary economic development.[9]

At Ebla in northern Syria, the palace archive yields details about trade in ca. 2500 BCE, including a 1:5 gold–silver ratio. Ebla produced linen and woolen textiles, and craftsmen worked gold, silver, and precious stones into objects for export. Palace texts describe merchants as 'messengers,' or purveyors, but they also traded at their own risk. Several cities in the region had a *karum* or colony of resident merchants, with a head-man appointed from Ebla. One text records a treaty by which the kings of Ebla and Assur (on the upper Tigris) granted facilities to each other's merchants; these two trading networks probably had counterparts, based on centers like Susa (Elam) or Dilmun (Bahrain). The destruction of Ebla (ca. 2300 BCE) has been attributed to King Sargon of Akkad (2335–2279).[10] Sargon's realm did not long survive him. Kings of Ur and Babylon strove to recreate his grandeur, but they too had to contend with warlike tribes from the Syrian desert or the Zagros mountains. As Mesopotamia's economy stagnated, Dilmun reached a peak.

Early in the next millennium (eighteenth century BCE) Kanish was a Hittite town with access to Anatolian silver mines. Here archaeologists have found the archive of a *karum* from Assur, about 850 kilometers distant. While packs of textiles sealed by the proprietor came on donkey caravans, *karum* members contracted with junior partners to accompany the silver back to Assur, where accounts were tallied for sending with the outbound caravan. Merchants might expect a round-trip profit of 100 percent, less 30 percent for taxes and transit.[11] From about 1600 BCE, various palace archives show diplomatic relations between the Hittite kings of south-central Anatolia and their counterparts in Assur, Baylonia, Elam, and Egypt. One ruler claimed to display his grandeur by bestowing gifts, which the other claimed to receive as tribute. Between the lines one may discern openings for the transregional trade that is well documented by archaeology. Merchants dared not cross a neighboring king's territory without permission, but this implied an undertaking to protect travelers. Around 1200 BCE a wave of invasions by land and sea struck the Middle East with sufficient force to dissipate the great kingdoms, and the commerce that depended on stability.[12]

Phoenicia—a truncated remnant of ancient Canaan—was perhaps the earliest trading region to recover. From about 1500 to 1200 BCE Phoenicia was ruled by Egypt. With little competition from the legendary 'thalassocracy' of Minoan Crete, Sidon and Byblos shipped the fabled cedar of Lebanon to Egypt in return for gold from Nubia, and papyrus, for which Byblos became the main distribution center, leaving to later ages a word for 'book.'[13] The report of an Egyptian emissary (ca. 1070) shows a resumption of trade, but now the king of Byblos boasted of having twenty ships for trade with Egypt, and fifty more hired out to a local merchant. Tyre, not mentioned until the reign of the Phoenician King Hiram I (969–936 BCE), soon became a center for Phoenicia's signature product—purple-dyed cloth.[14] The First Book of Kings records a treaty between Hiram I and King Solomon, for a Phoenician fleet to be sent to Ophir (Somalia?) for gold and precious stones; there is archaeological evidence that ships were built around this time in Solomon's Red Sea port, near modern Elath. The Phoenicians, erstwhile subjects of the pharaohs, were evidently out to break Egypt's monopoly on traffic down the Red Sea to the Horn of Africa. Tyre and Sidon came under Assyrian rule in the 800s BCE, but kept a measure of independence, in return for tribute in gold.[15]

Phoenician craftsmen needed precious metals for their workshops. Denied access to mines in Anatolia by Assyrian expansion, Tyre and Sidon planted colonies to the west, from the 700s if not earlier. Greek cities were sending out colonists at the same time, in much greater numbers. The commonplace contrast between Phoenician trading posts and Greek agricultural settlements is overdrawn; Greek colonies boosted the trade of their mother-cities, and Phoenicians too looked for farmland. But Phoenician expansion does reveal a mercantile strategy focused on the metals trade; Punic outposts were numerous in Iberia, important for both its gold and silver and as a transit point for tin from Cornwall. In the seventh century, when Tyre and Sidon were fully subjected, Carthage became the nerve center of an ongoing commercial empire. Passages to the western Mediterranean were guarded, and unwelcome intruders were kept out. But Carthage met its match when Rome took to the sea. At the end of the punic Wars (264–143 BCE), Carthage was a flattened ruin, still visible near Tunis.[16]

UNDER THE AEGIS OF EMPIRE, CA. 560 BCE–600 CE

Scholars once envisioned all empires as having a mercantile strategy, by analogy with modern European empires. But students of ancient empires have pruned back the number of military expeditions that can be seen as having commercial aims.[17] These empires did promote trade, but in the main indirectly, through greater security and the establishment of diplomatic ties. Persia's Cyrus the Great (560–530 BCE) brought many trading regions under his authority, from Khurasan in the east to Scythia (north of the Black Sea) and Egypt in the west. Darius I (522–486) introduced a uniform silver coinage and had a canal dug from the Nile delta to the Red Sea. Persia also governed its far-flung provinces wisely enough to keep the Achaemenids on their throne for two centuries—until Alexander the Great's conquering march (331–323).[18]

The city on the Nile that bears Alexander's name would be of great importance for trade, but later. Meanwhile, dynasties founded by his generals maintained contacts with the east. Egypt's Ptolemies re-dug the Nile–Suez canal, and encouraged a Red Sea trade that brought myrrh and frankincense from South Arabia, and cottons and jewels from the Indus delta. Late in the second century BCE, a certain Hippalus is said to have 'discovered' the southwest monsoon that enabled mariners to sail across the Indian Ocean from the Horn of Africa to the Malabar coast, instead of making for the Indus delta by keeping to the coastline.[19] At the head of the Persian Gulf, two Greek towns, Charax and Apologus, received traffic from India, as did Gerrha, a Chaldean town on the Arabian shore, from which caravans crossed the desert to Petra (Jordan), linked by another route to the Red Sea. The Seleucids of Iran and Mesopotamia, rivals to the Ptolemies and sovereigns of the Persian Gulf, paid more attention to overland routes to India, from which they obtained toll revenues, and prized war-elephants, brought over the Hindu Kush and west through Bactria (northern Afghanistan). From 247 to about 140 BCE Bactria had a separate Greek dynasty whose kings converted to Buddhism. Their successors, the Kushans, sent missionaries to China along routes used by merchants, over the Hindu Kush and the Pamirs and across the Taklamakan desert. One of the great stone Buddhas at Bamian, destroyed in this century by the Taliban, dated from the Kushan era.[20]

Silk fabrics had long been leaving China, albeit not as articles of trade: China fended off nomad attacks by 'filling the frontier with silk.' Tribute-silk traded far to the west, across the steppe; Herodotus tells of a Greek merchant who had traveled with a Scythian caravan from the Black Sea to the land of the 'Issodones,' possibly just east of the Tianshan mountains.[21] The opening of the Silk Road, well south of the steppe, was accomplished by China's Han dynasty (225 BCE–227 CE). In the 120s BCE Emperor Wudi (141–86) expelled the Xiongnu confederacy from the Gansu corridor, between the Qilian mountains and the Gobi desert, and extended the Great Wall west to Dunhuang. Meanwhile, an envoy was sent west to make contact with the Yuezhi (Kushans), known enemies of the Xiongnu. When he returned many years later, courtiers hailed this new and distant ally as confirmation of Wudi's mandate from heaven. 'Blood-sweating horses' from Ferghana (modern Uzbekistan), on the far side of the Pamirs, made excellent mounts for the imperial cavalry; when this traffic was interrupted Wudi sent an army across the Taklamakan Desert to Ferghana. For nearly a millennium the Han and their successors would battle the Xiongnu and their successors for control of oasis towns along the southern rim of the Taklamakan. Through these towns traffic ran south and west, across the Karakoram range to Ladakh (Kashmir) and the upper Indus; or down the Wakan Corridor and over the Hindu Kush to Bactria; or across the Pamirs to Ferghana and Sogdia (Samarkand). Kushan and then Sogdian merchants journeyed to China,[22] with precious adornments for thousands of new Buddhist temples, including gold, silver, lapis lazuli, and, from the distant Mediterranean, red coral.[23] Letters from the Gansu corridor (ca. 300 CE) show Sogdian merchants arranging the shipment west of silks (obtained from Chinese garrisons, who were paid in silk) and musk (which came from Nepal, and was worth more than its weight in gold).[24]

In the Mediterranean, Augustus Caesar's decisive victory over his foes (31 BCE) ushered in a long period of peace. In desert lands of the Roman east, goods now traveled more easily, thanks to an Arab saddle that balanced heavy packs from the back of one-humped camels. Rome built a trunk road from Petra to its port on the Gulf of Aqaba, and another, protected by garrisons, from Coptos on the middle Nile to Berenice on the Red Sea. In the second century CE, Strabo was told that 120 ships a year sailed down the Red Sea for India. The *Periplus* or *Circumnavigation of the Indian Ocean*, from ca. 50 CE, shows mariners using the western monsoon to sail to Malabar. Of the imperial silver *denarii* unearthed in the subcontinent, 99 percent have been found in southern India. The coin hoards point up an enduring characteristic of west–east trade. India, with no native sources of gold or silver, had a voracious appetite for precious metals. And Rome had a balance-of-payments problem, although the volume of luxuries from the distant east was still relatively small, mainly Malabar pepper and cloves and nutmeg from what is now Indonesia. Frankincense—for perfuming the powerful as well as for temple ritual—came from south Arabia and 'spices' for embalming came from east Africa, including myrrh. Although Romans now knew about silk, they preferred the diaphanous fabrics of Gaza ('gauze'); China's rich brocades, with gold thread woven in, were not popular until the late empire.[25] But contact with south India drew Greek- and Aramaic-speaking traders farther east. Parts of Southeast Asia were becoming cultural colonies of India, with Sanskrit as a chancery language. Romans too came to understand that one could reach south China by rounding the Malay peninsula. Chinese documents record an embassy from Marcus Aurelius, in 166 CE.[26]

Under the Parthians (247 BCE–224 CE) Persia fended off Rome's armies but permitted trade to the east to pass unhindered. Palmyra, a Roman city in northern Syria, sent caravans to Transoxonia and Sogdia and had a merchant colony in Susa, the Parthian capital.[27] But the Sassanian shahs (224–651) gave more attention to commerce. To promote traffic to India they built new harbors, including the fortress town of Siraf, opposite Bahrain; they also transferred trading communities from Oman to towns on Persia's Indian Ocean coast. Merchants of the Nestorian Christian community, banned from the Roman empire for their heterodox beliefs, flourished under Persia's Zoroastrian sovereigns, with important colonies on the Malabar coast and Sri Lanka, now the hub for trade with China. Persia's interests in Sri Lanka were important enough to call for a naval expedition to the island under Emperor Nushirvan (531–579), and another in the next century.[28]

Sassanian Persia also used the East Roman empire's growing demand for rich silks as a weapon. Eastward traffic from Roman Egypt and the Red Sea seems to have declined, perhaps because of a fall in the demand for frankincense; Christian sensibilities favored incense for the altar, but not for the homes of the rich. But when Yemen was conquered by the Negus of Christian Ethiopia (520s) Constantinople saw an opportunity. Until the 570s, when it was conquered by the Sassanians, Yemen was a base for Ethiopian merchants sailing to Sri Lanka, on their own behalf, and with commissions from Constantinople for buying silk. Overland trade was halted in 540, when Persia and Byzantium went to war; one *casus belli* was Constinople's refusal to pay a higher duty for Chinese silks. This was a blow also for Sogdian merchants. Near the eastern terminus of the Silk Road, in the Northern Wei capital of Luoyang, they lived in the city-ward reserved for aliens from the west, said in 528 to have 2,500 households, perhaps 12,500 people. Now under Turkish rule, the Sogdians persuaded their khan to send an embassy, but Persia refused to reopen trade. The khan then sent another Sogdian delegation across the steppe to Constantinople, where, in 568, they were warmly welcomed. As later embassies to China show, brocades for the Byzantine elite did not have to come via Persia.[29] Byzantines and Sassanians fought their last war between 610 and 628, even as another contender for dominion formed in the wings.

CHINA, ISLAM, AND THE MONGOLS, 589–1500

China under the Sui (589–618) and Tang (618–906) emperors has plausibly been described as 'the best ordered state in the world.' Fractious aristocrats in the councils of state were gradually displaced by civil servants, and revenue problems were assuaged by making the salt trade an imperial monopoly. As wet-rice agriculture spread to the south, the magnificent Grand Canal brought grain to cities and frontier garrisons in the north.[30] China's economy was now 'the largest in the world both in gross and per capita terms,' and its technology was the most advanced. High-temperature blast-furnaces produced steel of a quality not to be matched in Europe for centuries, and prototypes for the porcelain that would eventually set a fashion around the world. As demand grew for exotic goods—falcons and furs from the northern steppes, perfumes and horses from Iran, spices and pearls from Southeast Asia—the empire's big merchants, hitherto focused on domestic trade, turned to international commerce.[31] China's 'gravitational pull' may be gauged from the quarter for westerners in the Tang capital of Chang'an, which may have housed as many as 25,000 people.[32] Far to the south, the resident alien population of Guangzhou (Canton) was no doubt much larger. Peace and prosperity were interrupted when a rebel general of Sogdian-Turkish ancestry captured the capital (756), inaugurating a civil war. As imperial armies regained Chang'an a few years later there was a massacre of westerners. Meanwhile, in 758, 'Arabs and Persians' took advantage of the chaos by raiding Guangzhou from the sea.[33]

Traffic from the Persian Gulf to Guangzhou in the following century is described by an Arab geographer. Muslims had a *qadi* for settling disputes, but the Chinese sequestered incoming wares until all ships were in, and took 30 percent for duty; only then could foreigners trade for silks, spices, musk, and camphor. When a rebel army sacked Guangzhou in 878, the number of Muslims, Christians, Jews, and Zoroastrians massacred is said to have been not less than 120,000. This disaster temporarily shifted maritime trade to Southeast Asia, especially to the Buddhist kingdom of Srivijaya, based in southern Sumatra, which controlled both sides of the Straits of Melaka.[34] But foreigners soon returned to China's ports, and traffic increased as the Song dynasty (960–1279), centered in the south, restored order, giving particular attention to the safety of the sea lanes. This was the great age of China's commercial shipping, when many new commodities entered the international market, including porcelain, lacquerware, and steel.[35]

China's western partner was the trading *ecumene* of Islamdom. The Quran makes trade an honorable profession, and Islamic writers underlined the point by inflating the credentials of Muhammad's trader-clan, the Quraysh.[36] Yet commerce was not a priority for the Umayyad caliphs (632–749) who ruled from Damascus and faced Byzantine armies in Anatolia; they focused on further conquest.[37] Urban and commercial interests apparently had a part in the rise of the Abassid dynasty (750–945).[38] Baghdad, the new capital, soon became the largest city in the world outside of China. The Abassids kept the silver dirham uniform and stable, and where possible concluded treaties with erstwhile foes, like the Khazar kagans of Transcaucasia. The Caspian's narrow coastal plain, hemmed in by the Caucusus and the sea, and hitherto contested by the rival empires, now became a trade route for a people called the Rus', who transported northern furs down the Volga in exchange for precious dirhams.[39] Meanwhile, Omani merchants brought East Africa into the Indian Ocean circuit when they set up island colonies off the coast, trading for the gold demanded in India's markets, and also for ivory and slaves. This was the formative era for Islamic mercantile institutions like the *funduqs* that sheltered merchants and their wares, and a new instrument of payment whose name passed into European languages ('cheque').[40]

After the reigning Abassid was stripped of political authority by a Turkish mercenary chieftain (945) the caliphate survived in name only. But successor states used trade as a source of revenue and prestige. In Transoxonia, the Saminids (877–999) began as provincial governors for the Abassids. They made Bukhara a center for Persian literary culture, and an emporium from which huge caravans crossed the steppe to Itil, the city of the Volga Bulgars, to which furs, amber, and honey flowed from various parts of Russia.[41] On the Persian Gulf, a major revolt by African slaves (868–883) diminished Basra's standing as an entrepôt. Then the Buyids (932–1062) gained control of both sides of the Gulf, and built up Siraf as a successor to Basra, receiving merchant ships from Sofala (Kenya), south India, and south China.[42] The Fatimids, a Shi'ite dynasty from the Maghreb, claimed to revive the caliphate. Their conquest of Egypt (969) and foundation of Cairo apparently lent substance to the claim; many Jewish merchants seem to have left Baghdad for Egypt at about this time. Meanwhile, trade to the east from the Persian Gulf declined—especially after Seljuq Turks sacked Baghdad in 1055— as did caravan traffic from the Gulf to Beirut and Damascus. The Fatimids successfully promoted the Red Sea as an alternative, making Alexandria the favored Mediterranean terminus for goods coming from Asia by sea. Egyptian officials supervised *funduqs* for merchants of many nations, including the 'Franks'—Venetians, Genoese, and Catalans.[43]

In south India, still the hinge of east–west maritime trade, local rulers enjoyed important revenues from trade. Cognizant of Hindu sanctions against ocean travel, they granted concessions to seafaring newcomers—Persians, Greeks, Jews, Syrian Christians, and Arabs. The last of these groups—called *Mappilas*—grew in importance from the eleventh century. To the east, the Hindu Colas of *Colamandalam* (the Coromandel coast) took a serious interest in maritime trade. For the convenience of merchants from Srivijaya they helped build a Buddhist sanctuary in their capital. But they also launched two naval campaigns against the island kingdom (993, 1026) to secure free passage through the Straits of Melaka and on to China, or possibly to provide support for the overseas operations of their merchant guilds. Coromandel's *Mariyyakayars*, Tamil-speaking Muslims, joined in this new phase of Indian expansion. The Muslims who from about this time planted small colonies (e.g. in Java) seem to have come from south India and Sri Lanka.[44]

In the explosion of Mongol power under Chinggis Qan (d. 1227) many traditional centers of overland trade—like Balkh (capital of ancient Bactria)—were dealt a blow from which they never recovered. Yet, even before the great conqueror's death Mongol officials began identifying skilled craftsmen and forcibly relocating them so as to meet the empire's economic needs. For example, brocade was for the Mongols a matter of state—'an essential element of nomadic statecraft.' A khan's train included hundreds or even thousands of camels laden with rich fabrics, for regular distribution to generals who maintained their authority by rewarding subordinates in the same way.

Accordingly silk-weavers were rounded up and resettled in three locations near the Mongol capital. Chingiz's grandsons divided the empire into four khanates, based in Qaraqorum (Mongolia), Bokhara, Sarai (on the Volga), and Tabriz.[45] But lines of communication between the capitals were kept open, and regular diplomatic missions back and forth could also be trade ventures. Under the *pax Mongolica*, ca. 1245–1335, merchants and missionaries from the distant west traveled safely from the Black Sea to China; some brought back samples of the 'Tartar' brocade that quickly became a rage at European courts.[46]

During the fourteenth century trade suffered both from a broad economic contraction in many parts of Eurasia, and from internal struggles that convulsed the Mongol khanates. The Ming emperors (1364–1638), supplanting the Mongol or Yuan dynasty, ruled a China that was smaller and more focused on its Han heritage. The voyages of Admiral Zheng He (1405–1433) represented both a climax and a final act for China's presence in the Indian Ocean; thereafter, the Ming government turned its back on maritime trade and the overseas Chinese.[47] Tamerlane (r. 1370–1405) re-formed the Central Asian khanate and promoted a revival of the silk road from Samarkand, his magnificently embellished capital. But he also visited systematic destruction on rival trade centers, along the northern steppe route, and in northern Syria and Mesopotamia, where he targeted the Nestorian Christian minority.[48] In Iran the Ilkhanids revived trade in the Persian Gulf by making the island of Hurmuz into a port. But the peace and security of the realm did not survive the death of the last khan (1335).[49] By contrast, in the seas south of China trade seemed to flourish the more for not being under the control of a powerful state. By the mid-fifteenth century, Melaka had become the meeting point for merchants from south China, India, and the Indonesian archipelago. Foreign communities could regulate their affairs and conduct trade as they wished, provided they paid tolls and did not disrupt the sultan's peace.[50] Melaka was in fact such a magnet for trade that newcomers from the west saw it as a possible 'key' for dominating the sea-lanes.

EUROPE IN THE EAST, CA. 1100–1750

In medieval Europe, small princely territories and semi-autonomous city-states were thick on the ground, and merchants had a voice in policy. This combination of circumstances meant that cities and territories supported their merchants, if necessary by going to war. In the north, from about 1100, Novgorod controlled extensive hunting-grounds for black sable, sending furs down the Volga to the Bulgar Khanate and welcoming a merchant colony representing north Germany's Hanseatic League. From about 1300 the Hansa controlled traffic to the west. But in the 1440s, even as the Hansa blockaded Novgorod, leading Hanseatic cities were challenged in their home waters by merchants and warships from the county of Holland, then ruled by the dukes of Burgundy.[51] In Italy, Venice and Amalfi began trading in the east under Byzantine auspices. By the time of the Crusades, Venice and Genoa were maritime powers in their own right. If Venice sponsored the overthrow of the Byzantine emperor and his replacement by a Latin prince (Fourth Crusade, 1204), Genoa backed Michael Paleologus in his restoration of Byzantine rule (1268). Thereafter, Genoa planted colonies all across the northern shore of the Black Sea, profiting from the vitality of the steppe route under Mongol dominion. But then came Tamerlane's campaign of devastation along the steppe, and the conquest of Constantinople (1453), which soon made the Black Sea an Ottoman lake. The balance thus shifted to Venice, which had an arrangement with Egypt's Mamluk dynasty (1250–1517). While Venice controlled the sea-lanes to Mamluk Egypt and Syria, her Alexandria merchants had to buy pepper and fine spices from the sultan's officials.[52] From about 1500 the Ottoman war fleet eroded Venice's dominion of the seas. But the brocades and other rich textiles favored by the Ottoman elite came not from China but from Venice.[53] The real problem for Venetian trade— or so it seemed—was that Portuguese caravels started bringing Malabar pepper to Lisbon's wharves.

Portugal's voyages to India reflected the crown's ties to trade (the king had merchant ships), the ambitions of the court aristocracy, and the medieval Catholic dream of making contact with a legendary Christian king on the far side of the realm of Islam. Once in India (1498) the Portuguese grasped that goods from Europe would not buy pepper. Instead, one had to bring Indian cottons to Sofala (East Africa) for the gold demanded by pepper-traders. Later, taking advantage of Ming China's ban on direct trade with Japan, the Goa-based *Estado da India* found a further source of liquidity by bringing Chinese silks from Macao to Japan in exchange for silver. Over time the greatest commercial initiative was shown by private traders of the Portuguese nation, including men of mixed blood, who, forsaking the protection of the *Estado*, set up shop in ports all over the Indian Ocean. The aristocrats who governed the *Estado* had a simpler strategy: they used their warships to convert existing networks of trade into a system of tribute, by seizing and fortifying the choke-points of seaborne traffic, including Melaka (captured in 1511) and Hurmuz. Though the Portuguese never found the mythical Christian kingdom of the east—unless one counts their contacts with Ethiopia—the *Estado* supported the efforts of Catholic orders to make converts, as among the Paravas, a pearl-fisher caste in South India. They expected their Christian empire of the seas to be opposed by 'Moors,' and they were not disappointed. The Ottoman conquest of Aden (1538) effectively blocked the Red Sea to Portuguese shipping. The Ottomans also encouraged a distant ally, the sultan of Aceh (northern tip of Sumatra), who built war-fleets to fight the infidels, even as his merchants used the Straits of Sunda to sail from the Spice Islands (eastern Indonesia) across the ocean to Aden. This new connection revived trade to the Mediterranean through Alexandria, boosting Ottoman customs revenues, and allowing Venice to regain the lead in supplying Europe with pepper and spices.[54]

From 1580 until 1640 Portugal and its overseas dominions were ruled by Spain—just when the nascent Dutch Republic, centered on the maritime province of Holland, was fighting for independence from Spain. Patriotism and profit thus combined in Dutch assaults on the Asian sources of Spanish wealth. After several fleets from Holland and Zeeland had sailed through the Straits of Sunda to the Spice Islands, the Dutch States General in 1603 squelched local rivalries by chartering a *Vereenigde Oost-Indische Compagnie* (United East-India Company). With a permanent stock of capital, the VOC mapped out a long-term strategy. European ships and guns were now deployed not just to control sea lanes but also to control sources of supply. In the Spice Islands, Banda produced some 95 percent of the world's nutmeg; in 1621 the Dutch conquered and forcibly ejected native growers, replacing them with islanders who promised to trade only with the Honorable Company. As for the perennial problem of liquidity, the Dutch had access to silver from Spanish America, since they traded with Iberia even in time of war. But the VOC minimized outbound shipments of specie by developing the 'country trade' in Asian waters. In Surat, for example, the Dutch did their best to wrest from Gujerati merchants the transport to markets in Java of the Indian cottons that were customarily traded for spices (the VOC had its headquarters in Djakarta, renamed Batavia). The aim was to build a stock of capital in Asia, not just to buy goods for homeward voyages, but also to support the mounting costs of warships and fortresses in the east. Finally, to forestall the 'corruption' that they attributed to the Portuguese, the VOC decreed a strict ban on private trading. These policies brought some success against European rivals. The new English East India Company was compelled to give up trading in the Spice Islands, falling back on India instead, and the *Estado da India* was ejected from many strongholds, including Melaka. But the attempt to control the supply of pepper (as had been done for fine spices) was a costly failure; pepper was grown in too many places. Even more troubling was that the European market for pepper and fine spices showed signs of saturation by the middle of the seventeenth century. And the ban on private trading was just effective enough to discourage Company servants from engaging in the random initiatives that might have counter-balanced the VOC's heavy investment in the pepper and spice trades.[55]

In the English East India Company (EIC), chartered in 1600, stocks of capital were formed and liquidated for each voyage. Moreover, until the Anglo-Dutch wars began (1650s), rivalry with the VOC was a private concern, not a matter of state. English merchants doubted the cost-effectiveness of using warships to conduct trade, and in any case the EIC did not have funds to match the size of Dutch fleets—hence the EIC's failure to secure a foothold in the Spice Islands. Yet, falling back on India proved a blessing in disguise. The EIC, initially based in Surat, expended more of its trading capital on the calicos and other Indian cottons, for which, unlike pepper and fine spices, the demand in Europe seemed not to have any limits. The English also devoted more resources to Bengal, where food was plentiful and inexpensive, so that cotton-weavers producing for export could live cheaply. Early in the eighteenth century, as Europeans acquired a taste for tea, the VOC made its purchases from Chinese traders resident in Java, but the English went to Guangzhou, bringing (among other things) opium now grown in Bengal. Finally, though they complained about 'interlopers,' EIC directors never prohibited Company servants from trading on their own. Private traders thus filled in gaps left by the EIC, allowing English shipping to crisscross the whole Indian Ocean region.[56]

In the seventeenth century the combined activities of European companies accounted for only a fraction of the trade conducted through great ports like Surat, or (on the Coromandel coast) Masulipatnam. But in 1730 the English and the Dutch (in that order) were plausibly described as the greatest traders in Bengal.[57] However, there was still another European rival. After a false start in the 1660s, France's *Compagnie des Indes* was re-launched in the 1720s, with capital provided from the lucrative royal tobacco monopoly and subsequently from the crown. To obtain specie for India French ships called at Cadiz, for the proceeds of France's favorable trade balance with Spain. By 1740 France's exports of specie to the east—equivalent to about 265,000 kilograms of silver—equaled those of England. Officials at Pondichéry were also the first to train Indian *sepoys* with European weapons and tactics. But a shift in royal priorities soon reduced the needed flow of resources. The turning point came in 1757, when the *nawab* of Bengal occupied Calcutta, now the center of British trade. Facing the *nawab*'s large army and his French military advisers, two thousand sepoys and British regulars won the day at Plassey.[58] The English East India Company was not yet a territorial power in India, but from this point on there was no question about who commanded the seas.

One must not imagine that European power in the Indian Ocean went uncontested. In the east, the Bugis of Sulawesi attacked Dutch outposts in the Spice Islands. In the west, the Omanis ousted the Portuguese from Mombasa and other fortified settlements on the coast of east Africa.[59] In India, all the European firms depended, even against their will, on large loans provided by Hindu or Jain *shroffs*, for the timely purchase of homeward-bound cargo; in many cases the same men contracted with local weavers to supply Company orders for cottons, thus keeping foreigners out of the Indian countryside. Still, the contest among Europe's maritime nations represented a historical turning point, in one way in its outcome (the victory of the EIC), and in a larger sense from its very beginning. Scholars peering into the past will invariably have different ideas about when regional systems of trade can be said to have linked together in a unified network. But the best way to reconstruct what the world was like at a given moment is to start from the perceptions of contemporaries. In other words, we may say that the world of the Indian Ocean had a unified trading system from about 1500 (if not before), because from about 1500 successive waves of brave and avaricious newcomers discerned that there was such a system, and thought they could turn it to their advantage.

NOTES

* This chapter honors the memory of my late friend and colleague at the University of Minnesota, Professor Thomas S. Noonan, a pathfinder to the pathfinders of long ago.

1. S. H. Ambrose, 'Chronology of the Lower Stone Age and Food Production in Africa,' *Journal of Archaeological Sciences* 25 (1998), 377–92.

2. Paul Bahn, *Pyrenean Prehistory. A Paleoeconomic Survey of the French Sites* (Warminster: Aris & Philips, 1984), 85–90; Klaus Schmidt, *Sie bauten die ersten Tempel. Das rätselhafte Heiligtum der Steinzeitjäger. Die archäologische Entdeckungen an Göbekli Tepe* (Munich: Beck, 2006).

3. Colin Renfrew and John Dixon, 'Obsidian in Western Asia: A Review,' in G. de G. Sieveking *et al.*, eds., *Problems in Economic and Social Archaeology* (London: Duckworth, 1977), 137–50.

4. For the debate about when urban civilization may be said to begin, Mario Liverani, *Uruk: The First City* (London: Equinox, 2006), chapter 1.

5. Maria Eugenia Aubet, *The Phoenicians and the West: Politics, Colonies and Trade*, 2nd edn. (Cambridge: Cambridge University Press, 1994), 101–10; Liverani, *Uruk*, 41–2.

6. For lapis lazuli finds at 29 sites dated before 3000 BCE, Magarita Primas, 'Innovationstransfer vor 5,000 Jahren. Knotenpunkte an Land- und Wasserwegen zwischen Vorderasien und Europa,' *Eurasia Antiqua* 13 (2007), 1–13.

7. Liverani, *Uruk*; Samuel Mark, *From Egypt to Mesopotamia: A Study of Predynastic Trade Routes* (College Station, Tex.: Texas A&M University Press, 1977).

8. C. C. Lamberg-Karlovsky, 'Third Millenium Modes of Exchange and Modes of Production,' in Jeremy A. Sabloff and C. C. Lamberg-Karlovsky, eds., *Ancient Civilization and Trade* (Albuquerque, N.M.: University of New Mexico Press, 1975), 341–68.

9. Cf. Mario Liverani, *Antico oriente. Storia, società, economia* (Bari: Laterza, 1991), 151–6.

10. Liverani, *Antico oriente*, 213–19, 249–51; G. Pettinato, 'Il Commercio Internazionale di Ebla: Economia Statale e Privata,' in Edward Lipinski, ed., *State and Temple Economy in the Ancient Near East*, 2 vols. (Leuven: Department of Orientalistiek, 1979), I, 189–233.

11. Liverani, *Antico oriente*, 358–66.

12. Liverani, *Antico oriente*, 469–78, 629–42.

13. Chester G. Starr, *The Influence of Sea Power in Ancient History* (Oxford: Oxford University Press, 1989), 12–13; Robin Hägg and Nanno Marinatos, *Minoan Thalassocracy. Myth and Reality* (Stockholm: Svenska Institutet I Athen, 1984); Aubet, *The Phoenicians and the West*, 21–4, 30.

14. Aubet, *The Phoenicians and the West*, 6.

15. Aubet, *The Phoenicians and the West*, 29–45, 55–9.

16. Aubet, *The Phoenicians and the West*, 257–87; John Boardman, *The Greeks Overseas: Their Colonies and their Trade*, 4th edition (London: Thames & Hudson, 1999). Cf. Starr, *The Influence of Sea Power*, 29–49, 54–5.

17. E.g. S. A. M. Adshead, *China in World History* (New York: St. Martin's, 1988); Manfred G. Raschke, 'New Studies in Roman Commerce with the East,' in Hildegard Temporini and Wolfgang Haase, eds., *Aufstieg und Niedergang der römischen Welt*, 9: 2 (Berlin: G. de Gruyter, 1978), 604–1378.

18. George F. Hourani, *Arab Seafaring in the Indian Ocean in Ancient and Early Medieval Times*, revised by John Carswell (Princeton: Princeton University Press, 1997), 11–13; Pierre Briant, *Histoire de l'empire perse. De Cyrus à Alexandre* (Paris: Fayard, 1996).

19. Hourani, *Arab Seafaring*, 18–30.

20. Hourani, *Arab Seafaring*, 13–16; S. A. M. Adshead, *Central Asia in World History* (New York: St. Martin's, 1993), 37–41; Étienne de la Vaissière, *Sogdian Traders: A History*, tr. James Ward (Leiden: Brill, 2005), 17–20.

21. J. Ferguson, 'China and Rome,' in Temporini and Haase, eds., *Aufstieg und Niergang der römischen Welt*, 581–603, here 581.

22. Raschke, 'New Studies in Roman Commerce,' 606–21 (the quotation); Vaissière, *Sogdian Traders*, 73–84.

23. Ying-Shih Yü, 'The Hsiung-nu,' in Denis Sinor, ed., *The Cambridge History of Inner Asia* (Cambridge: Cambridge University Press, 1990), 118–50; Adshead, *China in World History*, 24–26; Peter Golden, *Nomads and Sedentary Society in Medieval Eurasia* (Washington, D.C.: American Historical Association, 1998), 14–24; Xinru Liu, *The Silk Road: Overland Trade and Cultural Interaction in Eurasia* (Washington, D.C.: American Historical Association, 1998), 11–13.

24. Vaissière, *Sogdian Traders*, 45–66.

25. Richard W. Bulliet, *The Camel and the Wheel* (Cambridge, Mass.: Harvard University Press, 1990), 87–106; Raschke, 'New Studies in Roman Commerce,' 634–67; Adshead, *China in World History*, 24–39.

26. Paul Wheatley, 'Sartyanarta in Suvarnadvipa: From Reciprocity to Redistribution in Ancient Southeast Asia,' in Sabloff and Lamberg-Karlovsky, eds., *Ancient Civilization and Trade*, 227–84; Adshead, *China in World History*, 28–30.

27. Raschke, 'New Studies in Roman Commerce,' 641–3; Vaissière, *Sogdian Traders*, 87–8.

28. André Wink, *Al-Hind: The Making of the Indo-Islamic World*, 3 vols. (Leiden: Brill, 1990–1995), 1: 47–51; Hourani, *Arab Seafaring*, 38–41.

29. Hourani, *Arab Seafaring*, 43–5; Raschke, 'New Studies in Roman Commerce,' 596–7; Adshead, *China in World History*, 72–3; Vaissière, *Sogdian Traders*, 199–211; Bulliet, *The Camel and the Wheel*, 104.

30. S. A. M. Adshead, *T'ang China: The Rise of the East in World History* (New York: Palgrave/Macmillan, 2004), chapter 2.

31. Adshead, *T'ang China*, chapter 3; Raschke, 'New Studies in Roman Commerce,' 637.

32. Adshead, *T'ang China*, 68, and *China in World History*, 76–7; Vaissière, *Sogdian Merchants*, 137–40.

33. Vaissière, *Sogdian Merchants*, 216–20; Hourani, *Arab Seafaring*, 61–3.

34. Hourani, *Arab Seafaring*, 64–78; Wink, *Al-Hind*, I, 84–5; Kenneth R. Hall, *Maritime Trade and State Development in Early Southeast Asia* (Honolulu: University of Hawai`i Press, 1985).

35. Wink, *Al-Hind*, I, 216–20, 225–30; Adshead, *China in World History*, 129–30.

36. Patricia Crone, *Meccan Trade* (Princeton: Princeton University Press, 1987).

37. Ira Lapidus, *A History of Islamic Societies*, 2nd edn. (Cambridge: Cambridge University Press, 2002), 38–40.

38. Thomas S. Noonan, 'Why Dirhams First Reached Russia: The Role of Arab-Khazar Relations in the Development of the Earliest Islamic Trade with Eastern Europe,' in his *The Islamic World, Russia, and the Vikings, 750–900* (Aldershot: Ashgate, 1998), II, 202.

39. Lapidus, *A History of Islamic Societies*, 56–68; Noonan, 'Why Dirhams First Reached Russia.'

40. Olivia Remie Constable, *Housing the Stranger in the Mediterranean World* (Cambridge: Cambridge University Press, 2003), chapter 2; Wink, *Al-Hind*, 1: 24–31.

41. Richard N. Frye, *Bukhara: The Medieval Achievement* (Norman, Okla.: University of Oklahoma Press, 1965), chapters 3–4; Janet Martin, *Treasure of the Land of Darkness: The Fur Trade and Its Significance for Medieval Russia* (Cambridge: Cambridge University Press, 1986), 12–17.

42. Wink, *Al-Hind*, 1: 20–1, 54–5.

43. Wink, *Al-Hind*, 1: 56, 86–90; Constable, *Housing the Stranger*, 107–13.

44. Wink, *al-Hind*, 1: 70–85, 315–30; Stephen Frederic Dale, *Islamic Society on the South Asian Frontier: The Mappilas of Malabar, 1498–1922* (Oxford: Oxford University Press, 1980), chapter 1.

45. For China's Yuan dynasty, the Chagatai khans of Central Asia, the Golden Horde, and the Ilkhanids of Iran, see the tables in David Morgan, *The Mongols* (Oxford: Oxford University Press, 1987), 222–4.

46. Thomas T. Allsen, *Culture and Conquest in Mongol Eurasia* (Cambridge: Cambridge University Press, 2001), 41–50, and *Commodity and Exchange in the Mongol Empire: A Cultural History of Islamic Textiles* (New York: Cambridge University Press, 1997), chapters 1, 5.

47. Adshead, *China in World History*, 197–200.

48. Adshead, *Central Asia in World History*, chapter 5.

49. Wink, *Al-Hind*, 2: 19–21; Morgan, *The Mongols*, 158–74.

50. Wink, *Al-Hind*, 3: 215–20.

51. Martin, *Treasure of the Land of Darkness*, 43–84; Klaus Spading, *Holland und die Hanse im 15en Jahrhundert* (Weimar: Böhlau, 1973).

52. Eliahu Ashtor, *The Levant Trade in the Later Middle Ages* (Princeton: Princeton University Press, 1984); Constable, *Housing the Stranger*, 234–6.

53. James D. Tracy, 'Il commercio italiano in territorio ottomano,' in Franco Franchetti, Richard A. Goldthwaite, and Reinhold C. Mueller, eds., *Il Rinascimento italiano e l'Europa*, vol. IV, *Commercio ne cultura mercantile* (Treviso: Angelo Colla, 2007), 455–84.

54. Giancarlo Casale, *The Ottoman Age of Expansion* (Oxford and New York: Oxford University Press, 2010).

55. F. S. Gaastra, *De Geschiedenis van de VOC* (Haarlem: Fibula van Dishoek, 1982); Niels Steensgaard, 'The Growth and Composition of the Long Distance Trade of England and the Dutch Republic before 1750,' in James D. Tracy, ed., *The Rise of Merchant Empires* (Cambridge: Cambridge University Press, 1990), 102–52; R. J. Barendse, *The Arabian Seas: The Indian Ocean World of the Seventeenth Century* (Armonk, N.Y.: M. E. Sharpe, 2002), chapter 8.

56. K. N. Chaudhuri, *The Trading World of Asia and the English East India Company, 1660–1760* (Cambridge: Cambridge University Press, 1978); Barendse, *The Arabian Seas*, chapter 9.

57. Chaudhuri, *The Trading World of Asia*, 16, 198–9.

58. Catherine Manning, *Fortunes à Faire: The French Trade in Asia, 1719–1748* (Aldershot: Ashgate, 1996).

59. Michael N. Pearson, *Port Cities and Intruders: The Swahili Coast, India, and Portugal in the Early Modern Era* (Baltimore: The Johns Hopkins University Press, 1996), chapter 6; Christian Pelras, *The Bugis* (Oxford: Oxford University Press, 1996), chapters 5–6.

REFERENCES

ADSHEAD, S. A. M. *China in World History*. New York: St. Martin's, 1988.

——, *T'ang China. The Rise of the East in World History*. New York: Palgrave Macmillan, 2004.

ALLSEN, THOMAS T. *Commodity and Exchange in the Mongol Empire. A Cultural History of Islamic Textiles*. New York: Cambridge University Press, 1997.

ASHTOR, ELIAHU. *The Levant Trade in the Later Middle Ages*. Princeton: Princeton University Press, 1984.

AUBET, MARIA EUGENIA. *The Phoenicians and the West: Politics, Colonies and Trade*, 2nd edn. Cambridge: Cambridge University Press, 1994.

BARENDSE, R. J. *The Arabian Seas: The Indian Ocean World of the Seventeenth Century*. Armonk, N.Y.: M. E. Sharpe, 2002.

HOURANI, GEORGE F. *Arab Seafaring in the Indian Ocean in Ancient and Early Medieval Times*, revised by John Carswell. Princeton: Princeton University Press, 1997.

LIVERANI, MARIO. *Antico oriente. Storia, società, economia*. Bari: Laterza, 1991.

MARTIN, JANET. *Treasure of the Land of Darkness: The Fur Trade and Its Significance for Medieval Russia*. Cambridge: Cambridge University Press, 1986.

RASCHKE, MANFRED G. 'New Studies in Roman Commerce with the East,' in Hildegard Temporini and Wolfgang Haase, eds. *Asufstieg und Niedergang der römischen Welt* 9: 2 (Berlin: G. de Gruyter, 1978), 604–1378.

TRACY, JAMES D., ed. *The Rise of Merchant Empires*. Cambridge: Cambridge University Press, 1990.

VAISSIÈRE, ÉTIENNE DE LA. *Sogdian Traders: A History*, trans. James Ward. Leiden: Brill, 2005.

WINK, ANDRÉ. *Al-Hind. The Making of the Indo-Islamic World*, 3 vols. Leiden: Brill, 1990–5.

CHAPTER 17

....

INDUSTRIALIZATION

....

PATRICK KARL O'BRIEN

DEFINITIONS, CONCEPTS, AND CONTEXTS
....

As an economic activity, industry is distinct from agriculture, forestry, fishing, mining, quarrying, transportation, finance, trade, and the myriad of services that make up separable tasks performed by the workforces of modern economies. Throughout history men and women have manufactured commodities for use or for trade and sale. No economy (family, village, urban, regional, or national) has operated without producing some range of industrial output.

Industrialization refers, however, to an economic transformation that is more recent and different in scale and scope from the mere making of artifacts and has involved the rapid rise in the significance of manufacturing in relation to all other forms of production and work undertaken within national (or local) economies.

Following the seminal work of Simon Kuznets, economists, historians, and sociologists have measured and compared how industrialization evolved historically for a sample of cases where the official data is available.[1] For most national economies in Africa, Asia, and South America, available and secure data relate to only recent decades. Nevertheless, tabulated and compared across countries, these familiar macro-economic indicators exemplify several universal features of industrialization.

For example, they show that as industrialization proceeds, the shares of national workforces employed in regional and national outputs emanating from agriculture, forestry, fishing, and mining decline and ratios of employment and output classified as industrial increases. Output and employment emanating from services which include all forms of non-commodity output sold (and/or supplied) either to consumers (e.g. as health care) or utilized as 'inputs' (e.g. distribution, legal advice, accountancy, etc.) in order to sustain both modern manufacturing and primary forms of production rise. As industry grows more rapidly than other forms of commodity output, then the demand for inputs from services shifts in favor of manufacturing. Trends in the shares of services delivered directly to consumers are, however, difficult to classify. At higher levels of industrialization, final service output becomes a more important component of national products and employment. Recent economic development in third-world countries has been marked by an early rise in the relative significance of jobs in services that are a concomitant of population growth, urbanization, and the slow growth of manufacturing. These trends exemplify high levels of urban under-employment among unskilled workers whose incomes are supported more by way of transfer payments than through purchases of goods and final services that add unequivocally to the sum of human welfare.

For real and sustained development there is no substitute for industrialization, which can also be observed in the reallocation of national stocks of capital (embodied in buildings, machines, equipment, tools, infrastructures, communications, and distribution networks) away from primary and towards industrial production. Furthermore, statistics for foreign trade also tracks the progress of industrialization over the long run in terms of predictable shifts in the composition of a nation's exports and imports. Sales of domestically produced manufactured exports normally grow in significance, and import substitution means that purchases of foreign manufactured goods usually diminishes as a share of total imports.

These essentially taxonomic and statistical exercises (derived from the work of Kuznets and his school) are important because they help to define and make concrete a process that has proceeded on a global scale for roughly four centuries. They expose national and regional variations from general patterns and contribute to the understanding of major economic variables that historically fostered or restrained industrialization in different parts of the world.

Industrialization is also a highly important process for the welfare of mankind because the reallocation of labor, capital, and other national resources towards industry has been accompanied by technological and organizational change, leading to: higher levels of output per man hour; rising living standards; population growth; urbanization; cultural changes; and shifts in the balance of power among nations. Industrialization has also been elaborated and analyzed in social, cultural, and geopolitical terms. For example, Talcott Parsons depicted industrial societies in terms of a set of interconnected social characteristics, hegemonic values, and legal systems that sociologists regard as functional modernities.[2]

Bert Hoselitz and his followers have taken Parsonian taxonomies further by elaborating upon the types of changes required in personal behavior and social institutions for modern industry to progress. Sociology proceeds (in the manner of Max Weber) to contrast 'traditionalistic patterns of action' defined as ascriptive, multidimensional, communitarian, familial, and authoritarian with types of individualistic, achievement-orientated, mobile, entrepreneurial attitudes and behavior that should somehow become more dominant in national or local cultures for industrialization to take hold.[3]

Unfortunately historical records constructed case by case are not often clear on whether social changes precede or accompany industrialization. Furthermore, sociological and socio-historical approaches have been more concerned with the disruptive, dislocative, and potentially negative consequences of industrialization for families, communities, villages, and regions than with its nature, origins, and positive effects on living standards. Read as a social process, industrialization has indeed often led to differentiation flowing from new divisions of labor, class formation, and uneven regional development. As industry diffused from country to country, it became, moreover, associated with deindustrialization, unemployment, and the economic decline of nations. The inspiration for writing in pessimistic ways about industrialization is derived from Karl Marx. Sociological understanding of industrialization is now changing under the impact of programs of research, which combine several traditions of theory with history and more processes centered on global perspectives.[4]

Modern research has exposed how complex, multifaceted, and variable the now universal process of industrialization has become since Marx wrote his critique. Numerous paths to an industrial society have been elaborated, and no foreseeable collapse of capitalism is now predicted.[5] Any 'general theory' or representation of industrialization at anything other than these meta levels of generalization based upon structural changes in output, employment, and the allocation of resources (pace Kuznets) or upon very broad changes concerned with the 'modernization' of societies and cultures (pace Parsons) remain taxonomic and aspirational.

INDUSTRIALIZATION AS A HISTORICAL PROCESS

'Modern industry' (i.e. industrial activity concentrated in particular regions and towns, organized in factories, firms, and corporations and using machinery and inanimate forms of energy) evolved gradually over time. It appeared in some national and regional economies before others. Industrialization studied as a long-term historical process has occupied generations of economic historians. Their analyses of the major forces that carried the growth of national industrial sectors forward from one stage to another at separable technological epochs in the evolution of modern industry on a global scale are usually distinguished between early and late industrialization. 'Early industrialization' refers to the histories of the developed economies of Western Europe and European economies overseas (the United States, Canada, Australasia). They deal mainly with the epoch which opens with the beginnings of European industrialization in Britain in the mid-eighteenth century and closes with the end of the long boom after World War II (1948–73). This period is often divided between the first and a second wave of industrialization associated with electricity and the internal combustion engine.[6] 'Late industrialization' covers the decades 1950–2010 when the process diffused to a sample of countries in East Asia led by Japan.[7]

Douglass North and Robert Thomas provide a succinct account of the largely private incentives, initiatives, and enterprise prominent during the first epoch of industrialization. As they summarize this history, the accumulation of capital in industry, the acquisition of skills needed for manufacturing, the diffusion of improved forms of organization, and the funds for research and development into the scientific knowledge and technologies, which raised the productivity of the labor, capital, and other inputs used to produce industrial outputs, all required private investment. That investment emerged as a response to incentives in the form of prospective but predictable material gains for the investors and entrepreneurs involved. It required politically enforced rules to mitigate the risks from instabilities, breakdowns, and failures that often occurred during the build-up of modern industry. Such incentives, together with insurance against avoidable risks, rested in large part upon institutions and laws for the conduct of all forms of economic activity (including industry) that were put in place and enforced by European states and by private voluntary associations between the twelfth century and the era of the French Revolution (1789–1815).[8]

With promotional institutions and legal systems in place, 'proto-industrialization,' the initial phase of an industrialization process destined to become global, proceeded to develop in many regions across the European continent. Thus, when it emerged after 1750, mechanized industry did not spread randomly across the map, but located within established regions already specialized in manufacturing.

Research by Franklin Mendels and other historians of pre-industrial Europe into these patterns and clustering shows that insights can be gained into modern industrialization by observing and explaining the background and conditions which led industry to grow (and decay) in some places before others. They warn us, however, that there was no linear progression from proto to modern forms of industry.[9]

Walt Rostow's controversial generalizations also remain heuristic to contemplate. They are derived from Marx and scholars from the German Historical School, who explored the origins of capitalism which led to industrialization over several centuries from the Middle Ages through to the nineteenth century. Rostow adheres to their assumptions, namely, that modern industrial market economies evolved in rather comparable ways but at different speeds through demarcated stages. In his model an evolutionary accumulation of capital and knowledge carried economies to a point of discontinuity or 'take-off,' from where they industrialized at a speed and on a scale that takes them forward into 'self-sustained' and irreversible growth.[10] Critiques of Rostow's stylized depiction of European industrialization are well taken, particularly Alexander Gerschenkron's equally contentious essay 'Economic Backwardness in Historical Perspective.'[11] Gerschenkron's enduring insight was to represent European industrialization as a process of 'unity in diversity.' Unlike Rostow (and Kuznets) he was more concerned to explain variations than similarities across nations. He expected that the study of carefully delineated contrasts in the strategies used by now-affluent countries to build up modern industry would help to explain the time they took to converge towards the highest attainable levels of industrialization and per capita income. Although many of his hypotheses have been confounded by subsequent historical scholarship, Gerschenkron's bold attempt to model variations across Europe has inspired an entire programs of research that seems more likely to lead to grounded theories than the concentration upon similarities and unavoidable stages in a growth process.[12]

Industrialization, in the Kuznetsian sense, can be represented statistically as a universal macro-economic process, but differentiation in the composition of outputs, great diversity in methods of production, and variety in modes and styles of organization characterized the historical development of European industry between the French Revolution and the 1950s. Viable alternatives to mass mechanized production persisted not only in numerous regions on the mainland but also within Britain, the leading industrial economy of the period before 1914. They survived because new technologies only provided substitutes for handicraft skills within a constrained (if widening) range of industrial production and because markets, particularly for high-quality consumer and capital goods, required flexible adaptations to changes in demand. Mass, large-scale, factory-based industrial production never became efficient for all manufactured commodities. Considerable segments of traditional industry survived. Sharp discontinuities with handicraft and proto forms of production never emerged. Instead, and while industry became the dominant sector in economy after economy, change and expansion within industry continued to represent a process of continuous adaptation. New technologies, tools, forms of power, and modes of organization emerged which extended the range of skill required for the differentiated range and manufacturing on offer.[13] An American, still less a British, paradigm for industrialization never emerged across the industrial regions of Europe until perhaps after the Great War and then only for, say, five decades or so before Asian competition reminded European industrialists of their traditional comparative advantages in small batch, flexible, and differentiated forms of production.

Furthermore, Alfred Chandler's seminal book really makes the same point by revealing that the competitive and discernable lead in productivity established by considerable segments of American industry (including steel, chemicals, pharmaceuticals, automobiles, oil refining, electrical goods, and fertilizers) during a second stage of Western industrialization (1893–1973) owed much of its international prestige to the fact that the United States embraced managerial capitalism more extensively than its European rivals. Chandler's approach reifies the organizational factor (the modern corporation) into the core of an explanation for American industrial success and for the relative retardation of other leading industrial economies over long stretches of the twentieth century. While his thesis is certainly relevant to some of the leading industries of the Second Industrial Revolution (where only large-scale corporations could realize the economies of 'scale and scope' and the scientific knowledge embodied in modern technologies), it has not been accepted as valid across the spectrum of manufacturing. There is far more to the competitive power of national industries (and even for the United States) in the twentieth century than Chandler's heuristic model suggests.[14]

GLOBAL DIFFUSION: PRESENT TENDENCIES AND FUTURE TRENDS

Moving beyond Europe and North America, Paul Bairoch has made a bold attempt to quantify the pace and geographical distribution of industrialization on a global scale from 1750 to 1980. His estimates will be revised but can meanwhile be used to support some broad and not implausible generalizations about the growth and distribution of manufacturing output for the world as a whole.[15] After 1750 (the point conventionally selected to mark the onset of the First Industrial Revolution in Britain) global, industrial output took more than a century to double. Between the mid-nineteenth century and the Great War it quadrupled. Over forty years dominated by depression and war, 1912 to 1953, output trebled and then trebled again over two decades that followed to the peak of the long boom in 1973. Thereafter the annual rate of growth of global industrial output has declined, but it remains rapid by historical standards.

Industrial production in third-world countries probably doubled over the two centuries after 1750. Nevertheless and over long cycles marking the sub-period down to the Great War, their combined output may have declined in both relative and in many places in absolute terms. It certainly fell sharply on a per capita basis as the populations of Africa, Asia, and South America purchased a rising share of the manufactured goods they consumed in the form of imports from the industrializing countries of Europe and North America. Over the long run and on a global scale, the share of world industrial output emanating from production located within third-world economies declined from around 70 percent, 1750–1800, down into the 10 percent range, ca. 1950. Thereafter it began to rise again; and rapidly over recent decades when industrialization accelerated in China and India. But for some two centuries from, say, 1750 onwards, industrialization (measured as industrial output per capita) has been pretty well confined to Europe and North America.

That is why until recently, discussions about the course and causes of industrialization have been overwhelmingly concerned with the scale, efficiency, and development of technologically advanced industries within industrialized countries of the West. For roughly two centuries before 1900, Britain remained the world's leading industrial economy (conspicuously so when measured in terms of industrial output per capita) before it was superseded by the United States around 1900 and later by other European economies and by Japan at the end of the twentieth century. Initially European and North American industries attempted to converge towards the standards of labor productivity, technological advance, and organizational efficiency displayed by many (but not all) British industries. Thereafter standards set for convergence shifted to the United States displayed at the top-of-league tables ranking national industries and entire industrial sectors in terms of a battery of productivity indicators purporting to tell businessmen and governments how well or badly a particular economy was performing within a global context. Britain's relative decline, the rise of America, Germany, Russia, Sweden, Switzerland, Belgium, Italy, latterly Japan and the newly industrializing countries of East Asia have all been measured and analyzed in relation to a range of indicators exemplifying industrial power and efficiency.[16]

For most of the twentieth century the overwhelming size of American industry and its persistent dominance, measured in terms of manufactured output per head of population, stands out. The United States retained its hegemonic position for longer than would have been the case without two global wars (1914–18 and 1939–45).[17] Its competitive advantages diminished during the long boom when productivity growth in several European economies and Japan exceeded that of the lead country. This phase of convergence has exposed the interactions between key variables such as technological opportunities, social capabilities, scale economies, initial natural endowments, and elastic supplies of under-employed labor as the impetus behind the rate of industrialization achieved by European economies after World War II. The convergence discussion has revealed that within the now-industrialized market economies of Europe and North America, industrialization has proceeded by exploiting the potential for productivity gains already embodied and clearly functioning in the technologies, organizational forms, and institutions of the lead or leading industrial economies. It is a perception that singles out similarities rather than contrasts or adaptations to the social and technical capabilities of particular countries.[18]

Among European nations, the attempt to homogenize the process in terms of a conceptual vocabulary drawn from economics and sociology carries more conviction than the transposition of similar analytical and taxonomical categories to the Asian and Latin American conditions and cultures of newly industrializing countries. For these so-called late industrializers, the roles their governments play, the strategies and organizational structures adopted by their firms, as well as their variable and different legal systems and cultures, are emerging as facets of a distinctive process that may well add up to a 'new paradigm' for industrialization.[19] This recent wave or what is euphemistically referred to as a 'Third Industrial Revolution' embodies an almost universal adaptation to the opportunities provided by new technologies and competitive challenges arising from the diffusion of industry to more and more locations and countries around the world.[20] Responses to the revolution in information technologies, high-speed transportation, biochemicals, genetic engineering, robotics, computerized control systems, as well as the relocation, diffusion, and integration of industries on a global scale do not look that dissimilar between later and earlier industrializers. Modern, rapidly growing industries have become knowledge-intensive and cater for increasingly affluent and discriminating bodies of consumers. Industries everywhere are being restructured to become more flexible and adaptable to volatile changes in consumer taste, accelerated technological change, and intensified international competition. Firms adapt by becoming smaller and less hierarchically ordered than prototype American corporations of the twentieth century. Their proclaimed missions are to mobilize the knowledge and intelligence, not simply of their scientific, professional, and managerial staff, but also the skills and commitment of their workforces in order to upgrade and differentiate manufactured goods and in order to exploit a continuous flow of product and process innovations.[21]

There may not be much that is really novel in the current phase of restructuring, reorganizing, and relocating industry, or in the rediscovery of sources of industrial innovation and efficiency gains among the skills and motivations of workers on factory floors.[22]

Instead, two general problems currently require more urgent academic and political attention. The first and most serious is how and when the remaining very poor third-world economies with small industrial sectors of limited potential might find a place in this new international division of labor.[23] Secondly, will the developed economies resort to even higher levels of protection in an attempt to delay what some politicians regard with dismay as 'deindustrialization,' which operates to erode the living standards of their citizens?

Deindustrialization is normally defined as a falling share of industrial employment and output in relation to gross national products. Some third-world economies (e.g. India and China) suffered from deindustrialization in the course of the nineteenth century. Nevertheless, current concerns with the size of the industrial compared to the service sector in advanced economies, particularly the United Kingdom and the United States, may be unwarranted because the distinction between services and industrial production is no longer clear cut. Furthermore, the adverse balances of industrial trade does not (as it did in centuries past) flow from rates of import penetration because affluent European and North American consumers are spending more upon a widening range of cheap manufactured goods from the industrializing countries of the third world. Rather, the core of contemporary adjustment problems can be located in trade and capital flows among industrialized and advanced economies themselves. Nevertheless, if the new protectionism in all its devious forms spreads, then the diffusion of industry to Asia, the Middle East, and South America, which gained momentum in recent decades, could be easily restrained.[24]

INTER-SECTORAL CONNECTIONS

Meanwhile industry continues to be perceived as the 'leading sector' for the long run development of national economies. When, where, how, and with what effect industrialization emerges to play that 'role' depends, however, upon support received from other sectors. Before economies industrialize, their resources are heavily concentrated within agriculture. In the absence of inflows from beyond the borders of domestic economies their primary sectors are called upon to supply much of the labor, capital, raw materials, and markets that industry requires for long-term growth. These connections have been formally modeled by economists, but the basic linkages can be understood and their significance measured by comparing the experiences of particular countries (cases) during the early stages of industrialization when agriculture could nurture or constrain the development of towns and industries.[25]

Forward and backward linkages between industry and transport are almost as important to appreciate. Demand for transportation widens and deepens when industries purchase inputs and sell their final outputs over wider spaces. The coordination of specialized, regionally concentrated but spatially dispersed centers and sites for industrial production depended upon the services supplied by an extended and increasingly efficient, network of transportation. Industrialization has been accompanied and actively promoted by a long series of innovations in that critical sector (including surfaced roads, canals, railed ways, steam-, oil-, and jet-propelled engines), which lowered the costs, speeded up, and regularized the delivery of the final outputs and the inputs required for the expansion of manufacturing industry. Transportation declined in price and grew more rapidly than commodity production. Transport not only provided a final output, travel, but it is connected through backward linkages to several major industries, including iron and steel, engineering, and construction. Without rapid and continuous technological changes in transportation, industrializa- tion on a regional, national, and global scale would have been severely constrained.[26]

No set of institutions supporting industrial firms (particularly smaller firms) is as important as banks and other financial intermediaries. This sector developed to collect savings and provide the loans that industrialists borrowed as threshold capital, as well as the credits required to sustain the day-to-day operations of manufacturing enter- prises. Industrial firms do not function unless they can be provided with ready and sustained access to finance. Banks also help firms through liquidity crises and provide some assurance of stability during downswings in the business cycle. Unfortunately, the framework of rules and regulations promulgated by governments in order to avoid inflation and maintain the international value of local currencies has also operated to repress the emergence and distort the activities of financial intermediaries. Regulating the money supply and the exchange rate while providing for access to loans that are helpful for industry, confronts governments with difficult choices as they try to balance the competing claims for industrial growth with financial, price, and balance-of- payments stability.[27]

Monetary and fiscal policies cover an important sub-set of a whole range of connections between the state and the industrialization of national economies. Famously for the command economies of Russia and China, the initial creation of modern industrial sectors was planned, funded, and executed by central governments. Historically most other states undertook a less comprehensive and directional role. They financed and set up certain industries and subsidized others but in general provided infrastructures of communications, energy supplies, education and training, information and technical advice, and security in order to promote private investment and private management of domestic industrial sectors.[28] States also established and enforced the laws within which industrial enterprises are organized, recruit labor, raise capital and credit, and sell manufactured goods.[29] In short, with some large exceptions (including the conspicuous failures of Russia and China) industrialization emerged, developed, and continues to be operated by private enterprise, but within frameworks of facilities, rules, and institutions established, supported, and sustained by governments.

Even among historians debates about connections between governments and indus- try are often suffused with ideological preconceptions about the effectiveness of private, compared to state, initiatives and management for the promotion of modern industry. Histories of industrialized economies have been written purporting to demonstrate the benign as well as the malign effects of state 'interference' with the operation of market forces and private enterprise.[30] Late (i.e. post-1945 or Cold War) industrialization became a confusing battleground of claims and counter-claims for market failures versus bureaucratic ineptitude behind the performance of third world industrialization in recent decades.[31] Fortunately, a more balanced view is beginning to emerge which seeks to analyze the kind of government strategies for industrialization that have proved either helpful, neutral, or a hindrance for long-term industrial development.[32] Historical research has exposed the structural and historical conditions that have, in large measure, predetermined successes and failures in national economic policies.[33] Intellectual discourse about the role of states has moved on from mere ideology into the realm of empirically based analyses and theories that now look more heuristic than ideological.[34]

INTERNATIONAL RELATIONS AND THE GLOBAL CONTEXT

Inferences and prescriptions can be drawn from a wide range of historical and contemporary analyses of several paths or patterns of industrial growth concerned with measured links between domestic industry and the international economy. While endogenous (internal) inter-sectoral connections matter, no country has ever industrialized without rather considerable recourse to assistance from societies beyond its borders. Furthermore, a major stimulus to the build-up of national industries can often be traced to prospective profits obtainable from the sale of manufactures on world markets or successful attempts to escape from the constraints of small or slowly growing home markets. In nearly every case some proportion (in many cases a large and/or indispensable share) of the inputs of raw materials, capital, skilled labor, professional know-how, and the technology required to establish and sustain industries emanated at least in initial stages from places beyond national frontiers. International flows of commodities (exports and imports), services (transportation, distribution, insurance, and other commercial assistance), and the factors of production (capital, credit, technology, and useful knowledge) have always been integral to the spread of industrialization around the globe, even before Britain emerged as the first industrial nation and exporter of capital and know-how in the nineteenth century.[35]

The significance of international trade and commerce for the timing, pace, and pattern of industrialization is encapsulated in statistics for a country's balance-of-payments accounts. International migrations of capital and labor have also been estimated and analyzed in order to reveal the pull and the push of foreign and domestic markets, as well as political and other forces involved in the diffusion of industrialization during the nineteenth and twentieth centuries and also (but without help from hard data) for several centuries before.

Between 1846 and 1914 globalization and industrialization went hand in hand, at least among European economies and European off-shoots overseas in the Americas and Australasia. Dramatic declines in the costs of transportation and integrated commodity markets stimulated trade and specialization. Massive migrations of labor, followed by capital, reallocated resources efficiently across frontiers and sectors of national economies. In the absence of governmental impediments to trade, labor and capital flows, underemployed and cheap labor moved out of the countryside towards the cities at home and abroad and into employment in industry and related urban services. Between 1914 and 1948 this benign process of globalization became severely restrained by tariffs, immigration controls, and two World Wars. It picked up (but not to the same extent) during the long boom from 1948 to 1973. Recently the diffusion of industrialization through trade, capital, and labor flows across frontiers has accelerated again, but alas may become endangered by the resurgence of a 'new protectionism.'[36]

Debate about the significance of 'endogenous' versus 'exogenous' forces in the industrialization of otherwise sovereign and ostensibly autonomous countries with modern domestic industries has persisted and covers the entire spectrum of national 'cases' from Britain (site of the first industrial revolution) to the Asian tigers and currently to China and India industrializing at great speed in the late twentieth and twenty-first centuries. Some economists see commodity trade as the 'handmaiden' rather than as the 'engine' of growth, but it is more likely that the role of exports and imports varied from place to place and also depended from cycle to cycle on the underlying buoyancy of the world economy as a whole and upon regulations but not restraints by states' international economic relations.[37]

Everywhere industrialization required high and increasing levels of investment not simply in buildings, machinery, inventories, and other assets that supported manufacturing activity, but in far greater value and volume in the infra-structural facilities needed for the transmission of energy for urbanization, housing, transport, and distribution networks and public services that accompanied the build-up of modern industry. Internally generated savings could be inadequate particularly when businessmen and governments wished to finance a rapid development of modern industry. Furthermore, the import content of local industrialization (particularly the machinery but also raw materials, intermediate inputs, and the recruitment of foreign professional and skilled labor) had to be funded in the form of foreign exchange which also became scarce and expensive when countries began to industrialize at speed.[38]

Loans and credit from abroad then became necessary to fill these two gaps particularly during the early phases of industrialization when local investors and financial intermediaries regarded industrial enterprises as risky and/or when balance-of-payments constraints dominated the allocation of foreign exchange for industrial development. Capital from beyond national boundaries became available at prices that governments and local businessmen often found excessive and on terms they regarded as constrictive for national autonomy and as potentially restrictive for longer-term industrial development. Before the era of decolonization (which occurred rapidly after World War II) an 'imperial component' also entered into payments made for inflows of metropolitan and foreign capital.[39]

After decolonization bargains continued to be struck, between investors and borrowers from more or less dependent but nominally sovereign economies, that nationalistic debtors have persistently regarded as intrusive and 'exploitative.' Yet most countries continued to rely heavily on international capital markets, and by the late twentieth century numerous industrializing economies in Latin America, Africa, Asia, and post-Cold War Russia and Eastern Europe accumulated levels of foreign debt that reached crisis proportions in relation to their capacities to earn the foreign currency required to satisfy debt-servicing obligations to creditors from overseas.[40]

Long-term growth in output and productivity in manufacturing continues to rest ultimately upon the discovery, improvement, and development of scientific and technological knowledge that can be profitably applied to industrial production. Most industrialized and industrializing countries (and to some extent this observation applies even to the first industrial nations) borrowed, emulated, adapted, and built upon manufactured products and industrial techniques initially developed outside their frontiers. Although there are certain competitive advantages to be reaped from being the locus of inventions and a first mover in new product lines, industrialization as a global process depends more upon adaptation, improvement, and further development of technically and commercially viable industrial technologies diffusing from place to place and across frontiers. Thus, it is the 'transfer' rather than the 'discovery' of industrial technology that has long represented the 'core' of industrialization. Problems investigated under the heading of diffusion are concerned with the development of the local and national capabilities required to diversify into new forms of manufactured output and to operate and to build upon imported technologies. Economies which somehow acquired the necessary skills, capabilities and complementary facilities to absorb modern technologies and to diversify their manufacturing activities industrialized before countries that for historical, political, and cultural reasons found this 'learning process' difficult. Societies arrive at plateaus of possibilities at different periods in their histories.[41] Meanwhile, the accelerated pace of innovation, the increasing complexity of new technologies, together with established (and often vested) cultures of resistance to change, makes the problem of convergence to the standards of efficiency set by leading industrial economies and powers ever more difficult to attain.

Multinational corporations (MNCs) claim to provide modern solutions to the diffusion problem, but their critics are not convinced that either their organizational structures or their basic objectives are adequate for the task of establishing more than a modicum of modern industry in most third-world economies. Nevertheless, over the past half-century, MNCs have in practice assumed the leading role in facilitating movements of investible funds and managing the transfer of industrial technologies around the world. These corporations and conglomerates are usually privately owned companies that are centrally controlled by an executive located in and recruited from a single country (overwhelmingly the United States, but including: Britain, France, Germany, Switzerland, the Netherlands, Japan, India, Korea, Taiwan, etc.). Multinational corporations produce and sell manufactured goods on a global scale. In origin such organizations are not new. In form, structure, and purpose their antecedents can be traced back to Dutch, English, and French corporations trading with the Americas, Asia, and Africa in the sixteenth and seventeenth centuries.

An impressive list of European and American corporations, making and trading in industrial commodities well beyond the frontiers of their own 'national markets' had certainly appeared before 1914. Their range and reach spread between the wars. They soon encompassed the globe and assumed control over a very large share of transnational trade, capital flows, and technology transfers before the end of the long boom from 1948 to 1973. American multinationals diffused modern technologies, new products, good managerial practices, and improved forms of industrial organization and thereby contributed positively to the recovery of European industries from World War II.[42]

Their role (along with European and Japanese MNCs) in the development of industry in the third world still remains more controversial. They stand accused of diffusing inappropriate products, exporting obsolete technologies, and recommending hierarchical or culturally biased managerial systems to the under-developed industries of South America, Africa, and Asia. They are said to under-invest in the training they provide to upgrade local workforces. They are perceived to exploit cheap labor around the globe and retain monopoly rights over modern technologies and best-selling product lines. Paradoxically, in developed countries 'national' multinationals are regarded (by those who take a less than sanguine view of the social problems involved in the adaptation to the forces of international competition) as unpatriotic agencies for deindustrialization.[43]

INDUSTRIALIZATION ON A GLOBAL SCALE OVER THE VERY LONG RUN

Since paleolithic times people have been engaged in making artifacts for use, decoration, and exchange. Supplies of industrial commodities increased in volume, range, and sophistication when settled agricultures emerged and generated the surpluses of food and raw materials required to support towns, specialization, trade, and the political orders associated with a succession of 'empires' or 'civilizations' which rose, flourished, and declined in the Middle East, Africa, Europe, Asia, and Mesoamerica between the onset of the neolithic era and the Industrial Revolution. Global historians divide this epoch of some five millennia from Sumerian civilization to the Middle Ages into a succession of ancient empires, and their books are preoccupied with the political, military, and cultural factors behind their rise and decline.[44]

For historians of industry who tend to periodize in terms of millennia before and centuries after the Industrial Revolution, an interest in ancient civilizations resides in understanding the range, amount, design, and above all the costs or values in exchange of the manufactured artifacts these empires bequeathed to posterity. Archaeologists have collected and arranged a great deal of the evidence required to appreciate the evolving variety and volume of industrial production that originated from urban sites that seem to have been spatially concentrated and specialized in manufacturing as far back as the Sumerian Empire (which flourished in the Tigris and Euphrates Valley between 3800 and 2000 BCE).

They have classified and recorded the endurable artifacts these empires produced and exchanged with other civilizations. Lists of the remains of such commodities are long, variegated, and increasingly sophisticated and testify to the existence of long-distance trade in manufactures within and across Asia, Europe, and Africa long before the heyday of those familiar empires of Greece and Rome. Although diffusion of industrial products and improvements to the knowledge involved in their design and manufacture clearly occurred long before the Industrial Revolution, it is impossible for historians to offer even contestable conjectures about the amounts of trade in manufactures or to begin to measure the volume of industrial production on local, let alone on global scales much before the beginning of the eighteenth century.

Yet neither industrial production nor trade in industrial goods could have been other than important. Thus, depictions of the Industrial Revolution in Britain as making a sudden and rapid transition from national or regional economies based overwhelmingly upon agriculture to industrial economies are now regarded as gross simplifications. Significant volumes of industrial products had been manufactured and traded in many parts of the world long before that famous conjuncture. Machinery, some of it driven by wind and water power, had been used for centuries. Examples of concentrations of labor under the roofs of workshops and factories or organized within the walls or yards to collaborate in the making of particular products can be found in numerous towns and cities of many empires and states of the Middle East, India, China, and Europe as far back as Sumeria. Workmen became proficient in a defined and evolving range of skills, crafts, techniques, or processes required to manufacture industrial goods long ago. In short, key features of industrialization that have transformed the potential for rapid economic growth over the past three centuries (including the manufacture of expanded ranges of useful artifacts, trade in industrial commodities, mechanical engineering, inanimate forms of energy, specialization, factories, and spatial concentration of industrial activity) can be found in archaeological and historical records that go back in parts of the world to neolithic times. Furthermore, and although such impressions cannot be validated with reference to statistical evidence, narrative histories of 'rapid' and 'impressive' growth in industrial production and trade that accompanied the rise of cities, towns, and regions in the Middle East, Europe, Asia, and Mesoamerica, now convince historians that the big question of what may be *new* about the industrialization of the past three centuries remains entirely heuristic to contemplate.[45]

This all implies essential contrasts between the modern industrialization of the past three centuries and previous epochs can only reside in the pace, pattern, and greater global diffusion and the intensity of integration of industries. For example, since the late seventeenth century, the volume and range of manufactured commodities used, consumed, and enjoyed by masses of people in nearly every part of the world has increased at a rate that looks unprecedented. Before our modern era upswings in the amount and variety of manufactured goods made for the affluent populations of particular empires and cities may well have been equally rapid, but they remained geographically confined, and the consumption of manufacturers, even within favored sites and places, was restricted to minorities of their populations with the money to buy or the power to appropriate something more than the food, shelter, and clothing required for subsistence. Furthermore, nearly all the towns and polities that contained significant concentrations of industrial activity remained entirely vulnerable to political and natural disasters (including breakdowns of internal order, warfare, plague, disease, and natural disasters of every kind). Industry and trade could be destroyed and permanently depressed by these exogenous shocks. Declines (serious and absolute), as well as dramatic accounts of the rapid rise of industry and commerce, seems to be an omnipresent feature of the histories of urbanized societies right down to the sixteenth century. Yet, short of a nuclear holocaust, nationwide vulnerabilities to political and natural disasters that afflicted the very survival of urban industry and commerce for millennia seems to have been replaced by those altogether less catastrophic problems of shocks, cyclical swings, and relative economic decline that has punctuated the history of industrialization since the eighteenth century.[46]

Something akin to Braudelian conjuncture seems to separate the history of industrialization considered as a global phenomenon from the growth of pockets of industrial activity as they appeared and disappeared around the world for millennia before 1750.[47] That is why a distinguished succession of famous scholars from economics, history, sociology, and anthropology began to investigate the origins and reflect upon the positive and negative outcomes of the Industrial Revolution even before the first example of that famous transition had run its course in Britain and diffused onto the European mainland over the nineteenth century.

Classic analyses of modern industrialization remain instructive to read because they expose how traditional many ostensibly modern concepts, approaches to and insights from its study really have remained.[48]

What inevitably impresses students of industrialization who read canonical texts as background to case-by-case, country-by-country studies with this vast subject is how repetitious and circular many modern discussions that attempt to explain and generalize about long-run pace and pattern of modern industrialization in various parts of the world have become.[49] Nearly three centuries of empirical investigation and reflection by a succession of the very best minds in history and the social sciences has not produced any kind of general theory of industrialization. It is simply understood as the core process of structural change behind modern economic growth as that process evolved country by country.[50] Sensible taxonomies and vocabularies defining the inputs and the inter-sectoral connections required to generate accelerated rates of industrial production have also been more tightly formulated and refined. For that all-important purpose of measurement, production functions have been fitted to macro-data for industry as a whole (and to particular industries) in econometric exercises which purport to separate out and estimate the precise significance that can be attributed to each and every one of a carefully specified range of inputs behind the growth of industrial outputs. Although the mechanisms through which these inputs impact upon growth are now appreciated, the sense in which they are separable and quantifiable components of a historical process of sustained industrial development remains elusive. Net capital formation, recruitment of better skilled and more highly motivated labor, improved management, more efficient technology, optimal scale and rational organization, aggressive marketing and closer integration into an increasingly competitive international economy, an enhanced framework of supportive governmental policies, and so on, will all be included in any discussion of the 'necessary inputs,' 'preconditions,' 'requirements,' or 'proximate determinants' for industrial growth. Yet how, when, and why they all interacted together and generated sustained industrial growth for particular places at particular times remain key questions for historians and social scientists pondering the large fact that, after roughly three centuries of industrialization, the highest levels of industrial output per capita are still concentrated in roughly twenty to thirty national economies that support satisfactory standards of living for just a minority of the world's population.[51]

Although several newly industrializing countries have recently, but clearly, entered the 'club' of industrialized market economies and their levels of industrial productivity begin to approach standards set by the early and leading industrial powers in Europe, North America, and Japan, there is no statistical evidence for any sustained worldwide process of convergence in levels of real wages on output per worker employed in the manufacturing industry. On the contrary, divergence between a somewhat larger group of national economies that can now be represented as industrialized and economically successful and those that are still developing more or less rapidly (like China and India) may if anything be increasing.[52]

Given that a great deal is now known about the process of industrialization and the proximate factors required to promote it, the frequently posed question of why the whole world is still not industrialized deserves to remain high on intellectual agendas, particularly as the industries of 'follower countries' are deemed to possess competitive advantages as and when they attempt to catch up. For example, countries with small and/or less efficient industrial sectors can, in theory, emulate and adapt the technologies and modes of organization that are demonstrably successful elsewhere in the world economy. They could borrow the funds and hire the technicians and managers required to establish modern industry on established international capital and labor markets. Their workers are cheap. Their natural resources and home markets are often under-exploited. Their governments remain keen to promote and subsidize the development and diversification of national industry. With misgivings they even welcome the plants and branches of multinational corporations.

It is now nearly three centuries since Britain passed through the First Industrial Revolution, yet convergence has been slow, painful, and geographically confined. Except at rather banal levels of generality, there is no parsimonious explanation of why many more countries are not industrialized. Students will be told that the small selection of national economies that followed Britain's lead (and particularly the twenty or so cases that eventually surpassed Britain's standards of industrial productivity) possessed or quickly built up something referred to as the 'social capability' required to industrialize. Manifestly most other countries (which include within their borders, the majority of the world's population) did not and have not acquired the requisite social capabilities. Social capability is, however, little more than a portmanteau category that refers to cultures, values, family systems, political and legal institutions, religions, motivations, education, and skills embodied in national populations that operated to inhibit or facilitate the development of modern and efficient industrial sectors. Over any period of time they operate as a heritage of national and/or local histories. Social capabilities can be pushed in required directions by governments, by other institutions, such as churches, schools, and industrial firms, and altered by material incentives to invest, develop, and work in industry. Beyond this conceptual level of generality there is no substitute for studying both successful cases of industrialization, country by country, and contrasting them with cases that came later to the endeavor and have found greater difficulty in converging towards the macro-economic structures and productivity levels of the world's leading industrial powers.[53]

Although there seems to be no substitute for history, there can be no expectation that any general model of industrialization could somehow be inducted by considering and aggregating the full variety of successful and unsuccessful case studies on offer. That pessimistic reflection is strengthened, moreover, by the observation that difficulties for the formulation of any general theory of industrialization have been compounded because the international context within which regions and countries industrialized has changed profoundly since the eighteenth century. This has occurred because the knowledge base and range of technologies used to manufacture industrial commodities has evolved at an accelerated rate since British industry pioneered the development of steam power, coke smelting, and mechanical engineering to raise the productivity of labor employed in the production of consumer goods, machinery, and transportation.[54] Furthermore, the geopolitical parameters for industrial development based upon trade, imports of investible funds from abroad, the diffusion of technology, and the hire of skilled and professional manpower on international labor markets has also changed dramatically. For example, a liberal international order from 1846 to 1914 succeeded the aggressive and war-prone mercantilism of previous centuries. Neo-mercantilism and the era of global warfare followed from 1914 through to 1948. Thereafter American hegemony, decolonization, and the rise of multinational enterprise reduced the obstacles to the spread and relocation of modern industry around the globe. Since 1989 the collapse of command economies, committed to forcing the pace of industrialization in Russia, Eastern Europe, and China (without any discernible records of success) has reduced the powers of states to check the geographical spread of private industry. Capitalism assisted by positive help, incentives, and regulation from governments have triumphed as so-called end to history. States everywhere are more or less committed to free enterprise, but it remains difficult to prescribe the right mix of policies for all national cases. Unless the current wave of protectionism intensifies, long-established trends in the interdependence and integration of industry on a global scale look set to continue, and industries will become ever and more cosmopolitan and dispersed in their locations. Although the range of technologies now on offer to late industrializers provide opportunities for unprecedented rates of structural change and rates of increase in labor productivities (*pace* China and India), no particular illumination is derived from labeling industrialization as it now proceeds at the beginning of this millennium as qualitatively different, or as a third or fourth industrial revolution.

For more than three centuries modern industry has adapted to opportunities provided by flows of new knowledge.[55] Telematics, biotechnologies, robotics, and other novel technologies are just the latest wave requiring industries to restructure, relocate, and readapt to possibilities to satisfy mankind's seemingly insatiable demands for manufactured commodities. In this current phase of technological development, knowledge, human skills, capacities for coordination, and flexible responses to volatile global markets seem to carry the kind of competitive advantages required during earlier phases of industrialization, before that process became synonymous with large-scale corporations, fixed capital, and mass production. In the twenty-first century success seems to require new and different political and social capabilities that are already shifting the concentrations of industrial activity away from Europe and North America and back to Asia.[56]

Notes

1. Simon Kuznets, 'Towards a Theory of Economic Growth,' in Simon Kuznets, *Economic Growth and Structure* (Cambridge, Mass.: Harvard University Press, 1965), 1–81.
2. Talcott Parsons, 'Some Principal Characteristics of Industrial Societies,' in Talcott Parsons, *Structure and Process in Modern Societies* (Chicago, Ill.: Free Press, 1960), 132–69.
3. Bert Hoselitz, 'Main Concepts in the Analysis of the Social Implications of Technical Change,' in Bert Hoselitz and William Moore, eds., *Industrialization and Society* (Mouton: UNESCO, 1963), 11–31.
4. Stephen Sanderson, *Social Transformations: A General Theory of Historical Development* (Oxford: Blackwell, 1995), and Marcel van der Linden, *Workers of the World: Essays Towards a Global Labor History* (Leiden: Brill, 2008).
5. References to a virtual library of sociological writings on industrialization are cited in the journal *Annual Reviews in Sociology*.
6. David Landes, *The Unbound Prometheus: Technological Change and Industrial Development in Western Europe from 1750 to the Present*, 2nd edn. (Cambridge: Cambridge University Press, 2003).
7. Alice Amsden, *The Rise of the Rest: Challenges to the West from Late Industrialising Economies* (Oxford: Oxford University Press, 2001).
8. Douglass North and Robert Thomas, 'An Economic Theory of the Growth of the Western World,' *Economic History Review* 21 (1970), 1–17.
9. Franklin Mendels, 'Proto-Industrialization: The First Phase of the Industrialization Process,' *Journal of Economic History*, 21 (1972), 241–61.
10. Walt Rostow, 'The Preconditions for Take-Off' and the 'The Take-Off,' in Walt Rostow, *The Stages of Economic Growth* (Cambridge: Cambridge University Press, 1965), 17–58.

11. Alexander Gerschenkron, 'Economic Backwardness in Historical Perspective,' in Alexander Gerschenkron, *Economic Backwardness in Historical Perspective* (Cambridge, Mass.: Harvard University Press, 1962), 5–30.

12. Richard Sylla and Gianni Toniolo, eds., *Patterns of European Industrialization in the Nineteenth Century* (London: Routlege, 1991).

13. Charles Sabel and Jonathan Zeitlin, 'Historical Alternatives to Mass Production: Politics, Markets and Technology in Nineteenth Century Industrialization,' *Past and Present*, 108 (1985), 133–76.

14. David Teece, 'The Dynamics of Industrial Capitalism,' *Journal of Economic Literature* 31 (1993), 1–45.

15. Paul Bairoch, 'International Industrialization Levels from 1750–1980,' *Journal of European Economic History* 11 (1982), 269–333.

16. Moses Abramovitz, 'Catching Up, Forging Ahead and Falling Behind,' *Journal of Economic History* 46 (1986), 385–406.

17. Gavin Wright, 'The Origins of American Industrial Success 1879–1940,' *American Economic Review* 80 (1990), 651–68.

18. Nicholas Crafts and Gianni Toniolo, *Economic Growth in Europe since 1945* (Cambridge: Cambridge University Press, 1996).

19. Toshio Hikino and Alice Amsden, 'Staying Behind, Stumbling Back, Sneaking Up, Soaring Ahead: Late Industrialisation in Historical Perspective,' in W. Baumol, *Convergence of Productivity* (Oxford: Oxford University Press, 1994), 285–315.

20. Daniel Bell, 'The Third Technological Revolution and its Possible Socio-Economic Consequences,' in *Dissent* 36 (1989), 164–76.

21. Richard Florida, 'The New Industrial Revolution,' *Futures* 23 (1991), 559–76.

22. Giovanni Arrighi, ed., *The Resurgence of East Asia* (London: Routledge, 2003).

23. Rolf Kaplinsky, 'Technological Revolution and the International Division of Labour in Manufacturing: A Place for the Third World,' in Rolf Kaplinsky and Charles Cooper, eds., *Technology and Development and the Third Industrial Revolution* (London: Frank Cass, 1989), 5–37.

24. Ajit Singh, 'Manufacturing and De-industrialization,' in John Eatwell, Michael Milgate, and Paul Newman, eds., *The New Palgrave Dictionary of Economics* (London: Macmillan, 1987), 63–78.

25. Giovanni Federico, *Feeding the World: An Economic History of Agriculture, 1800–2000* (Princeton: Princeton University Press, 2005).

26. Peter Hugill, *World Trade since 1431: Geography, Technology, and Capitalism* (Baltimore, Md.: The Johns Hopkins University Press, 1993).

27. Karl Born, *International Banking in the Nineteenth and Twentieth Centuries* (Leamington Spa: Berg, 1983), and Rondo Cameron *et al.*, eds., *Banking in the Early Stages of Industrialization* (Oxford: Oxford University Press, 1967).

28. Douglass North, *Institutions, Institutional Change and Economic Performance* (Cambridge: Cambridge University Press, 1990).

29. Stefan Epstein, *Freedom and Growth: The Rise of States and Markets in Europe, 1300–1750* (London: Routledge, 2000).

30. Robert Ekelund and Roy Tollison, eds., *Politicized Economics, Monarchy, Monopoly, and Mercantilism* (College Station, Tex.: Texas A&M University Press, 1997).

31. Robert Allen, *Farm to Factory: A Reinterpretation of the Soviet Industrial Revolution* (Princeton: Princeton University Press, 2003).

32. Ito Shapiro and Lance Taylor, 'The State and Industrial Strategy,' *World Development* 18 (1990), 861–78.

33. Charles Tilly, *Coercion, Capital and States* (Oxford: Oxford University Press, 1990).

34. Richard Wade, *Governing the Market: Economic Theory and the Role of the State* (Princeton: Princeton University Press, 1990), and Ha-Joon Chang, ed., *Institutional Change and Economic Development* (London: Anthem, 2007).

35. Jeffrey Williamson, 'Globalization, Convergence and History,' *Journal of Economic History* 56 (1996), 277–306.

36. Kevin O'Rourke and Jeffrey Williamson, *Globalization and History* (Cambridge, Mass.: MIT Press, 1999).

37. Irving Kravis, 'Trade as a Handmaiden of Growth: Similarities between the Nineteenth and Twentieth Centuries,' *Economic Journal* 80 (1970), 850–72.

38. Kevin O'Rourke, ed., *The International Trading System, Globalization and History* (Cheltenham: Elgar, 2005).

39. Herfried Munkler, *Empires* (Cambridge: Polity Press, 2007).

40. Alan Kenwood and Alan Loughheed, *The Growth of the International Economy*, 3rd edn. (London: Routledge, 1992).

41. Joel Mokyr, *The Lever of Riches: Technological Creativity and Economic Progress* (Oxford: Oxford University Press, 1990).

42. Ronald Findlay and Kevin O'Rourke, *Power and Plenty: Trade, War, and the World Economy in the Second Millennium* (Princeton: Princeton University Press, 2007).

43. Robert Casson and Ron Pearce, 'Multinational Enterprises in LDCs,' in Norman Gemmell, ed., *Surveys in Development Economics* (Oxford: Blackwell, 1987), 90–132.

44. Graeme Snooks, *The Dynamic Society: Exploring Sources of Global Change* (London: Routledge, 1996).

45. Andrew Sherratt, 'World History: An Archaeological Perspective,' in Solvi Sogner, ed., *Making Sense of Global History* (Oslo: Universitesfortlaget, 2001).

46. David Christian, *Maps of Time: An Introduction to Big History* (Berkeley: University of California Press, 2004).

47. Fernand Braudel, *Civilisation and Capitalism, 15th–18th Century*, 3 vols. (London: Collins, 1988).

48. Peter Stearns, *The Industrial Revolution in World History* (Boulder, Colo.: Westview, 1998).

49. Paul Bairoch, *Victoire et deboires. Histoire économique et sociale du monde du XVI siècle au nos jours* (Paris, Gallimard, 1997).

50. Nicholas Teich and Roy Porter, *The Industrial Revolution in National Context* (Cambridge: Cambridge University Press, 1996).

51. Angus Maddison, *The World Economy: A Millennial Perspective* (Paris: OECD, 2001).

52. Dilip Das, *China and India: A Tale of Two Economies* (London: Routledge, 2006).

53. François Crouzet, *A History of the European Economy, 1000–2000* (Charlottesville, Va.: University Press of Virginia, 2001), and Amsden, *The Rise of the Rest*.

54. Robert Allen, *The British Industrial Revolution in Global Perspective* (Cambridge: Cambridge University Press, 2009).

55. Arnold Pacey, *Technology in World Civilisation* (Oxford: Blackwell, 1990), and James McClelland and Harold Dorn, *Science and Technology in World History* (Baltimore, Md.: The Johns Hopkins University Press, 1999).

56. David Held *et al.*, *Global Transformations: Politics, Economics and Culture* (Cambridge: Polity Press, 1999).

REFERENCES

ALLEN, ROBERT. *The British Industrial Revolution in Global Perspective.* Cambridge: Cambridge University Press, 2009.

AMSDEN, ALICE. *The Rise of the Rest: Challenges to the West from Late Industrialising Economies.* Oxford: Oxford University Press, 2001.

BRAUDEL, FERNAND. *Civilszation and Capitalism, 15th–18th Century,* 3 vols. London: Collins, 1988.

CHRISTIAN, DAVID. *Maps of Time: An Introduction to Big History.* Berkeley: University of California Press, 2004.

CROUZET, FRANÇOIS. *A History of the European Economy, 1000–2000.* Charlottesville, Va.: University Press of Virginia, 2001.

FINDLAY, ROBERT, and KEVIN O'ROURKE. *Power and Plenty: Trade, War and the World Economy in the Second Millennium.* Princeton: Princeton University Press, 2007.

GERSCHENKRON, ALEXANDER. 'Economic Backwardness in Historical Perspective,' in Alexander Gerschenkron, *Economic Backwardness in Historical Perspective.* Cambridge, Mass.: Harvard University Press, 1962, 5–30.

KENWOOD, ALAN, and ALAN LOUGHHEED. *The Growth of the International Economy.* 3rd edn. London: Routledge, 1992.

KUZNETS, SIMON. 'Towards a Theory of Economic Growth,' in Simon Kuznets, *Economic Growth and Structure.* Cambridge, Mass.: Harvard University Press, 1965, 1–81.

LANDES, DAVID. *The Unbound Prometheus: Technological Change and Industrial Development in Western Europe from 1750 to the Present.* 2nd edn. Cambridge: Cambridge University Press, 2003.

MOKYR, JOEL. *The Lever of Riches: Technological Creativity and Economic Progress.* Oxford: Oxford University Press, 1990.

NORTH, DOUGLASS. *Institutions, Institutional Change and Economic Performance.* Cambridge: Cambridge University Press, 1990.

CHAPTER 18

....

BIOLOGICAL EXCHANGES
IN WORLD HISTORY

....

J. R. MCNEILL

ALL human history unfolds within ecological contexts. Culture, always and everywhere, depends on nature. But at the same time, humans have shaped ecosystems—their culture has altered nature—for many thousands of years. By and large, human impacts on ecosystems have grown over time, and today they play a governing role in ecological change and indeed in biological evolution. One important way in which people have altered environments, and thereby altered their own ecological contexts and their own history, is through biological exchange.

Biological exchange can refer to any number of things. Here it means above all else the long-distance transfers of crops, domesticated animals, and disease-causing microbes, or pathogens. This choice is intended to emphasize biological exchanges that carried the greatest and most direct historical significance. Thus, more attention will be paid to sugarcane and horses than to dandelions and squirrels. But it is in some respects an arbitrary choice. For one thing, it is anthropocentric, ignoring all manner of biological exchanges that (so far) have had no or negligible effects on human affairs. While this may be a dubious procedure from an ecological standpoint, it is legitimate within the discipline of history in which human concerns remain front and center. For another, the choice focuses attention on the movement of biological species rather than the movement of genes within and among species. It privileges sudden, long-distance, intercontinental movements, such as the arrival of maize in Africa, over more local and gradual ones such as Roman efforts to spread grape vines throughout Europe or Chinese endeavors to extend rice cultivation. It also underplays the transfers of weeds, pests, fungi, medicinal plants, insects, birds, and countless other creatures that have had some impact on human history. The chapter aims to explore the role of the most important biological exchanges for human history.

Biological exchange was sometimes carried out intentionally and sometimes accidentally. People carried animals and crops from one place to another by careful and conscious design, but normally also brought seeds, pests, weeds, and microbes inadvertently. Even intentional introductions often brought unexpected consequences, as in the famous case of rabbits in Australia. A few nineteenth-century immigrant rabbits, brought out from Britain to augment food supplies, multiplied into tens of millions of nibbling pests, destroying the grasslands on which Australian sheep and cattle grazed. An intentional introduction led to vast unintended consequences. Episodes such as this illustrate an important principle in biological exchange, or more strictly speaking in ecological invasions, one often called ecological release: exotic immigrant species can leave their predators and parasites behind, and thereby flourish in their new homes far more prolifically than in their old niches, generating great disruptions in the ecology of the lands that receive them. This happens in about one out of every hundred exotic introductions.[1] It has happened often enough that today governments make great efforts to prevent most forms of biological exchange. For most of human history, people experimented eagerly with it. Now fear of biological invasions and consequent crop damage or the marginalization or extinction of indigenous species has restricted experimentation. A biological protectionism has grown up. It has dubious intellectual underpinnings, since it is often unclear what is indigenous and what is not, and occasionally this bio-nationalism carries darkly chauvinist overtones.[2] Biological exchange still proceeds, indeed in quantitative terms faster than ever thanks to the recent surge in long-distance trade and travel. But now it is more furtive and more accidental than at any time in recent millennia.

EARLY DAYS (TO CA. 10,000 BCE)

For most of the four-billion-year history of life on earth, most terrestrial species stayed put. Natural barriers inhibited species' migrations and divided the earth into separate biogeographical provinces. Their frontiers changed very slowly. Only birds, bats, flying insects, and good swimmers consistently bucked the trend. A few earthbound species did so occasionally, thanks to continental drift and to sea-level changes and land bridges that temporarily united continents. The earliest hominids and humans exemplified this partitioning of the planet. They confined themselves to east and southeast Africa for many tens of thousands of years. They probably helped to rearrange the biota of their preferred range, at least from the time they domesticated fire. A more intensive fire regime favors fire-compatible species, often grasses. Early humans may even have purposely used fire to change ecology, if they understood that more fire and more grass led to more big and tasty herbivores.

When humans first left Africa for new horizons, perhaps around 100,000 years ago, they brought fire with them and presumably had similar ecological effects on the balance between forest and grasslands. They may additionally have accidentally brought some African species with them as they trekked into Southwestern Asia, maybe fleas, or lice, or other persistent hitchhikers. They probably brought some archaic pathogens with them. They walked eastward to south and Southeast Asia and by 40,000 years ago, if not before, made the open-water crossing to Australia. Others hiked northwestward into Europe. By 15,000 years ago, and perhaps before, a small group walked across the land bridge of Beringia to the Americas, probably following herds of caribou. (Abandoning anthropocentrism, one might consider the first American humans as exotic invaders inadvertently brought by caribou.)

Probably the first intentional intercontinental biological introduction occurred when people brought dogs to North America in the migration from Siberia. Somewhere in western Asia, sometime around 16,000 years ago, some wolves gradually became dogs, partnering with humans in the unconscious interest of mutual survival. Human–dog teamwork proved especially effective in high latitudes such as Siberia and Alaska. In America, dogs probably played a role helping humans in the rather sudden extinction of many large mammals (climate change may also have played a part). However that set of extinctions happened, it carried major consequences: the Americas were left with almost no native species suitable for domestication, pushing human history in the Americas onto different paths than it might otherwise have taken. People also brought one dog species, the dingo, to Australia about 3,500 years ago. The dingo, an able hunter, also helped sweep some native Australian species into the dustbin of natural history.[3]

Dogs notwithstanding, for the long span of history before 10,000 BCE—the Paleo-lithic—biological exchanges were rare and usually inconsequential. There were surely some that have left no trace, especially likely with pathogens. But in the absence of domesticates (other than dogs late in the Paleolithic) there could be no intentional biological introductions—other than of humans themselves.

DOMESTICATION, AGRARIAN SOCIETIES, AND OVERLAND BIOLOGICAL EXCHANGE TO 1400 CE

Towards the end of the last ice age, beginning about 11,000 years ago, people went on a domestication spree. Current opinion now holds that the process took place independently at least seven times in seven places, first in the so-called Fertile Crescent of Southwest Asia, and subsequently in both northern and southern China, New Guinea, Sahelian Africa, South America, Mesoamerica, and perhaps in North America and Southeast Asia as well. Thereafter, biological exchange, both intentional and unintentional, accelerated. Those species most easily domesticated and most useful for human designs were deliberately carried from one place to another. In some cases the transported species brought their own pathogens and parasites with them. Humans often moved less in their lives as they settled down to agriculture, but they took more with them when they moved.

As it happened, most of the easily domesticated and especially useful species lived in Eurasia. Those plants and animals sensitive to climate conditions or to day length (several flowering plants take their cues to bloom from day length) traveled fairly well on east–west routes within Eurasia. The plants and animals on which early agriculture and herding rested spread, almost instantaneously by the standards of the past, although in fact it took a few millennia.[4] This process no doubt proved highly disruptive biologically, as alien species invaded new biogeographic provinces. It also proved highly disruptive historically, obliterating peoples who did not adapt to the changing biogeography, the changing disease regimes, and the changed political situations brought on by the spread of farmers, herders, and eventually of states. Out of this turmoil of Afro–Eurasian biological exchange emerged the great ancient civilizations from the Huang He (Yellow River) to the Nile, in place by 1500 BCE. They all based their societies on intersecting but not identical sets of domesticated plants and animals, in which wheat, cattle, pigs, goats, sheep, and horses usually figured prominently. These societies and states were in effect the winners in a political shuffle created by the drift toward domestication: they were the ones who took fullest advantage of the novel opportunities for demographic growth, state-building, military specialization, and conquest.

The part of this ecological story that archeological and genetic evidence best (meaning: least incompletely) reveals is the spread of Southwest Asian crops and animals into Europe. Wheat, barley, cattle, pigs, sheep, goats, and horses formed the heart of the Southwest Asian agricultural complex, but peas, lentils, chickpeas, broad beans, and other garden crops were nutritionally important too. Via Anatolia and the Balkans this complex filtered into Europe, averaging about one kilometer per year, reaching Britain around 4000 BCE. It came to the Baltic later, to Mediterranean shores earlier. Recent genetic evidence implies that it came with human migrants who substantially replaced the previous occupants, but no doubt in many cases European foragers took up herding and farming when presented with the example. They were already in the habit of adjusting to rapid climate change, as the glaciers melted back and cold steppes became forests. All the important domestic animals and most of the crops of Europe as of 2000 BCE were exotics, almost all from Southwest Asia.[5]

As of 2000 BCE, New Guinea, Africa, and the Americas had experienced much more limited biological exchange. The scanty evidence suggests the cultivated zones of highland New Guinea remained highly isolated until modern times. In Africa, crops spread mainly along the Sahel, extending from Senegambia to Ethiopia. In the Americas cultivation spread more widely in tropical latitudes but nonetheless interactions of all sorts, biological and otherwise, remained modest in scale compared to Asia, especially the corridor from the Nile to the Indus, the world's most intensively interactive zone around 2000 BCE. One of the constraints on crop movements in the Americas was that the main cultigen of Mesoamerica, an ancestor to today's maize called *teosinte*, had to adjust genetically to different diurnal rhythms before it could prosper at different latitudes. This requirement slowed its northward migration from Mesoamerica, and slowed the diffusion of the concept and practice of agriculture.

Over the next 3,000 or so years, the pace of biological exchange sped up, but in fits and starts. When conditions became favorable for trade, for example when large states imposed peace over broad areas, biological exchange picked up. At the apogee of the Roman and Han empires, roughly 100 BCE to 200 CE, trans-Asian routes, collectively known as the silk road, saw heightened traffic, inevitably including plants, animals, and pathogens. China acquired grapes, African sorghum, camels, and donkeys, while Rome received cherries, apricots, peaches, walnuts, and possibly smallpox and measles too. The great plagues of the late second century, which reduced the population of the Roman empire by perhaps a third, probably included smallpox in a starring role.

In Eurasian history two further moments of heightened biological exchange followed, both thanks to propitious political conditions. The second (the Rome-Han era being the first) and least consequential came during the early Tang dynasty (in China), in the seventh and eighth centuries CE. The Tang rulers came from diverse ethnic and cultural backgrounds, and for a century and a half showed keen interest in foreign trade, technology, and culture (e.g. Buddhism), as well as plants and animals. The Tang court imported exotica: curious creatures, aromatic plants, ornamental flowers, and so forth. Much of this was inconsequential in social and economic terms, but some of it, such as the cultivation of cotton (imported from India), was not. Cotton textiles soon became a significant part of the Chinese economy, and they have remained so ever since. The Tang dynasts were culturally receptive to strange plants and animals, but at least as importantly their political power on the western frontier, and the geopolitical situation generally before 750, promoted the trade, travel, and transport that make biological exchange likely. For roughly a century and half (600–750) the numerous polities of Central Asia were frequently consolidated into only a few, simplifying travel and lowering protection costs. A handful of large empires held sway throughout Central Asia, making the connections between China, India, Persia, and the Levant safer than usual. This geopolitical arrangement fell apart after 751, when Muslims defeated Tang armies, and after 755 when rebellion shook the Tang to its foundations. Thereafter both the stability of the geopolitical situation and the receptivity of the Tang to things foreign changed, waned more often than waxed, and the opportunities for biological exchange diminished.[6]

The third moment came with the pax mongolica of the thirteenth and fourteenth centuries. The Mongols established their rule with liberal resort to brutality, but once in power enforced order so as to foment trade. By this time the most promising exchanges of plants and animals had already taken place. But the heightened transport across the desert-steppe corridor of Central Asia may have brought carrots and a species of lemon to China, and a form of millet to Persia. Quite possibly, it also allowed the quick diffusion from Central Asia, or perhaps from Yunnan in southwestern China, of the bacillus that causes bubonic plague, provoking the famous Black Death, the worst bout of epidemics in the recorded history of Europe, Southwest Asia, and North Africa. Plague may also have afflicted the heartlands of China in these centuries, and perhaps sub-Saharan Africa too, although the evidence is ambiguous.

Two further biological exchanges within Eurasia deserve special attention for their historical significance on regional scales. The first is the case of so-called champa rice, a strain first cultivated in Vietnam. By the deliberate policy of a Song emperor, champa grains were distributed widely to Chinese farmers beginning in 1012 CE. Champa rice was more resistant to drought than any older Chinese strains, and much faster to mature. With champa rice, farmers could double-crop or even triple-crop in a single year, or they could develop crop rotations, alternating rice and wheat for example. Within 150 years, champa rice was the commonest variety in many parts of China from the Yangzi River southward, opening up new terrain, especially poorly watered hill slopes, to rice cultivation. The enormous economic expansion of the Song, the emergence of a more commercial economy, and even the development of an iron and coal proto-industrialization in the north all depended on food surpluses that champa rice made possible.[7]

At roughly the same time, the expansion of an Islamic trading world that linked the Indian Ocean shores with those of the Mediterranean brought about a whole range of crop transfers within western Eurasia (and North Africa). Between the tenth and thirteenth centuries, overland and seaborne commercial networks facilitated by the relative peace supervised by the Baghdad-based Abbasid caliphate (750–1258), brought sugar, cotton, rice, and citrus fruits from India to Egypt and the Mediterranean. These plants, and the cultivation techniques that came with them, worked a small agricultural revolution on the hot and often malarial coastlands of North Africa, Anatolia, and southern Europe.[8] Many coastal plains could now be brought under cultivation on a regular basis, often for the first time since the Roman Empire. Sugar and cotton could flourish even with unskilled and unmotivated slave labor; their introduction and spread may have quickened the pace of the slave-raiding that kept Mediterranean and Black Sea populations anxious for centuries. Keeping armies of laborers at work on malarial coasts—in the Levant, Egypt, Cyprus, Crete, Sicily, Tunisia, and Andalusia, to mention a few centers of sugar production—required constant re-supply in the form of slaves snatched (or bought) from poorly defended (and poor) peasantries. Sometimes this quest took slave raiders to the Black Sea coasts, but it also took slave merchants across the Sahara and along Atlantic African coasts. Saadi dynasts, originally based in the Sous and Draa river valleys of Morocco, brought sugar and African slaves together in a profitable mix beginning around 1350. They extended their plantation economy and their state, taking over most of Morocco by 1550, by which time their economic formula of sugar and African slaves had been transplanted to Atlantic Islands such as the Canaries and Madeira, and then to the Americas.

While this process of Eurasian (and North African) biological exchange never truly came to an end, it slowed whenever political conditions weakened inter-regional contacts. It slowed after around 200 CE, with the erosion of the *pax romana* and *pax sinica* which had so encouraged long-distance travel and trade within Eurasia. It slowed especially after the end of the *pax mongolica* around 1350. But by that time, sugar cane had taken root in India and the Mediterranean; wheat had spread widely throughout most of its potential range, as had cattle, pigs, horses, sheep, and goats. In other words, less and less was left to do even when political conditions encouraged biological exchange.

Meanwhile, on other continents, similar if smaller-scale processes of biological exchange and homogenization were in train. In the Americas, maize spread from its Mesoamerican home both north and south, despite the difficulties in adapting to different day lengths at different latitudes. Maize cultivation allowed much denser habitations and underpinned almost every major concentration of population in North America—salmon-eating peoples in the Pacific northwest being the likeliest exception. Maize is superb at converting sunshine into edible calories, but as a staff of life it is deficient in important nutrients. So where Amerindians took up maize as their main subsistence crop, they tended to become more numerous, less healthy, and smaller in stature. By 1000 CE maize had migrated to the Atlantic seaboard of North America and as far north as Quebec.[9]

In Africa, connections along the Nile corridor brought domesticated cattle south of the Sahara allowing the development of pastoral societies from what is now Sudan to South Africa. By 500 BCE or so, traffic along the Nile corridor introduced malaria to the Mediterranean world, where it remained a scourge for the next twenty-five centuries. The Bantu migrations beginning some 2,000 years ago probably diffused several sahelian crops, mainly sorghums and millets, throughout eastern and southern Africa, and possibly brought infectious diseases that ravaged the indigenous, previously isolated, populations of Southern Africa. Sometime around 300 CE some unknown African Columbus inaugurated regular, if at first infrequent, travel across the western half of the Sahara, connecting the Sahel and the Maghreb. This gradually became a routine crossing, if always dangerous, and the route by which (linguistic evidence suggests) large horses entered West Africa. Large horses allowed cavalry, a new military format for West Africa, and aided in the construction of states and empires far larger than any before, such as those of Mali and Songhai (ca. 1230–1591). West Africa acquired an equestrian aristocracy. This aristocracy, and the states it spawned, were sustained economically in part by slave raiding, an activity that mounted warriors could pursue much more efficiently than could anyone on foot.[10] These biological exchanges in Africa and the Americas must have been ecologically and politically tumultuous, although the evidence concerning their impacts is very sparse except in the case of horses in West Africa.

SEABORNE BIOLOGICAL EXCHANGE AND BIOLOGICAL INVASION BEFORE 1400 CE

Intercontinental biological exchange has a long pedigree as the aforementioned example of the first human and canine arrivals in Australia and the Americas shows. Throughout the southwest Pacific, initial human settlement of unpopulated islands wrought major ecological changes, including numerous extinctions, especially of birds, from about 4,000 years ago through until the first colonization of New Zealand by Polynesians roughly a millennium ago. All these instances were cases of invasions of 'naive' lands, continents and islands that had no prior exposure to humanity and its fellow travelers, or to the intensified fire regime that human presence normally brought. This helps to explain the dramatic effects, particularly the rash of extinctions, that followed upon human settlement of Australia, New Zealand, and the Americas.

In one of the enduring mysteries in the history of biological exchanges, the sweet potato, a native of South America, somehow was transplanted to central Polynesia by 1000 CE and subsequently spread widely throughout Oceania. It is a delicate crop and could not survive a driftwood voyage. No one doubts that people transported it, although no one knows just when, how, or even who. It eventually became a staple food in the western Pacific, highland New Guinea, and to a lesser extent the East Asian archipelagos and mainland, although in the latter case probably more via other routes than across the Pacific. The legendary maritime skills of the Polynesians, and the paucity of useful native species on their islands, combined to make Polynesia, proportionally speaking, home to exotic plants and animals more often than almost anywhere on earth.[11]

Once mariners had figured out the annual rhythms of the monsoon winds, the Indian Ocean provided a reliable sailing environment and became another pathway for seaborne biological exchange. Some time before 500 CE, somebody brought bananas, Asian yams, and taro to East Africa. These Southeast Asian crops had much to recommend them, as they do well in moist conditions, whereas the millets and sorghum that Bantu expansion brought into central and southeastern Africa grew best in dry conditions. Plantains, of which bananas are one variety, had existed in the wild from India to New Guinea. Linguistic and genetic evidence suggests they arrived on the East African coast as early as 3,000 years ago, and reached the forest zone to the west of the great lakes (now Congo) around 2,000 years ago, just about the time of the Bantu migrations. Quite possibly the success of Bantu speakers, often attributed to their use of iron, owed something to their successful adoption of these exotic Asian crops. As relative newcomers to eastern and southern Africa, Bantu migrants had less invested in prevailing ecological patterns and fewer disincentives to experiment. Bananas, taro, and yams were probably introduced to East Africa more than once, and almost surely were brought again in the Austronesian settlement of Madagascar that took place soon before 500 CE. These Asian crops assisted crucially in the epic (but unrecorded) colonization of Central Africa's moist tropical forests by farmers, as well as in the settlement of Madagascar.[12]

Several other significant intercontinental biological transfers took place before 1400 CE, mainly between Africa and South Asia, a route that posed minimal obstacles to sailors. Africa's millets became important food sources in the subcontinent, beginning with the Bronze Age cultures of the Indus centered on Harappa and Mohenjo Daro, in which millet came to supplement wheat and barley. Pearl millet, derived from a West African savanna grass, today the world's sixth most important cereal, was brought to India some 3,000 years ago, and now accounts for about 10 percent of India's cereal acreage. East African sorghum entered India a few centuries later, and eventually became India's second most important grain after rice. Sorghum stalks were useful as fodder for India's cattle. Finger millet, also from Africa, made it to India only around 1,000 years ago, but became the staple grain in Himalayan foothill communities and in India's far south. The main effect of the transfer of African crops to South Asia was to provide India with more drought-resistant dry-land crops, opening new areas to settlement and providing a more reliable harvest where water supplies were uncertain. This effect mirrors that of Asian crops in eastern and southeastern Africa, in which the introduced species encouraged settlement of humid forestlands. These examples suggest a very lively world of crop exchange—and probably weeds, diseases, and animals too—around the Indian Ocean Rim from ca. 3,000–1,500 years ago. The regular monsoon winds of the Indian Ocean helped make this region of the world precocious in its maritime networks and hence in biological exchange.[13]

BIOLOGICAL GLOBALIZATION AFTER 1400 CE

After 1400, mariners, most of them Atlantic Europeans, linked almost every nook and cranny of the humanly habitable earth into a biologically interactive web. The world's seas and deserts no longer served to isolate biogeographical provinces. It became a world without biological borders, as plants, animals, and diseases migrated wherever ecological conditions permitted their spread, although how soon and how thoroughly they did so often depended on transport technologies and skills, and patterns of trade, production, and politics.

Columbus inaugurated regular exchanges across the Atlantic in 1492. On his second voyage he deliberately brought an ark-full of species new to the Americas. Over the next few centuries his followers brought still more in an ongoing process now known to historians as the Columbian Exchange, after the title of Alfred Crosby's 1972 book on the subject.[14] The most conspicuous result was that Amerindians acquired a large array of new plants and animals, as well as devastating diseases hitherto unfamiliar to them. Those diseases included smallpox, measles, mumps, whooping cough, and influenza, all of which had become fairly widespread in the sprawling interactive zone from Japan to Senegambia. They were endemic, childhood diseases (sometimes called 'crowd diseases' because they require large, interacting populations to stay in circulation) that contributed to high rates of infant mortality. But most adults in Eurasia and Africa were survivors, and either resistant or fully immune to most or all of these infections. In addition to the crowd diseases, the Columbian Exchange brought some lethal vector-borne African diseases to the Americas, such as yellow fever and malaria. In the Americas all these were new diseases, so no Amerindians carried any resistance. Thus, these infections ravaged the American hemisphere between 1500 and 1650, lowering populations by 50–90 percent in one of the two largest-scale demographic disasters in world history (the other being the Black Death).

In one important respect, this horrific experience was an extension of older patterns. Ever since the rise of dense human populations living cheek by jowl with domesticated herd animals, which means approximately since 3000 BCE, infectious disease has assisted some people at the expense of others. By and large, those who lived in close quarters with many others, and who routinely swapped bacteria and viruses with animals, developed stronger resistance to more infectious diseases than did others (and those in such populations who did not, tended to die in infancy). They maintained a quiver full of lethal infectious diseases, circulating among children, which they unwittingly launched against other populations with less extensive disease experience. This differential experience with, and resistance to, infectious disease goes a long way towards explaining why large, dense populations usually expanded territorially at the expense of smaller, more scattered ones.[15] In the case of the Columbian Exchange, this pattern asserted itself on the grand scale.

The Amerindians had little in the way of lethal infectious disease to export to Africa and Eurasia. When their forebears migrated to North America they passed through northeastern Siberia and Alaska during an ice age. Brutal cold is not conducive to the survival of most pathogens, so they arrived relatively free from infection. Beyond that, they left Siberia when no animals but dogs had been domesticated, so that the infections derived from cattle, camels, and pigs (e.g. smallpox and influenza) had not yet evolved. Once in the Americas, Amerindians did not domesticate any herd animals other than alpacas and llamas, which seem, by chance, not to have hosted pathogens that evolved into agents of human disease. As regards pathogens, the Columbian Exchange was a notably one-sided affair.

The same was true of domesticated animals. American turkeys spread to other continents, but nowhere did they become important. Alpacas and llamas never prospered outside their native Andes, although scattered populations do exist elsewhere. The Americas had little in the way of domesticated animals, and what they had did not travel well. On the other hand, Eurasian species flourished when transported to the Americas. Cattle, goats, sheep, pigs, and horses were the most important animal immigrants. They all found empty niche space in the Americas, especially cattle and horses on the vast grasslands of the pampas, the llanos, and the prairies. The new animals provided Amerindians with new sources of animal protein, of which they had comparatively little before 1492, and of hides and wool. Horses and oxen offered an important source of traction, making plowing feasible in the Americas for the first time, and improving transportation possibilities through wheeled vehicles and greater variety of pack animals. That extended the potential of commerce and specialization in production, which could be socially divisive but at the same time raised overall economic production. The new animals introduced new frictions to the Americas too. They habitually munched and trampled crops, provoking quarrels between herders and farmers of the sort familiar throughout Africa and Eurasia but hitherto almost unknown in the Americas.[16]

As in West Africa, horses in North America upset the political order. The Amerindians of the prairies acquired horses from Spanish Mexico in the seventeenth century, and some of them quickly mastered the equestrian arts. On horseback, they became far more adept as bison hunters, solving any subsistence problems as long as the bison lasted. Moreover, those with horses easily inflicted military defeat on those without, so by around 1850 peoples such as the Sioux and Comanche had built considerable territorial empires on the basis of mounted warfare.[17]

Horses and humans share an affinity that often affected human history. Horses are by far the easiest animals for people to ride (elephants and camels come far behind), and thus for the millennia between their first domestication and the advent of motorized vehicles, horses represented the apogee in human (terrestrial) mobility. Their speed and power helped make them militarily important until the early twentieth century. Horses and humans are the only species that can sweat profusely and thus sustain strenuous exercise for hours on end. Together they can chase other species— wild cattle, bison, deer, bears, kangaroos—until their quarry overheats and has to stop running. Together they can fight cavalry actions that last all day, something beyond the capacity of war elephants and camels (the other species often harnessed for military purposes). In their ability to cool their bodies by profuse sweat, horses and humans were made for each other. They made a formidable tandem wherever they went, often too strong for human populations without horses to withstand. (And, abandoning anthropocentrism once again, this tandem proved too strong for populations of horses without humans as well, i.e. for wild horses which by 1900 existed only in a few nooks and crannies of the biosphere).

The Columbian Exchange was more even-handed when it came to crops. The Eurasian staples of wheat, rye, barley, and rice found welcoming niches in the Americas. Sometimes those niches had to be created through human (and animal) labor, as for example with rice, both Asian and African, in Surinam and South Carolina. Some of the new crops could survive in cold and dry landscapes where the indigenous crops fared poorly: Saskatchewan does better growing wheat than maize. Aside from grains, the Americas also acquired citrus fruits, bananas, grapes, and figs from Eurasia, and millets, sorghums, yams, okra, and watermelon from Africa. So the new crops extended the possibilities of American agriculture somewhat, and allowed a more varied diet. But they did not constitute a vast improvement, because the Americas already had maize and potatoes and plenty of fruits and vegetables.

Drug crops such as sugar and coffee changed the Americas as profoundly as did the food crops. Sugar, originally a grass from New Guinea, but a commercial crop in South Asia, China, and the Mediterranean, came to Brazil and the Caribbean in the sixteenth and seventeenth centuries. Both a mild drug and a food, it became the mainstay of a plantation economy based on African slave labor. Coffee, from Ethiopia and Arabia, also became a plantation crop in the eighteenth century. Without these imported crops, the plantation complex of the Americas would have been a much smaller matter; and the Atlantic slave trade far smaller as well.

Maize and potatoes, together with cassava, tomatoes, cacao, peanuts, sweet potato, pumpkins, squashes, pineapples, and a handful of others formed the Americas' contribution to global food crops. South America also gave tobacco to the world. Some of these crops had revolutionary consequences in sizeable regions of Africa and Eurasia. Potatoes, for example, nicely suited the soil and climate conditions in northern Europe from Ireland to Russia. Their arrival and spread played a considerable role in allowing the surge of population growth there in the eighteenth and nineteenth centuries, which helped supply the manpower for both overseas empires and the labor for the industrial revolution. Potatoes stored well, especially in cold climates, and they contain excellent nutrition. In their native Andes, where production and storage had been raised to a high art, potatoes had helped fuel the expansion of the Inka empire in the fifteenth century. A few centuries later they played a broadly similar role in northern Europe. Their career in Europe, especially Ireland, also shows the dangers of over-reliance on a single staple. The Irish potato famine of 1845–52, a result of crop failure caused by a potato disease, cost Ireland a quarter of its population—a million dead and another million emigrated.[18]

The potato's impact on northern Europe's food supply required another biological migrant: clover. Clover, although not from the Americas, was essential to the impact of the Columbian Exchange in Europe. Clover hosts micro-organisms that have the rare capacity to fix nitrogen from the air in the soil, putting it where plant roots can absorb it. All plants need nitrogen, and for many it is the nutrient in shortest supply. Potatoes are especially nitrogen-hungry crops, and cannot yield well consistently without nitrogen supplements to the soil. While clover grew wild throughout Europe and Southwest Asia, the earliest evidence of clover cultivation comes from Islamic Andalusia in the thirteenth century. Castilians soon learned the value of clover cultivation, and the practice of using clover in rotation with food crops spread northward with Spaniards (in this respect the territorial expansion of the House of Habsburg proved a blessing to all Europeans). Lombardy and the Low Countries became centers of clover cultivation. By 1620, English farmers had begun to plant clover, and by 1850 it was in widespread use throughout northern Europe. Clover's nitrogen-fixing properties allowed the potato to have its nutritional and demographic impact. And because clover makes an excellent fodder crop, it also allowed higher cattle populations and helped raise milk and meat production levels throughout northern Europe. Although as yet unsung by historians, clover can claim an impact on European history as great as that of the potato.[19]

Maize had a more diffuse impact than the potato and clover. It did well in conditions as varied as those of southern Europe, China, and larges swathes of Africa. Maize allowed new lands to be brought under cultivation, because it prospered where grains and tubers would not. It undergirded population growth and famine resistance in China and southern Europe, but nowhere was it more influential than in Africa, where today it is the single most important food. In the two centuries after 1550, maize became a staple in Atlantic Africa, from Angola to Senegambia. Different varieties suited the several different rainfall regimes in Africa, and improved African chances of surviving drought. Maize stores much better than millets, sorghums, or tubers. It thus allowed chiefs and kings to maximize their power by centralizing the storage and distribution of food. In the West African forest zone, maize encouraged the formation of larger states than had existed before. The Asante kingdom embarked on a program of expansion after the 1670s, spearheaded by maize-eating armies which could carry their food with them on distant campaigns. Maize also served well as a portable food for merchant caravans, which contributed to commercialization in Atlantic Africa, including the slave trade. The slave trade could more easily reach well inland if merchants, and their human property, had an easily portable food supply. Storehouses of maize also made it more practical to imprison large numbers of slaves in the infamous barracoons of the West African coast. Just as sugar and coffee heightened the demand in the Americas for African slaves, so maize in Africa increased the practicality of the slave trade.[20]

Cassava, also known as manioc, was the Americas' other great contribution to African agriculture. A native of Brazil, cassava with its deep root system is admirably suited to drought and poor soils and resistant to many crop pests. It too did well in many parts of Africa, and like maize it provided a portable food that underlay state formation and expansion in West Africa and Angola. Cassava, like potatoes, need not be harvested at a particular season but may be left in the ground for weeks or more. It is an ideal crop for people who might need to run away for their own safety, for example people routinely subject to slave raiding. In this respect it served as a counter to maize: it helped peasantries to flee and survive slave raids, while maize helped slavers to conduct and extend their business.

The Columbian Exchange was the largest-scale, fastest, and most important intercontinental biological transfer in world history. But it was not the only one that followed upon the navigational exploits of Columbus' generation. A modest trans-Pacific exchange (or 'Magellan Exchange') resulted from Magellan's voyages, at first affecting chiefly the Philippines, and intensified in the wake of Captain Cook's meanderings throughout the world's largest ocean. The Pacific islands themselves, rather than the ocean's rim, felt the greatest effects, and as in the Americas (or in Australia after 1788) the most striking result was sharp depopulation in the wake of repeated epidemics.[21] Many American food crops became important in East Asia, such as sweet potatoes, maize, and peanuts in south China, but they probably arrived not across the Pacific in the wake of Magellan, but across the Atlantic and the Indian Oceans via Portuguese and Dutch traders.[22]

Taken together, the whirlwind of intercontinental biological exchange in the centuries between 1500 and 1800 brought astounding changes around the world. It led to demographic catastrophes in lands unfamiliar with the crowd diseases. It improved the quantity and reliability of food supplies almost everywhere. In cases where horses were new, it reshuffled political relations by providing a new basis for warfare.

All these early modern exchanges carried historical consequences. European imperialism, in the Americas, Australia, and New Zealand, simultaneously promoted and was promoted by the spread of European (or more usually Eurasian) animals, plants, and diseases. Europeans brought a biota that unconsciously worked as a team to favor the spread of European settlers, European power, and Eurasian species, and thereby to create what Alfred Crosby, the foremost historian of these processes, called neo-Europes—including Australia, New Zealand, most of North America, Uruguay, Argentina, and southernmost Brazil.

Beyond the neo-Europes, something of a neo-Africa emerged in the Americas. More than ten million Africans arrived in the Americas in slave ships between 1550 and 1850. In those same ships came yellow fever and malaria, which profoundly influenced settlement patterns in the Americas, because they were so lethal to people without prior experience of them. Slave ships also brought West African rice, which became the foundation of the coastal economy in South Carolina and Georgia in the eighteenth century and important in Surinam as well. Other African crops came too: okra, sesame, and (although not in slave ships) coffee. All this combined to create a neo-Africa from Bahia to the Chesapeake. It was a world of African people and culture, where indigenous peoples almost died out and indigenous culture, including foodstuffs, was partially absorbed into the neo-African matrix. In this it resembled the neo-Europes. But at the same time neo-Africa was profoundly different from the neo-Europes: until the Haitian Revolution (1791–1804), nowhere in the Americas were Africans and people of African descent politically, economically, or socially in control, whereas Europeans and their descendants soon dominated the neo-Europes.

A more nuanced picture of Atlantic America would include transition zones between the low-latitude neo-Africa and the temperate neo-Europes. Even Quebec had some African components in its biota and culture by 1750, and Barbados and Bahia had significant European inputs, but nonetheless may usefully be construed as neo-Europe and neo-Africa. But the stretch between Cuba and Maryland (roughly 22–38 degrees north latitude) blended African and European elements more evenly, creating creolized biotas and culture. The same held true in a corresponding southern transition zone in southeastern Brazil, in what are now the states of Minas Gerais, Espírito Santo, Rio de Janeiro, and São Paulo (roughly 16–26 degrees south latitude). In the Americas, the Columbian Exchange created 'neo-Afro-Eurasias' in which the proportions of African and European and (to a lesser extent) Asian components varied, depending partly on latitude, or climate, and partly on the accidents of biological and cultural history.

As the Columbian Exchange indicates, sailing ships brought the continents together as never before, at least since the final breakup of Gondwanaland about sixty-five million years ago. But they did not prove hospitable conveyances to every form of life. They filtered out a few species that could not for one reason or another survive a long journey. The age of steam, and then of air travel broke down such remaining barriers to biological exchange, accelerating the dispersal of old and new migratory species alike. Although its greatest impacts came in the sixteenth and seventeenth centuries, in a sense the Columbian Exchange never ended. American raccoons, grey squirrels, and muskrats for example colonized parts of Europe in the nineteenth and twentieth centuries. European starlings spread throughout North America. Nor did the Magellan Exchange come to an end. If anything, it sped up in the nineteenth and twentieth centuries, not least because of deliberate introductions of species such as the kiwi fruit (from China to New Zealand to Chile and California) and eucalyptus trees (from Australia to almost everywhere).[23]

In the eighteenth and nineteenth centuries deliberate introductions became an increasingly institutionalized enterprise. Botanical gardens undertook to spread useful plants far and wide, especially within the confines of European empires. In the most famous example, British plant prospectors took rubber tree seeds from their native turf in Brazilian Amazonia to Kew Gardens outside of London, and from there to British Malaya. A rubber plantation economy soon blossomed in Malaya, undermining the rubber tapping business in Brazil. Dutch authorities managed to get seeds of cinchona trees (native to the eastern slopes of the Peruvian Andes) to Java, where by the 1870s they were producing commercial quantities of quinine, a drug that offered protection against malaria. Cheap quinine made European empire, and in the early 1940s Japanese empire too, far more practical in malarial lands than it could otherwise have been. In Australia and New Zealand, settlers organized societies dedicated to the purpose of importing familiar plants and animals from Britain, typically regarded, by settlers at least, as superior to the native species of the Antipodes. Botanical gardens, plant prospectors, and acclimatization societies all combined with improved transportation technology to sustain biological exchanges in the nineteenth and twentieth centuries.[24]

Inevitably, accidental and unwelcome biological exchange continued as well. Pests such as coffee rust or phylloxera (a menace to grape vines) circulated around the world thanks to improved and intensified transport in the nineteenth century. Cholera escaped from its native haunts around the Bay of Bengal and became a global scourge in the early nineteenth century. At the end of the century rinderpest, an extremely lethal cattle virus, spread to east and southern Africa, wiping out as much as 90 percent of the herds, bringing destitution to pastoral peoples (and opening niche space for wildlife). The demobilization of millions of World War I soldiers and sailors in 1918, and their quick movements around the world by steamship, spread an influenza virus that killed from twenty to sixty million people, most of them in India. The influenza killed many more people than did the war itself.

CONCLUSION

Faster and more frequent transport and travel continue to promote biological exchange. Today there are some 44,000 regular air routes that constantly, if inadvertently, move insects, seeds, and germs around the world.[25] Aquatic species shuttle around the world's harbors in the ballast water carried by ocean-going ships. This was the path taken by the zebra mussel from the Caspian Sea to the lakes and rivers of North America, where its prolific colonization costs billions of dollars annually. Many governments try hard to keep out weeds, pests, and germs, but every success is provisional, valid only until the next arrival of invasive species. And some governments, having other priorities, do not bother. So the long-term process of biological globalization continues, and will inevitably continue.

Like cultural globalization, it will never be full and final. Rubber trees will not colonize Iceland, nor will caribou roam Borneo. But within the limits prescribed by climate, soils, and other ecological conditions—these limits change but they can never disappear—biological exchange will continue to take place and to affect human history. It may now seem that it will never again have the influence that it did in the era of the Columbian Exchange 400 and 500 years ago. As regards the exchange of economically useful plants and animals, this is probably true: almost all that can usefully happen has already happened, due to determined efforts over the centuries. But in the realm of pests and pathogens it could well be otherwise. In biological history four or five centuries is the merest flash. In the long run strange and unforeseen things will happen.

NOTES

1. M. Williamson, *Biological Invasions* (London: Chapman and Hall, 1996); N. Shigesada and K. Kawasaki, *Biological Invasions: Theory and Practice* (New York: Oxford University Press, 1997).
2. These themes are explored for the United States ca. 1870–1930 in Peter Coates, *American Perceptions of Immigrant and Invasive Species* (Berkeley: University of California Press, 2006).
3. Tim Flannery, *The Future Eaters* (Chatswood, Australia 1994); Flannery, *The Eternal Frontier* (New York: Atlantic Monthly Press, 2001).
4. Jared Diamond, *Guns, Germs and Steel: The Fates of Human Societies* (New York: Norton, 1997).
5. Luigi Luca Cavalli-Sforza, *Genes, Peoples, and Languages* (Berkeley: University of California Press, 2000); D. Harris, ed., *The Origins and Spread of Agriculture* (Washington, D.C.: Smithsonian Institution Press, 1996).
6. Edward Schafer, *The Golden Peaches of Samarkand: A Study of T'ang Exotics* (Berkeley: University of California Press, 1963).
7. Francesca Bray and Joseph Needham, *Science and Civilization in China. Vol VI. Biology and Biological Technology. Pt 2. Agriculture* (Cambridge: Cambridge University Press, 1984), 492–5.
8. Andrew Watson, *Agricultural Innovation in the Early Islamic World: The Diffusion of Crops and Farming Techniques, 700–1100* (Cambridge: Cambridge University Press, 1983). See also a challenge to parts of Watson's position: Michael Decker, 'Plants and Progress: Rethinking the Islamic Agricultural Revolution,' *Journal of World History* 20 (2009), 187–206.
9. James D. Rice, *Nature and History in the Potomac Country* (Baltimore: The Johns Hopkins University Press, 2009), 26–7.
10. Robin Law, *The Horse in West African History* (Oxford: Oxford University Press, 1980). Jack Goody, *Technology, Tradition, and the State in Africa* (Oxford: Oxford University Press, 1971).

11. J. R. McNeill, 'Of Rats and Men: A Synoptic Environmental History of the Island Pacific,' *Journal of World History* 5 (1994), 299–349.

12. John Iliffe, *Africans: The History of A Continent* (Cambridge: Cambridge University Press, 1995).

13. Kenneth Kiple, *A Moveable Feast: Ten Millennia of Food Globalization* (New York: Cambridge University Press, 2007), 46–8.

14. Alfred W. Crosby, *The Columbian Exchange: Biological and Cultural Consequences of 1492* (Wesport, Conn.: Greenwood, 1972).

15. William H. McNeill, *Plagues and Peoples* (New York: Doubleday, 1976).

16. Elinor Melville, *A Plague of Sheep* (New York: Cambridge University Press, 1994).

17. Pekka Hämäläinen, *The Comanche Empire* (New Haven: Yale University Press, 2008).

18. A recent summary of potato history is John Reader, *Propitious Esculent* (London: Heinemann, 2008).

19. Thorkild Kjaergaard, 'A Plant That Changed the World: The Rise and Fall of Clover, 1000–2000,' *Landscape Research* 28 (2003), 41–9.

20. James McCann, *Maize and Grace: Africa's Encounter with a New World Crop* (Cambridge, Mass.: Harvard University Press, 2005) is the starting point for the history of maize in Africa. On the relevance of introduced crops to the slave trade, see also Stanley Alpern, 'The European Introduction of Crops into West Africa in Precolonial Times,' *History in Africa* 19 (1992), 13–43.

21. J. R. McNeill, 'Of Rats and Men.'

22. For a review, Sucheta Mazumdar, 'The Impact of New World Food Crops on the Diet and Economy of China and India, 1600–1900,' in Raymond Grew, ed., *Food in Global History* (Boulder, Colo.: Westview Press, 2000), 58–78.

23. Robin W. Doughty, *The Eucalyptus: A Natural and Commercial History of the Gum Tree* (Baltimore: The Johns Hopkins University Press, 2000).

24. Richard Grove, *Green Imperialism: Colonial Expansion, Tropical Island Edens and the Origins of Environmentalism, 1600–1860* (New York: Cambridge University Press, 1994). Richard Drayton, *Nature's Government: Science, Imperial Britain, and the 'Improvement' of the World* (New Haven: Yale University Press, 2000). Warren Dean, *Brazil and the Struggle for Rubber* (New York: Cambridge University Press, 1987).

25. Andrew Tatem and Simon Hay, 'Climatic Similarity and Biological Exchange in the Worldwide Airline Transportation Network,' *Proceedings of the Royal Society. Biological Sciences* 274 (2007), 1489–96.

REFERENCES

BURNEY, DAVID. 'Historical Perspectives on Human-Assisted Biological Invasions,' *Evolutionary Anthropology* 4 (1996), 216–21.

CARLTON, J. H. 'Marine Bioinvasions: The Alteration of Marine Ecosystems by Nonindigenous Species,' *Oceanography* 9 (1996), 36–43.

CARNEY, JUDITH. *Black Rice: The African Origins of Rice Cultivation in the Americas.* Cambridge, Mass.: Harvard University Press, 2001.

CROSBY, ALFRED. *The Columbian Exchange: Biological and Cultural Consequences of 1492.* Wesport, Conn.: Greenwood Press, 1972.

——. *Ecological Imperialism: The Biological Expansion of Europe, 900–1900.* New York: Cambridge University Press, 1986.

CURTIN, PHILIP D. 'Disease Exchange across the Tropical Atlantic,' *History and Philosophy of the Life Sciences* 15 (1993), 169–96.

GROVES, R. H. and J. J. BURDON. *Ecology of Biological Invasions.* Cambridge: Cambridge University Press, 1986.

HOBHOUSE, HENRY. *Seeds of Change: Five Plants that Changed the World.* New York: Perennial, 1986.

KIPLE, KENNETH. *A Moveable Feast: Ten Millennia of Food Globalization.* New York: Cambridge University Press, 2007.

LELAND, JOHN. *Aliens in the Backyard: Plant and Animal Imports into America.* Columbia, S.C.: University of South Carolina Press, 2005.

McCANN, JAMES. *Maize and Grace: Africa's Encounter with a New World Crop.* Cambridge, Mass.: Harvard University Press, 2005.

McNEILL, WILLIAM H. *Plagues and Peoples.* Garden City, N.J.: Anchor Press, 1976.

MELVILLE, ELINOR. *A Plague of Sheep.* New York: Cambridge University Press, 1994.

MOONEY, HAROLD A., and RICHARD J. HOBBS, eds. *Invasive Species in a Changing World.* Washington D.C.: Island Press, 2000.

SHIGESADA, N., and KAWASAKI, K. *Biological Invasions: Theory and Practice.* New York: Oxford University Press, 1997.

WATSON, ANDREW. *Agricultural Innovation in the Early Islamic World: The Diffusion of Crops and Farming Techniques.* Cambridge: Cambridge University Press, 1983.

WILLIAMSON, M. *Biological Invasions.* London: Chapman and Hall, 1996.

CHAPTER 19

....

CULTURAL EXCHANGES
IN WORLD HISTORY

....

JERRY H. BENTLEY

SINCE the 1960s, when world history gradually began to emerge as a distinct field of professional historical scholarship, world historians have focused their attention and their analyses mostly on political, social, economic, demographic, and environmental issues with strong material dimensions. Processes of cross-cultural trade, large-scale migration, epidemic disease, and environmental change have all been popular issues for world historians, as have comparative economic analysis, processes of imperial expansion, and cases of colonial rule. One of the most fundamental assumptions of this contemporary world history is the notion that historical development does not take place exclusively within the boundary lines of individual societies or cultural regions. To the contrary, cross-cultural interactions and exchanges have influenced the development of all or almost all peoples and societies throughout the world's history. If this point is true, it stands to reason that there have likely been cultural as well as political, social, economic, demographic, and environmental implications of cross-cultural interactions and exchanges.

CULTURAL EXCHANGE AS A HISTORICAL PROBLEM
....

Under the banner of 'new cultural history,' the analysis of cultural issues has flourished in the larger discipline of history since the 1980s, yet world historians have been slow to address the cultural dimensions of cross-cultural interactions and exchanges. The inherent slipperiness of cultural analysis helps to explain this apparent disinclination toward global-historical analysis of cultural developments. It is certainly simpler to probe the cultural dimensions of historical developments within well-defined and tightly focused contexts than to explore them in large, comparative, transregional, and global contexts. This is particularly true given the far-reaching influence of Clifford Geertz's anthropology, in which cultural analysis takes the form of thick description based on local knowledge that focuses on webs of significance that humans weave for themselves within particular and distinctive communities. Geertz's anthropology has proven brilliant for purposes of understanding particular cultural environments, but it does not lend itself readily to the analysis of interactions, engagements, and exchanges between peoples of different cultural traditions.

When historians have turned their attention from individual communities to large-scale comparative, transregional, and global issues, they have found it much simpler to quantify bolts of silk, trace the effects of biological exchanges, or outline the structures of colonial rule than to evaluate the meaning of cultural borrowings, the depth of religious conversions, or the dynamics that help to explain cultural exchanges. There is no major paradigm for the analysis of cultural developments that flow from cross-cultural interactions and exchanges—no coherent body of theory and analysis, for example, analogous to the modernization or world-system school of thought on modern political economy. World historians have worked out no common approach to the study of cultural developments, nor have they even adopted any settled vocabulary or analytical convention for the investigation of cultural developments.

In spite of the inherent messiness of cultural-historical analysis, particularly when carried out on comparative, transregional, and global scales, the cultural dimensions of cross-cultural exchanges demand world historians' attention. The term 'cultural exchange' might refer to many kinds of developments, including the spread of scientific, technological, ideological, educational, philosophical, and religious traditions that reflect deeply held values and worldviews, with particular attention to the adaptations and other reactions that take place when representatives of different societies and advocates of different traditions interact intensively with one another.

When peoples of different societies and cultural traditions engage in systematic and sustained interaction, any number of cultural consequences can follow from their dealings. It is possible for peoples of different societies to interact over long terms with little exchange of cultural traditions. More commonly, though, different cultural traditions have provoked reactions or wielded influence beyond their own communities. Sometimes exposure to different traditions has generated disapproval, revulsion, or even active resistance to foreign and unfamiliar traditions. Other times the introduction to new views has prompted interest and led to the adoption of new traditions. Yet even in those cases when peoples have adopted new ways—by converting to a different religious faith, for example, or accepting a new set of ideological values—they have inevitably made cultural adjustments that bridge the gap between their inherited and adopted traditions. For this reason, when thinking about large-scale patterns of technological exchange, the historian Arnold Pacey has argued that it is less helpful to speak about 'technological diffusion,' as a process by which technologies have supposedly spread intact from one society to another, than about 'technological dialogue' or 'technological dialectic,' as a process by which technologies have undergone adaptations and adjustments as they have crossed and re-crossed the boundary

lines of societies and cultural regions.¹ Indeed, processes of cultural blending, translation, and syncretism have characterized cultural exchanges more generally.

In the absence of any generally recognized paradigms, theories, scholarly conventions, or even analytical vocabulary, how might historians best go about investigating
processes of cultural exchange in comparative, transregional, and global contexts?
When world historians and other scholars have turned their attention to cultural
exchanges, they have exhibited a strong tendency toward methodological individualism. They have drawn theoretical, analytical, and interpretative inspiration from a
broad range of sources, including anthropological investigations, social theory, and
postcolonial scholarship. The study of cultural exchanges is clearly an unruly endeavor.
At the same time, it is an endeavor that presents the stimulating challenge of seeking
disciplined ways to understand subtle and complex developments in cultural history
from global perspectives. In exploring this scholarly project, this chapter will review
some of the general visions of cultural exchange that scholars have sketched, discuss
the more prominent analytical approaches they have taken, and then outline the larger
patterns they have recognized in the historical analysis of cultural exchanges.

APPROACHES TO THE STUDY OF CULTURAL EXCHANGES

Compared to the global-historical study of economic development, the analysis of
cultural exchanges has resisted the allurements of general theory. Three distinct schools
of thought provide structure for a vast body of scholarship exploring large-scale
economic development and the rise of the west: the modernization school, the
world-system school, and the California school as represented by historians like
Kenneth Pomeranz, R. Bin Wong, Andre Gunder Frank, Jack Goldstone, Robert
B. Marks, and others.² Processes of cultural exchange have found a few general
theorists, but none has influenced the general understanding of cultural exchanges to
the extent that the modernization, world-system, and California schools have dominated conceptions of large-scale economic development and the rise of the west.

In his own quirky way, Arnold J. Toynbee recognized that processes of cultural
exchange merited attention. In one of the later parts of his massive *Study of History*,
Toynbee discussed the issue of 'Contacts between Civilizations in Space (Encounters
between Contemporaries),' where he looked for patterns of cultural exchange that lent
themselves to the possibility of general understanding. As in other parts of his work,
Toynbee took a rigid and unsympathetic approach to cultural exchanges. Like Johann
Gottfried von Herder and Oswald Spengler, Toynbee valued cultural purity—the
supposedly untainted cultural expression of an ostensibly coherent society—and
he regarded cultural exchange and cultural borrowing as disgusting promiscuity,
which he sometimes even characterized with the term 'miscegenation.' He held that

the spread of cultural influence ('cultural radiation' in Toynbee's parlance) took place most effectively when a society was in the state of disintegration, and he insisted further that the process had steep costs because as a given society spread its influence, it also opened itself to the intrusion of foreign elements that would taint its own supposed cultural purity.[3] This fastidious anxiety about cultural purity reflected a xenophobia that led Toynbee (along with Spengler and others) to tendentious and highly distorted analyses of cultural exchanges. *A priori* assumptions that cultural exchanges involve odious and obscene conduct undermined his efforts to investigate cultural exchanges as historical processes.

Two scholars—Mary W. Helms and Jerry H. Bentley—have taken more constructive approaches to the analysis of cultural exchanges as large-scale historical processes. Both reflect a concern in recent scholarship to take questions of power into account as historians turn their attention to cross-cultural interactions and exchanges. Interactions between peoples of different societies always took place in contexts of differential power relations, and power in its various forms influenced processes of cultural exchange. Thus, issues of power will figure prominently in this chapter's discussion of cultural exchanges.

The anthropologist Mary W. Helms explored the cultural significance of long-distance interactions in an important book entitled *Ulysses' Sail: An Ethnographic Odyssey of Power, Knowledge, and Geographical Distance*. Focusing primarily on travelers in preindustrial times, Helms held that cross-cultural interactions often had large social and political implications. Although it was certainly not unknown for preindustrial populations to view foreign peoples and customs as dangerous, distasteful, or threatening, Helms pointed out that it was also possible for the foreign to hold attractions. Distant knowledge could be powerful as well as threatening, a source of prestige as well as danger, and individuals like long-distance travelers who enjoyed access to foreign knowledge had opportunities to parlay their unusual experiences into social and political power. Either as visitors to foreign lands or as sojourners returning to their own societies, long-distance travelers had the potential to serve as cultural brokers who possessed exotic knowledge and carried authority from afar. Geographical distance actively encouraged cultural exchange—both because of the inherent power that distant knowledge could bring and because of the advantages that individuals were able to realize for themselves as cultural brokers with access to distant knowledge.[4] Thus a dynamic of power deriving from geographical distance was essential for the understanding of cultural exchanges.

While Helms concentrated on the cultural implications of geographical distance, Jerry H. Bentley focused on processes of interaction and cultural exchange themselves with an eye toward identifying patterns of cultural exchange and understanding the power dynamics underlying them by locating them in appropriate political, social, and economic contexts. While acknowledging Helms's point that foreign cultural traditions often held a certain appeal, Bentley drew attention also to the barriers that impeded the flow of foreign influences across cultural boundary lines. Foreign beliefs, values, and customs have often seemed alien and unappealing on numerous grounds, so the adoption of foreign ways and conversion to foreign beliefs have frequently been unanticipated or even surprising developments calling for special analysis and explanation. In an effort to understand the different trajectories followed by different processes of cultural exchange—why some cases of cross-cultural interaction led to widespread adoption of foreign traditions, for example, while others did not—Bentley looked to the political, social, and economic contexts in which cultural interactions and exchanges took place. Without reducing cultural developments to material causes, he argued that political, social, and economic circumstances have often had the effect of reinforcing cultural choices. This approach is particularly useful for purposes of analyzing cultural development at the social rather than individual level. Individual men and women ultimately make their own cultural histories, of course, even if not always under conditions of their own choosing, and individuals have certainly made commitments that run contrary to their immediate material or social interests. In many historical cases, however, it is quite clear that some kind of political, social, or economic advantage has accrued to individuals who made particular cultural choices. Only by viewing cultural exchanges in appropriate contexts is it possible to understand the complex dynamics of political, social, and economic power that have influenced cultural developments in processes of sustained interaction between peoples of different societies.[5]

Apart from Helms and Bentley, very few scholars have offered large-scale analyses of cultural exchanges as global historical processes. Many others, however, have focused attention on individual cases of cultural exchange, and in doing so they have developed analytical techniques and advanced interpretations that offer excellent guidance to those seeking to understand processes of cultural exchange on larger scales. Works by scholars of the Melbourne school of ethnographic history merit special mention here because they have probed the complexities of cross-cultural environments with particular insight and with attention to questions of power relations. Scholars associated directly with Melbourne included Greg Dening, Donna Merwick, Rhys Isaac, and Inga Clendinnen, and many others have reflected their scholarly influence. Beginning in the 1970s, the Melbourne school crafted distinctive applications of the anthropological turn in historical scholarship—first in the context of Pacific islands history, later in the contexts of North American, Latin American, European, and Australian histories as well. Melbourne scholars have generally framed their studies to concentrate on the historical experiences of tightly focused communities or societies, but they have also shown partiality to situations in which cultural differences and asymmetric power relations contributed to the tensions that their chosen communities and societies have had to deal with. Both cultural differences and power relations became salient issues in the context of cross-cultural interactions such as the encounters of European explorers and colonists with Marquesas islanders, Yucatec Maya, and the native peoples of New Holland (explored in works of Dening, Clendinnen, and Merwick, respectively).[6] Most written sources reflect the views of the more powerful European parties to these interactions, so Melbourne scholars have resorted to archaeological evidence, orally transmitted accounts, and the tactic of reading written sources against the grain in efforts to recover the perspectives of less powerful individuals and groups. The sophisticated analyses of Melbourne scholars have enriched the understanding of cross-cultural interactions not only by probing sensitively into cultural issues but perhaps even more so by bringing multiple perspectives into consideration and taking differential power relations into serious account.

Attention to power has been the hallmark of postcolonial scholars who have fashioned yet another approach to the historical analysis of cultural exchanges in modern times. Edward W. Said argued famously in *Orientalism* that European scholars constructed a body of knowledge defining the colonial 'orient' as the inverse of their own society, and further that the knowledge they produced had tremendous power because it was the filter through which policy makers and colonial administrators understood most of the world beyond Europe. In this view of things, European influence went well beyond the persuasion of foreign peoples to adopt religious and ideological views in that it established the fundamental categories for the analysis of societies and set the criteria for determining what counts as rational and irrational, civilized and uncivilized, cultured and barbarian, advanced and backward, active and passive, progressive and stagnant, modern and traditional.[7]

Said traced the origins of orientalist views to ancient times, when Greeks viewed Persians as irrational, inferior, subservient barbarians, but he focused attention principally on the era of global empire, when European and Euro-American peoples had the means to project their power in the larger world. Yet his insights into the construction of knowledge in colonial contexts clearly resonate in the cases of expansive and imperialist societies other than Europe. It is certainly possible to see that European peoples constructed a body of knowledge about sub-Saharan Africa, the Americas, and Oceania as well as Asian lands, and further that the resulting sense of intellectual control coincided neatly with programs of conquest, empire, and settler colonialism in these regions.[8] Yet similar projects unfolded elsewhere when Manchu and Chinese imperialists relied on cartography and ethnography to gain intellectual control over regions of southwestern China, central Asia, and Taiwan that they were trying to absorb into the Chinese empire.[9] Expansive societies like imperial Russia and Tokugawa Japan also carefully surveyed lands and peoples in regions of interest such as Siberia and Hokkaido, respectively. Indeed, from ancient times to the present, it would be possible to identify numerous cases in which powerful peoples have compiled bodies of knowledge that aided their programs of territorial expansion and colonial rule. Thus, construed broadly as knowledge serving the interests of empire, orientalism was neither a new development nor an exclusive possession of European peoples, even if Europeans perhaps raised the art of producing orientalist knowledge to a particularly high level. To the contrary, many versions of orientalism have aided numerous imperial projects at different times and places.

Methodological individualism remains the rule in the historical analysis of cultural exchanges. Yet several large-scale studies as well as insightful works focusing on individual cases of cross-cultural engagement offer useful guidance for the analysis of cultural exchanges. Recent efforts to take issues of political, social, and economic power into consideration are particularly helpful for purposes of understanding processes of cultural exchanges. The following pages will draw on recent studies in essaying a sketch of the main patterns in the global history of cultural exchanges.

CULTURAL EXCHANGES IN PRE-MODERN TIMES

Historical analysis of cross-cultural interactions and cultural exchanges has focused principally on early modern and modern times when written sources produced by European peoples became abundant. The sources are welcome in that they offer some documentation of cross-cultural engagements, even if they reflect partial and often skewed perspectives. Since Melbourne scholars, postcolonial critics, and others have clearly exposed the limitations of these European sources, it is possible for historians to develop techniques and adopt tactics to correct for biases and bring additional perspectives into consideration.

What about earlier eras lacking the abundance of sources generated by European peoples during the past half-millennium? To what extent is it possible to analyze cultural exchanges in pre-modern times? In the interests of considering cultural exchanges within their political, social, and economic contexts, my own preferred approach is to identify eras or periods of intense cross-cultural interaction and trace the patterns of cultural exchanges that took place under the different sets of conditions prevailing at different times.[10] It is not possible for a brief essay to consider all the periods of cross-cultural interaction that historians have postulated, so here I would like to discuss the nature of cultural exchanges in two broad eras—pre-modern times up to about 1500 CE and the modern age of the past five hundred years—in which processes of cultural exchanges unfolded according to somewhat different dynamics.

Although evidence has long since disappeared, there can be no serious doubt that cultural exchanges took place from the earliest days of coherent and recognized cultural communities. J. R. McNeill and William H. McNeill have suggested that animist and shamanist beliefs about a realm of spirits and human-spirit relationships may have circulated around much of the world in the era between about 40,000 and 10,000 years before the present. Although admittedly speculative, this suggestion is nevertheless plausible in view of the wide distribution of animist beliefs among hunting-and-gathering peoples and the strong likelihood that bow-and-arrow technology made its way to most parts of the world during the latter part of the same era.[11] In any case, long before the invention of agriculture and the establishment of settled societies, there were plentiful opportunities for early human groups to exchange beliefs and ideas as well as to trade exotic items, arrange marriages between different communities, and pass along technological discoveries as hunting-and-gathering peoples encountered one another during seasonal migrations.

With the establishment of settled societies, cultural exchanges figured prominently among the various processes of cross-cultural interaction that linked individual societies into larger networks of communication and exchange. Without reducing cultural developments to functions of other interactions, I would argue that cultural exchanges routinely accompanied processes such as the conduct of cross-cultural trade, encounters of different peoples during large-scale migrations, and interactions between peoples from different societies in the context of imperial expansion or colonial rule. In the absence of sources, it is impossible to know the details of these early cultural exchanges, but it is also impossible to doubt that cultural exchanges accompanied processes like long-distance trading during the Upper Paleolithic era or the migrations of peoples speaking Indo-European and Bantu languages.[12]

After the invention of writing, processes of cultural exchanges came into clearer light. In Mesopotamia, Egypt, the Indus River valley, and other regions, early cities and administrative settlements offered opportunities for those who visited them or ventured out and connected them with their contemporaries and counterparts in the larger world. Mesopotamians and Egyptians traded with one another at least by 3500 BCE, and by the third and second millennia BCE, commerce linked the whole region from Anatolia, Syria, and Egypt in the west to Afghanistan and the Indus River valley in the east. Although limited evidence bears directly on cultural as opposed to material exchanges, cultural exchanges certainly accompanied travelers and traders throughout the region. It is likely, for example, that Egyptians borrowed art motifs, boat designs, and writing from their Mesopotamian contemporaries.[13] In the western hemisphere evidence of early cultural exchanges is more sparse. Yet even there it has been possible for archaeologists to trace certain cultural exchanges by mapping the spread and distribution of culturally specific artifacts such as cultic and burial goods in ancient North America.[14]

With the emergence of the large imperial societies, the pace of cross-cultural interactions quickened again, and the organization of extensive trade, travel, and communications networks created a foundation for sustained and systematic engagement between distant societies. The silk roads network was the most extensive among the early networks of interaction, and after about 200 BCE, it facilitated cultural as well as commercial and biological exchanges. Best known as a cluster of roads and sea lanes over which merchants traded silk, spices, horses, glass, and other commodities, the silk roads also served as highways for the spread of religious and cultural traditions. Land routes linked societies from China and Korea to Bactria and India and beyond to Iran and the Mediterranean basin, while a complementary network of sea lanes enabled mariners to sail between China and Japan, Southeast Asia, Ceylon, India, Iran, Arabia, and East Africa. After the emergence of Islam, traffic over these highways and sea lanes increased dramatically in volume, and soon an additional network of roads crossing the Sahara Desert linked sub-Saharan Africa and the Mediterranean basin.

Though originally constructed for commercial and military reasons, the roads and sea lanes of the eastern hemisphere proved to be outstanding routes for the dissemination of religious and cultural traditions. Buddhism spread from its Indian homeland to Iran and central Asia, and later to China, Korea, Japan, and Vietnam as well. Christianity spread from Palestine along trade routes to all parts of the

Mediterranean basin and east to Mesopotamia, Iran, India, and parts of central Asia. Shortly thereafter, Manichaeism found a home in largely the same regions. The appeal of Islam extended in particularly dramatic fashion from its Arabian homeland to a broad swath of the Eurasian continent from Indonesia in the east to Morocco in the west and parts of sub-Saharan Africa in the south. Between the seventh and the sixteenth centuries, all these faiths continued their geographical expansion and also attracted large communities of enthusiastic supporters in distant regions. Scientific, mathematical, technological, and medical traditions also spread far from their original homelands.

How is it possible to account for the remarkable diffusions of these religious and cultural traditions?[15] The larger contexts in which cultural exchanges took place merit close attention for their potential to bring focus to the various kinds of power that influenced processes of cultural exchange. The political context was defined by several large imperial states that made long-distance travel feasible by pacifying much of the Eurasian continent and that in several cases also encouraged adoption of a particular religion in the interests of cultural unity. In the era of the ancient silk roads, these states included the Han dynasty in China, the Mauryan and Kushan dynasties in India, the Seleucid and Parthian dynasties in Iran, and the Roman empire in the Mediterranean basin and Europe. In the era from about 500 to 1000 CE, the major imperial states included the Tang and Song dynasties in China, the Abbasid dynasty extending from the eastern Mediterranean to northern India, and the Byzantine empire in the Mediterranean basin. Over the following half-millennium from about 1000 to 1500, the principal states included the transregional empires of nomadic peoples like the Saljuq Turks, the Ottoman Turks, and especially the Mongols as well as more traditional state formations such as the Ming dynasty in China. As for social and economic contexts, this premodern, preindustrial world featured a series of productive agricultural societies that generated enough surplus to support sizable industrial and commercial sectors and to send large numbers of merchants abroad in search of commercial and business opportunities while also offering opportunities to those whom itinerant merchants encountered on the roads. Indeed, the roads, sea lanes, and transportation technologies that facilitated the spread of religious traditions were explainable entirely as a result of the political, social, and economic conditions of the era.

Granting the significance of the larger contexts, organizational considerations also help to explain the spread of Buddhism, Christianity, Manichaeism, and Islam. All four were missionary religions that relied on impassioned believers who worked to persuade doubters to abandon or even reject their inherited traditions and undergo a conscious conversion to a new way of life. Except in a few cases, it is impossible to know precisely what individual converts were thinking, how they understood their cultural odysseys, or why they made their cultural choices. Yet the tactic of employing ardent missionaries to spread the message was a development of fundamental importance for the spread of the religious traditions. Once they were out in the field, missionaries were able to draw upon numerous techniques to attract converts. In a pre-scientific age, a reputation for working miracles was a favored and particularly effective trait for missionaries. Miracle-workers were able to attract broad notice, even among the wealthy and powerful, because of their apparent ability to tap supernatural forces for useful and desirable ends. Missionaries helped spread religious traditions also through more mundane services such as providing support and comfort for oppressed or downtrodden groups. By adopting an ascetic way of life, missionaries set high standards for lay believers to emulate while at the same time, paradoxically, relieving them of the burden of actually meeting those standards in their own behavior because they could contribute to the larger cause by providing financial support for missionaries and religious institutions.

For those who learned about new religious traditions from missionaries and other representatives, several options were available. It was possible to ignore or reject a new cultural or religious alternative, and this was perhaps the most common initial response to a new and strange teaching. Rejection sometimes went so far as to take the form of violent opposition and resistance. Another possibility was to tolerate a new cultural or religious arrival and make selective use of the opportunities that it presented: if the proponents of a foreign tradition introduced new knowledge as well as unusual doctrine, some degree of partial accommodation might seem desirable. Yet another option was to sever ties with an inherited cultural or religious tradition and adopt a new alternative in its place. This last possibility might seem improbable because wholesale conversion to a new cultural or religious tradition was often quite inconvenient. It could involve adoption of new languages, foods, and customs. It could require new and uncomfortable relationships with family, friends, acquaintances, and business partners. It could involve the cutting of hair, the growing of hair, the wearing of distinctive dress, or the mutilation of body parts. Yet conversion to new cultural or religious traditions has occurred frequently in world history. Moreover, conversion was often not simply a personal development undertaken by individuals but also a social phenomenon because large numbers of individual conversions had the potential to bring about the cultural transformation of an entire society.

In light of the barriers to conversion, this option merits particular attention and calls for at least two levels of analysis. One set of issues has to do with the meaning of conversion to a different cultural or religious tradition. It is certainly conceivable that many individuals who converted to new religious traditions made conscious, deliberate decisions on the basis of considerations that they deemed important, and I would not want to exclude the strong possibility that sincere acceptance of religious teachings drove or at least accompanied many conversions. This does not mean, however, that converts necessarily adopted new religions as understood by long-time practitioners. The simple translation or explanation of new religious concepts inevitably involved accommodation of foreign ideas to accustomed ways of thinking about the world. As a result, a process of syncretism inevitably accompanied conversion, so that in some greater or lesser measure, converts always viewed new alternatives through the filters of their inherited traditions as they negotiated their way from one cultural or religious position to another. Many studies have shown how major religious traditions have developed in anything but monolithic fashion as their proponents and converts in different lands have adopted them and adapted them to local needs and interests.[16]

A second set of issues has to do with the relationship between conversion and the political, social, and economic contexts in which it took place. In many cases there was a demonstrable sociology of conversion, in that individuals' cultural and religious choices coincided with their political, social, or economic interests. In some cases political authorities favored a privileged tradition or sought to repress a disapproved alternative, with implications for the cultural choices made by individuals. States commonly promoted a particular tradition (through sponsorship of religious institutions or by showing preference for a certain community when seeking recruits for important positions) or by contrast discouraged an undesired alternative (through discriminatory taxation, repression of religious institutions, or campaigns of persecution). These measures have rarely achieved total success in channeling individuals toward states' preferred cultural or religious alternatives, but over time they were able to exercise deep influence on the cultural landscape of entire societies. Quite apart from state policies, social and economic interests also had strong potential to shape individuals' cultural and religious choices. The historical record is full of cases in which individuals adopted new cultural or religious alternatives introduced by well-organized foreigners who also offered business and commercial opportunities. Conversion to a new religion was not necessarily a mercenary affair, but it had the potential to confer social and economic benefits by facilitating relationships between peoples of different societies. Over time, as families and communities passed their adopted traditions down through the generations, and as they continued to attract new adherents, introduced traditions could find solid footing and shape the cultural landscapes of entire societies.

Xinru Liu and Tansen Sen have recently offered sophisticated empirical studies that flesh out some of these general points by considering the spread of Buddhism from India to China in political, social, and economic contexts. Liu showed that the establishment of Buddhism in China between the first and seventh centuries CE took place squarely in the context of trade between India and China. Buddhism benefited directly from trade that initially brought ritual and symbolic items for a small community of Buddhist merchants and Chinese converts. By the seventh century, trade between India and China had burgeoned, and its benefits flowed both to the mostly Buddhist merchants who conducted it and to the expanding community of Buddhists in China, including local converts. For his own part, focusing on the period from the seventh to fifteenth centuries, Sen showed that this pattern continued well into the tenth century and that official embassies worked alongside commerce to reinforce the spread of Buddhism to China. After the tenth century, Sen found that trade continued, but the Chinese Buddhist community increasingly diverged from the Indian, which was in any case declining under pressure from exponents of Hinduism and Islam.[17] Thus, both Liu and Sen make it clear—without reducing the explanation of complex cultural exchanges to material terms—that trade and diplomatic activity were crucial features of the environment in which the influence of Buddhism made itself felt in the region from India to China.

Cultural Exchanges in Modern Times

The patterns of cultural exchange outlined here did not come to an end in 1500 CE. To the contrary, they survived well into modern times—not surprisingly, since a millennium-long period of hemispheric integration anticipated the era of global convergence that opened about 1500.[18] Sanjay Subrahmanyam and C. A. Bayly have both drawn attention to the circulation of cultural elements that represented strands of continuity linking premodern and modern times. Particularly in the eastern hemisphere, as merchants, ambassadors, and other travelers followed routes that had been in use since deep antiquity, they continued to introduce ideas, myths, religious teachings, and valuable foreign knowledge to peoples from other societies and cultural traditions—to the point, as Bayly has argued, that different societies adopted similar responses, such as reform movements, to common cultural problems.[19]

Yet the dynamics of global history changed after 1500. European peoples enjoyed opportunities to reap enormous benefits from their exclusive and unprecedented access to all the world's regions after 1500, and after 1800 they gained further economic, technological, and military advantages with the emergence of mechanized industry.[20] Even as some processes of cultural exchange continued to follow long-established patterns, others clearly reflected the enhanced power of European peoples after their remarkable round of geographical exploration and discovery followed by the even more extraordinary processes of industrialization and imperialism.

Perhaps even more than in pre-modern times, power was a central element in processes of cultural exchange during the centuries after 1500. Certainly there was more documentation than in pre-modern times, hence the foundation for improved understanding of the patterns. The practices of cartography, ethnography, and historiography, which enabled peoples who enjoyed the resources needed to construct bodies of knowledge about their less powerful contemporaries, figured among the most important intellectual tools of empire in early modern and modern times. Power did not grant European peoples the ability to impose their cultural choices on others, but it ensured that European cultural traditions would enjoy unusual opportunities for expansion. European cultural options, including modern natural science and business practices as well as several forms of Christianity, gained exposure throughout larger portions of the world than any alternative. Until the twentieth century, even massively popular religious traditions like Buddhism, Hinduism, and Islam remained largely confined to the eastern hemisphere. Meanwhile, by contrast, between about 1500 and 1800, European merchants, missionaries, explorers, colonists, settlers, and other travelers introduced their cultural preferences to most of the Americas and to parts of Asia, sub-Saharan Africa, Australasia, and the Pacific islands. Geographical exploration and expansion enabled European observers to chart the global cultural landscape and begin constructing a body of knowledge about other peoples and their cultural traditions. It of course also offered other peoples the opportunity to form views about European visitors and assess their cultural baggage. The process of observing other peoples and constructing ethnographies was, therefore, a reciprocal affair, but Europeans enjoyed asymmetric advantages in that they were able to compile a much more comprehensive body of global cultural knowledge than any other people.[21]

Political, social, and economic contexts remained crucial frameworks for understanding the flows of cultural influences in modern times. In the Americas, conquest and massive depopulation following the introduction of smallpox and other diseases often shook the confidence of indigenous peoples in their inherited cultural and religious traditions. By no means did they immediately reject their inherited traditions and adopt Christianity. To the contrary, traditional religious beliefs remained popular, and individuals sometimes mounted spirited resistance to European missionaries' efforts to win Christian converts. When indigenous Americans did adopt Christianity, they frequently assimilated the new faith to their earlier inherited beliefs.[22] Over time, however, as European colonists progressively extended their control over native societies and consistently suppressed observance of pre-Columbian religions, sometimes quite violently, the old ways gradually disappeared, leaving Christianity as the only institutionally organized religious alternative remaining. Australia and many of the Pacific islands experienced a similar combination of conquest and depopulation caused by introduced diseases, followed by subjugation at the hands of European settlers who forcibly suppressed native cultural traditions.[23] There, too, indigenous peoples frequently adopted Christianity—tepidly and tentatively at first, although over time, many Pacific islanders made deep commitments to an adopted faith that they interpreted and adapted to meet the needs and interests of their own communities.

Most parts of Asia and Africa did not experience epidemics caused by introduced diseases and consequently did not undergo the catastrophic demographic decline that afflicted American and Pacific islands societies. Nor, apart from a few regions in the Philippines, Indonesia, and central Africa, did they experience conquest and colonial rule by European peoples during the early modern era from about 1500 to 1800. Nevertheless, European Christianity drew interest in several Asian and African lands, where the reception of Christianity clearly reflected a process of syncretism bridging inherited and foreign religious interests. In the case of the Philippine Islands, where orthodox Roman Catholic Christianity ultimately found a large and enthusiastic following, early converts routinely assimilated missionaries' teachings to inherited views of social and cultural propriety.[24] Similarly, in the kingdom of Kongo, many took inspiration from the introduced faith and turned it in unexpected directions: the Kongolese prophetess Dona Beatriz Kimpa Vita, for example, claimed to be possessed by St Anthony, criticized witchcraft and slave trading, revised Roman Catholic liturgy to suit her views, taught that Jesus and Mary had been black Kongolese, and strived to fashion a Christianity that met the needs of her society. Her movement attracted fervent interest but dwindled after 1706, when political and church authorities executed Dona Beatriz for witchcraft and violently suppressed her followers.[25] Official suppression also accounts for the decline of a small Christian community in China and a sizeable movement in Japan, where a process of syncretism was again on conspicuous display. Following the brutal suppression of both European Christians and their Japanese converts, a small group of Japanese 'hidden Christians' secretly continued to observe their new faith. Out of communication with Christians in Europe, Asia, the Americas, or anywhere else, they transmitted their faith on the basis of memory rather than orthodox texts or religious authorities. The result was a syncretic tradition that blended basic Christian teachings with Buddhist, Shinto, and folk elements to create a distinctive faith with a hybrid amalgam of doctrines and rituals that addressed the needs and interests of believers in the rural fishing communities that were the principal homes of the hidden Christians.[26]

If geographical exploration and expansion increased European cultural influence in early modern times, the twin processes of industrialization and imperialism enhanced European and Euro-American cultural strength even further after the nineteenth century. Orientalist knowledge of the kind diagnosed by Edward W. Said took on new significance, as European and Euro-American peoples had better means to exercise power as well as better methods of exploring and constructing knowledge about the world beyond their own societies. Michael Adas, Bernard S. Cohn, and many others have explored both the characteristics and the effects of this orientalist knowledge. In charting the changing views of European commentators on their African and Asian counterparts, Adas held that on their first introduction to Indian and Chinese science in the seventeenth century, European travelers found much to admire. With the rapid development of Enlightenment thought, modern science, and mechanical industry, however, European appraisals of other peoples steadily and correspondingly declined. Over time, qualified admiration for Indian and Chinese accomplishments turned into contempt for stagnant societies, theories of European racial superiority to Asian and especially African peoples, an ideology of domination, and a sense that European peoples had an obligation to pursue a civilizing mission in African and Asian lands.[27] Meanwhile, Cohn focused attention on distinct ways in which British discovery, construction, and codification of knowledge about India contributed to cultural and colonial hegemony. Mastery of Indian languages, codification of law, and collections of artifacts all advanced a project to construct a body of knowledge that facilitated colonial rule.[28]

Global empire, mechanical industry, and orientalist knowledge never enabled European peoples to impose their cultural choices on colonial subjects at will. European missionaries relied on both imperial power and orientalist knowledge when sowing seeds of Roman Catholic and Protestant Christianity in Asia, Africa, the Americas, and Oceania. Yet subject peoples' responses varied enormously from outright rejection of missionaries' messages to skepticism about their motives and relationships with colonial authorities to creative misunderstandings and adaptations of European teachings.[29] Nevertheless, granting that Europeans did not enjoy absolute power abroad, a recent study of the German overseas empire found that orientalist representations held crucial implications for the real-world fates of colonized peoples. German ethnographers portrayed the Herero people of southwestern Africa as cruel and inhuman, the islanders of Samoa as noble savages, and the Chinese as a clever and practical people distinguished by a lustrous past but also as underachievers currently mired in corruption, poverty, and stagnation. Not surprisingly, perhaps, German colonial authorities subjected the Herero to a brutal slaughter, imposed a mild but paternalistic and exploitative protectorate on the Samoans, and sought to learn what they could from Chinese in the German sphere of influence in Qingdao while also viewing their semi-colonial subjects through racist lenses.[30]

Since 1900 and especially 1950, even as missionary efforts and the quest for converts has continued, secular cultural exchanges have dramatically increased in volume. European and American universities have emerged as prominent venues for the transfer of western natural science, technology, social science, and legal values to the larger world. European, American, and Japanese businesses have influenced business practices, business values, and even business dress (in the form of the businessman's suit of clothes) around the world. The phenomenon of globalization, driven largely by European and American capitalist interests, has facilitated the spread of sushi, commercialized sports, blue jeans, Bollywood movies, and world music. Historians have barely begun the effort to think about these cultural developments, chart their larger patterns, and analyze the large-scale dynamics that help to explain them. Yet it is clear that cultural exchanges continue to take place in the context of interactions between peoples of different societies and cultural traditions, and further that they continue to reflect the political, social, economic, and other kinds of power that are available to the world's peoples engaged in processes of cross-cultural interaction and exchange.

Notes

1. Arnold Pacey, *Technology in World Civilization: A Thousand-Year History* (Cambridge, Mass.: MIT Press, 1990).
2. See two essays by Jerry H. Bentley: *Shapes of World History in Twentieth-Century Scholarship* (Washington, D.C.: American Historical Association, 1996), and 'The New World History' in Lloyd Kramer and Sarah Maza, eds., *A Companion to Western Historical Thought* (Oxford: Blackwell, 2002), 393–416.
3. Arnold J. Toynbee, *A Study of History*, 12 vols. (London: Oxford University Press, 1934–61). See particularly Part IX, 'Contacts between Civilizations in Space (Encounters between Contemporaries),' 8: 88–629.
4. Mary W. Helms, *Ulysses' Sail: An Ethnographic Odyssey of Power, Knowledge, and Geographical Distance* (Princeton: Princeton University Press, 1988).
5. Jerry H. Bentley, *Old World Encounters: Cross-Cultural Contacts and Exchanges in Pre-Modern Times* (New York: Oxford University Press, 1993).
6. Greg Dening, *Islands and Beaches: Discourse on a Silent Land: Marquesas, 1774–1880* (Honolulu: University of Hawai'i Press, 1980); Inga Clendinnen, *Ambivalent Conquests: Maya and Spaniard in Yucatan, 1517–1570*, 2nd edn. (Cambridge: Cambridge University

Press, 2003); Donna Merwick, *The Shame and the Sorrow: Dutch-Amerindian Encounters in New Netherland* (Philadelphia: University of Pennsylvania Press, 2006).

7. Edward W. Said, *Orientalism* (New York: Pantheon, 1978). Said later modulated some of his views in publications such as *Culture and Imperialism* (New York: Knopf, 1993).

8. For somewhat overstated views along these lines, see Mary Louise Pratt, *Imperial Eyes: Travel Writing and Transculturation* (London: Routledge, 1992); and Tzvetan Todorov, *The Conquest of America: The Question of the Other*, trans. by Richard Howard (New York: Harper and Row, 1984).

9. Laura Hostetler, *Qing Colonial Enterprise: Ethnography and Cartography in Early Modern China* (Chicago: University of Chicago Press, 2001); Peter C. Perdue, *China Marches West: The Qing Conquest of Central Eurasia* (Cambridge, Mass.: Harvard University Press, 2005); Emma Teng, *Taiwan's Imagined Geography: Chinese Colonial Travel Writing and Pictures, 1683–1895* (Cambridge, Mass.: Harvard University Asia Center, 2004); Stevan Harrell, ed., *Cultural Encounters on China's Ethnic Frontiers* (Seattle: University of Washington Press, 1995).

10. See Bentley, *Old World Encounters*, as well as 'Cross-Cultural Interaction and Periodization in World History,' *American Historical Review*, 101 (1996), 749–70.

11. J.R. McNeill and William H. McNeill, *The Human Web: A Bird's-Eye View of World History* (New York: Norton, 2003), especially 17–18.

12. Philip D. Curtin, *Cross-Cultural Trade in World History* (Cambridge: Cambridge University Press, 1984); David W. Anthony, *The Horse, the Wheel, and Language: How Bronze-Age Riders from the Eurasian Steppes Shaped the Modern World* (Princeton: Princeton University Press, 2007); Christopher Ehret, *The Civilizations of Africa: A History to 1800* (Charlottesville, Va.: University of Virginia Press, 2001).

13. To cite only a single work of many that throw light on these issues, see Michael Rowlands, Mogens Larsen, and Kristian Kristiansen, eds., *Centre and Periphery in the Ancient World* (Cambridge: Cambridge University Press, 1987).

14. Jonathon E. Ericson and Timothy G. Baugh, eds., *The American Southwest and Mesoamerica: Systems of Prehistoric Exchange* (New York: Plenum, 1993); Timothy G. Baugh and Jonathon E. Ericson, eds., *Prehistoric Exchange Systems in North America* (New York: Plenum, 1994).

15. The following discussion draws on Bentley, *Old World Encounters*.

16. For only one example see Clifford Geertz's brilliant study of Islam as understood and practiced at the extreme ends of the Muslim world: *Islam Observed: Religious Development in Morocco and Indonesia* (Chicago: University of Chicago Press, 1968).

17. Xinru Liu, *Ancient India and Ancient China: Trade and Religious Exchanges, A.D. 1–600* (Delhi: Oxford University Press, 1988); Tansen Sen, *Buddhism, Diplomacy, and Trade: The Realignment of Sino-Indian Relations, 600–1400* (Honolulu: University of Hawai`i Press, 2003).

18. Jerry H. Bentley, 'Hemispheric Integration, 500–1500 CE', *Journal of World History* 9 (1998), 237–54.

19. Sanjay Subrahmanyam, 'Connected Histories: Notes towards a Reconfiguration of Early Modern Eurasia,' in Victor Lieberman, ed., *Beyond Binary Histories: Re-imagining Eurasia to c. 1830* (Ann Arbor: University of Michigan Press, 1997), 289–316; C. A. Bayly, *The Birth of the Modern World, 1780-1914: Global Connections and Comparisons* (Oxford: Blackwell, 2004).

20. Jerry H. Bentley, 'Early Modern Europe and the Early Modern World,' in Charles H. Parker and Jerry H. Bentley, eds., *Between the Middle Ages and Modernity: Individual and Community in the Early Modern World* (Lanham, Md.: Rowman and Littlefield, 2007), 13–31.
21. For a useful sampler of studies, see Stuart B. Schwartz, ed., *Implicit Understandings: Observing, Reporting, and Reflecting on the Encounters between Europeans and Other Peoples in the Early Modern Era* (New York: Cambridge University Press, 1994).
22. Clendinnen, *Ambivalent Conquests*; Serge Gruzinski, *The Conquest of Mexico: The Incorporation of Indian Societies into the Western World, 16th–18th Centuries* (Cambridge: Cambridge University Press, 1993); Patricia Lopes Don, 'Franciscans, Indian Sorcerers, and the Inquisition in New Spain, 1536–1543,' *Journal of World History* 17 (2006), 27–49.
23. For the case of the Marquesas Islands, see Dening, *Islands and Beaches*.
24. Vicente L. Rafael, *Contracting Colonialism: Translation and Christian Conversion in Tagalog Society under Early Spanish Rule* (Durham, N.C.: Duke University Press, 1993).
25. John K. Thornton, *The Kongolese Saint Anthony: Dona Beatriz Kimpa Vita and the Antonian Movement, 1684–1706* (Cambridge: Cambridge University Press, 1998).
26. Christal Whelan, trans., *The Beginning of Heaven and Earth: The Sacred Book of Japan's Hidden Christians* (Honolulu: University of Hawai`i Press, 1996).
27. Michael Adas, *Machines as the Measure of Men: Science, Technology, and Ideas of Western Dominance* (Ithaca, N.Y.: Cornell University Press, 1989).
28. Bernard S. Cohn, *Colonialism and Its Forms of Knowledge: The British in India* (Princeton: Princeton University Press, 1996).
29. Jean and John Comaroff, *Of Revelation and Revolution*, 2 vols. (Chicago: University of Chicago Press, 1991–97).
30. George Steinmetz, *The Devil's Handwriting: Precoloniality and the German Colonial State in Qingdao, Samoa, and Southwest Africa* (Chicago: University of Chicago Press, 2007).

REFERENCES

ADAS, MICHAEL. *Machines as the Measure of Men: Science, Technology, and Ideologies of Western Dominance.* Ithaca, N.Y.: Cornell University Press, 1989.

BAYLY, C. A. *The Birth of the Modern World, 1780–1914: Global Connections and Comparisons.* Oxford: Blackwell, 2004.

BENTLEY, JERRY H. *Old World Encounters: Cross-Cultural Contacts and Exchanges in Pre-Modern Times.* New York: Oxford University Press, 1993.

COHN, BERNARD S. *Colonialism and Its Forms of Knowledge: The British in India.* Princeton: Princeton University Press, 1996.

COMAROFF, JEAN and JOHN COMAROFF. *Of Revelation and Revolution*, 2 vols. Chicago: University of Chicago Press, 1991–97.

DENING, GREG. *Islands and Beaches: Discourse on a Silent Land: Marquesas, 1774–1880.* Honolulu: University of Hawai`i Press, 1980.

HELMS, MARY W. *Ulysses' Sail: An Ethnographic Odyssey of Power, Knowledge, and Geographical Distance.* Princeton: Princeton University Press, 1988.

SAID, EDWARD W. *Orientalism.* New York: Pantheon, 1978.

SCHWARTZ, STUART B., ed. *Implicit Understandings: Observing, Reporting, and Reflecting on the Encounters between Europeans and Other Peoples in the Early Modern Era.* New York: Cambridge University Press, 1994.

CHAPTER 20

......

PRE-MODERN EMPIRES

......

THOMAS T. ALLSEN

DEFINITIONS AND DIFFERENCES

......

EMPIRE is regularly defined as a political unit of large extent controlling a number of territories and peoples under a single sovereign authority. Of the three criteria, only one, sovereign authority, is quantified. Judgments concerning size and diversity are, naturally, arbitrary and tentative but unavoidable in any search for the general characteristics of empires.

As for size, how big is big enough, and when did political units first cross this threshold?[1] In Egypt, the New Kingdom (ca. 1550–1070 BCE) was the first unit comparable in size to modern states such as Spain or Turkey. In Mesopotamia, there were two notable leaps in the scale of political organization: the Akkad Dynasty (ca. 2360–2180 BCE) unified the entire region for the first time, and later the Neo-Assyrian Dynasty (935–612 BCE) expanded beyond 'The Lands between the Rivers,' extending its influence into Asia Minor, Syria, Phoenicia, and Egypt. The Assyrian state, with its program of territorial acquisition, diverse subject population, and political-ideological pretensions, is perhaps closer to the modern image of an empire. And whether or not it was the 'first,' it is an early example of the type and, of equal importance, Assyrian practice greatly influenced the political culture of its much larger Iranian successors, the Achaemenids (534–330 BCE), Parthians (247 BCE–227 CE), and Sasanids (226–651).

The Mauryans (322–187 BCE), who exercised suzerainty over much of the subcontinent, began the Indian imperial tradition, one continued by the Kushans (ca. 25–260 CE), invaders from Central Asia, and the Guptas (320–467), an indigenous dynasty. In northern China, the first well-documented states, the Shang (ca. 1520–ca. 1030 BCE) and Zhou (ca. 1030–221 BCE), were loosely structured polities, and by the reckoning of traditional Chinese historiography, the imperial age was inaugurated when the Qin (221–207 BCE) and Han (202 BCE–221 CE) dynasties restored order, established centralized government, created a sense of Chinese identity, and expanded into new territories.

The Xiongnu (ca. 209 BCE–87 CE) is normally viewed as the first steppe empire, the nomads' response to Qin and Han empires. It was followed, after a prolonged period of division, by the Türk Qaghanate (552–744) and its principal successors, the Khazars (ca. 650–965) in the west and the Uighurs (745–840) in the east.

For the Mediterranean world, despite several dramatic 'rehearsals,' those of Athens and Alexander the Great, the notion and nomenclature of empire is intimately tied to Rome. As Roman power spread, the Latin *imperium*, 'command,' gradually acquired the additional meaning of the territories under the Republic's authority, its 'empire.' And, like the Han, which became the model for East Asia, Rome long defined empire for Europe.

While the New World produced some impressive early civilizations, the Olmec (ca. 1200–400 BCE) and Classic Maya (ca. 300–900 CE), large, centralized states come later. The Toltecs (ca. 950–1200) were perhaps the first empire in Mesoamerica, followed by the Aztecs (ca. 1400–1520), who built upon and surpassed the achievements of their predecessor. In the Andes there were a series of expansive states culminating in the Incas (ca. 1400–1536), who fashioned the largest, most integrated empire in the Americas.

Although all ruled over heterogeneous populations, their diversity is partially obscured because empires are named after the dominant group and because long-lived empires leave an after-image of uniformity. The degree of ethno-linguistic diversity, however, varied greatly. The extremes can be seen in two East Asian empires, the Han, in which the ruling house and a majority of subjects were Chinese, and the Yuan (1271–1368), in which the ruling Mongols constituted little more than 1 percent of the total population. In general, it can be said that founders often became minorities and that the larger the empire, the more likely this was the case. This meant that conquerors had to take into account a number of distinct constituencies and that the rights and functions of subjects were often determined by ethnic and communal affiliations.

Empires have been categorized, or at least labeled, in many ways—as sedentary, nomadic, maritime, tributary, incorporative, absorptive, defensive, mercantile, informal, and the like. For our purposes, the most useful distinction is between the imperial regimes of recent origin and those that arose prior to 1500. While modern and traditional empires share some characteristics, noted where appropriate, their differences are stressed here.

First, traditional empires, which survived into the twentieth century, are predominantly land-based, while modern empires, which developed alongside them, are predominantly maritime.

As for agency, modern empires were initiated by commercial interests with government backing, and in their final, 'New Imperialism' phase, by nation-states. The earlier forms have their origins in city-states and other small polities, monarchies and republics, but some of the most spectacular imperial ventures were launched by 'military entrepreneurs,' who started out commanding personal armies and followings, not states.

Motives for expansion and methods of control also differed; modern empires began with the search for new materials and markets which entailed economic competition and indirect forms of dominance, while traditional empires began with the search for additional land and subjects which entailed military competition and outright conquest.

A further distinction is that modern imperialists expanded as a society, remained in contact with the metropole, and preserved their original identities, while traditional empire builders sometimes lost contact, acculturated with subject peoples, and changed identities. Put differently, the metropole in all modern empires held itself culturally superior to the subject population, while in the traditional it was not unusual for ethnically alien conquerors to recognize openly, and rely upon, the cultural-administrative superiority of subjugated peoples. Thus, in contrast to the 'civilizing' projects of modern empires, those in earlier empires were sometimes mounted by subject peoples for the 'benefit' of foreign ruling elites.

Next, discussions of 'disparities of power' that guide analysis of modern imperialisms have limited relevance to the older forms. The Soviet Empire's forcible seizure of the Baltic states in 1940 exemplifies such undeniable disparities in modern contexts, but what of the Mongols' conquest of China in the thirteenth century? By any calculation, based on current notions of national power, there was indeed a stark disparity, but one that strongly favored the eventual losers, the China-based dynasties of the Jin (1115–1234) and Southern Song (1127–1279). In this balance sheet, Mongolia had one million people and a pastoral economy, while together their adversaries had some 100 million people, controlled the most productive economy in the world, and had access to advanced military technology. Clearly, in earlier times, a very different calculus of power was in play.

This introduces the final difference, that concerning military technology. In the post-Columbian world, there were often disparities in weaponry that favored the imperial power; these, moreover, tended to grow over time, encouraging imperial projects by lowering costs. The conquests of traditional empires, on the other hand, rarely depended on technological advantage. There are several reasons for this. First, most innovations in military technology were not decisive during the initial phase of their development; in range and rate of fire, quality bows outperformed first-generation handguns. Second, when innovations such as gunpowder began to confer advantage, they diffused rapidly; technological monopolies are fleeting at best.

WARFARE AND EMPIRE

Since traditional empires were born in warfare, and their long-term success was dependant on force, the issue of military supremacy calls for comment. In wars between armies with similar armaments, the outcome was usually decided by the quality and quantity of their respective forces. Quality is determined by the methods of recruitment and training, the resulting discipline and skills of individual soldiers, the morale and cohesion of units, and the degree of command and control exercised over formations in the field. As a general proposition, this can be said of both ancient and modern armies.

The matter of quantity, however, is far more variable. Under pre-modern economic conditions, a society's demographic base is not a straightforward indicator of the number of troops it can mobilize. Commitment to intensive forms of agriculture found in China, for example, places limits on the recruitment of adult males. Further, some states demilitarize their interiors, and many hierarchical, aristocratic societies try to create monopolies over military service, thereby restricting the number and type of weapons in the hands of commoners. Such societies are characterized by low 'military participation ratios.'[2] In contrast, across northern Eurasia there were many pastoral and agricultural societies with lower population densities but with higher participation ratios; in some, virtually all adult males engaged in military training and warfare on a regular basis.

These warrior societies, quite literally 'nations at arms,' shared a number of characteristics: (1) economic production, maintained by women and children, was not greatly affected by the call-up of males; (2) social stratification was poorly developed; (3) hunting remained an important method of resource extraction and military training; (4) the right to bear arms was enjoyed by all; (5) weapons were made locally, often by the individual; and (6) mounted warfare, sustained by domestic supplies of horses, was the norm.

This, of course, meant that the balance of power, measured by the quantity, quality, and mobility of military forces, often favored smaller, marginal peoples. It is hardly surprising, then, that those societies inhabiting the warmer, more densely populated and productive hinterlands of Eurasia regularly sought to recruit and co-opt warriors from the northern forests and steppes as allies, auxiliaries, mercenaries, military slaves, march wardens, and royal guards. Sometimes, too, these northerners came south as raiders and traders and, under the right circumstances, transformed themselves into conquerors and empire builders.

Since expansive states continuously encounter new opponents and environments, military success also requires openness to change, modifications, and additions to the inherited methods of warfare. Flexibility of this sort is most clearly manifested in the adaptation of enemy weapons, tactics, organization, or even whole new modes of combat. The Romans, strongly committed to infantry, nevertheless developed an effective cavalry arm as a result of their encounters with the mounted forces on their eastern frontiers.[3] More impressive still, the Mongols, from the arid steppe, rapidly mobilized Korean and northern Chinese maritime skills to form a navy that was instrumental in the defeat of the Southern Song in 1279.[4]

In most cases, the fastest way of acquiring new military skills was to bring in foreign specialists, either as mercenaries or as drafts on the defeated, a practice that produced multi-ethnic armies. The Achaemenid forces invading Greece in 480 BCE and the Mongolian forces attacking Baghdad in 1258, like recent colonial armies, consisted mainly of foreign auxiliaries 'stiffened' with regular units from the homeland. At times, an empire's greatness was best communicated ethnographically, its diversity serving as a hallmark of its size and success. Sometimes, too, foreigners put on display around capitals as garrisons or royal guards became major players in imperial politics.

Adaptability also encompasses decision making, dealing quickly and effectively with the ever-changing fortunes of war. Besides technical knowledge, tactical and organizational abilities, successful military commanders have the capacity to identify and exploit unexpected opportunities and to anticipate and avoid sudden threats. All this, of course, is self-evident and applicable to military leadership in general. It is stressed here because many traditional empires were founded by individuals whom contemporaries believed were possessed of a very special good fortune. Such leaders were endowed with superhuman, sometimes supernatural, gifts that marked them off from mere mortals. And their special gifts, their charisma, attracted and inspired adherents, built confidence and morale, and, following military conquest, became a central element in efforts to justify imperial authority, a topic explored below.

In its initial stages, empire building is almost always associated with periods of intense conflict and the concomitant militarization of society. The Qin arose to power by incorporating states that had previously swallowed up other contenders, and the Inca did likewise. Imperial expansion is not, however, solely a matter of military natural selection or of blind aggression: it can also be sustained, directed, even initiated by outside invitation. The Greek city states repeatedly invited Roman intervention against internal rivals, and contending factions in North China repeatedly called in steppe peoples as allies, thus jumpstarting nomadic expansion southward. But however activated, imperial war machines, once engaged, ran continuously through a fairly predictable cycle: initial conquests, pacification campaigns to teach the habits of obedience, defensive operations along frontiers, and, finally, wars attending imperial disintegration.

ORGANIZING EMPIRES

Military triumphs, especially decisive ones, present victors with choices: depart with booty, negotiate a new relationship with the defeated, or permanently occupy the conquered lands, an option requiring the establishment of some type of governmental machinery. Depending on their stage of development, empires could import their own institutions and personnel, displacing local authorities over time, a practice followed by the Qin and Han. Or they might leave locals in place and rule new territories indirectly. The New Kingdom, Achaemenids, Romans, and Aztecs left native institutions intact, as did nomadic and semi-nomadic conquerors, who co-opted indigenous bureaucrats to help them control and exploit agricultural and urban populations. The Liao (907–1124), founded by the Khitans, and the Yuan, founded by the Mongols, followed this strategy in China, as did the Great Seljuqs (1038–1194) in Iran and Iraq. In these and similar regimes, there was an ethnic division of labor between the indigenous 'men of the pen,' who administered the locals, and the foreign 'men of the sword,' who controlled the occupying forces and their dependents.

There was also substantial variation in the administrative machinery at the center. In Rome or Tang (618–906) China, there were impersonal bureaucracies that loyally served successive rulers or even new dynasties. The situation was much different in empires established by northerners, whether nomads or sedentaries, for whom loyalty was primarily to the person of the ruler, not the state. In such regimes, the central administrative apparatus emerged from the household establishment of a successful warlord or tribal leader. Consequently, individuals who tended rulers' personal needs served simultaneously as the principal administrative and military officers of the realm. This often created an anomalous situation in which the central organs of the imperial government, informal and patrimonial in character, exercised authority over local organs of government that were far more formal and bureaucratic, a feature encountered in empires of Inner Asian origin, the Mongols (1206–ca. 1370), Temürids (1370–1506), and Mughals (1526–1858).[5]

The practice of combining radically different methods of governance, some direct, some indirect, some exported from the center, some borrowed from subjects, and others based on *ad hoc* arrangements, is a common feature of traditional empires. All were political conglomerates, complex hierarchies of metropolitan districts, home provinces, special military commands, client rulers, buffer states, and sometime allies.

Administration, by whatever means, implies some form of record keeping or writing. In the selection of official languages and scripts, as in methods of governance, multi-ethnic, multi-lingual empires always presented a range of choices. Perhaps the most economical was the solution arrived at by the Qin, who promoted an artificial literary-bureaucratic language, 'Classical Chinese,' and standardized the characters of the preceding era, thereby imposing graphic unity on diverse spoken and written dialects.

In this and other cases, the official language was closely related to the native tongue of the ruling elite. In many instances, however, conquerors, as a matter of convenience and respect, granted administrative status to a language of the subject population, as the Romans did wherever Greek was well established. Sometimes this occurred because the conquerors had no written language in their pre-imperial era; the ruling house of the Achaemenids, who spoke an Iranian language, used Aramaic as the principal language of administration, and later on, the Seljuqs, who spoke Turkish, relied on New Persian. In essence, both dynasties gave preference to a language used by the largest available pool of trained administrative personnel.

For conquerors without a written language there was another alternative—creating a written version of their native tongue, a solution favored by steppe peoples. The Türk, the first to do so, used the 'Runic' script, based loosely on Aramaic, the Khitans used modified Chinese characters, and the Mongols borrowed the Uighur alphabet. This, of course, did not preclude reliance on the written languages of subject peoples in the conduct of official business. In the Mongols' trans-continental empire, Chinese, per-sian, Tibetan, East Slavic, Mongolian, and various dialects of Turkic were in simulta-neous use. Multi-lingual people flourished in these milieus and such milieus served as arenas of intense linguistic interaction, borrowing, and change.

Because of their scale and diversity, empires adopted and promoted measures of standardization. These appear in many guises: introduction of court costumes and military uniforms to encourage group feeling; formalization of languages and scripts for clarity of communication; establishment of official weights and measures for ease of revenue collection; and the introduction of coinage, whose weight and composition is guaranteed by the state, as a medium of exchange. This began in Lydia (ca. 700 BCE) and was adopted, ca. 480, by the Achaemenids, who, however, never imposed a monopoly on minting, a policy not fully implemented until Roman times. East Asia had a similar history; money first appeared during the Era of Warring States (480–221 BCE), was standardized by the Qin, and became a monopoly under the Han. This suggests the development of official coinage is a slow, incremental process that has as much to do with the expansion of states as with the expansion of commerce.[6]

Time, too, was standardized. The management of time, through official calendars regulating ceremonial, administrative, and economic life, always confers great political power. Additionally, calendars, derived from the motions of the heavens, have impor-tant cosmological functions; they allow authorities to date and celebrate vital begin-nings and turning points in both natural and human history and are, thus, a means of affirming world views and inculcating ideological precepts. In Chinese regimes, the Han and its successors, calendars were treated like coinage and monopolized, while in others, the Achaemenid and Mongolian, multiple systems of time reckoning were tolerated for pragmatic reasons. But all imperial courts, in the Old and New Worlds, kept careful track of time.

Safe lines of communication were yet another imperial imperative and once opera-tive provided a measure of security and order, and perhaps the illusion of peace, and more certainly a vehicle for wide-ranging exchange. While solutions varied, all required the creation of extensive infrastructure.

Best known are the Roman roads and Inca highways but all first-generation em-pires—Achaemenids, Mauryans, and Qin/Han—made heavy investments in road systems. Inland water transport was also developed, most notably in China. Starting with the Sui (581–618), and continuing under the Tang and Yuan, great efforts were made to connect the economically productive south with political centers in the north through an intricate system of canals. Their purpose, of course, was to move soldiers, officials, and supplies. But courts, too, were in motion. Itinerant monarchy was the result of various factors: nomadic heritage, multiple capitals, and the need to inspect local conditions, mobilize scarce resources, display majesty, test loyalties, and reassert authority in the countryside.

While royal roads and waterways retained a public character, special and restrict-ed accommodations were built to accommodate official travelers. The Achaemenids and their satraps built numerous large 'paradises' across the country, supplied with living quarters, hunting parks, gardens, storage facilities, and garrisons. These constituted the principal outposts of governmental authority in the countryside and allowed the ruling strata to move through the realm in comfort and security.[7] On a more modest scale, the Carolingians built networks of villas and hunting lodges for similar reasons.

Another perennial concern of imperial courts was the rapid dispatch of orders and information. This encouraged the growth of government postal systems which in the Old World featured relays of dispatch riders and in the New World, which lacked riding animals, relays of runners. Besides conveying messages, these services had important security functions, collecting internal and external intelligence. Already mentioned in the Assyrian period, analogous institutions are found under the Achaemenids, Sasanids, Romans, and Byzantines. Drawing upon these traditions, the Umayyad (661–750) and Abbasid (749–1258) caliphates fashioned a sophisticated royal post (barid) that was taken over by other Muslim kingdoms. The culmination of these systems of imperial communication came under the Mongols, who organized a postal service (jam) that at one time extended from North China and Mongolia to Iran and the lower Volga.

The primary purpose of investment in administration, communication, and transportation was, naturally, the acquisition of resources needed by the imperial center. The proceeds of traditional empires came in several forms and sometimes in a set sequence: first, booty, typically a one-time but massive return collected by the imperial army; second, tribute, a more calculated and, therefore, repeatable source paid *and collected* by the defeated; and third, regular taxation following permanent occupation collected by agents of the imperial government. The initial costs of doing business were, thus, mainly military and later, mainly administrative.

Commonly, the first step in the economic exploitation of a newly occupied region was a census, a prerequisite for a transition from tribute to taxation. The actual collection, in kind or coin, might be assigned to imperial officials or farmed out to private entrepreneurs, a measure that saved costs and sped monies to the royal coffers, one that proved attractive to many empires from the Roman to the Mongolian. Census-taking was often accompanied by cadastral surveys that recorded agricultural lands and identified natural resources—everything from salt pans to metal deposits—of potential value to the state. In East Asia, many Chinese dynasties, as well as the Mongols, placed salt and other commodities under official monopolies with some degree of success.

Besides revenue collection, population registration had the goal of identifying human resources, most particularly to meet the open-ended demand for the military manpower needed to push forward and secure frontiers. Moreover, since empires were continually engaged in construction—palaces, public buildings, fortifications, transportation facilities, water control, and agricultural projects—there was a constant demand for general labor services. Registrations also found specialists, engineers, artisans, and artists, who adorned imperial courts with their skills as well as their presence.

JUSTIFYING EMPIRES

Although empires relied on military might, all sought ideological sanction for their conquests and rule. In attempting to gain subjects' acceptance, empire builders were aware that persuasion was often more cost effective than coercion. This is not to say that the dissemination of political messages involved no expense, since in societies with limited literacy much royal propaganda was conveyed visually and on a monumental scale, all of which strongly suggests that these appeals were directed toward the populace at large, not just elites.

Early examples of this technique are provided by the extensive reliefs recovered at Nineveh, the Neo-Assyrian capital, which depict, in serial episodes, their rulers' single-handed victories over rebels, foreign foes, and rampant nature. In their most mature form, these were accompanied by text detailing the exploits of their heroic, ever-triumphant sovereigns.[8] The basic elements of the Assyrian model were taken over by the Achaemenids, who communicated with their diverse subjects in Akkadian, Elamite, and Old Persian, for which they devised a special cuneiform syllabary. So far as is known, its sole purpose was to broadcast royal propaganda in public inscriptions.

In pursuit of legitimacy and majesty, the media was as important as the message. Splendid capitals—Persepolis, Rome, Chang'an, Baghdad, and Cuzco—with their monumental palaces, pleasure grounds, public buildings, and ceremonial centers, not only dominated human activity but imposed a human order on Nature. This impulse for the grand scale also found expression in public spectacles—parades, progresses, royal hunts, and victory celebrations—all carefully stage-managed to provoke awe and produce grandeur. These lavish expenditures of energy, a form of conspicuous consumption, dramatized a ruler's resources and reach, as well as organizational abilities. And such expenditures, for which there was no immediate, tangible return, were preeminently political acts, simultaneously inspiring and intimidating.[9]

Rulers exercised authority through special dispensations bestowed by cosmic forces—gods, Heaven, or Nature. Some, the Egyptian pharaohs and Inca emperors, claimed divine descent, but the majority, the Chinese 'Son of Heaven,' Kushan 'Son of God,' and Mauryan 'Beloved of God,' insisted only that they had mandates to rule on earth as part of some larger design. Cosmic kingship, in its varied forms, rests on the belief that the ruler, representing the forces of order, is the central figure in the eternal struggle against chaos, whether human or natural. In such a world, rulers ordered human affairs as chief lawgiver and defender of the realm and mediated the all-important relationship between the realms of culture and nature as builder, huntsman, and ceremonial head of state.

The writ of such sovereigns, from New Kingdom pharaohs to Roman and Inca emperors, was the known world. While empires regularly co-opted and manipulated pre-existing religious and ideological systems in support of such universalist pretensions, their public acceptance was closely linked to increases in the scale of political organization. The Achaemenid empire was approximately five times the size of its largest predecessor, Assyria, and the Mongolian five times larger again. To contemporaries, these vast empires *were* the world, and their assertion of universal dominion was eminently plausible and explicable only in terms of special dispensations and good fortune. Chinggis Qan is a household name because he founded the largest contiguous land empire in world history, surpassed only by the British dominions of the early twentieth century, and Alexander the Great achieved undying fame not for what he created but for what he destroyed, the Achaemenids' unprecedented universal state.

The special good fortune or charisma that underwrote the triumphs and achievements of dynastic founders and then passed to their heirs was an early attribute of kingship in West Asia. In ancient Iran this 'royal glory,' called *farnah*, was represented visually by a nimbus or crown around the ruler's head. The concept was in fact widespread among all the Iranian-speaking peoples, including the steppe-dwelling Scythians.[10] Later on, the same notion, *qut* in Turkic and *suu* in Mongolian, appears as the central element in the imperial ideologies of the steppe. In the Far West, this found expression in the *felicitas* of the Roman emperors, the good fortune or divine favor that guided their actions.

For nearly two millennia, ideologies of good fortune were associated with empires, supporting the view that they arose through chance, that most were 'accidental.' Interestingly, another long-lived political concept, *translatio imperii*, the transference of the right to empire from one dynasty or people to another, affirms the alternative interpretation, that empires arose by design.

Such transference was in fact common. The Mexica, founders of the Aztec empire, forged real and fictive connections to their Toltec predecessors in the quest for legitimacy. In Europe, the most famous instance of transfer is Charlemagne's coronation as 'Emperor of the Romans' on Christmas day, 800. Byzantium, too, embraced this inheritance and in the sixteenth century Muscovy proclaimed itself the sole heir to the Roman-Byzantine legacy. Earlier, the Achaemenids appropriated the Mesopotamian heritage, Alexander tried to appropriate the Achaemenid, and later the Sasanids, with greater success, cast themselves as heirs and restorers of this hallowed and mythologized imperial tradition. In its turn, the Abbasid Caliphate, while making use of Islamic ideology, took on the shape of the Sasanian state and borrowed many of its institutions and symbols of royalty.[11]

Perhaps the most formalized system of transference is found in China, where there was a chronologically continuous series of 'legitimate' dynasties. In order to accomplish this seamless transmission many small, short-lived, and non-Chinese regimes are included. While the resulting 'orthodox line' (*zhengtong*) was artificial, an *ex post facto* creation, it remained a major source of political legitimacy in East Asia for two millennia.

The steppe zone, with less system, presents a comparable picture of imperial succession. The Mongols were extremely sensitive to the political traditions of their Turkic predecessors, especially the Uighur, despite a 350-year gap between them, and replicated their ideology in all essentials, despite the fact that by the thirteenth century the Runic script could no longer be read. In his turn, Temür, who arrived on the scene when the Mongolian model was still very much alive, could only pretend to be restoring their faltering empire and rule through Chinggisid puppets. Next, the Mughals, descendents of Temür, laid claim to his territories and rights and took his title, 'Lord of the Auspicious Conjunction,' thereby appropriating his good fortune.[12] Here is another extended chain of imperial transfer, this effected by a kind of 'serial appropriation' in which each regime claims the mantle of its immediate predecessor.

In this vision of history, empires have a kind of immortality and all except the first arise from a model that provides inspiration and a template by which it can be reconstructed. These seemingly contradictory views on empire formation, one emphasizing chance, the other design, are in fact compatible. Within the historical memory of every cultural tradition there are a number of political options, alternative organizational, behavioral, and ideological models, some of which are manifest and some latent, some 'operative' and others 'held in reserve.'[13] Thus, whenever a bandit leader, nomadic chieftain, rebel general, or ambitious prince, through good management *and good fortune*, reached a certain threshold of military success, an alternative, imperial model was called forth and attempts made to recapture its earlier glory through emulation and ceremony. These alternatives are consequently means of adaptation to new circumstances and, because reconstruction is ever selective and always inexact, mechanisms of political change in traditional societies.

Successful empire builders took care to attract willing participants and collaborators with opportunities for personal advancement and with a wide repertoire of political doctrines and models—cosmic kingship, good fortune, and universal order—that was recognizable, sometimes even appealing to subjects; ideologies, it is important to remember, are intended to motivate as well as legitimate.

DECLINE AND FALL

Revealingly, internal, contemporary views of imperial decline lead back to the same models. From ancient times onward, indigenous commentators have sounded a similar refrain in periods of crises: we have lost the wisdom and spiritual strength of the founders, the model rulers, as a result of complacency, improper behavior, and preoccupation with personal gain. In empires of Inner Asian origin, the emphasis is usually on the erosion of martial vigor and ethnic identity, again because of the seductions of easy living. In both cases, therefore, efforts at revitalization take the form of revisiting and reinterpreting the original imperial model.

Modern commentators, in contrast, downplay moral decline and concentrate on economic factors. They sometimes assume that there is a mode of resource extraction or exchange system particular to imperial regimes. Some empires are described as tributary, extracting resources from the defeated through repeated demonstrations of military supremacy. In others, the economy, it is argued, was embedded in society, based on reciprocity and redistribution, not market mechanisms. Another model focuses on asymmetric core-periphery relations. Here a wealthy core, because of disparities of power, is able to exploit a poorer periphery.

Such systems do exist: the Aztec empire certainly had a strong tributary component, the Incas undoubtedly engaged in massive redistribution, and the rise of the Tang can be understood as a powerful core extending its sway over a periphery. Clearly, though, no form of exchange is common to all empires, nor is it clear that specific forms monopolize exchange within individual empires. Variation and mutability seem to be the norm. In the case of core-periphery relations, for example, imperial states repeatedly arise on the frontier.[14] In other words, *disparities of wealth* often prompt attacks toward the center and, therefore, the direction of military aggression in world history is commonly, if not primarily, from the poor peripheries to the rich cores. This is true in Mesoamerica, where outsiders, Toltecs and Aztecs, seized the core and in Eurasia, where a series of Inner Asian empires extracted resources from far wealthier centers in the sedentary world.

Given this variability, how, then, are we to understand the economies of traditional empires? The Mongols' economic 'system' is helpful in this regard. Their empire has been labeled as feudal, redistributive, and tributary, all of which are too limiting and miss an essential point: across Eurasia, the Mongols learned how to install, infiltrate, and dominate a wide spectrum of exchange and subsistence systems. At the Yuan court, the center, a redistributive system prevailed in which goods extracted from the sedentary sector were massively recycled among the ruling elite and their nomadic followers, all according to the social norms of the steppe. But this was not the only exchange mechanism operative. In the north, the Yuan obtained furs from the peoples of Siberia through tributary relations and the silent trade, a truly archaic form of exchange. At the same time, in the south, the growing international demand for blue and white porcelain produced what can only be described as a striking example of market-driven exchange. In the late thirteenth and early fourteenth centuries, independent Chinese entrepreneurs at Jingdezhen in Jiangxi began manufacturing 'chinaware' in response to West Asian tastes. Most tellingly, the Muslim merchants who supplied the critical marketing information also imported the cobalt pigment essential in the production process. This enterprise, enjoying government encouragement, was probably the largest, most sophisticated manufacturing complex of its day measured by the volume of production, range of distribution, and use of long-distance marketing techniques.[15]

The Mongolian example, with its amalgam of embedded, tributary, command, and market economies, suggests that there was no uniform or reproducible imperial mode of exchange or production. Since empires were always cobbled together from disparate ethno-linguistic groups and smaller polities, and held together by different methods of governance, it is hardly surprising that they were economic conglomerates as well, each with its own mix of subsistence and exchange systems. Indeed, this is a natural consequence of the fact that empires, to be empires, must combine the resources of distinctive cultural and natural areas—the Iranian plateau with the

Mesopotamian river valleys, the eastern steppe with the North China plain, and the Andean *altiplano* with the coastal zone.

Still, despite the variable character of imperial economic systems, several general points can be offered, at least as explanations for their failure. Empires are costly enterprises, ever hungry for resources, profligate in expenditures, exploitative, inefficient, and open to large-scale corruption. Perhaps the best way to couple their economic behavior with modern economic theory, as Joseph A. Tainter has argued, is with the law of diminishing marginal returns. As empires expand and the lineal miles of frontiers grow and the number of subjects multiply, increased inputs in defense, administration, and legitimation no longer produce proportional returns in security, resources, and loyalty. Only during the initial phases of expansion is an empire a profitable enterprise, and once 'plunder frontiers' are replaced by defensive frontiers, costs steadily escalate and efforts to meet them, through further expansion or intensified revenue collection, generate resistance and avoidance, enlarged bureaucracies and militaries, increased official corruption, heavier demands on the treasury, and ever declining marginal returns.[16] Since universalist pretensions were built into imperial ideologies, and since it was difficult and extremely dangerous to halt or demobilize imperial armies, which develop a vested interest in continuing warfare, this kind of self-defeating over-extension is only to be expected.

LEGACIES

Whether intentional or not, imperial regimes generate extensive political and cultural change, and such transformations constitute one of their primary legacies. Some regimes, Rome and the Han Dynasty, were consciously assimilative, striving to attract, civilize, and absorb 'barbarians.' But empires also fashion new peoples. In pursuit of frontier security, as a tool of diplomacy, and for convenience of administration, they divide, label, and reshape those they encounter and conquer. During the sixth and seventh centuries, Byzantine classification of frontier peoples, mainly in terms of their military and political potential to the empire, did much to shape Slavic ethnicity in the Balkans.[17] A similar kind of 'geopolitical ethnicity' was practiced on the Chinese-Inner Asian frontier, where Tang diplomacy, settlement policy, and categorization schemes reconfigured nomadic and forest peoples.[18]

Steppe empires engaged in an even more forceful, far-reaching version of these policies. The Mongols completely rearranged their nomadic subjects for purposes of military mobilization, with the result that following their decline the ethnic and tribal structure of the steppe zone was thoroughly transformed. These post-Chinggisid ethnic formations, further defined and refined by the Russian and Soviet empires, later emerge as the modern nations of Central and Inner Asia.

Imperial expansion transformed political and ethnic landscapes in a multitude of ways. Most obviously, it continuously stimulated secondary state formation. In some instances this was small scale and defensive, as in the emergence of the Frankish war confederation in the second century CE in response to Roman pressure.[19] In others, the response was large-scale and imitative. The First Bulgarian Empire (584–1018) can be viewed as a self-conscious 'counter-empire' to Byzantium, its rival and model. Decline produced similar results; following disintegration, territories, provinces, and military commands formed by empires served as the nuclei of new polities and tribes.

On many occasions, imperial expansion generated massive population movements, much of which was unplanned and extremely chaotic—the flights of people seeking escape from advancing armies as well as those seeking sanctuary within imperial borders. The experience of Rome and China in the period between the third and fifth centuries is a prime example of this kind of ethnic and demographic transformation. Empires also initiated more controlled movements. This was particularly common in West Asia and the steppe, where whole communities were deported to distant locales to secure lines of communication, revitalize desolate provinces, or punish disloyalty. The Inca, too, moved people around their realm for similar ends. While these may not have reached the magnitude of the programs of settler colonialism and population displacement that occurred in the post-Columbian Americas, the transfers and deportations of traditional empires were nonetheless massive and, by connecting peoples who did not necessarily wish to be connected, left in their wake innumerable cultural collisions and exchanges.

The intensification of cultural and economic contacts between faraway peoples is perhaps the most remarked legacy of empires. The promotion of cultural exchange was a natural byproduct of imperial policy. Rulers everywhere patronized the arts and sciences to enhance the majesty and to encourage cultural elites to proclaim their virtues to wider audiences. More importantly, the culture patronized was not limited to that of the royal house: the Achaemenids blended Iranian, Mesopotamian, and Greek traditions; the Romans, Latin and Greek; the Temürids, Turko-Mongolian and Perso-Islamic; and the Tang patronized Chinese, Central Asian, and Indian culture in its Buddhist garb.

Foreign products added mystery and majesty to courts; strange, eye-catching cultural and natural goods from distant lands were essential props for rulers claiming imperial status. Through a process of competitive emulation, imperial courts were sensitized to 'international' standards and were loath to be thought out of fashion or out of touch. The Tang eagerly adopted the hunting cheetah, then the rage of the royal hunt in West and Central Asia, to meet such standards. More consequential was the collection of plants from afar. From Shanglin Park in Han China, to Kew Gardens in England, imperial regimes have had a major hand in the circulation of botanical specimens across continents and later across the globe.

The presence of foreign specialists was equally persuasive in establishing a ruler's standing on the 'world' stage. This is why the Achaemenids advertised the array of imported materials and artisans employed in the construction of their royal palaces and why Temür put on public display the host of technical specialists collected during his campaigns of conquest.

While the urge to accumulate things foreign was inherent in the process of empire building, their transmission was made possible by improvements in transportation and security. Long-distance merchants, attracted to imperial centers to sell foreign wares, often stayed on as financial advisors, tax farmers, intelligence agents, and, in time of war, as supply specialists. It is not by chance that the silk route reached its first apogee at the turn of the first century CE when an alignment of four great empires, the Roman, Parthian, Kushan, and Han, held sway from the Mediterranean to the Pacific.[20]

Long-distance merchants were, moreover, instrumental in the promotion of religions; the spread of Buddhism, and later of Islam, is closely linked to overland and maritime commercial networks. These merchant-missionaries had particular success among the steppe empires: the Uighur empire accepted Manichaeism in 762, while the ruling elite of the Khazar empire converted to Judaism around 800. Besides enhancing legitimacy, conversion to a World Religion served as a means of adapting to changing external conditions. For one thing, it allowed these regimes to 'piggyback' on organizations that had their own information circuits and infrastructure, a useful tool in the hands of rulers attempting to attract and manipulate polities and peoples on and beyond their frontiers.

Some empires, however, enjoyed, on the strength of their own resources, a cultural reach that far out-distanced their sphere of political-military influence. There are several notable examples of political empires sitting at the center of even larger cultural empires. In East Asia, the Tang served as a model for many surrounding peoples—Koreans, Japanese, and Vietnamese—who borrowed its institutions, ideology, and intellectual and material culture. Its influence in these regions was largely created through appropriation, not imposition, because neighbors came to regard the Tang as a source of inspiration, prestige, and legitimacy.[21] In the West, the Byzantine empire, despite fluctuations in size and power, presided over an Eastern Orthodox 'Commonwealth' reaching from the eastern Mediterranean to Transcaucasia and northward to Russia. The center offered an attractive package of ideas, institutions, symbols, and ceremonies that could be selectively adapted to local needs.[22] It could also offer programs of technical assistance; the Byzantine court sent prized artisans to teach their skills to fellow communants in the Russian hinterlands as a gesture of goodwill and, of course, in hope of future returns.[23]

SUMMARY

In the early sixteenth century, maritime Europe, starting on its own path to empire, encountered large imperial regimes across the globe—the Ottoman, Safavid, Mughal, Ming, Aztec, and Inca—each of which had an identifiable genealogy and model. The remarkable persistence of these imperial traditions, exhibited in their location, configuration, and organization, is itself worthy of study. So, too, is the question of why, despite the lack of contact, there were similar imperial structures in the Old and New

Worlds. But the historical significance of empires is by no means limited to these weighty comparative and theoretical issues.

To a meaningful degree, global political history is simply the oscillation between universal empires and multi-state systems. In their expansive modes, empires destroyed and created states and were similarly productive in decline, devolving back into smaller polities, some entirely new and others merely refashioned. And long before there were anthropologists, colonial or otherwise, empires were in the business of identifying, classifying, and reordering peoples. In the complex process of ethnogenesis, imperial 'taxonomies' have long played a vital role.

Standard imperial policies had equally profound cultural consequences. Population transfers, garrisons, and colonies produced close encounters, while secure lines of communications and interest in things foreign produced long-distance exchange. Empires functioned, therefore, as huge catchment basins channeling, accumulating, and storing the innovations of diverse peoples and cultures, many of which they tested, adapted, validated, and propagated farther afield.

Traditional empires, though they presented themselves as sources of stability and order, and despite their modern-day reputations as bastions of conservatism and reaction, were persistent, long-term agents of historical change.

NOTES

1. For all comparisons, see Rein Taagepera, 'Size and Duration of Empires: Systematics of Size,' *Social Science Research* 7 (1978), 108–27, especially 116–17, 126.
2. Stanislav Andreski, *Military Organization and Society* (Berkeley: University of California Press, 1971), 33–6, 232.
3. Ann Hyland, *Equus: The Horse in the Roman World* (New Haven: Yale University Press, 1990), 170 ff.
4. Xiao Qiqing [Hsiao Ch'i-ch'ing], 'Meng-Yuan shuijun zhi xingchi yu Meng-Song zhanzheng,' *Hanxue yanjiu* 8 (1990), 177–200.
5. Stephen Blake, 'Patrimonial-Bureaucratic Empire of the Mughals,' *Journal of Asian Studies* 34, no. 1 (November 1979), 77–94.
6. Susan Sherratt and Andrew Sherratt, 'The Growth of the Mediterranean Economy in the First Millennium B.C.,' *World Archaeology* 24, no. 3 (February 1993), 363.
7. Pierre Briant, *Rois, tributes et paysans* (Paris: Belle Lettres, 1982), 451–6.
8. Irene J. Winter, 'Royal Rhetoric and the Development of Historical Narrative in Neo-Assyrian Reliefs,' *Studies in Visual Communication* 7 (1981), 2–38 and Pamela Gerardi, 'Epigraphs and Assyrian Palace Reliefs,' *Journal of Cuneiform Studies* 40, no. 1 (1988), 2–35.
9. Cf. Bruce G. Trigger, 'Monumental Architecture: A Thermodynamic Explanation of Symbolic Behavior,' *World Archaeology* 22, no. 2 (1990), 2–32.
10. Gherardo Gnoli, 'On Old Persian *Farnah-*,' *Acta Iranica* 30 (1990), 83–92.
11. Shaul Shaked, 'From Iran to Islam: On Some Symbols of Royalty,' *Jerusalem Studies in Arabic* 7 (1986), 75–91.

12. On this chain, see Thomas T. Allsen, 'Spiritual Geography and Political Legitimacy in the Eastern Steppe,' in Henri Claessen and Jarich Oosten, eds., *Ideology and the Formation of Early States* (Leiden: Brill, 1996), 116–35; Beatrice Manz, 'Tamerlane and the Symbolism of Sovereignty,' *Iranian Studies* 21, nos. 1–2 (1988), 105–22; and Lisa Balabanlilar, 'Lords of the Auspicious Conjunction: Turko-Mongol Imperial Identity on the Subcontinent,' *Journal of World History*, 18, no. 1 (March 2007), 1–39.

13. See Philip Salzman, 'Ideology and Change in Middle Eastern Tribal Society,' *Man*, n.s., 13 (1978), 618–37.

14. David Wilkinson, 'Cores, Peripheries, and Civilizations,' in Christopher Chase-Dunn and Thomas D. Hall, eds., *Core/Periphery Relations in Precapitalist Worlds* (Boulder: Westview, 1991), 157–60.

15. Robert Finlay, 'The Pilgram Art: The Culture of Porcelain in World History,' *Journal of World History* 9, no. 2 (1998), 150–8; and Chen Yaocheng, Guo Yanyi, and Chen Hong, 'Sources of Cobalt Pigment Used in Yuan Blue and White Porcelain Wares,' *Oriental Art* (Spring 1994), 14–19.

16. Joseph A. Tainter, *The Collapse of Complex Societies* (Cambridge: Cambridge University Press, 1990), 91 ff.

17. Florin Curta, *The Making of the Slavs: History and Archaeology of the Lower Danube Region c. 500–700* (Cambridge: Cambridge University Press, 2001), 335–50, especially 347.

18. Mark S. Abramson, *Ethnic Identity in Tang China* (Philadelphia: University of Pennsylvania Press, 2008), 108–49.

19. David Harry Miller, 'Ethnogenesis and Religious Revitalization beyond the Roman Frontier: The Case of Frankish Origins,' *Journal of World History* 4, no. 2 (Fall 1993), 277–85.

20. J. Thorley, 'The Silk Trade between China and the Roman Empire at its Height, circa A. D. 90–130,' *Greece and Rome*, second series, 18 (1971), 71–80.

21. Charles Holcombe, *The Genesis of East Asia, 221 BC.–A.D. 907* (Honolulu: University of Hawai`i Press, 2001), 215–28.

22. Jonathan Shepard, 'The Byzantine Commonwealth, 1000–1550,' in Michael Angold, ed., *The Cambridge History of Christianity*, vol. 5, *Eastern Christianity* (Cambridge: Cambridge University Press, 2006), 3–52.

23. Thomas Noonan, Roman Kovalev, and Heidi Sherman, 'The Development and Diffusion of Glassmaking in Pre-Mongol Russia,' in P. McCray and W. D. Kingery, eds., *The Prehistory and History of Glassmaking Technology* (Ceramics and Civilization, vol. VIII; Westerville, Ohio, 1998), 293–314.

References

ALCOCK, SUSAN E. *et al.*, eds. *Empires*. Cambridge: Cambridge University Press, 2001.

ALLSEN, THOMAS T. *The Royal Hunt in Eurasian History*. Philadelphia: University of Pennsylvania Press, 2006.

BARFIELD, THOMAS J. *The Perilous Frontier: Nomadic Empires and China*. Oxford: Blackwell, 1989.

CONRAD, GEOFFREY W. and ARTHUR A. DEMAREST. *Religion and Empire: The Dynamics of Aztec and Inca Expansionism*. Cambridge: Cambridge University Press, 1995.

DANDAMAEV, MUHAMMAD A. and VLADIMIR G. LUKONIN. *The Culture and Social Institutions of Ancient Iran*. Cambridge: Cambridge University Press, 1989.

DOYLE, MICHAEL W. *Empires*. Ithaca, N.Y.: Cornell University Press, 1976.

EISENSTADT, S. N. *The Political Systems of Empires*, vol. 1 New York: Free Press, 1969.

FARMER, EDWARD L. *et al. Comparative History of Civilizations in Asia*. Reading, Pa.: Addison-Wesley, 1977.

GARNSEY, P. D. A. and C. R. WHITTAKER, eds. *Imperialism in the Ancient World*. Cambridge: Cambridge University Press, 1978.

HELMS, MARY W. *Craft and the Kingly Ideal: Art, Trade, and Power*. Austin, Tex.: University of Texas Press, 1993.

LEWIS, MARK EDWARD. *The Early Chinese Empires: Qin and Han*. Cambridge, Mass.: Harvard University Press, 2007.

SCHWARTZ, GLENN M. and JOHN NICHOLS, J., eds. *After Collapse: The Regeneration of Complex Societies*. Tucson, Ariz.: University of Arizona Press, 2006.

SILVERSTEIN, ADAM, J. *Postal Systems in the Pre-Modern Islamic World*. Cambridge: Cambridge University Press, 2007.

TOYNBEE, ARNOLD J. *A Study of History*, vol. 7. London: Oxford University Press, 1954.

YOFFEE, NORMAN, and GEORGE L. COWGILL, eds. *The Collapse of Ancient States and Civilizations*. Tucson, Ariz.: University of Arizona Press, 1988.

CHAPTER 21

....

MODERN IMPERIALISM

....

PRASENJIT DUARA

THE renewed interest in imperialism after the wars in Afghanistan and Iraq has re-cast a vexed problem regarding the delimitation of the scope of the term imperialism. The urge to distinguish 'imperialism' from 'empire' has surfaced as some scholars seek to dissociate the United States' actions from the term imperialism and affiliate it with the less negative, if not positive, vision of empire. Whatever one's view of American activity, the distinction is worth considering in our delimitation.

EMPIRE AND IMPERIALISM IN HISTORY
....

'Empire' is the more enduring phenomenon in world history. It represents a political order which incorporates various political communities differentially or in a graduated hierarchy into the imperial center, as in the Roman or Ottoman empires. Empires were forged through violent *imperialist* projects of conquest but tended to transition to relatively stable orders often extending over centuries. 'Imperialism' is of course the process of building the empire, but it also represents a singular aspect of empire, one in which the conquered territory has not been incorporated—whether temporarily or not—into the metropolitan state framework and is retained in an entirely dependent and separated status, with or without a colonial state.

It is possible to see this difference as simply two phases of a single process, one in which empires were imperialist, and imperialisms become empires. But from the early decades of the twentieth century, much scholarship regarded contemporary imperialism as a distinct and perhaps even exceptional phenomenon that could not be compared to older forms of empire because of its close ties to capitalism. In the early twenty-first century, however, the view began to appear that these imperialisms were also beginning to transmute into more benign expressions of empire as a kind of 'extended protectorate' or federal structure.[1] Indeed, while Michael Hardt and Antonio Negri do not necessarily view it as benign, they believe that the contemporary world is in fact an 'empire' of global capital and transnational flows without an imperialist center.[2]

While recognizing that empire and imperialism cannot be fundamentally disassociated, certain historical conditions can predispose some rulers towards sustaining radical difference and subordination (imperialism) and others towards relative differences (empire). Indeed, European *colonialism* of the nineteenth and twentieth centuries may be viewed as imperialism built upon racial distinctions that found it very difficult to transition to empire. Let us review the different factors that are specific to modern imperialism.

Before the nineteenth century, *colonialism* referred to the settlement of conquered lands by metropolitan populations who violently cleared it of the pre-existing peoples as far as possible. This was clearest in the Americas and Australia, but also in parts of Africa. From the nineteenth century, rather than settlement *per se*, colonialism came to refer to a form of state control over native populations. The goals of colonial rule were radically different from those in the metropole as were the perceptions about native people. Typically, these differences were sustained by powerful racist theories informed by social Darwinist ideas of a hierarchy of backward and advanced races. As a form of state control sanctioned by, but separated from the conqueror's state system, colonialism became the distinctive expression of imperialism as a relatively long-term phenomenon.

Modern imperialism was not only based on colonial rule. Indirect or informal imperialism in the nineteenth and twentieth centuries took hold notably in China, the Ottoman empire, and Iran, where imperialists dominated not by direct control of state apparatuses, but by economic control and the actual and potential use of military violence—what in the Chinese context came to be known as 'gunboat diplomacy.' Typically, these societies were not colonized either because they were too expensive to administer or because of inter-imperialist rivalry over their control. Often imperialism in these societies reflected indirect rule by 'imperialist committee.' Indirect imperialism was also characterized by the separation of races. For instance, most Chinese were barred from residing in the foreign treaty port settlements, and citizens of imperialist nations were exempt from Chinese law in China.

Modern imperialism may also be distinguished from early modern Eurasian empires such as the Habsburg, Ottoman, Russian, Mughal, or Qing empires. These large land-based empires tended to conquer *contiguous* territories and incorporate them within the framework of the old state albeit with graduated differences. Some, notably the Russian empire, did seek to make the transition to modern imperialism in the later part of the nineteenth century. The Western European sea-based empires which expanded into the New World from the sixteenth to the eighteenth century, most notably Spain, pioneered many of the forms of modern imperialism—such as international law—but they were principally settler colonialisms and do not form a major part of this inquiry. The later sea-based empires of the Dutch, the French, and the British were distinct in that they created state structures responsible primarily neither to the settlers nor to the indigenous populations, but to the imperial metropole.

The two characteristics of modern imperialism identified so far—their maritime and colonial elements—were made possible by two other critical factors. The first of these is modern capitalism. The commercial revolution of the seventeenth and eighteenth centuries and more particularly the industrial revolution in Great Britain dating roughly from the 1770s set off the search for global resources and markets. What world systems theorists refer to as 'global regimes of capital accumulation' were created not simply by increasing trade but by integrating capitalism with ever growing technical and organizational capabilities *to control the social and political environment* of worldwide capital accumulation. Thus, nineteenth-century imperialism was distinctive because the drive for capitalist profit was yoked to highly complex organizational machinery which could mobilize resources and profits from afar without need to incorporate these distant lands into the metropolitan state.

These capabilities included not only the machinery of violence but the capacity to channel massive flows of labor and utilize racial ideologies to extract hyper-profits from this labor. For example, the slave labor brought to the plantations of the Caribbean islands were regarded as so sub-human that every means were sought to extend their work time and reduce the expenses for their bare sustenance. Captain Bligh, made famous by the movie *Mutiny on the Bounty*, brought the breadfruit tree to the Caribbean from Tahiti. Since the breadfruit tree required no cultivation as a food source, it was believed that slaves could simply pluck it off the tree and eat while at work. Thus, both expense and time could be saved to generate more profit. The grateful Jamaican planters awarded 'Breadfruit Bligh' 1,000 guineas.

The administrative machinery set up in the colonies also worked to create favorable conditions for capitalism by creating the infrastructure for the free flow of goods, primary resources, and capital between the colony and the metropole. This included not only the construction of ports, roads, and railroads connecting sources of raw materials and minerals to ports, but also the standardization of weights, measures, time, currency, and other means of creating a rationalized market economy. This was, of course, most evident in colonies such as British India, but it was also conducted in China where indirect imperialism prevailed. There, the Imperial Maritime Customs Agency, which came to be controlled by the British, deployed legions of native and colonial agents far and wide across the empire. They collected information and supplied reports on local currencies, weights, measures, administrative practices, levies, and the like in order to ultimately create measurable, standardized, and marketable objects of exchange—objects that were exchangeable not merely within China but with goods coming from distant places like Rio de Janeiro.

Finally, the fourth factor that shaped modern imperialism was nationalism. We have seen that the state was exceedingly important in modern imperialism. By the nineteenth century, the nation-state was already established in the major imperialist societies, Britain and France. Together with the national capitalists, the nation-state became the principal player in the inter-imperialist rivalry for colonies and resources. For over a hundred years after the defeat of Napoleon in 1815, British imperialism dominated the world. However, from the last third of the nineteenth century, British dominance came to be increasingly threatened by the rise of new nation-states with imperialist ambitions including Germany, Italy, Russia, Japan, and the United States. Most of these states sought to modernize and compete globally by creating and mobilizing the nationalist—even hyper-nationalist—sentiments of its citizenry.

Nationalism was deployed to rally the population and resources for war preparation and for war itself. State-administered mass organizations to mobilize civilian support for war were first developed by states such as Japan, the Soviet Union, and Italy which had observed the insufficiency of civilian support during World War I. Mass nationalist organizations in competitor nation-states were developed along the model of a con-script army and were elevated rhetorically to represent the will of the people. In this way they would call on the people to transcend immediate and particular interests, such as forgoing personal consumption or delegitimizing striking workers within the nation.

If during the nineteenth century, imperialism was largely the business of competitive nation-states, and nationalism was mobilized to further their interests, by the twentieth century *nationalism had become the driving force behind imperialism*. Hannah Arendt commented that imperialists appeared as the best nationalists because they claimed to stand above the reality of national divisiveness and represent the glory of the nation.[3] Imperialism had become fatefully intertwined with nationalism, and the core of modern nationalism at the heart of imperialism would make it very difficult to make the transition to empire or federation.

Nationalism also creates a new force of division not seen in the old type of empires. Unlike the empires that were based less on rights than on a graduated hierarchy of privileges and obligations, nation-states created a system of citizen rights for the national body politic but none for those in the empire. Thus was created a political-legal dualism which was reinforced by—and, in turn, reinforced—racialist and cultural theories and practices of difference. To some extent, it provoked nationalism in colonial societies to emerge in the mirror image of the imperialist nation of two communities pitted against each other. This binary continues to hinder the transformation of imperial relations into more federated or trustee-like relationships envisioned by scholars like Anthony Pagden.[4]

HISTORIOGRAPHY

The systematic study of imperialism begins with J. A. Hobson's critique of the economic bases of imperialism in 1902. In this study, we find the root causes of imperialism developed in later theories: the competition of industrial capitalist powers, the excess of manufactures over the consumption power of the domestic public, and the surplus of available capital that drove capitalists to secure distant lands for markets and resources. Thus were articulated the themes of over-production, under-consumption, and surplus capital that came to form the basis of Marxist theories of imperialism developed by Lenin, Rosa Luxembourg, and others. To be sure, unlike Lenin, Hobson did not believe that imperialism was an inevitable result of capitalism. He believed it was a coalition of classes, especially the finance capitalists, who pushed government policies towards a risky and hopeless colonialism. His alternative was to enhance the purchasing power of the national public.

For Lenin, imperialism represented the highest stage of capitalism, the outcome of the necessary logic of capitalism which can only thrive on the surplus value extracted from industrial workers. Simply put, higher profits entail lower wages which restricts the market for industry and forces capitalists to open new markets for their goods and investments. But more than the export of manufactured goods, it was the export of investment capital that explained imperialism. Not only did capital become truly global, it harnessed state power for its purposes and the profits and glory brought about by imperialism enabled the state to buy out the 'labor aristocracy' in its own society at the expense of the colony. In this new global context, the proletarian revolution would emerge not from the working classes of the mature capitalist countries, but from the weak links in the chain, such as Russia, where capitalism had its most devastating impact because of the relative weakness of capitalist political and social institutions.

It is difficult to overestimate the influence of Lenin's theory of imperialism on the subsequent understanding of the phenomenon, particularly as it penetrated the ideas of even non-Marxist leaders of the anti-imperialist movements in Asia and Africa, such as Sun Yat-sen and Kwame Nkrumah. Some of these ideas were also developed by left-wing intellectuals in Latin America as 'dependency theory.' As developed by Andre Gunder Frank and others in the 1970s, this theory held that modern imperialism has to be grasped in terms of an evolving and highly uneven capitalist world system with core regions and peripheries. The core regions represented the industrialized capitalist economies, and the peripheries the regions which the former exploited for raw materials and markets. While wage-based capitalism developed in the core, this same capitalist development produced capitalist *underdevelopment* in the periphery by perpetuating pre-capitalist forms of surplus extraction and unequal exchange between manufactured goods and primary products. According to dependency theorists, the problem was not that the periphery was insufficiently capitalist and modern. These areas of the world were well incorporated into the capitalist world; but the capitalism of the core produced the 'underdevelopment' of the periphery.

A closely related theory is world-system theory associated with Immanuel Wallerstein, Giovanni Arrighi, and others. These theorists argue that there has been a capitalist world-system since at least 1500 with changing cores and peripheries (leading to semi-cores and semi-peripheries as well). For instance, in the cores, Iberian mercantile capital was overtaken by the Dutch who were, in turn, overtaken by the British and in the contemporary world, by the United States. They too argued that the peripheries were kept underdeveloped through unequal exchange and older forms of labor mobilization. Thus, economic development in England, for example, was dependent on slave labor in plantation economies and low-cost agricultural production in the land- and resource-rich New World. But world-system theory had a more dynamic historical sense, not only in being able to see changing cores but in noting how certain political mechanisms—such as nationalism—could transform a periphery into a core region. The best instance of this in the nineteenth-century world was, of course, Japan.

Critics of Marxist, dependency, and world-system models often point to the 'metro-centric' nature of these understandings of imperialism. The periphery remains a passive object waiting to be molded according to the designs of the technologically superior powers. The earliest revision of this understanding came from the work of John Gallagher and Ronald Robinson, who argued that through much of the nine-teenth century, Britain operated the 'imperialism of free trade.'⁵ As the preeminent industrial power and, thus, the superior trading partner, Britain sought when it could to indirectly control the conditions of trade. Indirect control involved the participation of a range of indigenous partners or collaborators in the imperialist enterprise and thereby granted a greater role to actors in the periphery. Instead of focusing on policies and actions initiated from the metropolitan center, Gallagher and Robinson lay more stress on extrinsic and contingent factors shaping the nature and timing of imperial projects.

The volume *Tensions of Empire*, edited by Frederick Cooper and Ann Laura Stoler, perhaps best expresses the post-metrocentric turn in imperialism studies. The book not only seeks agency more locally but also emphasizes cultural and social as much as economic factors. Modern imperialism, the editors note, has been viewed in Mani-chaean terms as the monolithic imperial center dominating a periphery almost equally singular in its passivity.⁶ Nationalist movements in the empire also tended to see the imperialist versus the ruled in clearly demarcated ways. The scholarship suggests that this dualism is exaggerated. The new structures of power presented opportunities for many local elites and groups to ally themselves with imperialists and restructure society. These included newly empowered African chieftains (discussed below) and Chinese *compradors* or business agents of the imperialist powers who, however, also competed in certain areas with the imperialists.

Indeed, there were several different interests and ideologies among both the im-perialists and the ruled that created instabilities and uncertainties in the imperial project. Modern imperialism was accompanied by the universalist ideology of the Enlightenment, which advocated equal rights and universal citizenship for all. It thus contradicted the doctrine of imperialist rule founded on the unbridgeable difference between colonizer and colonized, a doctrine fostered by other Western theories of race and civilization. For the imperialists, this contradiction was often managed by argu-ments about the unpreparedness of colonial people for self-rule and the 'white man's burden' to carry out the civilizing mission in the unenlightened world. Of course, this argument was not always accepted by the colonized.

As early as the French revolution, there occurred the slave revolution in Haiti in which the slaves seized upon French revolutionary ideas to call for their liberation in the name of the Rights of Man. The French revolutionaries did not, however, support the movement, which was crushed. Still, the ghost of the Haitian revolution haunted French and British imperialists in subsequent years and also contributed to the movement to abolish slavery. More generally, the authors in *Tensions of Empire* argue that relationships between colonized peoples and imperialist powers were multi-faceted, and the former were often able to refashion colonial ideas of rule and superiority. For instance, conversion to Christianity was sometimes used by converts in the Philippines and Africa to entitle themselves to lead the mission. At other times, Christianity was itself reorganized to develop a movement of opposition to colonial rule.

Another school of thought represented in this volume is post-colonialism. While this scholarship too points to negotiation and appropriation on the part of colonized subjects, it emphasizes the *cultural and ideological production* of imperialism. The most significant contribution to this idea was made by Edward Said in *Orientalism*. Said argued that Western colonial power (in Egypt and the Middle East, in his case) was based not only on economic and political domination, but upon a vast and powerful apparatus of knowledge production of the 'Orient,' or the world of the colonized, which in turn was undergirded by claims to rationality and detached objectivity. In other words, colonial systems of power-knowledge produced the colonized subjects as objects of scientifically true knowledge through categories of 'the science of races' in a way that would advance or reproduce colonial domination. To be sure, these knowledge forms created in relation to the colonies also impacted self-conceptions of people back in the metropolis.

Soon after the publication of Said's *Orientalism*, other scholars began to observe that the colonized subjects often reproduced these very categories as ways of understanding the self, as when colonized intellectuals began to look down on extended families as 'tribal' or popular religion as 'unenlightened.' Partha Chatterjee argued that nationalism reproduced many of the categories and goals of colonial capitalism in its underlying assumptions. At the same time he showed how certain nationalists like Mahatma Gandhi overcame the deepest ideological roots of colonialism and experimented with alternative visions of community. In the end, however, these visions went unrealized as the nation-state conformed closely to the norms and imperatives of global capitalism propagated in the name of enlightenment and freedom.[7]

While the jury is still out on the extent to which the periphery was able to successfully *subvert* the imperialist system of knowledge and economic production, there is no doubt that the people from the periphery were much better able to *appropriate* this very system to compete with the imperialists and bring an end to formal colonialism, if not indirect imperialism. In the course of the nineteenth century, imperialism became the means of not only integrating the world, but homogenizing it much more than it had been heretofore. Imperialist enterprises and the state created new forms of economic organization, (legally sanctioned) private property, individual rights, new types of professional organizations, and large-scale political and social corporate entities such as the nation, the ethnic group, and even religious groups to replace or supplement ascriptive groups such as guilds, caste, lineage, or village community. To be sure, such groups were to be found more often in large cities, such as Shanghai, Mumbai, or Lagos, or in coastal or core zones of the empire, and the gap between these zones and the hinterland remains one of the legacies of imperialism that decolonizing nations grapple with.

Nonetheless, it was the new forms of social organization spawned by imperialist penetration that came to challenge imperialist rule. Thus, modern entrepreneurs, managers, accountants, educators, industrial workers, and lawyers not only experienced the limits on their careers and prospects imposed by colonial rule, as experts in modern knowledge, they also learned the means to challenge or circumvent these limits. These groups became the leaders of the new national and political movements that sought to mobilize the population in the hinterlands to challenge imperial rule.

Principal Developments in Modern Imperialism

Modern imperialism, associated with industrialization, capitalism, and the nation-state, begins with the industrial revolution around the 1770s and saw its heyday during the Pax Brittanica from 1815 to 1870. The rise of British power was connected to the collapse of the Spanish empire catalyzed by the outbreak of revolutionary wars of independence in the New World and the defeat of Napoleon in 1815. British industrial and naval might enabled it to rule the seas and control much of Asia, Africa, and Pacific Islands through the informal imperialism of 'free trade' and colonial rule.

Even as it lost its settler colonies in North America, Great Britain developed political control over India through the military activities of the mercantilist East India Company. The Company received the monopoly on Asian trade by royal charter in 1600 and reaped great profits by exporting the hugely popular Indian textiles into all of Europe until the end of the seventeenth century, when silk and wool merchants in France and England succeeded in restricting these imports. Finding its profits reduced, the Company increasingly intervened militarily in the declining Mughal empire, bringing the empire's provinces and autonomous Indian principalities under its own military control. Its penetration was facilitated by competing Indian governors and local rulers jockeying for control in the crumbling empire and by the Company's decisive defeat of the French in 1760. Political rule enabled control of revenues and profits of Indian and later Southeast Asian trade as well as the personal enrichment of company 'nabobs' such as Robert Clive and Warren Hastings. By 1773 high taxation and disruption of trade led to a famine in Bengal that wiped out one-third of the population.

Political control of large regions also enabled the Company to make up for lost textile profits by mandating the cultivation of opium in India. Opium was to be smuggled into China to reverse the large trade surpluses China was running with the Company because of Western demand for Chinese tea and other products. The opium trade was managed through a complex system known as the 'country trade,' in which

Company officials auctioned revenue acquired in opium to private traders from various countries who carried the contraband up the coasts of Southeast Asia to various Chinese ports. The opium trade rapidly changed the balance of payments with China. In the first decade of the nineteenth century, China saw an inflow of about $26 million in her international balance of payments. But in the decade after 1828, the net outflow from China was $38 million. Opium became the world's most valuable single commodity trade in the nineteenth century. Thus, by means of military and political control, the East India Company reversed earlier losses of silver to countries like India and China and developed the resources to pursue further colonization of India.

Meanwhile, the Chinese economy and large sections of the population were being ravaged by the spread of the opium trade, prompting China to declare war against the British in 1838. The defeat of the Qing in the Opium Wars led to a century-long period of informal empire in China where not only the British but many other Western powers received the same concessions as the British by inserting the most-favored-nation clause in the treaties they signed with China. Together, the treaties came to be known as the Unequal Treaties and imposed indemnity payments on the government, fixed low tariffs for Western goods, established extraterritorial rights for ordinary (i.e. non-diplomatic) citizens of the imperialist countries in China, spread missionaries into the interior, and intervened in many other ways. Non-compliance brought on threat of war—gunboat diplomacy—or the reality of it, which led to still more unequal treaties. The Western powers also opened up several large cities for trade and residence known as 'foreign settlements.' These settlements, especially in large cities such as Shanghai and Tianjin, became the source of Western cultural penetration and hybrid cultures that were to change China.

In part because the Company had acquired a colony in India much larger than Britain itself and in part because of the emergence of a new configuration of economic and political interests in Britain, the British Parliament gradually began to curb the power of the Company. Increasingly dominated by the industrial classes and 'free traders' from the last decades of the eighteenth century, Parliament passed various acts that sought to restrict the autonomy of the Company and transform the mercantilist bias in favor of free trade, including free trade in opium. The Company's monopoly on Asian trade was abolished in 1833, and British imperial power came to be represented by government officials.

During most of the nineteenth century, as we have seen, Great Britain engaged in the 'imperialism of free trade.' As the most efficient producer of industrial goods, it had a competitive advantage in world markets as long as access to markets and free and smooth exchange was possible. These latter conditions, however, often necessitated military and administrative intervention in societies where markets may have long prevailed but which did not necessarily conform to the British view of the sanctity of private property and universal exchange. In this period, British policy only applied formal controls when it was not possible to safeguard and extend British interest through the cheaper means of informal control.

By the early nineteenth century, the British economy had become effectively globalized, importing food and raw materials and exporting manufactures—mainly cotton and iron—and services to the world. Initially, most of its trade was conducted with Europe and North America, but the share of empire in British trade and investment grew steadily, especially in the latter half of the century. While in 1850, one-third of British investment was in America and the rest in Europe, by 1913, nearly half was in the empire. Between 1850 and 1860, British exports to the empire rose from one-fourth to one-third of its total exports.[8]

India was critical to British trade and empire. Its revenues and the vast and modern military enabled the British to maintain its military and trade supremacy in Southeast Asia and most of all in China. The bulk of the soldiers fighting for the British in every one of its wars in China came from India. To the west, British Indian troops were mobilized to fight wars in places like Turkey and Malta without need for sanctions from Parliament and at no cost to the British citizen. The empire also helped Britain balance about two-fifths of its deficits with the Americas and elsewhere by sustaining large deficits in the Indian accounts in Britain in balance of trade, interest income, (often guaranteed) return on investments, and colonial administrative charges—items Indian nationalists would call the 'drain' from India. As European competitors started to close off their colonies in the later part of the century, British trade and investment became more focused in the empire.

By the third quarter of the nineteenth century, British free trade imperialism came to be increasingly challenged by the rise of other imperialist powers. The fierce competition for resources and markets was heralded by the 'scramble for Africa.' Until the 1870s Europeans ruled only about 10 percent of African territory. By the time of World War I, only Ethiopia and Liberia (created by freed American slaves) remained independent. While particular policies and events may have triggered the scramble, such as Bismarck's colonial policies of the 1880s or the Belgian King Leopold's cruel private company in the Congo, it is best understood in terms of major changes within Europe. European industry was maturing, and like Britain at an earlier time, these—especially German—industries were now driven to find natural resources and overseas markets to overcome the limitation of domestic markets. The scramble also indicated that mature capitalist nation-states were beginning to act systemically: they were competing for the same resources, and their actions were closely conditioned by the others' behavior.

In the context of competition, Britain could no longer rely on indirect control through supportive indigenous organizations. Indeed, it often annexed territories to pre-empt control by its competitors. In order to protect the Suez Canal route to India, Britain seized Egypt in 1882 and established a virtual sovereignty over Sudan in 1899. After the discovery of gold and diamonds in South Africa, Britain declared war on the Dutch settlers (Boer War, 1899–1902) and eventually won all of South Africa. Britain's possessions included Gold Coast, Nigeria, and Sierra Leone in the west and Kenya and Uganda in the east. France got a foothold in Algeria as early as 1830, gradually extended control into Morocco and Tunis, and annexed most of northwest Africa from Algeria south to the Congo River. Germany became the third largest colonial power in Africa, and Italy annexed Eritrea and Italian Somaliland in East Africa.

The Great Powers issued the Berlin Act in 1885 to lay down rules for expansion in Africa. Although the Act issued pious proclamations about the well-being of the 'natives,' it also clarified the rules of African exploitation: a power with holdings on the coast had prior rights in the back country. The colonization was ruthless and rough. Often small groups of white men would enter the interior with a clutch of treaties, transform a village elder into a tribal chieftain, and bestow upon him all kinds of new powers, such as the right to convey sovereignty, sell land, or grant concessions in a mining area. Then came what amounted to forced labor and exploitation of the region. Terence Ranger has suggested that African tribalism and chiefdoms were a creation of imperialism.[9]

Many scholars refer to the last quarter of the nineteenth century as the period of 'new imperialism.' Except perhaps in Latin America, where both British and Americans competed for indirect control, the imperialism of free trade continued to unravel. This was most clear in China, where Britain too gave up the rhetoric of free trade and threatened to grab more special spheres of influence and territories of direct rule. After Japan defeated China in its first major imperialist war in 1895, it sought to colonize Chinese territories. It gained Taiwan and a leasehold in Manchuria, but the Russians, Germans, and French, fearing that Japanese control of the mainland would restrict their access, forced it to withdraw from Manchuria. Instead, Russia developed a special sphere of influence in Manchuria through the provision of loans to the Qing government. Although it was not full-fledged colonial rule, the exclusive imperial prerogatives in different parts of the country set off the scramble for China. The 'slicing of the Chinese melon' was opposed by the United States, which championed the Open Door policy in China. The threat of territorial division electrified Chinese nationalism, and this movement together with the Open Door policy and greater tensions within Europe stayed the imperialist division of China. From World War I until their defeat in 1945, Japanese imperialists occupied the greatest extent of Chinese territories.

While advocating Open Door in China, the United States also participated in the new imperialism in nearby Philippines when it took over the Spanish colony after the Spanish–American war of 1898. Elsewhere in Southeast Asia, the new imperialism was particularly evident in the French conquest of Indo-China, a territory much larger than France, in 1883. Siam survived colonial rule by emerging as a buffer between British power to the west in Burma and Malaya and the French to the east. The Dutch had been lodged in the Malay archipelago since the eighteenth century, and although they controlled the lucrative trade in products such as coffee, sugar, spices, timber, and minerals—often through slave labor in the Dutch 'culture system'—their control of local societies was indirect and tenuous until the twentieth century.

Most of the imperialist powers in Southeast Asia were toppled by the Japanese military after the outbreak of the pacific War in 1941, and this had a significant psychological impact upon the colonized about the invincibility of the Europeans. Japan, however, soon created its own 'anti-colonial' empire in the Greater East Asian Co-Prosperity Sphere, where nominally sovereign regimes formed Japanese puppet states. Although several of the European colonialists returned to reclaim their colonies after Japan's defeat, the decolonization movement had become sufficiently powerful to resist their return for any length of time.

MID-CENTURY TRANSFORMATION OF IMPERIALISM

If the last quarter of the nineteenth century witnessed the 'new imperialism' with competitive nation-states scrambling to divide up the world into spheres of exclusive control, the end of World War I led to yet another change in imperialism undertaken not by the old European imperialist powers but the new powers such as Japan, the United States, and the Soviet Union. This is an imperialism that I call the 'imperialism of nation-states,' and its first expression may be seen in the Japanese puppet state of Manchukuo established in northeast China (or Manchuria) from 1932 to 1945.

The inter-war era was characterized by a new environment for imperialist competition and domination. The barbarism of World War I exposed the ideal of the 'civilizing mission' as a sham to many in the rising nationalist movements in Asia and Africa. These movements often combined appeals to their own ancient civilizations with socialistic justice (suggesting the massive impact of the Russian revolution) to critique the imperialist, social Darwinist theories of ineradicable racial differences between Western peoples and the rest of the world. The anti-imperialist movement also made increasing demands for economic and political parity upon the imperialist powers.

Secondly, the new imperialist tendency to exclude other imperialist powers from access to one's own colony or sphere of influence took a new turn. The inter-war imperialists sought to create regional formations or economic blocs in which colonies or subordinate territories were often re-constituted as nominally sovereign nation-states, although they remained militarily in thrall to the metropole. The imperialism of nation-states reflected a strategic reorientation of the periphery to be part of an organic formation designed to attain global supremacy for the imperial power. As Albert Lebrun declared after World War I, the goal was now to 'unite France to all those distant Frances in order to permit them to combine their efforts to draw from one another reciprocal advantages.'[10] Yet France would find it very hard to implement this new formation. With the simultaneous rise of rights consciousness in the colonies and dependencies and the increased need for resource and social mobilization within them, it was more efficient for the imperialists to foster *modern* and *indirectly* controlled institutions in them. The goal was to control these areas by dominating their institutions of mobilization, such as banks, the transportation infrastructure, and political institutions, which were created to resemble those of the metropole (such as legislative councils, institutions of political tutelage, and political parties like the communist parties or the Concordia in Manchukuo). In short, unlike British free trade imperialism, the inter-war imperialists attended to the modernization of institutions and identities. They often espoused cultural or ideological similarities—including sometimes anti-colonial ideologies—even while racism and nationalism accompanied the reality of military-political domination.

Subordinate states were militarily dependent upon and economically mobilized for the sake of the metropole, but it was not necessarily in the latter's interest to have them economically or institutionally backward. Thus, this imperialism occasionally entailed a separation of economic and military-political dimensions. In some situations, as in the Soviet Union–Eastern Europe and the Japan–Manchukuo relationships, massive investments and resources flowed into the client states, thereby breaching the classical dualism between an industrialized metropole and a colony focused on the primary sector common to colonial imperialism.[11]

The older imperial powers of Britain and France recognized the value of economic growth in the empire for competitiveness during World War I when colonial troops and resources played a vital role. In Britain, Joseph Chamberlain's neo-mercantilist ideas of colonial development and of 'imperial preference' began to be taken more seriously after World War I. But as a consequence of entrenched ideas of colonial self-sufficiency, post-war capital needs at home, and, not least, demands for protection by British industry, only once before 1940 did expenditure on colonial development creep above 0.1 percent of British gross national product.[12] Similarly, while the French government extended imperial preference and implemented reforms during the 1930s, investments in economic and social development projects were insignificant until 1946.[13] The establishment of Manchukuo in 1932 marked the first major effort at the transformation of the metropole–colony relationship. Like China, Japan had also been subject to the unequal treaties by the United States and European powers. But the Meiji restoration of 1868 enabled it to build a strong nation-state that succeeded in abrogating these treaties. Indeed, to express its strength as a nation-state, Japan created an empire in Korea and Taiwan. At the same time, since the Japanese leadership also felt victimized by the Western powers, they identified with their weaker 'Asiatic brethren' in the very areas they were colonizing or seeking to colonize. This rhetoric of pan-Asianism curiously became still sharper as Japanese imperialism expanded in East Asia during World War I, when the Western powers were preoccupied. In 1919, after the Japanese encountered the first mass protest against their expansionist policies in the March First movement in Korea and the 4 May movement in China, groups of policy makers in the colonies and the military began to experiment with new forms of empire that crystallized in Manchukuo in 1932.

Manchukuo sought to reconcile the rhetoric of pan-Asianism with the military's quest for empire in Asia by creating a state that was integrated with the Japanese economy but had theoretically sovereign and modern institutions. Manchukuo had its own constitution and flag and was fashioned as a developmental state set upon creating a modern economy and an identification of the people with the state. The predominantly Chinese population could use their own language and occupy top positions in the government.

Behind the institutions was the reality of Japanese military control and close shadowing of Chinese officials by Japanese ones. Racial discrimination against the Chinese was pervasive despite the rhetoric of equality and brotherhood. However, in terms of economic and developmental indices, particularly in the areas of industrialization and municipal governance, the Manchukuo regime performed very well. It was especially after the establishment of Manchukuo that Japanese exploitation of colonies such as Korea was accompanied by sharp increases in their productive capacity. The accumulated per capita British investment in India was only $8 compared to Japanese investment in Korea of $38 in 1938.[14]

During the post-World War II era, the Soviet Union's creation of a regional system of militarily dependent states in Eastern Europe reflected many features of the new imperialism. A shared anti-imperialist and anti-capitalist ideology sanctioned a centralized economic and political system. The Soviet Union combined economic leverage and military threat to integrate states that were often more economically developed than itself into a regional economy. In some ways, the imperialism of the Soviet Union revealed the counter-economic consequences of this logic of empire. Not only were the client-states of the Soviet Union in Europe often more developed, the USSR may have subsidized their economies by supplying them with cheap oil and raw materials while importing finished products from their economies. This was the price paid by the imperial power to create and maintain dependence and assure its security.[15]

In part because of the consciousness of its own colonial past, and with the exception of a few places (most notably, the Philippines), the United States had long practiced imperialism without colonialism. After the Spanish–American War in 1898, the United States created a system of client states around the Caribbean basin in Central America. These nominally independent states became increasingly dependent on the United States, which accounted for more than three-fourths of the region's foreign trade as well as the bulk of foreign investment. During the decade of the 1920s, when Japan was experimenting with indirect imperialism in Manchuria, the United States too was seeking to develop and refine informal control over Central American countries especially as it faced revolutionary nationalism in the region. Officials, diplomats, and business groups stressed means such as American control of banking, communication facilities, investments in natural resources, and the development of education—particularly the training of elites in American-style constitutions, 'free elections,' and orthodox business ideas. But the threat and reality of military intervention remained close at hand.[16]

American imperialism was characterized not only by the Monroe Doctrine but also by the Open Door policy. Although there were contradictions and tensions between the two approaches, there were also continuities, most importantly in the practice of using sovereign or nominally sovereign polities to advance American interests. In 1917, President Woodrow Wilson pointed to the continuities when he declared that the nations of the world should 'with one accord adopt the doctrine of President Monroe as the doctrine of the world . . . no nation should seek to extend its polity over any other nation or people.' But just two weeks before, Wilson had sent troops to the Dominican Republic and committed American military forces in Haiti and Mexico as well.[17] The United States sought to foster an ideological and economic hegemony among its client states by creating them as reliable emulators subject to external economic and military constraints. Note, however, that this imperialism did not become developmentally oriented until the 1950s, when it was forced to respond to the Cuban revolution.

The tensions between American interests and global enlightenment were to be contained not only by military power, but perhaps more importantly by the notion of a *limited* self-determination, the idea of tutelage. As Secretary of Interior, Franklin Lane wrote in 1922: 'What a people hold they hold as trustees for the world . . . It is good American practice. The Monroe Doctrine is an expression of it . . . That is why we are talking of backward peoples and recognizing for them another law than that of self-determination, a limited law of self-determination, a leading-string law.'[18] Little wonder then that the Japanese representative at the League of Nations hearings on Manchukuo repeatedly insisted on the Asiatic Monroe Doctrine as Japan's prerogative in Asia. Indeed, the tension between enlightenment and self-interest paralleled the same tension in Japanese pan-Asianism.

In the post-World War II period, this combination of interest, enlightenment, and military violence has developed into what Carl Parrini has called 'ultraimperialism.' The latter refers to American efforts to maintain cooperation and reduce conflict among imperialist nations who were busily scrambling to create monopolistic or exclusive market conditions in various parts of the world during the first half of the twentieth century.[19] Ultraimperialism is secured by a chain of military bases around the globe—and structures such as the International Monetary Fund, General Agreement on Tariffs and Trade, and World Bank—to enable the conditions of cooperation among advanced capitalist powers and to facilitate the new (developmental or modernizing) imperialism in the decolonized world. Although the United States is hardly a regional power any longer, as a global empire it employs, in the words of Arrighi, Hui, Hung, and Selden, a vast system of 'political and military vassalage' and fosters a 'functional specialization between the imperial and vassal (*nation*) states. . . .' In this respect, the post-war United States represents the apogee of the 'imperialism of nation-states.'[20]

Imperialist competition in the first half of the twentieth century was catalyzed by a particular configuration of capitalism and nationalism. The nationalist foundations of modern imperialism have made it very difficult for the imperialist nation, whether Japan in Manchukuo or the United States in Iraq, to transition to a federated polity or cooperative economic entities or even 'empire.' The force of nationalist identity and interests from the earlier period has proved remarkably tenacious, particularly as they develop new linkages with competitive capitalism. The globalization and regional formations of our own time may have many new features, but the entrenched relations between capitalism and nationalism continue to create obstacles to global cooperation.

NOTES

1. Anthony Pagden, 'The Empire's New Clothes: From Empire to Federation, Yesterday and Today,' *Common Knowledge* 12, no. 1 (Winter 2006), 13–14.
2. Michael Hardt and Antonio Negri, *Empire* (Cambridge, Mass.: Harvard University Press, 2000).

3. Hannah Arendt, *The Origins of Totalitarianism* (New York: Harcourt Brace Jovanovich, 1973), 152–3.

4. Pagden, 'The Empire's New Clothes.'

5. John Gallagher and Ronald Robinson, 'The Imperialism of Free Trade,' *Economic History Review*, second series, 6, no. 1 (1953), 1–15.

6. Frederick Cooper and Ann Laura Stoler, eds., *Tensions of Empire: Colonial Cultures in a Bourgeois World* (Berkeley: University of California Press, 1997).

7. Edward Said, *Orientalism* (New York: Pantheon, 1978); Partha Chatterjee, *Nationalist Thought and the Colonial World: A Derivative Discourse* (London: Zed, 1986).

8. Michael W. Doyle, *Empires* (Ithaca, N.Y.: Cornell University Press, 1986), 264–6.

9. Terence Ranger, 'The Invention of Tradition in Colonial Africa,' in Eric Hobsbawm and Terence Ranger, eds., *The Invention of Tradition* (Cambridge: Cambridge University Press, 1983), 211–62.

10. As quoted in D. Bruce Marshall, *The French Colonial Myth and Constitution-Making in the Fourth Republic* (New Haven, Conn.: Yale University Press, 1973), 44.

11. See Prasenjit Duara, *Sovereignty and Authenticity: Manchukuo and the East Asian Modern* (Boulder, Col.: Rowman and Littlefield, 2003).

12. Stephen Constantine, *The Making of British Colonial Development Policy, 1914–1940* (London: Frank Cass, 1984), 25, 276.

13. Marshall, *French Colonial Myth*, 224–6.

14. Sub Park, 'Exploitation and Development in Colony: Korea and India,' *Korean Journal of Political Economy*, 1, no. 1 (2003), 19.

15. See Paul Marer and Kazimierz Z. Poznanski, 'Costs of Domination, Benefits of Subordination,' in Jan F. Triska, ed., *Dominant Powers and Subordinate States: The United States in Latin America and the Soviet Union in Eastern Europe* (Durham, N.C.: Duke University Press, 1986), 371–99.

16. Robert Freeman Smith, 'Republican Policy and the Pax Americana, 1921–1932,' in William Appleman Williams, ed., *From Colony to Empire: Essays in the History of American Foreign Relations* (New York: John Wiley, 1972), 273–5.

17. Andrew J. Bacevich, *American Empire: The Realities and Consequences of U.S. Diplomacy* (Cambridge, Mass.: Harvard University Press, 2002), 115–16, quoting from 115.

18. Quoted in Smith, 'Republican Policy and the Pax Americana,' 271.

19. Carl Parrini, 'The Age of Ultraimperialism,' *Radical History Review*, 57 (1993), 7–9.

20. G. Arrighi, T. Hamashita, and M. Selden, eds., *The Resurgence of East Asia: 500, 150 and 50 Year Perspectives* (London: Routledge, 2003), 301.

References

Bacevich, Andrew J. *American Empire: The Realities and Consequences of U.S. Diplomacy.* Cambridge, Mass.: Harvard University Press, 2002.

Cooper, Frederick, and Ann Laura Stoler, eds. *Tensions of Empire: Colonial Cultures in a Bourgeois World.* Berkeley: University of California Press, 1997.

Doyle, Michael W. *Empires.* Ithaca, N.Y.: Cornell University Press, 1986.

GALLAGHER, JOHN, and RONALD ROBINSON. 'The Imperialism of Free Trade,' *Economic History Review*, second series, 6, no. 1 (1953), 1–15.

HARDT, MICHAEL, and ANTONIO NEGRI. *Empire*. Cambridge, Mass.: Harvard University Press, 2000.

HOBSON, J. A. *Imperialism: A Study*. Ann Arbor, Mich.: University of Michigan Press, 1965 (originally published in 1902).

MÜNKLER, HERFRIED. *The Logic of World Domination from Ancient Rome to the United States*, trans. by Patrick Camiller, Cambridge: Polity Press, 2007.

SAID, EDWARD. *Orientalism*. New York: Pantheon, 1978.

STOLER, ANN LAURA, CAROLE MCGRANAHAN, and PETER PERDUE, eds. *Imperial Formations and their Discontents*. Santa Fe, N.M.: School of American Research Press, 2007.

WALLERSTEIN, IMMANUEL. *The Modern World-System*, vol. III: *The Second Great Expansion of the Capitalist World-Economy, 1730–1840's*. San Diego: Academic Press, 1989.

PART IV

REGIONS

CHAPTER 22

EAST ASIA AND CENTRAL EURASIA

PETER C. PERDUE

Since ancient times, East Asia and Central Eurasia have been connected to the world. Nationalist histories, however, have focused on the internal 'unity' of each of the nation-states of East Asia—China, Korea, Japan, and Vietnam—while Central Eurasia has been fragmented into 'Inner Asia' (Mongolia, Tibet, Xinjiang, and Manchuria) and 'Central Asia' (former soviet Central Asia). These arbitrary divisions ignore similarities and interactions within Asia, and they no longer fit the post-1989 world. Globalization and nationalism have now developed together. China insists that its Inner Asian territories have always been part of the Chinese nation, while the independent Central Asian republics seek to distinguish themselves from each other and from Russia. Nevertheless, East Asia and Central Eurasia have a much longer history of cultural and economic interaction than of nationalist isolation. This chapter will suggest ways to study the global connections of East Asia and Central Eurasia.

DEFINITIONS, REGIONS, AND ENVIRONMENTS

Seven horizontal climatic bands span Eastern and Central Eurasia: (1) the arctic tundra of the far north; (2) coniferous forests covering Siberia and northern Manchuria; (3) mixed and deciduous forests dominating North China, Korea, and Japan; (4) the steppe belt extending from northwest China through Mongolia to Ukraine; (5) high deserts and oases in the core of Central Asia; (6) subtropical rain forest in the rice paddy areas of South China and Taiwan; and (7) monsoon regions with high jungle in southwest China and Vietnam. Each of these ecologies supported a distinctive local culture, but their populations constantly migrated and exchanged goods with each other.

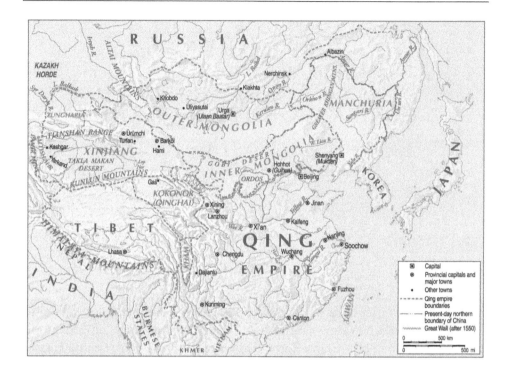

Determined pilgrims, warriors, or merchants could cross even the most barren deserts, highest mountains, and thickest jungles. No insuperable natural barriers blocked the expansion of empires or the networks of religion and trade.

In the temperate and subtropical regions, dense populations concentrated in river valleys and low foothills but avoided the swampy or malarial coasts. The Wei River (a tributary of the Yellow River), the central and lower Yangzi basins, the Kyoto plain, and the Red River delta supported the core areas of East Asia. The Selengge and Orkhon Rivers of Mongolia, the Liao River of Manchuria, oases at Khwarezm, in the Ferghana valley, and along the Syr Darya and Amu Darya rivers formed the core of Central Eurasia. Around the settled agriculturalists swirled nomadic pastoralists, caravan merchants, and other mobile peoples. Some of them had fled the hard life of tilling the soil to live off herds of animals. Others were warriors on horseback who raided and traded with merchants and peasants. Although their populations were smaller than those in the valleys, they replenished themselves from forced migrants and refugees, or they took captives. The constant conflict between mobile pastoralists and agriculturalists defined much of the evolution of culture across the region. Even in the Japanese islands, horse-riding invaders came down the Korean peninsula and left their traces in early myths.

Since the second millennium BCE, states and empires in China spanned several ecological zones. They included some of the steppe, most of the north China plain, and much of the central Yangzi; Japanese and Vietnamese states spanned lowlands and hills. The combination of cultures, more than the dominance of a single one, generated the vitality of these civilizations. States derived most of their revenue from the settled peasantry, but most of their warriors, horses, and forest and animal products came from the steppes and mountains.

Religious cultures crisscrossed the region. Unlike Europeans, East Asians generally did not polarize around religious divisions: synthesis and coexistence were more common. The ancestral cults of China, the basis of Confucian social ethics, thrived alongside popular Daoism, Buddhism, and the worship of local deities. Japan mixed its local cults, later systematized as 'Shinto,' with Confucian and Buddhist traditions imported from China and Korea. Buddhist missionaries moved out of India through Afghanistan along the silk routes, spreading the religion all across East and Central Eurasia. We may define much of the East Asian region as the land of Mahayana Buddhism (China, Mongolia, Tibet, Korea, Japan, Vietnam), but Buddhism never completely dominated anywhere. Central Eurasians mingled the cult of Heaven with shamanic practices and Buddhist institutions until the coming of Islam. Even monotheistic Islam was much less restrictive than in the Middle East, supporting cults of local revered figures that looked suspiciously like the worship of saints. Christianity took root only in Korea and Vietnam on the periphery.

Linguistic divisions also demonstrate complex mixtures. The Sinitic languages are a group of mutually incomprehensible languages, varying greatly by region. Now China and Taiwan have imposed the common language (*Putonghua*) as the only written version, but popular speech is still fragmented. The Altaic group, including Mongolian, Turkic languages, Manchurian, and most likely Japanese and Korean, spans most of the steppes and deserts of Central Eurasia. Tibetan is a distinct language with some Sinitic aspects. Vietnamese, also a separate language, borrowed over 70 percent of its modern vocabulary from Chinese. In Southwest China, hundreds of other languages are scattered across the mountains and valleys. This diversity of spoken languages contrasts with the unity of writing. The Chinese script, dating from the second millennium BCE, extended to Japan, Korea, Vietnam, and parts of Central Eurasia, supporting states and bureaucracies. The only other comparable written traditions are the Uighur script, used in Mongolia and Manchuria, and the Tibetan script derived from Sanskrit. Turkic peoples now use the Arabic or Cyrillic scripts or, most recently, the Roman alphabet. The Roman alphabet is now the official written form in Vietnam, while Koreans use their own alphabet. Thus, the region has created or adapted nearly all the major script traditions of the world.

In short, blurred boundaries and fluidity constantly undermined any efforts to establish clear, consistent, coherent unities on geographical, religious, or linguistic criteria.

ANCIENT CONTACTS

Recent archaeological finds demonstrate constant interaction between the ancient civilizations of Eurasia. Of the four major primary centers of civilization—Egypt, Mesopotamia, Indus valley, and China—China was the latest to develop. The cities of the Shang period appeared ca. 1500 BCE and the earliest writing in 1200 BCE. The discovery of a fifth major center in Bactria-Margiana (modern Turkmenistan and Afghanistan) shows that Central Eurasia had its own civilization linked to the Middle East, and it could have been a way station for cultural transmission farther East.[1]

China derived important cultural and technological elements from Central Eurasia. Chinese graves contain bronze chariots nearly identical to those found in the tombs of central Russia. Iron metallurgy definitely moved eastward across the steppe. The adoption of wheeled vehicles greatly increased mobility, further dispersing peoples across the steppes. Speakers of Indo-European languages spread from origins in Turkey or southern Ukraine eastward and westward, moving into Iran, India, and around the Tarim basin in Xinjiang, China.[2] One fascinating cultural symbol, called the Queen Mother of the West (Xiwangmu) in China, is derived from the Greek goddess Cybele.[3] The Chinese language even includes some words of Persian origin (like *shi* for lion). Many practices of Chinese Daoism are quite similar to those of Indian yogis.[4] These are only a few examples of extensive cultural interchange in prehistoric times.

But why is the Chinese script the oldest surviving writing system from this region, and why does Chinese not use an alphabet? The nomads, living mainly in small tribal groups, did not need writing until they formed an empire, and the small-scale oasis societies did not need it either. Writing in China is the result of the ferocious interstate competition that led to the creation of the Chinese empire. As competing kings built bureaucracies and armies, they recruited advisers to consult oracles and classic texts. The common scripts of the oracles began to diverge, as each warring state developed its own traditions, but the Qin emperor, who unified China in 221 BCE, banned the rival scripts, burned the rival history books, and imposed a single standard script. It has lasted nearly unchanged ever since. The Phoenicians and other alphabet users were trading peoples of the Mediterranean and Middle East; the Sogdians, the traders of Central Eurasia, in fact used a version of the Phoenician alphabet. The elites who ruled the East Asian states regarded the classical Chinese script, a written language distinct in vocabulary and grammar from any spoken language, as a convenient tool for holding their empires together.

Outside China, each East Asian state modified the script to fit its own linguistic needs. The Japanese developed two syllabic alphabets in the eighth century CE, the Koreans created their own alphabet in the fourteenth century, and the Vietnamese constructed their own versions of Chinese characters to write their native language. Several Central Eurasian regimes which occupied parts of north China also created their own scripts based on the Chinese characters. Classical Chinese writing tied the East Asian cultural world together on a greater scale than Latin in Europe.

STATE FORMATION AND EXPANSION

China created the first powerful bureaucratic state in Asia, when the Qin emperor conquered his enemies, the rival kings of the Zhou realm, in 221 BCE. The Qin state, at the western end of the Chinese cultural sphere, had adopted powerful military technologies from its nomadic neighbors. The emperor repressed contending schools of thought, standardized roads, administrative divisions, and currency, and expanded his control northward with military campaigns and large walls. The brutal Qin empire soon fell, but its successors, the two Han dynasties, endured for over four hundred years, from 206 BCE to 220 CE. Han armies expanded in all directions, establishing brief control of the Tarim basin of Xinjiang and conquering Vietnam. The Han emperors, however, could conquer the empire on horseback, but not rule it on horseback. Like many later imperial formations, the Han mixed together vigorous military men, often influenced by steppe nomadic horsemen, settled peasants, and literate officials and consultants.

The Han rulers stabilized agriculture based on Confucian precepts of low taxation and equal land holding and made Confucian philosophy the orthodox doctrine, but they encouraged religious syncretism. Missionaries arriving from India during the Han made Buddhism into a powerful rival scriptural tradition by translating Indian texts into Chinese. Up to the ninth century CE, Buddhism grew to become the dominant religious tradition in China, and it became even more dominant in Japan, Korea, and Vietnam. As a universal creed, Buddhism transcended local loyalties, and in the Mahayana version of East Asia, its monks encouraged support from lay believers, allowing Buddhism to penetrate deeply into daily life. Buddhist manifestations interacted with other local cults, so that in one temple people could worship famous officials, warriors, Daoist sages, and Buddhist monks. Buddhist texts brought many new words and concepts into the Chinese language; in Japan, Buddhists introduced the first written sources. The creation of the first states in Japan and Korea in the fifth to seventh centuries depended heavily on support of the Buddhist clergy.

The nomads of the Eurasian steppe, since the first millennium BCE, had formed a powerful military society that constantly contended with the Chinese states to the south. The Chinese despised these 'barbarians,' but depended on them for horses and weapons. The Han dynasty held back the nomads by combining military expeditions, controlled frontier trade, defensive walls, and divide-and-rule diplomacy. The Xiongnu confederation dominated the oases and steppes of Central Eurasia, but the Han rulers sent China's most valuable export—silk cloth—to the Xiongnu to be transported along the caravan routes to the west, in return for horses and guarantee of peace on the border. These trading relationships, when they flourished, kept China in steady contact with the Roman and Parthian empires in the far West.[5]

With the fall of the Han dynasty in the third century CE, Turkic peoples from the steppe conquered parts of China and cut off the silk routes. Disunity lasted until the reunification of China under the Sui and Tang dynasties in the seventh century CE. Under the Tang in its flourishing age, China extended its commercial and cultural influence even farther than under the Han, occupying the Tarim basin of modern Xinjiang, sending large amounts of silk and other commodities to the West, and obtaining respect from the Turk empire of the steppe, as the Tang emperor had himself declared a *kaghan*, or ruler of the Turks. As the Tang empire expanded, the Turks, originating in the Altai mountains, created their own expansive empire in its shadow. They used the wealth of the silk routes to support their military forces, while protecting trade across Central Eurasia. Tang China likewise strongly influenced Korea and Japan to copy its great bureaucratic model, and kept control of Vietnam as a province. Tang elites greatly enjoyed the exotic products of their far-flung empire, such as rhinoceroses brought as tribute gifts from the south, whirling Khotanese dancers from the far west, or lacquer from Japan.[6] Tang troops also fought with a powerful Tibetan state and fought off Arab armies at the critical battle of the Talas River in modern Kyrgyzstan. Muslims, Christians, and even Jews joined the Chinese and Buddhists as travelers and residents of the huge cosmopolitan empire.

After 750 CE, as Tang power declined, regions developed in independent directions. Military governors took over much of the periphery, while Turkic steppe rulers took control of Central Eurasian oases. Vietnam escaped permanently from Chinese domination in 939 CE; Korea established a new dynasty in 935, and Japan ceased sending tribute embassies to China. From 800 to 1200, population and economic centers shifted to the south, especially the lower Yangzi valley and southeast China coast. Intensive rice paddy cultivation in the river valley supported commercial networks, large cities, and booming maritime trade.

China, under the Northern Song and Southern Song dynasties (960–1279), did not even control all of its heartland. The partially nomadic Jin took control of all of North China in 1126, forcing the Song rulers to the 'temporary' capital of Hangzhou. Yet despite its military failures, the Song was a time of tremendous economic and technological advancement. Three of the crucial inventions of world history—the compass, gunpowder, and printing—all originated in China and developed most rapidly during the Song. Using the compass, large ships headed south from China's coast into the waters of Southeast Asia. Song military forces developed all the uses of gunpowder, from napalm to artillery; they lost battles because their northern neighbors used these techniques even more effectively. Printing, invented in the seventh and eighth centuries, developed into a large industry in the Song, producing cheap editions of classical texts for the millions of students cramming for the examination system, popular editions of Buddhist sutras, and the first mass editions of plays, stories, and graphic arts. The Song rulers created an iron industry whose output was not exceeded until the later stages of the British Industrial revolution, printed the world's first paper money, and Hangzhou became the largest urban society in the world. Unique among Chinese dynasties, the Song derived most of its tax revenue from commerce.

In Central Eurasia, the nomadic Uighurs settled in cities and created a large oasis-based and commercial empire, while propping up the declining Tang emperors with their military forces. They embraced the Manichaean religion derived from ancient Iran. Farther west, Iranian and Turkic rulers of the Samanid and Karakhanid states firmly implanted Islam in the oases of Central Asia. Vietnam, under its first independent dynasties, created a smaller bureaucratic state centered on the dense population of the Red River valley, while expanding trade along the coast to the south and north to China. Japan generated a glorious but isolated cultural life, centered on the sophisticated court in Kyoto, while rustic warriors gradually took control of the countryside.

In the thirteenth century, Mongols erupting from the steppes for the first and last time joined the fractured societies of Central and Eastern Eurasia under one giant empire, covering all of China, Central Asia, most of the Middle East, and Russia. The Mongol conquests at first devastated many agricultural regions, but the Pax Mongolica that endured for the fourteenth century revived the silk route caravans, turned the attention of Chinese once again toward Central Eurasia, and caused Central Asian cities to flourish. Timur, the last of the great nomadic conquerors, made his headquarters in Samarkand a treasure house of looted commodities, while wrecking much of the Middle East. Japan and Vietnam successfully fought off Mongol invasions, but the warriors of Japan soon turned against each other, tearing Japan apart in brutal internal battles.

China's Ming dynasty (1368–1644), founded by a peasant leader from the south, drove out the Mongols and established an agrarian-based, more isolationist regime in the fifteenth century. At first, the early Ming rulers expanded aggressively, staging campaigns in the northwest, invading Vietnam, and staking their claim to a military and commercial presence in Southeast Asia by sending large fleets there under the leadership of the Muslim admiral Zheng He. But the northwest campaigns failed, Vietnamese guerrilla warriors drove out Chinese troops, and threats from the northwest forced the cancellation of the maritime expeditions. Ming China contracted its geopolitical ambitions to the core of Han China, while on the frontiers, autonomous Mongol chieftains and oasis kingdoms grew. Korea, freed from Mongol domination, established the Choson dynasty, the longest lasting dynasty in Asia, lasting from 1392 to 1910.

In the sixteenth century, for the first time, the New and Old Worlds joined together, and the 'human web' expanded to global scale.[7] The Spanish and Portuguese maritime voyages and conquests made these connections possible, but it was the wealth of Asia that made them profitable. Silver from American mines flowed east across the Atlantic through Spanish and Dutch channels to India and China, in exchange for textiles, tea, porcelains, and spices. It also flowed west across the Pacific through Manila and Macao into China and Japan, fueling commercial networks extending from the Strait of Melaka, along the southern Chinese coast, to Taiwan and southern Japan. The global silver flow forced the Ming rulers to reopen the doors to trade, by allowing the

Portuguese a lease on Macao and permitting Chinese to travel overseas. The silver penetrated all of China in the late sixteenth century, dramatically transforming society. As the Ming tax system shifted to a silver basis, millions of dollars of silver moved to the northwest to pay the soldiers and their supporters on the garrisons on the Great Wall. A new consumer-driven society flourished in China and Japan, generating demand for large numbers of printed books, precious objects, gardens, and luxury leisured living. New philosophical currents and cultural movements supported the middle-class urban consumer over the landed elite.[8] Crops from the New World, like tobacco, maize, sweet potatoes, peanuts, and chili peppers, changed the Asian diet while supporting increased populations. By 1600, Ming China grew to at least 150 million people, still the largest empire in the world.

Central Asia, by contrast, fell behind. The decisive shift of trade routes toward the sea undermined the caravan trade, and constant warfare disrupted the oasis societies. Nomadic confederations fractured as the Russians advanced inexorably across Siberia. Several Mongol rulers briefly formed confederations, but none of them could recreate the huge empire of Chinggis Qan. Ming defensive strategies and trading licenses pitted the Mongols against each other, but trade across the Great Wall continued. It did not wall off the Chinese from the steppe, but it did disrupt nomadic economies.

The seventeenth century brought new military regimes to power in East Asia, each of which developed the maximum potential of their preindustrial societies. During the late sixteenth and early seventeenth centuries, Northeast Asia experienced violent state competition, as the four contending states, Ming China, Korea, Japan, and the rising Manchu state, challenged each other. The Japanese warrior Hideyoshi's invasions of Korea from 1592 to 1598 drew in Chinese intervention to drive him out, while the Manchus extracted revenues from Korea to build their state. Japan and Korea chose protective isolation, while China and Vietnam expanded energetically.

The Manchus, Central Eurasian warriors from the northeast, joined with Mongol cavalry and Chinese infantrymen to topple the Ming dynasty from its control of the Chinese heartland. They proclaimed the new Qing dynasty in 1636. They then took Taiwan, Mongolia, Xinjiang, and parts of Central Asia, and secured predominant influence in Tibet. Unlike the swift but ephemeral Mongol conquest, their rule lasted for over 200 years and laid the basis for the territorial claims of the modern Chinese nation-state. China became not just a Han-dominated empire, as it was under the Ming, but a vast multicultural structure of diverse peoples. Confucian scholars still espoused orthodox principles of government, but they had to manage Buddhists, Muslims, and local religions that flourished among the people and diverse ethnic elites of the expanded empire.

Expansion brought the final destruction of the independent Mongolian states and brought the Chinese into contact with new peoples like the Russians and Kazakhs in Central Eurasia. In the south, they faced the European trading companies, led by the Dutch and British. Under the name of 'tribute,' the Qing managed foreign trade relations with a flexible regime of controls in the eighteenth century, welcoming foreigners who brought gifts, but putting them under strict constraints. Russians met the Qing traders at the border town of Kiakhta, while the British and other Europeans were confined to a small part of the city of Canton. Despite their constraints, these arrangements brought profit to the foreigners and provided the Qing with two essential goods: horses (from Central Asian Kazakhs) and silver from the mines of Latin America.

Domestic commerce also flourished greatly under Qing expansion. The expanded scale of markets promoted division of labor, allowing farmers to specialize in their best crops and trade them for money with other regions. The lower Yangzi specialized in cotton and silk; the middle Yangzi in grain; hill regions of south China in porcelain and tea for export. North China grew cotton, and northwest China exported wool. The Grand Canal linking north and south China developed from a military transport route into a major artery of private commerce and communication.

Opportunities for clearing new land stimulated mobility. Migrants headed outward in all directions: from north China to southern Manchuria, from central China to Sichuan, from southeast China to Taiwan, from northwest China to Xinjiang, and from south China to Southeast Asia. Qing officials were ambivalent about this new mobility: they knew that migrants brought development and relieved pressure on poor regions, but the new arrivals could be unruly and difficult to control. Regardless of legal restrictions, however, the masses of Chinese traders and peasants continued to push toward the frontiers, as the population of the empire doubled to 300 million. Chinese established a firm and powerful presence in Southeast Asia, performing useful roles for the colonial powers as tax collectors, opium traders, and miners. Qing China, despite the reservations of its conservative elites, had definitively entered the world.

Meanwhile, Japan's rulers, tough samurai warriors who defeated their rivals and unified Japan after three centuries of chaos, took a different path, yet with surprisingly similar results. Sixteenth-century Japanese had participated actively in the vibrant trade routes of maritime East Asia, sending squadrons of merchants and soldiers (whom the Chinese called 'pirates') to trade along the coast, and establishing colonies in coastal Vietnam. In return, Europeans brought weapons, Christianity, and gold to Japan. The Tokugawa rulers, fearing the disruptive effects of foreign goods and religions, shut down nearly all foreign trade, except for the Dutch confined to a small island in Nagasaki and tribute missions from Korea. Yet they carefully observed China, requiring regular reports from merchants who traded on the coast.

Although Japan reduced its foreign contacts, within the country trade boomed in spite of Tokugawa repression. The authorities required the lords to spend large amounts of money to travel back and forth to Edo (modern Tokyo). The traffic on the trunk road to Edo generated great opportunities for merchants, innkeepers, porters, and entertainers, while the consumer demands of the rich population made the city expand. Kyoto, the center of the court, retained its aesthetic charm. Merchants who controlled the grain and money exchanges concentrated in Osaka. Between them, Edo, Kyoto, and Osaka made Japan one of the great urban centers of the world, and one with the most intensive communication networks. The Tokaido and the Inland Sea (Japan's

'Mediterranean') linked the three core islands together, while the Tokugawa lords expanded north into Hokkaido.

As elsewhere, Japanese actively promoted land clearance, intensification of agriculture, and greater division of labor and commercialization of agriculture. But three features set off Japan from most of Eurasia: the Japanese population did not grow rapidly in the eighteenth century, the shoguns demilitarized the entire country, and local rulers set about to preserve their forests from destruction. The tight village communities of rural Japan controlled births (partly through infanticide) to preserve their livelihoods. At the same time Japan gave up the gun, as the Tokugawa deliberately demolished hundreds of castles and disarmed the entire populace, allowing only swords for ceremonial use by the ruling samurai class. Villagers and local lords passed strict regulations to preserve forest production. Only an island country like Japan could enforce such environmental legislation. Yet Japan and China followed parallel paths in the eighteenth century of commercial development, integration of regions, and rising agrarian and urban prosperity.

GREAT DIVERGENCES

The nineteenth century, by contrast, ended with striking differences between the East Asian countries. China and Japan kept their independence, while the rest of the region fell under colonial domination. The Qing rulers, wracked by internal war and foreign invasion, lost territory and ultimately the dynasty itself, while Japan made itself into a major world power. Korea fell under Japanese colonial rule, Vietnam under French control, and Central Asia under Russian domination.

What accounts for this remarkable divergence? Both China and Japan faced similar onslaughts by European and American imperial powers, determined to open their markets for industrial manufactures. The British made China the first target, as they chafed under the restrictions of the Canton trade. Convinced that only mandarin obstruction blocked their textile sales, and determined to eliminate the silver drain, the British forced open Chinese ports to trade in two Opium Wars from the 1840s to 1860. France and the United States eagerly followed the British lead, seizing the chance to sell goods and send missionaries to the interior. Russia took advantage of China's weakness to occupy parts of Xinjiang and build the Siberian and China Eastern Railway across Manchuria to the Pacific, while the Germans established a leasehold in Qingdao, Shandong.

The Qing empire, afflicted with multiple rebellions generated by population growth, ecological devastation, heretical religions, and ethnic conflict, could not respond effectively until the 1860s, when several provincial governors launched a self-strengthening movement to build 'a strong military and a rich nation.' These leaders built arsenals, dockyards, and industrial establishments, translated Western technical and legal texts, and hired Western advisors. They successfully shored up the Qing regime, as Western powers realized they would profit by extracting concessions from the restored empire.

In 1854, when the United States sent gunboats to Japan, demanding a commercial treaty, Japanese activists learned from China's debacle. Responding to Commodore Perry's 'black ships,' they prepared to overthrow the Edo shogunate. After a turbulent decade, in 1868, they declared the 'restoration' of power to the Meiji emperor. The Meiji restoration carried out a more thoroughgoing pursuit of self-strengthening, wealth and military power. In China, conservative resistance stalled the reformist governors' efforts, but in Japan, the entire society threw itself into radical change. The samurai and their lords lost their privileged status, commoners embraced careers open to merit, and the new government sought knowledge throughout the world to strengthen imperial power, as Japan quickly industrialized and built new military forces.

But despite the modernizers' efforts to 'escape Asia'—weak and backward China— they could not avoid Eurasian geopolitics. Korea, 'a dagger pointing at the heart of Japan,' faced its own reform movement when Japan forced it open. Competing inter-ventions by Chinese, Russians, and Japanese culminated in Japan's war against China in 1895. In this final test of nearly thirty years of self-strengthening, Japan surprised most observers by winning a decisive victory over much larger Chinese forces. The British, engaged in the Great Game of geopolitical competition with the Tsarist empire in Asia, signed an alliance with Japan in 1902. Japan then astounded the world with its victory over Russia in 1905. Now Japan had put itself on the map as a major world power. Korea became a complete colony, and the Qing empire headed down the road to collapse.

We should not assume that deeply rooted differences between Japanese and Chinese culture caused such astonishingly divergent results. Japan and China shared roots in East Asian Confucian and Buddhist traditions, agrarian relations, market structures, and imperial authority. The warrior samurai of Japan, after 250 years of peace, had turned into bureaucrats like their Chinese counterparts, the literati. Yet Japan met the challenge because of its immediate response to the mortal threat of foreign imperialism. The new political leadership, calling their revolution a restoration of imperial power, mixed French, German, and British models to create a modern industrial state. Foreign loans and advisers gave Japan a boost, but the key to Japanese power was its agricultural population. The farmers paid the taxes and joined the armies, and peasant women toiled in the textile factories that led Japan's export boom.

China, by contrast, could not create a fiscal system that provided stable revenue, because its peasant population was too diverse and its local elites too powerful. After 1895, despite owing enormous indemnities to Japan, China sent thousands of young men there to learn the secrets of a modern state. A desperate effort by the young Qing emperor to promote radical reform, backed by students returning from Japan, failed in the face of determined opposition by his aunt and conservative forces in 1898. The Manchu conservatives then backed attacks on Christian Chinese and foreigners in north China by martial arts groups known as Boxers. This mass uprising brought intervention by foreign armies, the flight of the court from Beijing, further indemnities,

and humiliation. Then the Manchus themselves launched a last-gasp reform movement in 1905, abolishing the examination system and promoting new armies on the
Japanese model. It was too little too late. The Qing empire collapsed in the face of
radical nationalist movements in 1911.

Chinese and Japanese nationalism in the twentieth century also developed on
contradictory yet related paths. Each country could not escape the grip of the other;
each pursued similar goals, but tragically, for fifty years the two nations fought brutal
wars with each other. Overseas students in Japan and merchants in southeast Asia
generated the idea that China was not an empire but a nation-state. The students
picked up the powerful and seductive concept of *minzu* (*minzoku*), the Japanese
translation of the German *Volk*, for a 'people' united by deep emotional ties of blood,
soil, history, and language. They argued that the Han people, descendants of the
Yellow emperor, had formed a united race 5,000 years ago, but they suffered oppression
from the barbarian Manchus. Only a violent revolutionary nationalist movement could
throw off imperial despotism to establish a new republican government. They rejected
the arguments of reformers, inspired by England or Japan, who advocated a constitutional monarchy. Sun Yat-sen, the leader of the radical nationalists, raised funds
from the overseas communities of Southeast Asia and recruited his fighting men
from underground brotherhoods who had battled the Manchus ever since the fall of
the Ming dynasty.

After the fall of the empire and the declaration of the Republic of China on January 1,
1912, however, Sun Yat-sen realized that the new nation could not abandon its frontier
territories. He now embraced the 'five nationality' concept uniting Han, Manchus,
Mongols, Muslims, and Tibetans under a single political regime. The Republic's
political ideology blended Western constitutionalism, Japanese and German racialism,
and the socialist ideals of the Soviet Union. Ultimately, however, as Mao Zedong
predicted, political power came from the barrel of a gun. China dissolved into civil
war until the Nationalist army led by Chiang Kai-shek nominally reunited it in 1927.

Japan, despite defeating China and Russia, and controlling Korea and Taiwan, still
did not feel secure. The failure of the Republic of China to unify its territory left China
vulnerable to a free-for-all competition between the imperial powers, a competition in
which Japan had to engage. Many Japanese sympathetic to China advocated a grand
Pan-Asian alliance under Japanese leadership to expel Westerners from Asia. Some of
them respected China's classical culture, although they despised its weak modern state.
Others supported Japanese racial superiority based on the unique descent of the
Japanese people from the Sun Goddess. Still others endorsed Woodrow Wilson's
ideal of an open global order of equal nations.

But in the end, military concerns won out over economic and cultural ties. During
World War I, Japan took advantage of the European power vacuum to impose on
China its Twenty-One Demands, giving Japan predominant economic and political
influence along the Chinese coast. At the end of the war, the Versailles conference
awarded Japan Germany's leasehold territories in Shandong, enraging Chinese nationalists who had believed in Wilson. The French and British excluded all colonial

participation at Versailles (including the Vietnamese nationalist Ho Chi-minh), but recognized Japan as a fellow member of the imperialists' club. Chinese students, merchants, and urban citizens responded with the mass movement of 4 May, 1919, forcing their government to reject the Versailles treaty.

China and Japan remained locked in a tense embrace throughout the 1920s and 1930s, buffeted by the ups and downs of the global economy. Chinese boycotts of Japanese goods put pressure on Japan and promoted domestic products, but Chinese eagerly purchased fashionable Japanese exports. China and Japan competed to sell textiles and tea to the United States and Europe, but Chinese governments in Beijing financed themselves from Japanese loans. Japanese invested heavily in Manchuria's coal and iron industries, providing employment for Chinese migrants. Japanese looked to Manchuria as an enticing outlet for their impoverished rural population. Chiang Kai-shek, however, sought to extend control into Manchuria against Japanese influence.

The global depression beginning in 1929 tore apart the economic interdependency of the great powers of the world. Each of them now embraced autarky, clinging to their colonial territories and closing off their domestic markets with tariffs and immigration barriers. The United States had forbidden Asian immigration in 1924, and the Smoot-Hawley Tariff Act of 1930 sharply cut down foreign imports. Chinese and Japanese rural exporters suffered from the closure of the Southeast Asian and United States markets. China and Japan could not untangle their ties without war. In 1931, as Chiang's Nationalist government pressed on Manchuria, Japanese military forces staged a coup declaring the independent nation of Manchukuo, a puppet state of Japan. The League of Nations condemned Japan, and the United States and China refused to recognize Manchukuo, but Japan left the League of Nations to pursue an independent course.

Japanese still hoped to cooperate with China as part of a Greater East Asia Co-Prosperity Sphere that excluded Western imperial powers, but they seriously under-estimated the power of Chinese nationalism. As Chiang Kai-shek held tough against the Japanese presence in Manchuria, small border conflicts outside Beijing grew into full-scale war in 1937. Chiang's troops fought hard during their retreat to Shanghai, but Japanese military expertise once again decisively dominated China's numerically superior armies. Yet all of Japan's victories still failed to gain security or Chinese respect. When Chiang abandoned the capital of Nanjing in December 1937, Japanese troops committed an orgy of atrocities against a defenseless Chinese civilian population. Chiang retreated up the Yangzi river to the interior city of Chongqing, trading huge spaces of China for time to gather support for resistance.

At the same time, Chiang tried to eliminate his more serious enemy, the Communist Party. In 1921 a small group of students dedicated to a proletarian revolution founded the party in Shanghai. Even though workers in China were a tiny percentage of the population, they thought, like Marx and Lenin, that industrial workers would lead the revolution. Under orders from the Communist International, they joined a United Front with the Nationalists against the warlords, gaining substantial working-class support. On 30 May, 1925 they led major strikes against Japanese industrialists in Shanghai, invoking Sun Yat-sen's socialist ideals as evidence of their support for the Nationalist revolution. But when the Nationalists marched north in 1927, Chiang Kai-shek showed his true colors by unleashing criminal gangs, turning on the Communists and massacring their urban supporters.

Stalin and Trotsky, contending for leadership of the Soviet Union, furiously debated the causes of Communist failure in China. Mao Zedong, however, after the failure of urban insurrections, retreated with a small remnant to remote hills in southern China. In Jiangxi province, 1931–34, he created the first Soviet government, drawing support from poor peasants, bandits, underground brotherhoods, and refugees. Few thought that he would last long. Orthodox Communists attacked him as a mere peasant rebel.

But Mao and his party created a genuine peasant-led government, which fended off repeated attacks from Chiang's Nationalist armies. Chiang saw the Communist threat as even more dangerous than the Japanese invasion, a disease of the vitals as opposed to a disease of the skin. After five encirclement campaigns, he forced the Communists out of the Jiangxi base and into an 8,000 mile-long march to a new base area in northwest China, even more remote than Jiangxi.

If it had not been for the Japanese invasion, Mao's peasant guerrillas might have all perished in Yan'an. But when Chiang flew north to lead the final attacks on Mao, the warlord of the region instead kidnapped Chiang and forced him into a second United Front against Japan. To justify his nationalist claims, Chiang had to postpone the elimination of the Communists and grudgingly endorse joint action against Japan.

During the Second United Front, the Communists mobilized millions of peasants to support their base area in Yan'an and conducted guerrilla warfare against Japanese forces in North China. Yet they were not entirely cut off from the world. Soviet and American advisers visited them, and they supported much of the base area economy by smuggling goods through Japanese lines. Chiang Kai-shek, meanwhile, received substantial American aid after Japan attacked Pearl Harbor in 1941. To the great frustration of General Joseph Stilwell, the American military man who knew the most about China, Chiang hoarded most of his equipment to prepare for civil war after the end of the war with Japan. He preferred the uncritical support of the American air power leader, Claire Chennault, who did not press for serious reforms of the Guomindang party regime.

Both the Nationalist and Communist Parties originated as Leninist international revolutionaries, but both defied their foreign supporters. Chiang well understood the power of the American media. He and his wife, backed by Henry Luce, displayed themselves on the cover of *Time* magazine repeatedly. In 1937, they were named Man and Woman of the year, the second Asians (after Gandhi) to gain this honor. (Deng Xiaoping was the next one, in 1978.) But Chiang was not merely an American vassal. He had President Roosevelt dismiss the troublesome General Stilwell in order to preserve complete authority over conduct of the war in China. Mao, by contrast, received relatively little media or material support from the Soviet Union, because Stalin did not regard him as a genuine Communist. Mao developed his own distinct route to socialism in the caves of Yan'an.

Japan's defeat in 1945, followed by the Communist victory in China in 1949, realigned the major countries of East Asia, but tied them both to the powerful rivals of the Cold War. Chinese leaders endorsed the socialist bloc and accepted large amounts of aid from the Soviet Union, defying the American blockade. The United States occupied Japan until 1954, creating a demilitarized state which had to accept large American military bases to support the anti-Communist alliance. The Republic of China on Taiwan, the refuge of Chiang's regime, also needed the American military. But neither of the major powers in the Cold War could completely control their dependencies on their frontiers.

Koreans freed from Japan's occupation found their hopes for a unified country dashed, when the rival nationalists Kim Il-song and Syngman Rhee clashed in the Korean war of 1950. Kim Il-song's invasion of the south, backed by Stalin and reluctantly endorsed by Mao, was repulsed by United Nations forces under American leadership. When General Macarthur rashly approached the northern border, however, Chinese forces drove him back to the thirty-eighth parallel. The greatest losers in the Korean war were, besides the Koreans themselves, the Chinese, who lost thousands of men and, equally important, lost the chance to prepare for the conquest of Taiwan. The war was not a concerted plot by the Communist bloc. Kim Il-Song had dragged in his sponsors to fulfill his own ambitions.

In Vietnam, likewise, local actors pulled in great powers to serve their interests. When Japan defeated Russia in 1905, Vietnamese anti-colonialists rejoiced that an Asian power could defeat a Western nation. The French, however, successfully re-pressed all resistance movements, imprisoning large numbers of nationalists. The prisons themselves became nationalist breeding grounds by throwing together activists from all around the country.[9] The major anti-French organizing took place in neigh-boring countries, especially South China, Hong Kong, and Thailand. Ho Chi-minh, traveling with multiple aliases, constantly fleeing colonial police, was the classic border-crossing revolutionary activist, just the opposite of Mao Zedong, who never left China before his victory.

Germany's defeat of France in 1940 opened the space for Japan to free Vietnam from French domination. Ho Chi-minh took advantage of the Vichy government's paralysis to return to Vietnam and declare the August revolution of 1945, inaugurating Viet-nam's nationalist revolutionary struggle. Ho astutely garnered Soviet and Chinese support, while the French enticed the Americans to support the restoration of colo-nialism under the name of anti-Communism. The two rival regimes of North and South Vietnam battled with each other from 1954 to 1975, an essentially nationalist struggle fought under the ideologies of the Cold War. Americans and French suffered hundreds of thousands of casualties, while the Vietnamese sacrificed millions to create a united nation.

In domestic policy, China and Japan also pioneered new directions not anticipated by their great power sponsors. Although China first endorsed Stalinist economic planning centered on heavy industry, suppression of the market, collectivization of agriculture, and domination of the industrial proletariat in a single-party state, Mao soon deviated from Stalin's model. He realized that China could not simply sacrifice its peasant population for industrialization. The early collectivization campaigns succeeded where Soviet efforts had failed, giving Mao the confidence to push for giant communes uniting industry and agriculture. Mao rejected the agricultural engineer Khrushchev's warnings about limits to large-scale agricultural development, because he believed in the unlimited ability of humans to transform nature. At the same time, he challenged Khrushchev's fear of nuclear weapons and criticized his pursuit of peaceful coexistence with the capitalist West. Having confronted American forces successfully in Korea, and facing hostile Taiwan, he saw mortal threats to the socialist movement, but he embraced a Utopian vision of 'walking on two legs:' overcoming the rural–urban divide and promoting both agriculture and industry simultaneously.

Nature disagreed. The catastrophic famine of 1959–61, in which perhaps thirty million people died, the worst in world history, resulted from the clash between Mao's radical upheaval of agrarian production and the unavoidable realities of drought and flood. The famine discredited Mao's vision and allowed pragmatists led by Deng Xiaoping to free agrarian China from tight party control. Deng relied on market incentives and imported capital and technology, stating openly that black capitalists could catch mice better than white socialists. Orthodox Marxists had always rejected birth control, but the party in 1979 endorsed the world's most draconian birth control policy.

This irresistible trend toward internationalization won out over Mao's last effort to revive his vision in the Cultural Revolution of 1966–76, with the support of his last true believers, the young Red Guard movement. After Mao's death, China veered from Utopian visions of a classless society toward an equally fervent faith in the virtues of the capitalist free market, pioneering the move toward reform in the socialist world.

Japan, in its own way, also defied its main protector, the United States. In return for accepting the terms of the United States-imposed Constitution, which forbade major military forces, it gained unrestricted access to the enormous American market. Tariffs and regulations kept out foreign imports, while the state single-mindedly focused on developing world-class competitive export industries. Step by step, Japan climbed the ladder from low-cost consumer goods to the highest levels of technology and design, planning each stage, yet still calling itself capitalist. During this high-growth era, Japanese workers and unions supported company objectives instead of pressing for higher wages. When Japanese automobile exports rapidly penetrated American markets in the wake of the oil shocks of the 1970s, Japan still fended off American demands to open its own markets to imports and investment.

South Korea and Taiwan followed suit. The East Asian economic miracle, giving Japan, Korea, Taiwan, and Hong Kong growth rates of up to 10 percent per year and doubling per capita incomes in a decade, popularized theories of common Confucian values as the source of economic growth. But even though the elites of these countries often invoked shared values, the real factors were more mundane: an educated work force moving from rural to urban areas, high savings rates, substantial investment in technical education, and eager exploration of opportunities in foreign markets through personal visits, translation programs, and government planning.

This is not to say that history is irrelevant. Many of these features had roots in the preindustrial social formations of East Asia. China's rapid economic growth since the 1990s, following the 'four Asian tigers' boom in the early postwar period, indicates the close links among the countries of the East Asian region. Japanese technologies diffused throughout East Asia, and Hong Kong provided the key channel for overseas investors to get access to China. China's embrace of the global market marks a return to its historical role as a central actor in the world economy, which dates at least from the Tang dynasty. Many of the key elements of China's economic boom today have roots in the past. These include personal networks linking Chinese at home and overseas, peasants fleeing poverty to find jobs in cities or rural industries, and high savings rates directed by state banks into national investment programs.

During the past two centuries, Central Asia, by contrast, fell from being a crossroads of global trade into a colonized periphery. The Chinese and Russian empires had divided it in half by the mid-eighteenth century, eliminating the autonomous power of Mongols and Uighurs, and penetrating Tibet. The imperial powers now controlled the trade routes that crossed the region. During the nineteenth century, Chinese merchants entered Mongolia, subordinating its noble class with loans and developing wool exports to the coastal city of Tianjin. Russia created a purely colonial regime in Central Asia in the late nineteenth century, just when China made Xinjiang into a province of the empire. In the twentieth century, Outer Mongolia broke away from the Qing under Buddhist and Communist leadership, eventually putting itself under Soviet domination, while Inner Mongolia remained with China. Central Asians faced unappetizing choices between two kinds of Communist and nationalist regimes, both of which repressed their drives toward national autonomy. Tibet became the last of the vast Central Eurasian regions to come under foreign control after its failed revolt of 1959 and the Dalai Lama's flight to India.

China's greatest reform program began in 1978, two years after the death of Mao and eight years before Gorbachev initiated reform in the Soviet Union. Both countries had concluded that further growth depended on opening themselves to the capitalist world, downplaying class struggle, and encouraging individual incentives. Gorbachev and Deng Xiaoping both believed in improving socialism, not burying it, but in the critical year of 1989, the Soviet Union collapsed, while Deng authorized brutal repression to preserve the monopoly of the Communist Party.

Except for Fidel Castro's Cuba and Lukashenka's Belorussia, all the remaining Communist party-states are now in Asia. As the largest of them, China faces increasingly sharp contradictions between global incorporation and the maintenance of Party power. Remarkable economic growth has raised hundreds of millions of people out of poverty, but also created huge gaps in income, and given large shares of new wealth to corrupt party officials. Chinese who have gone abroad have returned entranced with all the trappings of cosmopolitanism, from Starbucks to the Internet, but the party-state nervously supervises their access to global culture. The government still promotes socialism, but it invites capitalists into the Party and seeks legitimacy from old-fashioned patriotism. It cooperates with international institutions on major issues like nuclear proliferation and global warming, but it tenaciously resists outside criticism on 'internal affairs' like human rights or carbon emissions. Although China has long been part of a larger world, the contradictions between outward orientation and parochialism are sharper than ever.

The other countries of East Asia have negotiated these treacherous waters in many different ways. North Korea remains the world's last unreformed Stalinist state, but Vietnam launched its own reform program, following China's lead, in 1986. Mongolia became an open democracy in 1996, which has voted the reformed Communist party back into power. The new Central Asian states range from complete dictatorships, like Turkmenistan and Uzbekistan, to states that experienced democratic revolutions, like the 'tulip' revolution of Kyrghyzstan in 2005.

On the other side of the Cold War, the legacies of bipolar conflict have become blurred. Japan is still a dependent ally of the United States but invests heavily in China. Its wartime record, however, fuels political polarization of Chinese patriots and Japanese conservatives against each other. South Korea also invests heavily in China, and South Korean male soap opera actors have become stars throughout East Asia, but relations with North Korea are tense. Taiwan's volatile politics caused it to swing from the Nationalist party to advocates of independence and back to Nationalist rule, while its economy grew and it increased its ties to the mainland. Some of these alliances repeat old patterns, going back fifty to one hundred or even five hundred years, while others are very new. The East and Central Asian societies will continue to respond actively to each other and the broader world in their own highly particular patterns, determined in large part by their previous history.

NOTES

1. Fredrik T. Hiebert, *Origins of the Bronze Age Oasis Civilization in Central Asia* (Cambridge, Mass.: Harvard University Press, 1994).
2. David Anthony, 'Horse, Wagon, and Chariots,' *Antiquity* 69 (1995), 264; and 'The Archaeology of Indo-European Origins,' *Journal of Indo-European Studies* 19: 3 (1991).
3. Elfrida Regina Knauer, 'The Queen Mother of the West: A Study of the Influence of Western Prototypes on the Iconography of the Taoist Deity,' in Victor H. Mair, ed., *Contact and Exchange in the Ancient World* (Honolulu: University of Hawai'i Press, 2006).
4. Victor H. Mair, introduction to Lao Tzu, *Tao Te Ching* (New York: Bantam, 1990).
5. Ying-shih Yü, *Trade and Expansion in Han China* (Berkeley: University of California Press, 1967).
6. Edward Schafer, *The Golden Peaches of Samarkand: A Study of T'ang Exotics* (Berkeley: University of California Press, 1963).

7. J. R. McNeill and William H. McNeill, *The Human Web: A Bird's-Eye View of World History* (New York: Norton, 2003).
8. Joseph Fletcher, 'Integrative History: Parallels and Interconnections in the Early Modern Period, 1500–1800,' in *Studies on Chinese and Islamic Inner Asia*, ed. by Beatrice Forbes Manz (Brookfield, Ver.: Variorum, 1985), 37–57.
9. Peter Zinoman, *The Colonial Bastille: A History of Imprisonment in Vietnam, 1862–1940* (Berkeley: University of California Press, 2001).

REFERENCES

BARFIELD, THOMAS J. *The Perilous Frontier: Nomadic Empires and China.* Cambridge, Mass.: Basil Blackwell, 1989.

BECKWITH, CHRISTOPHER I. *Empires of the Silk Road: A History of Central Eurasia from the Bronze Age to the Present.* Princeton: Princeton University Press, 2009.

BLUSSÉ, LEONARD VAN. *Visible Cities: Canton, Nagasaki, Batavia.* Harvard, 2008.

BROOK, TIMOTHY. *The Confusions of Pleasure: Commerce and Culture in Ming China.* Berkeley: University of California Press, 1998.

DOWER, JOHN W. *Embracing Defeat: Japan in the Wake of World War II and the Coming of the Americans.* New York: W. W. Norton, 1999.

GORDON, ANDREW. *A Modern History of Japan: From Tokugawa Times to the Present.* Oxford: Oxford University Press, 2003.

HANSEN, VALERIE. *The Open Empire: A History of China to 1600.* New York: Norton, 2000.

IRIYE, AKIRA. *China and Japan in the Global Setting.* Cambridge, Mass.: Harvard, 1992.

LEWIS, MARK EDWARD. *The Early Chinese Empires: Qin and Han.* Cambridge, Mass.: Belknap Press of Harvard University Press, 2007.

MAIR, VICTOR H., and University of Pennsylvania Museum of Archaeology and Anthropology. *Contact and Exchange in the Ancient World, Perspectives on the Global Past.* Honolulu: University of Hawai`i Press, 2006.

MARKS, ROBERT B. *The Origins of the Modern World: A Global and Ecological Narrative.* Lanham, Md.: Rowman & Littlefield, 2002.

PERDUE, PETER C. *China Marches West: The Qing Conquest of Central Eurasia.* Cambridge, Mass.: Harvard University Press, 2005.

ROSSABI, MORRIS. *Khubilai Khan: His Life and Times.* Berkeley: University of California Press, 1988.

SNOW, EDGAR. *Red Star over China.* UK, Black Cat, 1936, 1944.

SPENCE, JONATHAN D. *The Search for Modern China.* New York: Norton, 1999.

WAKEMAN, FREDERIC JR. *Strangers at the Gate: Social Disorder in South China 1839–61.* Berkeley: University of California Press, 1966.

WHITFIELD, SUSAN. *Life Along the Silk Road.* Berkeley: University of California Press, 1999.

WOODSIDE, ALEXANDER B. *Community and Revolution in Modern Vietnam.* Boston: Houghton Mifflin, 1976.

··

CHAPTER 23

SOUTH ASIA AND
SOUTHEAST ASIA

··

ANDRÉ WINK

For many centuries South Asia and Southeast Asia did not constitute two distinct regions of the world but one. This one region encompassed the bulk of the landmasses, islands and maritime spaces which were affected by the seasonal monsoon winds. Throughout its fertile and often extensive river plains it adopted recognizably similar patterns of culture and settled organization. Early geographers mostly referred to it as 'India.'

THE EXPANSION OF AGRICULTURE
AND SETTLED SOCIETY

··

The Neolithic transition from hunting and gathering to crop raising began in the relatively soft soils of what are now the Indo-Persian borderlands around 4000 BCE. Here the successful expansion of agriculture based on river inundation and irrigation gave rise to the Indus valley civilization of brick-built and walled cities which flourished between 3000 and 1500 BCE. Buried by mud, the prehistoric Indus valley cities of Harappa and Mohenjo-daro were, however, so thoroughly obliterated that hardly a trace or memory of them survived. The history of agricultural expansion and settlement elsewhere in South Asia, therefore, appears to have had no direct relationship to the precocious development of the Indus valley. In the alluvial plains of the Ganges and its tributaries such expansion began long after its demise, perhaps around 1000 BCE, when the Vedic Aryans mastered the metallurgy of iron and introduced heavy ploughs yoked to oxen and hafted axes. The use of iron equipment, probably in combination with slash-and-burn techniques, allowed land clearance to proceed eastwards, into relatively wet and thickly forested soils. It was only then that settled societies with Indian patterns of culture and organization began to emerge. Because of its unrivaled agricultural potential, the *Do-ab* or 'two-river' land of the Ganges and the Yamuna in due course came to be known as the 'heartland' of South Asia. It was here that Indian civilization began, not in the Indus valley.

In the peninsula wet rice cultivation emerged in the river deltas in the early centuries CE and soon overtook the central Tamil plain, converting it into a region of dense settlement closely resembling that of the northern heartland. In Southeast Asia too irrigated rice cultivation and settlement emerged in the drainage basins of great rivers, with similar Indian forms of culture and social organization, around the beginning of the Christian era, when the great prehistoric migrations of Melanesians, Indonesians, and Austronesians had come to an end.

By the early medieval centuries forest clearing and the process of agricultural expansion and settlement were beginning to give rise to a fragmented landscape of monarchies and lordships of varying dimensions and importance in the plains of all great river systems of South Asia and Southeast Asia. Everywhere peasant societies continued to grow in size and complexity and provided the foundation for a new political order.

At the same time peasants continued to live in the midst of immense forests and other sparsely inhabited lands, including deserts. Even at the end of the medieval centuries 'the wilds' still accounted for as much as 70–80 percent of the land surface of the region, while no more than 20–30 percent was settled. In both South Asia and Southeast Asia the expansion of agriculture and settlement would continue until the present. Europe, by comparison, reached its ecological limits much earlier and, due to deforestation, came to the brink of a nutritional and fuel disaster from which it was saved in the sixteenth century only by the introduction of coal and New World crops like potatoes and maize. South Asia and Southeast Asia demonstrated a potential for internal agricultural expansion and population growth far exceeding that of Europe and other parts of the Old World.

KINGS AND BRAHMANS

Superseding the thinly spread empires that integrated the trade routes of ancient times and were loosely Buddhist in orientation, the political order that emerged in the nuclear zones of agricultural settlement throughout South Asia and Southeast Asia in early medieval times typically consisted of a condominium of Hindu kings and Brahmans. This was a virtually new dispensation. None of the early medieval royal Hindu dynasties can be traced back to a period prior to the seventh century. Although their kings claimed to be reincarnates of the ancient kshatriya nobility (which we only know from the epic literature), they were more often than not of obscure, pastoral origins, sometimes from outside the subcontinent. The Brahmans too occupied a rather subaltern position as ritualistic priests prior to the seventh century. Now, in the emerging regional Hindu kingdoms they came to preside over monumental temple complexes, built with permanent materials like brick and stone, in which the gods and goddesses of the Hindu pantheon were enshrined for worship in elaborate cults and rituals. Early medieval Hinduism was the religious expression of the new vertical linkages that characterized the growth of settled monarchical states. Migratory movements of Brahmans from the older agricultural nuclear zones, especially those of the northern heartland, accompanied such growth everywhere in South Asia, and to a remarkable degree in Sri Lanka and the plains of Southeast Asia as well. In Sri Lanka, to be sure, the expansion of wet rice cultivation and agrarian settlement was accompanied by the spread of Buddhism among the rural population from the start. But here Buddhism developed as a peasant religion with a close resemblance to Hinduism in many of its basic social and political forms, quite unlike and in some essential respects the very opposite of the cosmopolitan Buddhism of the trading world of ancient India. Although they never acquired as prominent a role in Sri Lanka as they did in the subcontinent, there was a persistent and influential presence of Brahmans in Sinhalese society. Moreover, this presence appears to have expanded over time, and the Sinhalese Buddhist kings ended up making lavish donations to them, including land and villages. In the equally hybrid Hindu-Buddhist political formations of agricultural Southeast Asia the presence of large numbers of Brahmans is also attested everywhere. Even in those areas that went over to Buddhism in medieval times, such as Myanmar, Thailand, and Cambodia, Brahmans were not eliminated until as late as the sixteenth century. Here too Buddhism developed as a peasant religion.

Among the settled populations temporal and religious leadership and resources were inextricably intertwined. There is an almost limitless Hindu-Buddhist literature that made the absorption of the secular into the religious realm its central concern. This literature reflects a virtually universal and deeply-rooted belief in the innate divinity of kings in all medieval states. It was only in theory that divine incarnation was incompatible with the Buddhism of Sri Lanka and the mainland states of Southeast Asia. In the latter areas, in practice, the idea of divine incarnation of kings was replaced by the idea of rebirth through religious merit but never excluded the notion of a hereditary and quasi-divine right to the throne. In effect, the belief in divine incarnation of either Shiva or Vishnu survives in the coronation rituals of the Buddhist kings of Thailand and Cambodia of this day. The reason the Brahmans monopolized the sacerdotal functions and were regarded as indispensable at almost all medieval courts—whether Hindu or Buddhist—was always the same. Ultimate religious authority was vested in the Brahmans and not in the divine kings themselves. Since the temporal order upheld by the kings was fundamentally defective, the latter remained dependent on the spiritual power of the superior Brahmans. The texts, therefore, generally regarded the cooperation of kings and Brahmans as essential for the realization of the moral order or dharma.

The much expanded epigraphic record of medieval times thus points at the growth and advance of the agrarian economy and settled society, divine kingship in association with Brahman power, as well as a sharp increase in the size and importance of the Brahman caste in high positions, including pioneering ones in forest clearing. At the same time it provides evidence of the spread and consolidation of a much broader caste ideology in combination with an ever more minute division of labor. Caste came to prevail widely among the settled peasantry, ruling elites, and specialist mercantile and service groups in the zones of long-standing cultivation and dense populations in the Ganges plains, Tamil Nadu, and Malabar. Beyond such regions of early settlement, among the people of the forests and hills, martial pastoralists, inhabitants of the seaboard and domains not yet fully penetrated by agriculture, caste distinctions appear to have held little or no meaning. In the peripheral areas of Sind or Bengal caste existed but was not very elaborate or deeply rooted anywhere. In the Hindu-Buddhist countries outside the subcontinent it was not uncommon to find social hierarchies organized as caste systems but stripped of their religious connotations. In Sri Lanka the social hierarchy developed a mere formal resemblance to the theoretical scheme of the four varnas or social classes that is generally seen as the theoretical foundation of the Indian caste system. Here caste rules were much less rigid than in the subcontinent and religious notions of purity and pollution had no meaning for Sinhalese Buddhists, nor did untouchability. In practice it operated more like the customary law of the Buddhist laity, a secular code of conduct inseparable from the system of government that was maintained by the kings in cooperation with the Brahmans and the Buddhist sangha, and inseparable from the system of land ownership. The agrarian societies of the inland Hindu kingdoms of Java and Bali, however, developed profound and rigid caste hierarchies of their own. The fourteenth-century kings of the Javanese state of Majapahit, for instance, regarded themselves as the custodians of a religiously sanctioned social hierarchy based on tribute flows from the periphery to the center which was reminiscent of an Indian-style caste system and regarded all movement outside the control of the territorial state as subversive.

Even if caste was practically absent, as in mainland Southeast Asia, more or less formal social hierarchies emerged in the context of agricultural expansion and settled life. Hindu-Buddhist religious belief systems and practices sanctified the settled order of agrarian life everywhere. In Sri Lanka and mainland Southeast Asia long-distance trade, for this reason, was typically in the hands of Chinese or Muslim religious minorities. In South Asia itself, religious law books imposed severe restrictions on maritime travel for high-caste Hindus, especially if they were women. Hindu merchants, as well as their Jain counterparts, when away from home, appear to have remained women-less sojourners rather than to have settled abroad permanently. They virtually never intermarried with the local populations. Such were the conditions prevailing among Hindus and Jains in East Africa, the Red Sea, Central Asia, Persia, Melaka, and wherever else they were to be found in medieval and early modern times.

A GRAVEYARD OF CITIES

A wide-ranging new study concludes that 'the Mediterranean has probably been the most durably and densely urbanized region in world history.'[1] Cities like Athens, Rome, Alexandria, Antioch, Constantinople, Marseille, Cordoba, Barcelona, Pisa, Florence, Venice, and many others have been prominent centers of power and civilization over many centuries, and indeed, in some cases, millennia. More than anywhere, the political culture of the Mediterranean centered upon the city. For philosophers like Aristotle, there was no life beyond the limits of the *polis* or 'city,' except that of beasts and gods. From that original conception of the *polis* derives the entire European lexicon of 'politics.' Correspondingly, the long tradition of Mediterranean historiography has always privileged towns and cities, elevating them to a highly distinctive and supremely significant category, and the ultimate locus of change, progress and modernization. In Fernand Braudel's words, Mediterranean-European cities were 'electric transformers.'

The shifting mud and water masses of the immense and flat alluvial river plains of monsoon Asia, by contrast, were hardly conducive to urban development and continuity. Abrupt changes in the river courses and the retreat of the sea caused by heavy silting were a major source of urban disruption. So were earthquakes, particularly in the relatively young and still-moving northern mountain zone of the subcontinent, and in Sind and the Panjab. Indonesia's eighty-five volcanoes destroyed numerous cities—indeed, the annihilation in 1883 of the volcano island of Krakatau has become a byword for cataclysmic disaster. Add to this what we know of frequent cyclones, tsunamis caused by sub-oceanic tectonic plate movements, as well as desiccation caused by climate change, and a picture emerges of South Asia and Southeast Asia as the world region with possibly the most extreme environmental instability throughout recorded history—a graveyard of cities. Harappa, Mohenjo-daro, Ayudhya, Kanauj, Cambay, Cranganore, Gaur, Melaka, Angkor, Shrivijaya, Anuradhapura, and Polonnaruva are some of the most famous casualties on the list. There are many more. Archaeology provides evidence of abandoned settlements and dead cities—including many nameless ones—everywhere in the region.

In Sind, according to Richard Burton, 'Deserts spring up, cities, ports and towns fall in the space of time which it takes the Indus to shift its bed for a few miles . . . Except in a few cases, it is vain to speculate on the topography of the country fifty years ago.'[2] If the shifts and westering of the Indus River with all its tributaries, and the drying up of the Saraswati, played a key role in the destruction of the prehistoric cities of Harappa and Mohenjo-daro, the effects of later shifts of the same river system on the cities of medieval Sind—Debal, Alor, or the Arab capital of Mansura—as well as the early modern Muslim cities of Thatta, Multan, Lahore, or Muhammad Tor, while varied, were much the same and no less disastrous. Throughout the Indo-Gangetic plains river shifts have been so frequent that the sites of many cities and towns cannot be recovered. We know that the entire Bengal river system has moved to the east and underwent profound modifications between the twelfth and seventeenth centuries, and while this made vast new areas inhabitable in the delta, here too numberless cities have been buried in the marshes. In the lowlands of the peninsula the mutability of rivers was almost as great, as it was in the Gulf of Cambay, the Konkan, and on the Malabar coast. In Southeast Asia, all rivers that emptied out on the shallow Sunda platform are fringed with huge, flat marshlands with frequently migrating rivers and river bed sedimentation. The distribution channels of the Chao Phraya, in Thailand, have also changed their courses in medieval times; they once ran much further to the west, where there are now large areas of bush land and historic ruins along the former channels. Everywhere south of Thailand and outside Java, river-mouth city-states were the rule, and, ephemeral in their physical layout, rose and fell with striking rapidity. Shrivijaya, the epitome of these river-mouth city states, was situated in a coastal march produced by prolonged sedimentation of the tropical rivers flowing eastward from the Barisan mountains into the shallow sea of the Strait of Melaka. Such sedimentation, beginning at least five thousand years ago, was aided by volcanic eruptions, accompanied by mud-flows which swept down loose ashes, in inner Sumatra in medieval times, as well as by forest cutting, heavy rainfall, and tectonic movement, and produced very rapid changes in the coastline and the decline of many kingdoms in the eastern parts of the island, in the thirteenth century contributing significantly to the decline of Shrivijaya as well. As in Sumatra, in Java little kingdoms are known to have been wiped out in a few hours by volcanic eruptions, and hydrological instability, aggravated by these eruptions, had a destructive impact everywhere in the alluvial plains of the Solo and the Brantas rivers.

Such instability of the environment made urbanism labile and hence hard to sustain. To make it worse, historical cities in South Asia and Southeast Asia were almost entirely made of easily perishable materials (mud, bamboo, thatch, palm leaves, wood), with brick and stone reserved for religious architecture, palaces, and fortresses. With little or no permanent infrastructure, cities were barely distinguishable from extended villages, and historians have sometimes referred to them as 'rurban' rather than urban settlements. Rurban settlements could suffer depopulation with dazzling speed, complete desolation following in its wake. 'Labile rurbanism' was enhanced by demographic fluctuations related to the seasonal character of the monsoon, peripatetic elite mobility, frequent migrations caused by invasions, famines, epidemics, and droughts, as well as the general volatility of political life.

Without a continuous tradition of urban life anywhere, we look in vain for an ancient heritage that significantly shaped the medieval and modern cultures of South Asia and Southeast Asia. As mentioned, the prehistoric Indus cities of Harappa and Mohenjo-daro passed on little, if anything, to later settlement forms, urban, 'rurban' or otherwise. The marketplace orientation of Buddhism was becoming a thing of the past by early medieval times. There was no specific imperial legacy associated with the ancient dynasties of the Mauryas (326–184 BCE) and Guptas (320–550 CE). Virtually no ancient cities survived, no roads, and no monuments. Indian architecture began almost from scratch in medieval not ancient times. Even though the Indian lexicon of politics, religion, and social organization (including caste) can ultimately be traced to ancient times, its practical implementation had to wait until the beginnings of medieval times. It was not until then that the conditions of settled life—peasant culture, Brahman literati, and divine kingship—made such implementation possible on a general basis. Thus, while the European Middle Ages were a series of 'renaissances' of the ancient urban traditions of Athens and Rome—in the Carolingian period, then in the twelfth century, and finally at the dawn of the great Renaissance—India had to invent its ancient identity from rare surviving literary (mainly epic) sources, and there was no *translatio imperii* of the kind that made possible the establishment of a new order in Europe.

Geography and the World-Historical Context

The Indian historical experience is not defined by the bounded space of the ancient city or *polis* and its later imperial incarnations but by the proximity of the vast open spaces of desert and sea—the nomadic frontier and the maritime frontier.

South Asia is ecologically positioned at the southeastern end of the world's largest continuous arid zone. This 'Saharasian' arid zone runs from the Sahara to Arabia and the Levant, to the Persian plateau, then northwards to Central Asia, Mongolia, and parts of China, and connects with and extends deeply into South Asia itself—about half of the subcontinental landmass receives less than 3.28 feet of rainfall per year and can, on this account, be regarded as an extension of the great arid zone. Everywhere the ecology of the arid zone posed severe restrictions on settled agriculture, and hence its characteristic mode of production was pastoral nomadism of one form or another. This situation made South Asia a zone of transition between the pastoral-nomadic world of the 'Saharasian' arid zone and the humid, equatorial parts of Southeast Asia where intensive agriculture was practiced in river plains enclosed by rain forests. South Asia, but not Southeast Asia, was, as a result, exposed to the great nomadic movements and tribal migrations that occurred across the length and breadth of the arid zone through-out recorded history and especially in medieval times.

Among the earliest archaeological evidence of nomadic penetration into South Asia are *tumuli* found in Rajasthan, containing ashes and arms, which are reminiscent of the Scythian royal tombs or 'pyramids of the steppe' described by Herodotus. Sanskrit sources, in effect, point out how 'impure' nomadic Scythians (or *Shakas*, as they call them) have been moving from their steppe lands into South Asia probably as early as the third century BCE. Western Rajasthan was part of 'Indo-Skythia,' a nomadic territory coterminous with a large part of the arid zone of north-western India up to Sind and what are now the Afghan borderlands. This was also the territory that was absorbed in the empire of the Kushana 'royal horde,' an offshoot of the nomadic Yuezhi of Gansu, which reached deeply into the subcontinent in the early centuries CE. Still later, in the fifth century CE, the same territory was absorbed in the empire of the nomadic Hephthalites or 'White Huns.'

From its earliest beginnings, the presence of nomadic Scythians, Kushanas, and Hephthalites along the northwest frontier of the subcontinent was a crucial factor in the development of trade routes. The nomadic Turks, Mongols, and Afghans that came to South Asia in medieval times had a still bigger impact. The later part of the first millennium and the first half of the second millennium CE were a time during which the arid zone underwent important changes everywhere. Some of these changes were due to a combination of climatological and demographic factors associated with a medieval warming period.[3] Warm temperatures particularly affected horse-breeding nomads because horses, due to their inefficient digestive system, cannot easily survive on dried-out, low-protein grass, and even a slight rise in temperature could necessitate major migrations among the Turks and Mongols of the steppes that were entirely dependent on horse breeding. Changes in military capability and organization also provided part of the drive behind the medieval nomadic conquest movements and migrations into South Asia and other world areas with substantial sedentary populations such as Persia, China, and Russia. Among these were the enhanced effectiveness of mounted archery, the invention and spread of the stirrup, and improved body armor made of iron. Such factors, in combination with new modes of military and political organization that allowed them to overcome the limitations of their earlier tribal cultures, made horse-riding nomads militarily superior over sedentary people and hence hard to resist in their southward and eastward movements.

In the extensions of the arid zone in South Asia, however, pastoral nomadism as such quickly reached its natural limits because here it came to be closely associated with agriculture and settled society. These areas were exposed to the nomadic frontier but they were at the tail end of it and ecologically unable to accommodate large numbers of practicing pastoral nomads. Except in a few places in Afghanistan, Baluchistan, and Sind—ancient Indo-Skythia—pastoral nomads moving into South Asia had to adapt themselves to a mixed pastoral-sedentary environment and the overwhelming majority of them, for this reason, had to leave their nomadic mode of production behind. Effectively, these nomads turned themselves into a post-nomadic ruling elite in a society of settled peasants.

Turks, Mongols, and Afghans, while abandoning their nomadic life and becoming dependent on horse imports, boosted the importance of the extensions of the arid zone in South Asia in other ways, giving more power to previously marginal groups living on the peripheries of the old nuclear zones of settled cultivation. As a result, the mobilization of agrarian resources was vastly enhanced everywhere, while trade and the role of precious metals also increased again, and commercial and financial groups acquired a much higher profile. New military, political and commercial networks of unprecedented intensity came into play at the interface of arid zone and settled agriculture. Thus, even though the extensions of the arid zone in South Asia were of limited use for pastoral nomadism of any kind, and were especially unsuitable for horse breeding, they did provide increasingly important corridors for traffic and movement in an ecosystem that was otherwise primarily geared to settled agriculture. But, unlike Persia, China, or the Russian steppe, the influx of nomads into medieval South Asia did not bring about an increase of pastoral nomadism as such and over the long term did not bring agricultural expansion to a halt.

On the maritime frontier seafaring people played a similar role to that of pastoral nomads in the subcontinental extensions of the arid zone. In both cases unrestrained and rapid movement, the violent appropriation of mobile wealth by raiding, and long-distance trade were part of the normal adaptation to an ecosystem. The Indian Ocean was comparable in size to the great arid zone—an almost equally vast, uninhabited and dangerous second frontier of settled society which was easily accessible almost everywhere because of the prevailing monsoon winds (which were mastered by navigators as early as the first century CE) and a potential source of immense wealth. Both the nomadic and the maritime frontier were conduits of precious metals—the essence of mobile wealth—and a domain of unsociability. Just as Scythian nomads were regarded as 'impure' in the Sanskrit literature, the 'people of the sea' and 'sea nomads' of various stripes in the Malay-Indonesian archipelago were held in contempt as 'a low, vile people' prone to piracy and slave raiding by the land-based Malay. The seaboard—indistinguishable from a desert—was a place of extraordinary license and moral ambiguity, its fish- and meat-eating inhabitants occupying the bottom rungs of the caste order or simply regarded as outcasts and heretics. Only the vaguest distinctions prevailed here between trade, customs collection, slave raiding, and piracy.

AN INDO-ISLAMIC WORLD

This twofold frontier of mobile wealth—nomadic and maritime—largely developed under the aegis of Islam.[4] More than any other civilization before the onset of modern times, early Islamic civilization was founded on the unrestrained mobility of men and goods across great distances and the free circulation (*rawāj*) of precious metals. Athwart the most barren but strategically best situated parts of the arid zone, the Arabs, making use of the camel, were able to link the Mediterranean and the Indian Ocean in a single economic exchange network and thereby came to dominate all important maritime and caravan trade routes, with the exception only of the northern silk route (which remained contested by the Tang Chinese and the Tibetans) and one major trade center, Byzantium. Gold seized from the Sasanid palaces of Persia, the Byzantine churches and monasteries of Syria, and the Pharaonic tombs of Egypt, booty and newly minted gold and silver from supplies obtained in places as far afield as the Sudan (West Africa), the Caucasus, Armenia, the Ponto-Caspian steppe, Central Asia and Tibet, Southeast Asia, Sofala, Nubia, and northern Ethiopia, were brought into circulation and ensured the preeminence of a new and unified Islamic currency system based on the gold dinar and the silver dirham as a standard for global trade. All other institutions of the early Islamic world—from its extensive network of trade routes to its fiscal systems and slave armies—reflected, above all, the overriding importance of its cash nexus and mercantilist preoccupation with mobile wealth.

While Sind, Baluchistan, and the Makran coast, and Zabul and Kabul, were incorporated into the Umayyad (661–750) and early Abbasid Caliphates (750–1258), the first truly Indo-Islamic dynasty to straddle the divide between the nomadic arid zone and the settled river plains was that of the Ghaznavids (977–1186). In the medieval centuries the Ghaznavids were followed by the Ghurids (1186–1206), the 'Slave Kings' (1206–1290), the Khalajis (1290–1320), the Tughluqs (1320–1414), the Sayyids (1414–1451), and the Lodis (1451–1526). These were all dynasties which understood it to be their historic mission to extend or consolidate Indo-Islamic rule, rather than convert native populations, and made Delhi their capital. By the fifteenth century there was also a number of regional Indo-Islamic dynasties—notably in Bengal, Kashmir, Sind, Gujarat, Malwa, Khandesh, and the Deccan—that had gained strength at the expense of the Indo-Islamic dynasties of Delhi after Timur's momentous raid on the city in 1398. Releasing the dethesaurized wealth of Hindu temples and other treasure into a rapidly expanding money economy, this broad array of medieval Indo-Islamic states developed an unprecedented capacity to mobilize revenue and commercial resources. At first they had few formal and enduring institutions that can in any way be regarded as characteristic of an emerging but distinctive Indo-Islamic form of dominion and politically revolved around strife among competing horse warrior elites, many of slave origin, recruited from the nomadic frontier with cash, and ad hoc contests of strength. Administered by post-nomadic, poly-ethnic elites of Turks, Mongols, and Afghans without formal criteria of admission, and without fixed hierarchies of offices, these states for a long time continued to be immensely volatile, with dynastic succession in constant jeopardy. A watershed in the growth of specifically Indo-Islamic institutions was the immigration of numerous Muslim scholars and theologians from the Muslim lands devastated by the 'infidel' Mongols in the thirteenth century. These were not nomads even in origin but fugitive sedentaries. As a result partly of their presence, Iltutmish (ruled 1211–36) became the first Indo-Islamic ruler to receive sanction from Baghdad, receiving the Caliphal emissaries in 1228–29. From that date onwards the sanctification of a new Indo-Islamic homeland proceeded apace. Mosques were erected (often from the rubble of destroyed Hindu temples), Islamic prayer was introduced by cadres of religious clergy, Islamic law was dispensed by jurists. By the first decades of the fourteenth century the dynastic fortune of Indo-Islamic states came to be closely associated with the home-grown Sufi order of the Chishtis. Indo-Islamic rulers also promoted the immigration of dissident fringe groups of Mongols (Qara'unas, Nögödaris, Jurma'is, and the like) who were eager to take up military service and convert. Contemporary chronicles single them out for their extraordinary cruelty and unsubdued predatory instincts, the rapidity of their movements and general lack of discipline, and refer to such military converts as New Muslims. By contrast, contemporary historical chronicles say very little or nothing about the conversion of large numbers of Hindus. Up to the late thirteenth century, the conversion of Hindu 'infidels' enslaved during military campaigns, especially women and children, was probably numerically more important than the proselytizing efforts of Muslim mystics. In the fourteenth and fifteenth centuries native conversion was becoming more widespread, but mainly in the peripheral and still unsettled parts of the subcontinent and away from the Indo-Islamic capitals. The greater part of the population of the Kashmir valley converted in the reign of Sikandar Butshikan (1389–1413). In Bengal, conversion by Sufis and other Muslim religious elites occurred on an extensive scale on the frontier of settled society, among peripheral forest tribes gradually turning themselves into sedentary peasants during a period of land reclamation made possible by the eastward shifting of the Ganges and its tributary rivers.[5] The proliferation of numerous rural mosques in the countryside indicates this process was well under way by the later fifteenth century, and continued in the sixteenth and seventeenth centuries.

Newly emerging patterns of political dominance in the Deccan and the peninsula between the twelfth and thirteenth centuries strikingly resemble those of the emerging Indo-Islamic states. Here the most important dynasties were the Yadavas of Devagiri, ruling in the western Deccan and the Maratha country as far south as the Krishna River, the Hoysalas of Dvarasamudram in Karnataka, and the Kakatiyas of Warangal in Telangana. These dynasties had their origins in the ecologically marginal arid zone in the interior, where pastoral nomadism (of sheep, goats, and buffalo rather than horses) prevailed, and had levels of mobility not found in any of the settled parts of the peninsula but comparable, albeit on a much smaller scale, to those prevalent in the steppe lands. Across the peninsula, from the late twelfth and thirteenth centuries onwards, pastoral-nomadic people from the upland, arid zone, representing a relatively non-hierarchical and individualistic society of great dynamism and high risk tolerance sharply at odds with the conservatism of settled caste society, increasingly established their control over the fertile, densely populated kingdoms of the plains. Their rise to power was not accompanied by conversion to Islam but by the adoption of militant forms of Hindu devotionalism such as Virashaivism. The subsequent rise of the great Hindu empire of Vijayanagara in the fourteenth and fifteenth centuries followed similar patterns—its deities typically had the attributes of the fierce warriors of the pastoral communities of the inland southern Deccan. Everywhere in the peninsula the recruitment of large contingents of Muslim mounted archers from the north, which had started as early as the 1140s among the Hoysalas, reached a peak in the fourteenth and fifteenth centuries and was accompanied by stepped-up imports of superior horses through the seaports. An entirely new peninsular imperial order arose, with extensive forms of monetization and fiscalism closely resembling those of the Indo-Islamic states to the north and condemning the older areas of settlement in the plains to complete subordination. Throughout the subcontinent, the new capitals of the post-nomadic dynasties of the first half of the second millennium, including Delhi, Devagiri, Dvarasamudram, Warangal, and then Bijapur, Golkonda and Vijayanagara, were located on the fringes of the arid or semi-arid zone. On the interface of the world of the marches and the settled world, these eccentric new capitals could mediate between sedentary investment and the mobilization of the resources of pastoralists, military entrepreneurs, and merchants.

There were no ecological niches for pastoral nomads of any kind, let alone for horse nomads, in the mainland of Southeast Asia or the Malay-Indonesian archipelago. The

Mongol incursions into the mainland of Southeast Asia appear to have been mere incidents, with no lasting consequences except some reshuffling of power among local dynasties. The medieval development of the mainland was therefore characterized, above all, by the earliest territorial consolidation, administratively focused on the Buddhist sangha, of settled states and channeled through the region's north–south segmentation, with no sustained influx of nomadic or post-nomadic horse warriors anywhere. While South Asia went through a horse warrior revolution and incipient Islamization, mainland Southeast Asia did not participate in either of these processes. It is striking however that the medieval centuries which witnessed the emergence of post-nomadic Indo-Islamic states in South Asia also witnessed the rise and expansion of many important coastal centers and maritime people undergoing rapid Islamization throughout the Indian Ocean—in ports such as Kilwa, Hormuz, Cambay, Calicut, Melaka, Ayudhya, Phnom Penh, Samudra-Pasai, Gresik, Tuban, Demak, Jakatra, and Banten, among many others. The increased dynamism of the maritime frontier had much in common with that of the post-nomadic states in the subcontinent. Characterized by a high degree of unregulated and even lawless competition, the coastal centers were similarly open in physical and economic terms, pluralistic in political terms, and Indo-Islamic in cultural terms. Throughout the Indian Ocean this was an age of rapidly expanding commerce. Trade with China became overwhelmingly important, especially after 1277, when the Mongol emperor Kublai Khan established his power over the coastal provinces of southeastern and southern China and the drain of China's metallic currencies towards the Indian Ocean accelerated, at the same time that the presence of Chinese Muslim mercantile communities made itself felt everywhere. Indispensable in the formation of Indo-Islamic coastal states were also the 'sea nomads,' that is, the *orang laut*, *moken*, and *sama bajau*, in the Malay-Indonesian archipelago. Emerging on the frontier of settled society, like pastoral nomads, they were active in the primary arena of Malay political history and played a key role in the development of the naval power and communicative links upon which the hegemony of successive Malay states in the throes of Islamization was based, bringing together courts, subsidiary chiefs, and a developing peasantry in a zone of otherwise sparse population.

PATHWAYS TO EARLY MODERNITY

Historians have raised the specter of an early modern world, and of large-scale, often global or near-global, parallel and interconnected developments which define such an early modern world.[6] Even though disagreement remains about what constitutes an exact tell-tale list of these developments, a rough consensus has emerged about some of the most important ones.

Pastoral nomadism declined in importance between 1500 and 1800 CE and there was, due to a dual process of sedentarization of nomads and the spread of gunpowder weapons, a shift of power towards settled populations and increasingly large and well-integrated territorial states. These same centuries saw intensified land use and internal colonization accompanied by rural unrest and a decline of peasant prosperity as well as significant and at times rapid population growth (everywhere except in the Americas). European exploration and dominance of global sea passages created a true world economy for the first time. Everywhere the role of urban commercial classes increased substantially, and religious reformations, accompanied by wider literacy and the proliferation of vernacular texts together with new types of literature of humanist inspiration, among these urban classes completed the transition to early modernity in many, if not most, parts of the world.

The empire of the Mughals which successfully imposed itself on much of South Asia in the sixteenth to eighteenth centuries fits this paradigm of an emerging early modern world remarkably well. The dynasty claimed descent from the notorious Turko-Mongol steppe conquerors Chinggis Qan (died 1227) and Timur (1336–1405), but by the second half of the sixteenth century was turning its back on its nomadic legacy. The third Mughal emperor Akbar (ruled 1556–1605), his Indo-Afghan rivals overcome by tribal division, created an early modern 'gunpowder' empire that became legendary for its wealth and power. Akbar introduced a clearly articulated and enforced system of monetized 'ranks' (mansabs) and transformed the post-nomadic horde of Turko-Mongol horsemen of his immediate ancestors into a service nobility with a new uniformity, discipline, and cohesiveness. Awash in New World and Japanese silver, and in close collaboration with the ubiquitous Hindu banking and financier castes, a new fiscal system and bureaucracy were developed, based on scientific surveys, which became effective instruments for the sustained and regularized collection of unprecedented amounts of revenue—the imperial enterprise becoming a business enterprise. The closing of the nomadic frontier resulted in an increased emphasis on the Indian foundations of the empire, more specifically an alliance with the landed aristocracy of the Rajputs. This was a policy that went hand in hand with the adoption of a new political theology aimed as much at inclusion as intensified control of a multi-denominational subject population. Akbar, in effect, presided over the beginnings of an early modern reformation of religious thought which, across South Asia, emphasized restraint by reason, discipline, orderly conduct, the efficient management of time, and methodical work habits, while banning prostitution, hard drinking, and drug abuse.

Meanwhile the Portuguese, within fifteen years after their arrival, destroyed Muslim naval power in Indian waters, and their king could style himself Lord of the Conquest, Navigation and Commerce of Ethiopia, Arabia, Persia, and India. As Albuquerque wrote home in 1513, 'at the rumour of our coming the (native) ships all vanished and even the birds ceased to skim over the water.' The Portuguese, followed by the Dutch and English East India Companies, assumed the sovereignty of the sea, thereby bringing the medieval openness of the Indian Ocean to an end—a development made possible by the gunned ships introduced in Atlantic Europe in the course of the fourteenth and fifteenth centuries.

When these gunned ships arrived in the Indian Ocean hardly anything could resist them, although in practice the effects of the closing of the maritime frontier remained inconclusive and patchy until well into the seventeenth century. Over the long term they were fundamentally the same as those of the closing of the pastoral nomadic frontier. With their origins in the great medieval upheavals of the *orang laut* and similar people of the sea, a broad range of *pasisir* or 'coastal' principalities from Malabar and North Sumatra to Melaka, Java, and the Sulu archipelago, embraced Islam during the so-called 'spice orgy' which attended the world's recovery from the Black Death pandemic of the mid-fourteenth century. Then, in the later sixteenth century, the dynasty of the preeminent Javanese *pasisir* state of Demak conquered the last significant Hindu-Buddhist state of Pajajaran, in the interior of Java. Superseding Demak, two new states emerged in the central-Javanese interior, at Pajang and Mataram (located at the present-day cities of Surakarta and Yogyakarta). These states, with rich agricultural economies but with little involvement in maritime trade, completely disengaged from the increasingly Dutch-dominated *pasisir* of Java. Sultan Agung (ruled 1613–46) established the hegemony of Mataram in east and central Java, as well as in Madura, and devastated the coastal towns, forcing seafaring Javanese to move to Bantam, Palembang, Makassar, and Banjarmasin. From this time onwards, up to the early nineteenth century, central Java once again became the heartland of a powerful all-Javanese state and of a specifically Javanese courtly culture. Surrounded by the monumental Hindu and Buddhist relics of Borobudur and Prambanan, the Muslim empire of Mataram was deeply rooted in Indian and old-Javanese patterns. With the Dutch East India Company establishing itself as the dominant naval power in the archipelago, Javanese society turned inward and became relatively closed to cultural influences from overseas, although, in characteristically early modern fashion, there was considerable development of the money economy and tax-farming and toll-farming by Chinese middlemen became widespread, while intra-Javanese traffic by water and overland increased. Similar developments occurred slightly later in the mainland states of Southeast Asia, although here the break was less dramatic due to the relative marginality of maritime trade in this subregion. Muslim trade still played a role in Thailand and Cambodia in the sixteenth and seventeenth centuries. The Chams of Phnom Penh, Persians and Chulias from South India, and Malay traders dominated the overland routes then. But by the eighteenth century the mainland states had effectively fortified themselves against outside penetration and influence, re-organizing themselves around a territorially defensive Buddhist sangha and precluding Islam from making further headway here.

EUROPEAN IMPERIALISM AND ITS AFTERMATH

If the individual elements of early modernity varied in form, scale, and duration, while in many places one or more of its traits was entirely absent, it would not necessarily have led to full modernity anywhere. In 1800 neither South Asia nor Southeast Asia was on the verge of an industrial revolution. European imperialism decisively began to shape the further modernization of both regions in the nineteenth and twentieth centuries, but with lopsided results. With some simplification it can be argued that British imperialism in South Asia led to considerable political modernization but little economic modernization, while British, Dutch, and French imperialism in Southeast Asia led to some economic modernization but little political modernization. These lopsided results have begun to be redressed only in the most recent decades.

The British commercial presence in South Asia developed into full-scale imperial dominion or 'Company Raj' between 1757 and 1857/8. Throughout the second half of the eighteenth century great profits continued to be made in the trade of Bengal opium with China. By 1809, however, the Company had ceased to be a profitable commercial concern and began to look to land for revenue. Land revenue had been the foundation of the Mughal Raj, and it was to be crucial for the Company Raj as well. It remained so after the Mutiny of 1857/8, a significant challenge to British control in large parts of the subcontinent that was successfully overcome but led to the abolition of the Company and the introduction of an emphatically anti-reformist Crown Rule. Land revenue settlements provided the bulk of the financial resources to pay for British rule and were by far the most important administrative enterprise undertaken by the British-Indian government. But they were not revolutionary instruments of change. Everywhere in South Asia agriculture remained as much a gamble on the monsoon as it had always been. By the end of the nineteenth century nearly half of the agricultural acreage was under millet grains and pulses while the high-yielding and more dynamic rice was confined to the most populous areas of the north and east. Shortfalls in production remained inevitable, although there is evidence to show that the rate of expansion of cultivation matched the expansion of the population from under 200 million in 1800 to 285 million in 1901. There were frequent famines, particularly in the late 1870s and late 1890s. All that changed, to some extent, was the nature of production—a wide range of commercial crops was introduced and South Asia became a net exporter of raw cotton, rice, opium, wheat, tea, and raw jute.

Reflecting the Utilitarian assumption that improvement and modernization would follow judicial enactment, the main constructive impact of British imperialism in the early nineteenth century came with social and legal reform. Far from any spontaneous industrial take-off in 1800, there were still no modern factories in South Asia by 1850, and there was only some modern industrialization during the second half of the nineteenth century, pioneered by the Bombay cotton and Calcutta jute industry, next to a notable development of railroads and other technological infrastructure. Obsessed with its own security, the post-Mutiny government did not forge a wider fiscal base for itself. Unlike Japan or Russia, British India lacked the sense of national consent for a state-sponsored industrial development push. Moreover, in the face of persistent capital shortage throughout the nineteenth century and the early decades of the twentieth century, the volume of foreign investment was relatively tiny and fell far short of what was needed for industrial development.

In political terms the British Raj was collaborative rather than revolutionary from the beginning but at no time more so than in the decades after the Mutiny of 1857/8 and the late Victorian age (1837–1901). South Asia was not a plantation economy and never became a colony of white settlement, partly for reasons of climate and the nature of economic opportunity. There was also no widespread alien immigrant population, like the Chinese in Southeast Asia, that could serve as intermediary between the imperial overlords and the indigenous agricultural population. The 'steel frame' of the British Raj was the Covenanted Indian Civil Service, and this was a remarkably small, for most of the time entirely or almost entirely British elite corps—between 1858 and 1947 it seldom had more than 1,000 members. Because of its small size this imperial government had to make complex political choices about who could be desirable and effective collaborators. On the level of its day-to-day operations it could not have accomplished much without the aid of the much larger all-Indian Uncovenanted Indian Civil Service. The armies too were largely composed of Indians. Most importantly, after the Mutiny the British turned to the most conservative sections of society, the landlords and princes, as buttresses of the Raj. No longer the target of reformers, British India now became the hope of reactionaries.

Indirect rule through Indian princes set the British empire apart from the other European empires. After the middle of the nineteenth century the so-called Princely States formed about one-third of South Asia—there were well over 550 of them, some quite large and others small and insignificant. Concomitantly, by the time the Victorian era drew to a close, many British officials cultivated a Tory vision of India as a traditional, caste-ridden village society ruled by landed aristocrats in a spirit of benign paternalism that had to be preserved. Landlords, princes, elite Muslims, and other wealthy groups all collaborated in the new reactionary order that successfully put a brake on social and political reform. It was not seriously challenged until as late as the second decade of the twentieth century. Between 1914 and 1930 the subcontinent's exposure to World War I and its aftermath inevitably accelerated and deepened social and political change. The urban, Western-educated professional classes that had earlier been spurned for 'feudal' maharajas then began to emerge in a new subcontinental political arena and nationalism gathered momentum. Muslim separatism and the search for a Muslim homeland began in 1929. The end of the British Raj in 1947 coincided with the partition of the subcontinent and the creation of two independent states along religious lines, a Hindu-dominated India becoming the biggest democracy in the world, and Pakistan an Islamic republic mostly run by the military. Both states were marred by undeveloped national economies, but India came through with an arguably modern and secular political system.

For the British the South Asian subcontinent was only the nucleus of an empire that extended far beyond the borders of earlier Mughal rule. Most importantly, this involved complete domination of the Indian Ocean by British naval power as well as the conquest and occupation of contiguous areas that were deemed essential for the security of South Asia. The maritime provinces of Sri Lanka ('Ceylon') were held by the British from 1776, and the whole island was a Crown Colony from 1815 until 1948, after which it became a self-governing dominion in the British Commonwealth and, unable to forge unity as a modern state, fell prey to chronic civil war between its Sinhalese and Tamil communities. After the first Anglo-Burman war of 1824–6, Indians, along with a smaller number of Chinese, collaborated actively with the British in the development of Burma's economic resources and the completion of its conquest. British-Indian rule substantially disrupted Burma's indigenous social order. By 1914, as a result of its artificially stimulated economic development under an alien government, Burma had become an extremely fragmented society, with divergent ethnic groups interrelated only on the economic plane. Post-independence Burma (1948–) was renamed Myanmar and has been ruled by the military to the present day. Thailand and the Malay Sultanates lay outside South Asia's security perimeter but in time also gravitated towards British-Indian control. Thailand was able, in large measure, to maintain its juridical and territorial independence. On the Malay peninsula, Singapore was founded in 1824 as a counterweight against Dutch Batavia on the China route, to be joined two years later with Melaka and Penang in the British Straits Settlements. In 1867 the Straits Settlements became a Crown Colony under the direct control of London (and no longer ruled from British India). With the growth of the canning industry in America, the Malayan tin mines became a profitable asset, inviting deeper intervention. British residents were then appointed in the Malay Sultanates. In 1896 the Federated Malay States were created, with their capital at Kuala Lumpur, and by 1914 the British had established complete control over the Malay peninsula. 'British Malaya' consisted of three groups of states: the Straits Settlements, the Federated Malay States, and the Unfederated Malay States. Chinese labor was recruited for the tin mines, while Indian labor allowed British Malaya by 1920 to produce 53 percent of the world's rubber. Like all of Southeast Asia, Malaya was occupied by the Japanese in World War II. British authority was re-established in 1945 until the establishment of independent Malaysia under an authoritarian government in 1957.

The Dutch East India Company established its monopoly over the spice and pepper trade of the Indonesian archipelago in the seventeenth century, ousting the Portuguese, and by 1743–6 had brought the northern coastal territories of Java under its direct control. Having been formally dissolved in 1800, its territorial possessions became the property of the Dutch-French government. Under Governor-General Willem Daendels (in office 1808–11) an attempt was made to introduce revolutionary principles of government in Java and to extend control in the interior kingdoms of Surakarta and Yogyakarta. During the short British interregnum between 1811 and 1816, Stamford Raffles pursued the same policy, calling for European assumption of sovereignty throughout Java, and aimed to use, reform, or destroy indigenous institutions at will. In 1816, after the conclusion of the Napoleonic wars, Java was returned to the Dutch. Europeans and Chinese began leasing ever larger tracts of land for sugar, coffee, indigo, and pepper plantations in central Java. In the aftermath of the Java War (1825–30) political dominance was achieved throughout Java and the 'cultivation system' was introduced. Under this system each village was to set land aside for export crops (especially coffee, sugar, and indigo) for sale at fixed prices to the Dutch government.

Lasting profitability was thus achieved, and the system, which in practice knew wide variations, was kept in place until 1870. The cultivation system was not so much an appropriation of land as a tax in the form of labor. Exploitative as it was, the payments for labor did bring about a rapid expansion of money circulation in Java after 1830. The cultivation system also induced remarkable agricultural industrialization by introducing dozens of modern sugar factories in the Javanese interior. The latter remained the backbone of the Javanese economy until the depression of the 1930s. Moreover, the cultivation system led to a multiplication of Javanese exports. There was then, in this period, a definite rise of prosperity throughout Java and the purchasing power of the Javanese increased. It was a limited form of state-sponsored economic modernization unaccompanied by political modernization, not unlike what happened in Malaysia and, to some extent, Burma (Myanmar).

A year after the opening of the Suez canal, in 1870, the Agrarian Law opened Java to private enterprise, and the liberal period began. In contrast to British India, the number of European civilians in Java increased sharply, inaugurating an even more intensive exploitation of the agricultural resources of Java than had been achieved under the cultivation system. At the same time, a part of the surplus generated by the cultivation system was applied to finance the conquests of the Outer Islands—Madura, Bali, Lombok, Irian Jaya, Sumatra, and Kalimantan. It was, thus, only at the beginning of the twentieth century that Dutch rule in the Indonesian archipelago acquired a new territorial definition. After the Japanese occupation and two wars with the Dutch, independence was achieved in 1949, followed by the establishment of an authoritarian form of government.

Vietnam was the last of the important states of Southeast Asia to be brought under European control. Systematic development of governmental administration and the exploitation of economic resources by the French began after 1897 and was eventually extended throughout all of Vietnam, Cambodia, and Laos. The definitive French administrative system in Indochina was largely the work of Governor-General Paul Doumer (in office 1897–1902). Indochina was merely to provide jobs, trade, and investment opportunities for the mother country. Connections with neighboring Southeast Asian markets were severed to a degree not seen anywhere else in the region. Economic dependence bred social disequilibrium and cultural decline, affording no scope or encouragement to the expansion of native industry or agriculture. The results were even worse than in Burma (Myanmar), effectively delaying the modernization of the country by decades. Very large tracts of land were turned into tea, rubber, and coffee plantations by Europeans. The Communist Viet Minh took over from the Japanese in 1945. War with the French, who temporarily returned, followed. In the wake of the 1949 Communist revolution in China, there was a successful takeover by Ho Chi Minh. This was followed by the American war, and ultimately by the unification of North and South Vietnam by the Communist Vietcong in 1976.

Notes

1. Peregrine Horden and Nicholas Purcell, *The Corrupting Sea: A Study of Mediterranean History* (Oxford: Blackwell, 2000), 90.
2. Richard F. Burton, *Sindh and the Races that inhabit the Valley of the Indus* (1851) (Karachi: Oxford University Press, 1973), 3–4.
3. Brian Fagan, *The Great Warming: Climate Change and the Rise and Fall of Civilizations* (New York: Bloomsbury, 2008), xi–xii.
4. For a more extended treatment of this issue see André Wink, *The Making of the Indo-Islamic World*, 5 vols. (Leiden: Brill, 1990–2004 and forthcoming).
5. Richard M. Eaton, *The Rise of Islam and the Bengal Frontier, 1204–1760* (Berkeley: University of California Press, 1993).
6. Joseph Fletcher, 'Integrative History: Parallels and Interconnections in the Early Modern Period, 1500–1800,' *Journal of Turkish Studies*, 9 (1985), 37–57; John F. Richards, 'Early Modern India and World History,' *Journal of World History*, 8: 2 (1997), 197–209; the special issue devoted to 'Early Modernities' of *Daedalus: Journal of the American Academy of Arts and Sciences*, 127: 3 (Summer, 1998); and Jerry H. Bentley, 'Early Modern Europe and the Early Modern World,' in Charles H. Parker and Jerry H. Bentley, eds., *Between the Middle Ages and Modernity: Individual and Community in the Early Modern World* (Lanham, Md.: Rowman and Littlefield, 2007), 13–31.

References

Bayly, Susan. *Caste, Society and Politics in India from the Eighteenth Century to the Modern Age*. Cambridge: Cambridge University Press, 1999.

Bose, Sugata. *A Hundred Horizons: The Indian Ocean in the Age of Global Empire*. Cambridge, Mass.: Harvard University Press, 2006.

Charlesworth, Neil. *British Rule and the Indian Economy, 1800–1914*. London: Palgrave Macmillan, 1982.

Chaudhuri, K. N. *Trade and Civilisation in the Indian Ocean: An Economic History from the Rise of Islam to 1750*. Cambridge: Cambridge University Press, 1985.

Cipolla, Carlo. *Guns, Sails, and Empires: Technological Innovation and European Expansion, 1400–1700*. New York: Barnes and Noble, 1965.

Lieberman, Victor. *Strange Parallels: Southeast Asia in Global Context, c. 800–1830*. Cambridge: Cambridge University Press, 2003.

Pearson, M. N. *The Indian Ocean*. London: Routledge, 2003.

Reid, Anthony. *Southeast Asia in the Age of Commerce, 1450–1680*, 2 vols. New Haven: Yale University Press, 1988–93.

Wink, André. *Al-Hind: The Making of the Indo-Islamic World*, 5 vols. Leiden: Brill, 1990–2004 and forthcoming.

....

CHAPTER 24

THE MIDDLE EAST IN WORLD HISTORY

....

JOHN OBERT VOLL

THE Middle East is both a strategic concept and a geo-cultural region. As a concept and a specific label of identification, it is a product of analysts writing about twentieth-century world affairs. However, as a region, its peoples and cultures are associated with the history of humanity from ancient times, even though the label of 'Middle Eastern' may not have been applied to them until recently. This regional name itself shapes a way of understanding the history of the broad region of Southwestern Asia and Northern Africa. Both of the terms in the name—'Middle' and 'East'—identify the region in relationship to other world regions and reflect the importance of the region's involvement in broader global historical processes.

Understanding the place of the Middle East in world history requires examination of both the nature of the concept and the nature of the region. This dual effort means that along with examining the history of the region, it is important also to note how the concepts of the historical units involved in that history have changed in the presentations of the history of the Middle East.

THE MIDDLE EAST AS CONCEPT
....

The concept of the Middle East developed in the framework of imperialist strategic planning at the beginning of the twentieth century. Later in the century, the Middle East came to be understood as a major world cultural region rather than simply a strategic location. At the beginning of the twenty-first century, globalization and developments in communication reduce the sense of the Middle East as a region with distinctive characteristics and the term increasingly is used to identify a geographic location within broader networks of interaction. These changes illustrate the transformation from a world dominated by European imperialism to a world of increasing globalization.

In these changing concepts and historical conditions, the shape of what is called the 'Middle East' changed. It is not until the second half of the twentieth century that Northern African territories outside Egypt and Sudan were regularly included in what was called the Middle East. Northwest Africa was usually viewed within the framework of another important regional concept: 'the Mediterranean.' The Mediterranean basin is a clearly identifiable geographic unit that has for millennia been tied together by economic, military, and religious networks. The two regional concepts—Mediterranean and Middle East—are sometimes seen as complementary and sometimes competing. However, by the late twentieth century, all of Northern Africa was regularly defined as being part of the Middle East.

For a long time, Western Europeans identified the vast non-European spaces of Eurasia as the Orient or the East. In the nineteenth century, Western European leaders came to view strategic issues arising because of the weakening of the Ottoman Empire in Eastern Europe as 'The Eastern Question,'[1] and the regions involved came to be identified as the Near East. However, by the end of the century, as China and Japan became important in world affairs and new crises developed involving the Balkans and the Ottoman empire, 'Europe awoke to the fact that there were now two Eastern questions, Far and Near.'[2] As the terms Far East and Near East came into use, it was natural that someone would identify the region between as the Middle East.

The person usually credited with inventing the term 'Middle East' is Alfred Thayer Mahan[3] who, in an article in 1902 argued, 'Relatively to Europe, the Farther East is an advanced post of international activities, of very great and immediate importance; but from the military point of view . . . the question of communications, of routes of travel, underlies all others,' and in this context, the 'Middle East, if I may adopt a term which I have not seen, will some day need its Malta, as well as its Gibraltar.'[4] Although Mahan had not seen the term used before, it was in use as a term of convenience by analysts of international relations. General T. R. Gordon had already written an article on 'The Problem of the Middle East' in 1900, possibly reflecting usage of the term among British policy makers,[5] and some American analysts used the term as well. However, the term gained real visibility when Valentine Chirol, a widely-read journalist, published a series of articles in *The Times* and a book *The Middle Eastern Question*, in which he identified Mahan as the originator of the term. It was through Chirol and Mahan that the term came into popular usage.

These writers meant roughly the same thing when they spoke of the Middle East. It was the loosely-defined area between the Far East and the Near East. The Middle East, in these early strategic commentaries, included the territories in the western Indian Ocean basin, including the lands of the Horn of Africa and the Persian Gulf. Up until the middle of the century, the Middle East was basically conceived in terms of global imperial strategic characteristics and was not intended to be descriptive of characteristics of peoples and cultures within that region. That culturally-oriented definition only began to be developed following World War II.

The end of the Ottoman Empire following World War I resulted in a major change in what was identified as the Near East. The new Balkan states no longer were included in discussions of the Near East, and the term came most frequently to be applied to the eastern Mediterranean region, the Arabian Peninsula, and historic Mesopotamia. Increasingly, the term Middle East came to be used for discussions of this same region.

This trend in usage was strengthened during World War II, when the major Allied military command and supply centers in Cairo were identified as the Middle East Command and the Middle East Supply Centre. The shift to using the term Middle East rather than Near East was the work initially of British military officials. Politicians and scholars raised objections to this terminological shift, and the president of the Royal Geographical Society urged people to agree with Lawrence Martin, the head of the Division of Maps in the Library of Congress, that the Middle East was 'miscalled' in the current usage of the time, and both urged following the advice of Sir Percy Loraine 'to emphasize the proper limitations of the term "Middle East,"' even though Loraine admitted that by 1943 the term Near East 'appears to have become almost completely obsolete.'[6]

American usage did not shift as rapidly as in Great Britain. A British Under-Secretary of State for Foreign Affairs could affirm in 1951 during a parliamentary debate that the 'term "Near East"... is outmoded in this country and "Middle East" has superseded it for official purposes.'[7] By the late 1950s, however, American usage was changing and the emerging terminology used Middle East. As a result, when President Eisenhower used the term Near East in his speech to the United Nations General Assembly in 1958, it was necessary for the State Department to clarify that 'the department uses both phrases interchangeably to designate the same area.'[8] In the next year, the State Department Geographer, G. Etzel Pearcy, affirmed that Middle East was the most widely used term, even though the region was 'indefinable.'[9]

After World War II, the study of peoples and societies outside of Western Europe and North America gradually shifted from the approaches identified with imperial policy or strategic planning and Orientalism. By the 1950s, new methods of interdisciplinary research began to crystallize around the concepts of distinctive world regions, opening the way for the development of area studies. The study of these regions, *as regions*, was strongly encouraged in the United States by the passage in 1958 of the National Defense Education Act, which provided federal funding for language and area studies centers. Of the fifty-three centers receiving support in the first five years of the program, nine concentrated on the Middle East. The names identifying these centers reflect terminology of the time, with five being Middle East studies centers, three used the term Near Eastern, and one maintained the older Oriental Studies identification. The first criterion for a Center proposal to be successful was that it had to cover 'a clearly defined global area.'[10]

Following World War II, the concept of the Middle East as an identifiable cultural region rather than simply as a strategic geographic location began to be developed. W. B. Fisher observed in 1947 that in the Middle East, 'wartime experience in administration has shown that within this region there are common elements of natural environment and social organization,' and that on this basis 'one can postulate a unity for the region as a whole.'[11] By the late 1950s, the concept of the Middle East as a distinctive cultural region had developed to the point where a major anthropologist could assert that the Middle East 'is a culture area of its own, with a center and peripheries. The civilization which characterizes it, in various regional forms, is not only a unit, and not only intermediate between those of East and West, but in many ways ancestral to both.'[12] In the 1960s, this distinctive regional identity was affirmed by many scholars who, like Raphel Patai, would argue that 'beneath localized developments and variants, the observer familiar with the whole of the Middle East recognizes the same basic pattern, the same fundamental features whose presence sets Middle Eastern culture apart from the cultures of contiguous world areas.'[13] This reification of the areas being studied, changing them into seemingly objective entities, was a major part of the evolution of area studies in the 1960s and 1970s.[14]

The conceptual framework of regional studies involving a world divided into distinctive units shaped the way that scholars, policy makers, and other international professionals viewed the world outside of Western Europe and North America. In this framework, 'the Middle East' was one of the most important units of analysis. Initially the term was used primarily by outside scholars, but it began to be used increasingly by people from and within the region. In Arabic scholarship, the term was literally translated as *al-sharq al-awsat* and was soon integrated into the Arabic analytical vocabulary. In 1967, for example, Ayn Shams University in Egypt established a Center for Middle Eastern Studies (*Markaz al-sharq al-awsat lil-Buhūth*). By 1978 the term was sufficiently common so that when a major Arabic international newspaper was launched in London, it was called *al-Sharq al-Awsat*. It is an influential voice in the Arabic-speaking world. Most Arabic scholarly studies using the term deal with modern politics or strategic issues but as early as 1968, there were some medieval studies using the term as well.[15]

The boundaries of the Middle East, however, are not fixed, and by the 1980s it became increasingly clear that in at least some important aspects of political or social life, the Middle East was not the most effective unit of analysis. While this situation is partially a result of the artificiality of the concept of dividing the world into separate reified regions, it is also a reflection of major historic changes. As a result, the concept of the Middle East again gradually changed. While it was still imagined as a distinctive unit in many studies tied to the area studies paradigm, new images of the Middle East as a geographic location within broader networks of global relations also emerged by the beginning of the twenty-first century.

Globalization changes the nature of the world regions. Trans-regional networks of activities tended to reduce the importance of distinctive 'Middle Eastern' units. One important example is the experience of the petroleum industry. Oil companies had been international and multinational almost from the beginning of the twentieth century. However, following World War II, the governments of 'petroleum exporting countries' came to play important roles. In 1959 the Arab League hosted the first Arab Petroleum Congress in an effort to coordinate Arab policies. Within a year, this regional effort was transcended by the establishment of a global group of exporting countries, the Organization of Petroleum Exporting Countries (OPEC). Although the

Arab association continued in various forms, OPEC, not a regional association, became the major organization.

Major diasporas in the second half of the twentieth century also illustrate the shift from a distinctive Middle Eastern regional identity. Many people emigrated from the Middle East to other regions of the world. When these migrants became important minorities in their new societies, they were identified by their specific ethnic or religious identity. They were not identified as 'Middle Easterners.' One can see this in Western Europe, where, for example, Turkish guest-workers are identified as Turks, not as Middle Easterners.

The emergence of religion as a major unit of identification and analysis provides an important departure from the old area studies paradigm. The study of Islam in terms of history and the social sciences, as opposed to the study of Islamic theology and philosophy, tended to be concentrated within the framework of Middle Eastern Studies, despite the fact that the majority of the Muslims of the world live outside of the Middle East. This anomaly became important with what has come to be called the 'Islamic Resurgence.' The Islamic Revolution in Iran in 1978–9 made it clear that Islam was an emerging force in world affairs. The Soviet invasion of Afghanistan and the subsequent development of a jihad movement to oppose Soviet occupation provided foundations for the rise of a global movement of extremist Muslim militancy.

By the 1990s, the world of Islam was global, and the concept of the Middle East had little utility as a unit of analysis of Muslim affairs. In this new globalized context, important studies turned to the concept of the global Islamic community or *ummah* as an organizing unit for analysis.[16]

The concept of the Middle East had changed by the beginning of the twenty-first century. While the concept was central to regional studies, as the world regions themselves become less clearly separate in identity the conceptual units of analysis also change. Even in strategic planning, the original topic where the concept of the Middle East was developed, the boundaries have changed. In the structure of commands in the United States military, there is an interesting parallel to the old terminology. Much of what was originally in Mahan's Middle East is now in the Central Command, with 'middle' being replaced by 'central.' However, the Area of Responsibility (AOR) for the Central Command includes all of former Soviet Central Asia along with Pakistan and Afghanistan. In important ways, the Middle East as a concept has returned to what it was originally: a geographical term of convenience to identify specific territories.

FRAMING THE MIDDLE EAST IN WORLD HISTORIES

The evolution of the concept of the Middle East provides three general ways in which the region was analyzed and understood. These three ways cannot be precisely defined as separate methodologies but rather they can be seen as representing general modes of conceptualizing this important region.

The first mode was basically used for discussions of contemporary policies and military strategy in the first half of the twentieth century. The most frequently used terms in discussions of these subjects were the older terms of the 'Orient' or the 'Near East.' Neither Northern Africa nor the Balkans was included in these early discussions of the Middle East.

The second mode of conceptualizing the Middle East is the area studies approach. The key to this approach is the idea that the region is a socially and culturally identifiable unit, as well as being a geographical location. The special characteristics of Middle Eastern society and culture were emphasized. This mode fit into the broader development of scholarship in regional studies programs, in the context of global affairs in the decades immediately following World War II.

Under the pressures of globalizations, many assumptions underlying the area studies approach began to be disputed. By the beginning of the twenty-first century, while people still used the term Middle East extensively, the sense of it being a region distinct from other regions was replaced both conceptually and practically by analysis that emphasized the concept of the Middle East as a sub-unit in some broader unit of analysis, whether it was the practical world of petroleum markets or the globalized organizations of religious extremists.

These three modes can be seen in the ways that scholars throughout the past century presented the place of the Middle East and its history in the contexts of world history. Scholars have documented the history of the region over the past five to ten millennia. That historical narrative has been incorporated into world-historical narratives in ways that show the influence of the changing conceptualizations of the region itself. One of the key dimensions of these changing perspectives is the interactions in the usages of the terms Near East and Middle East.

A general consensus developed regarding the chronological periodization of the history of the region. The earliest era is the time of gathering-hunting peoples and peoples engaged in small-scale agriculture—in the old classical terminology, the paleo-lithic and neolithic periods. This period is studied by examination of specific locations and local groups, and terms like Orient, Near East, or Middle East are simply used to provide a general identification of the location of archeological sites.

Following that initial era, people discuss three broad periods before the early modern: the rise and development of ancient civilizations (large-scale urban-agricultural societies) from sometime in the fourth millennium BCE until around 700–500 BCE, followed by the development of 'classical' civilization from around 500 BCE until the rise of Islam in the seventh century CE, and then the era of the major Muslim states and societies from the seventh century through the sixteenth century.[17] Over the past century scholars have written the history of the region during these periods, and their historical narratives illustrate the changing conceptualization of the region and the evolving usage of the terminology applied to the region.

THE HISTORICAL NARRATIVES:
ANCIENT HISTORY

Scholars in the West and in the region have long been interested in the great historical narratives of ancient human history in the region. Studies of the ancient Middle East in the past century provide important foundations for the ways that the history of the region down to the present has been understood. The three modes of viewing the Middle East conceptually can be effectively illustrated by the evolution of the study of ancient history. In world-historical studies it is in coverage of the ancient period that the Middle East is most central.

Until the nineteenth century, understanding of ancient history was closely tied to the sacred narratives of Judaism, Christianity, and Islam. Hebrew and Christian scriptures presented the histories of major ancient societies, but within the framework of their own faith narratives. Early Muslim historians like Abu Ja'far Muhammad al-Tabari (839–923 CE) similarly framed their narratives in terms of the scriptural accounts of rulers and prophets. In these accounts, there was little sense of a regional identity. The complex societies within the region were covered as separate topics, sometimes within a broader category like 'ancient' societies.

This tendency to view the ancient history of the region as the history of a number of separate societies continued in the nineteenth century. By the time when Gordon, Mahan, and Chirol began speaking about the 'Middle East,' the histories of the ancient societies in the region were well-known. In the first decades of the twentieth century, people were beginning to utilize broader regional terms for discussions of these societies in the region. However, in discussing ancient societies, the initial major identifying label was that these societies were 'Oriental' civilizations, and then gradually terminology like Near Orient and Near East became more common.

Usage tended not to be consistent. An interesting example is the 1919 Presidential Address to the American Oriental Society given by James Henry Breasted, an influential leader in the development of modern scholarship on ancient history. The title of his address mentioned 'the Near Orient' but he also spoke of the Near East and the Nearer East and when he discussed the culture of the region, he called it 'Egypto-Babylonian culture.'[18]

In the two decades following World War I, the coverage of the ancient history of the region had a relatively standard form. Major scholarly surveys used 'The Orient' and Near East as broad labels identifying the region but the presentation concentrated on the separate 'civilizations' of Egypt and Babylonia/Mesopotamia. This structure is the basis for the presentation in the authoritative *Cambridge Ancient History*, in which the term Near East simply identifies the geographic location of the major civilizations being discussed. Similarly, M. Rostovtzeff spoke generically of 'ancient civilization' which 'first developed in the Near East,' but the presentation discusses separate societies. In his influential textbook on ancient history, Breasted used the term 'Ancient Near East' as a geographic location and identified the generic culture of the major societies as 'Oriental Civilization,' but there was little concept of the area being a unified region.[19]

In virtually no discussion of ancient history was the term Middle East used. However, in this scholarship, the conceptualization of the region as reflected in the usage of the terms Near East and Oriental was similar to the usage of the term Middle East. The concepts underlying the regional identifying terms were basically geographical. They referred to a location in the eastern hemisphere and did not involve conceptualizing a regional unit of cultural identity.

In the era of area studies following World War II, this situation gradually changed in the discussions of the ancient history of the region. The term Near East came increasingly to be used only in discussions of ancient history, and Middle East became the more common general term for the region. As a result, terminological usage was mixed. Major scholarly studies of the ancient world, like that of Chester Starr, continued from its first edition in 1965 through its third edition in 1983 to use the term Near East. An important Italian study spoke of 'Oriente Mediterraneo,' which became 'the Ancient Orient' in its English translation in 1960. At the same time important scholars of world history like William H. McNeill and Leften Stavrianos and Soviet scholars, among others, were speaking of the Middle East in their analyses of ancient historical developments.[20]

The most important transition, however, was the conceptualizing of the region, whether called the ancient Orient, or the Near or Middle East, as a significant historical-cultural unit. This new image of the region fit the pattern of area studies concepts. The basic narrative noted the rise of separate civilizations in the Nile and Tigris-Euphrates valleys. However, gradually, as a result of intensification of trade networks, important migrations of peoples, and the development of larger and eventually region-wide empires, the Middle East emerged as a world region. Chester Starr wrote of 'the unification of the Near East' and Sabatino Moscati describes those developments in the Ancient Orient which 'out of a multiplicity of disparate elements create an organic whole.'[21] In this process, the imperial unification of the region by the Assyrians and Persians is viewed as a culmination.

The ancient history of the region is not a history of the development of a homogeneous, culturally-cohesive unit like the emergence of Chinese civilization. Instead, the regional culture was viewed as a complex synthesis of relatively distinctive civilizations. The process was presented by William H. McNeill: 'Old geographical and cultural barriers had been broken through; and a cosmopolitan civilization, incorporating both Egypt and Mesopotamia into a larger whole, began to emerge in the Middle East.... [Despite] the survival of... cultural contrasts... an approximate uniformity of social structure gradually but unmistakably manifested itself in the Middle East.'[22] This conceptualization made it possible to utilize the area studies framework for framing the narrative of ancient world history.

By the end of the twentieth century, the realities of globalization changed the conceptual foundations of area studies as well as changing the nature of 'regional' identities themselves. The third mode of conceptualizing the Middle East as a geographic location within broader networks of global relations became important. This change reshaped the analyses of the ancient history of the Middle East. McNeill, whose conceptualization of the cosmopolitan Middle Eastern civilization was influential in the contexts of area studies, revisited his analysis of the ancient Middle East in 1990. In his critique, he argued that his earlier work 'assumes that separate civilizations form real and important groupings' and that 'discernibly separate civilizations were autonomous social entities whose interactions defined history on a global scale.' In McNeill's later assessment this analysis 'pays inadequate attention to the emergence of the ecumenical world system' as manifested first in the ancient Middle East.[23]

This concept of the ancient Middle East as a part of broader global networks of relations became central to narratives of ancient Middle Eastern and world history. One of the pioneers in this approach was Marshall Hodgson, who never accepted the area studies concept of distinctively separate regions. He argued that the great regional civilizations (China, India, the Mediterranean, and the Middle East) that were a core of emerging world historical narratives in the 1960s 'are imperfect historical abstractions. All regions formed together a single great historical complex of cultural developments.'[24]

In the early twenty-first century, much of the new scholarship emphasizes transcultural networks of relationships. This approach has had a major impact upon discussions of the ancient Middle East in world history narratives. Peter Stearns reflects this approach in his textbooks and in an important combination of an atlas and historical account of 'cultures in motion;' John and William McNeill provide a sweeping vision of 'the human web' of interactions in world history, placing the ancient Middle East in these broader patterns. Major new world history texts, like Craig Lockard's recent volume, emphasize 'societies, networks, and transitions' in understanding the 'ancient foundations of world history.'[25]

THE HISTORICAL NARRATIVES: CLASSICAL AND MEDIEVAL MIDDLE EAST

In the coverage of the classical and medieval periods, the concept of the Middle East as a region with a distinctive identity tends to be submerged in the discussions. Among Western scholars the central focus shifts from the ancient civilizations to the histories of Greece and Rome. In the first half of the twentieth century, many important studies were undertaken of the major classical societies, but these fit within the first mode of understanding. The Middle East was simply the geographic location of major separate states and societies. The most inclusive conceptual unit for analysis was 'Hellenistic civilization,' which built on studies of the cultural foundations laid by the conquests of Alexander the Great and the successor states.[26] Similarly, there were important studies presenting the history of the sequence of great Persian imperial states, which were viewed in the framework of the history of 'Persian Civilization' rather than as being regional.

The imperial focus of many of the histories of the Middle East opened the way for a major theme in the historiography of the classical era: the 'long war' between East and West, beginning with the accounts of the Persian Wars of the Greeks and continuing with accounts of the Roman wars against various Persian empires.[27] In this, the region—whether identified as the Orient, the Near East, or the Middle East—was basically presented as the geographic location for the events and not as a unit with distinctive identity.

In the era of twentieth-century area studies, the classical era of Middle Eastern history received remarkably little attention. Scholars important in the development of modern Middle Eastern studies, like Richard Frye, did not use the concept of the Middle East as a region when studying the classical era, instead emphasizing the significance of Persian civilization.[28] Similarly, scholars looking at the fragmentation of the Roman empire in late antiquity discussed the emergence of a distinctive Eastern Roman civilization that came to be conceived of as the Byzantine empire,[29] but even though they drew distinctions between the Byzantine East and the Latin West, Constantinople and the eastern empire were not included in a regional concept of the Middle East. The area studies concept of the Middle East had little impact on the study of the classical history of the region.

One important exception is the study of how the region interacted with all of the other major culture areas. The development of the concept of the cosmopolitan ancient Middle East by scholars like William H. McNeill was used to expand the study of the classical period beyond the histories of Greece and Rome. As the four regions of large-scale urban societies developed in the classical era, they were seen as maintaining distinctive identities but engaging in increasingly important interactions. McNeill used the term 'ecumene' to describe the band of societies stretching from the Pacific to the Atlantic, and described the later centuries of the classical era as a time of the 'closure of the Eurasian ecumene,' within which each civilization 'was complete and self-sufficient in itself.'[30]

In the era of globalization, important studies emphasized the place of the classical Middle East in the broader networks of human interactions. The general post-area studies approach is summed up in the chapter title for the classical era in a major world history textbook, 'Empires, Networks, and the Remaking of Europe, North Africa, and Western Asia, 500 BCE–600 CE.'[31] Interestingly, however, the older historiography of a clash between East and West, between 'civilizations' defined in old terms of area studies reification, continues in the twenty-first century in debates about the clash of civilizations. However, even in the historiography of clash, the Middle East is viewed as a location, but the clashing unit is more broadly defined as 'Islamic civilization.'

The historical study of the medieval era in the Middle East is closely tied to the broader field of Islamic studies. Whether in the early imperial mode, the area studies mode, or the globalization mode of conceptualization, the history of the Muslim peoples and the Islamic tradition is central. In the first half of the twentieth century, Western historians operated primarily within the concepts of Orientalist scholarship and studies were tinged with religious polemic. The basic unit of analysis was the

Muslim community, wherever it spread, rather than being tied to a regional concept like the Middle East. The area studies mode tended to view the Muslim world and the Middle East as being approximately identical. Writing in the early 1960s, Bernard Lewis, for example, affirmed that 'the term Middle East does nevertheless designate an area with an unmistakable character and identity,' and speaks of the evolution of 'Arab civilization' and 'Islamic' in the framework of 'the whole pattern of life and government in the Middle East.'[32] Many scholars recognized the distinction between the Middle East and the Muslim world and suggested that the Middle East 'roughly coincides' with the territories of the early Muslim empires.[33] In this way, the new society of medieval Islam provides a base for understanding the Middle East as a coherent unit.

By the end of the twentieth century, discussions of the region in medieval times tended to see the newly emerging Muslim community centered in the Middle East as part of larger networks or units. In this way, for example, Richard Eaton speaks of 'the integration of most of the population of the Middle East into a newly constituted Islamic society that had become by the tenth century a world civilization.' Other analyses viewed the medieval Middle East as part of the hemispheric 'Old World Web' in relations with other major urban societies or as a 'discourse-based' world-system which included a number of major regional societies.[34]

HISTORICAL NARRATIVES: THE MODERN MIDDLE EAST

Histories of the modern Middle East are, like ancient and medieval histories, shaped by the contexts of the historians as well as the developments which they are describing. Histories of the nineteenth and twentieth centuries tend to focus on relations between the Middle East and the major Western powers and on issues relating to the experiences of Middle Eastern peoples in the contexts of the global history of modernity. During the twentieth century a special challenge is faced by historians who are analyzing not only past developments but also the history of events in which they participate. In each of the eras of conceptualizing the Middle East, the scholars are living in the midst of the processes that they are describing.

In the first half of the twentieth century, the modern history of the region tended to be presented as histories of specific societies. The region was viewed as a single unit primarily in strategic and geographical terms. The parameters were already set by the time Gordon, Mahan, and Chirol were using the term. This view paid little attention to local political or cultural developments. Remarkably neither Gordon nor Mahan mentions the rise of nationalisms in countries whose strategic locations they discuss.

Following World War I, accounts of developments in Southwest Asia and northern Africa tended to be framed in terms of units of identity that were broader or more narrow than the regional concept of the Middle East. Valentine Chirol, who had popularized the term Middle East, wrote an essay on the impact of the abolition of the office of Caliphate by the new nationalist government in Turkey led by Mustafa Kemal. He spoke about responses in the broader Islamic world and in his conclusion used the term 'Near East,' rather than Middle East to describe the region in which the new Turks would be important.[35]

Current events in the region shaped the coverage. The broad framework for this coverage was frequently the Muslim world, with discussions like Chirol's suggesting that this world extended across the whole eastern hemisphere. The important survey by Arnold Toynbee in 1927 of 'the Islamic world since the Peace Settlement' presents an interesting conceptual combination. The volume's map identifies the Islamic world in extensive terms, but the coverage is almost exclusively of events in what is called 'The Middle East' and northwest Africa.[36] Generally in world history accounts written in this era, separate major themes like nationalism, imperialism, or reform and separate accounts of the histories of states were the format for the history.

Following World War II, the development of area studies changed the context in important ways. The concept of the Middle East as an appropriate unit for substantive analysis of major themes provided the foundation for many studies of important dimensions of modern Middle Eastern history. One of the most important themes was modernization. Important studies on this subject included historical analysis of the 'beginnings of modernization in the Middle East' as well as examinations of the transformation of 'traditional' society, or the roles of specific institutions like the military.[37]

As Middle East Studies programs became established parts of university programs, survey courses on the history of the region grew. As a result, textbooks for these courses were written and the existence of these texts helped to confirm the concept of the region itself. The historiography of the texts tended to be interactive with the market so that the nature of the coverage evolved. One of the early texts (1948) was by George Kirk, and by 1964 it had gone through seven editions. In its coverage of the modern era, this early text tended to emphasize great power policies and the politics of nationalism. The next generation of texts, like the one by Sydney Nettleton Fisher in 1959, gave greater attention to regional political and social developments and had its sixth edition in 2004. The text by Arthur Goldschmidt (1979) provided more complete coverage of Islam in the context of the Islamic resurgence, and its ninth edition (2010) has chapters on 'The Reassertion of Islamic Power' and 'The War on Terrorism' that cover material that would have been virtually inconceivable to textbook writers in the 1950s.[38]

In the final decades of the twentieth century, the nature of historiography of the Middle East changed significantly. Globalization encouraged transregional perspectives and new topics became important parts of scholarship. Major debates about methodologies in mid-century had been about issues raised by Marxists, but later, area studies and then 'postmodern' perspectives challenged many of the old approaches of Orientalism.[39] Important new areas of research included the study of women in Middle

Eastern history, both modern and pre-modern, as seen in the works of Nikki Keddie and the study of popular culture.[40]

The most visible new area of scholarship was created by the 'Islamic Resurgence.' By the 1980s, following the Islamic Revolution in Iran in 1978–9, much of the contemporary history of the region was written to cover the rise of Islamic movements. An important early example of this new scholarship is John L. Esposito's book on Islam and politics (1984), and his later book *The Islamic Threat: Myth or Reality?* (1992) reflects the debate in the 1990s about the clash of civilizations. In addition to the debates about 'political Islam' and the rise of militant groups, significant studies in the area of religion examined the modern history of Islamic law, devotional mystic organizations, and electronic communications that created the world of iMuslims and Cyber-Islamic environments. One important aspect of the new historiography in these fields is that the coverage is global rather than being confined to the Middle East of area studies.[41]

Discussions about global relations at the beginning of the twenty-first century reflect the new historiography in which the Middle East is conceived as a geographic region more than a reified cultural area. The debates, for example, about the 'clash of civilizations' show this change. The first person to use the term 'clash of civilizations' in a major public analysis (in 1990), Bernard Lewis, articulated the hypothesis in terms that basically remain within the area studies approach, the clash as being between the West and the Middle East.[42] However, the new conceptualization is reflected in the analysis of Samuel Huntington, who built on the work of Lewis. Huntington argued that the major tensions in world affairs would not be 'regional.' 'Regions *are geographical* not political or cultural entities. As with the Balkans or the Middle East, they may be riven by inter- and intracivilization conflicts . . . Divorced from culture, propinquity does not yield commonality.'[43] Huntington identified the major units in conflict as transregional 'civilizations.' In the debates that followed, even those who disagreed with the 'clash hypothesis' or who worked to redefine the conceptualizations of the clashing units did not use the concept of 'the Middle East.'[44] When they spoke of the Middle East, they, like Huntington, were basically identifying a geographical region.

CONCLUSIONS

The Middle East is a region, a concept, and a constructed term. As a label, it did not exist in any language before the nineteenth century. However, the lands and peoples to which the label refers have long histories. The territories between central Asia and northern Africa are the locations for major events in human history, and it is useful to have a term of convenience to designate this region. By the beginning of the twenty-first century, the 'Middle East,' even in translations to languages other than English, has become the most widely used term.

An examination of how the use of the term has changed since it was 'invented' at the beginning of the twentieth century provides both a summary of the main themes of the region's history and a reminder of the importance of the relationships between concepts used in analysis and the conclusions drawn by that analysis. In a general survey, three modes of usage over the past century of scholarship can be identified.

In the first mode, the term Middle East was simply an identification of a geographic location in the minds of European imperial strategic planners. The discussions involved policies of the European powers as they related to the region and the term (and these analysts) paid little attention to human life in the region. Discussions of history and society used a wide range of terms like the Near East or the Near Orient in discussing the evolution of urban-agricultural societies in ancient times and the establishment of major empires in classical and medieval times. Similar usage prevailed in discussions of local political and cultural developments in the modern era, with the broad regional concept being 'the Muslim world.' One can speculate that this terminological division helps provide an understanding of why the imperial planners frequently had difficulty in understanding the rise of nationalist movements or movements of religious activism and reform.

The second mode presents the move to the opposite pole of analysis. Following World War II, the development of area studies resulted in the near universal adoption of the old strategic term for the region, with such strong recognition of local cultural characteristics that the Middle East came to be viewed as a distinctive world culture. While the area studies approach provided an in-depth and interdisciplinary methodology for understanding human societies, it created an analytical framework in which the regions of the world were seen as qualitatively different. The interactions among the major societies received less attention, except for the interactions involving 'borrowing' from the West. The concept of the Middle East as a 'traditional' society in the process of modernization was one of the important themes in area studies analysis. This fixed and somewhat static nature of the concept of the Middle East opened the way for what critics came to call an essentialist approach viewing Middle Eastern culture as built on primordial roots—which was a new terminology for the old-fashioned vision of the 'unchanging Orient.'

The global and local transformations of the late twentieth century created the context for a conceptualization of the region that tended to view it as part of broader networks of interaction. This shift reflected the visibility of worldwide diasporas and transregional movements. However, the new mode was not tied to analysis of contemporary history; it also provided new frameworks for understanding the relationships among ancient and medieval societies as well.

Whether or not the specific term 'Middle East' is used, its adoption and widespread usage shows the utility of having a label for a region of significance in world history. The events of world history shape how the term is understood but the choice of term can also influence the way that those events are understood.

NOTES

1. A. L. Macfie, *The Eastern Question, 1774–1923* (revised edition; London: Longman, 1996), 1–4.

2. Roderic H. Davison, 'Where is the Middle East?,' *Foreign Affairs* 38: 4 (July 1960), 666.

3. See, for example, Davison, 'Where is the Middle East?,' 667–8; Roger Adelson, *London and the Invention of the Middle East: Money, Power, and War, 1902–1922* (New Haven: Yale University Press, 1995), 22–4.

4. A[lfred]. T[hayer]. Mahan, 'The Persian Gulf and International Relations,' *National Review* 40 (September 1902), 39.

5. Thomas E. Gordon, 'The Problem of the Middle East,' *Nineteenth Century* 47: 277 (March 1900), 413–24. For discussion of this article and usage of the term, see Clayton R. Koppes, 'Captain Mahan, General Gordon, and the Origins of the Term "Middle East,"' *Middle Eastern Studies* 12: 1 (January 1976), 95–8.

6. See Percy Loraine, 'Perspectives of the Near East,' *The Geographical Journal* 102: 1 (July 1943), 6; Lawrence Martin, 'Geographical Record, The Miscalled Middle East,' *Geographical Review* 43: 2 (April 1944), 335; George Clerk, 'Address at the Annual General Meeting of the [Royal Geographical] Society,' *The Geographical Journal* 104, Nos. 1 and 2 (July–August 1944), 4–5.

7. Quoted in Davison, 'Where is the Middle East?,' 672.

8. '"Near East" Is Mideast, Washington Explains,' *New York Times* (14 August 1958) <www.nytimes.com>.

9. G. Etzel Pearcy, 'The Middle East—An Indefinable Region,' *The Department of State Bulletin* 40: 1030 (March 23, 1959), 416.

10. Donald N. Bigelow and Lyman H. Legters, *NDEA Language and Area Centers: A Report on the First 5 Years* (Washington: US Department of Health, Education, and Welfare, 1964), 24, and Appendix E, 114–17 for a listing of the Centers.

11. W. B. Fisher, 'Unity and Diversity in the Middle East,' *Geographical Review* 37: 3 (July 1947), 417, 420.

12. Carleton S. Coon, *Caravan, The Story of the Middle East* (revised edn.; New York: Henry Holt, 1958), 2.

13. Raphael Patai, *Society, Culture, and Change in the Middle East* (3rd edn.; Philadelphia: University of Pennsylvania Press, 1969), Preface (1961), 4.

14. See discussions in John O. Voll, 'Crossing Traditional Area Studies Boundaries: A "Middle East" View,' *NewsNet: The Newsletter of the AAASS* 42: 2 (March 2002), 1, 4–6; John O. Voll, 'Reconceptualizing the "Regions" in "Area Studies,"' *International Journal of Middle East Studies* 41: 2 (May 2009), 196–7.

15. For an example of a global strategy study, see Abd al-Mun'am Imarah, *al-Istiratijiyyah al-Amrikiyyah fi al-Sharq al-Awsat ba'da al-Harb al-Alamiyyah al-Thaniyyah* ['American Strategy in the Middle East After World War II'] (Cairo: Markaz al-Mahrusah lil-Buhuth, 1997); for an example of a medieval study using the term, see Ibrahim Ali Tarkhan, *al-Nuzum al-Iqta'iyyah fi al-Sharq al-Awsat fi al-Usur al-Wusta* ['The Feudal System in the Middle East during the Middle Ages'] (Cairo: Dar al-Katib al-Arabi, 1968). Information about the newspaper *al-Sharq al-Awsat* can be found on its website at <www.aawsat.com>.

16. See, for example, Olivier Roy, *Globalized Islam: The Search for a New Ummah* (New York: Columbia University Press, 2004).

17. This periodization is similar to that presented in a number of major world history texts. See, for example, Jerry H. Bentley and Herbert F. Ziegler, *Traditions and Encounters: A Global Perspective on the Past* (4th edn.; Boston: McGraw-Hill, 2008).

18. James Henry Breasted, 'The place of the Near Orient in the Career of Man and the Task of the American Orientalist,' *Journal of the American Oriental Society* 39 (1919), 160–1, 180.

19. J. B. Bury, S. A. Cook, and F. E. Adcock, eds., *The Cambridge Ancient History* (New York: Macmillan, 1923), 1: v–x (Preface); M. Rostovtzeff, *The History of the Ancient World* (2nd edn.; Oxford: Clarendon Press, 1930), 1: 8; James Henry Breasted, *Ancient Times, A History of the Early World* (2nd edn.; Boston: Ginn & Company, 1935), iii, 279–82, and *passim*.

20. Chester G. Starr, *A History of the Ancient World* (3rd edn.; New York: Oxford University Press, 1983), 75 and *passim*; Sabatino Moscati, *Il profile dell'Oriente mediterraneo* (Torino: Edizioni Radio Italiana, 1956), and Sabatino Moscati, *The Face of the Ancient Orient: A Panorama of Near Eastern Civilizations in Pre-Classical Times* (Chicago: Quadrangle, 1960); William H. McNeill, *The Rise of the West* (Chicago: University of Chicago Press, 1963), chapter 4; Leften Stavrianos, *et al.*, *A Global History of Man* (Boston: Allyn and Bacon, 1964), 64 and *passim*; A.Z. Manfred, ed., *A Short History of the World* (Katharine Judelson, trans.; Moscow: Progress Publishers, 1974), chapter 2.

21. Starr, *A History*, chapter 6; Moscati, *The Face of the Ancient Orient*, 292.

22. McNeill, *Rise of the West*, 112–13.

23. William H. McNeill, '*The Rise of the West* after Twenty-Five Years,' *Journal of World History* 1: 1 (1990), 4, 7–8, 9–10.

24. Marshall G. S. Hodgson, 'The Interrelations of Societies in History,' *Comparative Studies in Society and History* 5: 2 (January 1963), 233. For more complete presentations of his views, see Marshall G. S. Hodgson, *Rethinking World History*, Edmund Burke, III, ed. (Cambridge: Cambridge University Press, 1993).

25. Peter N. Stearns, *Cultures in Motion: Mapping Key Contacts and Their Imprints in World History* (New Haven: Yale University Press, 2001); J. R. McNeill and William H. McNeill, *The Human Web* (New York: Norton, 2003); Craig A. Lockard, *Societies, Networks, and Transitions* (Boston: Houghton Mifflin, 2008), 104–14.

26. An important study of this type is W. W. Tarn, *Hellenistic Civilization* (London: Arnold, 1930).

27. A twenty-first century example is Tom Holland, *Persian Fire: The First World Empire and the Battle for the West* (New York: Anchor, 2005).

28. Richard N. Frye, *The Heritage of Persia* (Cleveland: World Publishing, 1963).

29. N. H. Baynes and H. St L. B. Moss, eds., *Byzantium: An Introduction to East Roman Civilization* (Oxford: Clarendon Press, 1948).

30. William H. McNeill, *The Ecumene: Story of Humanity* (New York: Harper & Row, 1973), 162, and *Rise of the West*, chapter 7.

31. Lockard, *Societies*, chapter 8.

32. Bernard Lewis, *The Middle East and the West* (Bloomington: Indiana University Press, 1964), 10, 12–13.

33. Nikki R. Keddie, 'Is There a Middle East?' *International Journal of Middle East Studies* 4: 3 (July 1973), 257.

34. Richard M. Eaton, *Islamic History as Global History* (Washington: American Historical Association, 1990), 7; J. R. McNeill and William McNeill, *Human Web*, chapters 4–5; John Obert Voll, 'Islam as a Special World-System,' *Journal of World History* 5: 2 (Fall 1994), 226.

35. Valentine Chirol, 'The Downfall of the Khalifate,' *Foreign Affairs* 2: 4 (15 June 1924), 582.

36. Arnold J. Toynbee, *Survey of International Affairs*, Vol. 1: *The Islamic World since the Peace Settlement* (London: Royal Institute of International Affairs, 1927).
37. See, for example, William R. Polk and Richard Chambers, *Beginnings of Modernization in the Middle East: The Nineteenth Century* (Chicago: University of Chicago Press, 1968); Daniel Lerner, *The Passing of Traditional Society: Modernizing the Middle East* (New York: Free Press, 1958); Sydney Nettleton Fisher, ed., *The Military in the Middle East* (Columbus: Ohio State University Press, 1963).
38. George E. Kirk, *A Short History of the Middle East, from the Rise of Islam to Modern Times* (London: Methuen, 1948; 7th edn.; New York: Praeger, 1964); Sydney Nettleton Fisher, *The Middle East, A History* (New York: Knopf, 1959; 6th edn.; with William Ochsenwald; Boston: McGraw-Hill, 2004); Arthur Goldschmidt, Jr., *A Concise History of the Middle East* (Boulder: Westview, 1979; 9th edn.; with Lawrence Davidson; Boulder: Westview, 2010).
39. An early critique of Orientalism is Hamilton Gibb, *Area Studies Reconsidered* (London: School of Oriental and African Studies, 1963), and the best-known critique is Edward Said, *Orientalism* (New York: Random House, 1978).
40. See, for example, Nikki R. Keddie, *Women in the Middle East, Past and Present* (Princeton: Princeton University Press, 2007), and Walter Armbrust, *Mass Culture and Modernism in Egypt* (Cambridge: Cambridge University Press, 1996).
41. For analysis of the transitions in Islamic law in the modern era see Tariq Ramadan, *Radical Reform: Islamic Ethics and Liberation* (New York: Oxford University Press, 2009). For modern mysticism, see Martin van Bruinessen and Julia Day Howell, eds., *Sufism and the 'Modern' in Islam* (London: Taurus, 2007); for cyber-Islam see Gary R. Bunt, *iMuslims, Rewiring the House of Islam* (Chapel Hill, N.C.: University of North Carolina Press, 2009).
42. Bernard Lewis, 'The Roots of Muslim Rage,' *The Atlantic* 266: 3 (September 1990), 56; Bernard Lewis, *What Went Wrong? Western Impact and Middle Eastern Response* (New York: Oxford University Press, 2002).
43. Samuel P. Huntington, *The Clash of Civilizations and the Remaking of World Order* (New York: Simon and Schuster, 1996), 130–1; emphasis added.
44. See, for example, Shireen T. Hunter, *The Future of Islam and the West: Clash of Civilizations or Peaceful Coexistence?* (Westport: Praeger, 1998); Hayward R. Alker, 'If Not Huntington's "Civilizations," Then Whose?' *Review* 18: 4 (Fall 1995), 533–62.

REFERENCES

BERKEY, JONATHAN P. *The Formation of Islam: Religion and Society in the Near East, 600–1800.* New York: Cambridge University Press, 2003.
CLEVELAND, WILLIAM L., and MARTIN BUNTON. *A History of the Modern Middle East.* 4th edn. Boulder: Westview, 2009.
DAVISON, RODERIC H. 'Where Is the Middle East?,' *Foreign Affairs* 38: 4 (July 1960), 665–75.
GERSHONI, ISRAEL, AMY SINGER, and Y. HAKAN ERDEM, eds. *Middle East Historiographies: Narrating the Twentieth Century.* Seattle: University of Washington Press, 2006.

IGGERS, GEORG G., and EDWARD Q. *A Global History of Modern Historiography.* Harlow, U.K.: Pearson, 2008.

KEDDIE, NIKKI R. 'Is There a Middle East?' *International Journal of Middle East Studies* 4: 3 (July 1973), 255–71.

LOCKMAN, ZACHARY. *Contending Visions of the Middle East: The History and Politics of Orientalism.* Cambridge: Cambridge University Press, 2004.

PEARCY, G. ETZEL. 'The Middle East—An Indefinable Region,' *The Department of State Bulletin* 40: 1030 (March 23, 1959), 407–16.

STIEBING, WILLIAM H. *Ancient Near Eastern History and Culture.* New York: Longman, 2003.

CHAPTER 25

AFRICA IN WORLD HISTORY: THE LONG, LONG VIEW

CHRISTOPHER EHRET

AFRICAN ORIGINS

HUMAN history began in Africa. Barely more than 50,000 years ago, the ancestors of every single human being alive today lived in Africa. World history to that point *was* African history. That is now becoming accepted knowledge. What seems less generally understood is that, just because a few Africans left the continent around 50,000 years ago and began to expand across the rest of the globe, history did not halt in Africa. The Africans who stayed behind in our common ancestral continent did not fall out of time into some kind of ahistorical stasis. They passed through the same big developments of human history, and did so in the same broad periods of time, as people elsewhere in the world.

The transformative shift in our ancestors to fully human intellectual and social capacities took place between 90,000 and 60,000 years ago. Human history began at that time, and it began in Africa. Earlier, by around 200,000 years ago, hominins in Africa developed many modern anatomical features, and sometime before 100,000 BP, in a period of interglacial climates, expanded their range from Africa to include adjacent warm-climate areas of the Levant. But this intrusion did not last. By around 70,000 years ago, when colder conditions returned, the cold-adapted Neanderthal hominins once again dominated this region, and the 'anatomically modern' populations had disappeared. The contrast of this history with human expansions after 50,000 BP could not be starker. Despite Ice-Age conditions, fully modern humans of that later time advanced right across the eastern hemisphere within a relatively few thousand years, even into periglacial climes. Neanderthal and other hominin populations everywhere eventually became extinct in the face of the advance of fully modern humans.

Clearly, a transformative evolutionary shift took place in Africa between 100,000 and 50,000 years ago. What was the crucial shift? A recent study gives the answer.[1] Critical anatomical changes in the vocal tract, allowing the articulation of the full range of sounds essential to human language, first appeared between 100,000 and 50,000 years ago. The crucial changeover was the development of two sound-producing cavities of relatively equal length—the mouth cavity with the tongue and the throat passage with the vocal cords—with the throat passage extending downward, fully perpendicular to the back of the mouth cavity. This feature is lacking in all other primates, including the anatomically modern humans of Africa and the Levant of 100,000 years BP. Among fully modern humans, language is everywhere the fundamental tool for creating and sustaining wider networks of relationship and, thus, community. The social and cooperative units of Neanderthals were very small, basically little more than nuclear families. The evolution of the full language capacity, in allowing early fully modern humans to form significantly larger cooperative and habitation groups, was perhaps the prime advantage of our common fully human ancestors over all other hominin species.

Archaeological finds point to the eastern side of the continent as the zone of the emergence of the mental and imaginative capacities that all modern humans share. In those parts of Africa, major new developments in tools, adornment, symbolic expression, and social relations took shape between 90,000 and 55,000 BCE. These include the making of deliberately fashioned bone tools in East Africa; shell beads in southern and eastern Africa; and very small backed stone blades, earliest in southern Africa but later also in East Africa. A striking signature of the emergence of the capacities of imagination and thought like those of modern humans was the making of the earliest symbolic representations, in the form of markings engraved in ochre, dating to 77,000 years ago in South Africa. Another signal development by the period was the exchange of valued kinds of stone or other goods over distance, indicative of the emergence of social relations of reciprocity and formal procedures for cooperation between otherwise separate communities.

By 50,000 BP humans were ready to embark on another new direction of history, spreading out from Africa into other parts of the world. Two initial outward movements may have taken place, one along now submerged southern Asian coasts and one across Sinai into the Middle East, branching westward toward Europe and east across Asia.

The First Great Transition

For 35,000 years human beings, wherever they spread in the world, continued to be gatherers and hunters of wild food. Then, separately in different parts of the world, the climatic shifts at the end of the ice age set off a long episodic 'First Great Transition' of human history, from foraging to food production—from the gathering and hunting of wild food to the deliberate tending and protection of animals and plants.

The initial warming of climate in the Bølling-Allerød interstadial, 12,700–10,800 BCE, brought increased rainfall and warmer conditions in many African regions. Three sets of peoples, speaking languages of the three language families that predominate across the continent today, probably began their early expansions in this period. Nilo-Saharan peoples spread out in the areas around and east of the middle Nile River in what is today the country of Sudan. Peoples of a second family, Niger-Kordofanian, spread across an emerging east–west belt of savanna vegetation from the eastern Sudan to the western Atlantic coast of Africa. In the same era, communities speaking languages of the Erythraic branch of the Afrasian (Afroasiatic) family expanded beyond their origin areas in the Horn of Africa, northward to modern-day Egypt.[2]

This last point needs special emphasis, considering how widespread the notion is that the Afrasian family somehow originated in the Middle East. The linguistic, genetic, and archaeological evidence combine in locating the origins of this family far south in Africa, in or near Eritrea or Ethiopia, and not at all in Asia.[3] A complex array of lexical evidence confirms that the proto-Afrasian society belonged to the pre-agricultural eras of human history.[4]

The return of colder, drier conditions in the Younger Dryas, 10,800–9500 BCE, set off a new round of subsistence innovation, before fully post-glacial conditions took hold in the tenth millennium BCE. In a few areas people began the first protecting of plants or animals, in this fashion laying the earliest foundations for agriculture. The rise of agriculture after 9500 BCE quantitatively transformed the directions of human history. The deliberate tending of plants and animals multiplies by magnitudes the amounts of food potentially obtainable from the same amount of land. The growth of human populations from a few hundred thousand to billions, social stratification, urban life, states, and the development of complex technologies all rest on the development of agricultural sources of food. In Africa peoples of two distant parts of the continent's middle belt independently set in motion developments leading toward agriculture.

In the tenth millennium in the savannas of modern-day Mali, communities speaking early daughter languages of proto-Niger-Congo, itself an offshoot of the Niger-Kordofanian family, began to intensively collect wild grains. Their Ounjougou culture is the earliest identified facies of the West African Microlithic, the archaeological complex of the early Niger-Congo peoples. Integral to their new subsistence system was their invention of possibly the earliest ceramic technology in world history, between 10,000 and 9400 BCE. Rather than grinding whole grains into flour, the Ounjougou people made the whole grains edible by cooking them in pots.

When did the shift from gathering to the cultivation of grains begin among Niger-Congo peoples? The archaeobotanical evidence is as yet unknown for the crucial periods. Provisional reconstructions of several early Niger-Congo verbs specifically connoting cultivation suggest, however, that the transition from collecting to cultivating grains in the grassland savannas of West Africa took place broadly in the period 9000–6000 BCE.[5]

West African agricultural history entered a new stage around the sixth millennium, with the cultivation of two new crops, Guinea yams and oil palms. The technological signature of this development was the adding of polished stone axes to the West African Microlithic toolkit. The new crops and tools opened the way for communities of the Benue-Kwa branch of Niger-Congo to spread between 5000 and 3000 BCE into the rainforest zones of West Africa, from modern-day Côte d'Ivoire to Cameroon. With polished stone axes they could clear forest for raising yams and oil palms, both of which require direct sunlight. An additional technological innovation probably dating to this period was the invention by the Benue-Kwa of broadlooms for weaving raffia-cloth. After 3000 BCE one offshoot of the Benue-Kwa group, the Bantu, carried the yam-based variety of West African agriculture farther southward and eastward through the equatorial rainforests of central Africa.

Far to the east, the Northern Sudanians, a Nilo-Saharan people of the southern eastern Sahara, took a very different first step toward agriculture. In the mid-tenth millennium BCE, a belated shift to wetter conditions spread Mediterranean climate, with cool-season rains and Mediterranean wild animals, most notably the cow, south to the middle of the Sahara. Contemporaneously, tropical grassland and steppe environments advanced north to the middle of the Sahara. The Northern Sudanians, following the climatic shift northward, encountered cattle at the interface of the two climatic regimes and, between 8500 and 7200 BCE, initiated the earliest herding of cattle in world history.[6] Like the Ounjougou people 2,500 kilometers to the west, they collected wild grains but, differently, they ground their grain into flour.

Around 7200 BCE a new development appeared in the eastern Saharan archaeology: neighborhoods of substantial homesteads, with thornbush cattle pens, round houses, and grain storage pits, and with sorghum as the notable grain. The linguistic evidence in this case strongly backs these indirect archaeological indicators that the Northern Sudanians of this era had begun to tend grain crops. They had important contacts, too, with the contemporary Afrasian communities immediately east of them in the Red Sea Hills region. These communities spoke early daughter dialects of the proto-Cushitic language. In the second half of the seventh millennium, the northernmost Cushites, ancestral to the modern-day Beja (the Medjay of the ancient Egyptians), were the intermediaries in the diffusion of sheep from the Middle East to their Northern Sudanian neighbors. Even earlier, the Cushites began, like the Northern Sudanians, to raise cattle, and they either collected or cultivated sorghum.[7]

The Northern Sudanians of the ninth millennium, along with a closely related set of Nilo-Saharan peoples, whom the archaeologist J. E. G. Sutton called the 'Aquatic Civilization of Middle Africa,' participated also in a second independent African invention of ceramic technology. The aquatic societies responded in a different fashion to the mid-ninth-millennium climatic amelioration. They became specialist fishing and hippopotamus-hunting peoples along the new rivers and lakes of the Sahara, and in the later ninth millennium they spread this economy westward across the southern Sahara.

Drier climates, 6500–5500 BCE, then shrank many Saharan streams and lakes, shifting the balance of advantage away from the aquatic communities. As a result, in the sixth millennium the descendants of the Northern Sudanians spread their agri-pastoral economy across the southern Sahara, displacing or assimilating many of the aquatic communities. Where perennial water resources existed, such as along the Nile, the aquatic livelihood persisted, but combined now with herding and probably cultivation. The inhabitants of the Khartoum Neolithic site of 5000 BCE along the Nile participated in a particularly notable invention, of cotton textile technology, attested by their possession of spindlewhorls.[8]

As with ceramic technology, here also African societies were leaders in innovation in the early agricultural eras. The history of cotton teaches a striking lesson as well—that peoples with no knowledge whatsoever of each other can and do arrive at parallel inventions. The domestication of cotton as a fiber plant for textile production took place separately in three distant parts of the globe: the eastern Sudan of Africa, India, and the New World. In each region the inventors of cotton weaving domesticated their own indigenous species of cotton. The evidence from Khartoum places this development as early in Africa as in India.

THE ERA OF AGRICULTURAL ELABORATION, 6500–3500 BCE

Parallel to trends in other world regions of early agriculture, so also in Africa the period 6500–3500 BCE was a time of growth in the variety and proportional contribution of agriculture to the diet. The Niger-Congo farmers brought two savanna legumes, the African groundnut (*Vigna subterranea*) and the black-eyed pea (*V. unguiculata*), into cultivation during this time. The Sudanic agripastoralists of the southern Sahara and the Sahel added melons and gourds of several varieties to their original emphasis on sorghum, and also began raising castor beans, spreading these crops to ancient Egypt by or before the third millennium BCE. Niger-Congo farmers and Sudanic agripastoralists separately domesticated an additional major grain crop, pearl millet (*Pennisetum glaucum*). In the Ethiopian highlands reconstructed early farming lexicon reveals that the Cushites during this time began to supplement their stock raising with two highland African grain crops, finger millet and t'ef.

The seventh to fourth millennium BCE was also a period of world history in which crops and animals domesticated in one seminal region first spread to other such world regions. In Africa between 6000 and 4000 BCE, Cushitic peoples domesticated the donkey, native to the Red Sea hills and the arid foothills of the northern Ethiopian highlands. Donkeys then spread via Egypt to the Middle East, where they became the earliest important beasts of burden. Sheep and goats, as noted, spread the opposite direction even earlier, in the second half of the seventh millennium, and rapidly became important animals in the Sudanic and Cushitic agripastoral traditions. From the Sudanic herders both goats and cattle spread west to the Niger-Congo societies of West Africa, again at a still uncertain period, but certainly before 3000 BCE. An early crop of the Sudanic agripastoralist tradition, sorghum, may have spread equally early to the Niger-Congo cultivators. African groundnuts and black-eyed peas diffused the other way, from Niger-Congo farmers to their Sudanic and Cushitic counterparts, reaching as far as northern Kenya by the third millennium BCE.

An especially interesting historical problem far from being solved is the question of how three important grain crops domesticated in Africa, sorghum, pearl millet, and finger millet, reached India between 3000 and 1000 BCE, without passing through the Middle East first. Might seagoing trade have already connected northwestern Africa and India by that time?

What may surprise is that Egypt was not an initiating region of these seminal developments. The indigenous Afrasian communities of the Egyptian Nile in the seventh millennium were still hunter-gathers. They gradually transformed their subsistence economy by adopting two staple crops, barley and wheat, along with sheep and goats from the Middle Eastern center of domestication. Melons, gourds, and donkeys reached them from the Sudanic agripastoralists to the south; surprisingly, cotton did not. Word borrowings in ancient Egyptian confirm that Sudanic herders also significantly influenced Egyptian beliefs and practices relating to cattle.[9]

THE SECOND GREAT TRANSITION: AFRICAN BEGINNINGS

By the fifth millennium BCE, the growing variety and productivity of agriculture brought about a growth in the size and density of human populations, such that a Second Great Transition, from villages and tiny local political units to towns and states, began to take place in several world regions. Historians have long identified Egypt as an early locus of this transition in the African continent. But because of the dominant Western idea of Egyptian exceptionalism, what historians have often not recognized is that the formative area of ancient Egyptian culture, southern Upper Egypt, was the *northern* outlier of a wider nexus of emerging complexity in the fourth millennium.

The first evidence of emerging complexity in the fifth millennium appeared not along the Nile itself, but in the then steppe country west of northern Lower Nubia. Three hundred kilometers from the river, the inhabitants of Nabta Playa erected an extensive megalithic archaeoastronomical array. The associated burials, of both cattle and people, reveal a wealthy pastoral society, with a complex ritual basis, in existence centuries before similar complexity in Upper Egypt.[10]

A further progression toward social and political complexity followed in the fourth millennium BCE, this time along the Nile itself, with states and the first towns appearing between the Nile–Abbay confluence in the south and southern Upper Egypt in the north. Town life along the river grew in importance, even as the drying of the Sahara in the fourth millennium brought the Nabta Playa culture to an end. Because of the relative archaeological neglect of Nubia, just two excavated sites, Shaheinab and Qustul, provide most of our knowledge of this era south of Egypt. The two towns lay respectively at the far northern and far southern ends of a thousand-kilometer stretch of cultural commonality along the Nile. On sites of ritual importance the people of this Middle Nile culture built large conical earthen mounds, reshaped since then by rain and wind into more formless-seeming tumuli. Ritual sites of this type represent a very long-lived cultural and political tradition, lasting in some cases down to recent centuries.

Qustul was the capital of wealthy kings from the mid-fourth millennium BCE up almost to the unification of Egypt late in the millennium. Like the earlier Nabta Playa pastoralist sites, the Qustul sites include numerous cattle burials. Pictorial documents in the royal graves explicitly depict the kings of the Qustul state as having conquered Upper Egypt. There is no *a priori* reason to reject these claims. If one sets aside the received notion of Egyptian exceptionalism, it is quite evident, as the archaeologist Bruce Williams argues, that here was a kingdom every bit as significant as its late pre-dynastic contemporaries in Upper Egypt.[11]

Behind the rise of the highly centralized kingship of dynastic Egypt may have been an additional factor, the adoption in late pre-dynastic Upper Egypt of elements of the rituals and royal ideology of the Qustul kingdom. Early Egyptian royal tombs, before the shift to pyramid building in stone, were covered with a conical mound of earth, mimicking the practice known as early as the fourth millennium in Nubia and still prevalent 2,000 years later in the kingdoms to the south. These outward resemblances accompany resemblances in ideology as well, from the special ritual significance accorded cattle to the claims of both Sudanic and Egyptian kings to a degree of personal sacredness unparalleled in the Middle East. Did Upper Egyptian rulers build their power in the later fourth millennium BCE by adopting legitimizing ideas from Nabta Playa and Qustul? The outward signs, at least, favor that proposal.

Two notable kingdoms persisted in Nubia through the Old Kingdom period. The more powerful state, Kerma, ruled the Dongola Reach in Upper Nubia and probably other lands farther south. The great fortifications at Buhen in Lower Nubia, built by the rulers of the Middle Kingdom, 2040–1700, after their conquest of the northern Sai kingdom, suggest an Egyptian concern with the potential threat from Kerma farther south. The placement of Kerma's capital at the northern end of its territories, closest to Egypt, may mean that the rulers of Kerma felt a similar concern about Egypt, or simply that they situated their court to better oversee trade with Egypt. The massive royal funerary sites at Kerma city give a sense of the power of this kingdom at its height. But as almost the sole excavations relating to the Kerma state, they leave us little idea of urban life more generally in Kerma and no knowledge of how much farther south Kerma's power might have extended.

In the late 1500s Thutmose I accomplished something new, a conquest that extended Egyptian power into the Dongola Reach between the third and fourth cataracts and imposed a thoroughgoing colonial rule over the region. A common historical presumption is that this conquest destroyed the Kerma kingdom. But was that the case? With the decline of Egyptian power in Dongola Reach in the twelfth and eleventh centuries BCE, many features of material culture reminiscent of Kerma's high era re-emerged in the archaeological record. Somewhere to the south, beyond the reach of Egyptian rule, the political and cultural traditions of Kerma apparently persisted.

In the ninth century BCE there arose south of Egypt a new major kingdom, called Kush by Egyptians. Historians today give this kingdom two names, Napata during the period up to the sixth century when its capital was at Napata city on the Dongola Reach, and Meroe after the sixth century, when the capital shifted to the southern city of Meroe. Around 750 BCE in the reign of Piye, Napata conquered Egypt, and Piye's successors ruled large parts of Egypt for much of the next hundred years. The future capital, Meroe city, already existed in the seventh century and surely lay within its southern territories.

The Western scholarly tradition of Egyptian exceptionalism obscures a startling fact. Piye's immediate successors ruled over an empire probably larger in territory than native Egyptian kings ever did, even at the height of the New Kingdom. In Egypt they tailored their religious relations and political propaganda to appeal to their Egyptian subjects, and for their efforts got recognition, from the parochial perspective of the Egyptians, as Egypt's twenty-fifth dynasty. From the record they left behind in Egypt, it is nevertheless evident that the Napata-Meroe rulers understood themselves as ethnically different and were not hesitant to represent themselves as such in royal art. Nor were they hesitant to make changes in the relations of political to religious power, with lasting effects even after Egypt regained its independence in the seventh century.[12]

The Napatan rule in Egypt from the mid-eighth to mid-seventh century was a conquest by a foreign power as much as the subsequent Assyrian and Persian conquests. The foreign power did not fade away just because it eventually lost the conquered Egyptian lands. The lands from the first cataract to the Nile–Abbay confluence remained the territory of one Napata-Meroe empire from the eighth century BCE until the third or fourth century CE, a period of more than 1,000 years. The empire became a manufacturing center of cotton textiles in its several cities along the Nile; Meroe city itself became a major iron-producing center. The kings built dams and encouraged new irrigation techniques to enhance animal husbandry and cultivation, and the state began to keep written records in its Meroitic language.

EARLY TOWNS AND STATES IN WEST AFRICA

A second early African development of towns and states began in West Africa in the second millennium BCE. In the Tichit region of today's Mauretania, along a low escarpment with reliable water sources, a 200-kilometer skein of large villages and small towns arose before the middle of the second millennium BCE. Each settlement seems to have specialized in a particular product for trade: one settlement produced grindstones, another arrowheads, still another beads, and so forth. At the middle of the skein lay one town larger than all the rest. Its location and greater size mark it out as the possible capital town of an early state ruling over that skein of settlements.

An additional region where the development of more complex polities appears to have been underway in the mid-second millennium was the Aïr Mountains of modern-day Niger. The archaeologist Augustin Holl argues for an independent invention of copper metallurgy in Aïr in the period 2500–1500 BCE. Five large megalithic elite burial sites existed in separate parts of the region during the early eras of copper production, indicative of the existence of several large chiefdoms or small kingdoms.[13] Were there also towns connected with these sites? That possibility remains to be archaeologically explored.

As early as the eleventh century, the centers of lasting urban development and commerce shifted south to the better-watered Sahel belt. Central in the new developments was the Inland Delta of the Niger River in modern-day Mali. Well before 1000 BCE peoples of this region specialized in different kinds of food production for trade. Farmers among the bayous of the Delta domesticated African rice (*Oryza glaberrima*) probably as early as the fourth millennium, while other communities became fishing specialists. Savanna farmers outside the Delta supplied sorghum and other savanna crops, along with domestic animals to the Delta communities. By the early first millennium BCE, the growth of manufacturing turned these long-existing trade relations into an emerging commercial revolution, with merchants, regular market centers, and long-distance transport of goods by both boat and donkey.

Urban life in the western Sudan and Sahel evolved in a unique fashion. The towns and cities developed out of earlier village clusters, in which each village had engaged in a different kind of production—cotton textile weaving in one village, potting in another, and leather working in still another. A fourth manufacturing specialization, ironworking, further diversified production between 1000 and 500 BCE, while the importation of copper from Aïr and from new mines in the far western Sahara greatly expanded the long-distance sector.[14] Another valued metal, gold, coming from upper Niger River goldfields, further enhanced these trends by the late first millennium.

Most intriguing, ironworking may have been separately invented in sub-Saharan Africa. Iron smelting is present in to the tenth and eleventh centuries BCE in sites as far apart as Rwanda and Lake Chad, too early and too far south to be reasonably explained as having diffused from an origin just 500 years earlier and 3,000 kilometers away in Anatolia, especially since iron did not reach the intervening lands, such as Carthage and Egypt, until *after* the tenth century BCE.

In the north-central parts of modern-day Nigeria, the new directions of economic change eventuated, between 700 and 400 BCE, in the emergence of the earliest significant state as yet known from West Africa, associated with the Nok culture. Around the central areas of this culture, excavators have unearthed many huge terracotta sculptures, broken and buried in the graves of high-rank persons. From the distribution of its cultural remains, the Nok state appears to have been as large as any kingdom of more recent centuries in the region. Iron was a major product, and it was probably a center for tin mining as well.

West Africa's commercial revolution was underway in the same broad time frame as the First Commercial Revolution of world history, which linked the Mediterranean and the Middle East via sea and overland trade connections to India and to Southeast Asia, Indonesia, and East Asia.[15] It is often assumed that the rise of the Garamantes in the Fezzan oases of the north-central Sahara after 900 BCE rested on their position as intermediaries between the two commercial revolutions. The evidence for a direct Garamantes role is still sparse, but contact of some kind did exist between the Inland Delta and Carthaginian commercial spheres: the peoples around the Delta acquired horses, along with the Punic name for the animal, sometime in the first millennium BCE.

Regular trans-Saharan trading networks likely did not develop, however, until the establishment of camels as beasts of burden and primary food animals among the inhabitants of the northern Sahara. Timothy Garrard has proposed that the opening of the Roman mint at Carthage in the late third century CE reflects the arrival for the first time of West African gold from across the Sahara. Most tellingly, he shows that the system of gold weight measures used by West African merchants right down to the nineteenth century preserved the particular system put into effect at the Carthage mint.[16]

EARLY TOWNS AND STATES IN
THE HORN OF AFRICA

Urban centers newly emerged also in the Horn of Africa in the first millennium BCE. Differently from the endogenous rise of towns and cities in the western Sahel and Sudan, the founding of urban centers in the Horn was owed in large part to the First Commercial Revolution. South Arabians from the opposite shore of the Red Sea, like the Phoenicians who founded Carthage and the Greeks who founded Cyrene, came to Africa seeking new commodities and new sources for old commodities—initially frankincense and myrrh, but subsequently tortoise shell and ivory—and their settlements took the form, like Carthage and Cyrene, of city-states, planted amidst the indigenous Cushitic pastoral and farming populations of the northern Ethiopian highlands.[17]

At first, the routes tying the Horn of Africa to the First Commercial Revolution passed overland through South Arabia to the Levant. After 300 BCE, the Red Sea itself became the central conduit of trade between the Mediterranean and the expanding commercial networks of the Indian Ocean. Sea routes passed from the Gulf of Aden across the Arabian Sea to India and from India to Indonesia, and south down the East African coast at least as far as modern-day Dar-es-Salaam in Tanzania. The terminus of this latter route at the close of the first millennium BCE was Rhapta, the earliest known East African town.

In the early first millennium CE, the kings of one far northern Ethiopian city-state, Aksum, brought all the towns and the countryside of the northern Horn of Africa under their rule. By controlling, protecting, and taxing commercial enterprise in the Horn and in the southern Red Sea, the Aksumite kingdom grew into a regional power, with hegemony extending to South Arabia as well. A notable effect of Aksum's dominant position along the main route linking the Mediterranean to the Indian Ocean was the spread of Christianity to Aksum, with King Ezana adopting it as the official religion about thirty years after Constantine had taken the same step for Rome.

The Sassanian conquest of South Arabia in the 570s undermined Aksum's predominance in the Red Sea trade, and the rise of the first Islamic Empire in the 630s to 750s completed Aksum's isolation from the main lines of commerce. In establishing Damascus as their capital, the Umayyad caliphs shifted the pivotal commercial sea link between east and west to the Persian Gulf. For a century the Red Sea became a commercial backwater.

From a comparative world history perspective, the significant consequence was that the Aksumite kings built a new material basis for their state, feudal in character. The transformation of Aksum from the later seventh to the ninth century strikingly parallels the course of change in contemporary, early medieval Western Europe. Urban life collapsed, with even the city of Aksum shrinking to an episcopal center of perhaps a thousand people. The kings created a horse-mounted military class by granting fiefs to their soldiers, with the peasants of each fief owing a portion of their product to their lord. The titles of provincial officials in late pre-feudal Aksum became the titles of the higher nobility. Monasteries became the principal centers of education and literacy. Kings granted fiefs of land to the monasteries to support their activities as religious centers, and the monks often acted as missionaries in spreading Christianity into the outlying areas of the kingdom.

One notable difference distinguishes the feudalisms of Europe and the Ethiopian highlands. Rights to land in pre-feudal Aksum were vested in the local peasantry, rather than in great landed magnates, as in the western Roman empire. As a consequence, a fief in feudal Aksum—and in its successor states, the Zagwe kingdom of the twelfth and thirteenth centuries and the Solomonic kingdom from 1270 onward—gave the lord a right to a portion of the peasant's production and certain other manorial privileges, but left the local farmers not as serfs, but as free people, able to bequeath the land they worked to their relatives and descendants.

THE ERA OF EMPIRES

Even as the northern Horn of Africa was entering into a long period of feudal governance in the later first millennium CE, in the savannas of western Africa an age of empires was beginning. Wagadu (Ghana), the earliest known large empire, rose to prominence before mid-millennium. Stretching from the Inland Delta of the Niger to

Senegal, Wagadu lay athwart the key trade routes linking the goldfields far to the south to the merchant networks of the Sahara. In an age when cities as such did not exist north of the Pyrenees, urban life flourished not just in Wagadu, but all across the western and central Sudan belt.

A series of other empires succeeded Wagadu in the centuries after its decline in the twelfth century: Susu from the mid-twelfth to early thirteenth century, with its power resting on control of the actual goldfields;[18] Mali from the 1240s to mid-fifteenth century, controlling access to both the gold sources and the northern outlets of the trade; and Songay from the mid-1400s to late 1500s, commanding the major Sahel trading cities and the salt trade of the Sahara. In the Chad basin the Kanem empire built its wealth and power, from the ninth to the fifteenth century, on a similar control over the access of neighboring states to the main trade routes of the central Sahara.

The commercial interests of these empires gave them strong ties to the Muslim world of those times. Islam had become established initially across North Africa following the early Muslim conquests between 642 and 710 CE. In the next several centuries it became the religion of the trans-Saharan trading networks. In the Wagadu and Mali empires as well, it became the religious allegiance of the merchants and the commercial centers. In the eleventh century the rulers of the Takrur kingdom of the Senegal Valley and the Kanem Empire of Lake Chad converted to Islam. The rulers of the later Mali and Songay empires also professed Islam, but the rural majority population in all those areas long continued to follow their older religions. Islam also spread with commercial relations along the East African coast, becoming integral to urban identity in the Swahili city-states by the twelfth century CE. In the Horn of Africa the spread of Islam, again among merchants, but also among the Cushitic pastoralist populations of the eastern Horn, provided religious backing for the military jihad of Ahmad Gurey (1527–43) against the Christian Solomonic kingdom of the Ethiopian highlands. In these various fashions Islam linked up large areas of Africa to major currents of world history between the seventh and fifteenth centuries. Timbuktu in the thirteenth century, for example, was not only a trade center intimately connected to the Mediterranean and Middle Eastern worlds, but a university town in the early sense of that term, with the university as a place where noted scholars gathered to write and teach.

West of the lower Niger River in today's Nigeria, a rich urban life developed in the second half of the first millennium CE. Ife, an early Yoruba city-state, grew into a major commercial entrepot, manufacturing glass beads and dealing in goods from the rain-forest and from the savannas to the north. Home to a splendid sculptural tradition of brass casting, using the lost wax method, it became, as well, the leading religious and ritual center of the Yoruba. An equally notable contemporary of Ile-Ife was the Igbo city of Igbo-Ukwu, also an artistic center for brass sculpture and the capital of a state, whose highly ritualized kings ruled the lands across the lower Niger, east of the Yoruba.

In the southern half of Africa, where agriculture did not arrive until 5,000 years ago, the first appearance of towns and states, not surprisingly, lagged behind areas farther north. In the equatorial rainforests of west-central Africa, long-distance commerce on the rivers of the Congo basin developed in the last millennium BCE out of an earlier trade in fish, farm products, products of the hunt, and stone tools among the Bantu societies, who had spread agriculture across the region 3000–1000 BCE, and the ancient foraging peoples of equatorial Africa, the Batwa ('Pygmies'). By mid-first millennium BCE the spread of iron across the Congo basin everywhere introduced a new manufacturing component to this trade. Other industries, notably raffia textile weaving and boat building, further fueled trade expansion. The Batwa carved out their own niche in the new economy by becoming specialist providers of honey, wax, skins, ivory, and other forest products.

In the Great Lakes region of East Africa, iron-using Mashariki Bantu settlers set off a different chain of developments in the early first millennium BCE. Encountering Sudanic and Cushitic agripastoralist communities, the Mashariki added sorghum and pearl millet from the Sudanic tradition and finger millet from the Cushites to their previously yam-based farming. The new crops, which required less rainfall than yams, allowed the Mashariki peoples to scatter out between 300 BCE and 300 CE across most of eastern and southern Africa. Iron technology spread with them, and the demand for iron helped stimulate new kinds of regional trade wherever they settled.

Mashariki communities who arrived at the East Africa coast toward the close of the first millennium BCE soon came into contact with the Indian Ocean developments of the First Commercial Revolution. The most salient and lasting effect of this encounter came not from the merchants who frequented East Africa's earliest town, Rhapta, but from Indonesian immigrants, who followed the Indian Ocean trade routes to East Africa and settled for a time at the coast before moving on to Madagascar around 300 CE. These ancestral Malagasy brought along several Southeast Asian crops, most importantly bananas, well suited to the wetter African tropical environments. Banana cultivation, which spread rapidly west to the Great Lakes and into the Congo basin, was far less labor intensive as well as more productive than yam raising. The historians Jan Vansina and Kairn Klieman have argued that the arrival of bananas in the Congo basin fostered a major leap upward in commercial activity in those areas, because reliance on the new crop freed up time for people to engage in trade and in the production of trade commodities.[19]

In the Congo basin political growth followed on the heels of these developments, with chiefdoms emerging between 500 and 1100 and, after 1100, kingdoms. The two earliest known kingdoms of the deep interior, the Songye and Upemba states of the middle Lualaba River region, date to roughly 1100–1400. In the lower Congo areas near the Atlantic coast, Kongo with its large capital city, Mbanzakongo, and several smaller provincial capitals flourished from around 1300 up to 1665. Both regions lay along major routes of long-distance trade and close to prime copper- and iron-producing areas.

In the African Great Lakes region, the earliest large states date also to 1100–1400. Supported by great wealth in cattle rather than trade, the rulers built extensive earthworks in their capitals. Several thousand people lived in these capitals, with their residential areas scattered over several square kilometers, interspersed with fields and pasture. These dispersed towns undoubtedly attracted trade in salt, iron, and food-stuffs, but their primary function was as political and ritual centers.[20]

In contrast, Southern Africa's first town, Mapungubwe, which flourished in the Limpopo Valley in the eleventh and twelfth centuries CE, was both a royal capital, with large stone structures, and the central entrepot connecting the source areas of ivory and gold in the interior to the sea routes of the Indian Ocean. The establishment of the Zimbabwe empire in the thirteenth century shifted the heartland of urban development north to modern-day Zimbabwe. The capital city of Great Zimbabwe, famous for its great stone buildings, had 15,000–18,000 inhabitants in the fourteenth century. Several provincial capitals in the empire, though smaller, appear also to have deserved the appellation of town.

AFRICA IN THE ATLANTIC AGE, 1440–1900

A third great transition in African history began in the fifteenth and sixteenth centuries, when western and southern Europeans, previously peripheral players in economic history across the eastern hemisphere, began to sail to every part of the world reachable by sea. The Spanish first, and then other Western Europeans, brought the Americas into continuous relation with the rest of the world, and the Portuguese, by sailing around Africa, directly linked up the farthest ends of the Old World. In so doing, Europe moved from the wings to center stage in a new global circulation of goods, people, and ideas.

For Africans the long-term changes set in motion by the new world historical dispensation fall into three periods—the early Atlantic age, from the mid-1400s to the mid-1600s; the middle Atlantic age, from the mid-1600s to 1800; and the late Atlantic age, from 1800 to the colonial 'scramble' for Africa at the end of the nineteenth century.

The early Atlantic age brought new prosperity to many Africans. Peoples of the Atlantic coast of the continent, previously only marginally connected to the thriving commercial and urban world of Africa's Sudan belt, became the central contributors to a new coasting trade. The Portuguese and Castilians in the fifteenth century established a pattern followed for two centuries, in which the European ships profited not just by obtaining products destined for European markets, such as gold, Malageta pepper, and tropical woods, but as transporters of African commodities from one coastal region to another. European ships, for example, carried cotton textiles of the Benin kingdom (ca. 1300–1897), located in today's southern Nigeria, to the Gold Coast to exchange for gold or to Sierra Leone to exchange for iron, which they then transported to Senegal to exchange for leather or slaves.

The commerce of the Sudan belt benefited as well, because African producers and merchants gained new outlets for their products and new sources of long-distance imports, and no longer depended solely on the trans-Saharan merchants and markets. The age of empire, it can be argued, came to an end in the western Sudan in the sixteenth century, not because of economic decline, but economic growth. The power of the empires rested on controlling access to two high-value commodities, gold and salt. The growth and spread even before 1500 of extended-family merchant firms, originally based in the Mali empire, stimulated demand for a new diversity of products and, over time, brought many new producing areas into far-flung networks of exchange. By the sixteenth century the diversity of products and multiplicity of centers of commercial production in West Africa undercut the ability of any one state to concentrate so much of the wealth and power. In place of the empires, numerous middle-sized kingdoms rose to prominence.

The middle Atlantic age, however, began a major realignment of Africa's trade relations with the rest of the world. In time one particular demand factor, with pernicious consequences over the long term, outstripped all the rest. The expansion of sugarcane planting in the Caribbean and Brazil in the seventeenth century immensely increased the call for a particular 'commodity,' human beings for slave labor. As European shippers turned more and more to slave trade and to paying for slaves with imports from Europe and Asia, the coasting trade shrank and African manufactures began to lose their distant markets.

Inland from the Atlantic coast, new states rose and old ones fell. The Asante and Oyo empires built their power in the later seventeenth and the eighteenth centuries as suppliers of war captives to the trade in human beings, although Asante, as a major producer of both gold and kola nuts, moved toward a more balanced economy in the eighteenth century. Dahomey in West Africa and the Kasanje kingdom in Angola prospered as essentially predatory states, always on a war footing. The old Kongo kingdom, in contrast, lost its former centrality in the trade networks of the Lower Congo and collapsed into thirty years of civil war in the last decades of the seventeenth century. The once-thriving urban centers of Kongo collapsed with it.

The late Atlantic period of the nineteenth century was an age of ironies for large portions of Africa. The British, after decades of profiting from slavery, became champions of suppressing the trade. Using diplomacy, stationing an anti-slaving naval squadron in West African waters, and establishing Sierra Leone as a colony for resettling freed slaves, the British very slowly cut into the Atlantic trade in human cargoes. But at the same time the slave trade simply expanded into new areas, as slave traffickers pressed their search for slaves deeper and deeper inland. Ovimbundu caravans from Angola traveled to the Lunda and Luba Empires of the southern Congo Basin, as well as to many chiefdoms and small kingdoms south of those empires. From the early 1800s onward, Yao and Swahili caravans carried slaves from east-central Africa states and from the East African interior to the Indian Ocean to meet a new demand for slave labor in the clove plantations of Zanzibar and the date plantations of Uman. In the second half of the nineteenth century, merchants from present-day Sudan allied with the Zande kingdoms of the far northeastern Congo Basin to raid for slaves destined for Egypt and the Muslim Middle East. In the last three decades of the century, mixed Swahili-Arab parties ravaged the eastern Congo Basin, also raiding for slaves. Adding to the terror in the 1880s and 1890s was the rapacious regime of the Congo Free State, essentially the private estate of Leopold, the king of Belgium. Leopold's concessionaires treated conquered communities no better than slaves, compelling them through mutilations and other brutal acts to produce rubber and other products desired in Europe.

Across the Sudan belt of western Africa, a different kind of ferment, Islamic in inspiration, reshaped the political landscape in the nineteenth century. Islam first became a vehicle for mobilizing popular sentiment against the existing political order in the seventeenth century in the lower Senegal Valley. Fulani immigrants from Senegal put these ideas into action in a new fashion in the early eighteenth century, raising a military jihad against the Susu kings in the Futa Jallon mountains of modern-day Guinea and establishing their own Muslim state in that region. The much wider Muslim political transformation of the Sudan belt in the nineteenth century began with a cleric, Usman dan Fodio, also Fulani, who lived far to the east in the nominally Muslim Hausa city-states of present-day northern Nigeria and southern Niger. In 1804 Usman, with a body of loyal adherents, raised the flag of jihad, and in the next decade and a half his forces and those of his followers conquered almost all of the Hausa areas, creating the caliphate of Sokoto. Inspired by this example, several other Fulani leaders farther west proclaimed their own jihads. The most important of these figures was Umar Tall, whose wars between 1836 and 1864 destroyed the non-Muslim kingdoms of Segu and Kaarta along the Niger River and created an unstable empire of shifting boundaries, brought to an end by French conquest in 1890.

Between 1880 and World War I European nations, step by step, imposed colonial rule all across Africa. The timing of the transformed power relations of Europe vis-à-vis Africa has a simple explanation: the Western invention in the second half of the nineteenth century of, first, repeating rifles and then machine guns destroyed a military balance that, as recently as the early nineteenth century, had been more nearly equal. Only Ethiopia and Liberia, the country established by freed American slaves in the 1820s to 1840s, maintained their independence. The kingdom of Darfur, so often in the news in recent years, held off colonial conquest until 1915.

Most Africans regained independence in the 1950s and the 1960s, and the rest in the 1970s, but they did so as citizens of new countries defined by colonial boundaries rather than by the very different political alignments of just eighty years earlier. Short as it was, the colonial era forever transformed the map of Africa. Islam took hold in the Sudan belt in rural populations who before colonialism had resisted adopting it; Christianity, often in highly Africanized forms, grew into the predominant religion across wide swaths of the continent. The historical memories and the social and ethnic allegiances of the previous age, however, did not disappear. In many of the fifty-three modern African countries the relevance of these factors greatly lessened over the past five decades. In other countries, including the Congo, Rwanda, and Burundi, they continued to generate conflict, factionalism, and violence. Everywhere the disincentives and disruptions to African production of the slave trade eras, deepened by the one-way extractive and single-product economic policies of the colonial era, have left the continent with a great deficit to make up.

AFRICA AND THE INTEGRITY OF WORLD HISTORY

To view Africa over the very long term is to discover that the notable developments of Africa's past followed similar pathways and proceeded at similar paces as comparable changes elsewhere in the world. Two great transitions of human history in the Holocene—from foraging to farming and, several thousand years later, from villages and informal governance to towns and states—not only were *not* late in emerging in Africa, but Africa was a continent of primary invention in those times. Cultivation of crops and herding of animals began in Africa as early as anywhere else except the Middle East, and only slightly later than there. The first domestication of cattle in world history took place in the southern half of the eastern Sahara 1000–1500 years earlier than the separate domestication of cattle around the eastern Mediterranean. The independent inventions by Africans south of the Sahara of ceramic technology twice, cotton textile weaving, raffia cloth weaving, polished stone tools, copper metallurgy, and probably ironworking reaffirm something historians have long understood—that particular advances in human technical capacities often arise more than once and in disparate parts of the world.

Within the overall progression of human history since the end of the latest ice age, the lag time between the earliest agriculture and the earliest towns and states in Africa accords with wider world history patterns. Typically, whether in the Middle East, Middle America, China, or Africa, the earliest urban centers and states came into being around 4,000–5,000 years after the first deliberate plant or animal tending. In the eastern Sahara the initial stage of the First Great Transition, from foraging to cultivation and herding, began around the mid-ninth millennium BCE. The second Great Transition in those areas, from localized political relations to states and from villages to towns, began in the fifth millennium at Nabta Playa and in the fourth millennium along the Nile itself, at such places as Shaheinab and Qustul in Nubia and Naqada in Upper Egypt. In West Africa the earliest towns and larger polities date to the second millennium. In those regions the span between first farming and first towns may have been as much as 6,000 or as little as 4,000 years, depending on how early the shift from gathering to cultivating wild grains came about.

On the other hand, exogenous factors may hasten the emergence of towns and states. The Zimbabwe empire and its capital, Great Zimbabwe, were founded in the thirteenth century CE, only about 1,400 years after the first farming and herding communities arrived south of the Zambezi River. External factors, in this case the demand for Zimbabwe's gold and ivory by the peoples around the Indian Ocean, created the wealth on which royal power was built. The kings controlled the major producing areas of these products and ruled over a much wider region as well, and the trade route giving the Swahili merchants access to these products passed from the coastal town of Sofala inland to the capital city.

African history cautions, as well, against the mistake of attributing all invention to the early regions of cities and states—to the cultural complexes historians have traditionally called 'civilizations.' Ironworking, for instance, rapidly established itself as a key productive sector in the commercial towns of West Africa in the first millennium BCE. But the men who innovated this technology lived elsewhere, in regions where village-scale residence patterns long prevailed; and ironworking spread equally rapidly across the non-urbanized, non-state parts of the continent.

Ancient Egypt exemplifies this point from an opposite standpoint. As important as Egypt became as a center of early state formation, it was not an initiating region in the first crucial transition of Holocene human history, to food production, but rather a crossroads in the subsequent diffusion of crops and animals. Its first large state, the Old Kingdom, took shape at one edge of a wider nexus of early complexity that included Saharan pastoralists, Nubian town dwellers, and the Qustul state to the south.

The events of the last 2,000 years deepened and extended the ways in which Africans participated in the wider compass of world history. The peoples of the Sudan belt and northern Africa already in the first millennium CE were more urbanized and more deeply intertwined economically with other world regions than were western and northern Europeans of the same period. Developments since 1500 CE, while transforming the place of Europe in world history, brought the rest of Africa equally deeply into the global sweep of events. Crops of both the Sudanic and West African agricultures, such as sorghum and black-eyed peas, crossed the Atlantic to the Americas. Native American crops, notably maize, cassava, broad beans, and peanuts, passed the other direction, to Africa. Niger-Congo Africans, forcibly brought to the Americas, carried with them the musical tradition that gave rise to both jazz and present-day styles of popular dance around the world. Uncovering the full body of African contributions is a historical work still in progress. It has only recently been appreciated, for example, that the Brazilian martial art *capoeira* carries forward a martial art tradition of the seventeenth-century Kasanje kingdom of Angola.[21]

Africa through all the earlier eras did not follow behind or lie outside the main trends and currents of human history. It is time to cease reading the economically destructive and socially disruptive encounters of the past few hundred years, and the enduring economic and political consequences of those developments for the continent, into the deeper African past, and to bring Africa directly and integrally, rather than as an afterthought, into world history.

NOTES

1. Philip Lieberman and Robert McCarthy, 'Tracking the Evolution of Language and Speech: Comparing Vocal Tracts to Identify Speech Capabilities,' *Expedition* 49, 2: 15–20.

2. C. Ehret, 'Reconstructing Ancient Kinship in Africa,' in Nicholas J. Allen, Hilary Callan, Robin Dunbar, and Wendy James, eds., *Early Human Kinship: From Sex to Social Reproduction* (Oxford: Blackwell, 2008), 200–31, 259–69.

3. C. Ehret, S. O. Y. Keita, and Paul Newman, 'The Origins of Afroasiatic,' *Science* 306 (3 December 2004), 1680–1, concisely summarizes the convergent findings of these three fields.

4. C. Ehret, 'Linguistic Stratigraphies and Holocene History in Northeastern Africa,' in Marek Chlodnicki and Karla Kroeper (eds.), *Archaeology of Early Northeastern Africa* (Posnan: Posnan Archaeological Museum, 2006), 1019–55.

5. C. Ehret, 'Linguistic Evidence and the Origins of Food Production in Africa: Where Are We Now?' in Dorian Fuller and M. A. Murray, eds., *African Flora, Past Cultures and Archaeobotany* (Walnut Creek: Left Coast Press, in Press).

6. Fred Wendorf and Romuald Schild, 'Nabta Playa and Its Role in the Northeastern African History,' *Anthropological Archaeology* 20 (1998), 97–123.

7. C. Ehret, 'Linguistic Evidence.'

8. For published plates showing the spindlewhorls, see A. J. Arkell, *Early Khartoum* (New York: Oxford University Press, 1949).

9. C. Ehret., 'The African Sources of Egyptian Culture and Language,' in Josep Cervelló, ed., África Antigua. El Antiguo egipto, una civilizatión Africana (Barcelona: Centre D'estudis Africans, 2001), 121–8.

10. J. McKim Malville, R. Schild, F. Wendorf, and R. Brenner, 'Astronomy of Nabta Playa,' in J. C. Holbrook, J. O Urama, and R. T. Medupe, eds., *African Cultural Astronomy* (Dordrecht, New York: Springer, 2008); M. Kobusiewicz and R. Schild, 'Prehistoric Herdsmen,' *Academia*, 3 (2005): 20–4.

11. Bruce B. Williams and K. C. Seele, *The A-Group Royal Cemetery and Qustul* (Chicago: University of Chicago Oriental Institute, 1986).

12. William Gordon, 'Cultural Identity of the 25th Dynasty Rulers of Ancient Egypt in Context: Formulation, Negotiation and Expression,' Ph.D. diss., University of California at Los Angeles, 2009.

13. Augustin F. C. Holl, 'Metallurgy, Iron Technology and African Late Holocene Societies,' in R. Klein-Arendt, ed., *Traditionelles Eisenwerk in Afrika (Köln: Heinrich Barth Insitut),* 13–54.

14. Roderick J. McIntosh, *The Peoples of the Middle Niger* (Malden, Mass.: Blackwell, 1998).

15. The characteristics of this 'First Commercial Revolution' are described in C. Ehret, *An African Classical Age* (Charlotteville, Va.: University Press of Virginia, 1998), 16–21.

16. Timothy F. Garrard, 'Myth and Metrology: The Early Trans-Saharan Gold Trade,' *Journal of African History* 23 (1982), 443–61.

17. C. Ehret, 'Social Transformation in the Early History of the Horn of Africa,' in Taddese Bayene, ed., *Proceedings of the Eighth International Conference of Ethiopian Studies* (Addis Ababa: Institute of Ethiopian Studies, 1988), Vol. 1, pp. 639–51; Peter R. Schmidt, Matthew C. Curtis, and Zelalem Teka, eds., *The Archaeology of Ancient Eritrea* (Trenton, N.J.: Red Sea Press, 2008).

18. Stephan Bühnen, 'In Quest of Susu,' *History in Africa* 21 (1994), 1–47.

19. Jan Vansina, *Paths in the Rainforests* (Madison, Wisc.: University of Wisconsin Press, 1990); Kairn Klieman, *'The Pygmies Were Our Compass': Bantu and Batwa in the History of West Central Africa* (Portsmouth, N.H.: Heinemann, 2003).

20. J. E. G. Sutton, 'Ntusi and Bigo: Farmers, Cattle-Herders and Rulers in Western Uganda, AD 1000–1500,' *Azania* 33 (1998), 39–72.
21. T. J. Desch-Obi, *Fighting for Honor: The History of African Martial Art Traditions in the Atlantic World* (Columbia, S.C.: University of South Carolina Press, 2008).

REFERENCES

EHRET, CHRISTOPHER. *The Civilizations of Africa: A History to 1800.* Charlottesville, Va: University of Virginia Press, 2002.
—— *History and the Testimony of Language.* Berkeley: University of California Press, 2011.
ILIFFE, JOHN. *Africans: The History of a Continent.* Cambridge: Cambridge University Press, 2007.
REID, RICHARD J. *A History of Modern Africa, 1800 to the Present.* Malden, Mass.: Wiley-Blackwell, 2009.

CHAPTER 26

....

EUROPE AND RUSSIA
IN WORLD HISTORY

....

BONNIE G. SMITH AND
DONALD R. KELLEY

EUROPA in Greek myth was a Phoenician princess who was raped by Zeus in the form of a bull, and her name became associated with the territories north of the Bosporus starting with the Balkans, set off from Africa and Asia. Later she was associated in a more complex mythical tradition with Noah's son Japeth, who in turn was associated with Europe (as was Ham with Africa and Shem with Asia); and this convention was reinforced by early cartographic tradition and by the empire of Charlemagne.[1] The subsequent 'Holy Roman empire' (later 'of the German Nation') survived for a millennium as a form of 'Europe,' especially under the Habsburgs, until it was dissolved by Napoleon in 1806 and succeeded by the Austro-Hungarian empire until 1918. Other expansive institutions in the modern period included the overseas empires of individual European nations, the Soviet empire after 1917, and the growing European Union of the late twentieth and twenty-first centuries.

ANCIENT EUROPA
....

The Roman empire was global in extent in that it incorporated territories from England to the Middle East and North Africa. Under Constantine, successor of Diocletian, it was Christianized and reunited. After Constantine's storied conversion, he summoned the first ecumenical council at Nicea, which issued the Western church creed. In the Byzantine empire based in Constantinople, Theodosius supported the orthodox faith and issued his own legal code. The empire continued to decline in the West, although the Papacy, successors of St Peter in Rome, emerged as a power in its own right and indeed a leader of the West. The Asian and Germanic tribes—Huns, Visigoths, Vandals, Lombards, Franks, and so on—moved into the territory formerly controlled by Rome and established their own governments and social institutions under the Christian faith and an overlying ecclesiastical government.[2] Justinian reconquered Italy and in the sixth century founded the great system of Roman law, which became a source and a model for legal systems around the world for centuries. Byzantium became the 'second Rome,' as Russia became the 'third Rome,' and both adopted the Greek orthodox religion which set them apart from Rome and laid foundations for the Great Schism in the fourteenth century.

The Holy Roman empire was established on the remains of the ancient Roman empire, having been overrun by various Germanic tribes, including Visigoths, Ostrogoths, Franks, Saxons, and Lombards, and Huns from Asia. All of them in classical tradition were regarded as 'barbarians,' although historians now prefer to talk of migrations rather than invasions. This 'new' empire, with Charlemagne's efforts at control through legislation and his agents (*missi dominici*), was from the first identified with Christianity and Christendom and so with the church, in a secular-spiritual partnership over 'Europe.' Empire and priesthood, *imperium* and *sacerdotium*—such was the organization of the Eurasian peninsula constituting what became the center of 'Western civilization,' resting on the ruin and remnants—and profound legacy—of Roman law.

In the seventh century, with the appearance of Mohammed and the Qu'ran, arose the religion and political power of Islam, and in the eighth century Muslims, having overrun northern Africa, began their conquest of the Iberian peninsula, defeating the last of the Visigothic kings but being defeated by Charles Martel at the battle of Tours (732), followed by Charlemagne's invasion of Spain.[3] Islamic culture flourished in Iberia, even as much of the later Middle Ages was taken up with the struggle with Spain and then the long Reconquista of the Moorish kingdom by Spanish monarchs, made just before the Columbian voyages supported by Isabella of Castile. In Syria and Mesopotamia, too, Islam long held sway. From the eleventh century, preceded by pilgrimages, eight Crusades were led by various European powers, which recaptured Jerusalem—and for a time Constantinople—and established a Christian Crusader's kingdom. In the thirteenth century the Mongols moved west and south, capturing Bagdad, while the Turks followed them, invading the Balkans and the Byzantine empire, capturing Constantinople in 1453, and becoming part of the international European state-system in the sixteenth century.

From the seventh century the Merovingian kings of Francia enjoyed military successes not only over various peoples in Frisia, Aquitaine, and east of the Rhine but also over the Arabs; and they formed a close alliance with the Roman church. In 771 Charlemagne became sole king, and after victories over the Saxons, Lombards, and Avars, he was elected Emperor in Rome and crowned by the Pope on Christmas Day 800, as a thousand years later was Napoleon, though defiantly holding the crown himself.[4] Meantime feudal and manorial institutions had developed, but the political structures of the empire were tenuous, and it fell into decay and collapsed, marked in 843 by the Treaty of Verdun. This treaty divided the territory between Charlemagne's sons, with Lothair keeping the imperial title and control of Italy and the 'middle kingdom' (Lorraine), Louis the German king of East Germany, and Charles the Bald king of the west Franks, basis of the future France. After Charlemagne Europe was a land of increasingly enserfed peasants and landed warriors, but the church provided another kind of government within feudal society through a network of bishoprics centering on Rome. In 1095 Pope Urban II celebrated the idea of a crusade based on the military initiative of 'Europe.' Such crusades for the recovery of the Holy Land against Arabs and Turks continued for two centuries, with diplomatic echoes for further generations.

Europe gained further self-definition through alien invaders from all sides: Scandinavians from the north, Islam from the south, and Mongols, Magyars, and Turks from the east. Cartographically Europe was best represented by the schematic T-O maps, with Asia above the cross bar, Africa to the right, and Europe to the left. The Crusades reinforced the division between East and West, as did the religious schism between Rome (western Catholicism) and Byzantium (Greek orthodox). According to Widukind of Corvey, 'the Italians, the French, and the Germans are the three outstanding races of Europe.' 'National' divisions were further emphasized by the universities and the Council of Constance. Economic activity and long-distance trade contributed further to the homogeneity of the European people. Out of the Conciliar movement came the semi-independent national churches, beginning with the Gallican and Anglican, which represented a main ingredient of the 'new monarchies' of the early modern period and the national churches, and their subsequent fusion in the modern state.

NATIONAL STATES

After the collapse of the Carolingian empire independent states began to form, such as Normandy (settled by Vikings), Aquitaine, and states in Provence and Italy. In Germany the four duchies of Saxony, Franconia, Swabia, and Bavaria moved toward independence.[5] Otto I of Saxony was elected king, made excursions into Italy, and claimed the imperial title by 'renovation' and support of the Papacy, but he died without issue. The relationship between empire and Papacy was disturbed by the Investiture Controversy, which began in the eleventh century. At this time the movement of Cluniac reform opposed clerical marriage and lay control of offices. In the east, Kiev, established as the first Russian state, adopted Christianity in its Byzantine form. The great Bulgarian empire was invaded by the Russians but enjoyed a revival in the thirteenth century and was invaded by the Muslims and Hungarians. In the thirteenth century the Mongols began invading Europe, while the Crusaders founded Christian states in the Middle East.

The twelfth century had seen a revival of ancient literature, especially Greek science and Aristotelian philosophy via Arabic translations, and through the new universities Latin became the lingua franca of modern scholarship, first through scholastic interpretations in theology, law, and medicine, and then through humanist attempts to restore ancient Latin language. Latin jurisprudence became the gate to careers in ecclesiastical and secular government. After this Latin stage came assaults on Greek and Near Eastern languages, especially those associated with the study of the Bible and with natural philosophy. Out of ancient logic and rhetoric developed the 'scholastic method' which infiltrated most of the other disciplines. The study of 'universal' history was pursued in the old Eusebian tradition, with non-Western traditions parallel to the development of Christianity, and the modern science of chronology, especially in the work of J. J. Scaliger, brought this up to date, with the addition of oriental languages in the seventeenth century, especially ancient Egyptian, which had fascinated scholars for centuries and produced modern 'Egyptomania.'

From the eleventh century the population of Europe began to grow and to promote agricultural expansion and the rise of urban commercial centers, which strengthened its position. Migrations and settlement were made into marginal areas in northern and eastern Europe, and manufacturing produced the first craft guilds and what used to be called 'primitive accumulation' of capital.[6] Peasant revolts and heresies accompanied this prosperity, as did the arrival of the Black Death from the east to Venice and the rest of Europe and Britain. Russia was conquered by the Mongols, and Kiev fell into ruins. Feudalism went into decline with the effects of the plague, but international trade continued to expand and so did high culture. The larger European nations developed royal and representative institutions and, driven by taxation, carried on wars as the primary function of the state, such as the Hundred Years' War between France and England. New states were founded in Bohemia, Hungary, and Poland, not to speak of the grand duchy of Lithuania; and Scandinavia achieved a union of the crowns of Sweden, Norway, and Denmark. In the later Middle Ages, too, arose the state of Moscow in the midst of Slavonic groups and following the Greek orthodox faith, which had long split Christianity, complicated by the invasions and settlements of Islam. All of these institutional developments prepared the way for Europe's relations with the wider world.

Europe's expansion eastward followed trade, but it proceeded more dramatically through the aforementioned Crusades from the late eleventh century accompanied by Muslim opposition and strong resistance. Contemporaneous to this was the drive westward by the Mongol empire and the conquest of North Africa by the Muslims. Throughout the middle ages European traders followed the silk road through Asian territories to China and Japan. The silk road was traveled first by Chinese traders through Central Asian middlemen by several routes, but Muslim expansion eastward led to the eventual closing of this road until the nineteenth century, when Western explorers and archeologists began again to travel it. Meanwhile Mongol conquests established an empire including China, Iran, Turkestan, and Russia. A century before Columbus, Chinese fleets ventured across the Indian Ocean to the rich ports of the Persian coast and Africa before retreating into isolation.

The western (Holy Roman) empire was restored under the Hohenstaufen, including Frederick Barbarossa and Frederick II, who concentrated on his Italian possessions to the neglect of Germany, which entered into its Interregnum in the mid-thirteenth century. A new phase of German history began with the election of the Habsburg emperors, the Golden Bull of 1356 having transformed the government from a monarchy to an aristocratic federation, with the principalities following their own political agendas on the road to independent statehood. In Spain the long movement of Reconquista was a more ambitious movement against the Muslims and their Moorish kingdom. England, abandoned by the Romans after Caesar, was similarly renewed under William the Conqueror of Normandy and the emergence of Parliament from the royal council and the institutions of monarchy, including the Common Law, Parliament, and the legal profession. By the fourteenth century Russia was emerging from the rule of the Tatars, and a century later Ivan (III) the Great became its first sovereign ruler and invaded Lithuania, which was reunited with the Polish kingdom. Kiev became the first Russian state and was converted to the Greek orthodox form of religion. The Islamic threat was replaced by that of the Ottoman Turks, who invaded the Balkans and finally conquered Constantinople in 1453, but the European and Russian states were preparing for their advancement outward.

EXPANSION WIDENS

The age of discoveries started earlier in the middle ages than has often been thought, being connected with the shift from Mediterranean dominance to the attraction of the western sea and Atlantic lands. From the eighth century Scandinavian sea raiders sailed south against British and European settlements and then west to the Faeroes, Iceland, Greenland, Vinland, and beyond. Blocked by Islam in the Mediterranean, Portugal, Aragon, Genoa, and other seafaring centers turned toward the Atlantic to reach the east, whether China, Japan, or the Indies. Portugal under Prince Henry the Navigator began the quest, first with the Canaries and other nearby islands, aiming for the gold reputed to be lodged with African rulers.

The Venetians and Genoese continued their contacts in the eastern Mediterranean, establishing their own trade routes and commercial empires. These contacts brought in new agricultural products, consumer goods, and influences in the arts. The later middle ages had seen the rise of trading centers both in Italy and the Netherlands, where self-governing communes appeared, whose ships expanded Europe's reach. The conflicts in Italy, especially between Florence and Milan, with Venice, Naples, and the Papacy joining the rivalries, drew interference from France with the invasion of 1494 and the response of Aragon and the subsequent 'Italian wars.' These intermittent wars dominated Europe until 1559, when they were succeeded by the civil and soon religious wars in France and the Netherlands, which began their own struggle of liberation from the expanding Spanish Empire. The Italian state-system and its diplomatic practices were continued by other states of Europe, and the experiences of the later fifteenth and early sixteenth century produced that 'politics Italian style' which was the basis of Machiavelli's and Guicciardini's conceptions of diplomacy and history and modern political thought continued by Bodin, Hobbes, and others that would in later centuries become influential around the world. The nation-state replaced the city as the central institution of European politics from the Reformation period, and the process of nation-building (or nation-invention) continued for centuries. Nation-building, European-style, would also become influential globally in future centuries.

In the West cities had begun as military or ecclesiastical foundations, but increasingly port cities grew as centers of regional and global trade and commerce as well as administration and religion, as seen in the case of the Netherlands and northern Italy. Venice in particular became the basis of a prosperous, commercial empire beyond Europe's borders and along with the other Italian city-states, including Florence and Milan, consolidated themselves and employed humanists like Leonardo Bruni and Coluccio Salutati in their governments. Humanists were those who studied and taught the humanities (*studia humanitatis*) and based their moral and political values on their understanding of classical antiquity. They were later drawn into politics and diplomacy. The early Reformers drew on humanism for their program, and Erasmus preceded Luther in his plans for a 'philosophy of Christ,' but Luther broke with him in moving toward a schism within the church, and the German princes took up his ideals in the name of political and religious independence from Rome. The Catholic Reformation, especially in its radical form of a 'Counter-Reformation' following the Council of Trent tried to preserve the old faith among the states of Europe but instead established a pattern of conflict and missionary expansionism that continued for centuries and outlived religious passions. The American frontier and Indian conflicts were later addenda to this process of movement outward from an 'old' center, from east to west.

Then Spain and England joined the explorations. English ships, especially from Bristol, crossed the Atlantic before Columbus, who drew on the information collected as well as common stories of Asiatic attractions. The Venetian citizen John Cabot started his voyages in 1496, made it to Newfoundland, and took formal possession of Nova Scotia (New Scotland) in 1497, while the Portuguese continued to explore the northern coast of 'America,' as it began to appear on maps. Last to enter the search was Spain, which benefited from the new art of printing to publicize the voyages of Columbus and later the conquistadores in Mexico and Peru. With these fifteenth-century voyages a new era of interaction between Europe and Russia and the rest of the world began.

The subsequent development of 'international law' extended the diplomatic and to some extent cultural arena of European activities and institutions, as European languages, religion, and certain values migrated with humans across the Atlantic, around Africa to Asia and beyond.[7] Disease moved with this expansion, even with the great ocean voyages of global discovery, especially because of Portugal, Spain, Italy, the Netherlands, and England. Closer to home, Emperor Charles V carried on a rivalry in the Mediterranean with the Ottoman empire, which became a participant in the European power struggles, before the Habsburg–Valois conflict came to dominate European politics during the Reformation.

RENAISSANCE INNOVATIONS

European diplomatic relations and institutions, increasingly important to Europe's place in the world, were creations of the Renaissance city-states of Italy, especially Venice.[8] At the end of the fifteenth century, they were adopted by the northern European states and Spain at the outset of the Italian wars and those between the houses of Valois and Habsburg, when Charles V was elected Emperor. In the 1530s the Ottoman Empire joined the European community of Christian nations when it established diplomatic relations with France. These diplomatic relations held the nascent European state-system together, eventually becoming the bedrock of European global empires. As an example, attempting to build alliances between states, in 1494 France invaded Italy, and Aragon responded, starting a series of wars that continued for centuries, as the dynastic struggles were joined by religious conflict, all of this shaped by diplomacy. In Florence Machiavelli developed his political insights in the context of these early wars and diplomatic efforts and promoted in effect a 'reason of state' beyond private morality.

In Germany Martin Luther was followed by Protestant princes—'protesting' imperial rule—who joined forces in a league against the emperor, the conflict continuing intermittently through the Thirty Years' War down to the treaties of Westphalia in 1648. Charles V's son Philip II of Spain headed a Catholic league against international Protestant forces, Calvinist as well as Lutheran, including England, which he tried to subdue by his grand armada in 1588. In France Francis I began the modernizing of the French monarchy. During the civil wars Henry of Navarre succeeded as Henry IV, bringing the Bourbon dynasty to the throne, and in England Elizabeth, daughter of Henry VIII, was succeeded by James VI of Scotland (James I of England). The subsequent conflict between the Stuart kings and Parliament degenerated into religious disputes, civil war, and the Puritan Revolution, succeeded by the rule of Oliver Cromwell, the 'Glorious Revolution' in 1688, and the rule of the Whigs. These exercises in power politics, inflected by diplomacy, underlay the growing competition for empire around the world.[9]

Western revolutionary patterns within states played themselves out in global terms and influence. The Dutch Revolt of the sixteenth century, when the Netherlands carried on resistance against the Spanish monarchy, continued off and on until Dutch independence in 1648. It was the first state created by revolution against a sovereign recognized in international law. In France evangelicals emigrated to Geneva, and some returned to establish congregations in France, which became centers of resistance protected by Protestant-sympathizing nobility, until resistance turned into active military Protest, establishing the foundation for worldwide networks. In the Protestant resistance, the Dutch, led by William of Orange, became associated with the French Huguenots, at least until the massacres of St Bartholomew in 1572, as part of the Calvinist international. After the wars the Edict of Nantes (1598) brought toleration to the French Protestants and an end to the civil wars, but the balance of parties was unstable, and the edict was finally revoked in 1688, resulting in the emigration of Huguenots to the east and west as far as South Africa and the New World.

At another corner of Europe, the Scandinavian powers struggled for control of the Baltic and its routes to global trade, while Poland waged its own fight for independence, and Lithuania and Muscovy were at war in the sixteenth century. Muscovy was ruled by Ivan III, who from the mid-fifteenth century undertook to conquer the non-Christian peoples to the northeast. Ivan IV ('the Terrible'), who was crowned Tsar of all the Russians, gained supremacy over the revolting Cossacks and pushed farther northeastward into Asia, finally subduing Kazan in 1552. Meanwhile, though Islam was pushed out of Spain by the Reconquista in 1494, the Ottoman Turks were expanding across Europe and the Balkans, already divided by Western and Eastern forms of Catholicism, almost to the gates of Vienna, including Hungary; and they produced what for centuries was known in diplomatic circles as 'the Eastern question.'

Imperial and colonial expansion produced Spanish dominance in the sixteenth century, and then slow eclipse alongside the rise of the Dutch and British empires from the seventeenth century. Spain provided the imperial model in 'New Spain,' especially in South America, the West Indies, and Mexico; the institutions of central-state rule, slavery, and international law proceeded from this experience. Spanish control provided jobs for *peninsulares* in the Caribbean and Latin America, while it led to an intermingling of peoples among those of European, African, and Native American heritage. The English and French in North America carried on imperial practices and state oversight along with political rivalry with Spain and between themselves. The Portuguese and Dutch founded their own imperial establishments in Asia and contributed further to global colonialism and state-building as well as trade.

Exploration and global expansion affected European culture and its ideas. With the Scientific Revolution and Enlightenment of the seventeenth and eighteenth centuries, some Europeans looked beyond the money to be made from the rest of the world. Elite leaders, like Louis XIV, borrowed heavily from non-Western styles: the king named himself the 'sun king' and garbed himself in feathers with a large Aztec sun on the front of his shimmering clothing. He built one of his mistresses a small palace entirely in imitation Chinese porcelain. Others went deeper: traveling Europeans such as the Jesuits provided clocks and telescopes to Chinese and other monarchs, and in return they studied foreign ideas of rational rule, free trade, and toleration. The Kangxi emperor of China was much admired not only by the Jesuits who had close-up knowledge of his way of life but by thinkers such as French author Voltaire, who saw Chinese monarchs as far more admirable than those of Europe because the former were instructed, accomplished, and intellectually curious. Frederick the Great wrote music for an opera in praise of Aztec ruler Monteczuma's religious toleration. Guidelines for good manners and examples of public education also came to Europe from the rest of the world, adding to the fund of other customs reported from around the world such as regular bathing and civilized sociability in coffee-houses.[10]

As Europe intensified its relationships with the world, Europeans gained new types of food, ending the subsistence economy in which they had lived until the eighteenth century. Foods such as apricots and melons had already entered Europe from beyond its borders, but now the diet became richer in nutritional value because of beans, tomatoes, potatoes, pumpkins, and squash, not to mention sugar, chocolate, coffee, and tea. The last four were stimulants, which helped advance the 'industrious revolution' of longer work hours and greater sobriety for Europeans who until that point had mostly consumed beer and other intoxicants. Opium from Asia relieved pain and stress much as chemical aspirin and tranquillizers would later do, also allowing people to work harder. Opium sparked poetry, such as Henrietta O'Niell's 'Ode to the Poppy,' and facilitated the writing of Samuel Coleridge, Sir Walter Scott, and other opium devotés.

From the seventeenth century on, European states fought one another for trading stations and other territorial rights in Asia and the Atlantic. The most bellicose were the Netherlands, Great Britain, and France, whose wars from the mid-seventeenth century until 1815—often called the great wars of empire—ended by toppling Dutch maritime hegemony, taming French ambitions, and signaling the ascendancy of Britain. Meanwhile, in the eighteenth century Russia continued its expansion by conquest in virtually all directions, and this expansion continued into the nineteenth century, as the empire came to control more than a hundred ethnicities across Asia and into Eastern Europe. The policy toward these ethnicities from Poland and Ukraine to the nomadic peoples of Siberia was Russification, which emphasized learning the Russian language and observing the Russian orthodox creed. For nomadic peoples in Siberia, Russian expansion ended their way of life, as the vast tracts of land needed for hunting and pasturing livestock were seized for mining, agriculture, and other ventures that would allow impoverished peasants from western Russia opportunity. None of these policies was completely successful; it was only after the Bolshevik revolution in 1917 that zealous Communists took up the cause of getting Muslim women to remove their veils and learn to read and assert their rights.

IMPERIAL EUROPE

Europe's expanding power around the globe never went unchallenged, but from the eighteenth century on, resistance and uprisings in North America, Haiti, and South America led to the creation of a series of new, independent nations in the western hemisphere that followed in the tradition of the Dutch revolt for independence. Additionally resistance to the European slave system involved uprisings and the formation of autonomous communities of escaped slaves. In 1776 the North American colonies began their armed resistance against Britain, becoming the United States of America under a Constitution adopted in 1789. In 1791, inspired by the grievances of both free blacks and slaves and by ideas coming from the Enlightenment and French Revolution, the French colony of Saint-Domingue revolted to become the independent state of Haiti. Finally, between 1810 and 1830 most parts of the Spanish empire in the western hemisphere achieved their independence, again influenced not only by the tradition of Native American uprisings in the empire and the successful creation of the United States, but also by theories of revolution, constitutionalism, and republicanism that had developed in Europe.

In India, the British, using troops from Europe, India, and other parts of the world were successful in expanding their base of operations in South Asia. The loss of the North American colonies made this expansion seem imperative. From having a few isolated trading posts on various parts of the long South Asian coastline, the East India Company inveigled, made deals, and fought its way into the heartland, where it negotiated with local rulers to serve as tax collector, military force, or business partner. In 1758 the Company's troops defeated Bengal's ruler and virtually took over the kingdom, gaining a base for its further incursions on other states. But the British hold on India was odd: even in 1947 on the eve of Indian independence, many states of the subcontinent's interior operated largely on their own.[11]

As the nineteenth century progressed, Europeans began to have their own products to trade with the rest of the world instead of relying merely on transshipping. While Russians could trade furs and England, France, and the Dutch could ship raw materials from their various trading stations and colonies, they did not have the rich stock of manufactured goods that much of the rest of the world had to offer. Their profits were mostly made by transshipping. That situation changed with the industrial revolution when they suddenly had cheap textiles, metal goods, weapons, and machinery of their own to sell. Developing alongside these were increasingly powerful European financial institutions funded in large part by the aristocracy, investing, making loans, and facilitating business transactions around the world. In the course of the nineteenth century Europe, and Britain in particular, developed as the world's pivotal financial center—a position it would hold long after it had lost its colonies in the mid-twentieth century. Financial power allowed Britain a great deal of indirect control in the newly independent countries of Latin America. Increasingly powerful in industry and trade, Japan for the nineteenth and even the twentieth century nonetheless allowed Britain dominance in finance.

Having more goods to sell and an increasing number of consumer desires made Europeans more exigent in their global relationships because the balance of payments was still not in their favor. In a specific example, Europeans had become great importers of tea—an item whose cost was still not met through sales of British manufactured goods. Instead Britain paid for its sales of tea from China with opium transshipped from India—a practice that drained China of its silver and that hurt its population. The Chinese outlawed trade in opium and seized imports from English ships. In 1839, the English fought back, blasting Chinese ports with its cannons and soundly defeating China's attempts at resistance. As a result of the Treaty of Nanjing, the Chinese had to open ports to British trade, which in practical terms meant their opening to all foreign trade. Somewhat later in 1853–4 the United States forced the Japanese to open ports to its ships, leading European nations to obtain the same access.

The French and British financed the building of the Suez Canal, while the French army fought its way to conquer Algeria as the last third of the nineteenth century opened. After the Indian Rebellion of 1857 the British government decided to take direct control of operations in India, declaring Queen Victoria Empress of India in 1876.

Meanwhile, deepening contacts with the rest of the world continued to reshape European society and culture. On the eve of the new imperialism and just after the Indian Rebellion, Charles Darwin published *Origin of Species* (1859) followed by *Descent of Man* (1871). Between 1831 and 1836, he had traveled aboard the Beagle around the coast of South America from Brazil to Chile, then across the Pacific, stopping at Micronesian islands, to South Africa, finally to arrive in England. Along the way he became adept at collecting fossils while also sending plants and other specimens back to scientists at home in England. Darwin argued that life had taken shape over countless millions of years before humans existed and that human life was the result of this slow development, called evolution. Though Darwin was hardly a social rebel, Darwin announced that the Bible gave a 'manifestly false history of the world.' The theory of natural selection, in which the fittest survive, suggested that human society was one where combative individuals and groups constantly fight one another.

Darwin's findings helped justify the intensification of Europe's attempted takeover of the world's resources and markets after the middle of the nineteenth century—sometimes called the 'new imperialism.' Inroads into the interior of Africa and land grabs in Asia were made easier by weather patterns that made for alternating floods and droughts in those regions. As these conditions led to famine and the attendant weakening of people's ability to resist invasions, the European takeover became possible. These so-called 'Victorian holocausts' affected China, India, and Africa among other places. Moreover, after 1870 two new European powers—Germany and Italy—joined in the race for empire, making the competition all the more intense and contentious. Germany became active in the Pacific, China, the Middle East, and on the east and west coasts of Africa. It also aimed to block the French in Morocco and elsewhere. German imperialism showed, however, lack of any consistency behind imperial policies: Germans indulged Samoans as the last remnants of a noble primitive civilization; wiped out many African ethnicities as unworthy of life; and conducted a vacillating policy toward the Chinese, at one time scorning their achievements and at another appreciating them. The same incoherence can be found in imperial motivation and practices around the world.

Although Europeans had been migrating for millennia, the movement of Russian and European peoples came to number in the millions as the nineteenth century drew to a close and remained high well into the twentieth century. Many settled in lands that had once been European colonies or that still were. The greatest number moved to the western hemisphere and to Australia and New Zealand, with tens of thousands of others crossing Asia and going into Africa to take up trade, agriculture, and other businesses. The British comprised the largest number leaving Europe, but Jews from Russia and Eastern Europe fled not only the weaker economies there but also the violent anti-Semitism that particularly characterized the Russian empire and was even sanctioned by its rulers. Scandinavia, late in industrializing, also sent a hefty percentage of its population. Many migrants, such as Sicilians, went to the 'New World' and, after sending funds back to the impoverished island, returned to live out the rest of their days, though many more settled permanently outside Italy.

TWENTIETH-CENTURY GLOBAL WARFARE

The intensification of interstate competition, however, was a constant among the European powers, causing them to arm to the teeth. Superior weaponry, alongside the decimation of the non-European population because of climate and famine, had helped Europeans make their inroads. By the end of the nineteenth century that weaponry was aimed additionally at rivals for direct imperial control in Asia, Africa, and the Pacific, heating up international antagonisms and imperial conflicts. The British put down the Boers with great difficulty in the South African War of 1899–1902, while it took a coalition of forces from eight imperial powers to defeat the Boxers in 1900, while also plundering China more generally. In 1904–5 the Japanese trounced the Russians in the Russo–Japanese War, bringing the first major defeat of a Western power in the twentieth century by a non-Western power and leading Russians to undertake the first of two historic revolutions. Another newcomer to overseas empire—the United States—defeated Spain, driving it from Cuba and the Philippines. Rebellions by colonized peoples erupted steadily in the pre-World War I years, not only in Africa and Asia but in Europe itself. In 1912 a cluster of Balkan states, which had already spun themselves off from the Ottoman empire in the nineteenth century, defeated the Ottomans during the First Balkan War in order to gain more land. In the Second Balkan War, however, they fought one another. The Third Balkan War, it is said, was World War I.[12]

Despite the force applied to the conquest of non-Western lands and despite the Darwinian rhetoric of white superiority, in fact the West continued its imitation of and engagement with the rich civilizations beyond its borders. Artists felt a strong influence from Japanese aesthetic values and created impressionist styles to express them. They gravitated to Asian and African philosophies, leading painters from Odilon Redon to Pablo Picasso to innovate in their art. Wassily Kandinsky invented non-representational art as part of his appreciation for African portrayals of a 'metaphysical principle' in their work instead of slavishly copying 'reality.' Composers such as Claude Debussy revolutionized music when they gravitated to non-Western musical values, while dancers invented so called 'modern dance' out of non-Western styles. Philosophers and other theorists were similarly drawn to non-Western ideas, shaping the writings of Nietzsche and Freud. The West created the major components of its culture by drawing on the rest of the world—and it would continue to do so down to the present.

World War I between the Allies (Russia, France, and Great Britain) and the Central Powers (Austria-Hungary and Germany) broke out at the end of August 1914 and saw its first major battles on the European continent. However, soon the Ottoman empire joined the Central Powers, while Japan, China, Australia, and Italy joined the Allies. The armed forces of still other nations joined the combatants, but the largest global contingents came from the colonial troops mustered to man the front lines both on the continent and across the empire. Germany, France, and Great Britain fought in various parts of Africa, uprooting villagers not only through conscription but through forced labor and seizure of resources. Colonial troops fought in the Middle East, to fulfill the Allies' goal of gaining Ottoman lands. In fact, the Allies induced famine to stir civilians to rise up against Ottoman rule. In addition, the French conscripted civilians in Southeast Asia into forced labor in France, replacing the men drafted for battlefront service. The war proved disastrous for most combatant countries, even for the victorious Allies. Four monarchies—German, Russian, Austro-Hungarian, and Ottoman—fell as a result of the war. While European production and agriculture declined, India, Australia, Japan, and the United States steamed ahead with replacement industries and farming. Germany's global holdings were divided among a range of allied nations including Japan, leaving general bitterness not only in Germany but in the new 'mandates' (colonies) themselves. Finally, veterans from the colonies often became the core of mass independence movements, having seen the barbarism of the so-called 'superior' nations of Europe.

Despite the atrocities and losses of World War I, Europe in the 1920s had reached the peak of its influence in the world, especially in organizations such as the League of Nations, which the United States Congress shunned. The Russian empire, which had collapsed with the Bolshevik Revolution of 1917, would later expand its reach and influence after World War II. Britain and France had bigger empires than before with new territories granted by the League of Nations in the mandate system. These included most of the Middle Eastern territories of the defeated Ottoman empire, among them oil-rich regions. Countries maintaining their independence, such as Iran, nonetheless felt the heavy hand of European influence. The Bolsheviks had more or less kept the boundaries of the old Russian empire, though they had lost control of Poland, Finland, and the Baltic states. From its territories, it welded the Union of Soviet Socialist Republics and like its imperial predecessor the USSR aimed at proselytizing and Russianizing (or Sovietizing) the inhabitants of Muslim and other territories.

Several global events destabilized Europe's and Soviet tranquility. First, an uprising in Egypt, the Gandhian mass movement against colonization, the rebirth of Turkey, and numerous other challenges from beyond the West threw the hegemony of Britain and France in particular into question. Second, Japan increasingly flexed its muscles with the aim of acquiring territory, not just in the adjacent regions but across Asia and the Pacific. By the late 1930s it had invaded China, set up the state of Manchuko, and proposed fighting and defeating the USSR, Britain, the United States, and other powers in the name of 'liberating' Asians from the West. Additionally, Italy and Germany also saw themselves as expanding, the former into Africa and the latter across Europe. Finally in 1929 the United States' stock market crashed, eventually losing 80 percent of its value. As the United States reined in credit, banks (most notably the Credit Anstalt in Austria) crashed around the world, trade plummeted, and agriculture suffered. The Great Depression of the 1930s, which caused suffering around the world, was a testimonial to the global interconnectedness of economies and the tenuous nature of European hegemony.

Global social order came under attack under the weight of economic collapse: imperial powers ratcheted up their demands on colonies; barter replaced trade and sophisticated financial mechanisms; unemployed men felt themselves better off following military leaders than upholding individual rights in a democracy. From Germany and Italy, through Eastern Europe to China and Japan, militarized politics, where one could gain prestige and good jobs following strongmen, captured people's allegiance. The spread of communications nationally and globally and the further development of weapons systems made the global situation tense, and nowhere more so than in Europe as the 1930s continued in the grip of economic depression. Mussolini and Hitler announced that expansion would right all wrongs and that military victory would fortify masculinity—so wounded by the Great War and by economic ups and downs. The Japanese also announced the need for expansion and a revival of the military spirit.

World War II broke out in East Asia when Japan invaded China in 1937 and in 1939 when Germany invaded Poland, producing a global war for empire that would last until 1945. Estimates as to the number dead vary, with a growing consensus that as many as 100 million perished. In this war, Germany and Italy allied primarily with Japan to form the Axis powers, while Britain and France allied at the outset until France was defeated in 1940. The British withstood the Battle of Britain, during which Germany used bombing in a future attempt to overwhelm it. Having failed, Germany then invaded the USSR in 1941, even though the two powers had signed a non-aggression pact in the summer of 1939. In December 1941, the Japanese decided to settle accounts with its Pacific rival, the United States, and bombed its assets in Hawai`i and the Philippines. At that point, Britain, the United States, and the Soviet Union along with dozens of smaller nations united to form a global alliance (the United Nations, it was initially called) to defeat the Axis. The former coordinated its efforts to a high degree in comparison to the Axis, whose heads of state never met in a threesome to plan strategy, align goals, and share resources. This was a fatal mistake, given the advantages in resources and manpower that the Allies enjoyed.

While the Japanese scooped up islands and Western holdings in the Pacific, German forces dashed across Europe, conquering most of Scandinavia and the west of the Continent. Before invading the USSR, it took over states and their financial and natural resources in southeastern and central Europe to add to its conquests in Austria, Czechoslovakia, and Poland in the 1930s. Germany's move to conquer the USSR in 1941, after initial victories, came to look increasingly foolhardy as its strategy of Blitzkrieg failed, given Hitler's refusal to concentrate Germany's forces, especially once winter set in. The Soviets had the advantage of vast Asian territory, to which it moved its wartime industries, while Germany had additional operations going against Allied colonies in the Middle East and North Africa. By this time, Britain had broken German codes, leading to the defeat of General Edwin Rommel's forces despite Rommel's innovative tactics. Like the Soviets, Britain benefited once again from Asian troops, as well as those from Africa, and from its greater experience conducting military operations around the world.

As the Soviet, British, and American military combined to crush Germany and Italy in Europe, the Mediterranean, and Africa, war in the Pacific, which had initially favored Japan, had by 1943 begun to turn in the Allies' favor, as they retook islands, aided resistance in China, and bombed Japan itself. It was symbolic of the turn taking place amidst the war that the effort to construct a super-weapon—the atomic bomb— took place in the United States with an international team of top scientists headed by Americans. Europe had been bombed to bits during six years of conflict; its moral leadership was obliterated by the German death camps, and its people were starving in 1945. As important for its standing in the world, nationalist leaders had mass backing in their demands for independence, and European wealth and other assets that might have held empires together had disappeared into the wartime effort. European hegemony had collapsed.

THE DOWNFALL OF EMPIRES

The USSR, however, remained a mighty world force, having led the effort against Germany and having enhanced its industrial capacity. People around across the globe respected the suffering of the Soviet people, whose casualties may have been as high as forty-seven million civilians and soldiers. However, the conduct of the war had made the Soviet leadership paranoid on two counts. First, the British and Americans had held off helping the USSR in the liberation of Europe until mid-1944, forcing the USSR to absorb the full brunt of the German army. Second, it appeared that the dropping of atom bombs on Japan was a warning to the Soviets. In that regard, the Soviets were not alone in wondering why the bombs had not been dropped on Germany. Joseph Stalin, who had led the effort to industrialize in the 1930s and then defeat Germany during the war, determined to create a buffer of loyal states in Eastern Europe. The expansion of European states—notably the USSR—thus did not end in 1945.

As for the other empires, the Dutch, British, French, and Belgians were in too pitiful a state to maintain their global reach at their prewar levels. Often with the assistance of Japanese forces, the United States helped these countries immediately after the war to put down independence movements, most notably in Indonesia and Vietnam. From 1947, beginning with the creation of the independent states of India and Pakistan, European empires devolved, sometimes with great bloodshed and brutality. Where there were fewer white settlers, decolonization was often relatively, though never entirely, peaceful. However, white settlers in Vietnam, Kenya, Algeria, and several other states enlisted armed help from the European metropole in futile attempts to prevent independence. The British set up concentration camps in Kenya, torturing Kikuyu and other ethnicities who wanted freedom. The French likewise tortured nationalists in Algeria, waging an equally brutal effort to prevent independence. Most independence movements were successful by 1980, in part by winning the battle with Europeans for public opinion.

The end of formal empire did not stop Europe's thriving relationships with the world. In the first place European businesses and Soviet manufacturers—including arms manufacturers—maintained a web of economic connections around the world once prosperity revived by the late 1950s. Second, European nations maintained ties with the rest of the world through Cold-War alliances that developed around the two superpowers—Russia and the United States. When six Western European nations signed the Treaty of Rome in 1957 setting up the European Economic Community or Common Market, it marked the creation of an economic unit that would develop its own global ties apart from both individual nations and the American bloc in the Cold War.

GLOBAL MIGRATION AND COMMUNICATION

Most important for the subsequent development of European culture and society—not to mention its internal politics—was the arrival in Europe of millions of immigrants from around the world. The migration began immediately after the war with the arrival of those seeking economic opportunity from such places as the Caribbean. Not only did the rising European welfare state need such cheap labor in hospitals and other growing institutions, because the European population had actually declined during the war with much of the continent devastated, construction workers could also find work. As a result, European governments made agreements with governments in Africa and other parts of the world for temporary laborers. Turmoil and uneven development also brought non-Europeans to Britain and the Continent because of the higher standard of living and greater safety. European politicians used the presence of migrants as key weapons in their platforms, and in the Netherlands, Austria, and other countries were successful in doing so. With the fall of the Soviet Empire and the outmigration from the region, there was in-migration to Russia, particularly among the Chinese who crossed the porous borders and set up businesses and farms. Xenophobic politics also shaped post-Soviet public debate.

Russia and Europe interacted with the world in new ways because of technological developments, specifically the beginning of telecommunications via satellites, computers, and a host of biological and medical breakthroughs that allowed for coordinated attacks on diseases, global trafficking in organs, and new approaches to reproduction. Global philanthropy such as Doctors without Borders started in Europe as did many anti-globalization movements. With globalization Europeans had to think harder about a range of issues such as North–South inequities, participation in global warfare, especially that mandated by the United States and the United Nations, and the beliefs and practices introduced by their new, non-Western citizenry such as genital cutting, veiling for women, and religious pluralism. It is hard to know whether Europe's and Russia's relationships with the world are any more difficult or complex than they were several millennia earlier, but they give historians and citizens an incredible tradition of interactions to consider.

NOTES

1. Denys Hay, *Europe: The Emergence of an Idea* (Edinburgh: University of Edinburgh Press, 1957).
2. Walter A. Goffart, *Barbarians and Romans, A.D. 418–584: The Techniques of Accommodations* (Princton: Princeton University Press, 1980).
3. Francesco Gabrieli, *Muhammad and the Conquests of Islam* (London: Weidenfeld & Nicolson, 1968).
4. Heinrich Fichtenau, *The Carolingian Empire* (Oxford: Blackwell, 1957).
5. Geoffrey Barraclough, *The Origins of Modern Germany*, 3rd edn. (Oxford: Blackwell, 1988).
6. Marc Bloch, *Feudal Society*, trans. by L. A. Manyon, 2 vols. (Chicago: University of Chicago Press, 1961).
7. Lauren Benton, *A Search for Sovereignty: Law and Geography in European Empires, 1400–1900* (New York: Cambridge University Press, 2010).
8. See the classic work by Garrett Mattingly, *Renaissance Diplomacy* (London: Cape, 1955).
9. Donald R. Kelley, *The Beginning of Ideology: Consciousness and Society in the French Reformation* (Cambridge: Cambridge University Press, 1981).
10. See, among many books on this topic, David Mungello, *The Great Encounter of China and the West*, 3rd edn. (Lanham: Rowman and Littlefield, 2009).
11. Of the thousands of books on imperialism, we chose two as examples of differing historiographies: P. J. Cain and A. Hopkins, *British Imperialism, 1688–2000*, 2nd edn. (Edinburgh Gate: Pearson Education, 2010), and Heather Streets, *Martial Races: The Military, Race, and Masculinity in British Imperial Culture, 1857–1914* (Manchester: Manchester University Press, 2004).
12. The following material comes from Bonnie G. Smith, *Europe in the Contemporary World 1900 to the Present* (Boston: Bedford St Martins, 2007).

REFERENCES

BROTTON, JERRY. *The Renaissance Bazaar from the Silk Road to Michelangelo*. London: Oxford University Press, 2003.

ELLIOTT, JOHN HUXTABLE. *Empires of the Atlantic World: Britain and Spain in America, 1492–1830*. New Haven: Yale University Press, 2006.

GOFFMAN, DANIEL. *The Ottoman Empire and Early Modern Europe*. Cambridge: Cambridge University Press, 2002.

GREENE, MOLLY. *A Shared World: Christians and Muslims in the Early Modern Mediterranean*. Princeton: Princeton University Press, 2000.

HIRSCH, FRANCINE. *Empire of Nations: Ethnographic Knowledge and the Making of the Soviet Union*. Ithaca, N.Y.: Cornell University Press, 2005.

HOERDER, DIRK. *Cultures in Contact: World Migrations in the Second Millennium*. Durham, N.C.: Duke University Press, 2002.

LIVINGSTONE, DAVID N. and CHARLES W. J. WITHERS, eds. *Geography and Enlightenment*. Chicago: University of Chicago Press, 1999.

MITCHELL, STEPHEN. *A History of the Later Roman Empire, AD 284–641: The Transformation of the Ancient World*. Oxford: Blackwell, 2007.

RINGROSE, DAVID R. *Expansion and Global Interaction, 1200–1700*. New York: Longmans, 2001.

SAHADEO, JEFF. *Russian Colonial Society in Tashkent, 1865–1923*. Bloomington, Ind.: Indiana University Press, 2007.

STEINMETZ, GEORGE. *The Devil's Handwriting: Precoloniality and the German Colonial State in Qingdao, Samoa, and Southwest Africa*. Chicago: University of Chicago Press, 2007.

WASWO, RICHARD. *The Founding Legend of Western Civilization from Virgil to Vietnam*. Middletown, Conn.: Wesleyan University Press, 1997.

CHAPTER 27

....

MEDITERRANEAN HISTORY

....

DAVID ABULAFIA

APPROACHES TO MEDITERRANEAN HISTORY

....

THE Mediterranean is both a place and a concept. We talk of *the* Mediterranean and refer to the waters that stretch eastward from the Straits of Gibraltar, linked to the Red Sea by the man-made channel of the Suez Canal and to the Black Sea by the natural channel of the Dardanelles and Bosphorus. More broadly, we speak of the Mediterranean as that sea, the islands within it, and the lands that border it, which in 2008 constituted twenty-five political entities including one Crown Colony, some military Sovereign Bases, a state recognized by only one other country, an enclave of indeterminate status, a microstate, and several powerful economies firmly ensconced within the European Union. Only two islands are independent states, Malta and Cyprus, and one of those has been divided in two since 1974. The large islands of the western Mediterranean all form part of bigger states whose center of economic activity is on the European mainland, even though most of those islands at one stage or another were closely linked to North Africa and were only drawn permanently into European political networks during the Middle Ages: Sicily, Sardinia, and the Balearics have at times been ruled from Africa.

Yet it is not very helpful to define the Mediterranean by way of the states and territories lapped by this sea. France and Spain look out to the Atlantic as well (and Portugal is sometimes treated as an honorary part of the Mediterranean). Maybe, then, one should define as 'Mediterranean' those parts of each territory that enjoy a 'Mediterranean climate'—whatever that is defined as being—or that lie south of the limits of olive production and enjoy a 'Mediterranean diet.' More rationally, perhaps, one could focus on those areas where daily life is bound up in some way with the Mediterranean Sea: towns such as Alexandria in the east and Ceuta in the west that have functioned as Mediterranean emporia, receiving and dispatching goods across the Mediterranean Sea, even when those goods originated beyond the Mediterranean; the tunny fisheries of Sicily and southern Spain; the great shipyards of Barcelona, Valencia, Genoa, Savona, and the forests behind them from which wooden ships were constructed.

Sometimes attempts have been made to draw a line about twenty kilometers inland as an arbitrary division between what can be defined as 'Mediterranean' and what belongs to the hinterland. Sometimes, too, attempts have been made to extend the Mediterranean world to include all areas that have fallen under the influence of the Mediterranean: its trade routes stretched into and beyond the Black Sea, beyond the Straits of Gibraltar, and down to the Red Sea. This 'Mediterranean world' might be stretched as far as Cracow in Poland or Bruges in Flanders. Or one could try to measure its cultural influence, creating a Mediterranean culture vigorously expressed not just in Spain but in Portugal and not just in Portugal but in Brazil, an approach favored by the Society for Mediterranean Studies.

This chapter will insist that the study of Mediterranean history encapsulates many important aspects of world history: it involves the investigation of connections between societies separated by extensive physical space, laying particular emphasis on commercial networks, the building of empires encompassing a variety of peoples, the movement of peoples, whether en masse or as pilgrims, slaves, and (latterly) as tourists, and the spread of religions into new continents. These phenomena can be traced across the surface of the sea across which Europe, Africa, and Asia meet one another and over which Christianity and Islam have vigorously competed for dominion. Setting aside for the moment its many islands, the sea itself has no permanent human occupants, other than the bones of those whose ships lie at the bottom of the sea; and yet it has a human history, which can, additionally, serve as a model for other maritime histories, of the Baltic, the Indian Ocean, or the Caribbean, or indeed for largely uninhabitable dry open spaces such as the Sahara Desert. The history of the Mediterranean Sea is not quite the same as the history of the Mediterranean lands, though the two have generally been confused. In this chapter, the emphasis is on the sea itself, in the belief that this permits a world-historical understanding of the Mediterranean.

To say this is to lay a different emphasis to the justly celebrated French historian of the Mediterranean, Fernand Braudel, whose study of the Mediterranean in the age of Philip II of Spain remains one of the most influential works of history of the last century. Braudel's emphasis was on the way the natural features of the Mediterranean molded human experience in a world where not much changed underneath the superficial violence of wars and empire-building: the book begins with a section revealingly entitled 'Mountains Come First.' On the other hand, the role of its many islands is not in doubt when considering the history of the Mediterranean, from Sicily, the largest, to the mass of tiny islands out of which Venice came to life, or the steep capes and peninsulas which depend largely on the sea for their existence—Ceuta and Gibraltar in the west, or Dubrovnik in the Adriatic.

Peregrine Horden and Nicholas Purcell, in their massive study of Mediterranean history entitled *The Corrupting Sea*, have emphasized the great variety of landscapes and physical conditions along the shores and amid the islands of the Mediterranean, and have pointed to the significance of 'connectivities,' systems of exchange necessitated by local shortages and excesses (for instance, exchanges of salt for grain in the early medieval Adriatic). At some periods in the history of the Mediterranean these exchange networks were greatly enlarged, encompassing the entire Mediterranean (as in the heyday of ancient Greek and Phoenician trade, or under the Venetians and Genoese in the Middle Ages). Merchants traded in goods that were as exotic on one side of the sea as they were commonplace on the other (say, southern French honey versus Levantine sugar in the late Middle Ages). It was differences, then, that generated trade; one would expect no less. To some extent these differences were determined by physical differences between the hot, dry climate of the southeastern Mediterranean and the more temperate climate of the shores of northern Italy and Provence (allowing for the existence of any number of micro-climates as well, such as Erice in western Sicily, with its vineyards high in the clouds above the flat saltpans of Trapani). But there were also cultural choices that determined what would be grown: medieval Western Europeans generally saw the land as fit for wheat, the staple crop, but their Islamic predecessors had cultivated cotton, dyestuffs, rice and other less humdrum products on the same land. And then there were products from far away that were traded across the Mediterranean, such as the spices of the East, seen as products of a quasi-paradise on the edge of the world, or the gold of Africa, or slaves from the Black Sea. Greed, the need for cheap labor, the wish to show off, made all of these into highly valued commodities within the Mediterranean. As still happens, the rich would go out and buy foreign articles not because they were necessarily much better in quality or design, but because of their rarity; 'sending coals to Newcastle' was a common Mediterranean enterprise even in the Bronze Age.

Classical and medieval cartographers understood the known world to revolve around the meeting-point of Europe, Asia, and Africa, in the Mediterranean Sea; this stylized concept of a world divided into three parts that met at the Mediterranean strangely survived even the discovery of the Americas, for it was still being repeated in late sixteenth-century works of geography. It was in the Mediterranean that religions, economies, and political systems met, absorbed one another, and clashed. Only in the sixteenth century did the Mediterranean gradually begin to become subsidiary to Atlantic networks of trade and politics. In a history of the Mediterranean Sea, rather than of Mediterranean lands, the agents of contact come to the fore: Phoenicians and Etruscans rather more than Pharaonic Egyptians and Hittites; Genoese and Venetians rather than popes and holy Roman emperors; Jews of Livorno and Smyrna no less than Ottoman janissaries. Yet these groups had an inordinate impact on the fate of empires as well: Carthage was a Phoenician foundation and blocked Roman attempts at expansion; Venice, once a subject of Byzantium, became 'lord of a quarter and half a quarter of the Byzantine Empire' after the Fourth Crusade in 1204; in the sixteenth century, the Genoese held the purse strings of the Spanish rulers. Religious cross-currents include the spread of the Jewish diaspora into the Hellenistic and Roman worlds (notably Alexandria), the underground Christian movement and its transforming role in the later Roman empire; the arrival of Islam and the conversion of the peoples of North Africa and parts of southern Europe to a dynamic new faith, while all the time the three religions (and, at earlier points, paganism) interacted and taught one another elements of theology, moral codes, even snatches of liturgical music. Singly and en masse, pilgrims moved back and forth across the surface of the Mediterranean. All this points to the importance of the theme of migration within and into the Mediterranean region: colonists from Greek and Phoenician cities heading westwards to Sicily (ninth century BCE onwards); Germanic peoples settling in Spain, Italy, and North Africa (third century CE onwards); Arabs from Yemen and Arabia, Berbers from the Maghrib, Copts from Egypt, settling in Muslim Spain (eighth century CE onwards); crusaders, Venetians, Catalans, and so on. Yet in the nineteenth century and particularly the twentieth we begin to see the reverse process on a massive scale, as Mediterranean peoples sought livelihoods in the New World or in northern Europe (with interesting cultural results such as the spread of the pizza). In the history of this sea, the lead actors are not necessarily the lead actors in the internal history of Spain, Italy, Greece, or the Levant.

The human presence on the shores and in the islands of the Mediterranean has altered the environment; just as wastes have been created, new land has been brought under cultivation (a recent example is the Pontine Marshes in Italy). Environmental degradation already occurred in antiquity, and ecological historians such as Oliver Rackham have debated how far the Mediterranean was capable of adjusting to the impact of humans by a process of what might be called self-correction. Gains in one area may have compensated for losses in another: the granaries of Tunisia declined precipitously in the Middle Ages, but other sources of supply (such as Morocco) came into their own. Under the general environmental heading, ports also have to be considered. Harbor facilities, natural or man-made, have had a substantial influence on the direction and character of trade. Take Corinth, for instance. The major port established by the ancient Greeks, as far back as the seventh century BCE, lay at Lechaion, on the Gulf of Corinth, facilitating contact with the Ionian Sea, the Adriatic, and Italy, and so it is no coincidence that the Corinthians also established colonies in Sicily, at Syracuse, and in the Ionian Sea, at Corcyra (Corfu). Ceuta, on the northern tip of Morocco, had ports on either side of the neck of land on which it stands, offering shelter to ships entering and leaving the Mediterranean in the face of unpredictable winds and heavy mists. It is important to remember what is in the sea, especially its fish and salt, and to relate these foodstuffs to human needs and the development of systems of exchange, even to religious practices: there is impressive evidence for massive consumption of fish in Barcelona during Lent in the fifteenth century. As John Pryor has shown, in the wake of Braudel, the currents and winds of the Mediterranean determined in significant degree who could arrive where and when, and thus both facilitated and blocked trade and the movement of navies.

Another major theme in the history of the Mediterranean is the changing means of communication across the sea. Relatively little is known about the design and efficiency of the earliest shipping, since the main evidence consists of rough images on pottery; discoveries in the Tyrrhenian and Aegean Seas have, however, greatly enlarged understanding of the capacity of Greek, Etruscan, Punic, and Roman ships, including shipwrecks off Giglio, a little island between Tuscany and Corsica, and off Sicily. There is the difficult question of whether improvements in ship design led to an increase in trade, as bigger ships became able to sail longer distances; an alternative view is that growing demand stimulated ship-builders to develop new designs, so that the improvements were determined in large degree by wider economic conditions. Looking at shipping, it is important to distinguish the role of fast, sleek vessels driven by wind and oar power from that of pot-bellied slow boats, full of grain, fish, salt, and timber which for millennia kept open the lifelines of many Mediterranean cities. It is a mistake to think of the trade of Genoa or Venice as in essence a luxury trade in silks and spices. Humbler items such as wheat and salt were traded in vast quantities; and in the ancient Mediterranean the evidence from discoveries of wine amphorae in southern France indicates, for example, how intensive the trade in Etruscan wine became. Linked to this theme there are important questions about the life of sailors, passengers, and (sometimes) galley-slaves; there is evidence for the duration of voyages at various periods, and for the degree of comfort or discomfort involved when people traveled by sea; this evidence often consists in merchant letters, such as the marvelous collection from the Jewish community of eleventh- and twelfth-century Cairo mainly preserved in Cambridge, the Cairo Genizah documents; out of these S. D. Goitein conjured up the image of a 'Mediterranean society' of traders, enjoying close ties of family, finance, and faith, with links right across and way beyond the Mediterranean.

One could also write Mediterranean history not as the history of the Mediterranean Sea but as the history of Mediterraneans, that is, of seas that act as bridges between cultures and peoples. Other 'middle seas' include the Baltic, the Caribbean, the Japan Sea, and (though a look at the map may not make this obvious) the Indian Ocean, which has been analyzed using the methods of Braudel. The Black Sea occupies rather a special position in this argument, since its own commercial networks often fed into those of the Mediterranean, providing revenues to those who controlled the narrow passage between the two great seas: the inhabitants of Troy in the Bronze Age, the inhabitants of Byzantion in antiquity, of Constantinople in the Middle Ages, and of Istanbul thereafter. Ancient Athens had already bought Black Sea grain, and the medieval Genoese exported cheap Ukrainian grain from Caffa in the Crimea, carrying it deep into the Mediterranean. They also exported large numbers of white Circassian slaves to Egypt, where many were recruited into the Mamluk guard. Yet the Black Sea also had a life of its own, for it was traversed by Varangians from Russia in the early Middle Ages who had no great ambition to penetrate beyond Miklegarð, 'the Great City' of Constantinople. Consideration should also be given to the 'sub-Mediterraneans' that existed within the Mediterranean Sea itself. There were networks within the Tyrrhenian Sea, linking Sardinia to Tuscany, southern Italy and Sicily. The Adriatic possessed a life of its own, for in addition to its function as a passage-way through which Mediterranean goods were channeled towards Venice, it possessed its own systems of exchange: the Dalmatian towns were perched on the edge of an inhospitable land-mass (that behind Dubrovnik is a limestone desert as reminiscent of the moon as of Earth). They, therefore, depended heavily on the supply of grain and vegetables from the facing shores of Italy. Venice too did not build its early fortunes on exotic trade with the East; rather, it was the fish and salt of the northern Adriatic, which provided a capital base from which the city's extraordinary expansion began.

These examples show how territories facing one another across an easily traversable waterway developed in very distinctive ways, but entered into contact with one another and transformed one another through trade, migration, and sometimes military conquest. A good example from the Mediterranean itself is the way medieval Sicily drew on the influence of both Byzantium and Islam, for it contained a mixed population of Greeks and Muslims, eventually conquered by Latin Christians, and the court culture of these new rulers was impregnated with Islamic and Byzantine motifs. Looking at other 'middle seas' we can see similar processes by which cultures across the water assumed a dominant role; a good example is the powerful influence of Korean and, in particular, Chinese culture on Japan, across the open spaces of the Japan Sea. This picture is not confined to watery open spaces. The dry open spaces of the Sahara and Gobi deserts also acted as metaphorical seas across which ideas, objects, and people moved—the famous gold trade across the Sahara heading north to the Maghrib, while the Maghrib exported, among much else, its dominant ideas, notably Islam. The oases such as the town of Wargla, in what is now Algeria, functioned as welcoming islands in the midst of a hostile environment where, just as on a 'wet sea,' humans needed to keep on the move if they were to survive. The Baltic displays some important features in common with the Mediterranean: like the Mediterranean, the medieval Baltic was a crusading theater, in which the crusading Military Order of the Teutonic Knights played a powerful part; like the Mediterranean, Christian merchants also established their dominance over its waters and trade routes, as the German Hansa created trading towns along the shores of the Baltic, notably at Riga, and as they exported grain, furs, and amber to consumers in the European heartlands. Finally, it is important to remember that new 'Mediterraneans' were created as the network of communications across the world grew. The great example here is the Atlantic. Before 1492 the eastern and western shores were not in contact (occasional Viking voyages apart); after 1492 not just Europe but Africa developed a fateful trading relationship with the Americas, based in significant measure on the tragic export of human cargoes to Brazil, the Caribbean, and North America. As Bernard Bailyn has pointed out, four continents entered into relations with one another, and what emerged was a system: African links to South America, in the form of the slave traffic towards Brazil, involved Portuguese entrepreneurs from Europe as well.

Yet the Mediterranean Sea is the 'classic Mediterranean,' not just because it carries the name but because it was there that the most intense contacts came into being, which saw the birth of Western civilization. Here, three continents meet in close proximity; a ten-minute boat ride takes a commuter from European Istanbul to Asian Istanbul; Algeciras in southern Spain is a half-hour from Ceuta, and Jebel Musa in Morocco stands clearly visible from the Rock of Gibraltar; on a clear day Africa can be espied from Erice in western Sicily. More importantly, the prevailing winds and the warm summers of the Mediterranean make navigation possible across its open spaces as well as its narrows, even if ancient and medieval shipping generally preferred routes that allowed captains to keep in sight of land. Good examples are the route from Genoa past eastern Corsica and Elba to Sardinia, though from there it was necessary to jump across the open sea to Sicily or Africa. Routes through the Greek islands also kept land in sight, though the trouble with small islands was that they could easily be seized by pirates and used as bases from which to harass shipping.

This is to speak of constants in the history of the Mediterranean. Braudel's Mediterranean was seen from the perspective of the late sixteenth century, even though this was combined with a view of the Mediterranean as a place where 'all change is slow.' The strength of Braudel's treatment lies in his mastery of the physical setting rather than of human activity; in his hands, even the history of trade becomes primarily the history of commodities. The human dimension is strangely lacking. This has established a tradition, most clearly visible in dozens of impressive works by French scholars of the *Annales* school, whose studies of Mediterranean cities such as Livorno in Italy, Bougie in Algeria, or Valencia in Spain have stressed the permanent structures underlying trade and social relations in whatever period they have been examining. The danger is that one then fails to demonstrate clearly changes over time—for instance, in the case of Valencia, the ups and downs of the trade in slaves or sugar. There is also a tendency to set aside political developments. A classic example of this is a rich and impressive study by Jacques Heers (who later broke with the *Annalistes*) of fifteenth-century Genoa, where the tumultuous politics of the city, which certainly had an impact on trade and social relations, are relegated to a few pages at the end, whereas the trade in grain and metals and slaves is given full exposure in the main text.

It is fair to state that, despite the proliferation of seminars and courses in 'Mediterranean history' at universities in the United States, Italy, Spain, Israel, Turkey, and Malta (to name just a few examples), there is little agreement on what constitutes 'Mediterranean history.' The approach adopted here emphasizes the sea itself rather than the lands around it, but even then it is necessary to take into account the many Mediterranean islands and the towns perched on the edge of the Mediterranean that created trade networks, whether local or pan-Mediterranean: Ceuta, Genoa, Dubrovnik, Syracuse, Carthage, Alexandria, Corinth, Salonika, Smyrna, Acre, Tel Aviv, to take examples from a variety of periods and places.

DEVELOPMENTS ACROSS TIME

In the second part of this chapter the focus is on the development of the 'classic Mediterranean' over time. The first inhabitants of the shores of the Mediterranean apparently had no means of crossing the sea. Neanderthal folk lingered in Gibraltar as late as 22,000 BCE, where their bones have been found in some quantity; but the lack of comparable evidence from Ceuta, across the Straits, suggests that they could only stare at the coast of Africa. The effective starting point of Mediterranean history, conceived in the terms applied here, is the moment when small boats from the mainland began to explore the Greek islands, searching for obsidian as early as the upper palaeolithic period, while the first settlers arrived in Sicily in around 11,000 BCE. From evidence for spasmodic navigation we move to the trade networks of the great civilizations of the eastern Mediterranean: so, not just Minoans and Mycenaeans in their own Greek and Cretan setting, but the appearance of the goods they manufactured in lands further west such as Italy, as well as their close contact, via Cyprus, with the Levant, and the role of the Trojan War as (possibly) a trade war for control of the entrance from the Black Sea into the Aegean, anticipating many later wars for control of Constantinople/ Istanbul. At the other end of the Mediterranean, the Straits of Gibraltar were already open to shipping, according to classical writers, from at least 1104 BCE, when Cádiz was supposedly founded by the Phoenicians, though this is almost certainly several centuries earlier than was actually the case. This link to the Atlantic, which was created so early, forms a constant theme throughout the human history of the Mediterranean Sea, and becomes a dominant one after 1492. The Mediterranean is not a closed world but one that, via the Black Sea, has links to the Eurasian steppes and, via the Atlantic, to northern Europe and West Africa. That, in essence, is why the Mediterranean is so important: what happens there has an economic, cultural, and political impact far beyond.

We can begin with a 'First Mediterranean' in which human beings opened up contact across the watery spaces, reaching the islands and even opposite shores, but not, at this time, drawing the entire space into a single system. The far west remained largely isolated from the eastern Mediterranean until the end of the Bronze Age, around 1100 BCE, or even later. In fact, the first evidence for trade across the Mediterranean takes us back to the late Stone Age or even earlier, when people first visited Melos in the Aegean in search of the volcanic glass known as obsidian, used in tool-making. Since Melos is an island we have immediate evidence for the regular movement of small boats, linking this island to the mainland of Greece and Asia. Even so, this was not trade: as far as can be seen, obsidian was simply collected, without, at first, any local intermediaries. It took many centuries for the complex trade networks of Minoan Crete and Mycenaean Greece to emerge in the eastern Mediterranean. The close of the period of the 'First Mediterranean' is marked by conflict and, possibly, by migration, by a breakdown in trade and by the fall of great cities. Here we can focus on an event which belongs at least as much to legend as to fact (but a legend whose persistence within and beyond the Mediterranean is itself an important feature of Mediterranean history): the Trojan War, most likely a battle for control of access to the straits leading out of the Mediterranean and into the Black Sea, an area that would remain of vital importance to the history of the Mediterranean through the Byzantine and Ottoman eras. The traditional date of 1184 BCE, furnished by classical authors, seems to stand up reasonably well. Homeric memories of the Trojan War were expressed in a wider Mediterranean legend: the story of the travels of Odysseus, which include what some consider to be descriptions of the waters around Sicily and southern Italy, a region in which many examples of Mycenaean Greek pottery from the time of the Trojan conflict have been found. Pirates, merchants, and migrants found their way gradually further and further west in this age of maritime pioneers. But the chaos ascribed by the Greek authors to this age extended further afield—this is the period in which we hear in Egyptian records of the Sea Peoples, among whom the most famous were the Philistines, probably of Greek origin, who settled the coast of Canaan and gave it their name, in the modern form of 'Palestine.'

The collapse of the great Bronze Age civilizations of the eastern Mediterranean marks the end of the 'First Mediterranean.' A 'Second Mediterranean' emerged as the Phoenicians and, later, the Greeks reopened the trade routes to the west, planting themselves in colonies in North Africa, Sardinia, Sicily, southern Italy, Spain, and southern France. Thus, in this phase the extent and scale of contacts was far greater than in the days when occasional Mycenaean traders had reached Taranto in southern Italy or eastern Sicily. Of course, the opening of these routes was a competitive business, and the Trojan War was only the first of many commercial conflicts, the predecessor of yet more aggressive campaigns which brought Greek fleets against Etruscan and Carthaginian ones in the waters round Sicily and southern Italy. Greeks also fought against Greeks, for ethnic loyalties were never paramount. The life of the inhabitants of Mediterranean Spain and northwest Africa was transformed from the eighth century BCE onwards by the coming of merchants buying local produce, food-stuffs, and raw materials in the main, and selling fine pottery and products of artisan workshops.

The major evidence for the creation of new networks is provided by the Phoenicians, who, from bases in modern Lebanon, established not merely commercial routes but daughter cities (colonies is a word better avoided, because it implies control from afar) as far afield as North Africa. There, they established the *Qart Hadasht*, or 'New City,' which later became known to the Romans as Carthago, and, eventually, further secondary centers in Spanish waters. The Phoenicians must be seen as vectors for the grander cultures of the Middle East, Egyptian and Mesopotamian, whose goods they distributed and, perhaps even more significantly, imitated in their own workshops. Commercial outposts came into existence. Typically, they were offshore islands, or at least perched on the edge of the territory with which the Phoenicians and others sought to trade: Motya, off the western coast of Sicily, was an important base for Phoenician and Carthaginian merchants. The need for safety and the wish to be masters of their own small enclave determined this behavior. There was an important link between merchants and writing. The Phoenician alphabet, ancestor of the Greek one, broke the near-monopoly of priests and other select groups on writing systems, until then very complex, even esoteric, so that a widely legible writing system suited to the needs of traders came into existence. The spread of the alphabet westwards is one of the great themes in early Mediterranean history.

The dominant theme in the history of the Mediterranean in the seventh to second centuries BCE is the struggle for political dominion in the east, between Athens and its rivals (a struggle that extended to the Adriatic and to Sicily), and conflicts in western waters in which Greeks, Carthaginians, Etruscans, and, later, Romans were the main actors. These struggles were largely effected through naval contests, because at their heart lay the opportunity to gain control of the trade routes, and the profits they brought. Especially important was the creation of the Greek 'colonies' (bearing in mind that they were largely autonomous) in such places as Syracuse, Taranto, and Cumae, the area known as 'Greater Greece,' *Magna Graecia*, while similar colonies developed along the shores of Asia Minor too. The Sicilian colonies furnished large amounts of grain to sustain growing cities such as Corinth. Beginning at Pithekoussai, on Ischia in the Bay of Naples, it was in Magna Graecia that the Greeks built trading and cultural ties to less sophisticated peoples who became heavily influenced by Greek practices; the adoption of forms of Greek script by the Italian peoples is just one example; another important example is the export of Greek religious ideas—anthropomorphic gods and goddesses, and a rich treasury of myths, which were grafted on to local gods in Italy and elsewhere. But in entering these waters the Greeks competed with others—the Phoenicians and the Etruscans in particular. Sometimes they worked side by side, as at Spina in the northern Adriatic, which became a great Etruscan centre for the import of Greek pottery. But there were violent clashes too, such as the great battle between the Greeks of Syracuse and the Etruscans at Cumae in 474 BCE. This, therefore, sets out a consistent theme: very many of the rivalries within the Mediterranean were rooted in commercial competition. Yet it was not necessarily a question of controlling gold and perfumes. More important to early Rome was salt, while the Etruscans were famous for their massive iron ore reserves, notably on and around Elba. Thus, we can see early on that the trade of the Mediterranean, contrary to the assumptions of many classic works, has to be understood not just as the exchange of luxuries, but as commerce in humdrum necessities such as foodstuffs and raw materials.

Competition and trade wars were a repeated reality. But there were also periods of relative stability. In such a period a hybrid culture developed in the eastern Mediterranean following the conquests of Alexander the Great and the establishment of Greek rule over Egypt and Syria. The Ptolemaic rulers of Egypt perpetuated ancient Egyptian notions of state control of the economy, but they also opened Egypt up to wider Mediterranean contacts (rather neglected under the Pharaohs), through the cosmopolitan city of Alexandria, home to Hellenistic Greeks, Jews, Copts, and many others. These contacts were economic—the Ptolemies maintained an impressive navy—and also cultural. The great Alexandrian library was an expression of the cultural unity that developed in the Hellenistic world, despite ethnic and religious tensions. The Hellenistic period was the period in which the foundations were laid for the Mediterranean empire of the Romans, and indeed of the Byzantines, as a Greek-speaking city-based civilization emerged in the eastern Mediterranean; meanwhile, real political power had shifted away from independent city-states into the hands of regional monarchs. The spread of cults, such as that of the Egyptian goddess Isis, provides evidence of the movement of people and of ideas across the ancient Mediterranean. Politically, it was Rome that triumphed: its political mastery of the Mediterranean was consolidated by the fall of both Greece and Carthage in the mid-first century BCE, and its economic interests were furthered by the establishment of Roman rule in Egypt. The famous wheat trade out of Egypt, Africa, and Sicily sustained Rome by the end of the first century BCE, though references to imports from Sicily reach as far back as the fifth century BCE. There existed a tension between attempts to protect the interests of the mother city, and the maintenance of a great commonwealth around the shores of the Mediterranean. Regions such as Gaul, Britain, and Western Germany were peripheral to an empire whose center of gravity was at first Rome, and then moved eastwards to Constantinople, thereby confirming the economic vitality of the old Hellenistic lands of the eastern Mediterranean. This was an area dotted with towns, long used to intensive commercial exchanges, which would continue even with the emergence of Islam and the loss of Byzantine Egypt and Syria in the seventh century.

The theme of the 'Second Mediterranean' is, then, the integration of the entire Mediterranean space into an interconnected trading area, culminating in the creation of something even more ambitious, an integrated political area, under the rule of the Roman emperors. The origins of the 'Third Mediterranean' must, not surprisingly, be sought in the political and economic fragmentation visible from fourth century onwards. Constantinople, the 'New Rome,' retained its mastery over the eastern Mediterranean until the rise of Islam, but what was lost, after a millennium of trans-Mediterranean trade, was intimate contact between the far west and the far east of this sea; and Byzantium too suffered from decline, as the depopulation of cities such as Ephesus (in modern Turkey) indicates, though collapse was less marked and recovery was much quicker than in the west. Moreover, in the seventh century Byzantium lost many of its most precious possessions in the Near East and in Western Europe, though in fact the rise of Islam did unify much of the Mediterranean in ways reminiscent of the Roman *mare nostrum*. To some extent Islam was able to restore the east–west contact, once most of Spain fell under Muslim rule (from 711 onwards); but north–south contact declined, and links between Christian Western Europe and the eastern Mediterranean weakened greatly. We enter the murky waters of the so-called Dark Ages; historians have argued passionately for and against the collapse of trade following the barbarian invasions of the fifth century onwards; the perspective from the Bay of Naples, a center of continuing trade, is different to that from the still-quiescent ports of northwestern Italy, partly because the merchants of Amalfi and Naples gained access to Byzantine and Muslim cities in the eastern Mediterranean and North Africa. 'Syrian' merchants, from the ancient trading centers of Phoenicia, and Jews are reported to have played an especially important role in trans-Mediterranean trade in this period.

Under Islam, a common market stretching from Spain and Morocco to Egypt and Syria was created, which also enjoyed close commercial ties to the Byzantine world in the eastern Mediterranean and southern Italy. There were significant bonds between the Greek and the Islamic worlds in the realms of high culture, where Arab translators helped preserve Greek texts by way of Aramaic translations, and lower down the scale, where Orthodox (and 'heretical') priests and monks formed part of a rich mixed culture within Islamic lands, alongside Jews and of course increasing numbers of Muslims. Here again we see one of the recurring themes of Mediterranean history: the Mediterranean as a theater for cultural and religious mixing, sometimes, as at this period, expressed through the emergence of a degree of mutual tolerance. This, however, was not automatically the case: eastern Christian monks arriving in early

Muslim Spain spurred local Christians to denounce Islam in public, setting off the crisis of the Martyrs of Córdoba that badly damaged Christian–Muslim relations in eighth-century al-Andalus.

From about 950 we observe unity within diversity. Sects multiplied, and so there rapidly ceased to be one Islam, just as there had rapidly ceased to be one Christianity. Yet this remained a relatively stable world, economically united despite sharp political divisions between Umayyads, Fatimids, Abbasids, and other claimants to caliphal power. Among those who crisscrossed the Mediterranean at this period were pilgrims of the three monotheistic faiths, some of whom, such as ibn Jubayr and Benjamin of Tudela, a Muslim and a Jew from Spain, have left vivid accounts of their travels in the age of the crusades. Large-scale Christian pilgrimage across the Mediterranean to the Holy Land preceded the First Crusade (launched in 1095), and was further stimulated by the crusade's startling success in capturing Jerusalem (in 1099). Into this world the Italian merchants and, alongside them, crusaders and other conquering knights irrupted aggressively at the end of the eleventh century. Their activities dominate the Mediterranean in the central Middle Ages. Yet this should not be presented entirely as a history of fragmentation. The rise of Italian trade is once again the history of the forging of commercial unity within the Mediterranean, the creation of the 'Third Mediterranean,' as the Italians, and later the Catalans and Provençaux, seized mastery over the trade routes from the Muslims and Jews and created their own trading bases in such cities as crusader Acre, Constantinople, Alexandria, Tunis, and Palermo. For, once they had gained their trading bases, the Pisans, Genoese, and Venetians sought peaceful relations with their Muslim trading partners, and were often criticized in Western Europe for the warmth of their ties with Muslim states such as Fatimid Egypt; Alexandria lived off the profits of the Levant trade, selling to Western merchants goods obtained from the Indian Ocean, notably pepper and other spices. The ties between the Catalans and the rulers of the Maghrib became so close that the Catalans even supplied mercenary armies to fight on behalf of the Muslim allies of the Christian kings of Aragon. On the other hand, the self-confidence of Christian Western Europe was expressed as well in the conquest of the Balearic islands and of the coastline of Spain (Majorca in 1229, Valencia in 1238, and so on).

As we move beyond 1200, the history of the Mediterranean increasingly becomes a history of vigorous and violent competition among Christians as well, seen in the struggle between Venice and Genoa for control of Crete at the start of the thirteenth century, or in the battle of Meloria in 1284, when the Genoese defeated their age-old rivals from Pisa and for a time gained control of Elba, rich in iron. Christians in the east were victims of the crusades as well as the Muslims, notably when the Fourth Crusade sacked Constantinople in 1204, a blow from which the Byzantine capital never really recovered. Further west, bloody battles between Catalans and Genoese for control of Sardinia, valued for its grain, cheese, and leather, spared no one, and resulted in gory massacres of sailors and passengers on enemy ships.

This third phase came to an end in the mid-fourteenth century, when the Black Death wiped out up to half of the population of the lands bordering the Mediterranean;

the whole economy of Christian Europe and the Islamic lands was reconfigured in remarkable ways. So a 'Fourth Mediterranean' began to develop at this stage. Some of the grand trunk routes declined and a new configuration came into being, as local trade routes came to the fore; and all this was related to major political events in the east, as the Turks gained control of the Aegean and interfered with access to such products as sugar, which Christian merchants now had to seek nearer home, in Sicily, Granada, and even outside the Mediterranean, in Madeira. There were fewer mouths to feed, and there was more money to spend on luxuries, so it was not just the routes that changed—it was also what was carried, and where it was carried. By the start of the fifteenth century, Valencia had become a boom town. We also begin to see the gradual emergence of the Atlantic as a destination for Mediterranean merchants and conquerors, with important results for the relationship between the Mediterranean and the wider world, even before Columbus crossed the Ocean in 1492, a year also of fateful importance for the religious history of the Mediterranean, since it saw the destruction of the Muslim kingdom of Granada and the expulsion of the Jews from Spain, many thousands of whom moved to Ottoman lands. The creation of a vibrant Atlantic economy transformed the Mediterranean as much as the Black Death. The 'Fourth Mediterranean' was increasingly linked to the Atlantic, and, as new spice routes were opened through the Atlantic, Mediterranean cities found themselves competing with Lisbon and eventually Antwerp in the spice trade. The decline in trade within the early modern Mediterranean encompassed a decline in grain production, for example in Crete, where vines and olive-trees now dominated.

The sixteenth and seventeenth centuries have always tended to be seen from the perspective of the conflict between Christendom and Islam, marked by the return of vicious piracy in the western Mediterranean (Hayrettin Barbarossa's 'Barbary Corsairs,' matched by Christian pirates such as the Hospitaller Knights of Rhodes and Malta), and by Spanish campaigns along the coast of North Africa. The siege of Malta in 1565 and the battle of Lepanto six years later to all intents divided the Mediterranean between Spanish and Turkish spheres of influence, since the Turks proved unable to establish mastery of the seas west of Malta. And yet, beneath this ruffled surface, the old unities still survived: trade between east and west, through Livorno, Smyrna, Dubrovnik, even cultural contact, as westerners expressed their fascination with things Turkish; and there was a degree of political accommodation in the seventeenth century, when Spain was preoccupied with political problems elsewhere (in America, Italy, and northern Europe), while the French king enjoyed remarkably friendly relations with the Sublime Porte from the early sixteenth century onwards. Even in this period, then, we need to think of the Mediterranean as a sort of unity. Livorno and Smyrna were opened up to merchants of all religions, cities in which political conflicts were often pushed aside to make way for exchange and profit; a significant role in the success of both cities was played by the descendants of the Jews exiled from Spain and Portugal at the end of the fifteenth century. Dubrovnik (Ragusa) is a particularly interesting case, for it functioned as a 'hinge' linking the Ottoman Balkans to Western Europe, and enjoyed a special degree of political autonomy within the Turkish sphere. Its rise to a position where it possessed one of the largest merchant fleets in the Mediterranean coincides to an uncanny degree with the decision of the Ragusan city-fathers to pay tribute to the Sublime Porte. However, these successes served as the prelude to the arrival of non-Mediterranean powers in the Mediterranean: English and Dutch pirates were already active in the Mediterranean at the end of the sixteenth century, and by the eighteenth century the Mediterranean was emerging as a battleground of powers whose main activities lay in the oceans beyond, beginning with the British capture of Gibraltar and Minorca at the start of the eighteenth century. At the end of the century, the Mediterranean was a major theater in the naval war between Napoleonic France and Great Britain.

This was all the prelude to extraordinary changes in the nineteenth century, which saw the radical transformation of the Mediterranean—the 'Fifth Mediterranean'—as Britain and France now worked together to make it into a Middle Sea in a new way, opening up the Suez Canal and permitting at long last the traffic of shipping from Europe to Asia without the need to circumnavigate the whole of Africa. Industrialization in northern Europe stimulated demand for raw materials from the east, which now passed straight through the Mediterranean. Thus, the Mediterranean gained a new importance as a passage-way, rather than as a region whose resources were valued in their own right; and yet, in a sense, an old relationship had been restored: the products of the Indies once again flowed in great quantities up the Red Sea, towards the Mediterranean ports of Egypt, as had been the case in the Middle Ages, before the Portuguese opened a route for pepper that bypassed the Mediterranean. Alexandria once again became an economic powerhouse after centuries of quite startling decline; its new inhabitants—Greeks, Jews, Italians, Turks, Copts—saw themselves as standing apart from the life of Egypt, and loudly recalled the classical description of their city as *Alexandria ad Aegyptum*, 'Alexandria on the way to Egypt,' rather than *in Aegyptum*. Meanwhile, the colonial powers gradually strengthened their hold on territories around the Mediterranean, starting with French Algeria from as early as 1830, and continuing to the eve of World War I, when Italy battled for control of Libya. Alexandria too was in effect managed by the great powers as a condominium.

At the same time, the Mediterranean entered the consciousness of Europeans in new ways, as the birthplace of Greek and, therefore, it was assumed, of European culture, notions which were confirmed by the discoveries of Heinrich Schliemann and Arthur Evans at Mycenae, Troy, and Knossos on either side of 1900. It became clear that the history of the Greek world receded further back in time than anyone had imagined. And the history of travel in the Mediterranean, from the time of Odysseus onwards, culminated in the coming of mass tourism during the late twentieth century, and the emergence of the Mediterranean as a playground for Europeans and Americans of all social classes. Take-off occurred, quite literally, in the 1950s with the first direct flights from England and Germany to Majorca; the rapid development, or indeed over-development, of the Spanish coastline was encouraged by the Franco government, in the hope of finding a way out of Spain's political and economic isolation from Europe. At the end of the twentieth century, the tourist invasion took on a new character as cheap flights made access to Mediterranean cities less costly, at least for the British, than a train ride within their own country. Travel was democratized, and it was not all concerned with viewing the ancient temples and medieval or baroque cathedrals scattered around the Mediterranean: in Majorca, Monastir, or Mykonos, beaches attracted more interest than museums. Two inventions, as far apart in technology as can be imagined, transformed the relationship between the Mediterranean and the north of Europe in the second half of the twentieth century: the airplane and the bikini.

Awareness of the damage that this has created has also grown. It is not simply a matter of ugly concrete hotels and apartments fringing the Costa del Sol; environmental abuse has also extended into the waters in the Mediterranean, with overfishing of bluefin tuna and other creatures, and with the dumping of harmful chemicals in areas such as the southern Adriatic. President Sarkozy of France has proposed a 'Mediterranean Union' alongside and overlapping with the European Union, and the 'Barcelona Process' has initiated discussion of environmental problems in a setting where old enemies such as Israel and Libya are encouraged to sit at the same table. It may be that the Fifth Mediterranean is also the Last Mediterranean, before the sea becomes denuded of its living creatures.

REFERENCES

ABULAFIA, DAVID. *The Great Sea: A Human History of the Mediterranean.* London: Allen Lane/Penguin; New York: Oxford University Press, 2011.

——, ed. *The Mediterranean in History.* New York: Oxford University Press, for the Getty Museum, Los Angeles, 2003.

BRAUDEL, FERNAND. *The Mediterranean and the Mediterranean World in the Age of Philip II.* 2 vols., trans. by Siân Reynolds. London: Collins, 1972–3.

COOKE, MIRIAM, ERDAĞ GÖKNAR, and GRANT PARKER, eds. *Mediterranean Passages: Readings from Dido to Derrida.* Chapel Hill, N.C.: University of North Carolina Press, 2008.

GOITEIN, S. D. *A Mediterranean Society: The Jewish Communities of the Arab World as Portrayed in the Documents of the Cairo Geniza,* vol. 1, *Economic Foundations.* Berkeley: University of California Press, 1967.

HARRIS, WILLIAM V., ed. *Rethinking the Mediterranean.* Oxford: Oxford University Press, 2005.

HORDEN, PEREGRINE, and NICHOLAS PURCELL. *The Corrupting Sea.* Oxford: Blackwell, 2000.

MATVEJEVIĆ, PREDRAG. *Mediterranean: A Cultural Landscape,* trans. by M. H. Heim. Berkeley: University of California Press, 1999.

PRYOR, JOHN. *Geography, Technology, and War: Studies in the Maritime History of the Mediterranean, 649–1571.* Cambridge: Cambridge University Press, 1988.

RACKHAM, OLIVER, and A. T. GROVE. *The Nature of Mediterranean Europe: An Ecological History.* New Haven, Conn.: Yale University Press, 2001.

TABAK, FARUK. *The Waning of the Mediterranean, 1550–1870: A Geohistorical Approach.* Baltimore, Md.: Johns Hopkins University Press, 2008.

CHAPTER 28

....

THE AMERICAS, 1450–2000

....

EDWARD J. DAVIES, II

THE AMERICAS BEFORE EUROPEAN CONTACT
....

HUMANS crossed over into the Americas as early as 22,000 years ago. As the glaciers, which covered much of North America, began to retreat around 9000 BCE and the climate warmed, hunter-gatherer societies slowly adopted agriculture and incorporated combinations of pumpkin, squash, maize, potato, or beans depending on the soil, altitude, and local ecologies into their diets. As sedentary peoples, they also began to live in villages at least part of the year.

By the beginning of the Common Era, several major civilizations emerged in the Americas in what is now labeled the classical age. These consisted of city-states that incorporated priestly and warrior classes, peasants, and craftsmen. They also developed extensive irrigation systems for farming and constructed large urban centers with populations ranging between 150,000 and 200,000, with impressive ceremonial structures and palaces. Building on precedents first established by the Olmecs, the mother civilization of Mesoamerica, in an earlier period, Teotihuacán became the dominant city-state in Mesoamerica for several hundred years. Eventually it fell to the Toltecs around 980 CE.[1]

Along the coasts of Peru, other civilizations put together successful ruling systems. Along the northern coast, the Moche earned a reputation for their engineering skills apparent in their road and irrigation systems and public works projects. The Nazca in southern Peru excelled in textile production, and their shrines attracted pilgrims from great distances. Inland, the Tiwanaku civilization emerged near Lake Titicaca around 100 CE and extended its rule south into present-day Chile. The Wari empire, northwest of Tiwanaku, appeared during the sixth century CE. Its rulers moved conquered peoples to secure their dominance. They also exercised tight control over all farm production and depended on an efficient road network to maintain their power. All these civilizations began to decline after 800 CE.[2]

In the Yucatan and in Guatemala, the Maya built numerous city-states adorned with great pyramids, huge palaces, and multistoreyed structures. Over sixty urban centers made up this complex society. Various combinations of drought, limited resources, barbarian invasions, and internal war unseated these civilizations.

Martial societies emerged in the post-classical age. The most notable, the Mexica in Mesoamerica and the Inca in the Andean world, built large tribute empires maintained by military power and effective political organization. These empires housed the largest concentrations of human beings in the western hemisphere, over 30,000,000 all together, and held vast wealth and power symbolized by their capital cities and their impressive armies.

In North America mound-building civilizations developed in the Common Era. The earliest of these, the Adena, and their successors, the Hopewell, thrived in the Ohio Valley before 500 CE. The Mississippians were the most enduring and impressive of the mound builders. They operated large-scale trading systems that covered much of the continent and moved high-value goods such as gold and obsidian over great distances. Of the urban sites, Cahokia, near present-day St Louis, emerged as the largest and dominant center by the ninth century CE. Massive mounds that served as temples and homes for rulers covered the landscape of Cahokia, where artisans and artists practiced their crafts. Cahokia and its civilization declined after 1150 CE.[3]

By the sixteenth century, a sizable number of peoples in North America lived in communities that depended on intensive agriculture. The Algonquian-speaking peoples in present-day tidewater Virginia provide an example of such social organization. In these centers, settlement and cultivation sometimes shifted either to exploit seasonal resources in various ecological environments or because the land no longer sustained the community.[4]

ENCOUNTERS: DISEASE AND DEATH
IN THE AMERICAS

The European arrival in 1492 posed a serious and ultimately deadly challenge to the peoples of the Americas and the Caribbean. The Europeans carried with them bacteria and viruses that were fatal to the peoples of the Americas. Isolated from the Eurasian disease pools, the indigenous peoples of the Americas lacked the immunities against these pestilences. Diseases such as smallpox, typhus, and measles struck early and consistently among the peoples first encountered by the Europeans.

Smallpox and other killers moved inland with Spanish expeditions. Smallpox engulfed the Mexica and Maya from 1519 to 1521. In 1545 typhus struck the valley of Mexico with the utmost severity. Each time an epidemic broke out, as much as 90 percent of the infected population perished. This pattern reduced the peoples in the Valley of Mexico from a high of 25,000,000 to barely 750,000 and in the Andes from 10,000,000 to 600,000 by the 1620s.

Similarly, epidemics came ashore in New England as European settlers and explorers landed and traded with the local populations. From 1616 to 1619 an epidemic killed some 90 percent of the 100,000 native inhabitants of coastal New England, and in the early 1630s smallpox struck New England carrying away a substantial part of the indigenous population. Such die-offs persisted into the nineteenth century. Beginning in 1837 smallpox raged among the Blackfoot in the northwest and killed some 40,000. This same outbreak all but exterminated the Mandan. As late as 1899, Pueblos were coping with a smallpox outbreak that threatened many in the United States' southwest.[5]

Conquest, Colonization, and Settlement

The Europeans who landed on the western shores of the Atlantic in the late fifteenth century were the first in a wave of conquerors and settlers exploring the globe. From coastal India and Japan to North and South America, European explorers and settlers founded colonies, set up trading stations, and conquered or lived under indigenous empires. In the Americas the Spanish built their vast empire by conquering the Mexica and the Inca. Spanish expeditions also extended the authority of the crown in Madrid over all of South America, Central America, and much of the North American continent.

In contrast the Portuguese and English found neither great empires nor immense wealth that fell to the Spanish after conquest. Failing in their quest, the Portuguese soon set up lightly populated colonies along the Brazilian coast where they developed economic relationships with the small populations of indigenous peoples such as the Tupian.

Similarly, the English who came in the seventeenth century settled in small communities hugging coastal Virginia or New England where they developed an uneasy relationship with the peoples such as the Powhatan and the Wampanoags. The English also settled in the Caribbean during the 1620s and 1630s in search of land, independence, and livelihood.

Last, the French moved into North America via the St Lawrence River (1602) and the Mississippi River (1718). They claimed sovereignty over large areas of North America, but their population remained small and their settlements few in number. The French, in part, came as trappers and explorers who worked closely with native peoples. They quickly acquired fluency in indigenous languages, married indigenous women and often spent part of the year in their communities.[6]

BUILDING TRANSATLANTIC ECONOMIES

The Europeans saw their new holdings as sources of raw materials and precious metals that would promote their economies in Europe. Slowly the Europeans began to build an Atlantic economy that rested on shipping, ports, raw materials, and precious metals. For the Spanish the silver powered their ambitions. The Spanish located the largest concentration of silver in the world in Potosí, in the Andes of present-day northern Bolivia. They used the forced labor system of the Inca, known as the *mita*, to mine the rich silver veins. The Spanish also developed extremely productive silver mines in northern Mexico at Zacatecas. Here, they relied on voluntary labor since the silver mines were distant from settlement. Silver integrated the emerging Spanish empire into an economic system that stretched across the Atlantic to southern Europe and paid for imperial Spain's many wars.

In the absence of precious metals, the Portuguese searched for agricultural products that appealed to European consumers. They opted for sugar, then immensely popular in British and European markets. To grow and process sugar they relied on the plantations worked by African labor that they developed off the west coast of Africa during the fifteenth and sixteenth centuries as their template. The Portuguese had first produced sugar in the Algarve region of Portugal and then mated this system of production with a seemingly inexhaustible supply of inexpensive labor from the African mainland on the small island of São Tomé. The men recruited for this task came as slaves. Veterans of the African slave trade, the Portuguese readily brought purchased Africans to Brazil. Anchored by the *engenho* or sugar mill, a plantation economy was soon flourishing along the Northern coast of Brazil in the Bahia and Pernambuco regions and generating substantial profits both for the plantation owners, Italian investors, and Italian and Portuguese merchants.[7]

The English in the Chesapeake and the Caribbean regions also looked to Europe and England as profitable markets. The English settlers in the Chesapeake (1607) chose tobacco and indentured labor as the basis of their plantation system. Tobacco won over many European consumers and created an intense demand for labor met by the steady stream of indentured servants. These men and women exchanged their freedom for land promised at the end of their service to the plantation owner who funded their voyage to the Americas. The recovery of a slumping English economy after 1680 reduced the number of bound servants willing to sign an indenture contract.[8]

Only African labor met the long-term demand for the English. Since Africans originally worked as temporarily bound labor, the shift to slavery occurred slowly over the course of the seventeenth century and accelerated after 1680. Ironically, the Portuguese, who nearly monopolized the early slave trade, brought the first Africans to the English colony. By the early 1700s a fully developed system of slavery embodied in the law met the labor demands of the colony's plantation owners. Tobacco and slavery were the keys to making the Chesapeake valuable both to the settlers and to London.

In the Caribbean, settlers arrived as free laborers to work small plots of land where they grew tobacco and cotton. In the 1650s, market-savvy settlers in the Caribbean shifted into the lucrative sugar markets. They adopted the model of the plantation worked by African labor that served the Portuguese so well, and by the 1700s, the sugar islands had become England's great sources of wealth. Experience in running plantations and in the harsh business of managing enslaved African labor traveled with these planters as they migrated to the Carolinas. There they built an economy around the staples of rice and indigo and the labor of enslaved Africans that fed European markets.[9]

For many English colonies neither slavery nor plantations were the direct means of livelihood. Certainly the English religious dissenters, the Pilgrims and Puritans who landed on the northeast coast of North America in the 1620s and 1630s, showed no inclination toward slavery. They sought to build religious utopias free from the interference of the Church of England. Eventually they turned to the sea where they constructed an economy based on shipping, the timber industry, and maritime insurance. New England ships would ply the Atlantic Ocean for many decades and profited from the slave trade as carriers and insurers. Similarly, farmers and merchants in Pennsylvania and other mid-Atlantic English colonies settled in the late seventeenth century produced and sent crops, meats, white-collar services, and other essentials to the Caribbean islands to sustain the highly specialized monocrop economies that grew and processed sugar and its by-products for the Atlantic trade.

Oceanic ports and fleets remained central to this Atlantic economy. Glasgow, Buenos Aires, Cartagena, Philadelphia, New York, Havana, and other major ports played a critical role as access points to European and British goods and as conduits for staples heading for the continent or Great Britain. Fleets connected Oporto and Lisbon with Rio de Janeiro and with African slave stations and factories. British colonial ships joined Philadelphia and Baltimore with Kingston, Jamaica, and Bridgetown, Barbados. Charleston and Buenos Aires served as key ports of entry for African slaves. London credit paid for the vital slave trade while Montreal and Quebec acted as gathering centers of the rich fur trade. Merchants lived in ports, and maritime centers such as Rio de Janeiro, Philadelphia, and Buenos Aires housed ship crews and maritime workmen that supplied the energy and skills to maintain and sail the vast shipping fleets of the Atlantic.[10]

REVOLUTION AND THE AMERICAS, 1760–1830

Revolutions dramatically transformed the political and economic realms of the Americas. The Seven Years' War (1756–63) marked the first step in this process. In winning this conflict with the French, the British established their supremacy in North America. Ironically, the victory was costly for the British government just as defeat was for the Spanish crown that had joined the losing side in this conflict. Both powers sought new ways to raise revenue in order to meet the debts incurred during wartime. These measures included more efficient means of collecting taxes and new institutions such as the Vice Admiralty courts in British territories or the Intendant in Spanish America to enforce new policies. In the process these reforms changed the relationship between the colonial governments in the Americas and the imperial centers.

Both empires seemed reasonably healthy on the eve of their revolutions. The British pushed through measures to centralize more power in the royal administration. These included revenue enhancement measures such as the stamp tax designed to give power to royal Vice Admiralty Courts to prosecute individuals who tried to evade the tax in its North American and Caribbean colonies. The Crown sent a new Lord Lieutenant of Ireland, another British possession, to challenge the power of the Anglo-Irish leaders who controlled the island. In both cases royal power intended to supplant colonial power. The Spanish empire also sought to enhance royal power and to make tax collection more efficient and productive. Census takers identified the population and the extent of its wealth while the new royal official, the Intendant, arrived with enhanced power and a train of assistants. Both the British and Spanish wanted to make the collection of taxes more efficient.

The British also faced a new and far more variegated empire. The French surrender brought the province of Quebec and its Catholic Quebecois under the Crown. The British also extended their rule over diverse indigenous peoples, especially those in the Ohio River valley. Placating their new subjects and satisfying the demands of their colonials exceeded the capacity of the British government. Policies that favored the French Catholics angered the colonials who had been bitter enemies of Quebecois for decades. At the same time, British efforts to preserve the integrity of the indigenous peoples in the Ohio River valley by prohibiting settlement also infuriated the British colonial subjects.

The Spanish ruling an ethnically and racially diverse population for over two centuries never faced the challenge confronted by the British. Indians, Africans, racially mixed peoples, subjects of Spanish descent, and Spanish transplants had long lived together and worked out accommodations, even if some of them were tenuous.

Both imperial powers met fierce opposition to their new policies. In the case of the British, the resistance turned to revolution and the loss of her North American colonies. These became the United States of America, a proclaimed self-governing republic dependent on elections, freedom of speech, an impartial judiciary, and a federal government with divided powers. The Spanish, on the other hand, contained the often violent protests such as the Tupac Amaru uprisings of 1781–3 in the viceroyalty of Peru and maintained the integrity of the empire.

The British Crown presided over a shadow of its former empire. Apart from a few islands in the Caribbean, only the territory of British North America remained. Wary of so many Loyalist refugees from the United States in Canada and the potential for another revolt, the British issued the Constitution of 1791 that incorporated many of the measures of the United States Constitution. In most ways, republicanism reigned in British North America.

REVOLUTIONS AND NEW REPUBLICS

The French Revolution and its successor Napoleon transformed the political landscape of the Americas via Ireland. The Revolution profoundly influenced young Irishmen who dreamed of independence from Great Britain. As important, they wanted to make Ireland a republic that would incorporate the ideals of the French Revolution. Needless to say, the British took a dim view of these aspirations and began a campaign to imprison or drive out those sympathetic to the French revolutionaries. As a result, Irish radicals forced out of their homeland during the turbulent 1790s and especially after the failed revolution of 1798 flocked to the United States, where they assumed key political positions such as editors of party newspapers and injected many of their ideas into the United States' political landscape. In the French-held island of St-Domingue, the repercussions of the French Revolution shaped the 1790 slave uprisings that eventually led to the Haitian Republic, freedom for the former slaves, and an end to the plantation system. In the Iberian Peninsula, the invasion of Napoleon's armies in 1808 ultimately led to revolutions in the Spanish-ruled Americas.[11]

In Spain, the French occupiers immediately removed the king. Under Spanish law, in the absence of a monarch, the people inherited the power to rule. *Cabildos abiertos*, open urban councils, convened across the Spanish world from Pamplona to Cartagena to set up juntas via elections. Eventually, a *Cortés*, or Parliament, made up of popularly chosen delegates from across the global Spanish empire, convened in Cadiz in 1812 where it drew up the Constitution. The Constitution proved to be a remarkably liberal document, for it ended Indian tribute in the Americas, gave citizenship and the rights inherent in this status to every male except those of pure African descent, established popular sovereignty, and placed severe limits on the Spanish monarch. It also gave citizens freedom of speech. In effect, it created a republican world.[12]

The monarch, Fernando VII, restored in 1814, rejected these measures and the limitations the Constitution placed on the king. He then sent an army to link up with loyal subjects in the Americas and brutally crush the republican forces. Few who suffered at the hands of his invading army forgot the violence of those years. After 1815, civil wars broke out across South America as royalist forces confronted revolutionary armies in protracted conflicts that would ultimately lead to the creation of new republics. The freedom and self-governing institutions promised in 1812 now became reality.

Ironically, to avoid dethronement the Portuguese monarch and his retinue fled to Brazil in the wake of the same invasion that led to the events in Spain. They ruled peaceably from Rio de Janeiro until the early 1820s when the monarch returned to Lisbon. Yet his son assumed the role of a constitutional monarch, much in the style outlined for the Spanish king, and remained in Brazil. His inheritors maintained a remarkable stability for Brazil for most of the nineteenth century.[13]

THE RISE OF INDUSTRIAL ECONOMIES
IN THE AMERICAS

Industrialization transformed the world in the nineteenth century. It integrated new technology into all aspects of national economies. It also created economies that cut across borders and relied on raw materials from distant locations. As the first industrial economy, Great Britain drove much of the early technological change and produced the first generation of highly skilled industrial workers and entrepreneurs. Other states, notably Belgium, France, and the German polities, recognized the immense material advantages of industrialization and looked to Great Britain for the skills and equipment necessary to build an industrial economy.

In the Americas, the United States copied this strategy. It relied on British knowledge, skills, and technology to build textile, railroad, and mining industries. British plant design, equipment, and even skilled British textile workers were crucial in the early history of United States textiles, lodged in New England. Eventually, United States skilled workers and entrepreneurs modified the imported technology and patented their own technology.

United States entrepreneurs also saw the possibilities of the railroad. Lacking either skills or the technology to manufacture locomotives, they turned to Britain. For some time, British technology drove the early rail industry in the United States. In due course United States manufacturers acquired sufficient knowledge and skills to produce iron track and the many parts that made up the locomotive. Railroads then served as a vital market for iron and later steel manufacturers in the United States.[14]

To power the railroad, the United States relied on coal, an industry dominated by British technology. The United States recruited skilled British miners and integrated British knowledge to construct early mining operations necessary to fuel the locomotives. By the 1850s United States coal entrepreneurs had adapted British technology to their own needs and introduced technological innovations suited to this environment. The railroad quickly became an important market for the developing coal industry and a far superior means of moving coal to industrial and home consumers. By the 1850s the rail industry also served as the basis for an integrated national market so vital to the industrializing United States' economy.

The United States plantation economy also sustained the vital British textile industry that made Great Britain the industrial pioneer. In the wake of the Revolutionary War the invention of the cotton gin enabled southerners to exploit the abundant short staple cotton that thrived in the climate and soil of the region. The tremendous growth of the cotton economy in the nineteenth century fueled British textile factories for decades. In New York City, where the cotton was auctioned to British buyers, merchants, banks, and a host of services made the cotton economy viable and an essential component of the British economy. Cotton developed into the major export of the United States, making up over 60 percent of United States exports as late as 1860, and gave the United States economy a powerful transatlantic character, different from the flow of British technology and skilled workers east across the ocean yet every bit as powerful.

Corporations first appeared in the United States rail industry, where scale created novel organizational problems. Handling a huge volume and diversity of freight, confronting distances of hundreds and increasingly thousands of miles, and employing huge workforces, railroads began to develop new schemes to monitor and control their sprawling enterprises. These demands created the first generation of corporate managers who imagined new ways of structuring their vast enterprises. Railroad leaders developed the notion of line managers who handled the day-to-day details of operating the railroad. The rail company owners and their advisors strategically oriented managers who handled the broader issues such as new markets, capital funding, and innovative technology.

The railroad industry provided a model for other industries including steel, electricity, and chemicals. These operations required sophisticated technology, benefited from large-scale production, and incorporated theoretical knowledge. These operations also capitalized on the capacity to produce diverse goods with similar production schemes. General Electric, for example, manufactured multiple products on a vast scale and relied on teams of superbly educated professionals and flexible production capacity to achieve this end. By 1900, the United States had developed the most diverse and dynamic economy in the world.[15]

Canada's industrialization began with railroads necessary to develop effective markets. Entrepreneurs began to build these in the 1850s, relying mostly on British capital and only secondarily on United States investments. The British investors saw these railroads as a necessity to export via ports and ships to Great Britain where the agricultural sector was insufficient to meet the exploding demand of the industrial cities.

The expertise of United States engineers, however, was essential in railroad construction while the organizational schemes pioneered in the United States became models for their Canadian counterparts. United States technology created the basis for modern Canadian industry, just as British technology had done in the United States during its early phase of industrialization.

Sensitive to the presence of the foreign companies, the Canadian political leaders developed an early version of import substitution industrialization. Labeled the National Policy, this strategy raised tariffs on products the Canadians intended domestic operations to manufacture and attempted to force out foreign imports. To counter this policy United States-based corporations began to deploy manufacturing branches within the borders of Canada. This decision was part of a larger strategy in which United States companies first looked to Europe and Great Britain as sites for their operations.[16]

Yet Canada surged to the head of the list because of its proximity and the quality of its workforce. United States corporations in the newer, science-based, large-scale production industries, namely chemical, electrical and automotive, saw Canada's educated workforce as a huge asset and moved there in sizable numbers. By World War I around 450 United States operations such as General Electric dominated the Canadian economy.

Canada would remain a prosperous country with a vibrant, if often foreign owned economy. Needless to say the United States replaced Great Britain as the major investor in the Canadian economy and was by far the dominant force in manufacturing. Canada also became the major trading partner and major source of investment for United States companies. Last, United States companies also used Canada as a platform from which to export high-value products to British dominions and colonies otherwise protected by British tariffs.

In the United States corporations looked south to Mexico for raw materials. Unlike Canada, where United States companies saw manufacturing possibilities and prosperous consumers, these same companies saw rich mineral deposits in Mexico. To the benefit of the United States, corporate leaders also found a regime led by Porfirio Díaz (1876-1910) that encouraged foreign investment as the most effective means to industrialize an overwhelmingly rural world. United States corporations built a rail system to guarantee essential transportation and a communications system to maintain daily contact between their operations in Mexico and the company headquarters. Copper and other mining operations, largely in the northern provinces of Sonora and Chihuahua, turned out millions of tons of vital metals, processed in smelters and refineries destined for the United States via major rail terminals in urban centers such as El Paso. Northern Mexico became an integral part of the United States industrial economy and a necessity for its continued prosperity.[17]

Bankruptcies, political instability, and the lack of demand for their exports had isolated Central and South America in the decades after the conclusion of their revolutions in 1830. British investments began the process of reintegrating these regions back into the international markets. These investments formed an important part of British global strategy from the 1850s into the twentieth century.

British money and mining companies exploited the rich nitrate fields of northern Chile in response to the demands of the industrial core in Western Europe and the United States. British money also flowed into Columbian coffee plantations to meet the industrial world's taste for tropical products. British capital also searched for food abroad given the decreasing capacity of her agricultural sector to feed her soaring industrial population. Argentina was irresistible. Its vast Pampas supported huge herds of cattle and offered soils highly suitable for wheat production, both of which Britain desperately needed. British money funded and maintained railroads and fleets of refrigerated ships to move these products to domestic and continental markets.[18]

By the end of the nineteenth century, United States industrialists also saw potential beyond North America and in areas where the British had already established their presence. Peru offers an ideal example. British investments brought Peru into London's orbit via investments in Andean mineral deposits used in heavy manufacturing. The mineral reserves also drew the attention of United States corporate interests. Having profited immensely from their Canadian and Mexican operations, they recognized potential in the Andean mineral reserves, especially in the large deposits of copper desperately needed by United States heavy industry. In 1902 the United States corporation Cerro de Pasco Copper Corporation, as it eventually became known, began buying lands rich with copper deposits. Cerro founders such as James B. Haggin brought their long experience with mining and smelting copper in Mexico to Peru. They and their successors built a large industrial complex in the remote central sierras east of Lima, much as they had in isolated, mountainous regions of Mexico. By the 1920s the political leadership of Peru under the guidance of President August Leguia fully welcomed foreign investment and corporations as a means to encourage the national economy, much as had occurred in Mexico. Such collaboration between United States corporations and local governments prevailed throughout Central and South America where United States private interests operated.[19]

The growing presence of the United States ultimately presaged the ending of the longtime dominance Great Britain held during the nineteenth century. World War I was decisive in this transformation. The war created a serious shortage of European-bound ships and cut off markets where the goods from Latin America ended up. Minerals and tropical products now shifted almost entirely to United States markets.

Migration and Labor Demands

The growth of economies in the Americas created intense demand for labor in both export-driven and industrializing economies. In the United States the immense size of its economy and its great diversity drew over 30,000,000 migrants from across Europe and several million from Asia. They came to work on the railroads and in the textile factories, as did the Chinese and Irish, respectively. Many came to work in urban construction or mines and steel manufacturing sites, typically Southern and Eastern Europeans. French speaking Quebecois from Canada filled the textile factories in Massachusetts from the 1870s and 1880s onward while Canadian English flocked to Michigan and Washington states in search of industrial jobs. Significant numbers of British, Central European, and Southern European migrants also crossed into the United States for more lucrative employment after short stays in Canada.[20]

The dramatic expansion of plantation economies in the late nineteenth century onward to meet the demands of consumers in industrial economies produced a desperate need for labor. German coffee growers in Central America hired contract labor from the Caribbean to satisfy the tastes of European and North American coffee drinkers. Similarly, British tea plantation owners in Assam, India recruited tens of thousands of Indian contract laborers to grow and harvest tea in volumes sufficient to soothe the palate of Britain's exploding population. French sugar growers in Réunion in the Indian Ocean depended on a steady supply of Africans workers for their plantations.[21]

This same pressure for tropical products appeared in exploding markets in the United States. The United States victory in the 1898 Spanish–American War resulted in the annexation of sugar-producing Puerto Rico and made sugar-rich Cuba a protectorate. The United States also made the sugar-dependent Dominican Republic a protectorate. To meet the intense demand for labor in these newly controlled territories, United States corporations recruited thousands of Jamaicans, Haitians, and Barbadians.[22]

The demands from overseas markets that transformed the labor supply in the plantation economies also appeared in export-driven ranching and farm economies. Argentina and Canada had vast expanses of land suitable for crops and grazing animals, the Pampas and Prairies, respectively, fully capable of responding to the nutritional needs of industrial populations. Yet neither country had sufficient domestic labor assets to develop these lands. The Canadian government opened up the Prairies by selling land cheaply to land-hungry immigrant families. By 1900, family farms covered the Prairies and were producing wheat that effectively competed in British and European industrial markets. In Argentina the *Estancieros*, the large landowners, preferred single young men to break the land, plant crops, and open up the range for cattle. Once the land was broken, the *Estancieros* both grew wheat and raised cattle intended for overseas industrial markets.[23]

THE GREAT DEPRESSION AND WORLD WAR II

The 1920s witnessed a resumption of global trade that benefited both exporting and industrial economies around the globe and in the Americas. Even in Mexico where a revolution directed, in part, against United States corporations had raged in the 1910s, leaders had worked out accommodations with many of these companies. The decade would end with the dramatic stock market crash in New York and the start of a long and painful depression for the Americas. United States corporations suspended their operations from Canada to the cone of South America and, in the process, severely damaged the export-driven economies of Latin America and North America. These, particularly the Latin American economies, would to a great extent remain cut off from the international economy until after World War II.[24]

In response Latin American economies turned inward, as did most economies across the globe. In lands where a developed industrial economy existed, such as the United States and Germany, the shift worked around reviving a wounded but developed industrial base. In Latin America the leaders faced the task of turning export economies into industrial economies. In a period of self-sufficiency, Latin American republics such as Chile began constructing an industrial-based economy during the 1930s into the 1940s.

THE GLOBAL COLD WAR 1941–2000

The end of World War II accelerated changes in the United States relationship with the world. Victor in 1945, the United States immediately faced a formidable enemy, the dedicated Communist state the Union of Soviet Socialist Republics (USSR), on a global scale. The tension between these two ideologically opposed states erupted into the Cold War. In the ensuing decades both camps sought to use their influence throughout the world, including the Americas.

This global scope appeared most dramatically in United States National Security Council order No. 68, which outlined the strategy for worldwide containment of the Communist threat. In this contest, the United States frequently relied on covert operations, espionage, economic pressure, and other means short of war and used the Central Intelligence Agency (CIA) as one of the main vehicles to deploy these assets. The United States had begun to use these tactics in the 1948 Italian elections. Massive United States-sponsored propaganda, financial aid to the pro-United States Party the Christian Democrats, and anti-Soviet films among other means turned out to be crucial in the defeat of the Communist candidates.[25]

At this time, Latin America sat on the margins of United States interests. The United States firmly believed the USSR intended to export her revolution to the regions where Communist parties vied for leadership, mainly Asia and Europe. Yet this perception would broaden as the Cold War assumed global dimensions. As early as 1947, when the Cold War erupted, the United States and republics in Latin America formed the Rio Pact, a regional military alliance and a model for the deliberately anti-USSR North American Treaty Organization. The United States also took the lead in establishing the Organization of American States designed to cope with any future Communist threats in the hemisphere and to afford security for the region.[26]

The United States also worried over the left-wing governments and their radical union supporters that had come to power during the Depression and World War II. The United States shifted its backing to military regimes, including that of General Manual Odria who seized power in Peru in 1948 and the long-ruling Marcus Pérez Jiménez in Venezuela, as a way to contain these seemingly anti-United States leanings. United States pressure also compelled states such as Peru to end trade with the USSR and in a few cases to sever diplomatic relations.

Worries over left-leaning government led to direct intervention in the early 1950s when populist José Arbenz won election as President in Guatemala. As a progressive left of center leader, he attempted to reduce the overwhelming dominance in Guatemala of the United Fruit Company, a United States corporation. In his most controversial move, Arbenz expropriated a significant amount of uncultivated land owned by United Fruit and redistributed it to 100,000 Guatemalan families whose lives were stalked by poverty.

The measures of the Arbenz administration stoked United States fear of the global expansion of Communism. The arrival of arms manufactured in Communist

Czechoslovakia enabled the United States to condemn the Arbenz government for its ties to a Communist regime and put into motion a CIA-directed clandestine operation to overthrow the Arbenz government. The covert tactics developed in Europe resulted in a successful coup, a reversal of Arbenz's reform measures, harsh anti-Communist laws, and installation of an authoritarian regime. Intervention became a regular feature of United States policies in Latin America.

The triumph of Fidel Castro in Cuba in 1959 over United States-backed dictator Fulgencia Batista represented a successful challenge to the United States, its corporations, and its anti-Communist policies. Castro's expropriation of largely United States-owned industry and land and his subsequent alliance with the USSR made him a formidable enemy.

The United States saw Cuba and Latin America as a central battleground in the Cold War. To cope with these threats, the United States relied on the covert tactics used so successfully in Western Europe in the late 1940s and Guatemala in the mid 1950s. United States administrations used propaganda, aid to anti-Castro forces both within and outside of Cuba, covert activities in Cuba, and intelligence gathering, all copied from the Guatemala operation, to topple Castro. These efforts came to no avail, and Castro remained in power and a significant danger to the United States and its capitalist system.[27]

Cuba reinforced this threat when it adopted the United States strategy of deploying military forces and civilian support to allies across the globe. From the 1960s onward Castro gave aid to countries in Africa battling what he termed imperialism. From Zaire to Morocco, Cuban troops and aid workers assisted forces ideologically in line with Castro's thinking. In the late 1980s South Africa-directed and United States-supported units conducted incursions into Angola, and again Cuba sent troops that were decisive in ending these forays.[28]

Central America and not Cuba would prove the decisive theater for ending the Cold War in the Americas. Here the global strategy of United States President Ronald Reagan intersected with the regional ambitions and fears of Argentina and other anti-Communist military regimes. The Civil War in Nicaragua, 1977–9, between the United States-backed dictator Anastasio Somoza Debayle and his opponents, the Sandinistas, precipitated the involvement of Argentina. Despite the long-time support of the Somoza regime, the United States under President Jimmy Carter withdrew its aid to the Somoza government in favor of a negotiated settlement.

The Argentinean government, already providing Somoza with weapons and other aid, mobilized a coalition of anti-Communist regimes from South Africa and Israel to Guatemala and Bolivia to save Somoza's failing regime. Argentina also gave resources to anti-Communist forces in El Salvador and Guatemala. Reaching for a major part in the worldwide assault on Communist regimes, Argentina demonstrated its hemispheric strength in opposing a Communist threat and its ability to draw in allies from across the Atlantic world. In the end the efforts of Argentina and its short-lived allies were unable to thwart the Sandinistas, and Somoza fled the country. Unwilling to concede defeat, the Argentinean military leadership switched its support to the thousands of former National Guardsmen whose military organization had kept Somoza in power.[29]

For the United States, Central America was a fundamental test of its global anti-Communist strategy. Reagan abandoned containment and adopted an offensive strategy of directly confronting Communist regimes. He saw this new approach as a direct counter to the Brezhnev Doctrine, which promised all means of support to Socialist regimes around the world. The United States would deploy its military, diplomatic, economic, and covert resources from Southern Africa to Afghanistan in an effort to defeat the USSR and its allies.[30]

Reagan saw the insurgency in Central America as part of the global threat posed by Cuba and the USSR. His fears overlapped with the regional concerns of Argentina, Chile, and other military regimes that saw the triumph of the Sandinistas as a mortal danger to their own existence. Argentina's cooperation with the United States in this effort ended when the United States backed Great Britain in the 1982 Falklands War; yet, Argentina continued to give support to the *Contras*, as the opponents of the Sandinistas were labeled.

The CIA assumed direction of the forces opposing the Sandinista. It trained the Contras and pumped in significant amounts of weapons and money. Similarly resources flowed into El Salvador. In the end the Sandinistas accepted free elections, and when defeated, they turned the reins of government over to a pro-United States government. Moderate though weak rulers held onto power in El Salvador. The wars in Central America marked the last phase of the Cold War, which ended with the collapse of the USSR in 1991.[31]

The Global Economy and the Americas, 1941–2000

During the Cold War the United States strenuously pushed for an international economy, yet it faced a stern challenge in the economic theory of Import Substitution Industrialization (ISI), formally articulated by Paul Prebisch, a member of the United Nations Economic Commission for Latin America. For Prebisch, the dominance of foreign corporations in the export industries that sustained Latin American states effectively subordinated them to foreign, usually United States interests. He rejected the export arrangements that trapped all of Latin America into a subordinate position selling cheap raw materials and importing expensive manufactured goods. To break this cycle, Latin American countries needed to raise tariffs and fees on major imported goods, promote industries that manufactured these goods, and develop healthy internal markets. His ideas gave Latin America a unified and logical philosophy with which to oppose the international trading system of the United States and its industrial allies. Mexico, Chile, and several other Latin American countries embraced his philosophy, often with positive results.[32]

As such, Latin America and the ISI strategy served the interests of developing economies in the post-1960 decades around the globe. Kenya, Iraq, Turkey, and many

newly independent states embraced ISI with demonstrable results: enhanced urbanization, industrial production geared to domestic markets, and rising levels of literacy. These
patterns repeated those that had occurred in Latin America several decades earlier.

Faced with high tariffs and the potential inherent in the developing economies of Latin
America, United States corporations developed a new market strategy. Before the 1960s,
the majority of the companies operating in Latin America consisted largely of metals and
raw materials producers. Corporations began to place branches of their manufacturing
operations in Latin America, much as had occurred in Canada in an earlier generation. In
a move anticipating this practice, General Electric shifted one of its product lines to Brazil
in the 1920s. Over the decades the corporation expanded its production sites and the
variety of products intended for the consumer market in Brazil. To acquire the parts and
accessories necessary for turning out finished products, General Electric linked up with
local manufacturers to whom the company gave technical education and quality control
to meet General Electric's exacting standards. In the process these local concerns
acquired the technological and knowledge assets of the major United States consumer
industries. As numerous United States corporations embraced this strategy, prosperity
began to reach consumers outside of the privileged classes.[33]

The global debt crisis of the 1980s ground the Latin American economies to a halt.
Countries in Latin America had borrowed heavily from United States banks to finance
infrastructural projects during this decade. By the latter part of this decade, states such
as Mexico and Argentina were unable to meet their debt obligations. The International
Monetary Fund (IMF) stepped in with massive loans to bail out these states. Created
near the end of World War II, the IMF became the chief lender to states in desperate
economic situations. It imposed a discipline that included deregulation, guaranteed
property rights for foreign companies, privatization of many government functions,
and severe cuts in government spending.

Recovery came slowly as states looked overseas for models of successful economies.
In effect, states in Latin America embraced the neoliberalism and open economy that
had well served Singapore, Taiwan, and other developing Asian economies. Adopting
their policies, Latin American countries now welcomed foreign investments, lowered
tariffs, cut duties imposed on exports, and sold off state-owned enterprises. Many of the
individuals who engineered this sweeping transformation in countries such as Chile
trained in United States universities such as the University of Chicago, which espoused
these policies. Inflation that had plagued Latin America dropped significantly, economies grew at a robust rate, and employment rose. Opening up the new global economy
and the potential for a hemispheric integration marked a new era for the Americas.[34]

The readiness of Mexico for such integration appeared in its joining of the North
America Free Trade Association (NAFTA), ratified in 1994. Mexico opened up its
economy in the 1990s both to United States financial institutions and to its
manufacturing companies. By the late 1990s some 700 United States companies had
located their factories in Tijuana, Mexico just beyond the southern Californian border.
Some 2,000 United States-owned factories employing 1,000,000 workers were doing
business in Mexico by the early twenty-first century.[35]

Canada, too, had long embraced an open economy as a way to bolster its small industrial base and to promote the export of raw materials to the United States. After World War II Canada experienced a huge increase in foreign, largely United States-driven, investments. Much of this capital appeared in the form of direct investments and mostly from the United States' largest 500 corporations. The United States long acted as Canada's main trading partner. For example, it bought some 70 percent of Canada's merchandise trade during the 1980s and 1990s, slightly more than Mexico. The intensity of such exchanges accounts for Canada's enthusiastic participation in NAFTA and its commitment to free trade.[36]

By the turn of the twenty-first century, the Americas seemed to be moving toward full economic integration. Nationalistic fervor had given way to more open economies that facilitated the movement of goods, services, and capital across borders. NAFTA and the assurance of integrating Central American republics into something similar promised rising levels of prosperity. In South America, Argentina, Brazil, and eventually Uruguay, Paraguay, Chile, and Bolivia formed the Southern Common Market either as full-time or associate members. It ranked fourth behind NAFTA, the European Community, and Japan in scale and volume.

GLOBALIZATION IN THE LATE TWENTIETH CENTURY

This trend was part of a larger global process of moving expensive production to cheap labor sites around the world. By 2000 the United States and other developed economies had opened up production sites in places such as the People's Republic of China, Indonesia, Malaysia, and Eastern Europe. Specialization also accompanied this global dispersal of production and made it fundamentally different from the branch strategy first developed in Canada and then used in Latin America. Chile capitalized on the specialization to sell salmon abundant in its coastal waters to Japanese markets heavily dependent on fish. It also produced summer fruits such as grapes and peaches harvested in what are the winter months of the northern climates and sold to hungry buyers in North America and Europe. Chile also spent a good deal of time and money to expand cultivation of arable soil and to make it far more productive.[37]

Even the United States saw its international orientation change. The production of the preeminent United States doll, Barbie, demonstrates the extent of this new global production scheme. The United States produced the molds and shipped them to factories in Southeast Asia. The plastics and hair parts came from Japan and Taiwan, while the Chinese made the cotton dresses. Plants in Indonesia, Malaysia, and China produced the finished product.[38] In this new global economy, even the United States, once the dominant economic power and home to the most powerful corporations, had dispersed many of its key manufacturing activities across the globe and had also contracted with foreign companies to make components of what was once a national product. At the same time, Latin American economies sought a new position in the reorganized global economy and began to assert their economic independence of the United States, most notably in Brazil with its energy independence and strong manufacturing base. The economic future is an open book, yet to be written.

NOTES

1. Benjamin Keen and Mark Wasserman, *A History of Latin America* (Boston: Houghton Mifflin, 1988), 13–21.
2. Cheryl Martin and Mark Wasserman, *Latin America and Its Peoples* (New York: Pearson, Longman, 2008), 19–23.
3. Alvin M. Josephy, Jr., *500 Nations: An Illustrated History of North American Indians* (New York: Alfred A. Knopf, 1994), 28–9 and 32.
4. Jay Gitlin, 'Empires of Trade, Hinterlands of Settlement,' in Clyde A. Milner II, Carol O'Connor and Martha A. Sandweiss, eds., *The Oxford History of the American West* (New York: Oxford University Press, 1994), 87.
5. For a discussion of smallpox see Sheldon Watts, *Epidemics and History: Disease, Power and Imperialism* (New Haven: Yale University Press, 1999), 84–108, and for smallpox, typhus, and yellow fever as well as regional outbreaks, see Noble David Cook, *Born to Die: Disease and New World Conquest 1492–1650* (New York: Cambridge University Press, 1998), 167–98.
6. John J. Bukowczyk, Nora Faires, David Smith, and Randy Williams, *Permeable Borders: The Great Lakes Basin As Transnational Region, 1650–1990* (Pittsburgh: University of Pittsburgh Press, 2005), 14–18.
7. James Lockhart and Stuart B. Schwartz, *A History of Colonial Spanish America and Brazil* (New York: Cambridge University Press, 1999), see chapter 7 for Brazil; Frederick Stirton Weaver, *Latin America in the World Economy* (Boulder, Colo.: Westview Press, 2000), 21.
8. J. H. Elliot, *Empires of the Atlantic World: Britain and Spain in America 1492–1830* (New Haven: Yale University Press, 2006), 54–5, 103–4, 94–7.
9. David Eltis, *The Rise of African Slavery in the Americas* (New York: Cambridge University Press, 2000), 136, 195, 199, 200–6; Edward J. Davies, II, *The United States in World History* (New York: Routledge, 2006), 6–7.
10. Davies, *The United States in World History*, 5; Elliot, *Empires of the Atlantic World*, 109–110; Jeremy Adelman, *Sovereignty and Revolution in the Iberian Atlantic* (Princeton: Princeton University Press, 2006), 10–11, 46–7; Eltis, *The Rise of African Slavery*, 219.
11. Lester Langley, *The Americas in the Age of Revolution, 1750-1850* (New Haven: Yale University Press, 1995), 87–99; David Wilson, *United Irishmen, United States: Immigrant Radicals in the Early Republic* (Ithaca: Cornell University Press, 1991).
12. John Charles Chasteen, *Americanos: Latin America's Struggle for Independence* (New York: Oxford University Press, 2008), 90–2; Jaime E. Rodriguez O, *The Independence of Spanish America* (New York: Cambridge University Press, 1998), chapter 3; Jeremy Adelman, 'An Age of Imperial Revolutions,' *American Historical Review* 113 (2008), 319–41. For a provocative discussion of representative institutions and citizenship in

Latin America, see Hilda Sabato, 'On Political Citizenship in Nineteenth-Century America,' *American Historical Review* 106 (2001), 1290–320.

13. Chasteen, *Americanos*, 126–8, 140–2, 145–7, 151–5.

14. Sean Patrick Adams, *Old Dominion Politics and Economy in Antebellum America* (Baltimore: Johns Hopkins University Press, 2004) for the transfer of British mining technology; Grace R. Cooper, Rita J. Adrosko, and John H. White, Jr, 'Importing a Revolution: Machines, Railroads and Immigrants,' in Carl Guarneri, ed., *America Compared: American History in International Perspective* (Boston: Wadsworth, 2005), 270–85.

15. For a comparative discussion of corporations in the United States, Germany, and Great Britain, see Alfred D. Chandler, Jr., *Scale and Scope: The Dynamics of Industrial Capitalism* (Boston: Belknap Press, 2004).

16. For an analysis of Canada's economy and its failed attempts to protect it from foreign companies, overwhelmingly US, see Gordon Laxer, *Open for Business: The Roots of Foreign Ownership in Canada* (Toronto: Oxford University Press, 1989), 5–6, 11–17, 37, 39, 41, 43–9, 123, 140; Glen Williams, *NOT FOR EXPORT: Toward a Political Economy of Canada's Arrested Industrialization* (Toronto: McClelland & Stewart, Limited, 1983), 16, 21–8, 36–9, 52, 96–104, 106–12.

17. John Mason Hart, *Empire and Revolution: The Americans in Mexico since the Civil War* (Berkeley: University of California Press, 2002), chapter 2.

18. Weaver, *Latin America in the World Economy*, 44–52, 55, 63–4, 66, 68; Jeffrey A. Frieden, *Global Capitalism: Its Fall and Rise in the Twentieth Century* (New York: W. W. Norton, 2006), 68–72.

19. Lawrence A. Clayton, *Peru and the United States: The Condor and the Eagle* (Athens, Ga.: University of Georgia Press, 1999), 86–8 and chapter 4; Thomas F. O'Brien, *The Revolutionary Mission: American Enterprise in Latin America, 1900–1945* (New York: Cambridge University Press, 1996), see chapters 5 and 6 for Peru and other chapters for the relationship between US corporations and the Latin American states.

20. For material on migration, see Walter Nugent, *Crossings: The Great Transatlantic Migrations, 1870–1914* (Bloomington, Ind.: Indiana University Press, 1992), chapter 15; Mark Wyman, *Round-Trip to America: The Immigrants return to Europe, 1880-1930* (Ithaca: Cornell University Press, 1993), chapters 1–3; Bruno Ramirez, *Crossing the 49th Parallel: Migration from Canada to the United States, 1900–1930* (Ithaca: Cornell University Press, 2001), chapters 1, 3, 4.

21. For a survey of German activities in Central America, see Thomas Schoonover, *Competitive Imperialism, 1821–1929* (Tuscaloosa, Ala.: University of Alabama Press, 1998), chapters 6–8; For a popular history of tea, see Laura C, Martin, *Tea: The Drink that Changed the World* (Boston: Charles E. Tuttle, 2007).

22. For the Caribbean see Cesar J. Ayala, *American Sugar Kingdom: The Plantation Economy of the Spanish Caribbean, 1898–1934* (Chapel Hill, N.C.: University of North Carolina, Press, 1999), chapter 6; O'Brien, *Revolutionary Mission*, chapters 8, 9.

23. For a comparative study of Canada and Argentina, see Jeremy Adelman, *Frontier Development: Land, Labor, and Capital on the Wheatlands of Argentina and Canada, 1880–1914* (New York: Oxford University Press, 1994).

24. Frieden, *Global Capitalism*, 220–8, 303; Weaver, *Latin America in the World Economy*, 117–27.

25. For an account of the outbreak of the Cold War see George Herring, *From Colony to Superpower: U.S. Foreign Relations Since 1776* (New York: Oxford University Press, 2008), chapter 14, and for the Italian elections, p. 621.

26. Herring, *From Colony to Superpower*, 625–8, 683–4.
27. Herring, *From Colony to Superpower*, 685–9; for a brief account of Batista and Castro as well as Castro's reforms see Thomas O'Brien, *The Century of U.$. Capitalism in Latin America* (Albuquerque, N.M.: University of New Mexico Press, 1999), 150–5.
28. Piero Gleijeses, 'The View from Havana: Lessons from Cuba's African Journey, 1959–1976,' in Gilbert Joseph and Daniela Spenser, eds., *In from the Cold: Latin America's Encounter with the Cold War* (Durham, N.C.: Duke University Press, 2008), 112–33.
29. For an account of Argentina's activities, see Ariel C. Armstrong, 'Transnationalizing the Dirty War: Argentina in Central America,' in Joseph and Spenser, *In from the Cold*, 134–70.
30. Herring, *From Colony to Superpower*, 862, 864, 881–5.
31. Herring, *From Colony to Superpower*, 886–9.
32. Frieden, *Global Capitalism*, 310–12, for ISI in a global context, see also 316–19 and for its flaws 351–6; Weaver, *Latin America in the World Economy*, chapter 5.
33. O'Brien, *The Century of U.$. Capitalism in Latin America*, 226–9.
34. For an account of neoliberalism, see Weaver, *Latin America in the World Economy*, 177–85.
35. For an account of Mexico's shift to an open economy, see Hart, *Empire and Revolution*, chapter 15.
36. Glen Norcliffe, 'Foreign Trade in Goods and Services,' in John N. H. Britton, ed., *Canada and the Global Economy* (Montreal: McGill-Queen's University Press, 1996), 25–47.
37. For account of Chile see Frieden, *Globalism*, 424–6.
38. Frieden, *Global Capitalism*, 417.

REFERENCES

ADELMAN, JEREMY. *Frontier Development: Land, Labor, and Capital on the Wheatlands Of Argentina and Canada, 1880–1914*. New York: Oxford University Press, 1994.

AYALA, CESAR J. *American Sugar Kingdom: The Plantation Economy of the Spanish Caribbean, 1898–1934*. Chapel Hill, N.C.: University of North Carolina Press, 1999.

ELLIOT, J. H. *Empires of the Atlantic World: Britain and Spain in America, 1492–1830*. New Haven: Yale University Press, 2006.

HART, JOHN MASON. *Empire and Revolution: The Americans in Mexico since the Civil War*. Berkeley: University of California Press, 2002.

HERRING, GEORGE. *From Colony to Superpower: U.S. Foreign Relations since 1776*. New York: Oxford University Press, 2008.

JOSEPH, GILBERT, and DANIELA SPENSER, eds. *In from the Cold: Latin America's Encounter with the Cold War*. Durham, N.C.: Duke University Press, 2008.

JOSEPHY, ALVIN M., JR. *500 Nations: An Illustrated History of North American Indians*. New York: Alfred A. Knopf, 1994.

NUGENT, WALTER. *Crossings: The Great Transatlantic Migrations, 1870–1914*. Bloomington, Ind.: Indiana University Press, 1992.

O'BRIEN, THOMAS. *The Century of U.$. Capitalism in Latin America*. Albuquerque, N.M.: University of New Mexico Press, 1999.

O'Brien, Thomas F. *The Revolutionary Mission: American Enterprise in Latin America, 1900–1945.* New York: Cambridge University Press, 1996.

Rodriguez O, Jaime E. *The Independence of Spanish America.* New York: Cambridge University Press, 1998.

Watts, Sheldon. *Epidemics and History: Disease, Power and Imperialism.* New Haven: Yale University Press, 1999.

Weaver, Frederick Stirton. *Latin America in the World Economy.* Boulder, Colo.: Westview Press, 2000.

CHAPTER 29

THE ATLANTIC OCEAN BASIN

ALAN L. KARRAS

MUSINGS FROM THE IRRITATED

IN general, historians ought to have two main goals: (1) reconstructing the past in a way that demonstrates how those who lived life in times before our own understood and interacted with the world that they inhabited *and* (2) ascribing meaning to these past experiences so that they are relevant to those of us in the present. These large questions do not require scholars to work solely within a particular national or linguistic boundary, though most historians are trained to do exactly that. Atlantic history can provide a cure for such nationalistic tendencies, though it will not be easy. Atlantic history, a once-promising field of study, has become a bit down-at-heel, suffering from malaise and, perhaps, terminal *ennui*. Despite this seemingly grim assessment of the patient's health, the longer-term prognosis might still remain promising.

Atlantic history, at least for the last several decades, has held out tremendous potential for modern world historians. Such scholars, who tend not to have had extensive training in the western hemisphere's history, nevertheless need familiarity with many historical processes that, arguably, first appeared during the modern period in the context of the Atlantic world. These world-historical processes, such as transoceanic migration, intercontinental and inter-imperial trade, religious proselytization, democratic revolution, and enlightened state-building point to a significance for Atlantic world history that cannot be underestimated; without the Atlantic world's history, in fact, there would be no global history.

The Atlantic world's vast spaces—four continents that border an ocean, in addition to the ocean itself—beg scholars to explore the interactions, exchanges, and connections between societies with an Atlantic shore. Moreover, the exchanges, interactions, and connections between these societies and others that are outside this geographic space, such as China, also affected the political, economic, cultural, and social developments within Atlantic societies. Tea, for example, played something more than a symbolic part in the American Revolution. It was also an essential product in the global spread of industrialization, as well as in commercial exchange within the Atlantic world's spaces, yet it generally remains unstudied.[1] Instead, to most scholars now working on the Atlantic world, tea appears as something that is dumped into Boston Harbor in the run-up to the War for Independence between Britain and its colonies.[2] Scholars' focus, in other words, generally remains on local and nationalist historical narratives, even when connections to a broader regional history like the Atlantic world, let alone to world history, are easy to make.

The reason that the historical focus continues to be fixed in place is worrisome. North American historians of mainland British North America, formerly known as early Americanists, have colonized Atlantic history. In doing so, they have hijacked the field's promising internationalist tendencies and turned them upside-down. They have minimized the role that more distant societies around the world played in the social, economic, and cultural life of those societies that border the Atlantic in North America, except insofar as that role can either be related to the development of a creole colonial identity *or* somehow connected to the metropolitan area in Europe that controlled a particular colonial society. Africa continues to be an afterthought, usually appearing in scholarship solely as a source of 'necessary' labor for plantation societies.[3] Studies of the flow of people, goods, and ideas in the Atlantic world are, therefore, limited—and they often tend to be written by those other than academic historians.[4]

To advance the field, then, and counteract its early American colonization, it is essential that historians of one of the other European countries to colonize the Americas begin to write histories that explore the interaction between *all* of the societies that bordered the Atlantic's shores. This does not yet appear to be happening: the Spanish world remains the Spanish world, so too does the Portuguese, and the Dutch, and the French. Historians are, in other words, limited by language and ethnicity.[5] When a work *does* appear from these quarters, such as J. H. Elliott's *Empires of the Atlantic World*, British North American historians immediately pronounce it 'magisterial,' while lamenting their own inability to produce such scholarship. Such lamentations do not help; rather scholars should simply devote more energy to engaging the Atlantic world's internationalist axes.[6]

The current situation is not entirely the fault of historians of colonial British America. Substitute Spanish or French or Dutch for British, and you will find scholars who are comfortable working with Spanish or French or Dutch historical sources, but who also remain unwilling or unable to approach neighboring geographic spaces that communicated in different languages. Most historians who do original archival research exhibit discomfort when writing about history that transcends national or linguistic boundaries; those who produce syntheses, moreover, are reticent to take on an existing literature with which they are relatively unfamiliar.

In a sense, who can blame them? Yet that is precisely the kind of risk that Atlantic history most requires. Until such time as training in world history becomes more widespread, if ever it does, it will be difficult to change the current state of affairs. The historical profession would need to be fundamentally reorganized, which seems increasingly unlikely, given both professional resistance and scarce budgetary resources. It is, then, no wonder that the field of Atlantic history is likely to continue drifting through the doldrums, much like many of the New World's first visitors from the Atlantic's eastern shores did centuries ago.

There is, moreover, an additional problem to be overcome. Just as language has proven to be a barrier for much Atlantic scholarship, so has chronological breadth. I argue here that Atlantic history has become synonymous with early American history; in a few cases, it has been pushed, somewhat uncomfortably, into the nineteenth century.[7] Within that time frame, three periods are usually ascribed to Atlantic world history. Though not all scholars agree on what dates the periods shift from one to the next, it nevertheless remains common for them to end in the nineteenth century, usually early, but sometimes middle or late. For example, in 1992, J. R. McNeill and I tried to push as far out as we could from the usual early American comfort zone. Given our own Caribbean and Latin American training, we got as far as the 1880s, when the last slave societies in the Americas were eliminated.[8] But even this now seems insufficient, given events of the twentieth century, and the role that a variety of interactions between the Atlantic-bordering societies have played in world history. In short, the Atlantic world concept needs to be pushed into the twentieth century, so that the region's transformation from a 'new world' to one that became integrated in various ways into other, shifting and sometimes opposing, regional blocs can be clearly articulated and explained, especially in relationship to existing national and world histories.

The political alliances between northern European states, like France and Britain, with the United States gave rise to a kind of north Atlantic world, not quite NATO, but something close, early in the twentieth century. The former colonies of Latin America continued their connection with Spain, and expanded contacts to southern Europe in, for example, the migration between Italy and Argentina. Africa, colonized in the post-slavery period by northern Europeans, also participated in the Atlantic world, but, as Peter Coclanis has indicated, this was *also* part of a newly expanding global history.[9] In other words, during the twentieth century the Atlantic world and its constituent parts became more closely connected to the rest of the world, using the Atlantic as one vector of connection among several. That this story remains largely untold except insofar as it can be related to a particular national historical literature is again understandable; it could easily be remedied with some innovative scholarly approaches.

Nevertheless, despite my general pessimism with the current direction of much Atlantic history, there are still reasons to argue for a coherent and expanded historical field. The first signs of such invigoration are even present. Textbooks and courses are dutifully appearing. But while these textbooks and courses generally grapple with the themes of Atlantic history, they generally read like a series of national and regional histories that are connected thematically.[10] They are not yet integrated into a single, or singularly distinctive, historical narrative. This is, of course, difficult to do, but it is absolutely essential if Atlantic history is to have a chance at overcoming the deeply ingrained temptation to tell the historical narrative of the United States (or any other society) through an Atlantic lens, while calling this revised national narrative Atlantic history. If historians can make this leap of faith, and accept a revised conceptual framework, Atlantic history indeed has a future. If scholars fail to rise to the challenge, Atlantic history will cease to provide a meaningful historical lens through which to view past societies.

EXPANDING TIME AND INTEGRATING SPACE

It is probably best to consider the Atlantic world as a single entity from the time that the four continents bordering the Atlantic Ocean became linked through exploration, migration, and commerce. This points to the late fifteenth century or the early sixteenth century. While there is no doubt that earlier interactions between parts of the Atlantic world, such as that between the Vikings and the Americas, took place, Africans were not included in this round of interactions. And, regardless of what one thinks about Ivan Van Sertima's work, *They Came before Columbus*, which boldly argues that interaction between Africa and the Americas took place long before Europeans arrived, clear connections between all four of the Atlantic's continents did not emerge before Columbus's voyages of the late fifteenth century. Indeed, this is why there is general agreement among scholars that the Atlantic world, as a unit of historical analysis, becomes possible only after 1500.[11]

Given the clear connections between the four continents that emerged after that date, the promise of Atlantic history was initially realized in works like Alfred Crosby's *The Columbian Exchange*. The concept is now so familiar that it needs almost no explanation; the book's title and argument refer to the exchanges of crops, animals, and diseases that took place among the various residents of the Atlantic's continents after the first European voyages of exploration. Other scholars have since taken up the important task of writing an Atlantic world environmental history, as a way of illuminating the interactions among the Atlantic's disparate peoples and explaining the dramatic decline of the indigenous American populations at the hands of those from across the sea.[12] From the Atlantic world's inception, demographics and environment can be easily used to illustrate the utility of the broad regional conceptualization.

The Atlantic world concept's historical utility was further expanded when the lack of an adequate labor supply in the Americas, a lack created by the imposition of European forms of social organization combined with disease explained by the Columbian exchange, required new sources of labor. Workers came initially, at least in some cases, from Europe, as well as from Africa but the vast majority of such labor was coerced, perhaps better known as slavery. Of course, the introduction of African slavery to the Americas, as well as its effects in Africa, was subjected to numerical analysis, most famously by Philip Curtin, whose estimates of the total size and scope of the slave trade have proven over time to be remarkably resilient.[13] The Atlantic slave trade, in fact, provided the labor that built large chunks of the Americas, making it especially important to Atlantic history. Moreover, through its monopoly system of labor, the slave trade yielded profits to Europeans that, if Eric Williams's general argument about slavery's profitability is correct, led to the availability of capital in Europe, which in turn fueled industrialization.[14]

Though the environmental and demographic approach to studying the Atlantic world has generally proven productive, especially in earlier historical periods, there is still much work remaining to be done. In particular, such avenues of inquiry need to be pushed forward into later chronological periods. For example, world historians have pointed to the role of industrialization in the Atlantic world in creating various kinds of pollution that have spread to other quarters. Greenhouse gases from North America and Europe have begun to demonstrate quite negative consequences in other places around the (Atlantic) world, especially those in the southern hemisphere.[15] Diseases, too, continue to spread from one part of the Atlantic world to others; HIV/AIDS is one prominent example, yet historical scholarship on these more recent human-pathogen interactions is generally limited.

If considering the Columbian exchange comes naturally, and has been clearly associated with Atlantic world history from its inception, it still remains somewhat more difficult for those other than world historians to imagine the roles that quinine or rubber played in shaping the nature of Atlantic historical interactions, especially after the abolition of the African slave trade. The growth of tropical medicine did after all allow the colonization of the rest of the world to proceed apace, which in turn changed the fundamental relationship between societies—including those in the Atlantic basin.[16] Yet, this story is often left out of Atlantic history, because of the general lack of attention to events and developments post-1800, let alone post-1900. Of course, this also means that these stories are not in the textbooks. That strikes me as unfortunate.

Pushing the story of Atlantic interactions into later periods ought also to have salubrious effects, especially concerning the role of Africa. Far too often, Africans are omitted from the Atlantic world's historiography. This seems a bit odd, since it was after all their labor, through slavery, that built much of the capital that circulated in the Atlantic basin. Though slavery in the Americas ended at various points in the nineteenth century (depending on both local and imperial conditions in each society), the role of Africa in the Atlantic did not end when the last slave had been freed. Instead, the role of African societies changed. New states created in the nineteenth century, such as Liberia and Sierra Leone, came into existence, in part modeled on the Enlightenment principles that the American, French, and Haitian revolutions attempted to codify and put into practice. The history of state building in this part of West Africa is not often connected to those earlier stories of revolution or the application of Enlightenment ideology that played so great a role in the Atlantic's history after 1760 or so.

Even so, this is not the extent of Africa's changing relationship with the rest of the Atlantic world. The British conquered the Dutch settlement at the Cape of Good Hope, making this southern settlement a base from where they could push into the African interior, paving the way for the eventual colonization of the African continent. Of course, this colonization was intimately linked to industrialization elsewhere in the Atlantic world, especially Europe and the Americas. In the few circumstances when Africans appear in the historical literature of the Atlantic world after 1850, they tend to be seen as participants in some kind of African diaspora, which is at least in part a misnomer. There was never any clear African identity that linked together people in Africa, let alone those of African descent who toiled in the rest of the continents and islands that bordered the ocean.

Paul Gilroy, in *The Black Atlantic*, makes a strong case for the cultural connections that existed among Africans who were scattered around the Atlantic world after slavery ended. Nevertheless, his work remains singular, as others have not generally attempted such an approach. The more important story, still largely untold, remains in the ways that the African continent changed its interaction with other Atlantic societies, especially after the slave trade ended and into the twentieth century.[17]

Community, Migration, and the Need for Political Economy

One of the great changes to the historical profession to come about after 1970 was a new focus on social history, especially in early (British North) America. This has all been well and good, as it has led to some important community studies which consider issues of demography, labor, social constructions, and even economic developments within these societal subsets. Such research tends to explore a particular place, for instance a town or region, at a particular time. Some historians also sought to expand such community studies by focusing on migration, and illuminating the relationships between societies in different places. A few of these migration studies even recognized that talking about migration required considering not just the westward migration of Europeans and Africans to the Americas, but also the eastward migrations of those in the New World to the Old World.[18]

In the Atlantic world, migration must be the starting point; there would be no Atlantic history, nor for that matter would there be global history, without it. Of course, there was migration of Europeans. The familiar story, at least familiar to those who studied British North American history, is that individuals migrated either for religious freedom (say, in Massachusetts or early Pennsylvania) or for new economic opportunities (say, everywhere else, but Virginia would be a good example). What the colonial migrants found was something rather different from what they expected and the rest, as they say, is history. The fact is that Europeans did migrate, but most of them, in all colonies including those from countries other than the United Kingdom, were single young men in search of greater economic opportunity than they would have had if they had remained at home. Not all of them were prepared for the hardships they would face in the mainland and island colonies and not all of them were even interested in working to improve their lives. Many of them wanted to earn quick profits and, when they could, return to live a more genteel existence in Europe. What this dictated was a certain kind of behavior in the colonies that might not have been tolerated at home, but which was just fine with an ocean between them and home. There has been a bit of work on this for all of the colonies, British and non-British, but an effective synthesis has yet to be produced.[19]

As importantly, the existence of all this transoceanic migration ought not to diminish the observation that there was plenty of indigenous migration, as a result of native displacement. The movement of peoples within Atlantic societies has largely fallen to those who study a particular area or territory; it has never been effectively linked to the larger processes that have been used to explain migration across the Atlantic World.[20] Moreover, there is a long tradition of arguing that blacks built America, as indicated earlier in this chapter, but there has not been a large-scale study of the ways in which Africans sacrificed themselves not just in the western hemisphere, but also in Africa, for the building of the Americas. Work by Walter Rodney, in the middle of the twentieth century, asserted that Europe underdeveloped Africa, but such work sometimes painted the Africans as purely passive, a fact that continues to make many social historians uncomfortable, just as it formerly provided succor for slavery's apologists.[21]

Parallel literatures for each of the various societies around the Americas exist. Some are even comparative, in that they look at two places, occasionally even in different regions. These studies ought to be considered building blocks for future Atlantic world scholarship; indeed it is essential for the field's health that broader thinking takes place. While local studies are often interesting, and demonstrate a particular author's research acumen, they demonstrate greatest utility as bricks that can be used in ways that the author might either have overlooked or not intended. This implies that they *can* be synthesized into larger historical narratives over broader geographical spaces. Such syntheses must, of course, traverse linguistic as well as geographical boundaries, just as residents of the Atlantic world themselves regularly did.

When one considers this broader transnational perspective, one has also to realize that there were entire groups of people who existed in the early Atlantic world as a kind of permanent migrant. I refer now to pirates; sometimes they were stateless, and at other times they were not. But all of them transgressed against not just their victims, but through their statelessness and far-flung wanderings, the various regional and demographic categories to which historians cling. In many ways, they connected the Atlantic world through their criminal political economy. A group of violent people who pillaged from European states, perhaps especially Spain, as they operated across the Atlantic basin, pirates managed to create societies because they had (stolen) money which just needed to be spent. Capital in these criminals' hands led to the formation of societies, such as English Jamaica, to service their needs and separate them from their

ill-gotten cash. Their actions attacked the operation of the region's political economy—
the relationship between the state, individuals who lived under its authority, and the
economy—just as those same actions led to new societies across parts of the Americas.[22] There has been some scholarly interest in this subject for the last couple of
decades, but perhaps none is more well known than Marcus Rediker's work in the early
Anglophone Atlantic world.[23]

Seeing pirates as a group of people, largely men, from European underclasses,
Rediker maintains that pirates created a kind of alternate reality to the miserable
European existences that they then had. The pirate ship became a kind of community,
a floating utopia, where both camaraderie and equality existed. Of course, there was
also violence—pirates were after all robbers on the high seas—but such brutality has
tended to be minimized in many such studies. Even so, pirates clearly *were* connected
to the state-building enterprise.

When the Golden Age of piracy ended in the first third of the eighteenth century,
pirates were fewer in number, but by no means eradicated. Indeed, they continued to
serve some of the same political economy functions that they had earlier, such as the
transfer of wealth from one state to another. There was, in fact, a thin line between pirates
and privateers, who were nothing more than pirates that the state licensed to attack their
enemies. A lack of systematic study of this phenomenon unfortunately exists; existing
scholarship does not generally relate pirates to an emerging transnational (and global)
political economy. Nor is earlier piracy usually connected to modern versions of the same
crime elsewhere around the world, though it ought to be.

Pirates and migrants, of all kinds, require additional study, but not just to characterize another community that operated in the Atlantic world. Instead, they are
significant for their roles in furthering a regional (and a global) political economy.
While it is true that some of the work done earlier in the twentieth century, again
largely focused on European empires, dealt with states, the mechanisms of government
and economic policies, there has not been much recent scholarship that has explicitly
dealt with the political economy of the Atlantic world. Lauren Benton's excellent work
on legal regimes is one recent effort and my own work on smuggling another step in
that direction, but more such transnational and synthetic work is long overdue.[24]

THE FINAL FRONTIER: GLOBALIZING
ATLANTIC HISTORY

The preponderance of early American (social) historians from North America in
Atlantic history, along with these historians' inability to see large historical processes
at work, led me to claim earlier that the field had itself been colonized. Just as
significantly, as I also claimed earlier, one of Atlantic history's biggest failings has
been its reluctance to move into the twentieth century. Compounding this, of course,

has been a general reluctance to transcend national and imperial boundaries. Even conceptualizing an English Atlantic, or a French Atlantic, or a Portuguese Atlantic does not allow scholars an adequate glimpse of the connections between people across the Atlantic world, which those people themselves understood.

Using at least two of the big ideas that now explain world history and its approach, religious proselytization and political engagement, it is possible to advance the field. I shall deal with each of these two ideas in turn. The first, proselytization, is certainly a subject that has already taken a great deal of space in Latin American historiography. Not only has there been work that looks at the spread of Catholicism and the missionary impulse into the Americas, but there has also been some scholarship that explores the ways in which syncretic beliefs have emerged, with both indigenous and African forms of religion. So too has there been similar work on the spread of some Protestant denominations, like the Quakers, Puritans, and Huguenots into some of the English colonies, especially those in North America.[25]

Moreover, proselytization has also been explored with later missionary impulses in the Atlantic world in the nineteenth century—first in the settlements of former slaves (Sierra Leone and Liberia), but also more broadly in the years before (and even after) the Scramble for Africa.[26] But these two missionary moments have not been effectively or systematically connected to each other, to the rest of the Atlantic world's history, nor even are they explicitly tied to world history. If connections are made, it is to the history of colonization and imperialism in a particular empire. Though this may well be a start towards connecting the theme to a temporally expanded Atlantic history, much work yet remains to be done. The same could also be said for the twentieth-century religious connections between Africa and the Caribbean, especially, say with regards to Rastafarianism. Similarly, there has been limited work on the Jewish Atlantic, though there are plenty of connections between Jewish networks in Europe, the Caribbean, and the Americas, both north and south. While not a proselytizing religion, Judaism can be another lens through which to see the transnational connections between Jews in Europe, the Americas (including the Caribbean and Brazil), and, later, those in South Africa.[27]

Just as discussions of religious diffusion need to be expanded and infused into an extended Atlantic world, so do the commercial and political connections, which are at the core of Atlantic world history, need bolder assertion. This is especially true given that so much of the work of those now practicing Atlantic history has been in social history. When ideology and politics do enter into their work, it tends to be in only a few places. These might include the American Revolution (or War for Independence, a much more accurate depiction), the slave uprising in Saint-Domingue (which is frequently called the Haitian Revolution), and the French Revolution. Some Latin American historians have written about their own country's independence movements, along with those in other Spanish speaking regions, but all of the western hemisphere's independence movements have not been tied to each other, let alone to the European Enlightenment ideology from which they derived.

The process of decolonization in the modern world began in the Americas, ca. 1776, and it proceeded around the Atlantic world in the Americas in the nineteenth century and in Africa in the twentieth, which oddly enough also saw the colonization of Africa. But few scholars of the Atlantic world seem to have noticed. In other words, the world-historical process of decolonization in the nineteenth and twentieth centuries needs to be more explicitly linked with the Atlantic's period of 'revolution' in the eighteenth century. Not only will this show the prevalence and persistence of Enlightenment ideologies as motivating factors for these revolts, but it will also show the ways in which the Atlantic's history can be neatly fit together—over a much longer period of time.

The problem is that the national historians, some more nationalist than others, avoid making these connections explicit, which eats away at the Atlantic world's constructive fibers. For example, Cuba's independence movement was long and drawn out; it involved multiple countries (Spain, Cuba, the United States, and others). It is deeply connected to the Enlightenment ideology and the early nineteenth-century indepen-dence movements but, at the same time, it is also deeply connected to North American history and, later, the Cold War (which is an Atlantic phenomenon, though it tends to get separated from the rest of the Atlantic world's history). Yet, far too often the story that gets told is one of Cuban independence from a Cuban nationalist's perspective. As a result, Cuba's connection to the Atlantic world seems tangential, even peripheral, especially after the abolition of slavery.

In fact, the Cold War's story ought to be a significant part of Atlantic history, but it is not. It is possible to assert that NATO and the Cold War have long played a central part in understanding geopolitics in the second part of the twentieth century; few would object to the Cold War as one of the central organizing principles of history and politics (or political economy for that matter) in the second half of the twentieth century. But in order to understand the ways in which the Cold War developed as it did in the postcolonial world, it becomes imperative to understand the relationships that predated it in the colonial world. This is no less true in the Atlantic world as it is in Vietnam or Eastern Africa.

Even so, only a few diplomatic historians, who work on NATO, have bothered to take on the Atlantic world concept as a twentieth-century phenomenon. Without a broader historical perspective, however, their work can appear to be somewhat paro-chial.[28] Its narratives are confined to particular places and institutions, without much contextualization of what came before. But it is precisely this story, the narrative of the rise of a former set of backwater colonies into a global superpower, which can be so instructive to other former colonies within the Atlantic world as well as former colonies elsewhere around the world. Yet historians regularly present the decolonization strug-gle and postcolonial states that emerged from it in purely nationalist terms. This is unfortunate.

After the American War for Independence ended in 1783 the new United States became a kind of mimic of European ways, even more so than the thirteen colonies were in the several decades before the war. Taxation policies, oddly enough, were not dissimilar in the United States from those in European states, for example—despite widespread merchant dissatisfaction with British taxation policies. And cultural forms clearly emulated those of Europeans, at least for a time. As a result, the relationship between the United States and Europe evolved to be more one of similarity than of difference. This marked a changed relationship with the colonies, one that emerged over time. Moreover, the former colonies, in the guise of the United States, would rise to the former colonial powers' defense, in the years during and after World War I. This marked the transition of the former colonies into major players on the world stage. Europe, in a sense, would have destroyed itself, at least without the help of its former colonial subjects. Rather than being a predictive model for other societies across the Atlantic world, either in Africa or the Americas, the story of the United States is much more an exception, an outlier.

I mean to suggest here that the former colonies in the Caribbean and in Latin America changed their economic relationship to their former colonial powers relatively little, despite having similar ideas about ending colonial rule. The independent states of Latin America developed transportation and communication infrastructures in the nineteenth century, it is true, but largely these were used to facilitate an export economy, one that was closely tied to European (and American) marketplaces. The Caribbean colonies remained sugar producers, or suppliers of other agricultural products, even after the demand for these products diminished with the introduction of the sugar beet in Europe and alternative sources for the other products were found elsewhere. After slavery ended, migrations from Asia, especially India and China, brought new migrants to these colonies, which had the effect of perpetuating racial and class divisions within the region. Economic development was, as a result, not especially great, which led to the exacerbation of the same kinds of racial problems that existed during the period of slavery and, perhaps, contributed to the underdevelopment of the region's colonies into the twentieth century. Moreover, the United States increasingly played the part of a neo-colonial power, one that took on the role that the European powers did, by providing capital to regimes and economies in exchange for economically beneficial commercial relationships and the products that they brought with them. Atlantic America, thus, increasingly became divided between those in the north and those in the south.

Atlantic Africa, for its part, went through a period of colonization while the western hemisphere was operating 'independently' or was being decolonized. When Africa's own decolonization took place in the second half of the twentieth century, as before, much of Atlantic Africa remained a supplier of minerals, fuels, and other raw materials necessary for industrial economies elsewhere in the Atlantic world, and even more recently in Asia, especially China. No longer was the continent forced to supply human capital. But, as in Latin America, the roads and other infrastructure that were built existed primarily to get extracted products from the interior to the coast, from where they could be exported by sea, just as they were before. This seems to me to be a new iteration of the very same idea of African sacrifice that Patrick Manning earlier used in his discussion of the African slave trade.

In short, the Atlantic world's patterns of development continued into the twentieth century more or less as they were before it. Slavery was replaced with other forms of formally free labor, much of it exploitative. Markets remained in the north, but now the United States was included in that category. Exports continued to dominate many of the economies on the Atlantic's western shores, at least in the south. Political and legal regimes resembled those in Europe and, where they did not, efforts to inculcate democracy, formulated and applied in the Atlantic world itself, were promulgated by, at the very least, the United States—along with several other Cold War allies as the individual cases dictated. It was, in a sense, as if little had changed. Roles seemed, at least superficially, to have been maintained.

The question, however, nevertheless must be asked: to what degree did the Atlantic world operate as a unit in the twentieth century? The answer is less than clear, but it is by no means completely opaque. By this I mean to suggest that the Atlantic world continued its patterns and relationships as have been described above. But where the Atlantic world began to change is that it became more integrated into the rest of world history, and global networks of exchange.[29] In short, the Atlantic world's story became quite clearly linked to the ongoing narratives that are associated with world history. Its distinctiveness, such that there ever was distinctiveness, faded, and its integration into a truly global economy continued apace. Commercial, cultural, and political relationships across the Atlantic world in the twentieth century became only a subset of those same kinds of relationships on a global stage. Where one ocean joined societies together at its inception, several oceanic spaces were now connecting the Atlantic's societies.

Perhaps it is for this reason that I find the Atlantic world's colonization by early American historians to be so deeply troubling. While it may well be useful for American historians to see the connection of their country to the rest of the world, especially in the early period and only marginally less so in later periods, it is nevertheless important not to think of the Atlantic world solely from this perspective or for that matter from any single national perspective. Instead, visualizing Atlantic history from a transnational perspective, that is one that clearly focuses on world-historical processes, will take the historian much closer to how people at the time understood their world. They knew from where their foodstuffs came, and they understood the relationships between the price they paid for consumables and the governments under which they lived. They might have, for example, purchased smuggled flour or slaves, and through that transaction participated in several legal transgressions that connected them to other legal regimes than the one in which they lived—and they surely understood what they were doing, in just the same way that people in 2010 purchase products whose provenance is unclear, for reasons that are very clear.

In other words, those who participated in the Atlantic world understood that they were contributing to a transnational enterprise with many of their actions in the same ways that those in the present do. Of course, it was clear when they embarked on a dock and disembarked on the other side of the Atlantic Ocean. But one did not have to travel in order to participate in the Atlantic world. One need only have been a consumer. And, it goes almost without saying—everyone *was* a consumer, just as everyone *is* now a consumer. People were never purely national consumers, despite efforts to make them so, and they knew it. It is, therefore, especially important for those of us who study Atlantic history to refrain from allowing any single country's historians from colonizing the field and making it a simple extension of a national history. The history of the Atlantic world is, by definition, transnational, and scholars must strive for it to remain so, even as they push to stretch its boundaries farther.

With this final plea, scholars should be moved away from conceptualizing the Atlantic as simply a study of European countries and their respective colonies, just as they should be reminded to include Africa more centrally in the Atlantic's story. World historians have a special role to play in these struggles, as they must remind those who study any of the colonies that would become the United States that the story of the Atlantic is much more than an effort to internationalize American history (which is, of course, its own worthy undertaking). World historians must do more to push forward the Atlantic's temporal boundaries, and grapple with the changes—as well as the continuities—that began to take place with industrialization and were furthered by the World Wars. Scholars of the Atlantic world must, for their part, do more to embrace the world historical enterprise, so that they remain relevant, insightful, and different from American historians. Atlantic historians must ask broader questions than has hitherto been the case, and they must be willing to use historical sources in multiple languages, or at least be willing to synthesize better the secondary literature that grapples with non-English-speaking places, in whatever language they might have been written. In this way, Atlantic world historians can better communicate what transpired in the Atlantic world's spaces, as well as in those that existed beyond it. In fact, Atlantic world historians must do everything in their power to relate the Atlantic world's history to that which took place around the world's other ocean basins.[30]

Notes

1. Brief references to tea and its association with sugar and industrialization can be found in David S. Landes, *The Wealth and Poverty of Nations: Why Some Are So Rich and Some So Poor* (New York, 1999), esp. 226, 426, 446. See also John Griffiths, *Tea: The Drink That Changed the World* (London: Andre Deutsch, 2008).

2. A perfect example of this point can be found in Thomas Benjamin, *The Atlantic World: Europeans, Africans, Indians, and Their Shared History, 1400–1900* (Cambridge: Cambridge University Press, 2009), 528–9.

3. I realize that this will be a somewhat contentious point, but I stand by it. The general point can be seen in Jack P. Greene and J. R. Pole's *Colonial British America: Essays in the New History of the Early Modern Era* (Baltimore, Md.: Johns Hopkins University Press, 1984), and more recently in Jack P. Greene and Philip D. Morgan's edited collection, *Atlantic History: A Critical Approach* (New York: Oxford University Press, 2009). The role of Africa is peripheral to much of this Atlantic history, except as it impacted slavery in the Americas. Scholars of African societies have responded with their own work. See, for example, John Thornton, *Africa and Africans in the Making of the Atlantic World,*

1400–1680 (Cambridge: Cambridge University Press, 1997) and Joseph C. Miller, *Way of Death: Merchant Capitalism and the Angolan Slave Trade, 1730–1800* (Madison, Wis.: University of Wisconsin Press, 1988).

4. See, for example, the work of Mark Kurlansky, *A Continent of Islands: Searching for the Caribbean Destiny* (Reading, Mass.: Da Capo, 1992) and *Cod: A Biography of the Fish That Changed the World* (New York: Penguin, 1998). Also see the important work by Sidney Mintz, *Sweetness and Power: The Place of Sugar in Modern History* (New York: Penguin, 1985); Mintz is not a historian at all, but an anthropologist.

5. This can certainly be easily demonstrated, for it is the way in which Greene and Morgan organized their recent *Atlantic History*. The essays turn around what seems an old-fashioned idea: that of a Portuguese Atlantic, or a Dutch Atlantic. In short, this totally obscures a basic point; people across the Atlantic, then as now, did not solely interact with those in their own national territory, even though it was the way in which their European states intended them to act. Moreover, this approach also fails the world historian's relevance test, in that what happened in the Atlantic world as a single unit directly bears on what is happening in today's globalizing world.

6. In Greene and Morgan, J. H. Elliot's *Empires of the Atlantic World: Britain and Spain in America, 1492–1830* (New Haven, Conn.: Yale University Press, 2006) is regularly referred to in these terms by multiple authors: see esp. 10, 57, 124, 309–10. The work is significant, but only because it accomplishes one part of what Atlantic history ought to do, and that is make broader arguments than the colonies of one country would otherwise generate.

7. See, for example, Philip D. Morgan and Jack P. Greene, 'Introduction: The Present State of Atlantic History,' in *Atlantic History*, esp. 18–21. The authors recognize the significance of this, even as they are aware that the field itself has not yet progressed there.

8. See J. R. McNeill, 'The End of the Old Atlantic World: America, Africa, Europe, 1770–1888,' in *Atlantic American Societies: From Columbus to Abolition, 1492–1888* (New York: Routledge, 1992), 245–68.

9. For a brief example of this, see Peter A. Coclanis, 'Beyond Atlantic History,' in Morgan and Greene, eds., *Atlantic History*, 337–56.

10. See Benjamin, *Atlantic World*, and Douglas R. Egerton *et al.*, *The Atlantic World, 1400–1888* (New York: Harlan Davidson, 2007).

11. Ivan Van Sertima, *They Came before Columbus: The African Presence in Ancient America* (New York: Random House, 1976). This in no way negates the idea that history did not exist within the various groups of people who lived in Atlantic societies, but it is their interaction with the ocean that must determine considering something Atlantic history.

12. See, for example, Alfred Crosby, *The Columbian Exchange: Biological and Cultural Consequences of 1492* (Westport, Conn.: Greenwood, 1973) and, for examples on the literature on demographic disaster, Noble David Cook, *Born to Die: Disease and New World Conquest 1492–1650* (Cambridge: Cambridge University Press, 1998) and Woodrow Borah and Sherburne F. Cook, *The Aboriginal Population of Central Mexico on the Eve of the Spanish Conquest* (Berkeley, Cal.: University of California Press, 1963).

13. Philip D. Curtin, *The Atlantic Slave Trade: A Census* (Madison, Wis.: University of Wisconsin Press, 1969).

14. Eric Williams, *Capitalism and Slavery* (Chapel Hill, N.C.: University of North Carolina Press, 1994); also see the debate that Seymour Drescher had with Williams in *Econocide: British Slavery in the Era of Abolition* (Pittsburgh: University of Pittsburgh Press, 1977) and Robin Blackburn's excellent series on Atlantic slavery, abolition, profitability and

industrialization in *The Making of New World Slavery: From the Baroque to the Modern, 1492–1800* (London: Verso, 1997) *and The Overthrow of Colonial Slavery, 1776–1848* (London: Verso, 1988). There is a large debate about the exact correlation between slavery, profitability, abolition, and industrialization around the Atlantic world. That debate is best explored by those who are most interested in it.

15. For a brief, and thoroughly depressing, examination of these subjects, see John R. McNeill, *Something New Under the Sun: An Environmental History of the Twentieth Century* (New York: Norton, 2000).

16. See, for example, Alfred W. Crosby, *Ecological Imperialism: The Biological Expansion of Europe, 900–1900* (Cambridge: Cambridge University Press, 2004); John R. McNeill, *Mosquito Empires: Ecology, Epidemics, War and Revolutions in the Great Caribbean, 1620–1920* (New York: Cambridge University Press, 2010); and Richard Sheridan, *Doctors and Slaves: A Medical and Demographic History of Slavery in the British West Indies, 1680–1834* (Cambridge: Cambridge University Press, 1985).

17. Paul Gilroy, *The Black Atlantic: Modernity and Double Consciousness* (Cambridge, Mass.: Harvard University Press, 1993), esp. chapters 5 and 6.

18. For an example of this kind of work, see Alan L. Karras, *Sojourners in the Sun: Scots Migrants in Jamaica and the Chesapeake, 1740–1820* (Ithaca, N.Y.: Cornell University Press, 1992). For another kind of approach see Bernard Bailyn, *Voyagers to the West: A Passage in the Peopling of America on the Eve of the Revolution* (New York: Vintage, 1986) and Alison Games, *Migration and the Origins of the English Atlantic World* (Cambridge, Mass.: Harvard University Press, 1999). All of this work is nevertheless incomplete; a fuller synthesis is clearly required.

19. See Edmund Morgan's 'The Labor Problem at Jamestown,' *American Historical Review* 76: 3 (1971), 595–611, as well as his *American Slavery, American Freedom* (New York: Norton, 1975). Also see Richard S. Dunn, *Sugar and Slaves: The Rise of the Planter Class in the English West Indies, 1624–1713* (Chapel Hill, N.C.: University of North Carolina Press, 1972). Others have done a bit of work on this in other areas: for example, see Ida Altman and James Horn, eds., *'To Make America:' European Emigration in the Early Modern Period,* (Berkeley, Cal.: University of California Press, 1991).

20. Indeed, this is exactly one of Amy Turner Bushnell's main points in 'Indigenous America and the Limits of the Atlantic World,' in Morgan and Greene, eds., *Atlantic History*, 191–222. Just because the internal migration did not take place across an ocean that does not mean the Atlantic did not affect the internal migration. There is, therefore, room in the national histories of large territories, such as Brazil, Mexico, Colombia, and the United States, for such migration studies to get connected to the Atlantic's processes, if they were, in fact, actually connected to them at the time.

21. This is an argument that was first made in Patrick Manning's *Slavery and African Life: Occidental, Oriental, and African Slave Trades* (Cambridge: Cambridge University Press, 1992). It has since been taken up elsewhere but not as widely, in my opinion, as the idea merits. Cf. Walter Rodney, *How Europe Underdeveloped Africa* (Washington, D.C.: Howard University Press, 1981).

22. I have discussed this in greater length in *Smuggling: Contraband and Corruption in World History* (New York: Rowman and Littlefield, 2009), esp. chapter 2.

23. See Marcus Rediker, *Villains of All Nations: Atlantic Pirates in the Golden Age* (Boston: Beacon, 2004), and *Between the Devil and the Deep Blue Sea* (Cambridge: Cambridge University Press, 1987).

24. The best recent treatment of this kind of problem is Lauren A. Benton, *Law and Colonial Cultures: Legal Regimes in World History, 1400-1900* (Cambridge: Cambridge University Press, 2002) and her article 'Legal Spaces of Empire: Piracy and the origins of ocean regionalism,' *Comparative Studies in Society and History* 47: 4 (2005), 700-24. My own work on smuggling attempts to build upon this: Karras, *Smuggling*.

25. For one example, see Nancy M. Farriss, *Maya Society Under Colonial Rule: The Collective Enterprise of Survival* (Princeton: Princeton University Press, 1984). For another, Gwendolyn Midlo Hall, *Africans in Colonial Louisiana: The Development of Afro-Creole Culture in the Eighteenth Century* (Baton Rouge, La.: Louisiana State University Press, 1992).

26. Some of this is discussed in Olaudah Equiano, *The Life of Olaudah Equiano, or Gustavus Vassa the African,* ed. by Paul Edwards (New York: Harlow, 1989). Other editions cover the same territory, and explore the connections between the anti-slavery movements in Britain and the colonization of Sierra Leone. Also see Alexander X. Byrd, *Captives and Voyagers: Black Migrants across the Eighteenth-Century British Atlantic World* (Baton Rouge, La.: Louisiana State University Press, 2008).

27. One example is Stephen A. Fortune's *Merchants and Jews: The Struggle for British West Indian Commerce, 1650-1750* (Gainesville, Fla.: University of Florida Press, 1984); another is Richard L. Kagan and Philip D. Morgan, eds., *Atlantic Diasporas: Jews, Conversos, and Crypto-Jews in the Age of Mercantilism, 1500-1800* (Baltimore, Md.: Johns Hopkins University Press, 2009).

28. For one example, see John Lewis Gaddis, *The Cold War: A New History* (New York: Penguin, 2005). Another could be found in Stewart Patrick, *Best Laid Plans: The Origins of American Multilateralism and the Dawn of the Cold War* (Lanham, Md.: Rowman and Littlefield, 2009). Also see Toyin Falola and Kevin D. Roberts, eds., *The Atlantic World, 1450-2000* (Bloomington, Ind.: Indiana University Press, 2008). This work is notable for pushing the Atlantic world into the twentieth century.

29. This is the argument that Peter Coclanis has made in 'Beyond Atlantic History' and elsewhere, and it is one that needs to be addressed for earlier periods. Even so, it is clear that the Atlantic world in the twentieth century was connected to non-Atlantic regions, such as Asia and, in terms of geopolitics of the Cold War, Russia.

30. See, for example, Jerry H. Bentley, 'Sea and Ocean Basins as Frameworks of Historical Analysis,' *The Geographical Review,* 89 (April 1999), 215-24. Also see Kären Wigen, 'Cartographies of Connection: Ocean Maps as Metaphors of Interarea History,' in Jerry H. Bentley, Renate Bridenthal, and Anand A. Yang, eds., *Interactions: Transregional Perspectives on World History* (Honolulu: University of Hawai'i Press, 2005), 150-66.

REFERENCES

BAILYN, BERNARD. *Voyagers to the West: A Passage in the Peopling of North America.* New York: Vintage, 1986.

BENTON, LAUREN A. *Law and Colonial Cultures: Legal Regimes in World History, 1400-1900.* Cambridge: Cambridge University Press, 2002.

BLACKBURN, ROBIN. *The Making of New World Slavery: From the Baroque to the Modern, 1492-1800.* London: Verso, 1997.

Coclanis, Peter A. 'Atlantic World or Atlantic/World?,' *The William and Mary Quarterly* 63: 4 (2006).

Curtin, Philip D. *The Rise and Fall of the Plantation Complex: Essays in Atlantic History.* Cambridge: Cambridge University Press, 1990.

Elliott, J. H. *Empires of the Atlantic World: Britain and Spain in the Americas, 1492–1830.* New Haven, Conn.: Yale University Press, 2007.

Games, Alison. 'Atlantic History: Definitions, Challenges, and Opportunities,' *American Historical Review* 111: 3 (2006), 741–57.

Greene, Jack P., and Philip D. Morgan, eds. *Atlantic History: A Critical Appraisal.* New York: Oxford University Press, 2009.

Karras, Alan L. *Smuggling: Contraband and Corruption in World History.* Lanham, Md.: Rowman and Littlefield, 2009.

McNeill, John R. *Mosquito Empires: Ecology, Epidemics, War, and Revolutions in the Great Caribbean, 1620–1920.* New York: Cambridge University Press, 2010.

Miller, Joseph. *Way of Death: Merchant Capitalism and the Angolan Slave Trade.* Madison, Wis.: University of Wisconsin Press, 1997.

Mintz, Sidney W. *Sweetness and Power: The Place of Sugar in Modern History.* New York: Penguin, 1985.

Rediker, Marcus. *Villains of All Nations: Atlantic Pirates in the Golden Age.* New York: Beacon, 2004.

Thornton, John. *African and Africans in the Formation of the Atlantic World.* Cambridge: Cambridge University Press, 1992.

Williams, Eric. *Capitalism and Slavery.* Chapel Hill, N.C.: University of North Carolina Press, 1944.

CHAPTER 30

OCEANIA AND AUSTRALASIA

PAUL D'ARCY

OCEANIA and Australasia are relatively recent and externally imposed terms. The term Australasia was coined by the Frenchman Charles de Brosses to refer collectively to the lands south of Asia, or present-day Australia and New Zealand. Oceania refers to the Pacific Islands east of present-day Indonesia and the Philippines across to Pitcairn Island in the southeast Pacific and also includes the western half of the island of New Guinea, which is now part of Indonesia. These islands are generally divided into three geographical areas: Melanesia, Micronesia, and Polynesia. These terms were coined by the nineteenth-century French explorer Dumont d'Urville, who deemed them to be racial and cultural classifications.[1] The majority of histories of the region focus on one of the three constituent parts: Australia, New Zealand, or Oceania.[2] Australasia and Oceania are generally afterthoughts in world history texts, lumped together and included at the end of global surveys as areas largely marginal to the main events of world history.[3]

Present-day national borders cut across previous indigenous exchange areas or unite peoples with little previous sense of collective identity, especially in the larger Pacific Island nations of southwest Oceania. Internal borders and cultural divisions are being increasingly challenged from within by the current generation as are those between Asia, Oceania, and Australasia. This re-evaluation is partly in response to increased mobility between geographical divisions and part of what the authors of the best survey of the region see as the most arresting feature of its societies: the local creation and transformation of identities that are often initially shaped by ideas generated elsewhere.[4] The region's value and prime relevance to world history lies in its comparative value in terms of European explorers and traders, and subsequent settler societies and their relations with, and impact upon, indigenous peoples,[5] and its distinct perspectives based on small size and being geographically peripheral to most events and processes covered in world history surveys.

INDIGENOUS EXPLORATION AND
COLONIZATION OF THE REGION

Oceania presented a number of environmental challenges and opportunities for the first peoples to explore and colonize from the Asian mainland. Two distinct bio-geographical zones are recognized within Oceania: Near Oceania and Remote Oceania.[6] These divisions map the progressive diminution of terrestrial and marine species' diversity eastward from their dispersal point into the Pacific as the gaps between islands increase.[7] Near Oceania is located in the western Pacific and demonstrates a great deal of environmental continuity with island Southeast Asia in terms of its large 'continental' islands and small gaps between islands. In contrast, Remote Oceania is characterized by large gaps between smaller islands and archipelagos.

Australia has become more arid since human settlement judging from the relatively larger size and greater diversity of its fauna 50,000 years ago compared to now. The northern tropical third has distinct wet and dry seasons. It is an old, weathered continent with few significant mountain ranges apart from that running just inland along the length of the eastern seaboard, but it is rich in minerals. New Zealand is geologically younger and less well endowed with mineral wealth, better watered and benign in comparison to Australia, although still prone to drought in the rain shadow area east of its high mountain spine that blocks the prevailing moisture-laden westerly winds.[8]

Aborigines came to Australia at least 50,000 years ago, most likely during times when colder climatic phases reduced the sea gap between it and Asian landmasses by locking up much of the earth's water in ice caps. Over the next 2,000 generations they spread across every ecosystem in this vast continent from humid coastal lowlands along the far northeast coast to the great sandy deserts of the western interior. They adjusted to each environment and modified them through use of fire to promote succulent new growth to attract wildlife for their semi-nomadic hunter-gatherer lifestyles. Each group controlled a territorial unit varying in size from 500 square kilometers in fertile areas to up to 100,000 square kilometers in desert country. Tribal groups were bonded by blood ties, intimate knowledge and deep emotional ties to their lands, and shared religious beliefs. Most territories were self-sustaining, although goods were exchanged between groups to end up as far as 1,500 kilometers away from their point of origin. Social exchanges also occurred, occasionally punctuated by armed clashes over resources and affronts to collective identities.[9]

Climatically temperate Aotearoa (New Zealand)[10] was settled much later than Australia by agricultural and seafaring peoples who also settled the islands of tropical Oceania. The exploration of the Pacific Islands was one of the greatest seafaring achievements of early humankind. Linguistic and archaeological evidence suggests the ancestors of the region's indigenous inhabitants came to the southwest Pacific from southeast China and Taiwan. The general consensus is now that Oceania was first settled by Papuan-speaking peoples more than 35,000 years ago whose penetration was limited to New Guinea and perhaps some nearby Melanesian islands. They were followed by Austronesian-speaking peoples 3,500 years ago whose main route from Southeast Asia was along the northern coast of New Guinea into Island Melanesia, and from there east to Polynesia or north to eastern Micronesia. Others sailed to the western islands of Micronesia directly from Southeast Asia. They were skilled seafarers and explorers who evolved sophisticated navigational techniques involving waves, swells, stars, and signs of land such as land-based seabirds to map the oceans as well as the lands they came across. Linguistic reconstructions of their proto-language suggest they came into the Pacific with canoes and food storage techniques capable of supporting long open-sea voyages into the unknown, which then evolved *in situ* over time.[11]

Most Islander societies developed some form of magazine economy and marriage or trade links with other communities to insulate themselves against climatic variability in rainfall, El Niño cycles, and natural disasters such as typhoons. One of the most densely populated areas of Oceania is the highlands of New Guinea. Archaeological excavations at Kuk swamp have revealed the beginnings of intensive agriculture in the highlands at least 7,000 years ago. While links between colonies and home islands were maintained and others forged between communities close at hand, most communities tended to be relatively self-sufficient in terms of their subsistence needs. Indeed, many localities were capable of producing far in excess of their subsistence needs for use in religious, social, and trade exchanges.[12]

Explanations of the evolution of social and political institutions in the Pacific, including Aotearoa, vacillate between environmental and cultural influences in attempting to explain why some developed complex hierarchical societies in which power was increasingly centralized under one ruler as in Tonga and Hawai`i, and others exhibited localized, more segmented socio-political organization such as in the New Guinea highlands. Environmental explanations emphasize the need for sufficient surpluses to support the specialist administrators and warriors associated with the sustained concentration of power, and cultural ones the driving force of collective and kin group status rivalry.[13]

THE INTERSECTION OF EUROPEAN
AND INDIGENOUS WORLDS

European encounters with the South Pacific began in 1519 when Magellan sailed westward across Oceania from South America. Other Spanish voyages of discovery followed in his wake. A series of violent encounters and the decimation of colonies in Melanesia from malaria soon ended Spain's South Pacific engagement. Henceforth, the Spanish focused on Micronesia and the trans-Pacific galleon trade carrying goods between the colonial ports of Manila and Acapulco. Their route bypassed most inhabited islands in the Pacific, while former links between Guam and the Caroline

Islands diminished with the violent establishment of Spanish rule in the Marianas and the subsequent loss of seafaring capacity within the island chain.[14]

European contact with the Pacific became more sustained from the late 1760s onwards as voyages of exploration by a number of European nations gradually mapped Australasia and Oceania, most famously and comprehensively through the three expeditions of Captain James Cook from 1768 to 1779. A large body of literature resulted which has inspired interpretation of first-contact situations to be a major theme in histories of the region. This body of material has been uniquely supplemented by movie-camera recordings of the indigenous reception of Australian prospectors as they penetrated the New Guinea highlands for the first time in the 1930s. These were also first-contact encounters for the coastal New Guineans who made up the majority of these gold-prospecting and government patrols into the interior in this period.[15]

First-contact histories have been prominent and controversial in national narratives and international academic debates in recent decades. While Cook's brilliance as a navigator and cartographer is undisputed, his transformation into a founding hero figure in New Zealand and Australian national narratives has been more controversial. Recently Gananath Obeyesekere characterized Marshall Sahlins' argument that Cook was revered and adopted into the Hawaiian pantheon as the god Lono as simply the transplanting of a long-standing western (or more correctly Anglophone-world) myth of the benevolent Enlightenment hero into the minds of non-western peoples by a western academic. A fierce academic exchange followed between Sahlins as an advocate of culturally specific worldviews as key determinants of actions in situations of culture contact and Obeyesekere arguing for more pragmatic, universally understood influences behind actions. Historian Ian Campbell argues that a distinct culture of contact arose as both sides realized they faced unusual circumstances and resorted to more flexible behavior themselves in an attempt to accommodate these circumstances.[16]

European encounters with the region's indigenous peoples seem to have been most problematic with Australian Aborigines. Both sides had little that the other desired, and the diversity and complexity of local languages acted as a further barrier to communication. The Aboriginal appearance and hunting-and-gathering economy did little to endear them to Europeans for whom the marks of civilization were intensive cultivation, productive enterprise, and appearance more akin to their own. Accommodations did occur on both sides of the cultural divide, but they were the exception rather than the rule.[17]

THE IMPACT OF PRE-COLONIAL EUROPEAN INFLUENCES

European colonial rule over most of the Pacific Islands came late and was preceded by decades of interaction between indigenous peoples and European explorers, traders, beachcombers, missionaries, and settlers. Although the Mariana Islands in Micronesia came under European rule in the last three decades of the 1600s, Europeans did not complete their colonial takeover of the Pacific Islands until the end of the nineteenth century. Most Micronesian islands were small and lacked resources sought by Europeans, so that colonial rule was characterized more by neglect than exploitation and settlement. Melanesia was also largely shielded from European inroads until after 1870 by the prevalence of malaria in its coastal zones. Only malaria-free New Caledonia and Fiji experienced significant Western settlement before 1870. Polynesia received more European attention than Melanesia and Micronesia in the immediate lead-up to the imposition of colonial rule. British government concerns about the consequences of unsupervised British settlement among Māori prompted it to take control of New Zealand in 1840. Concern about the growth of British influence in the region prompted France to secure control over the Marquesas Islands and Tahiti in the early 1840s. Most of Polynesia only came under direct European rule between 1870 and 1900, however.[18]

New ideas and experiences, goods, and pathogens are generally regarded as the most significant influences on indigenous cultures during this time of transition. Scholars are divided over the extent to which indigenous peoples exercised control over these influences. A number of individuals moved between cultures in the years following sustained European contact. From 1770 vessels themselves became zones of encounter, as Islanders took the opportunity to travel on Western vessels. What began as a trickle of invited guests in the late 1700s and early 1800s became a flood as Islanders eagerly sought employment on commercial vessels. Hawaiians, Tahitians, and Māori were particularly prominent as crew because of their islands' popularity as ports of call. Most Islanders who traveled on these vessels spent their time within Oceania, with occasional visits to ports on the Pacific Rim such as Sydney and Valparaiso. Some sailed into the Indian and Atlantic Oceans.[19]

Melanesians joined this outpouring from the 1860s when vessels began recruiting them as labor for the emerging plantation economies of settler colonies such as Queensland, Fiji, and New Caledonia.[20] Islanders traveled out of a sense of curiosity and adventure, or a desire to free themselves from constraints at home. They hoped to enhance their status through the exotic tales and goods they returned with. The Melanesian labor trade involved tens of thousands of people and has generated significant interest among historians. Interpretations broadly divide between those seeing it as exploitation and deceit and those seeing it as a process in which Islanders had a great deal of choice and control.[21]

Much scholarship emphasizes the fact that most Pacific Islanders were converted to Christianity by other Pacific Islanders as the sheer size of the task of conversion became apparent. Resources were already stretched as missions moved into Melanesia which consisted of many politically fragmented and linguistically diverse communities who required more missionaries on the ground for their diverse needs. Most Islanders, therefore, learnt about Christianity through the filter of Pacific Islander intermediaries. Aboriginal Australians were less willing recipients of the Christian message than Pacific

Islanders and Māori, which was also largely delivered through European clergy in mission stations.[22]

Introduced diseases are generally regarded as the most devastating influence of sustained Western contact on Oceanic societies. The magnitude of the ensuing depopulation remains controversial. This issue rose to prominence in 1989 when David Stannard, Professor of American Studies at the University of Hawai'i, published a book arguing that the indigenous Hawaiian population at European contact was at least double former estimates, so that post-contact depopulation until the first accurate census was truly catastrophic. While debate raged within the world of Pacific scholarship about Stannard's method for calculating contact populations and whether depopulation primarily resulted from epidemics or disease-induced infertility,[23] epidemiologist Stephen Kunitz argued that the key factors affecting the rate of depopulation were not so much biological as social, economic, and political. While epidemics could cause high death rates among populations with no exposure and immunity to them, the key was post-epidemic recovery which required social stability. Kunitz demonstrated that the areas with the most severe depopulation on record were areas where European colonization and dispossession disrupted indigenous societies. As historian Donald Denoon notes, 'Depopulation was for Stannard a cause, for Kunitz an effect, of dispossession.'[24] Denoon also makes the important point that specific localized circumstances such as diet and the presence of malaria led to variation in the degrees of Western contact and depopulation.[25]

The sheer size of Australia resulted in a great variety of local circumstances across time and space on the disease frontier accompanying Western expansion inland and north from the initial colonies in the southeast and southwest. Estimates of the Aboriginal population of Australia at the time of the first European settlement in the 1780s now generally range between 300,000 and 750,000. In general, communities further from the initial colonies retained closer ties to their land and suffered less from depopulation in direct proportion to the ever-decreasing density of Western settlement and economic activity away from the southeast and southwest population concentrations. Historian Keith Windschuttle recently questioned the methodology and conclusions of those who argued for massive depopulation of the Aboriginal population in the first decades of European encounters through violence and disease. Historian of Aboriginal Australia, Richard Broome, posits that perhaps 1,500 European settlers and 20,000 Aborigines in total were killed by violence on the moving frontier of European expansion.[26]

Other environmental influences have received less attention. A number of articles explore the decimation of flora and fauna for commercial profit by Europeans, most notably in regard to the whaling industry. The impact of Western food crops has also received some attention, particularly concerning Hawai'i and Aotearoa/New Zealand.[27] The devastating impact of introduced flora and fauna such as gorse, sheep, cattle, rats, possums, and rabbits on local species with few competitors or predators and fragile ecosystems has been detailed in a number of studies. While indigenous peoples changed their landscapes through burning to facilitate agriculture and hunting, the degree of deforestation and conversion of landscapes into pasture escalated dramatically after the arrival of Europeans, especially in Australasia.[28]

EUROPEAN SETTLER SOCIETIES AND PLANTATION COLONIES

British authorities conceived Australia as a legal *terra nullius* because Aborigines appeared to do little to cultivate or otherwise leave signs of occupation on the land with their essentially hunter-gatherer lifestyles and because it suited British interests to see the land as such.[29] This legal fiction prevailed until the modern era and sanctioned large-scale land alienation as settler numbers increased from essentially small convict colonies at a few coastal locations from the 1780s onwards into free settler colonies with an expanding pastoral frontier into the interior in the early 1800s. The tyranny of distance deterred large-scale free settlement until the discovery of gold in the mid-nineteenth century and large-scale, planned migration from 1860 to 1900 bolstered the population, aided by improved sea transport, shortened the effective distance between Europe and Australasia and in the second half of the nineteenth century. There were 250,000 Europeans resident in Australia by 1840 and 3.8 million by 1900. Most were English, but about one-quarter were Irish who gave Australia a much stronger anti-authoritarian and Catholic character than English-dominated New Zealand with its Scottish minority.[30]

Europeans settled New Zealand later than Australia and encountered more indigenous resistance. New Zealand's colonists were all free settlers and numbered only a few thousand in 1840 when the British Crown signed the Treaty of Waitangi with Māori. While the Crown believed New Zealand was now Crown land subject to British law, Māori continued to believe that they had only conceded partial sovereignty to the Crown.[31] Wars over control of land and destiny followed in the 1840s and especially in the 1860s. By the mid-1850s European and Māori numbers were on a par, and the discovery of gold in the South Island in the early 1860s led to a massive influx of Europeans. Māori were from then on a minority in their own land. European victory was followed by confiscation of both hostile and allied Māori land, and the registration and conversion to individual title of most Māori communal land along Western lines from the 1860s to the early 1900s through the Native Land Court did much damage to Māori social cohesion. The granting of four seats on the Legislative Council to allied Māori was little compensation.[32]

European settlement was more restricted in the islands of the tropical Pacific with the exception of the French convict settlement of New Caledonia whose indigenous population were also defeated militarily, outnumbered, and squeezed into reserves defined by Europeans and bearing little resemblance to traditional fluid and more expansive territoriality. Elsewhere, European discomfort with tropical conditions such as malaria resulted in much smaller European populations than in Australasia who supported themselves through plantation economies supplying European markets with copra especially and relying on indentured labor. The largest external flows of labor came from Japan for Hawai`i, Solomon Islands and Vanuatu (then New Hebrides) for Queensland, India for Fiji, and New Guineans moved internally by German authorities.[33] Military resistance to European colonial rule in the tropical Pacific was limited and largely unsuccessful as were attempts by the indigenous kingdoms of Tonga and Hawai`i to model their governments along Western lines to win support and recognition from European powers.[34]

Pacific Islanders remained the majority of the population in most plantation colonies in tropical Oceania despite the ravages of introduced disease. The limited European presence of European-run plantation enclaves, resident traders, and by and large poorly resourced and thinly stretched colonial administrations had a limited impact on most local communities beyond the collection of annual head taxes and perhaps periods of annual labor on plantations to earn taxes if the administration insisted on payment in cash rather than kind. Tensions sometimes arose between traditional authority figures and locals appointed to see to European interests in the absence of itinerant patrol officers, but the most influential and enduring external changes came from Christian churches which provided most of the Western education and services available in the colonial period. The result was a significant degree of continuity in local practice and indigenization of external elements such as Christianity well into this era and beyond.[35]

The economies of the Australasian settler colonies developed dramatically in the same era. Wool was Australasia's main export until 1850. Farming became increasingly important in the later decades of the nineteenth century as improvements in maritime vessels' carrying capacity and speed, and refrigeration in the 1880s, made the lucrative British market much more accessible, and meat and dairy products viable exports. Reduced shipping costs and higher returns saw demand for land increase, raising government revenue, further displacing indigenous communities, and converting more local ecosystems into pasture to produce wool, mutton, and beef, or wheat in certain areas with sufficient irrigation.[36] This boom also deterred diversification into other products and markets until Britain's joining of the European Economic Community in 1973 forced a search for alternatives. Economic expansion and a mood of optimism prevailed among Australian and New Zealand settler governments as their economic and communication ties to the world's financial hub London strengthened until the 1880s and 1890s when a series of natural disasters and a financial crisis hit hard economically and resulted in bitter confrontations between workers and their employers.[37]

The new settler colonies first affected the world economy in a significant way in the 1850s with the discovery of gold in Australia. Australian goldfields produced 40 percent of the world's gold output in the 1850s. The initial Australian gold discoveries in Victoria were followed by others in Queensland and Western Australia, and in New Zealand in the 1860s. At the peak, 150,000 goldminers descended on Victoria, including

40,000 Chinese. This bonanza of wealth and migrants saw the rise of Melbourne as a financial and urban center of 191,000 people by 1871. The easy gold was mined out by 1880 with subsequent mineral finds often larger than earlier finds but in more remote locations and requiring more advanced extraction methods. As a result, mining became dominated by large companies able to make large investments for large returns in inhospitable inland locations like Broken Hill and Kalgoorlie. The Australian economy benefited from immense mineral wealth from this time until the present day, particularly in Western Australia. Most profits ended up in London rather than Australia, however, as the majority of the big mining companies were British.[38] The same is true for New Caledonia and its nickel wealth from the 1890s, although New Zealand's gold wealth was less sustained, and farming was soon restored as the national economic mainstay.

Self-government by elected parliamentary majorities was granted to most Australasian colonies in the 1850s. Governors retained significant powers, however. Pacific Island colonies were ruled by administrators with prominent settlers consulted but not empowered. Indigenous peoples were politically marginalized across the whole region. The Australia colonies were federated into the Commonwealth of Australia on 1 January 1901 after a popular vote on the issue. New Zealanders declined federation with the Australian colonies, perceiving themselves to be a distinct and special people, superior to their trans-Tasman neighbors, and destined to set an example for the rest of the world in social justice.[39] Settler societies included many more men than women, particularly in rural areas. Masculine values pervaded public discourse on colonial identity, yet ironically, women secured the vote here in the 1890s as governments sought to secure social stability by improving the lot of women.[40]

Times of Anxiety: World Wars, Pandemic, and Economic Depression

The twentieth century ushered in new anxieties for the Australasian colonies. Japan's crushing victory over Russia in the north Pacific accentuated fears about their remoteness from Britain in the face of potential enemies much closer to home. Anglo-Japanese treaties in 1905 and 1911 did little to dissipate these fears, as suspicions remained about Japan's true intentions. A visit to Australia and New Zealand in 1908 by an American fleet at the invitation of the host governments was intended by all three parties as a warning signal to Japan not to intrude into this part of the European world.[41]

The next threat to Australasian security came from Europe rather than the Pacific with the outbreak of World War I. Japan fought as an ally of Britain and its empire against Germany and its allies. Australia and New Zealand easily secured German New Guinea and Samoa while Japan seized Germany's colonies in China and Micronesia. Small Pacific Islander units saw action in Europe, but most combatants from the region came from Australia and New Zealand and fought on the Western Front. However, it was the earlier campaign at Gallipoli in the Dardanelles that became the defining memory of this war as a rite of passage where the colonies proved themselves despite its smaller scale and failed mission. This campaign saw the birth of the ANZAC (Australian and New Zealand Army Corps) legend, where Australia and New Zealand defined themselves as unique and special.

The ANZAC myth emphasized their stoic pragmatism and bravery as true colonial frontier values and as a volunteer citizen soldiery (although most of their contingents were urban dwellers), embodied with an egalitarian streak and anti-authority bent, particularly in the case of Australians whose respect for their Turkish foes contrasted dramatically with contempt for the arrogant stupidity they perceived in British officers. The ANZACs believed themselves superior to British troops in combat. Yet, as colonies, there was no question of not supporting Britain in its hour of need. The Australian government failed in its attempt to introduce conscription, yet 400,000 volunteered out of the 1.5 million males aged between fifteen and sixty-four in 1914. Of the 330,000 servicemen who went overseas, 68 percent were either killed or wounded. New Zealand introduced conscription later in the war and enlisted 120,000 men—a remarkable achievement for a nation of only one million in 1914. About 80 percent were sent overseas, and 59 percent of these were either killed or wounded. These casualty rates were much higher than the average for British forces.[42]

The inter-war years were a time of economic anxiety and experimental response for Australia and New Zealand. All were affected by the 1918 influenza pandemic, with the highest recorded death rate of almost 20 percent occurring in New Zealand Samoa.[43] Both were extremely vulnerable to economic downturns because of their reliance on primary product exports subject to influences beyond their control, and Britain's crucial role and influence on their foreign relations, trade, and finance. Both suffered economic downturns in the run up to the Great Depression but responded differently. While New Zealand reinforced its dairy exports to Britain, Australia sought to diversify from farming into industry and manufacturing, albeit largely financed by British banks to the point where Australian interests became the largest clients of British financial institutions. The 1929 stock market crash led to primary commodity prices plummeting. Unemployment reached almost one-third of the workforce and national expenditures in both did not reach pre-1929 levels until a decade later. Both nations did commit to basic welfare to ensure a bottom line family wage was available to all through non-contributory social security being available to all citizens. Citizenship was unevenly defined however. Māori were paid less than Pakeha (Europeans), and Australian Aborigines were largely excluded from payment.[44]

New Zealand and Australia inherited new colonial roles in former German Pacific territories as part of the Versailles settlement. New Zealand faced a campaign of passive disobedience in Samoa in the 1920s, known as the Mau, when its officials sought to undermine traditional leadership roles for high chiefs. Matters came to a head when

New Zealand police opened fire on unarmed Samoan protesters on 28 December 1929. New Zealand clamped down on Mau members who fled into the bush. The resulting standoff was not resolved until a new Labour government came into power in New Zealand in 1936 and addressed Samoan grievances about their exclusion from government. On 3 January 1929 Australian authorities in Rabaul, the administrative center of Australia New Guinea, awoke to find most Melanesian workers on strike for better wages and conditions. The comprehensiveness and lack of warning of the strike shocked the Australians who meted out severe punishments on the strike's leaders who were drawn from the ranks of trusted indigenous occupations within the colonial regime—senior police and a ship's captain. The Ratana Church sprung up and thrived among Māori in the 1920s combining Christianity with Treaty of Waitangi principles. It turned to politics in the 1930s and secured designated Māori seats and allied with the reforming Labour government. Other Māori protested at the Eurocentric celebration of Waitangi Day as New Zealand's national day and Australian Aborigines staged a Day of Mourning in 1932 to coincide with Australia Day.[45]

The 1930s also saw mounting concerns about the inability of the international community to rein in the aggression of totalitarian regimes in Europe and East Asia. Australia and New Zealand committed themselves to the British war effort on the day Britain declared war, 3 September 1939. Their forces fought alongside British and Commonwealth forces in North Africa, Greece, Crete, and Italy from 1941 until the end of the war. France's Pacific colonies responded to the fall of France and its division into pro-Allied Free French and pro-German Vichy forces by eventually opting to join the Free French, with some serving in De Gaulle's Free French forces in North Africa and Western Europe.

Japan's stunning victories in the Pacific and Southeast Asia after their attack on Pearl Harbor on 7 December 1941 brought their forces almost half of Oceania and brought the frontline to the north coast of New Guinea and the northern Solomon Islands. Darwin was bombed by Japanese aircraft, and Japanese midget submarines were found in Sydney harbor in early 1942. The fall of Singapore exploded the myth of British power in the region and left Australia feeling vulnerable. With Britain stretched defending its own soil and Burma and India, the Americans filled the void and bore the brunt of the fighting in the Pacific. While more distant New Zealand felt less threatened by the Japanese and kept most of its forces in the North African and European theaters for the duration of the war, Australia focused on the Pacific, and Pacific events became the abiding memories of the war in their national consciousness: the first land defeat of the Japanese on the Kokoda Trail in Papua New Guinea and stoic survival as prisoners enduring appalling treatment from their Japanese captors.[46] The oceanic environment, vast distances involved, and ferocity of Japanese resistance led to many Japanese garrisons simply being bypassed and isolated through American aerial dominance, and their resistance was ultimately broken by the use of a new super weapon of unprecedented killing power—the atomic bomb.

POST-WAR THEMES: THE NUCLEAR PACIFIC, DECOLONIZATION, AND THE SEARCH FOR IDENTITY

Since World War II, New Zealand and Australia have been stable, socially and politically conservative nations largely electing right-of-center governments occasionally punctuated by brief periods of left-of-center government. Post-war Australia has benefited from mineral wealth and diversified its economy into manufacturing and industry more than New Zealand, and has also diversified its population more through immigration from continental Europe after the war and across the globe more recently, especially Asia. Almost one in four Australians were born outside Australia according to the 1996 census. New Zealand has become more Oceanic in its population base.[47] Māori rights have advanced immensely since the Waitangi Tribunal process gathered momentum in the 1980s to redress treaty grievances, with legal rights conveyed, wrongfully taken land restored, or economic compensation made. Land rights and recognition of past injustices in Australia have stalled somewhat since the landmark Mabo case in 1992 so that most Aboriginal Australians remain marginalized on the geographical and political fringes exhibiting social and health indicators only seen in nations that are recipients of Australian overseas aid.

Relative size and isolation have played major roles in Australian and New Zealand foreign policy. Smaller and more remote New Zealand feels more able to adopt neutral and idealistic stances over issues such as nuclear testing and environmental security, while Australia sees itself as a middle-ranking power with an interest in developing and maintaining a regional power projection and a capacity to support its close ally the United States in its global military actions. Both are strong supporters of free trade and democratic governance. They have been effectively a common market for services and goods since the signing of the Closer Economic Relations (CER) Agreement in 1983.[48]

Australasia and Oceania were directly affected by nuclear weapons' programs arising from Cold War tensions between the United States and Soviet blocs. The vast and relatively under-populated expanses of Oceania and western and central Australia proved ideal venues for nuclear testing by the Americans, British, and French, especially as their inhabitants were also politically marginal in essentially colonial relationships in American Micronesia, the British Gilbert Islands, French Polynesia, and Australia. Atmospheric testing of nuclear warheads was eventually replaced by first underground testing and then computer simulations and delivery system testing only as protests mounted within the region. A key watershed was New Zealand sending naval vessels into the French testing zone at Moruroa in 1973 to highlight France's intransigence over a World Court ruling on atmospheric testing. The South Pacific region was declared a nuclear-free zone in 1975 with only Australia qualifying its support out of concern for its military alliance with the United States which used nuclear-powered and nuclear-armed vessels. New Zealand made no such qualification, resulting in a rupture in the longstanding ANZUS Alliance that had formed just after

World War II in recognition of Britain's diminished capacity in the region and globally.[49]

Fears of economic viability as micro-economies in a global world and political coherence as arbitrary colonial boundaries united diverse peoples delayed independence until the mid- to late 1970s for most Pacific nations, despite the global mood of self-determination that prevailed with the formation of the United Nations after World War II. Coups in Fiji, civil war in Solomon Islands, and secessionist movement by Bougainville against Papua New Guinea have added to underlying concerns about economic viability in a number of Pacific states. Many now doubt the ability of states within the so-called 'Arc of Instability' to Australia's immediate north to make significant economic advances and secure political stability without external assistance. While many policy makers subscribe to this analysis, the majority of academic specialists on the Pacific have rejected or called for serious modification of the Arc of Instability paradigm.[50] The latter urge more acknowledgement of Pacific nations' highly inadequate preparation for independence as a fundamental reason for their current problems. They are also more cautious about the efficacy of applying foreign models to Pacific problems.

Independent Pacific Island states vary considerably in size from just over 20,000 in Tuvalu to approximately 6.1 million in Papua New Guinea. A variety of languages are spoken within larger nation states and the kin-based identity is the dominant affiliation of most citizens. Most inherited limited infrastructure from their colonial rulers and since independence have been unable to provide the transport, educational, health, and economic facilities needed to make their citizens willing and able to operate as citizens of a modern state. Most people still practice essentially highly localized subsistence lifestyles occasionally supplemented by cash crops. Despite poor communications and at times tense relations between social groups, a sizable minority of the population now travel beyond their kin-group area to work in the modern economy, especially in national capitals or large multinational undertakings such as mine sites. Such gathering places are sources of both identity formation and tension. While a new class-based urban identity has begun to take place in cities such as Suva, many if not most migrants to cities rely upon *wantoks*—networks who speak the same language and share cultural origins.[51]

Cold War certainties that placed the region firmly within the Western alliance have begun to break down. China's increasing prominence and influence in the world's economy has left its mark on the region. The late Ron Crocombe asserted that 'A spectacular transition is under way in the Pacific Islands. For the past 200 years, external influences, whether cultural, economic, political or other, have come overwhelmingly from Western sources. That is now in the process of shifting predominantly to Asian sources.'[52] China's rising presence and flow of aid and investment into the region has resulted in a similar expansion of aid and investment by its rivals Taiwan and Japan to protect perceived spheres of influence. The possibility of a three-way bidding war between China, Taiwan, and Japan for Pacific Island loyalties now looms, something which also threatens to drag Australia, New Zealand, and the United States into the race if it continues and intensifies. In 2006, the United States' Bush Adminis-tration declared 2007 the 'Year of the Pacific' as part of a move to re-engage with a region it perceives it has neglected since the fall of the Berlin Wall.[53]

CONCLUSION: EXTERNAL IMPOSITIONS AND INTERNAL MODIFICATIONS

Donald Denoon, Philippa Mein Smith, and Marivic Wyndham end their survey of the region's history with the following observation on the region's identity:

> Australians and New Zealanders of all descriptions feel comfortable with their Pacific neighbours. The extent and the warmth with which Islanders reciprocate is another question. In a critical sense, however, those sentiments hardly matter. It would be rash to suggest that the people of this region understand one (an)other. Quite the reverse: what gives the region some if its coherence is that communities identify themselves by misunderstanding their neighbours in a mesh of dubious analogies. It is the accumulation of perceptions, misperceptions and concerns which make ours such a dynamic region; and by reifying the region we make it a significant player in the layered impacts of, and reactions to, globalization.[54]

Despite the bidding war and rivalry looming in response to China's rising influence in the region, Oceania and Australasia remain on the margins of world history. Their destinies in this era of heightened, human-induced climate change are now even further linked to processes beyond its area over which they have no influence.[55] Now more aware of influences looming just over the horizon, the region's inhabitants must, nevertheless, still generally modify the impact of these external forces rather than hope to shape them.

NOTES

1. See Keith Sinclair, 'Introduction,' in Keith Sinclair, ed., *Tasman Relations: New Zealand and Australia, 1788-1988* (Auckland: Auckland University Press, 1987), 8, and Geoff R. Clark, ed., *Dumont d'Urville's Divisions of Oceania: Fundamental Precincts or Arbitrary Constructs?*, special issue of *The Journal of Pacific History* 38: 2 (2003).

2. The only comprehensive surveys covering Oceania and Australia are C. Hartley Grattan, *The South West Pacific Since 1900: A Modern History*, 2 vols. (Ann Arbor, Mich.: University of Michigan Press, 1963), and Donald Denoon and Philippa Mein-Smith with Marivic Wyndham, *A History of Australia, New Zealand and the Pacific* (Oxford: Blackwell, 2000). This chapter was heavily influenced by the latter.

3. The notable exception which emphasizes the Pacific and its cultures more than most world history texts is Jerry H. Bentley and Herbert F. Zeigler, *Traditions and Encounters: A Global Perspective on the Past*, 4th edn. (New York: McGraw Hill, 2008).

4. Denoon *et al.*, *A History of Australia, New Zealand and the Pacific*, 2.

5. The terms European and Western are used interchangeably to refer to influences and people emanating from European and North American Caucasian societies.

6. R. C. Green, 'Near and Remote Oceania: Disestablishing Melanesia in Culture History,' in Andrew Pawley, ed., *Man and a Half: Essays in Pacific Anthropology and Ethnobiology in Honour of Ralph Bulmer* (Auckland: Polynesian Society, 1991), 491–502, especially 493–5.

7. See E. Alison Kay, *Little Worlds of the Pacific: An Essay on Pacific Basin Biogeography* (Honolulu: Lyon Arboretum, 1980), 25, 33.

8. On the region's physical setting see Douglas L. Oliver, *Oceania: The Native Cultures of Australia and the Pacific Islands*, 2 vols. (Honolulu: University of Hawai`i Press, 1989), vol. 1, 326.

9. See Richard Broome, *Aboriginal Australians*, 2nd edn. (St. Leonards, NSW: Allen and Unwin, 1994), 9–21.

10. Aotearoa is the Polynesian word for New Zealand and is used here to refer to that landmass before a significant European presence occurred from the 1840s.

11. See K. R. Howe, ed., *Waka Moana: Voyages of the Ancestors: The Discovery and Settlement of the Pacific* (Honolulu: University of Hawai`i Press, 2007).

12. See Oliver, *Oceania*, vol. 1, 185–320, 501–89.

13. See, for example, the debate between Irving Goldman, 'Status Rivalry and Cultural Evolution in Polynesia,' *American Anthropologist* 57: 4 (1955), 680–97, and Marshall Sahlins, *Social Stratification in Polynesia* (Seattle: University of Washington Press, 1958).

14. See O. H. K. Spate, *The Pacific since Magellan: Vol. 1: The Spanish Lake* (Canberra: Australian National University Press, 1979).

15. There has been a spate of books recently on the voyages of Captain Cook. The best by far is Nicholas Thomas, *Discoveries: The Voyages of Captain Cook* (London: Penguin, 2004). On twentieth-century first-contact situations in the New Guinea highlands, see Bob Connolly and Robin Anderson, directors, *First Contact* (1983: DVD release 2005), and Bill Gammage, *The Sky Travellers: Journeys in New Guinea, 1938–1939* (Melbourne: Melbourne University Press, 1998).

16. The main attack against Sahlins was Gananath Obeyesekere, *The Apotheosis of Captain Cook: European Mythmaking in the Pacific* (Princeton: Princeton University Press, 1992), which prompted a robust defense from Sahlins in *How 'Natives' Think: About Captain Cook, For Example* (Chicago: University of Chicago Press, 1995). See also I. C. Campbell, 'European–Polynesian Encounters: A Critique of the Pearson Thesis,' *Journal of Pacific History*, 29: 2 (1994), 22231.

17. Henry Reynolds, *Frontier: Aborigines, Settlers, and Land* (Sydney: Allen and Unwin, 1987).

18. See Peter Hempenstall, 'Imperial Manoeuvres,' in K. R. Howe, Robert C. Kiste, and Brij V. Lal, eds., *The Pacific Islands in the Twentieth Century* (St. Leonards, NSW: Allen and Unwin, 1994), 3–28.

19. See David A. Chappell, *Double Ghosts: Oceanic Voyagers on Euroamerican Ships* (Armonk, N.Y.: M. E. Sharpe, 1997), especially 28–40, 158–63.

20. K. R. Howe, *Where the Waves Fall: A New South Sea Islands History from First Settlement to Colonial Rule* (Sydney: Allen and Unwin, 1984), 329–43.

21. See Doug Munro, 'Revisionism and its Enemies: Debating the Queensland Labour Trade,' *Journal of Pacific History* 30: 2 (1995), 240–9. For the impact of returning laborers, see Peter Corris, *Passage, Port and Plantation: A History of Solomon Islands Labour Migration* (Melbourne: Melbourne University Press, 1973), 111–25.

22. See Niel Gunson, *Messengers of Grace: Evangelical Missionaries in the South Seas 1797–1860* (Melbourne: Oxford University Press, 1978), Doug Munro and Andrew Thornley, eds., *The Covenant Makers: Islander Missionaries in the Pacific* (Suva: University of the South Pacific, 1996), and Broome, *Aboriginal Australians*, 101–19.

23. David E. Stannard, *Before the Horror: The Population of Hawai`i on the Eve of Western Contact* (Honolulu: Social Science Research Institute, 1989), and Andrew F. Bushnell, 'The "Horror" Reconsidered: An Evaluation of the Historical Evidence for Population Decline in Hawai`i, 1778–1803,' *Pacific Studies* 16: 3 (1993), 115–61.

24. Donald Denoon, 'Pacific Island Depopulation: Natural or Un-Natural History?,' in Linda Bryder and Derek A. Dow, eds., *New Countries and Old Medicine: Proceedings of an International Conference on the History of Medicine and Health* (Auckland: Pyramid Press, 1994), 324–39, quoting from 325.

25. Donald Denoon, 'Pacific Island Depopulation,' 332–4; David Stannard, 'Disease and Infertility: A New Look at the Demographic Collapse of Native Populations in the Wake of Western Contact,' *Journal of American Studies* 24: 3 (1990), 325–50; and Stephen Kunitz, *Disease and Social Diversity: The European Impact on the Health of Non-Europeans* (Cambridge: Cambridge University Press, 1994), 51.

26. See Keith Windschuttle, *The Fabrication of Aboriginal History* (Sydney: Macleay Press, 2002) versus Stuart Macintyre and Anna Clark, *The History Wars* (Carlton, Victoria: Melbourne University Press, 2003); and Broome, *Aboriginal Australians*, 50–1.

27. See Ross Cordy, 'The Effects of European Contact on Hawaiian Agricultural Systems—1778–1819,' *Ethnohistory* 19: 4 (1972), 393–418, on Hawai`i, and James Belich, *Making Peoples: A History of the New Zealanders from Polynesian Settlement to the End of the Nineteenth Century* (Auckland: Penguin, 1996), 152, on New Zealand.

28. See Alfred W. Crosby, *Ecological Imperialism: The Biological Expansion of Europe, 900–1900* (New York: Cambridge University Press, 1986), 217–68 for New Zealand; J. R. McNeill, 'Of Rats and Men: A Synoptic Environmental History of the Island Pacific,' *Journal of World History* 5: 2 (1994), 299–349 for Oceania; and, Geoffrey Bolton, *Spoils and Spoilers: A History of Australians Shaping their Environment*, 2nd edn. (St Leonards, NSW: Allen and Unwin, 1992).

29. See Henry Reynolds, *The Law of the Land* (Ringwood, Victoria: Penguin, 1987), and *Aboriginal Sovereignty: Three Nations, One Australia?* (St Leonards, NSW: Allen and Unwin, 1996).

30. Blainey, *Tyranny of Distance*, and Denoon et al., *A History of Australia, New Zealand and the Pacific*, 86–8.

31. Claudia Orange, *The Treaty of Waitangi* (Wellington: Allen and Unwin, 1987).

32. Denoon et al., *A History of Australia, New Zealand and the Pacific*, 130–4; Orange, *The Treaty of Waitangi*, 170–2; James Belich, *The New Zealand Wars and the Victorian Interpretation of Racial Conflict* (Auckland: Auckland University Press, 1986); and Belich, *Making Peoples*, 258–61.

33. See Donald Denoon, 'Plantations and Plantation Workers,' in Donald Denoon, ed., *The Cambridge History of the Pacific Islanders* (Cambridge: Cambridge University Press, 1997), 226–32.

34. I. C. Campbell, *A History of the Pacific Islands* (Christchurch: University of Canterbury Press, 1989), 83–91.

35. Campbell, *A History of the Pacific Islands*, 156–85.

36. Donald Denoon, *Settler Capitalism: The Dynamics of Dependent Development in the Southern Hemisphere* (Oxford: Oxford University Press, 1983), 100–6.

37. Luke Trainor, *British Imperialism and Australian Nationalism: Manipulation, Conflict, and Compromise in the Late Nineteenth Century* (Cambridge: Cambridge University Press, 1994), 123, 138; N. G. Butlin, *Investment in Australian Economic Development 1861–1900* (Canberra: 1976); and Denoon, *Settler Capitalism*, 71–6, 82–5.

38. See Geoffrey Blainey, *The Rush that Never Ended: A History of Australian Mining*, 2nd edn. (Melbourne: 1969); and John Salmon, *A History of Goldmining in New Zealand* (Wellington: Government Printer, 1963).

39. Helen Irving, ed., *The Centenary Companion to Australian Federation* (Cambridge: Cambridge University Press, 1999).

40. See Patricia Grimshaw, *Women's Suffrage in New Zealand*, 2nd edn. (Auckland: Oxford University Press, 1987) and Audrey Oldfield, *Woman Suffrage in Australia: A Gift or a Struggle?* (Melbourne: Cambridge University Press, 1992).

41. Neville Meaney, *A History of Australian Defence and Foreign Policy 1901–23: Volume 1, The Search for Security in the Pacific, 1901–1914* (Sydney: Sydney University Press, 1976), 51–2, 120; and M. P. Lissington, *New Zealand and Japan, 1900–1941* (Wellington: Government Printer, 1971), 8–9.

42. Bill Gammage, *The Broken Years: Australian Soldiers in the Great War* (Canberra: Australian National University Press, 1974), Chris Pugsley, *Gallipoli: the New Zealand Story* (Auckland: 1984).

43. Sandra M. Tompkins, 'The Influenza Epidemic of 1918–19 in Western Samoa,' *Journal of Pacific History* 27: 2 (1992), 181–97.

44. Denoon *et al.*, *A History of Australia, New Zealand and the Pacific*, 290–8.

45. On resistance to colonial rule see Peter Hempenstall and Noel Rutherford, *Protest and Dissent in the Colonial Pacific* (Suva: University of the South Pacific, 1984). For the examples cited above, see Malama Meleisea, *The Making of Modern Samoa: Traditional Authority and Colonial Administration in the Modern History of Western Samoa* (Suva: University of the South Pacific, 1987), 124–8; Ian Campbell, 'New Zealand and the Mau in Samoa: Re-assessing the Causes of a Colonial Protest Movement,' *New Zealand Journal of History* 33: 1 (1999), 92–110; Bill Gammage, 'The Rabaul Strike, 1929,' *Journal of Pacific History* 10 (1975), 3–29; J. M. Henderson, *Ratana: The Man, the Church, the Political Movement* (Wellington: Allen and Unwin, 1972); and Denoon *et al.*, *A History of Australia, New Zealand and the Pacific*, 312–13.

46. Stewart Firth, 'The War in the Pacific,' in Denoon, ed., *The Cambridge History of the Pacific Islanders*, 291–323; Hank Nelson, *P.O.W. Prisoners of War: Australians under Nippon* (Sydney: Australian Broadcasting Corporation, 1985); and, 'Kokoda: the Track from History to Politics,' *Journal of Pacific History* 38: 1 (2003), 109–27; and Geoffrey M. White and Lamont Lindstrom, eds., *The Pacific Theater: Island Representations of World War II* (Honolulu: University of Hawai`i Press, 1989).

47. Denoon *et al.*, *A History of Australia, New Zealand and the Pacific*, 349–51.

48. See Australian High Commission, Wellington, New Zealand website <http://www.australia.org.nz/wltn/CloseEconRel.html>.

49. Stewart Firth, *Nuclear Playground* (Honolulu: University of Hawai`i Press, 1987). Algeria's independence from France in 1962 removed the desert interior of Algeria as a nuclear testing ground for France.

50. See, for example, Ben Reilly, 'The Africanisation of the South Pacific,' *Australian Journal of International Affairs* 54: 3 (2000), 261–8 versus Jon Fraenkel, 'The Coming Anarchy in Oceania? A Critique of the "Africanisation of the South Pacific" Thesis,' *Journal of Commonwealth and Comparative Politics* 42: 1 (2004), 1–34.

51. On contemporary social and economic circumstances, see Karen Nero, 'The Material World Remade,' in Denoon, ed., *The Cambridge History of the Pacific Islanders*, 359–96.

52. Ron Crocombe, *Asia in the Pacific Islands: Replacing the West* (Suva: University of the South Pacific, 2007), vii.

53. On Taiwan see Jim Hwang, 'What Really Counts,' *Taiwan Review*, 30 November 2006, <http://taiwanreview.nat.gov.tw/ct.asp?xItem=23510&CtNode=128>; on Japan, see The Ministry of Foreign Affairs of Japan, 2006, *The Fourth Japan–Pacific Islands Forum Summit Meeting*, <http://www.mofa.go.jp/region/asia-paci/spf/palm2006/index.html>); on the United States, see Congressional Research Service, 'The Southwest Pacific: U.S. Interests and China's Growing Influence,' US Congress, April 2007, <http://www.fas.org/sgp/crs/row/RL34086.pdf>.

54. Denoon *et al.*, *A History of Australia, New Zealand and the Pacific*, 470.

55. The low-lying atolls of the Pacific are particularly prone to sea level rises and increased typhoon activity and intensity associated with global warming.

REFERENCES

BELICH, JAMES. *Making Peoples: A History of the New Zealanders from Polynesian Settlement to the End of the Nineteenth Century.* Auckland: Penguin, 1996.

BLAINEY, GEOFFREY. *The Tyranny of Distance: How Distance Shaped Australia's History.* Rev. edn. South Melbourne: Sun Books, 1982.

BROOME, RICHARD. *Aboriginal Australians.* 2nd edn. St. Leonards, NSW: Allen and Unwin, 1994.

CROCOMBE, RON. *Asia in the Pacific Islands: Replacing the West.* Suva: University of the South Pacific, 2007.

DENOON, DONALD. *Settler Capitalism: The Dynamics of Dependent Development in the Southern Hemisphere.* Oxford: Oxford University Press, 1983.

——, PHILIPPA, MEIN-SMITH, with MARIVIC WYNDHAM. *A History of Australia, New Zealand and the Pacific.* Oxford: Blackwell, 2000.

FIRTH, STEWART. *Nuclear Playground.* Honolulu: University of Hawai`i Press, 1987.

HOWE, K. R., ed. *Waka Moana: Voyages of the Ancestors: the Discovery and Settlement of the Pacific.* Honolulu: University of Hawai`i Press, 2007.

KUNITZ, STEPHEN. *Disease and Social Diversity: The European Impact on the Health of Non-Europeans.* Cambridge: Cambridge University Press, 1994.

OLIVER, DOUGLAS L. *Oceania: The Native Cultures of Australia and the Pacific Islands.* 2 vols. Honolulu: University of Hawai`i Press, 1989.

SINCLAIR, KEITH, ed. *Tasman Relations: New Zealand and Australia, 1788–1988.* Auckland: Auckland University Press, 1987.

CHAPTER 31

....

THE PACIFIC OCEAN
BASIN TO 1850*

....

RAINER F. BUSCHMANN

THE Pacific Ocean is the world's largest and deepest ocean, spanning about one-third of the earth's surface. Nearly twice the size of the Atlantic Ocean, its area of approximately 64,000,000 square miles (166,000,000 square kilometers) can easily accommodate all seven continents. As the name indicates, Oceania is by and large a waterlogged world; its roughly 25,000 islands range from New Guinea, earth's second-largest island, to the Republic of Kiribati (formerly known as the Gilbert Islands), with a land surface of a mere 275 square miles. Despite its size, the Pacific has received only scant global historical attention when compared to the Atlantic and the Indian Oceans.[1] To be sure, the Pacific played a prominent role intermittently in world history, highlighted by the Austronesian expansion, the Manila Galleon trade, the eighteenth-century European exploration, and the intense island-hopping military campaigns of World War II. At the same time such historical interest did not translate into a familiar timeline integrating this watery geographical feature into a larger world historical framework.

The continuities of historical events linking the liquid spaces of the Atlantic and the Indian Oceans are well explored and documented in prominent world historical texts. For the Indian Ocean, the decoding of the monsoon system in the first millennium BCE was crucial to establish an exchange system linking Africa and Asia that lasted well into the eighteenth century.[2] A smaller but equally continuous time-frame can be encountered in the historical development of the Atlantic Ocean. Generally originating with Columbus's voyages in the late fifteenth century, the Atlantic stayed central to global history throughout the revolutions in North and South America, Haiti, and France.[3] On a global historical scale, the Atlantic has become synonymous with the early modern world shedding light on both voluntary and involuntary migrations that greatly influenced the Americas, Africa, and Europe.

If one were to read the history of this colossal Pacific Ocean against its better studied Atlantic and Indian counterparts, some apparent differences quickly start to emerge. Apart from the most obvious element, size, one also needs to recognize that the Pacific is a world of islands. Of course, both the Atlantic and the Indian Oceans are spotted with islands. Yet these geographical features are, with a few noticeable exceptions, located in close proximity to nearby continents that greatly influence their historical development. The Pacific Ocean basin, on the other hand, is in the words of the late Tongan writer Epeli Hau'ofa 'a sea of islands'—a world dominated by many islands rather than large-scale continental features.[4] Besides the superficial geographical comparison among the oceans, the Pacific immediately invites a concern about periodization. Clearly there is more discontinuity than continuity to this ocean, and its history is best broken down by three distinct periods of exploration and settlement.

THREE PERIODS OF SETTLEMENT

The first period began approximately 50,000–40,000 years ago during the Pleistocene when lowered sea levels linked island Southeast Asia (referred to as Sunda comprising most of Indonesia and the Philippines today) with the rest of the Asian continent. Similarly, New Guinea and Australia were linked in a landmass that is referred to as Sahul. Archeologists argue that anatomically modern human beings crossed the still significant water gap separating Sunda and Sahul and gradually came to occupy the area they like to call Near Oceania. Besides Australia, this area is equivalent of a geographical feature generally known as Melanesia. Pacific historians currently eschew this term due to its racial stigmatization—*melas*, meaning 'black,' refers to the skin color of its inhabitants—opting instead to name the area according to settlement history. Despite the racial connotations, however, the term remains widely in use. The settlement of Near Oceania took a better part of 20,000 years until at the end of the Pleistocene rising sea levels greatly increased the water gaps between insular Southeast Asia and Oceania.

Approximately 6,000 years ago another wave of migrants braved the vast Pacific. Emerging out of the somewhat more sheltered waters of Southeast Asia, these settlers possessed sophisticated open watercrafts and spoke languages related to a group of tongues called Austronesian. A distinctive form of pottery, known as Lapita for the first site of its discovery on New Caledonia, aided archeologists in tracing their expansion. After leaving New Guinea and the Bismarck Archipelago about 5,000 years ago, these settlers broke out of the bounds of Near Oceania to settle what archeologists call remote Oceania—the vast expanses of the Pacific. About 3,000 years ago these settlers reached the triangle of Fiji, Samoa, and Tonga where the expansion came to a prolonged halt due to increasing water distances and upwind sailing directions in the eastern Pacific. It is roughly around this time that Lapita pottery disappeared from the archeological record. While the exact reason for this disappearance will never be fully known, archeologists postulate that the vanishing of pottery might be related to the cumbersome task of carrying clay containers on a seafaring vessel. Their tendency to break and lack of buoyancy might have influenced the Austronesian-speaking colonizers to forgo such means of transportation opting instead for more perishable items. From this triangle, the mariners ventured into the vast expanses of the eastern Polynesia settling Hawai`i, Aoetearoa (New Zealand), and Rapa Nui (Easter Island) by about 500–1000 CE. One major unresolved issue is whether or not these Austronesian mariners made contact with the societies living in the Americas. When Norwegian anthropologist Thor Heyerdahl drifted in a balsa raft from South America to the archipelago of the Tuamotos in 1947, many scholars accepted that accidental drift voyages from the Americas came to settle the many islands of the Pacific Ocean. Yet four decades of archeological research and experimental voyaging between 1960 and 2000 shifted the origin of Oceania's settlement to Asia.[5] Currently there is a small but growing minority of linguists and archeologists who argue that Polynesians might have reached California. Their main argument is based on the similarities between plank canoes of the Chumash people and Polynesians. The word employed for this canoe is *tomol*, which shares similarities with Polynesian words for a useful piece of wood. Many Pacific archaeologists tacitly accept such contacts, while their counterparts on the North American continents fear that accepting this diffusion in naval technology might minimize Native American accomplishment. More research is needed, of course, to shed additional light on this intriguing matter.

The third major incursion into the Pacific Ocean, referred to by some historians as the true beginning of globalization, originates with Ferdinand Magellan's circumnavigation (1519–22). Yet this incursion occurred a good 500 years after the settlement of Oceania had been concluded, leaving a major gap in the historical record that should, for the lack of a better term, be called 'the black hole.' Hau'ofa argued that Euro-American scholars tend to regard the 25,000 islands of Oceania as islands in the sea, isolated from resources and markets as well as prominent historical events. The Pacific region, thus, became the 'hole in the donut' in a world where social scientists tend to look closer at developments along the Pacific Rim.[6] Yet ignoring the 500–1,000 years between the settlement of the Pacific Islands and the entrance of Europeans into Oceania also means forgetting about important exchange networks that existed in the region. Historians all too often exaggerate the impact of Europeans on the Pacific Islands, arguing that the island communities were relatively self-contained and isolated from each other. Some archeologists add to this belief by emphasizing that cultural development in these societies was essentially an internal process driven almost exclusively by the urge to adapt to a newfound environment. This concept, however, contradicts Polynesian mythology, which abounds with tales of valiant navigators traveling between distant islands. Moreover, the ocean allowed for a symbiotic relationship between societies on high volcanic or continental islands and those living on relatively smaller coral islets.[7] If one is willing to pay any credence to the contact between the Chumash and Polynesian navigators, then one must acknowledge the reach and ability of these mariners.

There were indeed a number of existing exchange networks. In the Caroline Islands, the *sawei* network linked the high islands of the Palauan archipelago and Yap with the low islands over a distance of a little less than 1,000 miles. The island of Yap stood at the center of this exchange system, with its society utilizing important forms of currency, the most prominent one being the famous 'money' discs to forge alliances. In the past this exchange network has sometimes been labeled a 'Yapese Empire' where supposedly Yapese overlords extracted tribute from the coral atolls of the Caroline Islands by means of sorcery. This 'tribute' involved elaborate gift exchanges and frequent disaster relief following tropical storms in the region. Most of the long-distance voyaging performed in that area was actually performed by the atoll dwellers, which explains why traditional navigation in the Carolines has survived into our century.

The Tongans too established a semblance of an empire shortly before Europeans caught a glimpse of this vast ocean. Archaeological finds and oral traditions speak of an expansion of Tongan power about the year 1400 CE from the island of Tongatapu, first to other islands in the Tongan chain and later into Fiji to the west and Samoa to the east. The emerging Tongan maritime empire built its strength by placing junior members of the Tongan elite in outlying islands; through strategic marriages they enforced head island Tongatapu's authority. Control within the Tongan 'empire' rested—much like in the Yapese case—on reciprocity. While tribute from Fijian and Samoan isles went to Tongatapu, the Tongan chiefs depended on redistribution of wealth—a concept integral to Polynesian chieftainship. Identity based on gift exchange not only provided regional contacts throughout the Pacific, but also created societies that avoided the rigid ethnic categorization that followed European invasion into the area.[8]

These regional connections, however, did not establish supra-regional links. There is no indigenous name for the Pacific—nor was there one for the Atlantic or Indian Oceans for that matter—lending credence to the assertion of historian O. H. K. Spate that the Pacific was, much like the Atlantic, a European 'artifact.'[9] Although this assertion has experienced much criticism as of late, it remains true that the incursion of Europeans into the Pacific following the sixteenth century connected the islands of the Pacific to the continents of Asia, as well as North and South America with a degree of permanence that they had not experienced earlier.

The third incursion into the Pacific figured then as an important step into the direction of globalization and derived from a sustained European incursion into the area. European motives to enter the Pacific shared similarities with those guiding Oceanian mariners. Clearly, adventurous undertakings guided European and Austronesian exploration. Both ventures, however, differed in one major aspect— resources. Population pressure and limited resources figured as major movers for settlement of new islands in the Pacific. Likewise, interdependence and reciprocity were major incentives to create supra-regional exchange systems in the Pacific. It took, however, the search for other resources, beyond mere subsistence, to forge global connections.

PACIFIC GLOBAL CONNECTIONS

The exploration of the Pacific was very much related to the motives that drove Europeans across the Atlantic and the Indian Oceans. The lure of gold from African shores and a quicker and safer route to the spices of South and Southeast Asia proved important in this regard. Such reasons for exploration were further compounded by geographical fables arguing for the existence of unknown continents in the southern hemisphere. Geographers had since antiquity based their assumptions on arguments of the earth's equilibrium, continental symmetry, and the impossibility of an imperfect world following God's creation. Magellan's circumnavigation dispelled some myths, in particular the notion that all the earth's seas were encompassed by landmasses. At the same time, he gave rise to an increasing investigation of two obsessions, Terra Australis Incognita (the unknown southern continent) and the Northwest Passage, linking the Atlantic with the Pacific Oceans.[10] The mythical continents proved illusionary, but islands of the Pacific provided convenient stopover locations to rich Chinese markets or whaling grounds. In short, the islands had the same quality for Europeans as they had for Austronesian explorers several centuries before. The main difference between the two expansions was that the Austronesian originated in Asia, while the European venture departed mostly from the Americas.

This third, European, wave of settlement can only be understood with some sort of reference to the Atlantic and Indian Oceans. The lure of riches along the African coast and the Indian Ocean provided major incentives for sustained European contact with these regions and ultimately unveiled two new continents with seemingly untold wealth. It was in the Atlantic too, that oceanic space became increasingly politicized on a global scale.[11] The Treaty of Tordesillas signed in 1494 following a papal bull divided the Atlantic world into a Spanish and Portuguese sphere. It was only a matter of time before a similar partition had to be drawn in the Pacific Ocean when Magellan's circumnavigation revealed an alternative route to the Spice Islands in Island Southeast Asia. The ensuing Spanish claim over Maluku led to a dispute with the Portuguese that ultimately resulted in another treaty—Zaragoza—that settled matters in 1529. It almost goes without saying that the majority of European nations failed to accept these treaties' provisions, and nobody bothered to ask the indigenous peoples of Africa, the Americas, Asia, and Oceania. Voices, most prominently that of the Dutch legal scholar Hugo Grotius (1583–1645), clamored for a concept of the freedom of the sea (*mare liberum*), a concept that would increasingly gain currency when more scientific-ally minded expeditions entered the Pacific Ocean.

The establishment of European entrepots in Southeast and East Asia extended these areas into the Pacific. Melaka (1511), Macau (1535), Manila (1571), and Nagasaki (1571), became important ports of call for a growing, even if volatile, Iberian maritime empire. Manila in particular has received much attention by global historians over the last two decades. The survival of this Spanish enclave depended very much on the ability to master the return voyage to the Americas, an endeavor that took the better part of three decades. Once Spanish mariners revealed favorable winds in the northern Pacific, it resulted in a paramount trade route linking Manila with the port of Acapulco in New Spain. This trade exchanged Chinese goods, prominently silk and porcelain, with precious South American bullion and lasted until 1815. Economic historians have extolled the significance of this trade over the past two decades. Spanish desire for exotic silk and porcelain merged with the Ming Chinese official demand for silver. The resulting global interconnection forged true global connections linking all the continents for the first time.[12] The founding of Manila is also credited with another event of import. The city became an important settlement for a dispersal (diaspora) of Chinese individuals into the region who much to the chagrin of the Spaniards, started to dictate Manila's economic landscape. Following the Spanish example, the Dutch eagerly encouraged Chinese settlement in the East Indies.

The maritime road from Acapulco to Manila led through the Mariana Islands, an archipelago that aroused Spanish attention in the seventeenth century. The Jesuit Order, which exposed a growing interest in an expansion into the Pacific Ocean basin, decided to employ the island of Guam as a secure base for their endeavors. Interested in the fables about the southern unknown continent, Guam became in the eyes of the Jesuit Order a convenient launching pad for a large-scale conversion effort into the Pacific. The missionaries soon realized that they had overextended themselves. Indigenous uprisings against Spanish rule decimated the inhabitants through reprisals and disease. Consequently, the Jesuit attempt to establish themselves in the Caroline Islands remained limited and was abandoned in the early eighteenth century following the martyrdom of several of their members.

For the Spaniards, the Pacific Ocean basin remained essentially a source of wealth and souls. Fearing overextension beyond the Americas, Spanish officials kept their explorations to a minimum. Spanish expeditions between 1567 and 1606 located multiple islands—including the Solomons, the Marquesas, Santa Cruz, and the New Hebrides (better known as Vanuatu), but failed to return with promised riches. While many ecclesiastical officials pleaded to continue the exploratory ventures, the Spanish monarchy decided against the costly endeavor concentrating their attention mostly on the northern Pacific. Jealously guarding their discoveries against other European interlopers, Spanish authorities would ultimately be blamed for retarding the unveiling of the Pacific Ocean by the eighteenth century.[13] If one was to eliminate the religious fervor, Spanish journeys to the Pacific differed little from those of the Dutch in the seventeenth and early eighteenth century. When the search for easy riches evaporated, Dutch officials, much like their Spanish counterparts, quickly turned against mounting costly expeditions to the Pacific.

NEW EXPLORATORY MOTIVES

It was in the second half of the eighteenth century that political and economic motives were supplemented with scientific ones. The many wars that had been fought on the

Atlantic side of the Americas increasingly started to affect Pacific shores as well. George Anson's circumnavigation (1740–44) figured as a watershed event in this regard. On one hand it was a continuation of the privateering actions against Spanish possessions during the War of the Austrian Succession. Anson's incursion into the 'Spanish Lake' increasingly illustrated the vulnerability of the Iberian hold on the region. On the other hand, Anson's endeavor also raised the difficulties of Pacific exploration, as an estimated 1,300 out of 2,000 members of his expedition died of scurvy. Lastly, the lavish publications resulting from Anson's expedition raised the awareness of the Pacific as a new region for exploratory ventures.[14] Spanish secrecy and purported abuses against the Native American population now underscored the birth of a whole new genre of travel literature that turned its gaze on the Pacific. Charles de Brosses's *Navigations aux Terres Australes* (1756) and Alexander Dalrymple's *Historical Collection of Several Voyages and Discoveries in the South Pacific Ocean* (1770–1) navigated through published accounts to stimulate a renewed commercial interest in the region.[15] Similarly, when British troops from India captured the city of Manila in 1762, the British Admiralty, encouraged by such events, commissioned increasing exploration of the Pacific following the Seven Years' War. These endeavors no doubt carried political overtones, but they also sustained an enlightened spirit that sought to increase knowledge about the region. The isolation of the Pacific Ocean encouraged Europeans to envision Oceania as an isolated world that had little to no contact with the outside world.[16] Consequently, they expected a radical departure from known animals, plants, and human societies. The imagined fabrication of the Pacific Ocean basin greatly influenced the departing expeditions. Similarly, learned individuals eagerly awaited news from these novel regions.[17] Historian Bronwen Douglas put it best: 'The decades between 1760 and 1840 saw the indigenous peoples of Oceania assume an empirical symbolic significance in the natural history of men and the emergent science of anthropology out of all the proportion to their limited political, material and demographic import to Europe.'[18]

In the past, the Euro-American incursion into the Pacific Ocean experienced a two-fold historical interpretation. The first and more global approach explored how the arrival of Euro-American explorers to the Pacific Ocean basin contributed to the expansion of commercial and military maritime empires. Likewise, such an approach also concerns itself with the scientific and intellectual transformations that emerged from the encounter between said navigators and the societies of the Pacific Ocean basin.

The second, more recent approach, has gained in acceptance over the past three decades. Practitioners of this research direction were less concerned about the Euro-American 'discovery' of a new world in the Pacific. Instead, such studies focused on examining the numerous and contrasting encounters between outsiders and Oceanian agents. Since most Oceanic societies did not possess an extensive writing system, anthropology became the discipline most engaged in this approach. Anthropologists, experts in the interpretation of human remains and the cultural make-up of societies, assisted historians in their quest for alternative sources that included dance, material culture, and tattooing as well as a rich body of oral traditions. They also suggested that historians read the more traditional Euro-American accounts in a novel way, so as to reveal hidden indigenous meanings and actions. In all of their interpretive nuances, such approaches bore one major drawback for the more globally oriented historian. Ethnographic historians maintained that Pacific history, to be more meaningful for the peoples residing in the basin, could only be interpreted locally. The categorical rejection of global interpretations also resulted from a fear that the individual Oceanic societies might fade into footnote trivia when compared to other polities on a global scale.[19] The gulf between anthropological and global histories has seemingly widened over the last decade.[20] Anthropological approaches in the Pacific are now successfully exported to historical studies in other regions with the dialogue between African and Pacific studies serving as a particularly lively example. At the same time, the continuous emphasis on local manifestations is partially responsible for retarding the global historical appreciation of the Pacific Ocean basin.

Considering the nature of the present collection, this chapter will limit itself to the global or transnational aspects of Pacific encounters between 1760 and 1840. As hinted at earlier, encounters with indigenous societies had major implications for natural and social science. Such innovations are generally associated with the three voyages of James Cook (1768–80), although this illustrious navigator was neither the first nor the last to roam through Pacific waters. Ironically, Cook's main accomplishments were less in the realm of traditional discoveries. Indeed, his accolades were based on his ability to dispel long-held geographical chimeras. His exploration of Australian shores and the southern Pacific led to the dismissal of the Southern Continent. His third voyage did much to undermine the existence of the Northwest Passage linking the Atlantic with the Pacific Oceans. James Cook also carries the distinction of historical controversy. His rapid rise from obscurity, his egalitarian dealings with the indigenous peoples he encountered, and his acclaim even among countries who were sworn enemies of the British Crown make him the perhaps most celebrated discoverer of the eighteenth century, if not of all times. On the other hand, there are those historians who highlight his despotic character that left few marks on the indigenous cultures he encountered other than the introduction of violence and venereal diseases.[21]

The new world Cook encountered became part of numerous and richly illustrated volumes that more than reinforced the British claim to the Pacific. Cook's claim to the eastern shores of Australia would ultimately lead to colonial annexation only a few years after North American territory was lost following the Treaty of Paris in 1783. In the meantime, the French government had by no means been idle. The disastrous campaigns of the Seven Years' War (1756–63) had greatly reduced their empire, and the Pacific became a much welcomed region for novel annexations. Louis de Bougainville's circumnavigation (1767–9) solidified the romantic images of Tahiti and its enchanting inhabitants. Jean-François de Galoup, Comte de La Pérouse attempted to eclipse Cook's accomplishment through an ambitious expedition. When his two vessels vanished in the Pacific Ocean basin a year prior to the French Revolution, the dream of a French maritime empire had to be placed on hold.[22]

British and French publications did much to erode the century-old Spanish claim over the Pacific Ocean. Spanish officials, however, hardly resigned themselves to their fate. Concurrently engaging Cook's and Russian expansions into this area, Spanish vessels frequented Pacific waters between Tahiti and Tonga as well as Nootka and San Blas.[23] Moreover, Spanish intellectuals labored hard to deny the novelty of the Pacific societies, arguing instead that the newly encountered polities were a mere extension of the Americas. This Spanish idea of linking the old new world of the Americas with that of the eighteenth-century Pacific influenced the works of Alexander von Humboldt and Charles Darwin.[24]

ETHNOGRAPHY AND RACIAL CLASSIFICATIONS

The arrival of a more scientific inquiry also coincided with an increasing need to classify the cultures and societies encountered. Already during Cook's first voyages on the *Endeavour* (1768–71), he brought scientists who tinkered with innovative ways of classifying the objects of natural history they collected. Joseph Banks, the journey's official naturalist, brought along Carl Solander, who was one of the best students of Carl Linné (better known as Linnaeus). Linnaeus's method of classifying plants based on their reproductive systems was conveniently applied in the Pacific.[25] Cook's second voyage (1772–5) proved equally significant in that it tested chronometers in the determination of longitude on the open ocean. Such devices greatly assisted in the mapping and charting processes in the Pacific Ocean and supported political claims over contacted islands.[26]

Cook's second voyage was also responsible for a whole new way of 'seeing' contacted indigenous societies. The two German naturalists, Johann Reinhold Forster and his son Georg, accompanying Cook on this particular voyage became instrumental in this regard. Upon their return, the younger and elder Forster competed with Cook over publication rights. The British navigator easily won the contest since his volumes were richly illustrated with numerous engravings. The Forsters sought to make up the lack of illustrations with a reflection on the common humanity displayed by the societies they had encountered in Oceania. Cook's own rendition of the second Pacific voyage resulted in a largely descriptive account, as he disdained learned musings. Cook's misgivings with philosophical renditions emerged through the reading of John Hawkesworth's interpretation of his first voyage. Hawkesworth's liberal handling of the events elicited not only the navigator's scorn but also that of the learned British public. Johann and Georg Forster, on the other hand, were more concerned about placing Oceanic societies within a comparative framework. Their work maintained an existence of a common human origin (monogenesis) and attributed obvious differences to variable environmental rather than static innate factors. Such descriptions allowed for fluid ethnic boundaries and were thus akin to the indigenous systems based on kinship and reciprocity dominating social hierarchies in the Pacific. At the same time Cook's voyages also carried with them the kernel of ethnic reification, better known as 'race.' The Western construct of race is in itself a product of the Atlantic world, emerging out of the dreadful exchanges of the Atlantic slave trade. There are numerous studies of how the concept permeated the lowbrow as well as highbrow world of the Atlantic.[27] For the Pacific, such studies are just beginning.[28] It can be argued that the concept of race developed in the Atlantic Ocean basin, yet developed maturity in the Pacific worlds of the eighteenth and nineteenth centuries. By the time the Pacific came into focus, however, human migration in the Atlantic had mixed the region's ethnic groups, erasing the much-desired boundaries. The Pacific, on the other hand, was more promising. The concept of insularity, mentioned earlier in this chapter, is again helpful in this regard. Surrounded by large watery expanses, the islands of the Pacific formed convenient laboratories where ethnic intermixing was supposedly kept to a minimum. This island world then provided smooth categories much desired by European intellectuals. Pulling it all together was a French naval officer turned geographer by the name of Jules Sébastien César Dumont d'Urville who built on earlier suggestions to insist on a tripartite division of the Pacific Ocean basin. Adopting the existing terms of Polynesia and Micronesia, he added his own—Melanesia—a region based on racial appearances rather than geographical realities. European theorists found such constructions much to their liking and soon classified Australian Aborigines on the bottom as the most debased of all human societies quickly followed by Melanesian peoples. As such, the Pacific played a sad role in the formation of scientific searchers of racial hierarchies in the nineteenth-century world.

This attempt to capture fluid ethnic identifications into static racial categories was paralleled by an equally vicarious endeavor to reap economic benefit from the islands in the Pacific Ocean basin. The Dutch and the Spaniards were largely unsuccessful in such endeavors in the sixteenth and seventeenth centuries. The novel fauna and flora uncovered by the eighteenth-century exploration of the Pacific, however, provided new avenues for commercial exploitation. Cook's voyages were again highly instrumental in this regard. His identification of new plants and animals proved useful for the burgeoning China trade that had frustrated European traders for centuries. The Pacific Rim had provided the silver bullion to keep this exotic trade afloat, but from a European perspective it proved a costly investment.

Perhaps the best example tying in commercial and intellectual designs on the Pacific Ocean basin was the infamous mutiny on the *Bounty*, a mere decade after Cook's voyages. The *Bounty* combined the needs of an expanding Atlantic economy with the potential of the Pacific's novel discoveries. The breadfruit tree (*Artocarpus altilis*) newly described by the naturalists on Cook's voyages became a prospective food source for the growing African slave population in the British Atlantic world. William Bligh commanded the vessel and its promising mission to return the breadfruit seedlings from the island of Tahiti. Bligh's obsession with a perfect voyage, involving a lesser amount of casualties among the ship's crew, experienced its first setback when he failed to round Cape Horn due to stormy conditions. The alternative passage via the Cape of Good Hope upset the *Bounty*'s tight schedule, forcing the vessel to remain in Tahiti a great deal longer than originally planned. Moreover, Bligh found ways of alienating himself from the sailors. Forced periods of exercise through the addition of a fiddler to the ship's roster may have worked well for the numerous slave vessels crisscrossing the Atlantic Ocean. On the *Bounty*, however, such a practice elicited anger and resentment. When the ship finally edged to its Tahitian destination, European Romantic writings had greatly permeated the sailors' imagination. Such images were further reinforced when the seamen spent several months on the island waiting for the breadfruit seedlings to hatch. They grew accustomed to the lush and enchanting life on Tahiti that contrasted greatly with the harsh reality of the British Navy. Desertions were thus common when Bligh decided to depart Tahiti, and discipline was never quite restored upon the ship. Only a few months after leaving the Island, a majority of sailors under the leadership of Master's Mate Fletcher Christian rose up against their captain. Sparing his life, the mutineers placed Bligh in conjunction with his dwindling supporters in a tiny skiff, casting him adrift in the Pacific. Bligh and his motley crew accomplished the virtually unthinkable feat of covering 3,600 miles of open ocean to reach the safety of Dutch Timor. Bent on revenge, he quickly alerted the British Admiralty to dispatch warships in pursuit of the mutineers. In the meantime, Christian and the rest of the *Bounty*'s contingent had returned to Tahiti. Sensing that the island was too popular a destination to guarantee a comfortable living, Christian pushed on with eight fellow mutineers, eleven Tahitian women, and six Tahitian men. Reaching desolate Pitcairn, Christian decided to burn the *Bounty* and to establish a community on this island. The paradisiacal setting, nevertheless, soon descended into an orgy of violence and murder leaving a single mutineer, John Adams, as Pitcairn's last male resident. The Tahitian women who devised a successful blend of Christian and Tahitian values ultimately held this small society—now supplemented by numerous children—together. In the end, the mutiny turned out to be a story of failure. The transplanted breadfruit did not become a popular staple among the slaves of the Atlantic world, nor did the mutineers succeed in establishing a successful counterpart to the hierarchical shipboard societies of the Royal Navy.[29]

Exploiting the Pacific

By the time the *Bounty*'s story became a prominent parable in history books, commercialization had deeply engulfed the Pacific. The aging Manila Galleon exchange had been replaced by a burgeoning exchange with Chinese officials centering on the port of Guangzhou (Canton). Factories representing all major Euro-American nations sought to reap profit from this lucrative trade. The search for alternatives to silver uncovered North American furs, especially along the northwest coast then taking shape through the writings of Cook and his successors. The Pacific Ocean basin also offered valuable trade goods. Sandalwood, a fragrant wood much desired in China, established an expanding frontier, sweeping through the islands of the Pacific from east to west until the resource was all but exhausted by the second half of the nineteenth century.[30] Likewise, *beches de mer* (also known as trepangs or sea slugs) became popular due to their medicinal quality and delicacy status in China. Dried and cured, they were much sought after, and numerous traders quickly flocked to the Pacific to establish residency. Pearls and tortoise shell were additional items that found Chinese buyers in Guangzhou. To be sure, the emergent trade in the Pacific Ocean basin catered to the demand of Asian markets, yet it could not fail to have an impact on the islands that were now drawn into the exchange. When the last Manila Galleon sailed in 1815, the capital of the Spanish Philippines had long ceased to be a major hub for commercial exchange. The English East India Company had successfully expanded its commerce into the Pacific, partially aided by a novel expanding settlement at Port Jackson, Australia (1788), whose residents scoured the Pacific for budding economic possibilities. Their main competitors were not the traditional foes from France, Holland, or Spain, but a new nation that following the War of Independence (1783) saw itself cut off the lucrative trade with the British West Indies.[31] The Pacific offered new possibilities, for the China markets and the furs that could be obtained in North America, but also for novel resources that included whale and seal oil widely used as a source of artificial lighting and commercial lubricant. Managing to stay clear of the European conflicts resulting from the French Revolution (1793–1815), the American whaling fleets departing Nantucket and New Bedford soon eclipsed the British and French contingents and continued to dominate the hunt until its collapse in the second half of the nineteenth century.[32] Such commercial possibilities also triggered an additional wave of exploration that was less concerned about geographical discoveries. Instead, ventures such as Charles Wilkes's three vessels of the United States Exploring Expedition (1838–42) investigated emerging commercial possibilities of the Pacific which included a scientific mapping of the whales' annual migratory paths.[33]

The many islands located in the Pacific provided convenient stopover points to Asian trade markets and supply centers for the seasonal whaling fleets descending on Oceania. Bustling port towns developed in Honolulu, Pape'ete, and Koror that soon attracted both the best and the worst of Euro-American societies. The arrival of foreigners and their technological insights provided opportunities for enterprising indigenous peoples.Fire weapons and strong traditional ties became part of an important unification process soon creating a number of kingdoms in the Pacific Ocean basin. Best-known examples are the Kamehameha dynasty in the Hawaiian Islands, the Pomare monarchs on the island of Tahiti, and the succession established by Taufa'ahau (George Tupou I) in the Tongan Archipelago.[34] Historians examining the centralization processes occurring in Polynesia are quick to point out that the arrival of new European military technology and strategy was but one variable that should not be overestimated. While the effect of fire weapons cannot be ignored in the historical events unfolding on many Pacific Islands, traditional institutions and practices, most prominently marriage alliances, played equally prominent roles in the emergent consolidation of state power in Polynesia.[35]

Such unification processes divided, once again, global and anthropologically orient-ed historians. World historians see the commercial frontier sweeping through the Pacific as a forerunner of a Western controlled world system that soon encompassed the whole globe. They received additional support from environmental historians who studied closely the arrival of similar pathogens that had decimated the populations of the Americas centuries before. The spread of diseases throughout the Pacific differed from similar processes in the Americas. Oceania's insular world made the pathogen's pandemic spread of venereal diseases, smallpox, and others difficult. Those islands, however, that experienced an epidemic outbreak had similar losses as in the Americas.[36] Absolute numbers of this population decline are difficult to ascertain. Yet, researchers agree that in some regions, for instance the Hawaiian Islands, the decline could have been as much as 90 percent of the total population. Contrary to the global vision, anthropologically oriented historians are concerned about preserving of the indigenous peoples' agency. Rather than being at the receiving end of dehumaniz-ing economic or epidemiological forces threatening the Pacific Ocean basin, islanders made conscious decisions in the unfolding historical events.

The sandalwood trade and the arrival of the whaling fleets provide good examples to underscore the above assertions. When the aromatic wood scored high prices in Chinese markets almost by chance, scores of traders descended on the Pacific in search of the new commodity. The scattered inland growth of the sandalwood tree, however, made a foreign monopoly over the fragrant material nearly impossible. Traders were thus forced to make alliances with local chiefs to get access to the desired merchandise. Such alliances gave chiefs, especially in eastern isles of Polynesia, great leverage in their negotiations. On the flipside, the introduction of Western goods, ranging from billiard tables to rotten schooners (ironically the very items that Chinese buyers refused to purchase), induced new levels of indebtedness among the chiefs. Increasing levels of debt affected the relationship between chiefs and commoners when the latter bore the brunt of the labor. Spending many days in remote mountainous regions to fetch the sandalwood made them more liable to succumb to Western introduced diseases. Likewise, their absence from planting and fishing tasks had a noticeable impact on daily community subsistence.[37] The trade began in Polynesia in the late eighteenth century and exhausted itself by the 1830s. Further forays into Melanesia kept the sandalwood frontier active until the 1860s, but alternative Indian sources of wood lowered its expected prices.

The arrival of the whaling fleets in the Pacific Ocean was also a mixed blessing for the local communities. On one hand the whaling ships required water, provisions, fire-wood, shelter, and entertainment, thus providing new sources of income for the island societies. On the other hand, whaling was highly seasonal following the migratory paths of the mammals and could, therefore, not support a stable economic environ-ment. Whaling crews frequently comprised rowdy elements that gave way to political instability in the smaller communities. Lastly, their sheer insatiable desire for sexual entertainment led to a rapid increase of prostitution coupled with the spread of venereal diseases that further contributed to population decline. Historians are equally ambiguous about the historical impact on the many Polynesians who decided to enlist on such whaling expeditions. While the arrival of these ships provided additional possibilities for Polynesians to explore new horizons in the United States, Australia, and beyond, the departure of thousands of able-bodied individuals could only negatively affect the development of their Oceanic states.[38]

Similar debates can also be found at the root of the expanding mission frontier in the Pacific Ocean basin in the late eighteenth century. The Portuguese and Spanish Catholic frontier had considerable success along the Pacific Rim, which included the Americas, Southeast Asia, China, and Japan.[39] In the Pacific Basin, however, the ecclesiastical frontier remained localized to a few islands in Micronesia along the Manila Galleon track to New Spain. The Anglo-American Protestant expansion following a century later was the result of a renewed religious revival emerging at the time of the industrial revolution. Here the reading of James Cook's accounts took a different turn. Rather than emphasizing commercial potential or romantic paradises, the missionaries examined such writings for evidence of infanticide, incest, and general idolatry. Deeply concerned about the salvation of Oceanian natives, the Protestant frontier centered on the islands of Polynesia. In 1797 the London Missionary Society focused their attention on the island of Tahiti before expanding elsewhere. A generation after their arrival, the American Board of Commissioners for Foreign Missions took a precarious hold over the Hawaiian Archipelago, from where they ventured into the isles of Micronesia. Anglicans and French Catholics followed the Protestant missionaries and made their mark on the indigenous peoples of Polynesia and Melanesia.

By 1850 the Pacific Ocean basin was no longer an unknown territory on European maps. Following the Austronesian intrepid expansion into the region, the Euro-America expansion firmly tied the region to the Asian and American continents. Despite disease, commercialization, and missionization, most of the island territories maintained a high degree of independence that would soon come to an end. With the arrival of imperialism in the second half of the nineteenth century, all island territories would fall under Euro-American control. This important global tale is chronicled in detail in Chapter 30.

NOTES

* The author wishes to acknowledge Laura Dunlap's keen editorial advice.
1. Comparative studies on oceans are rare. Some exceptions are the forum on 'Oceans in History,' *American Historical Review* 111 (2006), in particular Matt K. Matsuda, 'The Pacific,' 758–80; see also Rainer F. Buschmann, *Oceans in World History* (Boston: McGraw-Hill, 2007).
2. Michael Pearson, *The Indian Ocean* (New York: Routledge, 2007); for a fascinating work that attempts to read similar connections in the nineteenth and twentieth centuries, see Sugata Bose, *A Hundred Horizons: The Indian Ocean in the Age of Global Empire* (Cambridge, Mass.: Harvard University Press, 2007).

3. See for instance Paul Butel, *The Atlantic* (New York: Routledge, 1999).

4. See Epeli Hau'ofa, *We Are the Ocean: Selected Writings* (Honolulu: University of Hawai'i Press, 2008).

5. For an accessible introduction to Oceania's settlement consult Patrick V. Kirch, *On the Road of the Winds: An Archeological History of the Pacific Islands* (Berkeley and Los Angeles: University of California Press, 2000).

6. Hau'ofa, *We Are the Ocean*.

7. One historian who has paid significant attention to existing exchange networks in Oceania prior to and during European expansion is Paul D'Arcy, *The People of the Sea: Environment, Identity, and History in Oceania* (Honolulu: University of Hawai'i Press, 2006).

8. D'Arcy, *People of the Sea*.

9. O. H. K. Spate's trilogy on European exploration *The Pacific since Magellan* (Canberra: Australian National University Press, 1979–88) is worth consulting in this regard.

10. For an overview of the concept of a mythological continent consult Glyndwr Williams and Alan Frost, eds., *Terra Australis to Australia* (New York: Oxford University Press, 1988).

11. Elizabeth Mancke, 'Early Modern Expansion and the Politicization of Oceanic Space,' *The Geographical Review* 89 (1999), 225–36.

12. See for instance the essays contained in Dennis O. Flynn, James Sobredo and Arturo Giráldez, eds., *European Entry into the Pacific: Spain and the Acapulco-Manila Galleons* (Brookfield, Ver.: Ashgate, 2001).

13. Mercedes Maroto Camino, *Producing the Pacific: Maps and Narratives of Spanish Exploration (1567–1606)* (New York: Rodpi, 2005).

14. Glynn Williams, *The Prize of All the Oceans: The Dramatic True Story of Commodore Anson's Voyage Round the World and How He Seized the Spanish Treasure Galleon* (New York: Viking, 1999).

15. Tom Ryan, '"Le Président des Terres Australes": Charles de Brosses and the French Enlightenment Beginnings of Oceanic Anthropology,' *Journal of Pacific History* 37 (2002), 157–86.

16. On insularity see John Gillis, *Islands of the Mind: How the Human Imagination Created the Atlantic World* (New York: Palgrave, 2004).

17. Bernard Smith, *European Vision and the South Pacific* (New York: Oxford University Press, 1960).

18. Bronwen Douglas, 'Seaborne Ethnography and the Natural History of Man,' *The Journal of Pacific History* 38 (2003), 3–27.

19. For some important representatives of such approaches see Marshall Sahlins, *Islands of History* (Chicago: University of Chicago Press, 1985); Greg Dening, *The Death of William Gooch* (Honolulu: University of Hawai'i Press, 1998); Nicholas Thomas, *Entangled Objects* (Cambridge, Mass.: Harvard University Press, 1991); for a succinct overview consult David Hanlon, 'Beyond "the English Method of Tattooing": Decentering the Practice of History in Oceania,' *The Contemporary Pacific* 15 (2003), 19–40.

20. It is quite probable that it will never be resolved. See also Rainer F. Buschmann, *Anthropology's Global Histories: The Ethnographic Frontier in German New Guinea, 1870–1935* (Honolulu: University of Hawai'i Press, 2009).

21. Gananath Obeyesekere, *The Apotheosis of Captain Cook: European Mythmaking in the Pacific* (Princeton: Princeton University Press, 1992); for a wider interpretation of James

Cook and his death at Kealakekua Bay see Glyn Williams's recent *The Death of Captain Cook: A Hero Made and Unmade* (Cambridge, Mass.: Harvard University Press, 2009).

22. John Dunmore, *French Explorers in the Pacific*, 2 vols. (Oxford: Clarendon Press, 1965–9).

23. Mercedes Maroto Camino, *Exploring the Explorers: Spaniards in Oceania, 1519–1794* (Manchester: Manchester University Press, 2009).

24. Rainer F. Buschmann, *Examining Pacific Chimeras: Spain and Oceania's Eighteenth-Century Exploration*, forthcoming.

25. A good point of departure for the scientific transformations that accompanied these voyages is Harry Liebersohn's *The Travelers' World: Europe to the Pacific* (Cambridge, Mass.: Harvard University Press, 2006).

26. The implications of this mapping process are best explored in Brian W. Richardson's *Longitude and Empire: How Captain Cook's Voyages Changed the World* (Seattle: University of Washington Press, 2005).

27. See for instance Marcus Reidiker, *The Slave Ship: A Human History* (New York: Penguin, 2007).

28. Bronwen Douglas and Chris Ballard, eds., *Foreign Bodies: Oceania and the Sciences of Race* (Canberra: Australian National University Press, 2008).

29. Perhaps the most ingenious of all rendition of the famed mutiny remains Greg Dening's *Mr. Bligh's Bad Language* (New York: Cambridge University Press, 1988).

30. A classic study is Dorothy Shineberg, *They Came for Sandalwood* (Melbourne: Melbourne University Press, 1967).

31. Arrell Morgan Gibson and John S. Whitehead, *Yankees in Paradise: The Pacific Basin Frontier* (Albuquerque: University of New Mexico Press, 1993).

32. Granville Allen Mawer, *Ahab's Trade: The Saga of South Sea Whaling* (New York: St. Martin's Press, 1999).

33. Nathaniel Philbrick, *Sea of Glory: America's Voyage of Discovery, The U.S. Exploring Expedition, 1838–1842* (New York: Penguin, 2004).

34. Consult K. R. Howe, *Where the Waves Fall: A New South Sea History from First Settlement to Colonial Rule* (Honolulu: University of Hawai'i Press, 1984), 125–97.

35. For the Hawaiian Islands consult Paul D'Arcy, 'Warfare and State Formation in Hawai'i: The Limits of Violence as a Means of Political Consolidation,' *Journal of Pacific History* 38 (2003), 29–52.

36. David Igler, 'Diseased Goods: Global Exchanges in the Eastern Pacific Basin, 1770–1850,' *The American Historical Review* 109 (2004), 693–719.

37. On a local impact of the sandalwood trade on Hawai'i see Patrick V. Kirch and Marshall Sahlins, *Anahulu: The Anthropology of History in the Kingdom of Hawai'i* (Chicago: University of Chicago Press, 1992), vol. 1 (Historical Ethnography), 55–97; for the whaling period consult 99–170.

38. David Chappell, *Double Ghosts: Oceanian Voyagers on Euroamerican Ships* (Armonk, NY: M. E. Sharpe, 1997).

39. Neil Gunson, *Messengers of Grace: Evangelical Missionaries in the South Seas, 1797–1860* (Oxford: Oxford University Press, 1978).

REFERENCES

BUSCHMANN, RAINER F. *Oceans in World History.* Boston: McGraw-Hill, 2007.

D'ARCY, PAUL. *The People of the Sea: Environment, Identity, and History in Oceania.* Honolulu: University of Hawai`i Press, 2006.

DENING, GREG. *Mr. Bligh's Bad Language.* New York: Cambridge University Press, 1988.

DENOON, DONALD, *et al.*, eds. *The Cambridge History of Pacific Islanders.* New York: Cambridge University Press, 1997.

—— and PHILIPPA MEIN-SMITH with MARIVIC WYNDHAM. *A History of Australia, New Zealand and the Pacific.* Malden, Mass.: Blackwell, 2000.

DOUGLAS, BRONWEN, and CHRIS BALLARD, eds. *Foreign Bodies: Oceania and the Sciences of Race.* Canberra: Australian National University Press, 2008.

EPELI, HAU'OFA. *We Are the Ocean: Selected Writings.* Honolulu: University of Hawai`i Press, 2008.

GILLIS, JOHN. *Islands of the Mind: How the Human Imagination Created the Atlantic World.* New York: Palgrave, 2004.

HOWE, K. R. *Where the Waves Fall: A New South Sea History from First Settlement to Colonial Rule.* Honolulu: University of Hawai`i Press, 1984.

KIRCH, PATRICK V. *On the Road of the Winds: An Archeological History of the Pacific Islands.* Berkeley and Los Angeles: University of California Press, 2000.

LANDSDOWN, RICHARD. *Strangers in the South Seas: The Pacific in Western Thought.* Honolulu: University of Hawai`i Press, 2006.

LIEBERSOHN, HARRY. *The Travelers' World: Europe to the Pacific.* Cambridge, Mass.: Harvard University Press, 2006.

SMITH, BERNARD. *European Vision and the South Pacific.* New York: Oxford University Press, 1960.

SPATE, O. H. K. *The Pacific since Magellan,* 3 vols. Canberra: Australian National University Press, 1979–88.

WILLIAMS, GLYN. *The Death of Captain Cook: A Hero Made and Unmade.* Cambridge, Mass.: Harvard University Press, 2009.

Index